HISTORY

OF

THE INDIAN NAVY.

(1613—1863).

HISTORY

OF

THE INDIAN NAVY.

(1613—1863).

BY

CHARLES RATHBONE LOW,
LIEUTENANT (LATE) INDIAN NAVY,
Fellow of the Royal Geographical Society.

AUTHOR OF

"THE LIFE OF F.M. SIR GEORGE POLLOCK, BART., G.C.B., G.C.S.I."
"TALES OF OLD OCEAN," "THE LAND OF THE SUN," &c.

IN TWO VOLUMES.
VOL. I.

The Naval & Military Press Ltd

Published by

The Naval & Military Press Ltd
Unit 5 Riverside, Brambleside
Bellbrook Industrial Estate
Uckfield, East Sussex
TN22 1QQ England

Tel: +44 (0)1825 749494

www.naval-military-press.com
www.nmarchive.com

Front cover illustration:
This painting by Thomas Buttersworth depicts Mahrmatta pirates attacking the sloop *Aurora*, of the Bombay Marine, 1812.

Back cover illustration:
European sailors of the Indian Navy breaching the Delhi Gate, 1858.

In reprinting in facsimile from the original, any imperfections are inevitably reproduced and the quality may fall short of modern type and cartographic standards.

THESE VOLUMES ARE DEDICATED

(BY SPECIAL PERMISSION, GRACIOUSLY ACCORDED)

TO

His Royal Highness the Prince of Wales,

TO WHOM ARE RESPECTFULLY TENDERED,

ON BEHALF OF HIS BROTHER OFFICERS,

WHO HIGHLY APPRECIATE THE HONOUR PAID TO THEIR

OLD AND DISTINGUISHED SERVICE,

THE GRATEFUL THANKS OF HIS ROYAL HIGHNESS'S

HUMBLE AND OBEDIENT SERVANT,

THE AUTHOR.

PREFACE

CHARLES RATHBONE LOW, like so many servants of the East India Company, came from an Anglo-Irish ascendancy family, with estates in county Galway. His grandmother was a daughter of the 4th Viscount Boyne, his grandfather served in H.M. 76th Foot, his father was a Major in the Bengal Native Infantry, and he himself married the daughter of a General. Charles was born at Dublin on 30th October 1837. He entered the East India Company's Indian Navy in 1853 and saw active service against pirates and slave traders in waters ranging from Zanzibar to the China Seas, only to have his career cut short in 1863 when the Indian Navy was abolished – hence the terminal date of the present work.

Returning to England, he was appointed the first Librarian (and Assistant Secretary) of the Royal United Services Institution in 1865, leaving the post in 1868 to concentrate on a career as a gentleman author and representative of the past glories of the Indian Navy. Beginning in 1866 and continuing until his death in 1918, he published a stream of monographs which included histories of the Royal Navy, the British Army, the First Afghan War, maritime discovery, and African exploration, and biographies of Field Marshal Pollock and Captain James Cook, while at the same time contributing hundreds of articles and shorter pieces to *The Times* and to literary and learned journals.

The work which has lasted longest, indeed which still has no rivals, is his History of the Indian Navy, published in 1877 – coincidentally the year when the two post-1863 local non-combatant marine services based at Bombay and Calcutta were reorganised as H.M. Indian Marine, eventually the Royal Indian Navy. An in-depth history of this second phase of the Indian Navy's existence has yet to appear but at least we have the mass of information accumulated by Low for the East India Company period. Copies of the original edition have now become both scarce and expensive, so the present reprint is most welcome. It also provides the opportunity to partly remedy the annoying lack of an index in the 1877 work. Low contented himself with detailed chapter summaries (which can still stand for a broad subject approach). The London Stamp Exchange has added indexes of ships and officers, compiled by Captain Kenneth Douglas-Morris R.N. (Retd.), whose enthusiasm for the Indian Navy — and its medals — is largely responsible for this reissue of Low.

Anthony Farrington
Deputy Director
India Office Library & Records

PREFACE.

MACAULAY, speaking of the indifference of the English public to Indian affairs, wrote that "a disturbance amidst the Spitalfields' weavers excited more attention in the Senate than the legislating for one hundred millions of its native subjects." But though the Indian Budget, annually brought before the House of Commons, excites a more languid interest among our legislators than a debate on a "breach of privilege," or a "personal explanation," yet the degree of interest this country attaches to Indian subjects has greatly increased since the time of the great Essayist. Hence I venture to hope that the records of a Service, which has been abolished and consigned to oblivion, may interest the British public sufficiently to be my apology for laying the story of its eventful career before the world.

Historical works have been written detailing the services of the Army in every Indian War of importance, generally by military writers of repute, as Wilkie, Thorn, Snodgrass, Kaye, and others, while naval historians, like James and Marshall, have narrated the deeds of the British Navy in Eastern waters; but, between the two, the Indian Navy has been forgotten, and accounts have actually been written of such events as the capture of Mauritius, and the Java War, in which no mention appears even of the presence of a squadron of ships of the Service, while the official reports make the barest reference to them. It is, therefore, a weighty, no less than a pleasing, task, that of doing justice to the dead, and to the survivors of a Service which, though uniformly treated with neglect and contumely, took a noble revenge by ever doing its duty.

It will be understood that, in confining myself in these pages to recording the services of the Indian Navy in the wars and other hostile operations in which they participated, I do not claim for the Service, by reason of this prominence, a preponderating share in the successes achieved.

I would point out that, irrespective of whatever interest may attach to this work as an Historical Record of the Indian Navy, many episodes of our conquest of India and the consolidation of our rule in our Eastern Empire, are, for the first time, disentombed from musty records and despatches, and brought before the public in the form of a connected narrative. Of such a nature are many passages in the early history of the Service, such as the operations against the Joasmi pirates and, generally, in the Persian Gulf, against the Beni-Boo-Ali Arabs, in the Eastern Islands preceding, and during, our occupation of Java, at the capture of Kurrachee and Aden, and the repulse of the repeated attacks of the Arabs in their desperate attempts to recapture that stronghold; also the part played by the Service in the First China War, in New Zealand, at the siege of Mooltan, in the First and Second Burmese Wars, the Persian War, the occupation of Perim and the Andaman Islands, and, finally, the services of the Indian Naval Brigades during the Sepoy Mutiny, which have been quietly ignored by all historians and

dinner, held in June, 1875, that the proposal was made to me, and, at first, I shrank from the task; but, encouraged by offers of assistance from the late Commander Heathcote, I.N., and other friends, I, as I have said, consented, with some diffidence, and many misgivings as to my ability, to prepare this record of the history of a Service in which were passed some of the best years of my life.

In writing of places so familiar to my brother officers, I have adopted the orthography in vogue before the abolition of the Service, ere the Hunterian system vexed the unlearned soul; not that I would, for a moment, seek to controvert the theories of its advocates, that the latter is an adaptation of an old system and may be more strictly correct. Far be it from me to discuss the knotty subject, upon which doctors " have agreed to differ;" I am content, with a due sense of humility at the confession, to class myself with the unlearned aforesaid.

The arrangement of the work is, as far as practicable, consecutive as to dates, but where distinct episodes, stretching over a period of years, require separate treatment, a chapter is devoted to the subject. This course is followed in such instances as the narrative of the dealings of the Service with the Joasmi pirates, and the records of the Surveys, events which, being of an episodical character, and ranging over a period of years, are more intelligible to the reader when thus treated. This explanation may be considered necessary to account for the absence of sequence as regards dates in the headings of the chapters.

Almost without exception, the entire body of surviving officers of the Service have responded to my appeal, and placed at my disposal details of their own services and such other information as they might

other authorities. If I have made public some of these events and shed new light on others, this work will not be without some value in the opinion of those to whom the services of the Indian Navy, *per se*, are of small moment. A point to which also I have devoted special attention is the surveys made by the Service. Mr. Clements Markham has written an admirable and succinct sketch of the hydrographical labours of the Indian Navy, in his " Memoir on Indian Surveys," but, in the succeeding pages, I have given a detailed account of each Survey, including the names of the officers engaged, from the time of Lieutenant McCluer, in the year 1773, to the date of the abolition of the Service.

The Indian Navy ceased to exist in 1863, but, though a period of fourteen years has elapsed since its extinction, not even the briefest sketch of its services has been given to the world. Mr. Clements Markham, in his work above mentioned, expresses an opinion that some officer of the Indian Navy " should gather together the recollections of his colleagues, and, with the aid of such fragments as have survived the general destruction, give to the world a history of the work done by the Indian Navy in war and during peace." Agreeing as I do with that accomplished geographer, I could have wished that some senior, and more competent, officer of the Service, had undertaken the task of writing a connected History of the Indian Navy, but as so many years have elapsed since the fatal day when our flag was hauled down in Bombay Harbour, and no person, qualified by familiarity with India, and imbued with the traditions of the Service, has come forward to accomplish the arduous, but honourable, duty, I reluctantly consented to undertake the work. It was at the annual Indian Navy

possess, and I here tender to them all,—from the senior officer, Captain Boyce,* a name honoured in the Service, as the following annals will show,—my hearty thanks for their co-operation.

But the difficulties that stand in the way of compiling a reliable and connected History of the Indian Navy, are of no common order, and this chiefly through an act of Vandalism more worthy of the days when the Alexandrian library was committed to the flames, than of the present century,—though, perhaps, we do the ancients scant justice when we instance this memorable deed as peculiarly typical of that age, for there are men still living who can recall the destruction by fire of the Public Library at Washington, when our troops entered that city in 1814. The act of Vandalism, mentioned above, was the destruction of the public records of the Indian Navy, and is thus referred to by Mr. Markham :—" Before the Indian Navy had become a thing of the past, there was a destruction of the materials for its history. Previous to 1860 there were many and most valuable records of that Service in the India Office, but in that year nearly all were reduced to pulp." Again he writes :—" The official records of the Bombay Marine and Indian Navy have been almost entirely destroyed. Its history can now only be traced in fragmentary memoirs, papers, and reports."

Horace has said:—" *Vixere fortes ante Agamemnona multi;*" but, as the bard adds, these heroes have gone down to oblivion, "*carent quia vate sacro.*" It is to rescue the names, " unhonoured and unsung," of

---

* This gallant veteran, who entered the Service so far back as the year 1802, and lost his legs in the memorable action fought on the 30th of June, 1815, between his brig, the 'Nautilus,' and the United States ship 'Peacock,' still survives, and wrote to me in excellent health and spirits on the 9th of April, 1877.

forgotten worthies of a Service consigned to obscurity by those formerly in power at the India Office, with studied intent, as would appear by the extracts from Markham's work, that I take up the pen.

The sphere of duty of the Indian Navy was remote, the operations, oftentimes, insignificant, and the results of small import to the destinies of the world. Though these reasons may, perhaps, militate against this record being received with interest by the countrymen of the gallant seamen whose achievements it registers, I would submit that this should not be so. It is both more glorious and less exacting on one's sense of duty, to participate in some great European conflict, with such incentives as "all the world" for spectators, the applause of an admiring people, and a grateful sovereign ready to shower rewards on the victors, than to serve through a "little war," such as many we shall detail, the very name of which is forgotten, a war waged in an obscure inland sea or gulf, in a deadly climate, against a bloodthirsty foe who gives no quarter, and with the depressing knowledge that success brings no honours to the survivors who, too often, carry away with them the seeds of disease and premature death. By its works, now for the first time made public, let the Indian Navy be judged at the bar of History, and let the stern arbiter decide whether it failed in its mission in those distant Eastern Seas during the two and a half centuries of its existence, or whether it has acted a part worthy the country of its birth.

If the people of these isles, and the world in general, are agreed in extolling one achievement of our race as pre-eminently greater than any other, without doubt that achievement is the acquisition of our magnificent Eastern Empire. It is an episode of the first magnitude in the history of the human race, for it has exerted a great and an abiding influence, not only on the two hundred and thirty millions of souls in Hindostan, but on the teeming population of China, with which its conquest has mainly brought us into contact, and of Asia generally. That we are now a first-rate Asiatic, as well as European, Power, is due to our Indian Empire, and my readers will, I trust, concede, after perusing this work, that the Service, whose history it records, had no inconsiderable share in acquiring this glorious inheritance, and achieving this renown for our beloved country.

Any one now visiting the Red Sea, the East Coast of Africa, and the Persian Gulf, would fail to realise the fact that, up to within the latter half of this century, the British flag was seldom seen in these waters, except from the peak of the cruisers of the Indian Navy. The steamers of the Peninsular and Oriental Company —the pioneer of which, the 'Hindostan,' was commanded by Captain Moresby, I.N.—were the first to break the spell in the Red Sea, then the telegraph lines were laid, and, lastly, the construction of the Suez Canal made it the highway to all the Eastern world, and led to the establishment of lines of steamers from Aden and the Cape to Zanzibar. Officers of the Service, to whom the Persian Gulf was familiar ground, can remember how, not more than twenty years ago, the only postal communication the squadron had with the outer world, was when a ship-of-war arrived from Bombay to relieve another, or a steam-frigate was despatched on a special service. A British merchantman was seldom seen, and a steamer never, in this inland sea, which bore a bad name as the haunt of pirates from time immemorial, and by reason of the intricate navigation of the Arabian littoral; but, since the establishment of the telegraph, in 1864, regular lines of steamers, between Bombay and Bushire and Bussorah, and London and these ports, *viâ* the Suez Canal, have sprung into existence, and the Persian Gulf is no more a *mare incognita* than the Red Sea and the East Coast of Africa. The romance has long departed from all these places, and the Nile and Bagdad have become well nigh as vulgarised by the inroad of excursionists as the Rhine or Venice.

But service in these inland waters a quarter of a century ago, meant expatriation, and letters from friends in England were usually nine months old. Hence it was, perhaps, that echoes of the doings of the Indian Navy, in their encounters with the warlike maritime Arab tribes of the Persian Gulf, and with the truculent races of the African coast and Red Sea, were long in reaching Bombay, and died away before they fell upon English ears.

As the historian of the Indian Navy, I have received many letters from officers of the highest rank and distinction, who have served with us, testifying to the efficiency of the Service and ability of the officers, but the exigencies of space and the patience of my readers forbid a reference to them. I feel, however, I shall encroach neither on the one nor the other, by extracting the following generous panegyric from a letter addressed to me, under date the 18th of April, 1877, by Vice-Admiral Sir F. Beauchamp Seymour, K.C.B., Commanding the Channel Squadron, an officer deservedly held in high esteem in the noble Service he adorns:—

"No person regretted more than I did the abolition of that gallant Service. In my opinion no greater mistake was ever made. It was a Service which ranked among its officers some of the finest and best fellows I have ever met during a career of over forty-three years, and during its existence I ever endeavoured to show to the officers of it my appreciation of its merits wherever we met. Campbell, Rennie, Lynch, and many others, will always be remembered by me. From many of them I have received great hospitality and kindness, while their knowledge of Eastern languages, and of the countries in which they served so continuously, countries never or rarely visited at that time by my brother officers, was of the greatest possible service to us all."

One other extract I shall make from a letter, dated the 14th of March, 1877, from Sir James D. H. Elphinstone, Bart., M.P., one of the Lords of the Treasury in the present Government:—

"I have taken the greatest interest in a Service which I had no hesitation in stating in my place in the House of Commons, had in a short time produced more men of varied ability as diplomatists, surveyors, navigators, and explorers, than any Service of similar dimensions in the world, and I could only wonder at the fatuity of a Government in breaking up such an establishment, a proceeding not only foolish in itself, but which has been attended by expensive and disastrous consequences, as I distinctly prognosticated."

Though the records of the Indian Navy do not show a roll of great actions won by fleets in line of battle, the Service was seldom at peace, and displayed the traditional heroism of British seamen in ship duels, boat actions, and other unpretentious affairs, in which species of combat courage and devotion have ever found their most remarkable opportunities for display, as is evidenced in the history of the Royal Navy. The Company's ships have, in olden times, been engaged in sanguinary conflict with Portuguese, Dutch,

and French ships-of-war, and with the pirate fleets of
Arabs, Sanganians, Coolies, and Malwans. In such
actions, in the capture by bombardment, or storm, of
strong forts—as Ormuz, Surat, Tannah, Severndroog,
Gheriah, and Mocha, and in good service rendered
ashore and afloat in Burmah, China, New Zealand,
Persia, and India—the honour of the Indian Navy as
a war marine has been vindicated, while, as the nursery of an unsurpassed band of scientific marine surveyors, its services to commerce and civilisation have
been universally acknowledged. I therefore appeal
with confidence to the verdict of History as to the
conduct and career of the Service, judged from these
public records, and, if the task has been inadequately
discharged, the blame must be equally divided between
my shortcomings as a narrator, and the paucity
and want of continuity of the available materials.

And here I would thank the Secretary of State for
India, the Marquis of Salisbury, for having permitted
me to consult such records of the Service as still
remain. I have also had access to detached MS.
notes collected by the late Commodore Brucks, I.N.,
who designed to write a history of the Indian Navy;
while, I may observe, that personally I was familiar
with the subject, having from time to time during the
past ten years, treated of episodes of the Service in
magazine articles. That portion of my materials
derived from published sources, was acquired in the
libraries of the British Museum, Royal Geographical
Society, Royal United Service Institution, and India
Office, the two latter, owing to the courtesy of the
librarians, being of special value. Lastly, I have received the cordial assistance of brother officers, and
relatives of those deceased, who have placed at my

disposal a vast amount of matter, including journals and correspondence, official and private.

The majority of English readers, in speaking of the victories achieved by British arms in India, regard Clive as if he was the first to cause the name and flag of England to be respected in that country; but though, in the marvellous story of the founding and building up of the magnificent fabric of Eastern Empire, the name of the hero of Plassy shines conspicuous as, perhaps, the greatest Englishman of his time, and the master-mason, under whose inspiring genius the work gave promise of assuming its present imperial proportions,—yet even in those far-distant times when the East India Company was a feeble commercial corporation, struggling against the competition of the Dutch and Portuguese, there were gallant seamen in their service, as Best and Downton, who upheld the honour of this country, and testified to their European and Asiatic enemies that they were not degenerate descendants of the race from which had sprung Raleigh and Drake. In those early days, when the Company contended for very existence with rival associations and hostile nationalities, they found in their Marine the only champion to fight their battles. Those forgotten worthies did "yeoman's service" for their honourable masters, and now that the Indian Navy, which was the last titular transformation undergone by the original Service, no longer exists, it is only just that, equally with their military brethren, they should receive the meed of credit which is their due; for, as a writer says of them, "in their early struggles with the Moguls and Mahrattas, the Dutch and Portuguese, they displayed an energy, perseverance, and courage, as indomitable as that which subsequently conquered at Plassy and Assaye—albeit they have not been so fortunate as to be praised by a brilliant essayist."

This, therefore, has been my self-imposed task, and though, in literary style and defective treatment of the theme, I may halt at an immeasurable distance behind the great masters who have written on cognate Indian subjects, at least it has been my endeavour, in treating of events and of the actions of men, to

> "Speak of them as they are;
> "Nothing extenuate, nor set down aught in malice."

Personally I have no interests to serve, no grievance to air; the furtherance of truth and justice has been my only object, and I venture to affirm that this plain speaking is the wisest course in the interests of the Service, notwithstanding the averment of Bacon, that " a mixture of a lie, doth ever add pleasure."

C. R. LOW.

Chelsea, November, 1877.

LIST OF SUBSCRIBERS.

	No. of Copies
DERBY, The Right Hon. Earl, K.G. (*First Secretary of State for India*)	1
LAWRENCE, The Right Hon. Lord, G.C.B., G.C.S.I. (*late Viceroy of India*)	2
LYTTON, The Right Hon. Lord, G.M.S.I. (*Viceroy of India*)	2
NAPIER OF MAGDALA, General the Right Hon. Lord, G.C.B., G.C.S.I. (*late Commander-in-Chief in India*)	1
NORTHBROOK, The Right Hon. Earl, G.C.S.I., D.C.L. (*late Viceroy of India*)	1
SALISBURY, The Most Noble the Marquis of, K.G. (*Secretary of State for India*)	1

Abbott, Major-General Sir Frederick, C.B., R.E. (*late Governor of Addiscombe*)	1
Abbott, General James, C.B., R.A.	1
Abbott, Major-General, S.A. (*late Commissioner in the Punjaub*)	1
Adams, Major-General E.	1
Adams, Captain G. N., I.N.	1
Alcock, Lady	2
Allen, G. W., Esq.	1
Allenby, H., Esq., J.P.	1
Andrew, W. P., Esq., F.R.G.S.	2
Anstruther, Major-General Philip, C.B., R.A.	1
Antram, J. P., Esq., I.N.	1
Applegath, Major-General F.	1
Aylesbury, Commander T., I.N.	3
Balfour, General Sir George, K.C.B., M.P., R.A.	1
Barker, Lieutenant W. H., I.N.	1
Barron, Lieutenant T. H., I.N. (*Commissioner of Police, Brisbane*)	5
Barrow, John, Esq., F.R.S.	1
Bates, Major C. E. (*Private Secretary, Lieutenant-Governor of the Punjaub*)	1
Bathoe, Mrs. M.	1
Baxter, Robert, Esq.	1
Bayley, Sir E. Clive, K.C.S.I. (*Council of the Governor-General*)	1
Bayly, Lieutenant-General R.A.	1
Becher, General J. R., C.B., R.E.	1
. R.*	1
Beresford, Captain Lord William L. De la Poer, 9th Lancers (*A. D. C. to the Viceroy*)	1
Berthon, Commander C. H., I.N.	1
Birdwood, Lieutenant-General C.	1
Bishop, E., Esq., I.N.	1
Blowers, Major Charles E., late of the I.N. (*Bombay Staff Corps*)	1
Boileau, Sir Francis M., Bart.	1
Boileau, Major-General J. T., R.E., F.R.S.	1
Boileau, Lieutenant-Colonel Geo. W. (*late of the Bengal Army*)	1
Boileau, Major Charles L. (*late of the Rifle Brigade*)	1
Bond, Reverend Alfred	1

* Widow of an Officer of the Indian Navy.

	No. of Copies
Bone, Frederick G., Esq., I.N. (*late Secretary to the Commander-in-Chief, Indian Navy*)	1
Booth, Lieutenant W. C., I.N.	1
Boyce, Captain C., I.N.	1
Brazier, Lieutenant E. J, I.N.	1
Brechin, the Right Reverend the Bishop of (Dr. Jermyn)	1
Bridge, Captain Cyprian A. G., R.N.	1
Brownlow, Rev. W. R. B.	1
Buckle, Rev. J. (*late Lieutenant I.N.*)	1
Buckler, C. D., Esq.	1
Bullock, Fred., Esq.	1
Burne, Lieutenant-Colonel O. T., C.S.I. (*Private Secretary to the Viceroy*)	1
Burne, Colonel H. K., C.B. (*Military Secretary, Government of India*)	1
Burt, Lieutenant Turner, W., I.N. (*late of the 15th Regiment*)	1
Burton, Captain Richard F., F.R.G.S. (*late 18th Bombay N.I.*)	1
Butt, H. G., Esq.	1
Buxton, the Hon. Mrs. F. W.	1
Bythesea, Rear-Admiral J., V.C. (*Consulting Naval Officer to the Government of India*)	1
Caldwell, W. B., Esq.	1
Campbell, General G., C.B., R.A.	1
Campbell, Captain C. D., I.N.	6
Carey, Lieutenant Henry C., I.N.	2
Carpendale, Rev. W. H. (*late Lieutenant I.N.*)	1
Cavenagh, General Orfeur (*late Governor Straits Settlements*)	1
Chapman, M., Esq., I.N.	1
Chesney, Mrs. F. R.	1
Child,* Mrs. S.	1
Chitty, Commander A. W., I.N.	2
Clark, Lieutenant A. J., I.N.	1
Clarke, Colonel Sir Andrew, K.C.M.G., C.B., R.E. (*Council of the Governor-General*)	1
Cleghorn, George, Esq. (*late Captain Scots Greys*)	1
Coghlan, General Sir William M., K.C.B., R.A. (*late Brigadier and Political Resident at Aden*)	1
Cole, W. T. Esq., I.N.	1
Coles, George, Esq.	1
Colley, Colonel G. Pomeroy, C.B. (*Military Secretary to the Viceroy*)	1
Collingridge, Captain, (*late H.E.I.C. Maritime Service*)	1
Collingwood, Lieutenant W., I.N.	4
Combe, J., Esq.	1
Connolly,* Mrs. C. M.	1
Constable, Captain C. G., I.N.	2
Conybeare, Major-General F., R.A.	1
Cookson, Commander A. A., I.N.	1
Cousens, Rev. R. R. (*late Lieutenant I.N.*)	1
Crofton,* Mrs.	3
Crookshank, Captain A. C. W. (*Assistant Secretary, Military Department, Government of India*)	1
Cruttenden, Captain C. J., I.N.	1
Curtis, Major-General W. F.	1
Daniell, Captain E. W. S., I.N.	2
Davies, Commander W. H., I.N.	1
Davis, Lieutenant, H. H., I.N.	1
Dawes, Lieutenant Edwin, I.N.	1
Dawes, Richard, Esq.	1
Dawes, George, Esq.	1
Dawes, N., Esq.	1
De Montmorency, Mrs R. H.	1
Dent, Lieutenant T. W., I.N.	1
Draper, Commander J. S., I.N.	3
Drought, Captain H. A. M., I.N.	1

* Widow of an Officer of the Indian Navy.

	No of Copies
Du Boulay, Lieutenant J. G., I.N.	1
Edlin, Lieutenant H. R., I.N.	1
Edwards, Lieutenant H. J., I.N. (*Emigration Officer and Nautical Surveyor, Board of Trade*)	1
Egerton, Robert Eyles, Esq., C.S.I. (*Lieutenant-Governor of the Punjaub*)	1
Elliott, Mrs. W.	1
Ellis, Captain Frederick (*late of the 9th Lancers*)	1
Ellis, Lieutenant Henry, I.N. (*Master-Attendant, Singapore*)	4
Elphinstone, Sir James D. Horn, Bart., M.P. (*Lord Commissioner of the Treasury*)	4
Etheridge, Captain H. W., I.N.	2
Evans, Captain Frederick J., R.N., C.B., F.R.S. (*Hydrographer*)	1
Evans, Colonel W. E. (*late of the 103rd Royal Bombay Fusiliers*)	1
Eyre, Major-General Sir Vincent, K.C.S.I., C.B., R.A.	1
Fayrer, Surgeon-General Sir Joseph, K.C.S.I., F.R.S.	1
Flack, Mrs. W. S.	1
Forsyth, Sir T. Douglas, K.C.S.I., C.B. (*Council of India*)	3
French, Lieutenant-Colonel P. T.	1
Frere, The Right Hon. Sir H. Bartle E., Bart., G.C.B., G.C.S.I. (*late Governor of Bombay*)	1
Frushard, Captain J. J., I.N.	1
Fry, Lieutenant F. W., I.N.	1
Gardner,* Mrs. Alan Hyde	2
Garrett, Lieutenant H.'H., I.N.	1
Giles, Commander E., I.N. (*late Master-Attendant, Kurrachee*)	1
Girdlestone, F. B., Esq., I.N. (*late Assistant Superintendent, Topographical Survey of India*)	1
Glen, Physician-General Joseph (*late of the Bombay Army*)	1
Glynn, Rear-Admiral Hon. H. Carr, C.B., C.S.I.	1
Godwin-Austen, R. A. C., Esq., J.P., F.R.S.	1
Gomm, Lady	1
Gordon, Captain, A. H., I.N.	10
Grant, Mrs. John	2
Grant,* Mrs. George	1
Green, Major-General Sir W. Henry R., K.C.S.I., C.B.	1
Green, Colonel Malcolm, C.B.	1
Greig, Lieutenant-Colonel I. M., R.E.	1
Greig, Lieutenant, J. G., I.N.	3
Greig, Major P. H., R.A.	1
Greig, Captain P. H. (*14th Bombay Native Infantry*)	1
Grounds, Captain H. W., I.N.	1
Haines, General Sir Frederick Paul, G.C.B. (*Commander-in-Chief in India*)	1
Hall, Vice-Admiral Sir William King, K.C.B. (*Commander-in-Chief, Sheerness*)	1
Hall, Colonel E.	1
Hall, Major John	1
Hall, Lieutenant A. H., I.N.	1
Halliday, Sir Frederick J., K.C.B., (*Vice President, Council of India, late Lieutenant-Governor of Bengal*)	1
Hamilton, Lord George, M.P. (*Under-Secretary of State for India*)	1
Hamilton, Sir Robert N., Bart., K.C.B.	2
Hamilton, Captain B., I.N.	3
Haughton, Colonel J. C., C.S.I., (*late Superintendent of Port Blair*)	1
Hawkins, Reverend B. D., M.A.	3
Hawkins, Miss S. C.	3
Hay, Rear-Admiral the Right Hon. Lord John, C.B. (*Commanding the Channel Squadron*)	1
Hayman,* Mrs. W. R.	1
Hellard, Commander S. B., I.N.	2
Helsham, Mrs. J.	1
Hewett, Prescott G., Esq., F.R.S., (*President, College of Surgeons*)	3
Hodge, Gen. Sir Edward C., K.C.B. (*late of the 4th Dragoon Guards*)	1

* Widow of an Officer of the Indian Navy.

	No. of Copies
Hogg, Lieutenant Colonel Sir James M. McGarel, Bart., K.C.B., M.P.	1
Holl, Lieutenant-General C.	1
Holt, Commander G. T., I.N. (*Nautical Assessor, Board of Trade*)	1
Home, Mrs. R.	1
Hope, Admiral Sir James, G.C.B., A.D.C. (*late Commander-in-Chief, China and East India Station*)	1
Hopkins, Captain F. W., I.N.	2
Hopkins, Mrs. S.	1
Hora, F. H., Esq., I.N.	1
Hordern, R. O., Esq., I.N.	1
Howell, A. P., Esq. (*Under-Secretary, Home Department, Government of India*)	1
Hudson, Robert, Esq., D.L., F.R.S.	1
Humphry, Captain E. W., R.E.	1
Hunter, Lieutenant T. R., I.N.	1
Hurlock, Lieutenant R. G., I.N.	1
Huyshe, General Alfred, C.B., R.A.	1
Ibbs, Miss	1
Jackson, Lieutenant H., I.N.	2
Jacob, Major-General Sir George Le Grand, K.C.S.I., C.B.	3
Jacob, Captain S. S. (*Bombay Staff Corps*)	1
James, Commander H. H., I.N.	1
Jefferis, Major John	1
Jenkins, Captain Griffith, C.B., I.N.	12
Jermyn, Lieutenant R. F., I.N.	1
Johnson, Lieutenant-General Sir Edwin B., K.C.B., R.A. (*Council of the Governor-General*)	1
Johnson, Colonel Allen (*Military Secretary, India Office*)	1
Johnstone, Mrs.	1
Jones, Captain J. Felix, I.N.	3
Joynt, Surgeon-Major C. (*Bombay Army*)	1
Kane, Surgeon-Major M.	1
Kemball, Lieutenant-General Sir Arnold B., K.C.S.I., C.B., R.A.	1
Kennedy, Mrs. H.	1
Kennelly, Acting-Master D. J., I.N.	1
Keys, J. A., Esq., I.N.	1
Kiell, G. M., Esq.	2
Kinchant, Commander R., I.N.	1
Kinchant, Mrs. R.	1
King, Lieutenant Duncan B., I.N.	1
Lake,* Major-General Edward, C.S.I., R.E. (*late Commissioner in the Punjaub*)	1
Lake, Mrs. Edward	1
Lakes, Lieutenant J. Gould, I.N.	1
Lamb, Lieutenant H., I.N.	1
Lambarde, Lieutenant T. M., I.N.	1
Lambert, Rear-Admiral Rowley, C.B.	2
Lamborn, Mr. (*late Engineer, I.N.*)	1
Lawrence, Lieutenant-General Sir George St. P., K.C.S.I., C.B.	1
Lawrence, Major-General R. C., C.B. (*late Political Resident at Nepaul*)	1
Leishman, Lieutenant W., I.N.	4
Le Messurier, Major A., R.E.	1
Lewis, Lieutenant G. L., I.N.	1
Leycester,† George P., Esq. (*Bengal Civil Service*)	1
Liardet, Lieutenant H. M., I.N.	1
Library—Army and Navy Club	1
,, Army Head-Quarter's Book Club (*Simla*)	1
,, Consulting Naval Officer to the Government of India	1
,, East India United Service Club	1
,, Foreign Department, Government of India	1
,, Junior Carlton Club	1
,, Kurrachee Club	1

* Deceased on the 7th of June, 1877. † Deceased on the 3rd of November, 1877.

	No. of Copies
Library—Madras Club	1
,, Madras Literary Society	1
,, Mess of the 10th Regiment Bombay Light Infantry	1
,, Military Department, Government of India	1
,, Oriental Club	1
,, Persian Gulf Telegraph, Kurrachee	1
,, Royal Engineer Institute	1
,, Royal Geographical Society	1
,, Royal Indian Civil Engineering College, Cooper's Hill	1
,, Royal Naval Club, Portsmouth	1
,, Royal United Service Institution	1
,, St. Stephen's Club	1
,, Simla Library and Reading Room	1
,, Trinity House Corporation	1
,, Viceroy's Book Club (Simla)	1
Litchfield, E. S., Esq., I.N.	2
Little, Lieutenant-General Sir Archibald, K.C.B. (*late of the 9th Lancers*)	1
Lloyd, Captain R., I.N.	1
Lloyd, Commander C., I.N.	1
Loch, Captain W. (*A.D.C to the Viceroy*)	1
Low, S. P., Esq., J.P.	1
Low, Captain H. (*late 40th Bengal N.I.*)	1
Low, Hamilton L., Esq.	1
Low, Augustus F., Esq.	1
Low, Gustavus J., Esq. (*Bengal Civil Service*)	1
Lowder, George G., Esq., I.N. (*Chinese Imperial Customs, Shanghai*)	3
Lugard, General the Right Hon. Sir Edward, G.C.B.	1
Lumsden, Major-General P. S., C.B., C.S.I. (*Adjutant-General in India*)	1
Lushington,* Admiral Sir Stephen, G.C.B. (*late Commander-in-Chief, Indian Navy*)	2
Lynch,† Mrs. H. B.	4
Lysons, Lieutenant-General Sir Daniel, K.C.B. (*Quartermaster-General, Horse Guards*)	1
McConnell, Jas. E., Esq., J.P.	1
Macgregor, Major-General Sir George H., K.C.B., R.A.	1
Mackenzie of Seaforth, Keith Stewart, Esq. (*late of the 90th Regiment L.I.*)	2
Mackenzie, Lieutenant R., I.N.	1
Mackinlay, John, Esq. (*late Engineer-in-Chief, Indian Navy*)	1
Maisey, Colonel F. C. (*Examiner in Military Law to the Government of India*)	1
Malcolm of Burnfoot Langholm, W. E., Esq	3
Manners, Commander F. E., I.N.	1
Marshall, Mrs. C.	1
Marshall, Mrs. J.	1
Marshall, Lieutenant W., I.N.	10
Martin, James, Esq.	1
Mason, Commander G. N. P., I.N.	1
Maughan, William, Esq.	1
May, Lieutenant E. R., I.N.	1
Mayo, Lieutenant Arthur, I.N., V.C.	1
Mayo, Rev. Herbert H.	1
Melvill, Major-General Sir P. Melvill, K.C.B. (*late Military Secretary, Government of Bombay*)	1
Merewether, Colonel Sir William L., K.C.S.I., C.B. (*Council of India*)	1
Mickleburgh, Frank H., Esq., I.N.	1
Mignon, R. J., Esq., I.N.	2
Milman, Major-General G. Bryan, C.B. (*Major of the Tower of London*)	1
Mitcheson, Commander P. W., I.N.	1
Morgan, Mrs.	1
Morland, E. H., Esq. (*Bengal Civil Service*)	1
Morton, C. H. E., Esq., I.N.	1
Nisbett, Commander A., I.N.	1

* Deceased on the 28th of May, 1877. † Widow of an Officer of the Indian Navy.

	No. of Copies
Nolloth, Rear-Admiral M. S.	1
North, Colonel J. Sydney, M.P., D.C.L.	1
Nott, Captain A. H., I.N.	1
Ogilvy, Lieutenant W. H., I.N.	1
O'Neill, W. Lane, Esq.	1
Ottley, R. B., Esq.	1
Ouseley, Colonel J.	1
Parker, Lieutenant G. C., I.N. (*Master-Attendant, Kurrachee*)	4
Peele, Surgeon-Major R. De C. (*late of the Bombay Army*)	1
Pelly, Colonel Sir Lewis, K.C.B., K.C.S.I.	1
Pendlebury, A. A. Esq., I.N.	1
Pengelley, Commander W. M., I.N.	1
Pepper,* Mrs. G. A.	1
Percy, General Lord Henry H. M., K.C.B., V.C.	1
Peters, C. H., Esq.	1
Phillimore, Rear-Admiral A., (*Admiral-Superintendent, Naval Reserves*)	1
Playfair, Lieutenant-Colonel R. L. (*H.M.'s Consul-General in Algeria*)	1
Polwhele, General T.	1
Poole, J. W., Esq.	1
Porter, Captain J. P., I.N.	1
Potts, Arthur, Esq.	2
Powell, Osborne C., Esq.	1
Pratt, F., Esq., I.N.	1
Quanbrough, F. W., Esq.	1
Rawlinson, Major-General Sir Henry C., K.C.B., F.R.S., D.C.L., LL.D. (*Council of India*)	1
Rawstorne, E. C., Esq.	1
Reid, Lestock R., Esq. (*Late Member of Council and Acting-Governor, Bombay*)	3
Rennie, Captain J., C.B., I.N.	1
Rennie, Miss	1
Rennie, John, Esq.	3
Revell, Lieutenant-Colonel Joseph L. (*late of the 2nd Bengal Europeans*)	2
Revell, Lieutenant-Colonel Blackett (*late of the 31st Madras N.I.*)	1
Richards, Rear-Admiral Sir George H., C.B., F.R.S. (*late Hydrographer*)	1
Righy, Lieutenant-General H., R.E.	1
Ritherdon, E. Esq.	1
Robbins, Reverend Dr. Jno, D.D.	1
Roberts, Major-General F.S., C.B., V.C., R.A., (*Quartermaster-General in India*)	1
Robinson, Captain G., I.N.	1
Robinson, F., Esq., I.N.	6
Rogers, Lieutenant T. R., I.N.	1
Rose, Surgeon-Major H. Cooper, M.D. (*Royal East Middlesex Militia*)	1
Russell, Dr. William Howard, LL.D.	1
Sanders,* Mrs. J. P.	1
Sawyer, Captain John, I.N.	1
Sconce, Lieutenant G. C., I.N. (*Emigration Officer and Nautical Surveyor, Board of Trade*)	2
Scott, Major W. (*late 2nd Bengal Light Cavalry*)	1
Seaton, Lieutenant Frank L., I.N.	1
Seymour, Admiral Sir Michael, G.C.B. (*late Commander-in-Chief, China and East India Station*)	1
Seymour, Vice-Admiral Sir F. Beauchamp P., K.C.B. (*late Commanding the Channel Squadron*)	1
Selwyn, Rear-Admiral Jasper H.	1
Shand, Livingston, Esq.	1
Sharp, Commander C., I.N.	1
Sheppard, Lieutenant J., I.N.	1
Skottowe,* Mrs. R.	1
Smart, J. D., Esq., I.N.	1
Spratt, Rear-Admiral Thomas A. B., C.B., F.R.S.	1

* Widow of an Officer of the Indian Navy.

	No. of Copies
Steel, Major J. P., R.E.	1
Stephens,* Mrs. John	1
Stiffe, Lieutenant A. W., I.N. (*Director, Persian Gulf Telegraph*)	2
Stradling,* Mrs. R. A.	1
Stradling, Reverend W. L.	1
Sulivan, Admiral Sir Bartholomew J., K.C.B.	1
Sutherland,* Mrs. A.	1
Sweny, Lieutenant M. A., I.N.	1
Tarleton, Vice-Admiral Sir Walter, K.C.B. (*late Admiral Superintendent, Naval Reserves*)	1
Taylor, Commander A. D., I.N. (*Superintendent, Marine Survey Department, Calcutta*)	10
Taynton, R. W., Esq., I.N.	1
Templer, Lieutenant C. B., I.N.	1
Ternan, Colonel A. H.	1
Tobin, Sir Thomas, Knt.	1
Tozer, Lieutenant M. P. S., I.N.	6
Tribe, Captain T. (*late Acting-Master I.N.*)	1
Trollope, Lieutenant J. H., I.N.	1
Tronson, Captain J., I.N.	1
Tuckwell, E. Esq., I.N.	1
Turner, Lieutenant-General H. Blois, R.E.	1
Turner, Major W.	1
Turner, Frank, Esq.	1
Twynam, Captain T. S. H., I.N.	1
Umphelby, Mrs. M.	1
Vaughan, Surgeon-Major J. (*late of the Bombay Army*)	1
Walford, Reverend J. Stewart	1
Walker, General Sir E. Walter F., K.C.B. (*late Scots Guards*)	1
Walker, Mrs. A. S.	1
Ward, Commander C. Y., I.N.	2
Webb-Peploe, Major D., M.P.	1
Wellesley, Admiral G. G., C.B. (*Senior Naval Lord Commissioner of the Admiralty; late Commander-in-Chief, Indian Navy*)	1
Wetherall, Lieutenant W. A., I.N.	2
Whalley, Captain J. Lawson (*1st Royal Lancashire Militia*)	1
White, Lieutenant-General W. G.	1
Wilkie, Colonel David	1
Williams, W. H. D., Esq., I.N.	1
Williams, Surgeon-Major Lloyd (*late of the Bombay Army*)	1
Wilson, Lieutenant C. P., I.N. (*Professional Member, Harbour and Marine Department, Board of Trade*)	1
Wilson, Sidney, Esq., I.N.	1
Winn, Lieutenant F. D. W., I.N.	1
Wollaston, Frederic W., Esq.	1
Wolseley, Major-General Sir Garnet J., G.C.M.G., K.C.B. (*Council of India*)	1
Wood,* Mrs.	1
Wood, Captain A. (*late of the Bombay Army*)	2
Woods, Mrs. E.	1
Young,* Mrs. J. W.	1
Yule, Colonel H., C.B., R.E. (*Council of India*)	1

Total Subscribers 371
„ Copies subscribed 504

* Widow of an Officer of the Indian Navy.

CONTENTS

OF

THE FIRST VOLUME.

CHAPTER I. (1600—1622.)

Introduction — Early Voyages of the East India Company's Ships — The Company's first *Firman* from the Great Mogul — Formation of a Local Marine at Surat — Captain Best's Victory over the Portuguese Fleet in Swally Roads, and consequent extension of the Company's Trading Privileges — Captain Downton's Defeat of the Portuguese Fleet — Action between the Company's Ships and the Portuguese Carrack — First Appearance of the Company in the Persian Gulf — Some Account of Ormuz — Capture of Ormuz by the Company's Ships and Expulsion of the Portuguese from the Persian Gulf 1

CHAPTER II. (1623—1698.)

Proposals regarding the Occupation of Bombay — Position of the Company at Surat and in the Persian Gulf — Courten's Association — Effect of the War with Holland on the Company's affairs — Bombay, its cession to the King, and subsequent acquisition by the Company — Gallant Defence of the Town and Factory of Surat by the Marine — Privileges granted to the Company by the Mogul Government — Development of the Surat Marine and Formation of the Bombay portion of the Service — Their Defence of the Surat Factory against the Mahrattas — Threatened Attack on Bombay by the Dutch — The Mogul and Mahratta fleets in Bombay Harbour — Reduction of the Bombay Marine — Gallant Actions fought by the Service — Rebellion at Bombay — Aggressive Conduct of the Company against the Mogul — Heavy Losses incurred by them during the War with France — English Pirates on the Coast of India — Affairs at Surat 46

CHAPTER III. (1699—1754.)

Contentions between the Old and New Companies—Precarious Condition of Bombay—Gallant Conduct of the Company's Seamen at Surat and Bombay—Depredations of the Arab Pirates—Duties of the Indian Marine—Prowess of the Company's Seamen at Carwar—Rise of the Pirate Chief Kanhojee Angria—Expeditions against Angria in 1717 and 1722—Gallant Defence of the 'Morning Star'—Piratical Proceedings of the Angrias—The Mahrattas and the Portuguese—Missions of Captains Gordon and Inchbird of the Marine to the Rajah of Sattara and the Peishwa—Loss, with all hands, of three Ships of the Marine—The Malwan and Cooly Pirates—The Bombay Marine at Tellicherry—Reduction of the Service in 1742, and Increased Depredations of the Pirates—The War with France—Mutiny of the Crew of the 'Bombay'—Increase of the Marine 84

CHAPTER IV. (1754—1759.)

Early Career of Commodore James—His Defeat of Angria's Fleet—Expedition against Severndroog—Capture of the Castle—Surrender of Bancoot—Operations against Gheria, and Destruction of the Power of Angria—Subsequent Services of Commodore James; his Retirement and Death—Operations during the War with France—Actions with the French Fleet—Affairs at Surat—Capture of the Town and Castle of Surat—Assumption by the Marine of the Tunkha and Duties as Mogul's Admiral 125

CHAPTER V. (1759—1790.)

Loss of Gombroon—Operations against Hyder Ally's Seaports—Capture of Tannah and Death of Commodore Watson—Commodore Moore's Action with the Shumsher Jung—Desperate Action between the 'Ranger' and Mahratta Fleet—Affairs in the Red Sea and Persian Gulf—Operations against Kharrack—The Bombay Marine at the Siege of Bussorah by the Persians—A Retrospect of the Bombay Marine—Construction of the Dry and Wet Docks at Bombay—Services of the Bombay Marine during the War with France and Hyder Ally 152

CHAPTER VI. (1772—1795.)

Surveys by Officers of the Bombay Marine—The First Surveying Expedition—Lieutenant Blair's Survey and Administration of the Andaman Islands—Lieutenant McCluer's Surveys in the Persian Gulf and West Coast of India—The Loss of the 'Antelope' on the Pelew Islands and Escape of the Crew—Captain McCluer's Mission to the Pelew Islanders—His Surveys on the New Guinea Coast—Adventures and Death of Captain McCluer—Estimate of his Career and Character—Lieutenant Hayes' Surveys in the Eastern Archipelago . 185

CHAPTER VII. (1793—1810.)

Gallant Action of the 'Vigilant,' Lieutenant Hayes, with Sanganian Pirates—Lieutenant Hayes' Services Ashore and Afloat—Services of the Company's Ships during the Revolutionary War—The Reduction of Ceylon and the Eastern Islands—The 'Bombay' frigate at Coupang—Brilliant Defence of the 'Intrepid'—Reduction of Ternate by Captain Hayes, and Action with Magindanao Pirates—Reorganization of the Bombay Marine—Strength of the Service in 1802—Occupation of Perim—The Expedition to Egypt—Services of the Marine in Sumatra and in the Persian Gulf—Loyalty of the 'Aurora's' Marines—The Reduction of Mauritius—The Services of Lieutenant D. Macdonald . 202

CHAPTER VIII. (1811—1816.)

Services of the Marine at the Reduction of the Island of Java and its Dependencies—The Expeditions to Palimbang and Samarang—Gallantry of Lieutenant Deane in the Sambas River—Expedition against the Rajahs of Sambas and Boni—Services of Lieutenant Deane—Gallant conduct of the Marine at Macassar—Rescue of the crew of H.M.S. 'Alceste,' by the 'Ternate' . 237

CHAPTER IX. (1811—1820.)

Operations against the Pirates of Kattywar and Cutch—The 'Malabar,' Captain Maxfield, in Burmah—Expeditions against Malwan and Dwarka—Gallant Services of Lieutenant Grant in Kattywar—Action between the 'Nautilus' and 'Peacock'—Services of the Bombay Marine during the Mahratta War—Shipbuilding in Bombay Dockyard—Operations at Mocha . . 273

CHAPTER X. (1797—1820.)

The Joasmi Pirates; their origin and early history—Attack on the 'Viper'—Their Defeat by the Imaum of Muscat, and Aggressions on the British Flag—The Treaty of 1806—Attack on the 'Fury'—Capture of the 'Minerva' and 'Sylph'—Their Repulse by the 'Nautilus'—The Expedition of 1809; Capture of Ras-ul-Khymah, Luft, and Shinaz—Recognition by Commodore Wainwright and the Bombay Government of the gallantry of the Marine—Renewed Depredations of the Joasmi Pirates—Action between the 'Aurora' and a Joasmi squadron—The Abortive Demonstration before Ras-ul-Khymah in 1816 —Repulse of a Piratical Fleet by the 'Antelope,' and other actions with the Joasmis—The Expedition of 1819; Siege and Capture of Ras-ul-Khymah and Zayah—Complimentary Orders on the Services of the Marine—Final Pacification of the Joasmis, and Signature of the Treaty of the 8th of January, 1820 310

CHAPTER XI. (1820—1824.)

Loss of the 'Ariel'—Repulse of a British force by the Beni-Boo-Ali Arabs—Historical Sketch of the Bombay Marine Battalion—Success of the Second Expedition against the Beni-Boo-Ali—Changes in the Uniform of the Bombay Marine 367

CHAPTER XII. (1804—1828)

Proposed Survey of the Red Sea—Lord Valentia and Captain Keys—Resumption of the Survey by Lieutenants Court and Maxfield—Survey of the China Seas by Lieutenants Ross, Maughan, and Crawford—Services of Lieutenant Court, first Marine Surveyor-General in Bengal—Surveys by Lieutenant Maxfield—Examination of the East Coast of Africa by Captain Smee and Lieutenant Hardy—Death of Captain Court and Appointment of Captain Ross as Surveyor-General in Bengal—His Resignation and Appointment of Captain Lloyd—Surveys by Lieutenants Dominicetti and Collinson—Survey of the Persian Gulf by Lieutenants Maughan, Guy, Brucks, Haines, and other officers 389

CHAPTER XIII.

(THE BURMESE WAR. 1824—1826.)

The Bombay Marine in Burmah—The 'Mercury' at Negrais—Capture of Rangoon—Defence of Kemmendine—Actions up the Irrawaddy of the 8th of July and 4th of August, 1824—Capture of Tavoy and Mergui—Repulse of the Burmese on the 5th of September by the Flotilla—Capture of Martaban—Gallant attack by two Cutters of the Hon. Company's ship 'Hastings'—Operations by Captain Barnes at Ramree on the 17th and 18th of July, and 15th and 16th of October, 1824—Unsuccessful Attack on Ramree on the 3rd of February, 1825 —Repulse of the Burmese by the Hon. Company's brig 'Vestal,' Lieutenant Guy—Commodore Hayes in Arracan—The Attack on Chamballa—Capture of Arracan—Occupation of Ramree and Sandoway—Gallant Conduct of Lieutenant Greer—Repulse of the Enemy at Kemmendine in November and December, 1824—Expedition to Tantabain—Capture of Bassein—Advance up the Irrawaddy—Repulse at, and subsequent Capture of, Donabew—Occupation of Prome—Actions of 1st, 3rd, and 5th of December, 1825—Occupation of Meaday—General Order of Sir James Brisbane—Capture of Mellown—Action at Pagahm Mew—Conclusion of Peace—General Order by the Governor-General—Votes of Thanks by the Court of Directors and the Houses of Parliament—Honours for the Bombay Marine 410

CHAPTER XIV. (1826—1830.)

Changes in the Constitution of the Bombay Marine—The succession of Superintendents—The Flotilla on the Arracan Coast—The Blockade of Berbera—The *matériel* and *personnel* of the Service in 1827—Discussion at the India House on the Condition of the Marine—Remodelling of the Service—Appointment of Captain Sir Charles Malcolm, R.N., as Superintendent—Formation of the Service into a Marine Corps, and its anomalous position as regards Martial Law—The Report of the Finance Committee—Trial of Commander J. C. Hawkins for Slave Dealing—Steam Navigation, and Overland Communication with the East—Commander Wilson and the First Voyage of the 'Hugh Lindsay'—Titular Change of the Service to "Indian Navy" . . 474

HISTORY OF THE INDIAN NAVY.

CHAPTER I.

1600—1622.

Introduction — Early Voyages of the East India Company's Ships — The Company's first Firman from the Great Mogul—Formation of a Local Marine at Surat—Captain Best's Victory over the Portuguese Fleet in Swally Roads, and consequent extension of the Company's Trading Privileges —Captain Downton's Defeat of the Portuguese Fleet—Action between the Company's Ships and the Portuguese Carrack—First Appearance of the Company in the Persian Gulf—Some Account of Ormuz—Capture of Ormuz by the Company's Ships and Expulsion of the Portuguese from the Persian Gulf.

NOTWITHSTANDING all that has been said to the contrary by some English writers, who appear to delight in detracting from their country's merits, there can be no doubt in the minds of those who study the history of our annexations in India, that a more pacific race of Proconsuls than our Governor-Generals, with the exception, perhaps, of Warren Hastings and Lord Ellenborough, never administered the destinies of an empire; but though at the memorable farewell banquets, always given by the Court of Directors to their representatives, on the eve of their departure for the East, "peace, retrenchment, and progress" formed the burthen of the valedictory address of the guest of the evening, yet events were always too strong for them, and, setting out with an honest intention to study the welfare of the many millions committed to their care, they found themselves embroiled in wars, none of their own seeking, and forced to effect annexations from which they were conscientiously averse. And it was so from the beginning. Had the East India Company, in the early years of their existence at Surat, where, as a corporation of traders, they lived from year to year on sufferance, the humble dependents of the Great Mogul and his Governor—had they, in those far off days, not been subjected to "the whips and scorns of time, the oppressor's wrong, the proud man's contumely," they would never have developed into the gigantic political corporation which overshadowed the East and made the name of Briton as respected throughout the length and breadth of the Asiatic continent as ever was that of the Roman legionary in the proudest days of Rome's ascendancy in Europe.

From the time of their first setting foot in India, and establishing a factory under the firman of the Emperor Jehangire, given in December, 1612, in acknowledgment of the gallantry of Captain Best, the commander of the 'Dragon,' they lived in a constant state of alarm, which acted as the best provocative to the military proclivities that only lie dormant in the breasts of all Englishmen. The clamours of a ferocious populace, endeavouring to beat down the gates of their factory, first induced them to engage the services of a small establishment of "peons;" then the necessity they were under of protecting their trading craft from the aggressions of pirates, with which those seas swarmed, compelled them to build, equip, and man a small fleet of "grabs" and "galivats," the germ of the Indian Navy, whose seamen were landed, when necessary, to defend the factory against the hostile assaults of fanatical mobs or the attacks of Sevajee's wild Mahrattas; later on, convinced of the necessity of having an insular emporium for their trade, whence they could carry on their peaceful avocations without being subjected to the oppression of native rulers, the President and Council of Surat accepted the offer of the King's government, and acquired the island and port of Bombay; and lastly, now being a territorial power, they required soldiers to garrison the fortress, and, as they acquired other possessions on the Coromandel Coast and in Bengal, continued their enlistments until the "Company of Merchants trading to the East Indies" developed into a political organization with enormous standing armies, which overcame all military rivals, European and Native, and, finally, overran the entire peninsula from Peshawur to Cape Comorin, and even carried the British flag to the Hindoo Koosh on the one side, and to the confines of Ava on the other.

Surat, the earliest of the British settlements in India, was also the first home of the Bombay Marine, which, in process of time, developed into the Indian Navy; and this being so, it will be necessary that we should briefly recapitulate the events that led to the formation of this, the first of the factories of that famous Company, which was destined to rival the military achievements of the most powerful empires of ancient and modern times, but, nevertheless, after defying the sword of Sikh, Mahommedan, and Mahratta, succumbed to the stroke of a pen of a Minister of State. Passing strange as is the story of the rise and progress of the greatest of corporations, nothing in its marvellous career is more astonishing than the manner of its disappearance. Burke, speaking in the latter part of the last century, said :—" The commission of the Company began in commerce, and ended in Empire ;" but had this eloquent censor of its first Governor-General lived to the year 1858, he would have regarded as an avenging Nemesis the fate that ended "the commission" of the great Company, not "in empire," but in its annulment by that still mightier power, the will of the British nation as expressed by the majority of the House of Commons.

On the 8th of July, 1497, Vasco Da Gama sailed from Belem on a voyage, the successful result of which was destined to open a new world of commerce and conquest to the maritime nations of Europe. The Cape, first doubled by Bartholomew Diaz, was passed on the 20th of November, and, on Christmas Day, he first saw the land which he called Tierra de Natal in honour of the day. The shores of India were sighted on the 17th of May, 1498, and, a few days later, he cast anchor in Calicut, the capital of the Zamorin. Further expeditions followed in rapid succession, under Cabral and other admirals, and the Portuguese, led by Almeida and Albuquerque, established themselves not only at Goa in 1510, but in the island of Ormuz, or Hormúz, in the Persian Gulf, though the latter great Viceroy suffered defeat in his attack on Aden. After the death of Albuquerque, the Portuguese power began visibly to decline in the East, and though his countrymen defeated the Guzerat fleet at Choul, in 1527, and levied contributions upon Tannah and Bassein, which they sacked and burned, they were forced to stand a siege at Diu, where, led by Antonio de Silveira, they displayed the most conspicuous valour and resolution. Until the middle of the sixteenth century, Indian productions reached England through the hands of the Venetians, who carried on an extensive and lucrative trade with Hindostan, viâ Egypt and the Red Sea, thus anticipating the route by which trade now pours into Europe. A commercial expedition, viâ Russia and the Caspian Sea, to Bokhara, was undertaken in 1558, by Mr. A. Jenkinson, but the venture failed commercially, and Jenkinson reported "that the merchants are so poor, and bring so few wares, that there is no hope of any trade worth following."[*] During the sixteenth century attempts were made by the Cabots, Frobisher, Davis, and others, to reach India by the North-West passage, and Sir Hugh Willoughby attempted the North-East passage by Norway. In December, 1577, Drake set out on his celebrated voyage to the Pacific by the Straits of Magellan, during which he visited the Moluccas and Java, and, laden with the plunder of the Spanish possessions in South America, returned to Plymouth by the Cape of Good Hope

[*] Mr. W. D. Cooley's "History of Maritime and Inland Discovery."

route, after an absence of two years and ten months. Inflamed by his great success, Raleigh, Gilbert, and other Englishmen, fitted out expeditions at their own expense; and Thomas Cavendish explored the Indian Ocean, and, having visited the Ladrone and Philippine groups, returned by the Cape, and cast anchor at Plymouth on the 9th of September, 1588, after an absence of two years and two months. But these were little better than buccaneering ventures, and it was nearly a century after the voyage of Vasco Da Gama that an effort was made to reach the East Indies for purposes of trade.*

On the 10th of April, 1591, three ships, the 'Penelope,' commanded by George Raymond, the 'Royal Merchant,' by Abraham Kendal, and the 'Edward Bonaventure,' by James Lancaster, sailed from Plymouth for India by the Cape route. The 'Royal Merchant' returned home, with the sick, from Saldanha Bay, the 'Penelope' was supposed to have foundered in a hurricane off Cape Corrientes, and the 'Edward Bonaventure' continued her voyage, and, passing Cape Comorin in May, 1592, carried on privateering in the Bay of Bengal and the neighbouring waters against Portuguese ships with much success. At length the crew mutinied, and, while on the return voyage to England, Captain Lancaster was deserted by the ship in the West Indies, but ultimately made his way to England, where he landed on the 24th of May, 1594, after an absence of three years and six weeks. In the following year a Dutch expedition of four ships, under Houtman, sailed from the Texel, and, after establishing the fact that a direct and lucrative trade with the East was possible, of which the Dutch subsequently took advantage, returned to Amsterdam in August, 1598.†

In the last year of the sixteenth century, the English East India Company made its first appearance on the stage of history. On the 22nd of September, 1599, an association of Merchant Adventurers was formed in London for the purpose of prosecuting a voyage to the East, the aggregate sum embarked being £30,000. Queen Elizabeth directed Fulke Greville, afterwards Lord Brooke, to report upon the memorial of the English merchants, and, this report being of a favourable character‡—though Greville makes the egregious error of confounding Taprobane, or Ceylon, with Sumatra—the Queen signified her approval of the projected voyage. The manage-

---

* Four gentlemen, members of the Turkey, or Levant, Company, journeyed to India by Aleppo, Bagdad, Ormuz and Goa; and one of the number, Ralph Fitch, who alone returned in 1591, published an account of the journey, which appears in Vol. IX. of Pinkerton's "Collection of Voyages and Travels."

† The history of the rise of the Dutch East India Company, may be perused in Vol. I. of Harris' "Collection of Voyages and Travels."

‡ Fulke Greville's Report, as also the Memorial of the Merchants, appears in Bruce's "Annals of the Hon. East India Company," Vol. I., pp. 115–126.

ment was intrusted to twenty-four directors, exclusive of Alderman (afterwards Sir James) Smith, the first Governor. The fleet consisted of the four following vessels:—the 'Red Dragon,' two hundred men, 600 tons, commanded by Captain James Lancaster, with the title of General, or Admiral, of the fleet; the 'Hector,' one hundred men, 300 tons, Captain William Davis; the 'Ascension,' eighty men, 260 tons; the 'Susan,' eighty men, 240 tons; and a pinnace, forty men, 100 tons.

The charter, which occupies twenty-six pages of printed quarto type, was granted on the 31st of December, 1600, and specifies that "Our most dear and loving cousin, George, Earl of Cumberland,* and our well beloved subjects, Sir John Hart, of London, Knight, Sir John Spencer, of London, Knight, Sir Edward Michelborne, Knight, William Cavendish, Esq.," also nine Aldermen of London, and other individuals specially named, to the number of two hundred and eighteen, have petitioned that they "at their own adventure, costs, and charges, as well as for the honour of our realm of England, as for the increase of our navigation, and advancement of trade and merchandize, within our said realm, and the dominions of the same, might adventure and set forth one or more voyages, with convenient number of ships and pinnaces, by way of traffic and merchandize to the East Indies, in the countries and parts of Asia and Africa, and to as many of the islands, ports and cities, towns and places, thereabouts, as where trade and traffic may, by all likelihood, be discovered, established, or had." In accordance with their memorial, Her Majesty constituted the petitioners, "a body corporate and politic, in deed and in name, by the name of *The Governors and Company of the Merchants trading unto the East Indies*," empowering them and their successors, in that name and capacity, to exercise all the rights and privileges of a body corporate. The charter prescribed the mode of management, and the countries within the limit of which they possessed the exclusive traffic, which embraced all ports, islands, and places of Asia, Africa, America, between the Cape of Good Hope and the Straits of Magellan; while the Queen bound herself and her heirs not to grant trading licences within the limits of the charter to any person whatever "without the consent" of the Company. Other privileges declared the exports of the first four voyages free of duty, credit to be given on the payment of import dues, and permission to export annually the sum of £30,000 in bullion or coin.

The four vessels above-named, together with the 'Guest,' victualler, of 100 tons, left Woolwich on the 13th of February, 1601, and finally quitted Dartmouth on the 22nd of April. The

* The narrative of this Earl's voyage to the Azores appears in Vol. I. of Pinkerton's "Voyages and Travels."

Cape was doubled on the 1st of November, and, without sighting India, they continued their voyage to the Nicobar Islands, and thence for Acheen, on the north-west extremity of Sumatra. They now commenced privateering operations against Portuguese shipping, which appeared to be more to their liking than peaceful trading. The 'Ascension' and 'Susan' were sent to England with cargoes of cinnamon, cloves, and pepper, and Lancaster continued his cruise with the 'Dragon' and 'Hector;' having taken valuable cargoes at Bantam, in the Island of Java, where he established a regular factory, Lancaster sailed for England, and cast anchor in the Downs on the 11th of September, 1603. The pecuniary results were eminently satisfactory, the returns being no less than ninety-five per cent. on the capital invested. On a second voyage the same ships were employed, though Captain Henry Middleton sailed in the 'Red Dragon' as admiral, and Captain Sufflet in the 'Hector' as second in command. The ships sailed on the 25th of March, 1604, and arrived in Bantam Roads on the 20th of December, whence the 'Hector' and 'Susan,' having completed their cargoes, set sail for England, the two other vessels proceeding to the Moluccas. Owing to the intrigues and opposition of the Dutch, Captain Middleton returned to Bantam, whence he sailed for Europe on the 6th October, and cast anchor in the Downs on the 6th of May, 1606. Notwithstanding that the 'Susan' was lost, and, that of the £60,000 adventured on this voyage, only £1,142 was expended in goods, the returns nearly doubled the capital, a result which was rather due to successful privateering than to honest trading.

The third voyage, for which £53,000 was subscribed, of which sum £7,280 was expended in goods, was undertaken in 1607, the ships being the 'Dragon,' Captain Keeling, who acted as admiral; the 'Hector,' Captain Hawkins; and the 'Consent,' of 115 tons, Captain David Middleton. The latter, who left England on the 12th of March, made the voyage alone, and reached Bantam on the 14th of November, whence he proceeded to the Moluccas, where he was unsuccessful in procuring a cargo; but he was so fortunate as to fall in with a Java junk from Amboyna, whose cargo of cloves he purchased for £2,948 15s., and, on his arrival in England in the following December, sold for £36,287. It was no wonder that such enormous profits excited the cupidity of adventurers, and that the Company jealously resented the granting of licenses by King James I. to any other parties. The 'Dragon' and 'Hector' sailed from the Downs on the 1st of April, 1607, and proceeded in company to Socotra, where the two ships separated, Captain Keeling proceeding to Sumatra and Bantam, and Captain Hawkins direct to Surat—the 'Hector' being thus the first of the Company's ships that anchored in an Indian port,* the previous voyagers having only visited the islands in the Indian Ocean, as Sumatra, Java and Amboyna. Hawkins, considering that there was a good opportunity of benefiting himself as well as his masters, resolved to remain at Surat for the purpose of founding a factory, and accordingly ordered his chief officer to proceed in the 'Hector' to Bantam and join Captain Keeling. He had brought a letter from King James to the Great Mogul, and thought he could not do better than proceed to Agra and deliver it in person. This was the first occasion on which an Englishman, representing the Company, made his appearance at the Court of the Mogul, and, apart from its political importance, considerable interest attaches to it in connection with this narrative, as Hawkins was an officer of the Indian Marine. Little thought that mighty potentate, Jehangire,† when he graciously received the ship-captain at the foot of his throne, that, in the humble suppliant for permission for his fellow-countrymen to trade with a distant port of his Empire, he saw before him the representative of the nationality which, by its maritime supremacy chiefly, grew gradually from a "puny infant"—as, a few years later, the Agent of the East India Company called their commercial settlement in Gombroon, or Bunder Abbas—to the strong-limbed giant who was to subvert the dynasty that Baber had founded, and Akbar and Aurungzebe built up and strengthened with such assiduous care.‡

* This is the account given by Beveridge in his "History of India," Vol. I., page 245. According to other writers, Captain Keeling proceeded to Surat, and having landed Mr. Finch to form a factory, sent Captain Hawkins to the Great Mogul at Agra. Orme speaks of an Englishman named Mildenall, who was the bearer of a letter from Queen Elizabeth to the Emperor Akbar, and arrived at Agra in the year 1603. After a residence there of three years, having obtained a firman for freedom of trade from the Emperor Jehangire, he proceeded to Persia, whence he again repaired to Agra, where he died.

† Jehangire means the "Conqueror of the World," though, unlike his great father, Akbar, this prince was a great tyrant and debauchee, without either talent or courage.

‡ From a pamphlet published in 1615, called "Trade's Increase," we gain information as to the number and size of the ships in that year belonging to the East India Company. "You have built," says the writer, apostrophizing the Company, "more ships in your time, than any other merchant's ships, besides what you have bought out of other trades, and all those wholly belonging to you. There hath been entertained by you since you first adventured, one-and-twenty ships, besides the now intended voyage of one new ship of seven hundred tons, and happily some two more of increase. The least of your shipping is of fourscore ton, all the rest are goodly ships of such burthen as never were formerly used in merchandise; the least and meanest of these last is of some hundred and twenty ton, and so upward even to eleven hundred ton. You have set forth some thirteen voyages; in which time you have built of these, eight new ships, and almost as good as built the most of the residue, as the 'Dragon,' the 'Hector,' &c." The same writer thus describes a ship, called, like the pamphlet, the 'Trade's Increase.' "It was a ship of eleven hundred tons, for beauty, burthen, strength, and sufficiency surpassing all merchant's ships whatsoever. But, alas! she was but shown; out of a cruel destiny, she was overtaken with an untimely death in her youth and strength."

Soon after Hawkins' arrival at Agra on the 16th of April, 1609, Jehangire, after promising to grant all the trade privileges solicited for the Company, proposed to him to remain permanently at his Court as the English representative, on a salary which was to begin at £3,200 a-year. Hawkins consented to the proposal, as he quaintly said in a letter to his employers giving his reasons:—" Trusting upon his promise, and seeing it was beneficiall both to my nation and myselfe, being dispossessed of the benefit which I should have reaped, if I had gone to Bantam, and that after halfe a doozen of yeeres, your worships would send another man of sort in my place, in the meantime I should feather my neast and do you service; and, further, perceiving great injuries offered us by reason the King is so farre from the ports, for all which causes above specified, I did not think it amiss to yield unto his request." But the Court nobles and some Portuguese Jesuits intrigued against this new Court favourite, whom they regarded as an interloper, and Hawkins, fearful of being poisoned, appealed to the Emperor who proposed that he should marry " a white mayden out of his palace," the orphan daughter of an Armenian Christian Not long after his marriage, Hawkins found that the fickle monarch had got tired of him, and, so far from " feathering his nest," he did not receive even the promised salary, while all the commercial privileges conferred on the English were cancelled; he, accordingly, left Agra, and made his way to Surat.

In the meantime the 'Hector' had proceeded to Bantam to join Captain Keeling, who assumed command of her, having sent the 'Dragon' to England with her cargo. Captain Keeling first proceeded to the Moluccas and then to Bantam, whence having placed the factory on a more satisfactory footing, he sailed for England, which was reached on the 9th of May, 1610 During the absence of the 'Hector,' two other ventures had been fitted out, the first consisting of two vessels, the 'Ascension' and 'Union,' which proved a total failure, the former being lost in the Gulf of Cambay, and the latter, while returning in the Bay of Biscay. The second venture, consisting of one ship, called the 'Expedition,' Captain David Middleton, was more fortunate; she sailed on the 24th of April, 1609, and returned to England with a valuable cargo obtained at the Moluccas, the profits of which, even including the losses of the previous voyage, amounted to no less than two hundred and thirty-four per cent.

As, owing to the opposition of the Portuguese at Surat, it became evident that the Company's ships must be prepared to repel force by force, for which more ships would be required an application was made to King James in 1609, when only six years of the original fifteen granted by the charter remained unexpired, for a new deed. This was granted, the number of members being increased from two hundred and eighteen to two hundred and seventy-six, and the provisions against "interlopers" being made more stringent, while the charter was made perpetual, with a clause reserving to the Crown power to recall it "after three years' warning." Three vessels were now fitted out for a sixth voyage at a cost of £82,000, of which the goods cost £21,500. The command of this expedition was given to Sir Henry Middleton, the leader of the second voyage, who hoisted his flag on board the 'Trade's Increase,' a vessel of 1,100 tons burden. In consequence of the report of the factors at Bantam and the Moluccas, that the cloths and calicoes imported from India were in great request in those islands, and their recommendation that a trade should be opened at Surat and Cambay to supply them with those commodities for exchange for the spices and other products of the islands, Sir Henry Middleton was directed to steer for the western coast of India. He sailed in the spring of 1610, and proceeded to Aden, where he left the 'Peppercorn,' the second largest of his vessels, and then steered for Mocha, where the native pilots ran his flagship aground. Sir Henry Middleton, fearing that she could not be got off, sent ashore a portion of her cargo, and landed with some of his crew, when he was taken prisoner by the Arabs. After a long detention and the loss of many of his men, he obtained his release, recovered his ships and sailed for Surat, where he anchored on the 26th of September, 1611. Here he found a Portuguese squadron, consisting of seven ships lying outside the roads, and thirteen smaller vessels inside the bar. They had heard of his arrival in the Red Sea, and, though the English were not then at war with Portugal, now made him aware that they disputed his right to trade at Surat, and would not even allow him to communicate with the Englishmen who had been left there by Captain Hawkins. This arbitrary proceeding the Portuguese admiral justified on the ground that he was invested with the office of Captain-Major, an office which made him guardian of all the northern coast of India, and warranted him in seizing all vessels which presumed to trade without his carta or permit. Such a right would have made the Company's charter little better than waste paper, and Sir Henry Middleton at once declared his determination not to recognise it.

In the correspondence which ensued, he told the Captain-Major that he had been sent by the King of England with a letter and rich presents to the Great Mogul, in order to establish the trade which his countrymen had already commenced; and that, as India was a country free to all nations, and neither the Mogul nor his people were under vassalage, he was determined to persevere, at all hazards, and, if necessary, to repel force by force. When he gave this answer, he was in the belief that an extensive and lucrative trade had been, or was about to be, established by the Company at Surat; but the information which he shortly after received, convinced him that for the present all idea of establishing such a trade must be abandoned.* Captain Hawkins, by the information he imparted on his return from Agra, made it evident that no trading privileges were to be expected from Jehangire while the Portuguese, being able to support their pretentions by force, appeared to him the European Power whom it was most conducive to his interests to propitiate. If he had any doubts as to the impossibility of trading at Surat in the present position of affairs, it would have been dissipated by the natives themselves, who confessed that so long as the Portuguese retained their ascendency, they durst not venture to incur their displeasure. Their advice, therefore, was that the English vessels should quit Surat for the port of Gogo, in the Gulf of Cambay, where it was said the Portuguese would be less likely to interfere. Sir Henry Middleton had another plan in view; and, after taking on board Captain Hawkins and his wife, who had arrived from Agra, and the Englishmen who had been left at Surat, he called a council for the purpose of determining their future course. "At this council," says Sir Henry, "I propounded whether it would be best to goe from hence directly for Priaman, Bantam, &c., or to returne to the Red Sea, there to meet with such Indian shippes as should be bound thither; and for that they would not deal with us at their owne doores, wee having come so far with commodities fitting their countrie, nowhere else in India vendable, I thought we should doe ourselves some right, and them no wrong, to cause them barter us; wee to take their indicoes and other goods as they were worth, and they to take ours in lieu thereof." The latter proposal was carried unanimously, and Sir Henry Middleton returned to the Red Sea and continued his course of compelling the traders to barter their goods for those he could not dispose of at Surat; and it is very probable that many acts of violence were committed under the pretence of legitimate trading. But seamen of the school of Drake, Frobisher, and Hawkins, were not likely to be very squeamish; as the Scotch proverb has it, "it's a far cry to Loch Awe," and there was small chance of their being called to account on their return to England.

In the meantime the Company fitted out another expedition consisting of three vessels, the 'Clove,' 'Hector,' and 'Thomas,' which sailed from England on the 18th of April, 1611, under command of Captain John Saris. As his destination was the ports in the Red Sea, a firman was obtained from

* See Beveridge's "History of India," Vol. I., page 248.

Constantinople, through the intervention of the British Ambassador, which was addressed to all the "great Viceroys and beglerbegs who are on the way, both by sea and land, from my most happy and imperial throne, to the confines of the East Indies," who were strictly enjoined "kindly and courteously to entertain and receive the merchants and subjects of Great Britain, coming or passing through or by any of our dominions, with a view to trade to the territories of Yemen, Aden and Mocha, and the parts adjoining, by assisting and relieving them with all things necessary for themselves, their men and ships;" and, in general, by yielding unto them "such offices of benevolence and humanity as shall be meet and convenient to be yielded unto honest men and strangers undertaking so long and painful a voyage." But Captain Saris, like Sir Henry Middleton, was doomed to disappointment, and on his arrival at Socotra, received a letter which had been left by Sir Henry Middleton, acquainting him with his proceedings, and warning him against Turkish treachery. Though his hopes of peaceful trade were now faint, he determined to test the efficacy of the firman, and with that view sailed directly for Mocha. His reception was encouraging, and, by judicious management and the exercise of forbearance, past jealousies and fears might have been forgotten; but there seems to have been little sincerity on either side, and Saris, on meeting with some obstructions, hastily quitted the port and returned to the Straits of Babelmandeb. Here he found Sir Henry Middleton engaged in pillaging, and instead of repudiating his proceedings, was tempted to become a sharer in them. Sir Henry's account of the compact for "romaging the Indian ships," is as follows:—"At last we agreed, and sealed it in writings interchangeable, that he should have one-third part of what should be taken, paying for the same as I did, for the service of his three ships in the action; leaving the disposing of the ships afterwards to me, who had sustayned the wrongs."

When by means of these violent proceedings, flimsily disguised under the name of barter, the depredators had possessed themselves of a sufficient quantity of Surat cloth and other Indian goods, for which a ready market could be found in the Indian Archipelago, they set sail in that direction. Sir Henry Middleton was again unfortunate; and, on learning that the 'Trade's Increase,' which he had ordered to follow while he went in advance with the 'Peppercorn,' had been wrecked on a coral reef, died of chagrin at the Isle of Machian, one of the Moluccas. Captain Saris, after spending some time in the same group, sailed for the Isles of Japan, where the Company had resolved to establish a factory. On the 11th of June, 1613, he cast anchor near Firando. Though he found the Dutch already installed, and disposed, not only to watch, but to thwart, his proceedings, a letter from the King of England, and a valuable present to the Emperor, procured him a favourable reception, and he had little difficulty in making arrangements for permanent trade. The voyage commanded by Sir Henry Middleton, notwithstanding the loss of the 'Trade's Increase,' yielded one hundred and twenty-one per cent; that by Captain Saris, two hundred and eighteen per cent. But it is evident, from the above account of their proceedings, derived from Beveridge's "History of India," that these returns have no title whatever to be classed, as they usually are, under the head of mercantile profits. About the same time that Captain Saris set out on his voyage, a single vessel, the 'Globe,' had been despatched from England, under the command of Captain Anthony Hippon. Instead, however, of proceeding to Bantam or the Red Sea, the 'Globe' sailed for the Coromandel Coast, being the first Company's trading vessel to visit these shores, to which the Portuguese and Dutch had long before repaired. But the Dutch, who were in superior force, would not permit Captain Hippon to trade at Pulicat, and, after visiting Masulipatam, near which, at a place called Petapoli, he left some people to form the nucleus of a factory, he proceeded to Bantam, and thence to Patany on the east coast of the Malay peninsula, and Siam, at both of which places he established factories.

To Captain Hippon, therefore, belongs the honour of having been the founder of those factories in the Bay of Bengal, which developed into magnificent trading establishments, and, ultimately, gave place to our Presidency cities of Calcutta and Madras.

Owing to the opposition experienced from the Dutch and Portuguese, it soon became apparent to the Directors of the East India Company, that, if they were desirous of continuing and developing the trade, which, notwithstanding all losses and obstructions, gave clear profits, seldom below one hundred, and often more than two hundred, per cent., on the capital invested on the voyage,* they must be prepared to oppose force by force. As a result of this determination they equipped their vessels for fighting, as well as trading, purposes, and despatched a squadron sufficiently powerful to repel aggression. The ships consisted of the 'Dragon' and 'Hoseander' (or 'Osiander,') afterwards joined by the 'James' and 'Solomon;' and the command of the squadron was entrusted to Captain Thomas Best.

The two first vessels sailed from Gravesend on the 1st of

---

* Bruce's "Annals of the Honourable East India Company," Vol. I., pp. 152-163. In this valuable work, published in 1810, a full account may be found of the early proceedings of the Company, whose historiographer Mr. Bruce was.

February, 1612, and arrived in the Swally,* or roadstead of Surat, on the 5th of September. Notwithstanding the discouraging account given by Captain Hawkins, little difficulty was found in opening a communication with the town; and Mr. Kerridge, who appears to have been a factor, or supercargo, on board the 'Hoseander,' was soon able to put Captain Best in possession of a sealed certificate, giving the English authority to trade. As it wanted some of the requisite formalities, some doubts were entertained of its validity, and, before these were solved, the Portuguese made their appearance.

The Portuguese fleet consisted of four galleons, and more than twenty armed vessels, which had come with the avowed determination of expelling the English. The Admiral's ship mounted thirty-eight guns, and the three others twenty-eight and thirty. The armed vessels, called by Orme, "frigates," had no cannon, but seemed intended for boarding and for service in shoal water. This fleet appeared off the bar of Surat, on the 28th of October, and, on being joined by other ships in the river, the number of so-called frigates now amounted to forty sail. Captain Best was well prepared for them; and, deeming it unnecessary to wait till he was attacked, at once assumed the offensive.

"On the 29th of October," says Orme, "Captain Best bore down from the roadstead of Swally, and engaged the Vice-Admiral's ship, separated by the tide and sands from the others. Placing himself in the 'Dragon,' at a distance of two cables' length, 'I began,' he says, 'to play upon him with both great and small shot, that by an houre we had well peppered him.'" A shot from her sunk his long boat and another wounded his mainmast. The day after he engaged all four of the ships; and three of them, either from ignorance or confusion, grounded on the sands, where they would have upset, if the crews of the "frigates" had not shored them up with their yards until the tide and further assistance got them afloat again. On the 31st the fight was renewed, and with still more success on the part of the English, who again defeated the Portuguese, and drove "three of their foure shippes on ground on the sands thwart of the Barre of Surat."

* Swally, which formed the seaport for Surat, at which vessels of great burden discharged their cargoes, was a village situated about twelve miles west of the city. The anchorage was in a road, seven miles in length, and one and a-half in breadth, between the shore and a sand-bank which was dry at low water; about midway up this channel was a cove called Swally Hole, where a fleet could lie in tolerable security. We are told that later on, the English and Dutch Companies built warehouses and laid out pleasant gardens at Swally, though Fryer, with his usual pungency of style asserts that the place was infested by "two sorts of vermin, fleas and banyans." During the months between September and March, when the Company's ships usually arrived from Europe, the "bunyas," or native merchants, congregated at Swally, when they pitched tents and built other temporary residences.—*See* Anderson's "English in Western India."

At night a frigate, prepared as a fire ship, bore down on the 'Dragon,' which discovered her in time and sank her. Eighty dead bodies floated to the shore; of the English only two were killed in the three fights. The four succeeding days passed without action, in the repair of damages. Captain Best, not doubting that the Portuguese would follow him, now resolved to try them in the open sea; and, crossing the Gulf of Cambay, anchored on the 9th at Madrasabad, which, at this time, was invested by the Mogul army. From hence he continued cruising along the shores on each hand, in order to learn the soundings, during which, having received several invitations from the Mogul general, who sent guarantees of safe conduct, Captain Best went ashore on the 21st, to his camp, and was much pressed by him to assist in the siege with two pieces of cannon; this, however, he refused, notwithstanding which presents were exchanged, and he was dismissed with civility.

The next day, being the 22nd of November, the four Portuguese galleons again appeared, and at night anchored within gunshot. Early in the morning Captain Best stood towards them, when they weighed and put before the wind; both sides opened fire, until, owing to their superior sailing qualities, the Portuguese got out of range. The next morning, at sunrise, Captain Best stood towards them again, and maintained the fight until noon, when both sides retired. Best, then finding, on examination, that both his ships had expended more than half their store of ammunition, resolved to reserve the remainder for defence, and steered towards Damaun. The Portuguese followed, but did not venture near enough to renew the fight.

On the 27th the two ships, no longer dogged by the Portuguese, anchored at Swally, and renewed the intercourse with their factors at Surat, where the result of the recent fighting had greatly raised the English reputation, even in the opinion of their enemies.

The confirmation of the Articles* by Jehangire, which arrived a few days after, were sent to Swally as a common letter of business, but Captain Best, aware of the intended contempt and its consequences, refused to receive it unless delivered with

* The principal clauses in this treaty were, "that the English should have full freedom of trade in his dominions, that their persons, while ashore, should be protected from the Portuguese; that their imports should pay only three and a-half per cent. as customs; that in cases of death no fees should be demanded, and the goods of the deceased should be delivered up to the first English ship which might subsequently arrive; that in cases of wrong, redress should be speedily obtained; and that an English Ambassador should be received and permitted to reside at the Mogul Court." According to Bruce, this important treaty was finally delivered with much pomp to Captain Best at Swally, on the 6th of February, 1613. Mill makes the date of the battle, November, 1611, and of the treaty, 1612.

the usual formalities. This show of spirit brought the Governor and his son-in-law, the Custom-master, to Swally, who presented it in state on the 11th of December, and congratulated the English Captain on his victory. The goods intended for the factory were immediately landed, and those provided there, received on board. On the 14th the four galleons appeared again, but anchored at a distance. Captain Best sailed in the night of the 17th, and was followed by them for two hours, when they parted company without firing. Near Cannanore he discovered the southern portion of the Portuguese fleet, and took a merchant ship from amongst them, which he sunk, after he had removed the cargo of rice and sugar. He then continued cruising down the coast until the end of February, 1613, when he sailed from Cape Comorin for Atcheen.

The principal factors left by Captain Best at Surat, were Aldworth, Canning, Kerridge, and Withington, and A. Starkey to proceed overland to England, with advices of the settlement of the treaty. Canning was sent with the King's letter and the present, which was of little value, to Agra; and, encountering much opposition, was attacked by robbers, who killed some of his escort, and wounded others, including himself and another Englishman. He arrived at Agra on the 9th of April, and was asked by the Mogul whether the present he brought was sent by the King; upon which he replied, that it was from the merchants. He continued in daily dread of poison from the Portuguese Jesuits, and died on the 29th of May, which confirmed the suspicion of foul play. Andrew Starkey also was poisoned somewhere on the way by two friars. Kerridge was sent from Surat, on the 22nd of June, to supply the place of Canning at Agra.*

From this date the Company assumed a definite position as a trading Corporation, recognized by the Great Mogul, and not as mere interlopers picking up the crumbs of commerce, under sufferance of their European rivals, the Portuguese.

The Company obtained permission to establish factories not only at Surat, but at Ahmedabad, Cambay, and Gogo, which were selected as the best situations.† After these concessions

* Orme's "Oriental Fragments," pp. 329-333.
† In the year 1612, the Company came to a resolution to trade in future as a joint stock corporation only, and a sum of £429,000 was raised, which the Directors apportioned out for four voyages. These expeditions which sailed in the four years, 1613-16, and were termed the tenth, eleventh, twelfth, and thirteenth voyages, consisted respectively, the two first of eight ships, the third of six ships, and the fourth of seven ships, but whereas the average profits of the preceding eight voyages, excluding the fourth, which was wholly unfortunate, amounted to 171 per cent., these four averaged only 87½ per cent.—Bruce, Vol. I., p. 166. A second new joint stock company was started in 1617-18, with a capital of £1,600,000, the number of ships being thirty-six, of 100 to 1,000 tons burden. After the death, in 1616, of Richard Hakluyt, the first historiographer of the East India Company, the journals of the East India captains were handed over

had been obtained, and the establishment of regular trading factories was resolved upon, it became necessary to afford them protection from the aggressions of the Portuguese and the pirates who infested those seas. Hence was formed the nucleus of the service that developed, first into the Bombay Marine, and, ultimately, into the Indian Navy; and which, after an existence of exactly two centuries and a half, terminated its existence, with scanty acknowledgments from its new masters in Westminster. In this year, 1613, when the Indian Marine was first formed, the Company had not a single European soldier, or Sepoy, in their pay, and the British Army had no existence, as the earliest of the regular regiments, whether belonging to the Guards or the Line, was not raised until 1660, the first year of the reign of Charles II.

The Agent at the Surat factory established a small local force of grabs and galivats,* mounting from two to five or six guns,

to Samuel Purchas, who published "Purchas, his Pilgrimes," in 1625, which included the logs of the first twenty voyages, which were, however, set forth in an abridged and mutilated form. Several of the originals have disappeared, and only two, Sir John Lancaster's first voyage in 1601, and Sir Henry Middleton's voyage in 1606, have since been published. Speaking of these journals, Mr. Clements Markham writes in his "Memoir on the Indian Surveys:"—"The rest are still preserved at the India Office, and are numbered in two series; the first, consisting of sixty-eight volumes, extending from 1606 to 1708; and the second, containing the logs of the East India Company's ships, from 1708 to 1832. The Journals of Lancaster, Middleton and Saris are missing, though a copy of the latter is now in the Topographical Depôt of the War Office. The oldest logs at the India Office, are those of Captain Keeling in 1606, and Captain Sharpey in 1607. Among the other journals of the first series, there is a curious treatise on map-making in Thomas Love's log, kept on board the 'Peppercorn' in 1610; Downton's memorial of his second voyage in 1613; the Journal of the junk, 'Sea Adventure,' on her voyage from Firando to Cochin China; the Journal kept in 1621, during a cruise off Manilla, on board a ship in the combined English and Dutch fleets, which sailed from Firando; and journals of other voyages to Aden, Surat, the Persian Gulf, and the Malabar and Coromandel Coasts. Only one of the Arctic voyages set forth by the East India Company has been preserved, and is about to be printed and edited by Sir Leopold McClintock. It is that of Captain Knight, who sailed in 1606, and landing on some frozen shore, was never heard of again." Unhappily among the Indian Records burnt in 1860, were the Minutes and Reports of the Committee of Shipping, "containing a rich mine of information relating to all that concerned the Marine branch of the Company's affairs, as well as the Indian Navy logs, that had been sent home."

* Orme describes as follows the grabs and galivats of his day:—"The grabs have rarely more than two masts, although some have three, and are about 300 tons; but the two-masted grabs are not more than 150 tons. They are built to draw very little water, being very broad in proportion to their length, narrowing, however, from the middle to the bows, where they have a prow, projecting like that of a Mediterranean galley, and covered with a strong deck, level with the main deck of the vessel, from which, however, it is separated by a bulkhead which terminates the forecastle; as this construction subjects the grab to pitch violently when sailing against a head sea, the deck of the prow is not enclosed with sides as the rest of the vessel is, but remains bare, that the water which dashes upon it may pass off without interception. On the main deck, under the forecastle, are mounted two pieces of cannon, nine or twelve-pounders, which point forward through the port-holes cut in the bulkhead and fire over the prow; the cannon on the broadside are from six to nine-pounders. The galivats are large row-boats built like the grab, but of smaller dimensions, the largest rarely

and officered by volunteers from the Company's ships, who traded as well as fought. The Service was very popular. This force, which from the character of the vessels, was long known as the " grab service," was employed for the purposes of affording protection to the Company's trade in the Rivers Taptee and Nerbudda, and in the Gulf of Cambay; and for the convoying, and also the carrying, of goods within the same limits. The Service was not long organised before it had an opportunity of proving its metal, and it is gratifying to add that its first action was a signal victory.

The Portuguese had become so arrogant and overbearing, that they openly quarrelled with the Mogul sovereign, an event favourable to the Company, who at once made common cause with the Emperor Jehangire. Since the departure of Captain Best's squadron, a period of two years and eight months, none of the Company's ships from England had made their appearance at Surat; but, on the 12th of October, 1614, a fleet of four ships was sighted off the factory, commanded by Captain Nicholas Downton, who had been one of Sir Henry Middleton's captains. These ships, named the 'New Year's Gift,' 'Hector,' 'Merchant's Hope,' and 'Solomon,' were respectively of 650, 500, 300 and 200 tons, with crews amounting in the aggregate to six hundred men, of whom many were sick. They had left England on the 11th of March, and had learned off Socotra of Captain Best's successes, and of the firman he had thereby secured from the Mogul Emperor. On his arrival, Downton was first of all saluted with the intelligence that the Portuguese Viceroy of Goa was determined to attack his small squadron with all the ships he could collect, which was not unacceptable news to a man of the temper of the gallant officer. Jehangire was only too glad to have the assistance of such doughty allies, for his ships and commerce were absolutely at the mercy of the Portuguese navy; and, powerful as he was on land, he was helpless on the sea. On the 9th of December, the son of Mocrib Khan, the principal Mogul general and Nabob,* met Captain Downton on the strand at Swally, and cemented the alliance between the two Powers; and, four days later, appeared in sight the Portuguese fleet of twenty-two "frigates," which passed unmolested, although

exceeding seventy tons. They have two masts, of which the mizen is very slight, the main-mast bears only one sail, which is triangular and very large, the peak of it when hoisted being much higher than the mast itself. In general the galivats are covered with a spar deck, made for lightness of split bamboos, and these carry only 'petteraroes,' which are fixed on swivels in the gunwale of the vessel; but those of the larger size have a fixed deck on which they mount six or eight pieces of cannon, from two to four-pounders; they have forty to fifty stout oars, and may be rowed four miles an hour."—Orme's "History of Hindoostan," Vol. I., page 408.

* The word Nabob is a corruption of Nawaub, which, again, is derived from Nayib, and means "deputy;" he was an officer of lower rank than the Soubahdar, who was the Mogul Emperor's viceroy.

near the sands of Swally, for Downton adhered to his resolution of not commencing hostilities. The fleet crossed the Gulf to the road of Gogo, where they burnt one hundred and twenty trading boats, and several ships, of which one was the 'Rehemy,' at this time the largest in the Indian seas; after this the soldiers landed and destroyed several villages, but Gogo, being walled, was safe. The news of this devastation arrived at Surat on the 16th of December, and renewed the suspicion of Mocrib Khan that the English were in league with the Portuguese, because they had not fired on their ships as they passed.

Before their return, Captain Downton weighed from Swally, and anchored off the bar of Surat, in order to protect the communication of his boats with the city. The roadstead is seven miles from the shore; and everywhere along the coast are sands, which afford refuge to vessels of light draught against the approach of heavy ships, of which the "frigates" availed themselves, anchoring much nearer the shore, from whence they chased, even into the river, every boat which appeared, either coming in or going out, whilst others cruised around without let or hindrance. On several nights some bore down, as if they intended to set the English ships on fire, "which," says Orme, "were kept in continual alerts, either of guard, defence, or chase, with very little detriment done or received, until the 29th, when Captain Downton, finding that he could not prevent the cruises of the 'frigates' at the mouth of the river, returned to Swally." On the 16th of January, a second fleet of nearly forty sail appeared from the south, and, joining those already at the bar, went in company into the river to get water, and came out on the following day. Within forty-eight hours there arrived a further reinforcement of nine ships, which were followed by two galleys.

The crews of the Portuguese Marine* in India were composed

---

* What the naval power of the Portuguese in the East was in those days, may be gathered from the "Life of Albuquerque," and from an interesting record of a Portuguese expedition to the Red Sea, which may be found in the "Log-book of Joao de Castro." This Portuguese admiral sailed, in January, 1541, from Goa with seventy-two sail, including twelve ships of war of great size, and two thousand picked soldiers, for the purpose of punishing the Turks who, four years before, had captured Aden and laid siege to the Portuguese settlement at Diu, but were repulsed by Governor Silveira. Joao de Castro was completely successful, and having visited Socotra, Aden, Massowah, Suakim, Toro, near Mount Sinai (which he visited), and Suez, arrived at Goa on the 21st of July, after an absence of seven months and twenty-one days. The original Log-book was sent to his family, but a fair copy, accompanied by drawings, he sent to his patron, the Infante Dom Luiz, at Lisbon, and on the accession of Cardinal Henry in 1578, it was deposited as a national heirloom in the library of the University of Evora. This invaluable work, however, disappeared, but a Portuguese professor, Dr. Carvalho, in 1828, while examining the catalogue of Cottonian MSS. in the British Museum (called after the donor, Sir R. Bruce Cotton), discovered this copy, consisting of sixty folios with fifteen drawings, of which a transcript was published in Paris in 1833. The first notice of the Red Sea, derived from other than ancient records, made its appearance at Venice in 1538, but it only conof two different orders. The fighting men were rated as genuine Portuguese, who, proud of this pre-eminence, refused, unless in cases of extremity, to take part in the services necessary to navigate the vessel, but reserved to themselves the management of the guns and small-arms. The mariners were either slaves or Hindoos of the meaner castes, or Christians born in the country, and considered unworthy of military service. The armament, which now appeared at the bar of Surat, was commanded by the Viceroy of Goa, Don Jeronimo de Azevedo, who hoisted his flag as Admiral, in the 'Todos Santos,' of 800 tons, having on board two hundred and sixty fighting men, of whom thirty were of family and distinction; and twenty-eight pieces of ordnance, which, probably, were of large calibre, for two are expressly said to be 42-pounders. Five others of the ships were from 700 to 400 tons, with from one hundred and eighty to one hundred and forty men, and carrying from twenty to fourteen guns. These six were rated as galleons. The two next in force were each of 200 tons, fifty men, and eight guns; and there was also a pinnace of four guns and eighty fighting men, and two galleys, each having fifty men. The "frigates" had eighteen oars on a side, and were manned with thirty fighting men, besides the rowers, who were probably two to an oar. The numerical strength of the crews of this armament, accordingly, amounted to four thousand three hundred and twenty, and, with the mariners in the larger vessels, made a total of six thousand natives serving with the fleet. The number of Portuguese, or Europeans, was two thousand six hundred, whose duty it was to work* one hundred and thirty-four pieces of cannon, against eighty of much inferior calibre in the English ships and Surat galivats.

Captain Downton considered the success of this armament as involving the certain destruction of English commerce in the Mogul's dominions, reasoning that, if his own ships should be driven from their station in the roads of Surat and Swally, the Portuguese Viceroy, by ravaging the city itself, would compel the Nabob to refuse the English all future resort and intercourse; Captain Downton, therefore, regarding the loss of his ships as of much inferior moment to such a result, deliberately resolved

sisted of two quarto pages. Exclusive of the logs of the Company's ships visiting the Red Sea, our own earliest work was published in 1750, and called "Navigation and Voyages to the Red Sea." The next embraced a series of "Instructions for Sailing from Cape Guardafui to Babelmandeb, and through the Straits," by Captain Norton Hutchinson, of the 'Doddington,' 1753; and, five years later, appeared a "Journal of the 'Latham' to Jeddah." Before the expedition of Sir Home Popham, and the surveys of Captain Court, a few years later, the Red Sea was a *mare incognita*.

* Orme, from whom the above calculation is derived, says, "We have endeavoured to compute the force of the Armada from the depositions in Purchas, of a Portuguese who served in one of the galleons. Faria de Souza relates this campaign; and although differing in some particulars from the English accounts, without partiality to the Portuguese."

to perish with them rather than recede. But like his prototype, Lord Howard of Effingham, who defeated the great Spanish Armada, in 1588,—and we do not deem the comparison unworthy the high renown of that great Admiral,—Captain Downton, we are told, "did not despair that stratagem might avail to supply the defect of force."

The Nabob, terrified by the appearance of the armament, sent his Shabandar, or Custom-master, and several other principal men, to the Viceroy, with a large present of provisions, and many promises to obtain peace; this the haughty Admiral refused, not doubting, like the Spanish Duke of Medina Sidonia, that he could destroy the English ships; after which he intended to exact much severer terms, or the full price of remission.

Early in the morning of the 20th of January, 1615, at low water,* Downton sent the 'Merchant's Hope,' called in the accounts, the 'Hope,' of 300 tons, to anchor at the south entrance of the channel, where the galleons would not have sufficient depth to come near her until the flood was high; the three other ships soon after came out of the cove, but anchored again in the channel. These manœuvres produced the intended effect, which was to induce the Portuguese Admiral to believe that the English ships had quitted Swally, in order to put to sea and avoid an action. The 'Hope' had scarcely anchored, before the whole fleet of the enemy were under sail, in order to stop the channel; the two smaller ships, with the pinnace, which were foremost, simultaneously grappled and boarded the 'Hope,' but the attack, being expected, was well met. Downton, cutting the cables of the three other ships, came down and fired into the enemy's ships entangled with the 'Hope,' the men of which had thrice beat off the Portuguese who had boarded. In despair at finding themselves between two fires, from which they suffered severely, the crews set fire to all the three and took to the water. Upon this a number of the "frigates," which had hitherto given no assistance, came upon the scene, and saved many of the drowning men.

In the meantime the 'Hope' had taken fire in her main and fore rigging, but, nevertheless, her crew managed to disengage her from the three ships, which were blazing fiercely and drove on the sands, where they burnt until overwhelmed by the flood. All this while the galleons kept on the outside of the spit, across which they cannonaded the English ships within the channel, which was answered, but with little loss on either side.

* The Channel of Swally is about a mile and a-half in breadth, and seven in length, and lies between the shore and a sand-bank of this length, which is dry at low water. The ships, when Swally used to be the station, anchored in a cove called Swally-hole, which runs into the land about midway in the channel.

The Portuguese galleons, which had all this while continued at anchor to the northward, fell down the next day to the bar of Surat, where Captain Downton caused them to be watched, suspecting the Viceroy might land and march on the city, in which case he resolved to attack the galleons, deprived of their fighting men; but the Viceroy saw the danger, and only sent the "frigates" into the river, to give moral force to the negotiations which he renewed with the Nabob, who, however, answered as before, that he could not abandon the English. On the 13th, the Viceroy sailed away with all his fleet, except twenty "frigates," a step which created various conjectures concerning his future intentions. Notwithstanding the alarms to which the English ships had been lately exposed, they had continued landing their cargoes and receiving on board the goods provided for England; when all were shipped, as well as the water and provisions, Captain Downton, deeming the fair season too far spent to permit of the enemy's fleet attacking the city, signified his intention of departing to the Nabob, who entreated him to defer it for fifteen days; and, after much seeming objection, he consented to a delay of eight. The Nabob now sent his tents and equipage to Swally, and arrived there himself with a great train on the morning of the 24th of February. On hearing of his arrival, Captain Downton landed with one hundred and twenty armed men, and proceeded to the Nabob's tent, where he was received and entertained with much courtesy. The Nabob returned the visit on board Captain Downton's ship, which he examined with intelligent curiosity, and was escorted to the shore by the Captain; two days after, the Nabob's son and son-in-law came on board to take leave, and, on the following day, several of the principal men of the town.

On the 3rd of March, the English ships weighed from Swally, and saw a fleet of "frigates" coming from the westward into the river, most of which passed in shoal water, out of shot; but the ships fired on the nearest, to give the last testimony of goodwill to their friends on shore. At daybreak, the Portuguese fleet, which was discerned at anchor nearer the shore, weighed and stood after the English ships throughout the day, but lost ground by not anchoring, as they did, on the flood.*
The next day, the 5th of the month, both fleets stood on to the south; but the Portuguese did not gain, although the 'Hope' sailed so ill that the 'Hector' was obliged to take her in tow. The succeeding day, Downton, thinking he had led the enemy's fleet far enough from their own ports and Surat, resolved to let them come up, and then, putting about suddenly, to attack them unexpectedly. He, accordingly, went in his

* Vessels going from Surat to the South, save their ground by anchoring on the flood, unless the wind is very stiff.

The Portuguese galleons, which had all this while continued at anchor to the northward, fell down the next day to the bar of Surat, where Captain Downton caused them to be watched, suspecting the Viceroy might land and march on the city, in which case he resolved to attack the galleons, deprived of their fighting men; but the Viceroy saw the danger, and only sent the "frigates" into the river, to give moral force to the negotiations which he renewed with the Nabob, who, however, answered as before, that he could not abandon the English. On the 13th, the Viceroy sailed away with all his fleet, except twenty "frigates," a step which created various conjectures concerning his future intentions. Notwithstanding the alarms to which the English ships had been lately exposed, they had continued landing their cargoes and receiving on board the goods provided for England; when all were shipped, as well as the water and provisions, Captain Downton, deeming the fair season too far spent to permit of the enemy's fleet attacking the city, signified his intention of departing to the Nabob, who entreated him to defer it for fifteen days; and, after much seeming objection, he consented to a delay of eight. The Nabob now sent his tents and equipage to Swally, and arrived there himself with a great train on the morning of the 24th of February. On hearing of his arrival, Captain Downton landed with one hundred and twenty armed men, and proceeded to the Nabob's tent, where he was received and entertained with much courtesy. The Nabob returned the visit on board Captain Downton's ship, which he examined with intelligent curiosity, and was escorted to the shore by the Captain; two days after, the Nabob's son and son-in-law came on board to take leave, and, on the following day, several of the principal men of the town.

On the 3rd of March, the English ships weighed from Swally, and saw a fleet of "frigates" coming from the westward into the river, most of which passed in shoal water, out of shot; but the ships fired on the nearest, to give the last testimony of goodwill to their friends on shore. At daybreak, the Portuguese fleet, which was discerned at anchor nearer the shore, weighed and stood after the English ships throughout the day, but lost ground by not anchoring, as they did, on the flood.*
The next day, the 5th of the month, both fleets stood on to the south; but the Portuguese did not gain, although the 'Hope' sailed so ill that the 'Hector' was obliged to take her in tow. The succeeding day, Downton, thinking he had led the enemy's fleet far enough from their own ports and Surat, resolved to let them come up, and then, putting about suddenly, to attack them unexpectedly. He, accordingly, went in his

* Vessels going from Surat to the South, save their ground by anchoring on the flood, unless the wind is very stiff.

boat to the three other ships, to give his instructions; but during his absence the flood set in, when his own ship, which carried his flag as Admiral, fell astern of the others. At this time the Viceroy's galleon, sailing well, was far ahead of the rest of his fleet and near enough to have brought Downton to action. The Portuguese gunner, says Orme, proposed to sink the 'Hope' with the two 42-pounders, which seem to have been the pride of the armada; but the officers warned him that the English Admiral had fallen astern with no other intention than to tempt the Viceroy to the trial, when the three other ships would bear down and overwhelm him. Acting upon this discreet advice, he hauled his wind towards the shore, was followed by his fleet, and all were soon out of sight, when the English ships continued their course.* When the Viceroy was afterwards arraigned for various crimes perpetrated during his government, his conduct on this day was one of the articles of accusation, and the very hidalgos, in deference to whose opinion he had refrained from the attack, bore witness against him. The English ships proceeded down the coast, and, on the 10th of the month, the 'Hope' was despatched to England; the other three doubled Cape Comorin on the 19th, and arrived on the 2nd of June at Batavia, where Captain Downton died on the 6th of August, as Orme well adds, " lamented, admired, and unequalled."†

In this affair the Portuguese lost three hundred and fifty men; and, says Mill, "the splendid achievements of the English against an enemy whom the Governments of India were ill able to resist, raised high their reputation for prowess in war." On the other hand, the Mogul fleet took little or no part in the action.

The Emperor Jehangire had already received a request that the English might be permitted to fortify their factory at Surat, which he had referred to his minister, Mocrib Khan, through whom the original firman for trade had been obtained; but there appeared to be no desire to grant the boon, which must have appeared, and rightly, the thin end of the wedge that was to make the Company a territorial power. Mr. Edwardes—the Company's factor at Ahmedabad, who, with Mr. Kerridge, the agent at Surat, may be regarded as the first representatives of the Company in India—proceeded to Agra, and was presented to the Emperor, on the 7th of February, by Asaph Khan, brother of the Empress Noor Mahal, so celebrated in Indian history for her beauty and goodness. During his stay, after the arrival of the news of the Portuguese defeat at Swally,

* Faria De Souza says that the English ships made their acknowledgments to the Viceroy for this resolution of not fighting them, by a salute of blank cartridge as an ironical compliment.
† Orme's "Oriental Fragments," pp. 346 to 356.

Jehangire expressed his satisfaction with the gallantry of the English, and presented him with a firman, directed to the Governor of Surat and Cambay, allowing the English to trade in his dominions. From this circumstance, it may be gathered that the East India Company achieved their first victory and gained their earliest privileges in Western India, through the skill of their naval officers and the valour of their seamen.

In 1615 the Local Marine force appears to have consisted of ten grabs and galivats, and, from this time, may be dated the permanent establishment of the Service. On the 18th of September in this year, a squadron of four of the Company's ships, under the command of that experienced seaman, Captain Keeling, arrived at Surat, having on board Sir Thomas Roe,* appointed Ambassador from King James to the Great Mogul, who was then holding his court at Ajmere. Sir Thomas was successful in obtaining the dismissal of the Governor of Surat, whose conduct had been arbitrary towards the English; and also a treaty, ratified by Jehangire, conceding the privileges already granted to Mr. Edwardes, by which the Company could establish factories in any part of the Empire, specifying Bengal, Scinde, and Surat. Sir Thomas Roe's advice to the Company shows him to be a man of sound sense and sagacity. He says:—"At my first arrival, I understood a fort was very necessary; but experience teaches me we are refused it to our advantage. If the Emperor were to offer me ten, I would not accept of one." His reasons for this opinion are, "firstly, that it be prejudicial to their trade; and secondly, the charge is greater than the trade can bear, for to maintain a garrison will eat all your profit—war and traffic are incompatible. By my consent you shall never engage yourselves but at sea, where you are like to gain as often as to lose." After instancing the Portuguese and Dutch, who "are beggared by keeping of soldiers," he continues—"Let this be received as a rule, that if you will profit, seek it at sea and in quiet trade; for, without controversies, it is an error to affect garrisons and land wars in India." The factors at Surat, being desirous of opening a trade with Persia, sent agents to the court of Shah Abbas, though contrary to Sir Thomas Roe's advice, who said that as the Portuguese were in possession of the ground, it would cost the Company more to protect themselves than they could hope to gain by the speculation. At this time, Surat and Bantam continued to be the chief seats of the Company's factories; but, although agents were sent to Amboyna, Banda, and other islands, they were unable to establish a factory,

* This embassy was sent in compliance with the wishes of the Company, who agreed to defray the expenses. The four ships forming the squadron were the 'Expedition,' 'Dragon,' 'Lion,' and 'Peppercorn.' The fleet was commanded by Captain Keeling, and the account of the voyage was written by Captain Peyton of the 'Expedition.'

owing to the jealousy of the Dutch, who seized two of the Company's ships—the 'Swan' and 'Defence.' This ill feeling eventually culminated on the 27th of February, 1623, in what is known in history as the Massacre of Amboyna, when Captain Towerson, the Company's Agent, and nine Englishmen, were seized and executed, on the pretence that they had entered into a conspiracy for the purpose of taking possession of the Castle of Amboyna.* This sanguinary deed was avenged in 1810, when the place surrendered to the British, just previous to the outbreak of the Java war.

On the 25th September, 1616, four ships arrived at Surat from England, which had left the Land's End on the 13th of March, in company with two others; of these latter one separated, during a violent gale of wind, in the Bay of Biscay, and the other remained behind at the Cape, but both at length got safe to Bantam, whither they were bound. These four ships—the 'Charles,' 'James,' 'Globe,' and 'Unicorn'—were under the command of Captain Benjamin Joseph, a brave and experienced seaman, and made their course, like all which had hitherto come to Surat† through the Mozambique Channel, between Madagascar and the mainland of Africa. Here, amongst the Comoro Islands,‡ they descried, at daybreak of the 5th of August, a Portuguese ship of enormous size,§ known

---

* These events took place notwithstanding the agreement arrived at in London on the 17th of July, 1619, between Commissioners appointed by the Dutch and English Governments, by which free trade was declared in the Eastern islands and on the Coromandel coast, and each Company was to furnish ten ships of war to be employed exclusively in India, for purposes of mutual defence, while a court, consisting of four members of each Company, was also appointed to sit at Batavia.

† Up to this date the ships that had sailed for Surat, all of which, however, did not arrive there, were the following :—The 'Hector,' Captain Hawkins, in 1607-8; the 'Ascension,' Captain Alexander Sharpey, in 1608-9; the 'Trades' Increase,' the 'Peppercorn,' and the 'Darling,' under Sir Henry Middleton, in 1610-11; the 'Dragon' and 'Hoseander,' under Captain Best, in 1612; the 'Expedition,' Captain Christopher Newport, which went to Guadel and Diu, but did not come on to Surat, in 1613; the 'New Year's Gift,' the 'Hector,' the 'Merchant's Hope,' and the 'Solomon,' under Captain Nicholas Downton, in 1614-15; the 'Expedition,' 'Dragon,' 'Lyon,' and 'Peppercorn,' which brought Sir Thomas Roe, and were commanded by Captain Keeling, in 1615-16.—Orme's "Oriental Fragments," p. 375.

‡ The four Comoro Islands lie nearly midway between the north extreme of Madagascar and the African coast. Comoro, the largest and highest of these islands, gives its name to the group, the others being Mohilla, Mayotta, and Johanna; they are all very high, and may be seen from fourteen to twenty leagues in clear weather. The inhabitants are Mahomedans, descendants of Arabs mixed with Africans, and are generally found to be courteous and hospitable; but the natives of Comoro appear not to have merited this character when the Indian ships first traded to India, for the 'Penelope' had part of her crew enticed on shore, and destroyed by the inhabitants of this island.

§ Edward Terry, who was chaplain to Sir Thomas Roe, sailed in the 'Charles,' which he calls "a new built goodly ship of a thousand tons; the 'Unicorn,' a new ship likewise, and almost of as great a burthen; the 'James,' a great ship too; three lesser, the 'Globe,' the 'Swan,' and the 'Rose.'" He likewise says, that "seven hundred men sailed in the carrack, for she was a ship of an

as a "carrack," bearing the flag of Admiral Don Manuel de Meneses at the main-top-mast-head, proceeding from Lisbon to Goa, and steering the same course as the English ships. Then ensued an action, which was highly honourable to the Portuguese. The 'Globe,' which, though the smallest ship, sailed the best of the English squadron, chased, and, having come up at noon to windward, hailed, but received for reply a command to fall to leeward, which was immediately followed by a dischare of five round shot from the carrack's heavy guns, each of which went right through her, when she returned the compliment with a broadside, and then fell astern. At three in the afternoon, Captain Joseph came up in his ship, the 'Charles,' and hailing, bid the commander of the carrack come on board to account for his attack on the 'Globe.' To this summons the latter answered that he had no boat; on which Captain Joseph sent his own, which returned with three officers bringing a message, "that Don Meneses had promised his master, the King of Spain, not to quit his ship; out of which he might be forced, but never commanded." Captain Joseph repeated his summons in writing; and said to the officers "that he would sink by his side or compel him," Meneses persisting, the fight began; and, in a few moments, a shot killed Captain Joseph. The master continued the engagement half-an-hour, when, night falling, he called a council, Captain Pepwell, of the 'James,' who was senior officer, now took command of the squadron. Meneses hung out a light to direct his enemies; but, when morning broke, was found at anchor so near the shore, that Pepwell did not deem it prudent to attack him in that situation. In the evening Meneses set sail, leading out to the open sea; and, when it was dark, again hoisted his light, which led to an encounter at sunrise.

Captain Pepwell had instructed his ships to engage by turns, and began himself in the 'Charles.' After the action had lasted half-an-hour, a shot from the carrack struck one of the iron guns, which shivered it, when the fragments, besides dangerously wounding three seamen and tearing the master's arm, struck out the eye of Captain Pepwell and wounded him in the jaw and leg. The mate now took command, and maintained the fight with spirit beyond the specified time. The other ships now took their turn with the same ardour, the carrack resisting until three in the afternoon, by which time her main-mast and mizen-mast had gone by the board, her fore top-mast was shot away, and her sides fearfully shattered,

exceeding great bulk and burthen, our 'Charles,' though a ship of a thousand tons, looking but like a pinnace when she was beside her." Sir Thomas Roe writes, that the carrack was of fifteen hundred tons burthen, and that Don Emanuel de Meneses had twice been general of the Portuguese forces, but not in India, where he neither appears before or after this voyage.

presenting several breaches. The island of Angazecha was not far off, to which she turned with what little sail she could set, and stood in so near the shore that the English ships would not venture to follow her close. The English commander, respecting the courage shown by the Portuguese admiral sent a boat with a flag of truce. Meneses received the officer but was not moved, either by the offers or the admiration expressed for his valour, to alter his first resolve; and said that, if able, he would get out to sea again on the morrow and renew the fight, when, if taken, he expected the treatment of a gentleman. In the night the wind and surf grew high the carrack drove, and, for want of sail to weather the danger struck and was jammed between two rocks : on these the crew landed, when they set fire to the carrack, which blazed fiercely all night. The Portuguese seamen carried off what they chose of the treasure, and all the jewels. The English ships kept near throughout the next day, when they bore away for supplies to the neighbouring island of Mohilla, where they arrived on the 10th of August.

The natives of Angazecha regarded the shipwrecked crew as invaders, and assailed them with stones; on which the Portuguese employed their firearms, and lost, in the retreat of the natives, their only hopes of sustenance. In this distress Meneses yielded to the advice of his gunner, and threw the arms into the sea, when the natives returned in great numbers and overpowered them : after stripping them of all their clothes we are told they threw away the dollars in order to put their heads into the empty bags. The Portuguese wandered about in parties to procure food—many endured great hardships, and some died. The pilot and a few men went in a boat, and coasted to find a more hospitable shore, when they fortunately met two junks belonging to a Mahomedan, which traded between the mainland and Madagascar. This man took up the boat, and having influence with the chief of that part of the island where the ship was wrecked, sailed thither, collected all the Portuguese, clothed them, gathered their treasure, secured their jewels, and sent them away in his own vessels to the Portuguese port of Mombaza, where they arrived on the 4th of September, and were afterwards conveyed to Goa. Here the valour and misfortunes of Meneses ensured a warm welcome from the Viceroy, Azevedo, and the citizens. He was sent back to Lisbon in an advice boat, and arrived in safety, to receive the same acknowledgments in his own country. And, indeed, his defeat merited a trophy of victory, for his force bore no proportion to the English ships. Orme, in detailing this action, does not fail to pay a just tribute to the fine spirit that animated the crews of the Company's ships. " Either of the strongest of these," he adds, " would probably have main-

tained an equal conflict against the same superiority, for a
this time the highest spirit of military honour animated all the
officers and seamen of the Company's Marine."*

* The following account of this famous sea-fight by Edward Terry, is in the
highest degree quaint, and the reverend gentleman moralizes, and quotes texts in
the midst of his discourse as if he were in a pulpit:—" About noon the 'Globe,
our least ship, by reason of her nimbleness, sailing better than her fellows, came
up with her on her broadside to windward, and according to the custom of the
sea, hailed her, asking her whence she was? She answered indirectly, of the sea
calling our men rogues, thieves, heretics, devils; and the conclusion of her rude
compliment was, in loud cannon language, discharging seven great pieces of artil
lery at our 'Globe,' though she had very little reason to do so, we having fou
ships in company, and she alone, whereof six pierced her through the hull
maiming some of her men, but killing none. Our 'Globe' replied in the same
voice, and after that fell off. About three o'clock in the afternoon, the 'Charles,
our Admiral, came up with her, so near, that we were within pistol-shot. Ou
commander, Captain Joseph, proceeded religiously, in offering them a treat
before he proceeded to revenge, so we saluted her with our trumpets, she with
her wind instruments, then we showed our men on both sides aloft; this done
our commander called to them, requiring theirs to come on board, to give an
account of the injury they had lately before offered us; they answered they had
never a boat, our commander replied that he would send them one, and imme
diately caused his barge to be manned, and sent off to them, which brought back
one of their officers and two others of inferior rank, with this message from the
captain, how that he had promised the King of Spain, his master, not to leave his
ship, and therefore forced he might, but never would be commanded out of her
Captain Joseph received the message, and used those that brought it civilly, and
then ordered that they should be showed in a broadside of great guns that lay
already primed to be fired against them, how we were prepared to vindicate our
selves, which put the poor Portuguese in a fit of trembling, and upon it desired
our commander to write a few words to them, that happily with their persuasion
might make him come. Captain Joseph, willing to preserve his honour, and to
prevent blood, consented, and forthwith caused a few lines in Spanish to this
effect to be sent unto him.

"'That whereas he, the commander of the carrack, had offered violence to our
ship that sailed peaceably by him, he will'd him to come presently, and give
reason for that wrong, or else at his peril.' So he discharged those Portuguese
sending one of our master's mates with them with these few words, and this
further message, 'that if he refused to come he would sink by his side, but that he
would force before he left him;' his word came to pass, for he himself fell suddenly
after by a great shot that came from the carrack's side. The commander of the
carrack, notwithstanding the message and menace sent to him, was still peremp
tory in his first answer; so our men returning, Captain Joseph himself made the
three first shots at them, all which (the mark being so fair and near) hit them
this done, the bullets began to fly on both sides. Our captain cheering his com
pany, immediately ascended the half-deck, the place where commanders used to
keep in those encounters to show their own gallantry and to encourage the com
pany under their command; where he had not been the eighth part of an hou
ere a great shot from the carrack's quarter deprived him of life in the twinkling
of an eye. For this Captain Joseph, he was certainly one who had very much o
a man in him for years antient, who had commanded before in sea-fights, which
he met withal within the streights in the Midland sea, and near death many time
in them, which took others round about him while himself went off untouched
and the reason was because his appointed time was not yet come. Certainly there
is never a bullet flies, that carries not a commission with it to hit or miss, to kil
or spare; the time, the place, and every circumstance besides of a man's dissolu
tion, is fore-determined." After further moralizing on his theme, he proceeds
"The bullet which carried away his life, hit him on the breast, beating out of hi
body his heart, and other of his vitals, which lay round about him, scattered in hi
diffused blood.

"After Captain Joseph was slain, the master of our ship continued the figh

In 1618 the Surat factors opened an intercourse with Mocha, and despatched a trading vessel to the port of Jask, situated not far from the entrance to the Persian Gulf; and, the ven-

about half an hour, then knowing there was another to be admitted into that prime place of command, the night approaching, for that time gave over, putting out a flag of council to call the captain of the Vice-Admiral, Captain Henry Pepwell, who was to succeed, and the other commanders, aboard, to consult about the prosecution of this encounter. The night being come, we now proceeded no further. The carrack stood still on her course, putting forth a light in her poop for us to follow her, and about midnight came to an anchor under the island of Mohilla, which when we perceived, we let fall our anchors too.

"The 7th, early before it began to dawn, we prepared for a new assault, first committing ourselves in prayer to Almighty God; towards the close of which exercise, I spake some words of exhortation and encouragement to all the people of the ship there together assembled, but was presently out-rhetorick'd by our new commander, who spake to the company thus, ' My masters, I have never a speech to make unto you, but to speak to the cooper to give every one of you a good cup of sack, and so God bless us.' Here was a speech indeed, that was short and sweet, that had something following it to make it most savoury, that it might be tasted as well as heard. Mine was verbal, without any such relish, and therefore I forbear to insert it. The morning come, we found the carrack so close to the shore, and the nearest of our ships at least a league off, that we held our hands for that day, expecting when she would weigh her anchor and stand off to sea, a fitter place to deal with her. And that afternoon we chested our late slain commander, putting some great shot with him into it, that he might presently sink, and without any ceremony of guns, &c., usual upon such occasions, because our enemy should take no notice, put him overboard against the island of Mohilla, where he made his own grave, as all dead bodies do, buried not in dust but water. A little before night that present day the carrack departed again to sea, we all loosed our anchors, opened our sails, and followed. The day now left us, and our proud adversary, unwilling as it should seem to escape, put forth a light as before for us to follow him, as afterward we did to purpose. The night well nigh spent, we commended again ourselves and came to God, when I observed more seeming devotion in our seamen that morning, than at any time before or after, while I kept them company, who, for the generality, are such a kind of people, that nothing will bow them, to bring them on their knees, but extreme hazards. When this exercise was ended, the day began to appear in a red mantle, which proved bloody unto many that beheld it. And now,we entered upon a second encounter, our four ships resolving to take their turns one after the other, that we might compel this proud Portuguese either to bend or break." The chaplain then describes the death of a seaman named Raven, " who immediately before we began to engage, came to me and told me that he had a desire to follow his master;" also of a tailor, " who, while the company he sailed with were engaged, brought his pressing-iron to one of the gunners, and desiring him to put it into a piece of ordnance already laden, telling him that he would send it as a token to the Portuguese, withal swearing that he would never work again at his trade; it pleased God immediately after to sentence him out of his own mouth, and to let his tongue to fall upon himself, for that great piece was no sooner discharged, but a great bullet was returned from the enemy, which struck him dead."

"And now, reader," he continues, "thou may'st suppose us speaking again to our adversary and he to us, in the harshest and loudest of all dialects, no arguments being so strong as those that proceed from the mouths of guns and points of swords. Our 'Charles,' the Admiral, played her part first, and ere she had been at defiance with her enemy half an hour, there came another great shot from him, which hitting against one of our iron pieces mounted on our half-deck, brake it into many little parts, which most dangerously wounded our new commander and the master of our ship, with three others besides who received several hurts by it. Captain Pepwell's left eye, by a glance of a piece of that broken bullet, was so torn, that it lay like rags upon his cheek, another hurt by a piece of the same bullet he received on his jawbone, and by another on the head, and a fourth

ture proving successful, a regular trade was established between the Gulf ports and Surat and Bantam.

As was foretold by Sir Thomas Roe, who returned to England in 1619, this traffic could not be conducted without exciting the jealousy of the Portuguese, who had enjoyed a monopoly in the Persian Gulf since the days of Albuquerque. The event justified the prediction, and "the Gulf" (as it was familiarly called in the Indian Navy) afforded to the Service a fresh field for the display of those qualities of enterprise and skill which they had already exhibited on the West Coast of India.

On the 19th of March, 1620, King James addressed a letter to Shah Abbas thanking him for the favours he had shown to English merchants, requesting a continuance of this protection, and that the additional privilege of having a factory near the port of Jask* might be conferred on them, when they might enjoy the liberty of trade already conceded to them in Persia through the influence of his Ambassador, Sir Thomas Shirley.

hurt he received in his leg, a ragged piece of that broken shell sticking fast between the two bones thereof, grating there upon an artery, which seemed by his complaining to afflict him so much that it made him take very little notice of all the rest of his hurts, it being most true of bodily pains, that the extremity of a greater pain will not suffer a man to feel much or to complain of that which is less; as that tormenting pain by the toothache makes a man insensible of the aching of his head, and when the gout and stone surprise the body at once together, the torture by the gout is as it were lost in the extremity of the stone. And thus was our new commander welcomed to his authority, we all thought that his wounds would very suddenly have made an end of him, but he lived till about fourteen months after, and then died as he was returning to England. I told you before that this man suffered not alone by the scattered pieces of that broken shot, for the master of the ship had a great piece of the brawn of his arm struck off by it, which made him likewise unserviceable for a time, and three others of the common sailors received several and dangerous hurts by it likewise.

"The captain and master both thus disabled, deputed their authority to the chief master's mate, who behaved himself resolutely and wisely, so we continued *alternis vicibus*, one after the other, shooting at our adversary, as at a butt, and by three of the clock in the afternoon had shot down her mainmast by the board, her mizen-mast, her foretop-mast, and moreover had made such breaches in her thick sides, that her case seemed so desperate, as that she must either yield or perish." He then describes the loss of the carrack, and concludes:—"Our 'Charles' in this opposition, made at her adversary for her part, three hundred and seventy-five great shot—as our gunners reported—to these we had one hundred musketeers that plied them with small shot all that while, neither was our enemy idle, for our ship received from him at least one hundred great shot, and many of them dangerous ones through the hull. Our fore-mast was pierced through the middle, our main-mast hurt, our main-stay almost spoiled, and many of our main-shrouds cut asunder. Thus, reader, thou hast the sum of that sea encounter, which I did the rather insert, because I believe that of all warlike oppositions there are none that carry more horror in them than sea-fights do, if the parties engaged be both very resolute, as very many who use the sea are, who will desperately run upon the mouth of a cannon, rush into the very jaws of death, before they have at all learned what it was to live; that being most true, which was antiently observed in the generality both of soldiers and seamen, that they fear neither God nor man."

* The town of Jask is situated about six miles to the north of the cape of that name, which bears about NNW. from Muscat distant forty-two and a-half leagues. The bay of the same name is to the west of the cape.

In November, 1620, the 'Hart' and 'Eagle,' two of the Company's ships, having proceeded to Jask with Surat goods for trading purposes, found it blockaded by a Portuguese fleet, consisting of four galleons, one large galley and sixteen vessels of smaller size, under the command of Admiral Ruy Frere. The Company's ships attempted to enter the port, but, being opposed by the Portuguese, returned to Surat for reinforcements. Here they were joined by the 'London' and 'Roebuck,' and again set sail for Jask, off which an indecisive action was fought, resulting in the Portuguese giving way and permitting the English ships to enter the port. The former, however, only retired to Ormuz to refit, and soon returned to renew the action with a force superior in strength. The fighting that ensued was obstinate and prolonged, but it terminated in favour of the Company's ships, which lost their Commodore, Captain Shillinge,* an able an energetic seaman. This success raised the English name throughout the Gulf, and facilitated the purchases of Persian silks which the factors were making.

Mr. Monnox, the Company's agent at Ispahan, had, at this time, sent a caravan, with several hundred bales of silk from that city to Jask, but it was stopped on the journey through Persia by the Khan of Shiraz, with the object of forcing the English to assist him against the Portuguese. In December, 1621, on the arrival of the Company's ships at Jask, the Persian Governor refused to permit them to embark their cargoes unless they would previously agree to assist his nation in repelling the Portuguese aggressions; and, as the ships had lost the monsoon, they were compelled to accede to this condition to avoid the interruption of the trade.† Under this stipulation an expedition, consisting of a Persian army and a squadron of the Company's ships and smaller vessels from Surat, was sent against Ormuz early in 1622.

At this time Ormuz was one of the chief emporiums of trade possessed by the Portuguese in the East. During its prime, when under native rulers, it was said to have boasted a population of forty thousand souls; looking, however, to its lack of water, and the natural capabilities of the island, there can

---

* This officer, on his outward-bound passage with the squadron of Company's ships that sailed in the season of 1620, touched at Saldanha Bay, and, on the 23rd of July, 1620, took possession of it and the adjacent country, in the name of the King of England, on the condition expressed in the Company's charter, that no other European Power had at this time claimed a right to this part of the Coast of Africa, reserving to His Majesty the right of assuming the sovereignty of those districts by proclamation, the original of which may be found in the MSS. of the India Office. By this act, the right of the Crown of England to the Cape 'of Good Hope was established by actual possession, many years prior to the Dutch occupation of it as a colony. Saldanha Bay reverted to this country by conquest in the year 1798.

† See Bruce's "Annals," Vol. I., p. 230.

be no doubt that this estimate is an exaggeration. From the references to its wealth and grandeur by Sir Thomas Herbert, and other travellers, and by our great poet, Milton, the place was doubtless of sufficient importance to excite the envy of the reigning Shah of Persia; while the injudicious conduct of the Portuguese in excluding the English Company's ships from trading to the Persian Gulf, or even entering its waters, raised against them a powerful enemy, who, entering into an alliance with the Persian potentate, supplied the naval part of an expedition which struck a fatal blow against Portuguese ascendancy in the East.

Milton refers in noble verse to the grandeur and opulence to which Ormuz attained under its native kings:—

> "High on a throne of royal state, which far
> Outshone the wealth of Ormuz or of Ind;
> Or where the gorgeous East, with richest hand,
> Show'rs on her kings barbaric pearl and gold."

Merchants from every quarter of the globe proceeded to a city where their property and persons were secure against the injustice and oppression to which they were subjected in the Native states of the mainland; and to this small, barren, island they carried their goods, and bartered them with traders from Persia, Turkey, Arabia and India, without being subjected to the impositions attendant on a residence in those politically unsettled countries.

The name of Ormuz, or Hormuz, says Fraser in his "Travels in Khorassan," appears formerly to have been applied to a state on the Persian shore opposite the island now known by that name. The chiefs were Arabs, and the fifteenth in the succession, pressed by his enemies, retired, first to Kishm and thence to Ormuz, then called Gerun, of which he received a grant from the Sovereign of the island of Kais, or Kenn, the extensive ruins in which attest the former existence of a considerable city. For two hundred years the new city of Ormuz enjoyed a high degree of prosperity, and, we are told, extended its sway along both sides of the Persian Gulf nearly to Bussorah; indeed, by one account, we find its limits described as reaching from Cape Ras-ul-Had, including many considerable cities, and that the chiefs, even those of Bahrein, were all tributary to the King of Ormuz."*

---

* In the work of the Abbé T. G. F. Raynal, entitled "A Philosophical and Political History of the Settlement and Trade of Europe in the East and West Indies," translated by J. Justamond, appears the following description of Ormuz before its occupation by the Portuguese:—"Ormuz became the capital of an empire which comprehended a considerable part of Arabia on one side, and Persia on the other. At the time of the arrival of the foreign merchants, it offered a more splendid and agreeable scene than any city in the East. Persons from all parts of the globe exchanged their commodities, and transacted their business, with an air of politeness and attention which are seldom seen in other places of

The following account of the early history of Ormuz, and its capture from the Portuguese by a Persian army and a fleet of the Company's ships, is chiefly derived from a paper in "The Geographical Magazine" for April, 1874, from the pen of Lieutenant Arthur W. Stiffe, I.N., an officer well known in the Service as an accomplished surveyor, and who now holds a high appointment in connection with the telegraph lines in the Persian Gulf, whose waters he and Captain Constable, I.N., have, by their surveys, done so much to render accessible to navigators of all nations.

The earliest settlement of the island, which had previously been uninhabited, was made about A.D. 1301, and an account of it was written by Turan Shah, the king of the island in 1347-48. Before the above date the kingdom of Ormuz was on the mainland, and, according to this history, it was founded by Arabs, who crossed over from Arabia; this is highly probable, as nearly all the cities on the Persian coast have been thus founded. The site of the city on the mainland, has been conjectured to be on the Minab river, where it possibly succeeded an older settlement of the same name, for Arrian tells us that Nearchus found a town called Hermozia at the mouth of the river Anamis, in a fertile district. The island was then called Gerun, and the name Ormuz was only applied to the kingdom and city on the main.

But, on an evil day for Ormuz, its wealth excited the cupidity of the Portuguese, then commencing their career of empire under the inspiring genius of that remarkable man, Alfonso Albuquerque,* or, more properly, Dalbouquerque. In 1508, after performing several exploits on the African coast, and taking Muscat and other places in Arabia, he entered the Persian Gulf with a squadron of seven ships, having on board a small force of soldiers, and resolved to make himself master of the island of Ormuz, which his great military and political

trade. The streets were covered with mats and in some places with carpets, and the linen awnings which were suspended from the houses, prevented any inconvenience from the heat of the sun. Indian cabinets inlaid with gilded vases, or china filled with flowering shrubs, or aromatic plants, adorned their apartments. Camels laden with water were stationed in the public squares. Persian wines, perfumes, and all the delicacies of the table were furnished in the greatest abundance, and they had the music of the East in its highest perfection. In short, universal opulence, an extensive commerce, politeness in the men and gallantry in the women, united all their attractions to make this city the seat of pleasure." This description has been characterised as an exaggeration by Fraser, but, nevertheless, all accounts agree in averring that Ormuz was great, wealthy and populous, before it fell into the hands—first, of the Portuguese, and then of the Persians.

* For details of the achievements of this great statesman and warrior, see "The Commentaries of the great Alfonso d'Albouquerque, second Viceroy of India, translated from the Portuguese Edition of 1774, with Notes and Introduction by Walter de Gray Birch," of the British Museum, Hon. Secretary of the British Archæological Association. This work forms the volume of the Hakluyt Society for 1875.

sagacity showed him would place the whole trade with India at his mercy. But his designs had been anticipated, and he found that the city was defended by a large fleet and army, the former said to consist of four hundred vessels, sixty being of great size, the latter of thirty thousand men. To a haughty summons to pay tribute to the King of Portugal, the Persian governor, Khoja Attah, who had not completed the fortifications of the city, made a temporizing reply; but Albuquerque was not to be cajoled, and, after some further negotiations, commenced a heavy cannonade, which is said to have inflicted terrible losses on the garrison and population. At length, having sunk or burnt all the ships, he received the submission of the governor, who agreed to pay £2,000 a-year annual subsidy to the King of Portugal, and to permit the erection of a fort. But the force at the disposal of Albuquerque, was only four hundred and sixty men, and Khojah Attah, seeing his weakness, and availing himself of a mutinous feeling that manifested itself among the Portuguese commanders, made preparations to renew hostilities. Albuquerque, thereupon, quitted Ormuz for Socotra, which had fallen to his arms, but returned in the following year, when the governor informed him that the stipulated tribute would be paid, but that he would not be permitted to build the fort. Albuquerque would, probably, have repeated the lesson of the previous year, but being apprized of his nomination to the Viceroyalty in succession to Almeida, proceeded to Cochin, and, after some opposition from his rival, who refused to deliver up the insignia of office, and even threw him into prison at Cannanore, he was installed Viceroy on the arrival of a large Portuguese fleet from Europe.

In 1510, Albuquerque attacked Calicut, where he was repulsed, and captured Goa, which he made the capital of the Portuguese possessions. From thence he turned his victorious arms against Malacca and Aden, where he suffered defeat, and, in 1514, made his third attempt against Ormuz. His name was now so dreaded over the East, that when he renewed his request to build a fort, the King complied; and Albuquerque, not only completed the works, but forced him to lodge his cannon within its walls, thus establishing Portuguese supremacy in the Persian Gulf; and they maintained their position in the island, in spite of an extensive and determined conspiracy to oust them.*

---

* The following is a description of the present appearance of Ormuz, from the pen of Lieutenant A. W. Stiffe, I.N., who visited the place in 1873 :—

"The island, which is rather more than four geographical miles across, and roughly circular in shape, presents a mass of hills from 300 to 700 ft. in height, occupying a space of about three miles each way on the south and south-west sides, the shores of which part are quite precipitous, the north and east sides presenting a low plain. Its surface is, therefore, pretty equally divided between hills and plains.

"The hills are of somewhat remarkable geological character. There are

After the occupation of Ormuz by the Portuguese, says Fraser, the King retained only the insignia of power, and was

some stratified rocks, forming the cliffs at the south-east angle, but the whole of the rest are probably of volcanic origin, and consist chiefly of rock salt, which is raised to a height of 300 to 400 ft., and presents the most fantastic outline conceivable, owing to the dissolution of the salt. They are encrusted with bright coloured earths, red, purple, and yellow, and are almost impassable, owing to the ruggedness of the surface. With these salt hills are associated several peaks of white or light grey-coloured rock of trachytic character, the highest of which rises to 700 ft., and all are of sharp precipitous outline. A view from the top of the high peak presented a perfect wilderness of pointed and rugged ridges, separated by abrupt valleys and singular funnel-shaped holes of various sizes, some of very large dimensions, possibly 200 ft. in depth, and others only a few feet deep, but all at a very steep slope. The trachytic rock is studded with iron pyrites and other minerals, often in most beautifully developed crystals.

"The valleys or ravines opening out of this mass of hills, and carrying off the rain-water which is not absorbed in the funnel-shaped pits, have in their course through the plains all the appearance of frozen rivers winding down to the sea. I walked about a mile up on the salt incrustation and the illusion was perfect, except as regards the temperature. This salt incrustation is collected and exported to Bandar Abbasi and Maskat.

"The plain on the north point terminates in a low sandy point on which stands the old Portuguese fort, and near it is the modern village, consisting chiefly of mat huts, and containing possibly two hundred men, who have a few boats and export salt fish, salt, and a red earth called by them gairn, which is used for staining and seasoning wood, and is sent to Maskat and thence to Calcutta. A few soldiers or armed men hold the fort as a sort of military post for the Governor of Bandar Abbasi. The place is rarely visited by a European vessel.

"The fort is a quadrilateral bastioned work, about 750 feet long by 620 broad. It has casemates under the ramparts, and the two southern or landward bastions are built with orillons; the entrance gate is in one of these recesses, and leads successively into two small courtyards before giving admission to the body of the place. In the *enceinte* is a fine, large, underground water cistern with a groined roof, supported by two rows of pillars. The south-west bastion, and west face are much undermined by the sea and partly ruinous; many of the arches and vaults inside the fort have been blocked up with stone to prevent their falling. It was separated from the island by a moat now filled up; the remains of a bridge across the moat are visible. Many rusty old iron guns lie about the interior of the fortress; the mortar used was excellent, and much more durable than the stones. The only other remains of the Portuguese town are the foundations of buildings along the sea-shore, and the ruins of a sort of outwork in the landward face of the town, which has embrasures and has been defended by a moat. The space occupied by the town is about half a mile by a quarter of a mile, as far as can be judged by the appearance of the ground. The most important ruin is a minaret about 70 feet high. It is of brick, and has been coated with glazed tiles, in a manner which renders the mosques of Bagdad such striking objects. It has two spiral staircases inside, much broken at the foot, and the whole structure is in a tottering state, the lower courses of bricks, to a height of six or eight feet, being much weathered away, thus undermining the building.

"Of the rest of the city nothing remains except mounds strewn with broken pottery, and a vast number of water cisterns, mostly choked with earth, in many of which small crops of vegetables are now raised. At about half a mile to three quarters of a mile to the southward of the minaret, are a number of Arab tombs of some pretensions to architecture, some of which have been of two stories. They are all more or less ruinous. In addition to the ruins of the Portuguese town already mentioned, there are the remains of a chapel with a zigzag road up to it, on a peak of the nearest range of salt hills; also of a small chapel or hermitage, on a little hillock on the north-east coast. One other ruin of the Arab city remains to be mentioned, viz.—the King's palace, or Turun-bagh, in the south-east corner. This is described as 'fairest of all; there, upon a

forced to request the assistance of his enemies in subduing the territory, of which Lahsah, or Lachsa, now known as El Kateef, near Bahrein, was the capital. In 1552, the Turkish Government sent from Bussorah an expedition of sixteen thousand men against the Portuguese, under the command of Peer Bey, described by Fraser, as " a veteran pirate;" but though he took Muscat, after a month's siege, and sacked Kishm, (Kesm) he was foiled at Ormuz, and had to retire from the fort, after plundering the town.

During Albuquerque's tenure of power he received, at Ormuz, an embassy from Ismael, the founder of the Sophi dynasty in Persia; and here, when in his sixtieth year, he was seized with the illness which carried him off, when within sight of Goa, though his biographers attribute his death chiefly to mortification on receiving notice of his supersession in the viceroyalty by his mortal enemy, and a denial from his sovereign of the title of Duke of Goa, which he had solicited. Albuquerque died on board his ship off the city he had captured, which the Portuguese still retain as the capital of their Indian possessions.

For upwards of one hundred years the Portuguese trade with Bussorah, and the ports of the Persian Gulf, flowed through Ormuz; but the year 1622 was destined to see the extinction of their power and commercial greatness in this inland sea, for there was no officer of the genius of Albuquerque to uphold the flag, and the sun of a race, rivalling his in maritime greatness, was rising in the East.

The succession of the native kings, whose power soon became quite nominal, was preserved during the Portuguese occupation of the island, but they were forced to take the oath of fidelity to the King of Portugal, and could not quit the island without the consent of the governor. The commerce and importance of Ormuz, commenced to decline from the date of its conquest by Albuquerque, chiefly owing to the rapacity of its rulers. Notwithstanding this decadence in its prosperity, Shah Abbas, King of Persia, saw with envy the opulence of Ormuz. He could not understand the source from whence it was derived, and looked to its conquest as an event that would add both to the glory and wealth of his country. Emaum Kooli Khan, Governor of Fars, called, in the accounts, Prince of Shiraz, received orders to undertake this great enterprise; but the King was well aware that it would be impossible to succeed without the aid of a naval force. The Company's agents at Surat were accordingly applied to, and consented to co-operate on the

plain between the hills and the sea, you see a country seat of the old Kings of Ormuz, adorned with groves of palm trees and two large cisterns for water.' The ruins of buildings and of water channels for irrigation are to be seen here, which is the only point in the hilly part of the island where stratified rocks are found and which is free from the all-pervading salt deposits."

following terms:—that they were to share the plunder, and that half of the Custom dues of Gombroon, on the mainland, was to be guaranteed to them, as well as exemption from payment of all duties at that port.

Dr. Fryer, a quaint writer who visited India and the Persian Gulf between the years 1672-1681, says:—"Shau Abbas the Great, when he had enlarged his dominions from the Persian Gulf to the Caspian Sea, and lastly, when he was about to wage war with the sea itself, having not one port in the Bay of Persia, sent down Imaun Cooly Caun, the famous warrior-general of his forces, against Ormuz, and all the harbours the Portuguese had in possession of this side the Gulf; and a ship of our nation coming in, Captain Wedal was implored to assist the Persians against his and their enemies, which, the general asking, the sea-captain consented to, first stipulating that the Persian soldiers should not meddle with the spoils before the English mariners were satisfied." Dr. Fryer then enumerates the terms of the treaty, the Company engaging "to keep two men-of-war constantly to defend the Gulf," while they, in return, "should have the first seat in the Council, and their agents be looked on with equal grace to their prime nobility."

The arrogant conduct of the Portuguese, in declining to permit foreign ships to navigate those seas without a pass from the captain of one of their forts, and then only under oppressive conditions, aroused the opposition of the Company's agents at Surat, who, confident in the discipline and valour of their sailors, resolved to take the earliest opportunity of wresting from their rivals the supremacy of the Persian Gulf.

At a consultation held in Swally Roads, a Commission was given by the President and Council at Surat, to Captains Blythe and Weddell, who were bound for Jask, near the entrance of the Gulf, with five good ships—the 'London,' 'Jonas,' 'Whale,' 'Dolphin,' and 'Lion,' and four "pinnaces,"* which formed the nucleus of the newly-formed local Marine. As the Portuguese had disturbed the trade, and committed depredations upon our ships, the commander of the British squadron was authorized to capture any vessels flying the Portuguese flag, and make reprisals on other ships. Information was received that the enemy, under Ruy Frere de Andrada, was waiting on the coast of Persia, probably to attack the Company's fleet, who were directed to use "all advantage" against the Portuguese, even in their own ports, if approved by a general council of war. On the 23rd of December the squadron arrived in Costack

---

* The pinnace of that day was a schooner-rigged vessel of two or three masts, which was also propelled with oars. Shakespeare, in his play of Henry VI., makes the pinnace an independent vessel, though Falstaff speaks of it as a tender. The pinnace was used for war purposes and mounted guns.

Roads, an open roadstead on the Persian coast near Minab, Ormuz being in sight, about ten leagues, W.N.W. The English factors at Jask informed the captains that the Portuguese had erected a fort at the town of Kishm*—whence they drew their supplies of water in seasons of drought—to which the Persians had laid siege ineffectually, and had lost a great many men. The Persian general had received orders from the Shah to take Ormuz at any cost, "wherefore the Prince of Shiraz had demanded the aid of our ships against the common enemy, the Portuguese," threatening otherwise, says the account from which we are quoting, to detain all the goods and money belonging to the Company in Persia.

In a consultation on board the 'Jonas,' articles of agreement were drawn up and signed by the captains, for giving aid to the Persians, and sent to the Khan of Shiraz, then on his way towards Minab. The English consented to act under fear of an embargo being laid on their goods, and also because they considered it would be "for the public benefit, and the securing a peaceable and profitable trade." The agreement was ratified by the Persian governor, subject to some points reserved for the Shah's decision. A new difficulty, however, arose, for we are told "when news of this agreement became known among the ships' companies, they refused to take any share in the business, but after much pains, they were reconciled to it."

On the 19th of January, 1622, the fleet anchored before the town of Ormuz, expecting that the enemy's armada would come out to fight. In this they were disappointed; but, as they learned that Ruy Frere de Andrada was in a fort in the neighbouring island of Kishm, which the Portuguese had constructed in the preceding year, the fleet sailed to that place, where it arrived on the following day. The Portuguese were soon reduced to extremities, and surrendered the fort to the English on the 1st of February. Among the killed on board the Company's ships, was the famous Arctic navigator, William Baffin, who acted as pilot. Seventeen guns and about one thousand prisoners, including the Portuguese Admiral, were taken in the castle. On the 4th of February the fleet proceeded to Gombroon, whence Ruy Frere was sent to Surat, in the 'Lion,' escorted by two pinnaces, so that only four ships and two pinnaces were left for the attack on Ormuz.

On the 9th of February the squadron arrived at Ormuz,

---

* Kishm, the largest island in the Persian Gulf, was called by the Portuguese "Quexome," "Kish" by El-Idrisy, and by Arrian, in his Voyage of Nearchus, "Oarakta." The Rev. G. P. Badger, in his "Introduction and Analysis" to his translation of the "History of the Imâms and Seyyids of Ormuz," makes the mistake of confounding the island of Kaish, which is a small islet generally known as Kenn, with the larger island of Kishm near Ormuz. (See his notes to pages three and four of his "Introduction and Analysis.")

accompanied by about two hundred Persian boats, and, on the following morning, disembarked the Persian army of thirteen thousand men,* who marched to the town "in a confused manner." They penetrated without resistance to the market-place, where they found further progress barred by barricades. The Portuguese, however, appeared to be afraid of being intercepted in their retreat to the castle, and also anticipated treachery on the part of the Mahomedan inhabitants, for they were quickly dislodged and retired into the castle. The Persians then sacked the town, breaking into all the shops and houses, and "wearied themselves with carrying away plunder all day;" and at night slept out without any military precaution, "so that had the Portuguese made a sally, they might have slain numbers."

The Persians now threw up trenches, and the English erected batteries, and also "sconces," and other works for protecting the trenches. The Company's vessels, meantime, engaged the Portuguese fleet, and sent in fire ships, which, on the 24th of February, destroyed the 'San Pedro,' formerly flagship of Admiral Andrada's fleet.

On the 17th the Persians exploded a mine under one of the bastions, charged with forty barrels of powder, by which a practicable breach was made in the salient angle. They then tried to assault the works, and about two hundred men made a lodgment in the bastion, but were eventually repulsed by the Portuguese, who fought with great bravery. By command of Emaum Kooli Khan, the Persians also set fire to the city, declaredly because his soldiers skulked in the houses, and could not be rallied to the attack.

The Persian army,—now forty thousand to fifty thousand strong, according to Captain A. Hamilton, though this estimate is probably exaggerated,—was soon reduced almost to a state of famine, and the little water found in the cisterns in the city was soon consumed, so that had our ships been driven off by a Portuguese squadron, whose arrival was expected, the situation of the besiegers would have been very critical, as they had to send daily for supplies to the mainland; they were also badly provided with arms, "having only small pieces, with bows and arrows, and swords; some of their chiefs had coats of mail." The patience of the English was much tried by the fraudulent behaviour of the Persian general, who "broke conditions with them in several things," and held conferences with the Portuguese without communicating with the English, and were guilty of other breaches of faith.

* Accounts differ as to the strength of the Persian Army. According to Captain Alexander Hamilton, who served in the Company's Marine, and may be regarded generally as a trustworthy authority, the army, when reinforced, numbered between forty thousand and fifty thousand men.

On the 2nd of April, officers from the ships, acting as engineers, exploded two other mines, forming a practicable breach, but the Persians would not take advantage of it. The garrison were now getting short of provisions, and suffering from sickness. On the 14th and 17th other mines were exploded, when the besiegers assaulted with two thousand soldiers. A few Portuguese held them in check, while a flanking battery did great execution among the Persians, who clustered on the breach like a flock of sheep, until, at length, they made a rapid retreat. Another assault on the 18th was also unsuccessful, but, on the 19th, the allies got possession of the entire outer wall, forcing the Portuguese to retire further within the castle. On this night a Portuguese frigate escaped the blockading ships, as was supposed, richly freighted.

On the 21st of April the Portuguese made overtures to the English, who received letters from the military commander and the Admiral, requesting their mediation with the Persian general, and saying that "if forced to surrender, as they soon must be, they would call upon the English for that purpose, as it were not reasonable for us to capitulate with the infidels when you are present." The English commanders guaranteed that their lives should be saved, and obtained a truce for two days to draw up conditions. On the 23rd the Portuguese surrendered themselves to the English on condition of being sent to Muscat or India. This was agreed to, and English and Persian officers were stationed at the gate to pass the garrison out and see that they took nothing with them. But the Persians escorted the King of Ormuz, together with all the Mahomedans and their treasure, out of the castle by the breach, and, contrary to the stipulations, whole bales of goods, with boxes and caskets full of treasure to an unknown amount, were conveyed at the same time over the trenches. On the 24th both English and Persians began to pillage "in a shameful manner." In the evening the Khan of Shiraz came over from Gombroon, and made a triumphant entry into the castle, in which were found three hundred pieces of brass and iron ordnance. The English were employed protecting and embarking the garrison, who, to the number of two thousand five hundred, left for Goa, on the 27th, in two ships the English gave for the purpose, being probably some of the captured vessels. Before embarking, these unfortunate men were ill-treated and stripped by the Persians.*

* Sir Thomas Herbert (the historian of a mission sent by the King of England in the year 1626, under Sir Dodmore Cotton) writes as follows in his quaint work, "Travels in Persia," of the greatness and downfall of this celebrated city. "Ormuz is an isle within the Gulf, in old times known by the name of Geru, and before that, Ogiris, 'but I dare not say from a famous Theban of that name.' Its circuit is fifteen miles, and it procreates nothing noteworthy, salt excepted, of which the rocks are participant; and the silver shining sand expresseth sulphur.

Captain Alexander Hamilton, in his "New Account of the East Indies," speaking of the reduction of the Island of Ormuz,

"At the end of the isle appears yet the ruins of that late glorious city built by the Portugals, but under command of a titular king, a Moor. It was once as big as Exeter, the buildings fair and spacious, with some monasteries and a large bazaar or market. Of most note and excellence is the Castle, well seated, entrenched and fortified. In a word, this poor place, now not worth the owning, was but ten years ago the only stately city in the Orient, if we may believe the universal proverb:—

'Si terrarum orbis, quaqua patet, annulus esset,
Illius Ormusium gemma, decusque foret.'
'If all the world were made into a ring,
Ormuz the gem and grace should be therein.'

"This poor city was defrauded of her hopes and continuing glory, such time as Emaun Khooli Khan, Duke of Shyraz or Persepolis, took it with an army of fifteen thousand men, by command of the King of Persia, who found himself bearded by the Portuguese. Howbeit, they had never triumphed over them had not some English merchant ships (then too much abused by the bragging Lusitanian, and so exasperated), helped them, by whose valour and cannon the city was sacked and depopulated. The captains serving the East Indian merchants were Captains Weddell, Blyth, and Woodcocke. Their articles with the Persian Duke were to have the lives of the poor Christians at their disposal, some cannons, and half the spoil; and accordingly when the city was entered, after a brave and tedious resistance, forced to yield by superior numbers and famine, every house of quality, magazine, and monastery, were sealed up with the signets of the Duke and merchants; by which good order the Company had, no doubt, been enriched with two millions of pounds (though but their share) had it not been prevented by a rascal sailor's covetousness, who, though he knew the danger of his life, and the loss of the Christian's credit, yet stole in a monastery sealed with both consents, commits sacrilege upon the silver lamps, challices, crucifixes, and other rich ornaments, and stuffed so full that in descending his theft cried out against him, was taken by the Persians, led to the Duke, confessed, and was drubbed right handsomely.

"But the greatest mischief came hereby unto the English, for the perfidious pagans, though they knew the merchants were not guilty of his transgression, and consequently had not broke the order—notwithstanding, the soldiers went to the Duke, saying, 'Shall we sit idle while the English, by stealth and secrecy, exhaust all our hopes of benefits and riches?' Whereat, the Duke, glad of such advantage, replied, 'If so, then go and have your desires.' Whereupon they broke open the houses and stores of what was valuable, and made themselves masters of all they found; whilst the confident sailors lay bragging of their victories a-shipboard. And when they were possessed of what was done, they exclaimed as men possessed; but the Persians understood them not, or cared they what their meaning was, seeing they verified the adage, Give losers leave to prate. Yet they found enough to throw away, by that small, sufficiently showing their luxurious mind and prodigality if they had gotten more; dicing, whoreing, brawling, and tipling being all the relics of their husbandry and thankfulness.

"Only Captain Woodcocke had good luck and bad; lighting upon a frigate that stole away unwitting to the enemy, loaden with pearls and treasure, that he took for a prize and kept all to himself, perhaps worth a million of rials or better. But see ill-fortune. The 'Whale,' of which he was captain, rich laden with his masters' and his own goods, hard by Swally Road without the bar, sunk, and was swallowed by the sands, occasioned by a hole neglected by the carpenter, and failing to carine or mend her, the ports were open and took in water, which, to prove that mere whales are subject to destruction, perished in that merciless element; Woodcocke, not long after, overwhelming his life with too much care, too unable to moderate so great misfortunes.

"This poor city is now disrobed of all her bravery: the Persians each month convey her ribs of wood and stone to aggrandize Gambroone, not three leagues distant, out of whose ruins she begins to triumph.

"Ormuz island has no fresh water, save what the fruitful clouds weep over her

says that Sir Thomas Roe, the British Ambassador to the Persian Court, and Shah Abbas, agreed that if the latter " would defray the charges of the ships that should come to his assistance, give the English a free trade all over the Persian dominions, custom free, and grant them one moiety of the customs raised by merchandize in the Gulf, they would not only help to drive the Portuguese out of Ormuze, but keep two ships in the Gulf, to protect trade. All which was agreed to by both parties, and sealed and signed by the King of Persia."

Of the expedition and the incidents of the siege, he says:—
"The English forces consisted of five ships, about forty guns one with another, and were well mann'd. The King of Persia sent an army of forty or fifty thousand, with trankies for transports, to land them on Ormuze. The English soon destroyed the Portuguese armada of light frigates and gallies, which were hal'd dry on the land near the castle. The castle firing briskly on them, sunk one of the English ships, whose artillery was carried ashore, and put in batteries to annoy the castle, which in sorrow of her desolation, late so populous; these are preserved in urns or earthen jars, and are most comfortable to drink in, and to give bedding a cool and refrigerating sleeping place, to lenify scorching Phœton, who is there potent in his flames and sulphur."

Shah Abbas the Great received at Ispahan the embassy sent by James I., of which Sir Dodmore Cotton was the head, and Sir Thomas Herbert the historiographer; but both the former and Sir Robert Shirley, appointed by the Shah to proceed as his envoy to the King of England, died within a few months. Sir Thomas Herbert, whose Memoir is published in the "Biographia Britannia," is, according to Sir John Malcolm, a reliable authority on Persian subjects, but his religious intolerance is frequently apparent in his writings, which are couched in quaint terms. As an instance, we would quote his description of a Mahomedan saint, whose grave denoted him to be a man of great stature, "as a long-named, long-boned, and long-since-rotten saint;" and again, speaking of one of the Persian ministers, whose foreign title irritated him, he displays his intolerance in the following language: "If God does not damn him for his heresies, He will assuredly do it for his long name, which always puzzled my Lord Ambassador."

Fryer, the writer already quoted, gives another version of the capture of Ormuz, which, however, is at variance with fact in all its details, but we lay it before our readers, as his curious and little-known work (which we were unable to procure in the library of the Royal Geographical Society) is generally accurate and reliable. He says:—"The articles being ratified on either side, the enterprise is undertaken; though of itself it was too great an action for one ship to perform, or even a well-appointed navy, had they been upon their guard (or any commander to promise without the consent of the King, his master), wherefore the English betake themselves to stratagem, and gaining leave to careen their ships under their guns, whilst the Portugals dreamt nothing less, they poured in men (the Persians being hid under deck) at unawares, that they were put into a consternation before they could think of their defence; whereby they became masters presently of the castle, strengthened both by sea and land, by this unexpected attempt vanquished, which otherwise was invincible; being possessed whereof by this rape, the rest of the island soon fell prostrate to the lust of the surprisers, and the English, having got their booty, left the Christians to be despoiled by the infidels, which thing, as it gained us esteem among the Persians, was the utter ruin of the Lusitanian greatness, it ever since declining, and is almost at its fatal catastrophe, for immediately upon this, their fleet before Muscat is defeated, and they were driven out of all their strong places in the Gulf, so that the loss was greater than if they had lost Mozambique, from whence they have their gold."

the shipping and batteries did so effectually, that in less than two months, the Portuguese capitulated to leave Ormuze, with all the fortifications intire, and to carry nothing away but their noble selves."

The Persians evaded the promised payment of a sum of money, and also of a share of the booty, alleging counter representations of the embezzlement of plunder on the part of the English, and also the necessity of referring the matter to the King. The account continues:—"After business was ended our miseries began, occasioned by the insufferable heat of Ormuz and the disorders of our own people by drinking arrack and other excesses no less injurious." Owing to these causes the ships lost many men, and eventually left Ormuz on the 1st of September, arriving at Swally Roads on the 24th.

As to the once famous city of Ormuz, it was given over to the Persians, by whom it was soon stripped of all that was of value and left to a natural decay, so that at the present day, if the "abomination of desolation" is to be found anywhere, it may be seen at Ormuz, which yields to the moralist a striking example of the vicissitudes of mundane greatness. That old and well-worn apothegm, "Sic transit gloria mundi," may be applied to Ormuz with not less force than it has served to point the tale of the decline of Tyre, Babylon, or any of the great cities of antiquity. The small island, whose luxury and wealth were once proverbial, which is said to have boasted a population of forty thousand souls, and was one of the chief marts for the commerce of the "gorgeous East," is now a barren rock, inhabited by some two hundred souls, who eke out a precarious existence by the sale of the salt which forms the sole staple of commerce.

Shah Abbas was overjoyed at the conquest, but all the magnificent plans which he had formed for having a great seaport, terminated in his giving his own name to Gombroon, which he commanded to be, in future, called Bunder Abbas, or the Port of Abbas. The hopes which the servants of the East India Company had cherished from the expulsion of the Portuguese from Ormuz and their other possessions, were also doomed to disappointment. The agreement, made by Shah Abbas to obtain their aid, by which it was stipulated that all plunder should be equally divided, that each should appoint a Governor, and that the future customs, both of Ormuz and Gombroon should be equally shared, was disregarded, as regards the two first clauses, from the moment the conquest was completed.

Another article of the treaty entered into between the allies was that all Mahomedans made captive were to be given up to the King of Persia, and all Christians to the English. Mr. Monnox, the agent of the East India Company, in reporting the fall of the island, boasted of his humanity to the prisoners, but added, "I must trust to Heaven for my reward, for the Portuguese are but slenderly thankful." He also soon found how illusory were the sanguine anticipations expressed in a letter from Ispahan to his masters in England, "that their dear infant," (a term applied to their commercial factory at Gombroon) "would receive new life if the King would but keep his word;" and, after the fall of Ormuz, we find the same gentleman stating that no benefit whatever can be expected from that possession unless it be held exclusively by the English. But any expectation of even partial advantage, was soon dispelled by the positive refusal of Abbas to allow the English either to fortify Ormuz or any harbour in the Gulf, though the Persian monarch renewed the treaty made in 1615 by Mr. Connock, and granted an additional firman, allowing the English to purchase Persian silks and bring them to Ispahan without payment of duties.

The chief advantage, therefore, gained by the Company in the destruction of Ormuz, beyond the grant of half the customs levied at the port of Gombroon,—which, in 1632 yielded £1,650, though it gradually decreased in amount—lay in their having broken the power of a hated rival in the Persian Gulf, in the waters of which they were now supreme; for they were only permitted to occupy two houses at Gombroon "lest they should give a building the strength of a castle." In other respects, the great success achieved by the Company's sailors, brought their masters much trouble and pecuniary loss, for a general impression prevailed in England that vast booty had been acquired by the Company and their officers at the capture of Ormuz, which had been carried to their account by their factors at Surat. When, therefore, the Company's home fleet of seven ships was fitting out for the venture of 1623, claims were made by the King, as "droits of the crown," and by the Duke of Buckingham, Lord High Admiral, for a proportion of the prize money which their ships were supposed to have obtained at Ormuz and elsewhere. For the purpose of establishing a ground for these claims, references were made by the King and the Duke of Buckingham to Sir Henry Martin, Judge of the Admiralty, and other civilians, to ascertain the King's and the Lord Admiral's rights; the former to a proportion of prize money belonging to the Crown, the latter to one-tenth of the prize money in right of his office. The first question appears to have been admitted, the governor and directors not feeling it to be their duty to dispute any point with His Majesty; the second demand they resisted on the plea that they had not acted under any letters of marque from the Lord High Admiral, but only under their charter, and contended that he had not any right to a tenth of the prize money, which had arisen from their having made prizes of ships, or taken plunder from their enemies.

In order, however, to substantiate the claims, both of the King and the Lord High Admiral, Captains Weddell, Blyth, Clevinger, and Beversham, were examined, also the several officers of the Company's ships which had made prizes in the East Indies from the Portuguese, and, particularly, those officers who had been employed at the taking of Ormuz, from which it appeared that the total amount of prize money was about 100,000 dollars, and 240,000 reals of eight; but this calculation was made without taking into view the charges and losses incurred by the Company in their equipment, or by their ships being called off from commercial engagements to act as ships-of-war.

While the suit was pending the ships of the season were stopped at Tilbury, the Company "put in arrest," and all their solicitations to the King and to the Lord High Admiral rejected. Eventually they were obliged to compound by paying £10,000 to the Duke of Buckingham to discharge his claim, and received an order from Sir Edward Conway, the Secretary of State, to pay also £10,000 to the King.* Thus terminated this episode of the conquest of Ormuz, but though it caused immediate pecuniary loss to the Company, the gallantry displayed by their seamen, and the skill and conduct of their officers, raised the British name in the estimation of Oriental Governments, which recognised in the new aspirants for maritime ascendancy in the East, a race whom it would be advisable rather to conciliate than to drive into hostility. Further, the Company gained a footing at Gombroon, which they maintained for a century and a half, when their factory was removed to Bushire. During the past forty years our Government have twice occupied the island of Karrack—the importance of which, from a military point of view, as commanding Bushire and the Shatt-ul-Arab river, is manifest by a glance at the map—but, on both occasions, have evacuated the island on the conclusion of peace, and, at the present day, the British flag flies only over the coaling depôt at Bassadore, in the island of Kishm, ceded to us as a station for the cruisers of the Indian Navy, by the great Imaum of Muscat, Seyyid Said, who rented it from the Shah of Persia.

* Bruce's "Annals," vol. i. p. 241.

CHAPTER II.

1623—98.

Proposals regarding the Occupation of Bombay—Position of the Company at Surat and in the Persian Gulf—Courten's Association—Effect of the War with Holland on the Company's affairs—Bombay, its cession to the King, and subsequent acquisition by the Company—Gallant Defence of the Town and Factory of Surat by the Marine—Privileges granted to the Company by the Mogul Government—Development of the Surat Marine and Formation of the Bombay portion of the Service—Their Defence of the Surat Factory against the Mahrattas—Threatened Attack on Bombay by the Dutch—The Mogul and Mahratta fleets in Bombay Harbour—Reduction of the Bombay Marine—Gallant Actions fought by the Service—Rebellion at Bombay—Aggressive Conduct of the Company against the Mogul—Heavy Losses incurred by them during the War with France—English Pirates on the Coast of India—Affairs at Surat.

IN 1624 the Company petitioned the King for power to authorise their commanders and agents abroad to try their servants and ships' crews by common and martial law, which was granted by His Majesty;* and, on the 6th of December, in the same year, an additional order was issued, authorising them to build forts in the East Indies for the security of their trade. In 1625 James I. was succeeded by his son, the unfortunate Charles, and, two years later, Shah Jehan came to the throne in succession to his father, Jehangire. At this time the affairs of the Company were in a state of depression; their factories at Ahmedabad and Broach were closed in consequence of the anarchy prevailing after the death of the late Mogul Emperor, while at home the £100 shares were selling at £80. The Company's trade in the Persian Gulf, also, was not prosperous, owing to the caprice and extortion of the Persian authorities, while their agents in the Eastern islands, thwarted by the Dutch, had abandoned both Bantam and Jacatra, (now known as Batavia, where their rivals had established their chief seat of government)

---

* It appears, however, that before the issue of this order, the Company were invested with legal powers for the punishment of criminals, for we find that in the year 1616, "a formal trial was held, and sentence of death passed against one Gregory Lellington, who was charged with murdering Henry Barton in Surat. The Court assembled on board the ship 'Charles' at Swally. The prisoner, having confessed his guilt, was sentenced to be taken ashore the next day, and there shot to death by the musketeers of the guard."

whence they had retired to Lagundy, in the Straits of Sunda, which had been taken possession of by Captain Swan, of the Company's ship 'Charles,' who gave it the name of Prince Charles' Island, though, owing to its unhealthiness, they were forced to abandon it, and returned to Bantam and Batavia. On the Coromandel Coast the Company had factories at Masulipatam and Pulicat, which were, however, both abandoned; and, in 1628, they established themselves at Armagaum, and, in 1640, Fort St. George was erected at Madrasapatam, now known as Madras.

In consequence of the increasing importance of Surat, the Government at Bantam was reduced to an agency dependent upon the Presidency of the former city, which became the chief seat of the Company's Government in India. The English had to sustain at this time the commercial rivalry of the Dutch, who outbid them at Surat, selling European goods cheaper than the Company's agents, and, to conciliate their rivals, they engaged to co-operate in a joint expedition against the Portuguese possessions at Bombay—called by Pepys and other old writers, Bombaim—and in the Red Sea. In the year 1627 the combined fleet sailed from Surat for Mocha, but the Dutch Admiral, Harman van Speult, a man of infamous character, died at that port, when the expedition returned, the Dutch having lost their largest ship, mounting forty-four guns. His successor, instead of supporting the English against the Portuguese, refused them his assistance in carrying into execution the orders of the Court, who had directed the formation of an establishment at Bombay, though the Dutch President proposed that, upon its reduction, the island should be equally divided between the two nations, and fortified, to make it independent of Native Powers. This circumstance is of interest, as the first notice we have of the Company's desire to obtain possession of Bombay, which, subsequently, played so important a part in their history, and was, for two centuries, the home of the Indian Navy. In 1628, the President and Council at Surat granted a commission as commodore to Captain Swanley, who was ordered to proceed to the Persian Gulf with a squadron of five ships, for the purpose of endeavouring to revive and increase the trade with Persia, and also of carrying on naval operations against the Portuguese.

At this time the most amicable relations existed between the English at Surat and the Mogul Government, for Bruce records that Captain Swanley was ordered to take on board his ship, Kherat Khan, who had been appointed by Shah Jehan, to proceed as his ambassador to the King of Persia, and to treat him, and the Mogul subjects in his suite, with attention and respect. Captain Swanley was further ordered to seize on all Portuguese vessels which he might meet on his voyage, and, in the first instance, to go to Jask,* and if, on reaching that port, he should obtain information that the Portuguese had any force in the neighbourhood of Ormuz, after landing the Ambassador and his suite at Jask, he was to immediately attack them in that quarter. Having effected the mercantile and naval purposes of his voyage in the Gulf of Persia, he was to return to the Malabar coast, and go down as far as Dabul, the principal town on a river of the same name, also known as the Anjenwil River, and there seize on any vessels belonging to ports not subject to the Mogul Government; one-sixth part of the prize-money was to belong to the captain and ships' crew, and the remainder to be carried to the Company's account.†

To obtain the assistance of the English against the Portuguese, the Mogul Emperor, who entertained a high opinion of the prowess of the officers and crews of the Company's ships, granted a firman to the President at Surat on April 5, 1629, authorising him to make reprisals on all ships of that nationality, both at sea and in port, within his dominions; and also intimated that he would require the assistance of the Company's ships in the following season. In September, 1630, a squadron of five sail arrived from England, having on board large supplies, which had been solicited by the President at Surat, to enable him to carry out the wishes of the Mogul Government. But the Portuguese Viceroy, having also received, in the preceding April, a reinforcement of nine ships and two thousand soldiers, resolved to anticipate the Company in their hostile intentions, and projected the recapture of Ormuz.

His first measure, says Bruce, was to request the Governor of Surat, to use his influence with the Mogul Emperor, to expel the English and the Dutch from his dominions, to admit the Portuguese to settle at Surat, and to have the exclusive trade of that port granted to them. On the rejection of this application, he resolved to employ forcible measures, in which, however, he was not more successful. The Portuguese fleet, commanded by Don Francisco Coutinho, tried to prevent the entrance of the English ships into Swally, when a sharp action ensued, in which the Company's ships had the advantage. This action was followed by frequent skirmishes, both at sea and on shore, the English still being successful in maintaining their ground. Irritated by failure, the Portuguese Admiral made an unsuccessful attempt to destroy the English ships, by fire; but, notwithstanding all his efforts, the latter succeeded in landing their cargoes.

* In Arrian's account of the voyage of Nearchus' fleet from the mouth of the Indus up the Persian Gulf, Cape Jask is called Bardis. It was while Alexander's fleet lay here that the controversy arose between Nearchus and Onesicritus, the "Captain of the Royal galley," as the historian calls him, who proposed that they should steer for Cape Mussendom, and coast along the shores of the Indian Ocean.

† "Bruce's Annals," vol. i., p. 289.

HISTORY OF THE INDIAN NAVY. 49

Captain Alexander Hamilton, in his "New Account of the East Indies," where he served between the years 1688 and 1723, says of this action:—" One season the English had eight good large ships riding at Swally, which is about ten miles from Rannier, where the President and his Council then resided;* and Swally was the place where all goods were unladed from the shipping, and all goods for exportation were then shipp'd off. The Portuguese thinking it a fit time to give a deadly blow to the English commerce, came with a fleet of six large ships, ten small, and ten or twelve large gallies, and anchored to the northward of the English, in a narrow channel, not musket shot wide, and a tide generally of six or seven miles an hour. The Portuguese landed near three thousand men, and seized some carts laden with the Company's goods. The English could not bear the insults they daily received, held a council, wherein it was resolved to land eight hundred men out of the ships and attack the Portuguese, while they were lulled in security of their own strength and numbers, and if they were overpowered, that those left on board the English should try if they could cut a Portuguese ship's cables that lay near them, and her driving on board of another, might, with the force of the tide, put them all aground on the shore, or a sand bank that they lay very near to. Accordingly, by break of day, the English were all landed, and every ship's crew led by their own commander. As they had conjectured, so it fell out, the English were among the Portuguese before they could get in a posture of defence, and put them in confusion. Those on board had done as they were ordered, one being cut

* According to Hamilton, the present city of Surat had no existence at this time, there being a neighbouring place called Rannier. He says:—"Surat was built about the year 1660, on the banks of the river Tapta, or Tappee, which being incommoded with banks of sand at Rannier, the then mart town on this river, the English removed about two miles further down the river, on the opposite side, near a castle which had been built many years before, to secure the trade from the insults of the Malabar pirates, who used to lord it over all the sea coast between Cape Comerin and Cambay. In a little time after the English had settled there, others followed their example, so that in a few years it became a large town, but without walls, and so it continued till about the aforesaid year, that Rajah Sevajee, who had never submitted to the Mogul's domination, came with an army and plundered it, except the European factories, who stood on their guard. Them he complimented with the proffer of his friendship, because perhaps he apprehended that he could not plunder them without bloodshed and loss of time. However he carried away a very great booty, which made the inhabitants petition Aurengzeb to secure them for the future by a wall round their town, which favour he granted, enclosing about four miles to build their city in; but trade increasing, the town was too small within the walls to contain the people that came about commerce, therefore several large suburbs were added to the city for the conveniency of mechanicks. The wall was built of brick, about eight yards high, with round bastions, two hundred paces distant from one another, and each had five or six cannon mounted on them. And the rich men of the town built many summer-houses in the fields, and planted gardens about them, to solace themselves and families in the heat, which was pretty violent in April, May, and June."

VOL. I. E

loose, soon made all the rest run aground, and most of them lost, especially the great ships. The little English army pursued the Portuguese, and killed many in their flight; but at a point of land, about three miles from the ships, the Portuguese made a stand, and rallied; but the little victorious army soon made them take a second time to their heels, and so the English got an entire victory, with small loss, for there were not twenty killed on the English side, but above fifteen hundred of the Portuguese. In anno 1690 I was on the field of battle, and saw many human skulls and bones lying above ground, and the story of the battle I had from an old Parsee, who was born at a village called Tamkin, within two miles of the field, and could perfectly remember the action." By this account it will be seen that the officers and seamen of the Company's ships, well maintained the reputation for valour they had acquired by their deeds under Best and Downton, and at Ormuz in 1622.

The Surat President represented to the Directors in England, the absolute necessity of sending out stores and reinforcements, to enable them to defend their houses of trade and ships against the superior force of the Portuguese; for, though the Dutch were also at war with that nation, no reliance could be placed on any assistance they would afford, and, indeed, all their efforts were turned to weakening the connection between the English and the Mogul Government, and striving to ruin the Company by actually selling European goods at a loss, and paying such high prices for Indian goods as to paralyze the markets. The urgency was the greater, from no shipping having arrived from Bantam at Surat, and from the naval power of the Portuguese being solely directed against the English.*

The Viceroy of Goa having failed at Surat, now directed his attention to reviving the Portuguese influence in Persia, where all previous firmans, even those to the English, were abrogated by the death of Shah Abbas; but in this his efforts were doomed to disappointment, for the new Sovereign, Shah Sophi, whose reign terminated by his death, in May, 1642, renewed previous firmans, and a body of two hundred Persian soldiers were sent to Gombroon to protect the English factory and shipping against the hostility of their rivals.

It having become an important object to conciliate the friendship of the Governor of the province of Fars, on whom their trade more immediately depended, the Agents had been obliged to offer the assistance of the English ships to co-operate with him in an expedition which he was preparing, to dislodge the Portuguese from Muscat. This offer was made, because the Agents had the alternative either of incurring his displeasure, or of giving an opportunity to the Dutch (who would readily have embraced it) to regain the favour of the Shah and of the Governor. The Agents, to avoid similar embarrassments, suggested to

* Bruce's " Annals," vol. i., p. 301.

the Court the expediency of having power to take possession of some place on the coast of Persia, to which they could retreat, in the event of any emergency, which was the first intimation we have of the policy which, ultimately, resulted in the permanent occupation of Bassadore, in the Island of Kishm, and of Karrack, during war time, in 1838 and 1856.

In May or June, 1634, a truce, to continue for six months—till after the notification of the decision of the Sovereigns of England and Spain, from whose Crown Portugal was not separated until 1640—was signed by the President of Surat and the Viceroy of Goa, by which the Portuguese ports were to be open to the English, whose factories were to reciprocate friendly relations with the Portuguese traders. Explanations having taken place between the Crown of England and Spain, on this basis, the Company's Agents in Persia were directed to avoid becoming parties in the state of hostilities then existing between the Portuguese and the Persians, and King Charles wrote a letter to the Shah, soliciting his protection of his subjects. In January, 1635, the truce between the rival European Powers in the East, gave place to a regular Convention, which was concluded, in person, at Goa between the Viceroy and Mr. Methwold, the President at Surat, who, writing home to the Court a few days later, proposed, says Bruce, in future to limit the English trade to four annual ships, two of which would find a lading at Goa, while the other two would either complete their investments at the other Portuguese ports, or at the English factories on the Coromandel coast, or Sumatra.

In prosecution of this plan of trade, the Presidency formed a factory at Scindy, and solicited a firman for settling a factory at Dabul. They built two "pinnaces" at Damaun, and two at Bassein, for the coast trade, and tried a new experiment, that of sending a pinnace, with a small investment, to Bussorah, which, being a Turkish port, was not liable to any interference from the Persian Government.

About the close of the year the Company were involved in great difficulties, owing to a number of persons, with Sir William Courten at their head—excited by prospects of gain, owing to the arrangements with the Portuguese—having succeeded in procuring a grant from the King, and forming an association which was known as "Courten's Interlopers." They sent ships out to Surat, whose arrival seems to have thrown the factory into the greatest confusion, and caused a suspension of trade for the season on the part of the Company.* Notwith-

* In the year 1636 occurred the first instance of the good offices of a successful physician effecting what the diplomatists could not gain by presents and fair promises. In that year the chief and factors of Surat, on the application of a nobleman at the Court of Shah Jehan, sent Gabriel Broughton, surgeon of the Company's ship 'Hopewell,' to Delhi to attend the Emperor's daughter, and so much were his skill and attention appreciated, that Imperial favours were liberally

standing a petition to the Crown against this infringement of their privileges, presented by the Court in 1637, Courten's Association received a new trading license for five years, which, however, was withdrawn on the 10th of December, 1639, on the Company affirming their intention to abandon the trade altogether, if the protection for which they prayed was not afforded to them. For many years after this withdrawal, the ships of Courten's Association seriously injured the Company, whose affairs languished owing to the Civil War raging in England between Charles I. and his Parliament, during which the cargoes sent home were but small. In the Persian Gulf the Dutch, having attained an ascendancy over the Persians, sent eight ships to Bussorah, where they almost ruined the English factory; also by their extortionate demands at Gombroon, the factory at that port likewise fell into so precarious a situation, that the Company's property was removed thence, and sent to Bussorah in June, 1645. The Gombroon factory, however, still continued a small business, and, on the outbreak of war between the Mogul and the King of Persia, there was a great improvement, the carrying trade being exclusively conducted by the Dutch and English ships; it was necessary to retain a footing at Gombroon, in order that the Company might realize the moiety of the customs acquired by their seamen at Ormuz, which varied every year, and, in 1648, amouted to 635 tomans, or about £1,900, though their fair proportion was estimated at £15,000 per annum.

In 1652 war was declared between Holland and England, and, in the following March, intelligence of the event was received at Surat. The East India Company had vainly sought for assistance from the Home Government, to repel the anticipated aggressions of the Dutch, who had a powerful fleet in the East Indies—that in the Persian Gulf alone consisting of fifteen sail. The Dutch factory formally declared war against England, and soon a fleet of eight large ships appeared off Swally. Though not deeming it prudent to attack the English factory and shipping in the river, which would have been considered an aggression by the Mogul Government, they set sail for the Persian Gulf. Off Jask they captured the Company's ships 'Roebuck' and 'Lanneret,' and, soon afterwards, seized the 'Blessing,' and drove the 'Supply' on shore, where she was

bestowed on him, and, in particular, he obtained a patent permitting him to trade, without paying any duties, throughout the Mogul's dominions. The benefit of this would probably have been doubtful if his good fortune had not followed him to Bengal, where he cured a favourite mistress of the Nawab, who, in gratitude, confirmed all his privileges. The generous surgeon did not, in prosperity, forget his former employers, but advanced the Company's interests by contriving that his privileges should be extended to them. Having done so, he wrote an account of his success to the factory of Surat, and, the next year, a profitable trade was opened in the rich province of Bengal.—Anderson's "English in Western India."

totally lost. These losses were heightened by the necessary cessation of the trade between Persia and Surat, owing to the Dutch fleet, having, by their vast preponderance, the command of the seas. After the conclusion of peace a commission was appointed, consisting of four representatives of the English and Dutch Companies, to regulate the compensation of damages which each asserted they had sustained between the years 1611 and the 18th of May, 1652; but the claims being nearly equal, after long deliberations, the commission awarded that there should be oblivion of the past by both parties; that the Island of Polaroon should be restored to the English Company, who should also receive from their rivals £85,000,* and a further sum

* Cromwell requested the loan of this sum, and the Company, afraid to disoblige so powerful a personage, lent him £50,000 for eighteen months. In this year, 1655, the Protector invaded their privileges and permitted the "Merchant Adventurers" to fit out ships and trade to the countries within their limits. In the following year the Company prayed for a renewal of their charter, which request was referred to a commission, among whose names there appears that of Sir Charles Wolseley, an ancestor of the successful leader of the Ashantee Expedition. The application resulted in the confirmation of the Company's rights and privileges by Cromwell and the Council of State, which were renewed by Charles II. on the 3rd of April, 1661.

In the old India Office in Leadenhall Street, among records of interest there was a letter from Oliver Cromwell, in reply to a petition addressed to him by the Company of Merchants in connection with the East India trade. The original petition, a copy of which was enclosed with the reply in a glass frame in the old Museum, was addressed to "His Highness Oliver, Lord Protector of England and Scotland," and it asks for a convoy of ships of war for some vessels which are expected to arrive with merchandise from the East. The signatures to the petition of the Indian merchants are almost all of them in clear, bold, and legible writing, and speak very highly for the art of penmanship among the merchant classes of the country, at a time when royal and aristocratic autographs were the most wretched of scrawls or cyphers. The following is the copy of the Lord Protector's reply:—"Oliver, Protector. We recommend the answerynge of this peteon to the Commyssioners of our Admiraltye desiringe them to doe herein what they may for the encouragement of the East India trade. Given at Whitehall this 6th of November, 1657." Another document of great interest, a letter written by Lord Nelson with his left hand, might be seen framed near this short letter of the Protector. Immediately on receipt of the news of the battle of the Nile, the Directors convened a Court for the purpose of expressing their opinion of the important service rendered by his lordship to the Company; and it was resolved unanimously—the original resolution being in the same frame as the letter of the gallant Nelson—"That in further testimony of the high sense the Court entertains of the very great and important benefits arising to the East India Company, from his Lordship's magnánimous conduct upon that glorious occasion, this Court requests his Lordship's acceptance of the sum of £10,000." This resolution having been conveyed to Nelson, he replied in the following terms:—"Foudroyant, Bay of Naples, July 3rd, 1799. Sir, I am this day honoured by your letter of May 3rd, conveying to me the resolution of the Hon. East India Company. It is true, Sir, that I am incapable of finding words to convey my feeling for the unprecedented honour done me by the Company. Having in my younger days served in the East Indies, I am no stranger to the munificence of the Honourable Company; but this generous act of their's to me so much surpasses all calculations of my gratitude that I have only the power of saying that I receive it with respect. Give me leave, Sir, to thank you for your eloquent and flattering letter, and I am, with continued respect, your obliged and obedient servant, NELSON.—Sir Stephen Lushington, Bart., Chairman of the Court of Directors of the Hon. East India Company."

of £3,615, to be paid to the heirs and executors of the sufferers at Amboyna in 1623.

In 1658 the factory at Surat was placed in peril by the feuds between the four sons of the Emperor Shah Jehan; but, ultimately, Aurungzebe, the third son, was successful, and, having cleared the field of all rivals, confined his father in his palace, where he survived seven years, and established his rule over almost the entire Peninsula. In these contests the general of one of the rival competitors took possession of the Castle of Surat, and another pillaged part of the town; but the English factory escaped molestation, owing to the prudent neutrality observed by the Company's servants. At this time, besides their factories at Surat and Fort St. George, which had been constituted into a presidency in 1653-54, though subordinate to Surat, they had stations at Agra, Ahmedabad, Mocha, Bussorah, Gombroon, Scindy, Rajahpore, Carwar, and Caile Velha; also inferior agencies at Cossimbuzar, Ballasore, and Patna, which were subordinate to the factory at Hooghly, which, again, was placed under the Presidency of Fort St. George. The stations in what were termed the Southern Seas, remained, as heretofore, dependent on the President and Council of Bantam.

At this time of weakness and partial eclipse as regards the Company's successful prosecution of trade with the East, an event happened which ultimately proved of vast importance to their fortunes, and which gave a new home for the Service whose history we are inditing. We refer to the acquisition of Bombay by the East India Company. Charles II., having married the Infanta Catherine of Portugal, by the 11th Article of the treaty of marriage, obtained as part of her dowry, "the Port and Island of Bombay in the East Indies, together with all the rights, profits, territories, and appurtenances thereof whatsoever." The extent of the island is small, only some eight miles, by about three in width, and neither Charles nor the Portuguese King could have dreamt of the great future before this obscure dependency of the House of Braganza; but it enclosed a land-locked bay which, for beauty and extent, is unsurpassed, while as regards its capabilities for sheltering a large fleet, it is one of the finest harbours in the world.

The Company had long cast an envious eye on Bombay. In 1653 the subject of its acquisition was brought to their notice by the President and Council of Surat, and, in the following year, the Directors addressed a letter to Cromwell, requesting that, while the treaty with the Dutch was pending, and he was endeavouring to settle the national trade to India, the town of Bassein, and port of Bombay, as well as the town and castle of Mozambique, might be acquired for them, as convenient stations for their trade and factories; and, five years later, they renewed the application to the Government, but without effect.

In March, 1662, the English Government despatched a fleet of five men-of-war, commanded by the Earl of Marlborough, having on board a Portuguese Viceroy to see to the execution of the treaty, with five hundred troops, under Sir Abraham Shipman, to receive possession of Bombay; but the Governor, taking advantage of some ambiguities in the treaty by which the island was ceded, refused to deliver it up, on the pretext that it was contrary to the usages of Portugal. The English understood that the neighbouring Portuguese stations, with the Island of Salsette, which is eight times larger than Bombay, were included in the cession; but the Governor peremptorily declined yielding up even the Island of Bombay. Sir Abraham Shipman applied, in this emergency, to the Company's President at Surat, to receive his troops, as they were dying from disease, caused by protracted confinement on board ship; but that official was unable to accede to this request, owing to the jealousy and suspicions that would be aroused in the mind of the Native Governor. Under these circumstances, the Earl of Marlborough, having landed the troops on the Island of Anjedivah, situated about twelve leagues to the south of Goa, returned in his ship to England,* and reported the refusal of the Portuguese Viceroy to comply with the terms of the treaty, upon which the British Government remonstrated with that of Portugal for want of faith, but only obtained evasive explanations. Meantime Sir Abraham Shipman—who made an offer of the island to the President at Surat, which was declined—and the greater part of troops, died at Anjedivah; and, at length, Mr. Cooke, his secretary, on whom the command devolved, in November, 1664, accepted the cession of Bombay on the terms prescribed by the Viceroy of Goa, by which the English renounced all claims to the contiguous islands, and allowed the Portuguese resident at Bombay, exemption from the payment of customs.† This convention King Charles refused to ratify, as contrary to the terms of his treaty with Portugal, and sent Sir Gervase Lucas in the Company's ship 'Return,' to assume the government of the island. This officer's first step was to institute an inquiry into Mr. Cooke's conduct, and, finding that he had been guilty of peculation, he dismissed him. Sir Gervase Lucas soon discovered that the Government of Bombay cost more than it

* This officer, James Ley, the third Earl of Marlborough, was killed by a cannon shot on the 3rd of June, 1665, on board the 'Old James,' in a great battle with the Dutch. He was buried in Westminster Abbey, and was succeeded in the peerage by his uncle, the fourth and last Earl.

† From an original return signed by Mr. Cooke, and dated Anjedivah, 3rd of December, 1664, it appears that the King's troops, who, on their embarkation from England in March, 1662, numbered four companies of one hundred each, exclusive of officers, were reduced by deaths to one hundred and three privates: and, on their arrival in the following February at Bombay, they mustered only one ensign, one surgeon and his mate, ten non-commissioned officers, four drummers, and ninety-seven privates.

produced, and, at length, the King, by letters patent, dated 27th of March, 1668, transferred the island from the Crown to the Company. By this Charter, Charles granted the Port and Island of Bombay to the London East India Company, "to be held to the said Company and their successors of the Crown of England, as the Manor of East Greenwich, in perpetuity and in free and common soccage at a fee farm rent of £10 payable on the 30th of September yearly at the Custom-house." With the island were conveyed all stores and arms, and the Company were empowered to make laws and take the necessary steps for the defence and government of Bombay.*

Under instructions from the Court of Directors, the President at Surat, Sir George Oxenden, took formal possession of Bombay on the 23rd of September, 1668. Six years before, this energetic and able officer had been appointed Director of their affairs "at Surat, and all other factories in the north parts of India, from Zeilon to the Red Sea;" and he now proceeded with a fleet of the Company's ships, accompanied by the squadron of men-of-war despatched to India under the command of the Earl of Marlborough, to take possession of Bombay. Sir George Oxenden sent three members of his Council and Captain Young, one of the Company's naval officers, as special Commissioners, to accept the cession of the island, and, on the completion of the transfer, the garrison, which had been strengthend by reinforcements from England, entered the Company's service, as the Bombay European Regiment, which became the nucleus of their military establishment. Captain Gary, who had succeeded Sir Gervase Lucas as Governor on his death, in May, 1667, was now displaced by Captain Young, of the Company's Marine, who became Deputy-Governor under the orders of the President and Council at Surat, though he did not long retain the post.

In 1664 the Marine was afforded an opportunity of distinguishing itself. Sevajee,† the famous chieftain who founded the Mahratta power in India, assumed the title of Rajah on the death of his father, Shahjee, and, having turned his attention to naval affairs, collected, according to the account of the Company's factors at Carwar, a fleet of eighty-seven vessels, manned with four thousand men.

* Bruce's "Annals," vol. ii., p. 200.
† Sevajee was, according to Orme, Sir Thomas Roe, Bernier, and others, descended from the Rajahs of Chittore, who trace their lineage from Porus, whom Alexander overthrew in his famous invasion of India. The first time this prince of freebooters came into conflict with the English was in the year 1661, when, after assassinating the King of Beejapoor's general, and defeating his army, he captured the town of Rajapoor, plundered the English factory, and refused to release the Company's agents, whom he confined for two years in a hill fort, until a ransom had been paid for them. Sevajee committed this act to revenge himself on the English, whom he accused, and possibly with truth, of supplying shot and shell to his enemies while laying siege to Panala, from which he had just escaped.

With these he took many Mogul ships, made descents upon the coast, and carried off much plunder from the ports belonging to the King of Beejapoor. Declaring his intention to attack the Portuguese at Bassein and Choul, he advanced rapidly upon Surat with four thousand horse, and arrived within fifteen miles of it on the 5th of January, 1664, before any tidings of his movements had been received. On his approach, the Mogul Governor left the town to its fate, and retired into the castle, while the inhabitants fled either in boats, or into the surrounding country. In this emergency, Sir George Oxenden and the Company's servants shut themselves up in the factory with their property, being of the estimated value of £80,000, and, after fortifying the building, called in the ships' crews for its defence, while the grabs and galivats in the river took up positions enabling them to act with effect. " When attacked," says Bruce, " they made a brave and obstinate resistance, and this opposition not only preserved the factory, but the town from destruction." On the arrival of the Mogul army, after the retreat of Sevajee, Sir George Oxenden received the thanks of the Commander for his fidelity and the gallantry of his men.

Horace Hayman Wilson, the historian, in referring to Mill's meagre narrative of this event, says:—" Scant justice is done to the Company's servants in this brief notice of a conduct highly remarkable for cool and resolute courage. Sevajee's approach to within fifteen miles of Surat was announced on the morning of the 5th of January, upon which the Governor retired into the castle, and the inhabitants fled from every part of the city except that adjacent to the factory. In the evening the Mahrattas entered, and part blockaded the castle, while the rest plundered and set fire to the houses. During that night and the following day repeated demands and menaces were sent to the factory, but they were all met with terms of defiance."

" We replied to Sevajee," writes Sir George Oxenden in his despatch to the Court, dated 26th of January, 1664, " we were here on purpose to maintain the house to the death of the last man, and therefore not to delay his coming upon us."

It does not appear that any organized attack was made upon the factory, but the Mahrattas assembled in considerable numbers before it, and broke into an adjoining house. To prevent their establishing themselves in a situation from which they might offer serious annoyance, a sally was made from the factory, which had the effect of dislodging the assailants, and putting them to flight with some loss and three men wounded on the part of the English; this success was followed up with spirit, the plundered house was occupied, several sorties were made, and pushed even to the gates of the castle, and the neighbourhood, for about a quarter of a mile round, was cleared of the enemy. No further attempts were made to molest the factory or its vicinity during the three days that Sevajee continued in possession of the town, and the inhabitants of the quarter in which the factory was situated, "were very thankful in their acknowledgments, blessing and praising the English nation," to whose valour they ascribed their exemption from the calamities which had desolated the rest of the city. The Governor presented Sir George Oxenden with a dress of honour, and recommended the interests of the Company to the Emperor Aurungzebe, who, subsequently, granted to the English a perpetual remission of a portion of the duties.* The Company also showed their approval of the conduct of their servants, by presenting the President with a gold medal and a gratuity of £200, and distributing £400 among his subordinates.

Soon after this event, Surat being again menaced with the approach of Sevajee's army, Sir George Oxenden seized the opportunity, while the Mogul's officers were again looking for the assistance of the English, to send a mission to Broach, to solicit from Aurungzebe's uncle, at this time Governor of Guzerat, the further confirmation of the Company's privileges. To this application he received a "Perwanna" from the Mogul, granting to the English the whole of the customs of Surat for one year, and an abatement on the rate from that time forward.

The President, seeing the importance of the Marine as a protection to the factory, and the service it rendered the Company's material interests by extracting further concessions from Aurungzebe, paid great attention to its efficiency. Hence it was enabled to cope successfully with the Company's numerous enemies, both European and Asiatic; for it was a peculiarity of our position in the East during this century, that while England was at peace with Continental States, their respective marines abroad maintained a state of rivalry which often found vent in acts of hostility.

During the year 1668 the 'Bantam,' pink, mounting eight guns, was employed as convoy to the Surat vessels belonging to the Mogul Government, which annually carried pilgrims to Jeddah, the factory receiving for this service the continuance, if not the extension, of the Company's privileges at Surat. The year 1669 witnessed a further development of the Indian Marine, hitherto only located at Surat. The trade of Bombay had been so much exposed to the depredations of the Malabar pirates and the fleet or armed boats of Sevajee, that the Council at the island intimated to the Court that it would be necessary to construct three small armed vessels to protect the merchant craft trading to and from the island, and to serve as convoys to those engaged in trade with the Gulf of Persia and Arabian Sea. In

* Mills' "History of India," vol. i., p. 98.

consonance with this proposal, the Court of Directors appointed, as their shipbuilder at Bombay, Mr. Warwick Pett, a descendant of the famous Sir Phineas Pett, celebrated for his talents as a shipbuilder at Deptford, in the reigns of Elizabeth and James. Mr. Pett was directed to proceed to Bombay and construct two ships, for which equipments and stores were sent from England, and, in the following year, directions were given for the construction of two other small brigantines. These orders may be regarded as the first links in the chain of events that, ultimately, ended in the withdrawal of the Marine forces of the Company from Surat to Bombay, which gave to the Service the name by which it was known until the year 1830.

In this year, also, the Council at Surat were directed to fortify Bombay, two military officers being appointed as engineers; and indeed, at the time of the lamented death of Sir George Oxenden, which took place on the 14th of July, 1669, the Council suggested the desirability of transferring the Presidency altogether from Surat to Bombay, as the proceedings of the Governor in banishing the shroffs, or native bankers, and the banians, or merchants, on account of some religious differences, affected the Company's trade, which was still further depressed by the alarm consequent upon an apprehended attack by Sevajee, when Mr. Aungier, the President, placed the factory in a state of defence.

In 1670 affairs at Surat again assumed a critical aspect. Bahadar Khan, the General of Aurungzebe, arrived, with three thousand horse, to defend the city against Sevajee,* who appeared at its gates at the head of fifteen thousand men. The great Mahratta Chief effected an entrance on the 3rd of October, and pillaged the city of an immense amount of booty and treasure. On this occasion, the Company's servants and the seamen of the Marine, did good service. Mr. Streynsham Master, one of the Council, who had acted early in the year as the Deputy of Mr. Aungier during his temporary absence at Bombay, proceeded with a party of seamen from Swally to defend the factory, and, notwithstanding the repeated and desperate assaults of the Mahrattas, succeeded in making a successful resistance. At length Sevajee, seeing the futility of his efforts, tried what persuasion would do, and endeavoured to induce the agent to return to Rajahpore for purposes of trade, but, of course, without effect. During the conflict many men were killed and wounded, and some goods, stored in detached warehouses, were lost; but the factory remained unscathed, and the most valuable

* At this time Sevajee was possessed of the greater portion of the Concan, by which is denoted the narrow strip of territory between Goa and Damaun, extending between the sea and the mountains, or Ghauts, (Sanskrit *Ghatta*) so called because they recede like steps from the seashore. Excepting Choul, which remained in the possession of the Portuguese, Sevajee was master of the sea coast from the river Rajahpore to Bombay harbour.

part of the Company's property had, on the first report of Sevajee's approach, been sent to Swally, or put on board the ships. The gallantry of the seamen of the Marine contrasted favourably with that of the French in their factory, who compounded with the Mahratta robber, and furnished his troops with the means of capturing the Persian factory, with its vast stores of gold and silver, which was defended by a Tartar Prince, called by the English factors, in their report, "The King of Kascar," who had returned by way of Surat from a pilgrimage to Mecca. The Dutch factory, being in a retired quarter, escaped pillage.*

President Aungier again recommended the withdrawal of the factory from Surat to Bombay, as apprehensions were felt of another attack by Sevajee's army; but the Mogul Governor deprecated the step, though, in the following year, on some Dutch seamen, who had insulted the servants of a chief, taking refuge in the English factory, he ordered the people to discontinue their services to the Europeans, whether English, French, or Dutch, and to put them to death if found with arms. The difficulty arising from this affair, was, at length, settled amicably, when another arose with the French, who, on the arrival of a large fleet of twelve armed ships, besides merchantmen, commanded by Admiral De la Haye, had the arrogance to demand that the English ships at Swally, as bearing the flag of a commercial Company, should pay their fleet, bearing the Royal colours, the honours of the flag. The President, however, with becoming spirit, resisted these preposterous pretensions, both because the Company's flag was authorised by the King of England, and from the fact of the distinction between the Royal and Company's flags being unintelligible to the Native Governor and people.

At this time affairs were complicated in the East, by this country being at war with Holland, and Bombay was placed in a state of defence, to resist the attack of a Dutch fleet, numbering twenty-two sail, having on board five thousand seamen, with one thousand regular troops, which appeared off the Malabar coast in February, 1673. The Dutch Admiral had solicited the alliance of Sevajee, for which he proffered his aid in reducing Jinjeera; but, fortunately for English interests, the alliance was rejected. In this crisis, President Aungier exerted himself, as Orme says, "with the calmness of a philosopher and the courage of a centurion." Besides his European force of

---

* See Bruce's "Annals," vol. ii., p. 285, and James Grant Duff's "History of the Mahrattas," vol. i., p. 247. The latter historian says that at the time of Sevajee's attack there were only a few hundred of the Imperial troops in the city, the greater portion having been withdrawn, either by accident or design, shortly before the arrival of the Mahrattas. In February, 1665, Sevajee had attacked Carwar, when the English defended their factory with courage and success.

four hundred soldiers, he raised a Portuguese Native Militia of one thousand five hundred men, and equipped and prepared for service his small squadron, which consisted at this time of two ships, carrying sixteen guns, the 'Revenge' and 'Hunter,' a Dutch prize, the 'Mayboon,' of twenty-two guns and three armed sloops, which had been built to protect the trade against the Malabar pirates. To this force a valuable addition was made by the arrival of four French ships, which had sailed from Surat. The Dutch Admiral and Governor of Ceylon, Rickloff van Goen, stood into Bombay Harbour in the night of the 20th of February, but, after closely examining the dispositions for defence, was so impressed with these preparations, that he decided to give up the projected attack, and sailed for Surat.*

* See Orme's "Oriental Fragments," p. 33.

A quaint account of Bombay in 1672, and of the Dutch attempt to surprise it, is given by Dr. Fryer, he says :—" The Dutch attempting to surprise the islanders, found them and the fort in so good a condition that they were glad to betake themselves to their boats without any booty, and the next day hoisted sails (for, said they, Bombaim being as stark as de deel) and not without good reason, for within the fort were mounted one hundred and twenty pieces of ordnance, and in other convenient stands twenty more, besides sixty field-pieces ready in their carriages upon occasion to attend the Militia and Bandarines. To the fort there belonged three hundred English and four hundred topazes, or Portugal firemen ; to the Militia, out of Portugal musters, five hundred under English leaders, all well armed ; of Bandarines (that look after the woods of cocoes) with clubs and other weapons, three hundred. Besides some thousands more would make a show, but not to be relied on should it come to the push. Moreover, in the road were riding three men-of-war, the best of thirty guns."
The town of Bombay he describes as follows :—" It is a full mile in length ; the houses are low and thatched with oleas of the cocoe-trees, all but a few the Portugals left, and some few the Company have built ; the Custom house and warehouses are tiled or plastered, and instead of glass use panes of oister-shells for their windows (which as they are cut in squares and polished, look gracefully enough). There is also a reasonable handsome buzzar. At the end of the town looking into the field, where cows and buffaloes graze, the Portugals have a pretty house and church, with orchards of Indian fruit. The English have only a burying place called Mendam's Point, from the first man's name there interred, where are some few tombs that make a pretty show on entering the Haven ; but neither church or hospital, both of which are mightily to be desired." He then describes the surburbs of Mazagon, Parell, Mahim, and Malabar Hill ; also the Government, and concludes with a patriotic outburst and his estimate of the bitterness of expatriation to such a place and climate, of which he says :—" I reckon they walk but in charnel houses, the climate being extremely unhealthy."
" Happy certainly then are those," he says, " and only those, brought hither in their nonage, before they have a gust of our Albion, or next to these, such as intoxicate themselves with Læthe and remember not their former condition. When it is expostulated, Is the reward of our harsh and severe pupilage? Is this the Elysium after a tedious passage ? For this will any thirst, with any content, will any forsake the pleasures of his native soil in his vigorous age to bury himself alive here ? Were it not more charitable at the first bubbles of his infant sorrows to make the next stream over-swell him ? Or else, if he must be fullgrown for misery, how much more compassionate were it to expose him to an open combat with the fiercest duellists in Nature, to spend at once his spirits, than to wait a piece-meal consumption." This tirade against the country and climate will not be endorsed by most old " Ducks," nor the concluding passage by any of those who return to England to enjoy their " off-reckonings." Speaking of the survivors, he says :—For in five hundred, one hundred survive not : of that hundred, one quarter get not estates ; of those that do, it has not been recorded above one in ten has seen his country."

All danger from this source ceased the following year, by the Treaty of Peace signed at Westminster, and the marriage of the Prince of Orange with Mary, daughter of the Duke of York. Before this was known in India, the Dutch Admiral encountered on the Coromandel coast, ten of the Company's trading ships which, notwithstanding the disparity of their force, maintained an obstinate conflict, in which two, being dismasted, were captured, and a third ran ashore rather than strike her colours.*

But anxiety was again felt for the safety of Bombay, owing to the hostile attitude assumed by the fleet of the Seedee. Early in 1673, Mr. Aungier first gave permission to four ships of the Mogul fleet to pass the Monsoon in Bombay harbour, which was due to a desire to conciliate the Emperor, as the Company's chief trade was derived from Surat; but, at the same time, he resolutely refused to allow the allied, and more powerful, fleet of the Seedee,† or Abyssinian Admiral, of Jinjeera, to remain in the harbour. In October, however, much alarm was occasioned in Bombay by the sudden arrival in the harbour of the allied fleets of the Mogul and of the Seedee, which, landing a large force, devastated the Corlahs‡ belonging to Sevajee, from which the English drew all their supplies. In the following April, the Seedee's fleet again appeared in the harbour, and landed at Sion, in the island, but were driven out by part of the garrison, and one of the Company's frigates. Another attempt to land five hundred men at Mazagon was likewise repelled by force;

* Orme, in his "Historical Fragments," gives an account of this action, principally derived from Mr. Fryer, who was physician in the Company's ships between 1672 and 1680.

† The Abyssinian Admiral in the service of the Mogul, who conferred on him the Jagheerdar of the southern portion of the province of Kalliannee, was generally known by the name of Seedee, and was under the authority of the King of Viziapoor, but received a stipend from the Mogul. The condition of his tenure was the maintenance of a Marine for the protection of the Mogul's subjects trading to the Gulf of Persia and Arabia, from the Malabar pirates and Portuguese, and his possessions were not considered hereditary, but were conferred on the most deserving officer of the fleet, and the chief so selected was styled Seedee and Wuzeer. The "Hubshee," as he was also called, from his nationality, became independent on the subversion of the Mogul power, though he owed semi-allegiance to the Peishwa of the Mahrattas. Upon the overthrow of Bajee Rao in 1817, his allegiance was transferred to the British. The crews of his vessels were in part composed of his countrymen, and a small African colony was thus formed in the Concan. The great maritime depôt was Dhunda Rajapoor, within half a mile of which stands the small fortified island of Jinjeera, and though the former was captured by Sevajee, the Seedee's fleet enabled him to defy the Mahratta army. The name of the Admiral or Seedee at this time was, says Grant Duff, "Futih Khan," though Orme calls him Sambole, who gave place, in 1676, to Seedee Cossim. The Seedee had charge of several forts, amongst which were Tala, Gossala, and Rairee, which also fell into the hands of Sevajee. The name Seedee is probably an adaptation of the word "Syud," or Lord. In the vulgar language of the Deccan all the natives of Africa were called Seedees, and the coal-trimmers in the steamships of the Indian Navy, who were negroes, were rated on the ships' books as "Seedees," and always so called.

‡ The Corlahs, meaning "districts," is a tract of land on the main extending from Thull, the south point of the harbour, to the river Penn. The word, which is frequently found in the ancient records of Bombay, has long become obsolete.

and, at length, they were glad to make a truce, by which three hundred of them were permitted to land at a time without other arms than their swords. But Bombay was alarmed, in the following year, by a descent made by ten thousand Mahratta troops, opposite the Island of Salsette, and a demand was made at Bassein, for the payment of the "chout," or tribute, of which we now hear for the first time.

Apprehensions were also entertained for the factory at Surat, from which, on an expected attack by Sevajee, the goods were removed for safety to Swally, the Company's frigate 'Hunter' being moored off Surat for the protection of the Establishment.

After many failures, Mr. Aungier, who declined to ally himself with Sevajee, so far as to undertake hostile operations against the Seedee's stronghold of Jinjeera, concluded a treaty on the 12th of June, 1674, with the Mahratta Prince, by which privileges of trade were conferred on the Company. On this occasion, the diplomatic agent, Mr. Henry Oxenden, who was introduced to the great Mahratta Chief, and his son, Sambajee, was present at the coronation of the former, which was conducted with great pomp and magnificence.

In the same year the Company exercised their privilege of enforcing martial law on the occasion of a mutiny among their garrison at Bombay. Mr. Aungier brought the ringleaders to trial, and, on being convicted, three were shot on the 21st of October, two were pardoned by the President, and Captain Shaxton, the Commander and Deputy-Governor, was found guilty on some of the charges, and sent to England to be dealt with by the Court. After an absence of nearly three years at Bombay, owing to the unsettled state of the Government in that island, Mr. Aungier returned to Surat in September, 1675, and, immediately, found himself compelled to place the factory in a condition to resist the apprehended attacks of Sevajee and his generals, who also extended their conquests into the Carnatic.*

* Dr. Fryer gives an amusing account of a conflict in which he participated, between a small galivat belonging to the Company and a Malabar pirate. In the latter part of 1675, he accompanied the agent of Carwar down the coast on a visit to Goa. He says:—"In our passage at Serapatan to the south of Dan de Rajapoor, a strong castle of Seva Gi's, descended a deep bay, where rode his navy, consisting of thirty small ships and vessels, the Admiral wearing a white flag aloft." Having left Carwar he visited Goa, and, while proceeding to Vingorla, the action we have alluded to took place. "The next day we passed the bar for Vingorla; half way we put ashore to refresh our men, and at ten in the morn set out again; at twelve we came close up with a Malabar that had seized a grab, but we soon made him yield his prize to engage with us, which they did briskly for two hours, striving to board us, casting stink-pots among us, which broke without any execution, but so frightened our native rowers that we were forced to be severe to restrain them; they plied their chambers and small shot, and slung stones, flourishing their targets, and darting long lances; they were well-manned in a boat ten times as big as our barge, and at least sixty fighting men besides rowers; we had none to manage our small gun, the gunner running away after sluts in brothels; one of the sailors undertaking it, was blown up by a cart-

Mr. Aungier sent two armed ships into the Persian Gulf for the protection of the Company's trade, and intimated to the Shah of Persia that the charges of these ships must be paid, in addition to the moiety of customs raised at Gombroon, otherwise the English ships would cease to protect the port; and the President declared, in terms which showed the independent position he assumed, that any refusal of this demand would be considered as equivalent to hostilities. This was one of the last public acts of Mr. Aungier, the able and high-spirited President of Surat, who died on the 30th of June, 1677, to the extreme regret of his colleagues. He was succeeded by Mr. Rolt,* the agent at Gombroon, Mr. Henry Oxenden assuming the Government of Bombay.

During the past few years the fleet of the Seedees, Cossim and Sambole—for there were two contending for the post of admiral to the Mogul—had passed the monsoon in Bombay harbour, and, by their lawless conduct and faction-fighting, caused much annoyance to the garrison and squadron in the harbour. In 1678 two admirals of Sevajee's fleet, which numbered, according to Orme, "fifty-seven sail, of which fifteen were grabs, and the rest galivats, all crowded with men," came down to Panwell with four thousand men, with the object of crossing over and attacking the ships and quarters of Cossim, who was now the recognised chief Seedee. But the steps taken by the Company's military and naval commanders, assisted by the Portuguese Governor of Bassein, who was alarmed for the safety of Salsette, were happily successful in warding off a collision. The Soubadar, or Native Governor, of Upper Choul, who had claims on one of the Company's factors, relying on the support of Sevajee, on the frustration of his hopes of burning the Seedee's fleet, seized thirty Bombay boats trading in the ports and rivers under his jurisdiction. Upon this being known at the Presidency, four armed vessels, having sixty European

ridge of powder, and squenched his cloaths aflame in the ocean, so that they were fully bent to board us; but they rising to come in, we all this while having sculked under our targets, discharged our blunderbusses, which made them sheer off, never to come near us again; after which we chased them, they flying afore us." The spectators of this encounter were the Dutch chief and governor on the shore, and a ship of twelve guns in the road. "By three," he says, "we came ashore with light hurts, but cried up mightily by the people, who are continually infested by these pirates without any resistance." During his passage from Surat to Gombroon in one of the armed ships of the Company's Marine, in 1676, Dr. Fryer saw some of the pirates that infested those waters, "but," he says, "they were not so foolhardy as to come nigh us, being content to gaze on what they durst not seize, and to wish us impotence instead of force." Of the pirates infesting the seas between Surat and the Persian Gulf, he says:—"Here in this large piece of water the Sindanian pirates wreak their malice on the unarmed merchants, who, not being able to resist their unbounded lust, become tame slaves to their lawless rage. These are alike cruel and equally savage as the Malabars."

* In 1681, Mr. Rolt was succeeded by Mr. Child, brother of Sir Josiah Child, Governor of the East India Company.

seamen on board, attacked the guard placed over these boats, and brought most of them back to Bombay.* In the following year (1679) the Court of Directors, in a review of their affairs at Surat during the past sixteen years, resolved to reduce the charges for the factory in that city, and the civil and military establishments at Bombay, which were to be henceforth limited to an annual charge of 71,900 Rs, while the factories at Carwar and Rajahpore were to be represented by native agents. The small Marine force was likewise reduced to a point that rendered it utterly incapable of taking the offensive against the powerful Mahratta or Mogul fleets. These reductions caused great dissatisfaction at Bombay, which was placed in a position of extreme danger, owing to the threatening conduct of Sevajee, who had now collected a fleet of twenty grabs and forty galivats. It cannot, however, be a matter for surprise that Sevajee was incensed against the English for permitting the Mogul fleets to have shelter and protection in Bombay harbour, thus, at the same time, evading an encounter with his own powerful fleet, and making a neutral port their base of operations. He, accordingly, directed his admiral to occupy Kenery, a small and uninhabited, but well-wooded, island, situated about two and a half miles from the mainland, and thirteen from Bombay, being just discernible from the deck of a ship lying in the

---

* The following wild freak is told of a Mr. Thorpe, described as "an ensign in the Company's Navy:"—

Mr. Thorpe, having quitted the harbour of Bombay in his manchua, (a) was one day cruising off Danda Rajapoor, and there descried a vessel belonging to the Seedee's fleet making towards him. The Seedee's people had taken him for a Malabar pirate, and he did not choose to undeceive them until they came pretty near. Then his colours were run up to the masthead, and they, perceiving their mistake, began to sheer off; but Thorpe was determined not to let them off so cheaply, so he invited some of the Seedee's crew to pay him a visit. On their coming on board he charged them with a design of seizing the Honourable Company's manchua. They stoutly declared that they had no such intention, but he nevertheless, with most reprehensible cruelty, ordered the hands of two of the men who had come on board, to be fastened behind their backs, and in this condition they were hoisted up to the vessel's yard. They soon admitted that their captain had intended to make the manchua his prize, which was probably the truth. Acting upon information thus unjustifiably wrung from his victims, Ensign Thorpe made the captain and two of his men prisoners, and continued his cruise down the coast. This affair involved the English in no little trouble, for the Seedee demanded satisfaction, and of course sent in an exaggerated statement of losses sustained. He maintained that he had been robbed of two thousand six hundred rupees, but the Bombay Government declared that only forty rupees were in his vessel; and excited his indignation by offering to restore that sum. The offending ensign, we are further informed, was deprived of his commission, but afterwards re-instated.

(a) Manchua, for manchava, a small vessel of ten or twelve "candies." Other craft used on the coast of India are, shybar or shebar, a large vessel; balloon for balyauv, a state barge; prow for parav, a small botella or batille, seldom exceeding thirty "candies;" ketch or dorish, meaning "one and a half," from having a main and mizen masts. (Hamilton's "History of Hindostan," vol. i. Paper by J. Vaupell, in the Seventh Volume of the Bombay Geographical Society's Transactions.) Grabs and galivats have already been described.

VOL. I. F

harbour. At the end of August, Sevajee sent three hundred soldiers and as many labourers, with arms and materials from the main, to the island, and, immediately, began to raise breastworks at the landing places. The Bombay Council apprehended the consequences of this occupation, and recollected a pretension to the island. This, however, was denied by the Portuguese at Bassein, who were equally alarmed, and now asserted an ancient right of their own; they having formerly attempted to settle on Kenery, which they quitted on finding that the wells only supplied salt water.

Owing to the cold fit of economy, the Bombay Government were without any galivats, which are vessels constructed for quick sailing, and, therefore, fitted three trading boats, which they manned with forty Europeans of the garrison, with orders to prevent the landing of any men from Sevajee's vessels, and to summon his admiral to evacuate the island. But this officer, contrasting the peremptoriness of the demand with the weakness of the armament sent to enforce it, answered that he never should quit his station until recalled by his master. After cruising ten days about the island, hard weather drove the trading vessels back to Bombay, whence they proceeded again to the island, reinforced by the 'Revenge,' carrying sixteen guns. The next day, which was the 19th of September, a lieutenant commanding one of these small craft, who was induced to land with his men, was treacherously killed, together with six other Europeans, the rest being made prisoners, and the vessel being hauled up on the shore. This took place, says Orme, "before any assistance could be given by the other vessels working against the wind and tide, which the enemy's boats, by their construction and oars, were much better able to surmount; and for several nights following passed to and from the island without being interrupted. The officers on the service imputed their ineffectual watch to the fewness of their vessels, and the whole of Sevajee's armada were assembling at Choul under the command of his admiral, Dowlet Khan." Upon this the Government of Bombay increased their force by hiring the vessels they wanted, and, on the 6th of October, the fleet off Kenery consisted of the 'Revenge,' as flagship, two grabs, and five armed trading vessels, only eight sail in all. On board of these were two hundred European soldiers, which amounted to two-thirds of the garrison of Bombay, besides the seamen forming the crews. On the 16th of October Dowlet Khan's fleet anchored close to the shore a little to the north of Choul, in sight of Kenery, to which a number of his galivats passed over in the ensuing night, and, on the next, returned to the main. At daybreak on the 18th their whole fleet bore down, firing from their bows, and advancing so fast that the English vessels, at anchor near the island, had scarcely time to get under weigh; in less than half-an-hour one of the grabs, called the 'Dove,' was surrounded and obliged to strike, and the other only avoided this danger by keeping aloof, while the five trading vessels set sail in retreat; so that the 'Revenge' was left alone in the midst of the enemy. She was commanded by Captain Minchin, having also on board Captain Keigwin, the commander of the garrison, both men of conspicuous gallantry. After a determined and desperate fight they beat off the enemy's galivats that attempted to board, and sunk five of them; on which the whole fleet, fifty vessels, fled before this single ship, and were pursued into shoal water to the bar of Negotan. Several of their galivats, with recruits and stores, succeeded in getting into Kenery during the fight. Two days later the enemy's fleet came out again from Negotan, but, when the English advanced to meet them, returned into the river.

At this time five thousand of Sevajee's troops, in expectation of better success from their fleet, came down from Rairee to Gallian, and demanded, as once before, permission of the Portuguese Government at Bassein, to pass at Tannah, in order to cross at Mahim into Bombay; but they were again refused. Nevertheless, their continuance at Gallian created much solicitude lest the Portuguese should change their mind, or they should succeed in procuring boats and passing down from Gallian in the night, while so large a portion of the garrison was absent in the fleet. Notwithstanding the increase of the English vessels watching Kenery, it still continued impossible to prevent the enemy's boats from reaching it in the night; thus, twelve landed supplies on the 25th, and five a few nights after; and, although not so readily, all got away in safety. Cannon were now mounted on the island, and fired at the English vessels, but they inflicted little loss; while several of the enemy's galivats were driven on shore near Negotan, at different times, by the Company's armed trading vessels. The 'Hunter,' which had come from Surat, and brought the President's guard of thirty-six Europeans to reinforce Bombay, was now sent to reinforce the fleet, which then quitted their station near Kenery, and anchored to block up the river, called by Orme, Negotan; but, as they could not do this effectually, owing to its having two outlets, the Commodore proposed to enter, burn the enemy's fleet, and ravage the country. The Council at Bombay, however, and, still more, the Presidency at Surat, were unwilling to risk provoking Sevajee's resentment. The Mogul Government at Surat were as much alarmed as either the English or Portuguese, at Sevajee's attempts to gain the command of the sea; for, hitherto, they had only dreaded him on shore. The Seedee, having obtained from the Government at Surat the necessary supplies, for the first time without grudge or regret, proceeded to Bombay with his fleet of two large ships, " three frigates of three masts," and fifteen stout galivats, in which, besides the Lascars, were seven hundred picked soldiers. They arrived at Bombay on the 10th of November, and, after conference with the Council there, joined the Company's fleet off Kenery, whose officers, at the same time, received instructions to be cautious.

Seedee Cossim, having rowed round the island, proposed to assault it with his own men, if the Company's vessels would cover the landing; but Captain Keigwin discovered that he intended to keep it, if carried, and, as Bombay might receive more detriment from the island being in his possession than that of Sevajee, evaded giving assistance. On this the Seedee cannonaded the island from his two ships for several days, which was returned, but with little effect on either side; during this time no firing passed between the Company's fleet and the island. This wariness confirmed the intelligence the Seedee had gained concerning the negociations between Bombay and Sevajee, and, in order to break them off, he sent his galivats in the night to ravage the neighbouring towns. Dowlet Khan prepared to come out of Negotan with a numerous convoy, laden with provisions and ammunition, and all his grabs appeared one morning at the mouth of the river; but, on the approach of the English and Mogul fleets from their stations, retired again. The smaller vessels were then left to block the outlets; but the Seedee, fearing his own might be surprised, withdrew them, and the watch was continued by only two of the Company's.

The Seedee continued firing at Kenery until the 9th January, 1680, when, says Bruce, " without intimating his design to the English captains, he anchored his fleet at Henery, a smaller neighbouring island, from which it is separated by a shallow channel, on which he landed men and cannon, and declared his intention of fortifying it, as a check on Kenery. Four days later, Dowlet Khan came out, with all his vessels, from the river of Negotan, and a general engagement ensued, with little damage, for it was over before the English could take any share in it. Dowlet Khan then brought guns to a rising ground on the mainland opposite Henery, against which they fired, and were answered as well by the Seedee's ships as the guns in the island. This cannonade continued several days. On the 27th Dowlet Khan came out again with his whole fleet and engaged the Seedee's for four hours, until he had lost four grabs, and as many of the smaller vessels, with five hundred men killed and wounded, besides the prisoners, and was himself severely wounded. The Seedee lost no vessels, and had only ten men killed. After the engagement the grabs, leaving the galivats to guard the neighbouring rivers, bore away to refit at Rajahpore, which is one hundred miles to the south of Negotan.

The Bombay Council were, at this time, negotiating a treaty

with an ambassador sent by Sevajee from Rairee, and, fearing he should think that this success of the Seedee was acceptable to them, they immediately recalled their own fleet. The Seedee, against whom they were much incensed at his having so treacherously occupied Henery, tried again to break off the treaty then being negotiated with Sevajee, by sending the grabs he had taken to be sold in Bombay, and, on being refused the permission, he entered the harbour on the 27th of February with his whole fleet, and detached his galivats, crowded with men, into the River Penn, which they went up as far as the depth permitted, burning all the towns and villages on either hand. Nevertheless the treaty was concluded in the middle of March; it confirmed that of 1674, made by Mr. Oxenden, and promised, on the part of Sevajee, immediate payment of what remained due of the compensation then allowed for the Company's losses at the sack of Rajahpore in 1673. The English, on their part, agreed to permit the Seedee's fleet to winter in the harbour, only on the condition of abstaining from any attack on the opposite shore. But Seedee Cossim made little account of treaties, and, on the 5th of May, came into the harbour with the main body of his fleet, and anchored off the fort without permission or firing the customary salute. Upon this guns were fired on his ships, which forced them to a further distance and produced a discussion, which, at length, terminated by the Seedee's consenting to refrain from the invasion of the "Corlahs," conformably to the engagements lately made by the Council with Sevajee; but their continuing in the harbour gave great umbrage to Sambhajee, the son and successor of the latter, who despatched troops to the shore, with the object of burning their fleet, though he continually deferred the attempt.

On the 1st of August, the night being dark, two hundred Mahrattas landed on the Island of Henery, and got within the works before they were discovered; but the Seedee's men attacked them with resolution and either took or killed the greater part. Eighty heads were brought in baskets to Mazagon, where Seedee Cossim prepared to fix them along the shore on poles, but was interdicted by the Council. This ill-success increased the resentment of Sambhajee, who sent more troops to the Corlahs, and threatened the invasion of Bombay, upon which the Council reinforced the outposts towards Gallian. At length the Seedee put to sea on the 2nd of December, and, after again returning to Bombay in April, 1681, proceeded to Surat on the 3rd of May.*

Notwithstanding the treaties and agreements made with the Moguls and Mahrattas, the hostile attitude assumed by these two parties in retaining possession of the Islands of Henery and Kenery, and the ill-judged orders for the reduction of the guard at Surat and the Military and Marine establishments at Bombay,

* Orme's "Oriental Fragments," pp. 79 to 97.

rendered the Company's position on the Malabar coast extremely precarious, for, with such reduced establishments, they were absolutely at the mercy of both Mahrattas and Moguls, and only escaped annihilation by showing a bold face, and hiding their weakness. It was not without many protests that the Deputy-Governor and Council at Bombay, and the officers of the Marine, submitted to the indignity of seeing the islets of Kenery and Henery in the possession of their warlike neighbours. The Bombay Government had addressed the Court of Directors, requesting permission to expel these intruders, a task they expressed their willingness to undertake with the means at their disposal; but the Court replied, on the 22nd of April, 1681, declaring themselves opposed to such an undertaking; and then, expounding their peace policy, added:—"Although we have formerly wrote you that we will have no war for Henery and Kenery, yet all war is so contrary to our constitution as well as our interest, that we cannot too often inculcate to you our aversion thereunto." In May of the following year, the same injunction is repeated in still stronger terms, although the inconvenience of allowing these islands to be occupied by the sailors of another nation is fully acknowledged.*

The death of Sevajee, on the 5th of April, 1680, and the succession of his son, Sambhajee,† from which hopeful auguries were drawn, made no difference in the position of affairs. Sambhajee, who had raised his fleet by great exertions to fifteen grabs and one hundred and twenty galivats, enraged by the constant depredations of the Seedee's fleet—which made Henery the base of their operations, whence they ravaged the coast, and seized his trading vessels—threatened to punish the English and Portuguese for maintaing a neutrality towards them; and, on the 5th of October, 1682, a portion of his fleet, numbering thirty sail, proceeded to attack that of the Mogul commander, which was lying at anchor, off Mazagon, in Bombay Harbour. The Seedee Cossim weighed with fifteen sail, having on board his best men, and stood up towards the Tannah River, where a sanguinary action took place, which resulted in a complete victory for the Seedee, who took four ships, including the flagship of the Mahratta Admiral, who was mortally wounded. Sambhajee, exasperated at his defeat, began to fortify the Island of Elephanta, in Bombay Harbour, for the purpose of annoying the English, but, alarmed at the hostile designs of the Moguls, who appeared determined to oust the English from Bombay, and the Portuguese from Goa and Damaun, he changed his plans,

* Anderson's "English in Western India."
† This brave but unfortunate prince was captured by Aurungzebe's forces, and in August, 1689, was publicly decapitated, after having a red hot iron drawn across his eyes, and his tongue cut out. On his death, Rajah Ram, son of Sevajee, and half brother of Sambhajee, by whom he was confined, was declared Regent during the minority of Shao, then a child in his sixth year.

and sent an ambassador to Bombay to propose an alliance against the Imperial Government; but the negotiations ended abortively.

Taking advantage of the disturbed state of affairs, pirates swarmed along the Malabar coast, and even had the temerity to attack one of the largest ships of the Company, when they met with so warm a reception as to discourage any attempt at repetition. Early in 1683, the 'President,' Captain Hyde, who had commanded her in the action with the Dutch fleet at Metchlepatam, arrived on the Malabar coast, and, proceeding to Bombay, was attacked by two ships and four grabs. Three of the latter grappled, when the crew of one boarded, but were beaten off, and the grab itself sunk close alongside. On getting clear of the other grabs, she maintained so hot and well-directed a fire that one of them blew up so near that the flash scorched many of the 'President's' men on the lower deck, and set her on fire in several places. Soon after, the other grab was also sunk, on which the remainder of the squadron sailed away. Of the floating men, some cut the 'President's' long-boat from her stern, and others were received into the ship. Most of them were Arabs, and all the fleet hailed from Muscat; they pretended to have mistaken the 'President' for a Portuguese ship which they were waiting for, but it was afterwards discovered at Rajahpore that they had all been hired by Sambhajee. The 'President' had eleven men killed and thirty-five wounded, and was obliged to put into Goa to repair her damages. As soon as this affair was known at Bombay, an envoy was sent to Rairee;* but Sambhajee denied any knowledge or complicity in the attack.†

About this time the Company despatched from England, on a trading speculation to Mocha, Bussorah, and Gombroon, the 'Dragon,' of 180 tons, carrying eighteen guns; and, in the following year, sent a squadron of armed ships to the East under Sir Thomas Grantham, who was also invested with the king's commission, with orders to proceed, in the first instance, to Java, and thence to the Persian Gulf, in order to demand payment of the arrears of Customs due from the Persian monarch, computed at thirty thousand tomâns, agreeably to the treaty concluded when the Company's ships expelled the Portuguese from Ormuz; and, in default of payment, he was directed to seize the Persian ships as prize, the amount realised being carried to the credit of the treasury at Surat.

During this same year (1683) Bombay was exposed to danger from a source where it might least have been expected. Captain Richard Keigwin, commanding the Company's garrison at Bombay, in conjunction with the other military officers, seized Mr.

---

* The remains of the strong fort of Rairee, or Raree, still form a conspicuous object from seaward.
† Orme's "Historical Fragments," p. 120.

Charles Ward, Deputy-Governor, and such members of Council as were in his interest, and, having annulled the Company's authority by a proclamation, dated the 27th of December, 1683, secured his own election as Governor by the inhabitants of the island and the garrison, consisting of one hundred and fifty European soldiers, and two hundred "topasses," as the native Portuguese soldiers were then called. He then proclaimed the authority of the King, to whom and the Duke of York, afterwards James II., he addressed letters stating his reasons for his conduct, and also seized on the Bombay Marine ships 'Revenge' and 'Hunter.' The President and Council at Surat, conscious of their inability to reduce the island by force, sent three commissioners in three of the Company's ships, with promises of redress of grievance and a general amnesty. The conferences, which lasted more than a month, were fruitless, and, in January, 1684, Mr. Child proceeded to Bombay with three of the Company's ships; but Captain Keigwin and his adherents were obstinate, for their resentment was mainly directed against the President and his brother, Sir Josiah Child, to whose influence they attributed the grievances of which they complained. As the crews of the Company's ships refused to act against the mutineers, Mr. Child and his council returned to the Presidency without having accomplished their object, though the ship 'Return,' sent to Surat, fell into their hands. On intelligence being received in England of these events, the Court of Directors appealed to the King, who issued an order, under sign manual, to Captain Keigwin and his associates, directing them to deliver up the island to the Presidency at Surat, and a commission, under the Great Seal, dated the 25th of August, 1684, was directed to Mr. Child, the members of Council at Bombay and Surat, and the commanders of the Company's ships, empowering them to receive the island from Keigwin and his associates, and to offer a general pardon to all —except the four ringleaders, Captain Keigwin, commanding the troops, Captain Alderton, commanding the 'Hunter,' which had gone over to the rebels, and Lieutenants Thornton and Fletcher—who should, within twenty-four hours' notice, return to their duty.

Under these commissions President Child was appointed Captain-General and Admiral of the Company's sea and land forces; Sir Thomas Grantham, a Company's officer, vice-admiral; and the senior captain of the Company's ships, rear-admiral. The fleet, under command of Sir Charles Grantham, whose flagship was the 'Charles II.,' of eighty guns, had proceeded direct to Surat before the news of the revolt was known in England. From Surat, Sir Thomas sailed in his flag-ship to the Persian Gulf; but, finding that the Dutch were in great force off Gombroon, he returned to Surat, whence he immediately proceeded to Bombay, where he arrived on the 10th of November, 1684. With great promptitude and resolution he landed without any attendants, and demanded a conference with Captain Keigwin, the result of which was that the latter agreed to deliver up the fort to him, as a King's officer, (Sir Thomas having also the King's commission), on condition of a free pardon to himself and his adherents. Accordingly, on the 19th of November, the surrender took place to Sir Thomas Grantham, who immediately transferred the island to Dr. St. John, the Judge-Advocate, also bearing the King's commission, by whom it was again delivered to Mr. Zingan, as the Company's Governor, till the arrival of the President. Sir Thomas Grantham then returned to England in his ship, the 'Charles II.,' having Captain Keigwin on board as his prisoner, together with twelve other sail from Surat and Gombroon; and thus terminated an episode that appeared fraught with disaster to the Company, but out of which they were extricated by the promptitude and ability of one of their Marine officers, whose situation was, at one time, no less trying to his courage, for, during the negotiations, one of the soldiers was on the point of shooting him, and, for a few days, the island was again in the possession of the mutineers.*

In the year 1685 Mr. Child (now Sir John Child, Bart.) was appointed, by the King's patent, Captain-General and Admiral of the Company's sea and land forces between Cape Comorin and the Gulf of Persia, Sir John Wyborne being created Vice-Admiral and Deputy-Governor of Bombay; and, in the following year, the seat of Government was transferred from Surat to Bombay, the Company's stores being kept in the 'Castle,' and the larger ships lying in the harbour. Surat was also reduced to an agency, with a Council subordinate to the new Presidency, which was clothed with unlimited power over the rest of the Company's settlements. Sir John Child, having left Mr. Harris as his agent at Surat, arrived at Bombay on the 2nd of May, 1687, and his first measures appear of a doubtful character; for, acting under instructions from the Court,* he ordered the 'Charles II.,' Captain Andrews, with the 'Modena,' Captain Wildey, two of the Company's largest ships, to proceed to Mocha and Bussorah, with secret orders to seize all Mogul and Siamese vessels at those ports, and also sent two ships to China with similar instructions.†

* Bruce's "Annals," vol. i., p. 541.
† The Company also entered on a course of active hostility in Bengal, which was abandoned as a trading station, and so greatly exasperated the Emperor Aurungzebe that he issued orders to expel the English from his dominions, which were only cancelled on their making a humble submission. In the course of these transactions, Captain Heath, commanding the Company's armed ship 'Defence,' accompanied by another vessel, on the 29th of November, 1689, landed some troops and seamen at Ballasore and took a battery of thirty guns. In 1698 the Company obtained a grant of the towns of Chattanuttee, Govindpore, and Calcutta, and constructed Fort William, when the station was constituted a Presidency.

It was intended, before any intelligence could reach Surat of the captures which these vessels might make, to endeavour, by address, in the first instance, and, in the event of failure, by force, to bring off the remaining factors, and the Company's property; and, for this purpose, Captain Wright was sent to Surat in his ship, the 'Cæsar,' with orders to lay off the river's mouth, and endeavour, by every possible scheme, to release the agent and factors; but, should that be impracticable, and the design of Sir John Child in sending the expedition up the Gulf of Persia, be discovered, then to seize on all ships belonging to the Mogul, or King of Siam, notwithstanding they might be under French, Dutch, or Spanish colours, and to detain the principal persons on board as hostages for the safety of the agent and factors at Surat.

The incident of the 'Dragon' having seized a Surat vessel going to Siam, gave an alarm that the English intended hostilities, and rendered impracticable the escape of the agent and factors, who were carefully watched and detained by the Governor, though no violence was as yet offered to their property or persons. On receipt of intelligence of the seizure of these officers, Sir John Child detained, by way of reprisal, all the Surat vessels which were then in the port of Bombay. This decisive conduct convinced the Governor of Surat that conciliatory measures must be resorted to, or open war be inevitable; for, as yet, he had not learned that any captures had been made by the English ships sent to the Persian Gulf and Red Sea.

Affairs were in this critical situation when Captain Andrews, in the 'Charles II.,' returned from the Persian Gulf to Bombay with six Mogul vessels, under Dutch colours, detained during his voyage. This event rendered it impossible to conceal actual hostilities, and, therefore, Captain Andrews was despatched to Surat to act in conjunction with the 'Cæsar,' to seize on all Mogul vessels he might meet with on his passage, or attempting to enter the port, and to watch the Seedee's fleet, reported to consist of two hundred galivats, which it was not the intention of Sir John Child to destroy, if they kept in port, as this would irritate the Mogul, who had recently been victorious in Viziapoor and Golcondah; but in the event of this fleet attempting to put to sea, presumably under the order of the Mogul, and with intentions hostile to Bombay, the 'Charles II.' and the 'Cæsar' were to attack them while crossing the bar of Surat. In the event of Captain Andrews conceiving the force of the Seedee to be too great, he was to retire to Bombay, where he would be joined by five ships, which were equipping to oppose the lesser fleet of grabs, fitting at Cambay for the invasion of the island.

At this crisis Muchtar Khan, a nobleman of the highest rank, and related to the Mogul, was appointed Governor of Surat, and he opened a conference with Mr. Harris for the accommodation of differences. On these negotiations ending abortively, Sir John Child embarked at Bombay on the 9th of October, 1688, and again appeared off Surat with a fleet of seven ships; and, though on this occasion he might have taken, or destroyed, the whole of the fleet of Yakoob Khan, the Seedee, from political considerations he avoided hostilities. Thus, as has so often happened when civil commissioners have hampered the action of military or naval commanders, the honour of the Service and of the British name, and, as eventually appeared in this instance, the interests of his master, were sacrificed to political exigencies. Muchtar Khan soon threw off the mask of friendship which he had assumed, seized and imprisoned Mr. Harris and Mr. Gladman on the 26th of December, 1688, ordered all the Company's goods in Surat to be sold, and offered a large reward for Sir John Child, alive or dead.

Sir John continued with the fleet off Swally, in the hope of finding some means of rescuing Mr. Harris and the Council; but, on the 16th of January, 1689, finding all his attempts at negotiation ineffectual, he returned to Bombay, and, on his passage, fell in with a Mogul convoy of trading vessels, of which he captured forty.

Hamilton, writing from a personal knowledge of events, says, in his "New Account," that before seizing this fleet, which he did against the advice of most of his council, Sir John Child asked the opinion of some sea officers, "and one, Captain Hilder, being the eldest, advised him not to meddle with the corn fleet, because it would straiten the army, and force them to look abroad for provisions, where it might best be procured, and perhaps might affect Bombay, which was in a great measure beholden to their neighbours for sustenance and firewood;" however, with the presumption and fatuity that marked all his proceedings, Sir John refused to act on the advice of this experienced officer.

While matters were in this situation, the fleet of the Seedee, Yakoob Khan, consisting of eleven ships and seventy galivats, were at Danda-Rajahpore, whence they put to sea and appeared off Bombay. Owing to the absence of part of his fleet, which had proceeded to Europe, Sir John Child was unable to persevere in his resolution of attacking the Seedee's ships; on the contrary, this fleet, disembarking a large force, made several descents on the island, and, having got possession of Mahim, Mazagon, and Sion, the Governor and his garrison were besieged in the castle.* The Company's troops amounted to only two thousand five hundred men, of whom only a small proportion were Europeans; and they would have been starved into a surrender, but that the Company's cruisers put to sea,

* Bruce's "Annals," vol. ii., p. 601 to 641.

and supplied the wants of the garrison by the capture of provision ships belonging to the Mogul and his subjects.

Captain Hamilton who was serving in the Company's Marine at this time, says:—"We passed the months from April to September very ill, for provisions grew scarce by the addition of three thousand Sevagees that were employed as auxiliaries in the military service of the Company. When the winter months were over, at September we went to sea with our small ships, to cruise on the Mogul's subjects, and had pretty good success. I was employed in that service, and had the command of a small privateer, with twenty fighting men, and sixteen rowers. In three or four months I brought nine prizes into Bombay, laden most with provisions and clothes for the enemy's army, which was increased to forty thousand; but we were not allowed any plunder, but were rather plundered ourselves, for when we brought our prizes in, our chests were severely searched, and if we had saved any of our pay, it was seized for the Company's use, as money we had found in the prizes, which made us careless in pursuing the enemy at sea."

The depth of humiliation to which Sir John Child had brought the Company's affairs at Bombay by his mismanagement and by the false economy which reduced the military and naval establishment to a state of inefficiency, may be imagined from the following passage from Hamilton's work:—"And now, the Seedee being master of the whole island, except the castle and about half-a-mile to the southward of the castle, he raised batteries on Dungeree Hill, which overlooked the fort wall, and disturbed the garrison very much; then he put four great guns in the Custom House, commonly called the India House, and raised at the Moody's House within two hundred paces of the fort, and another in the lady's house that he had been so unkind to, so that it was dangerous to go out or in at the castle gate till we got up an 'half moon' battery before it."

In this critical condition of affairs, Sir John Child* died at Bombay, on the 4th of February, 1690, when the office of President devolved on Mr. Harris, at this time a prisoner at Surat, Mr. Vaux succeeding to the Deputy-Governorship

* Sir John Child's administration of the affairs of Bombay was the most disastrous of any in the history of the Western Presidency. He committed the fatal mistake of undertaking nothing less than an arduous war with utterly inadequate means, with the result of bringing the Company's affairs to the verge of ruin. And yet Sir John, who had a powerful relative at headquarters in England in the person of his brother, Sir Josiah Child, commanded the confidence of his masters, who pronounced his conduct "faithful and honourable," and, early in the course of his arrogant proceedings, when success appeared to smile on him, voted him a reward of a thousand guineas. The two most able and honourable of the Company's Pro-consuls in Western India, were decidedly Sir George Oxenden and his successor Mr. Gerald Aungier, who by their courage, conduct, and high-mindedness, were remarkable in an age when profligacy and peculation reigned supreme from the Royal Court downward.

of Bombay. In the meantime, two commissioners, sent by the late President to the Mogul at Viziapoor, had succeeded in negotiating a peace, and, on the 4th of April, 1690, Mr. Vaux received the Imperial firman, by which Mr. Harris was released, the island of Bombay evacuated by the Seedee's army on the 8th of June, on payment of a fine of £15,000, and a reconciliation effected between the Company and Aurungzebe. By the terms of this firman, which may be perused in Bruce's Annals, the Company were admitted to their former trading privileges, though under conditions which can only be described as humiliating. President Harris afterwards said, writes Bruce in his "Annals," that "the real cause why the Emperor granted peace, was that he might continue to avail himself of the protection afforded to his pilgrim ships by the Bombay Marine."

Seedee Yakoob left behind him at Bombay, says Hamilton, a pestilence "which in four months destroyed more men than the war had done." According to this author, "of seven or eight hundred Europeans not above sixty were left by the sword and plague." To add to the embarrassments of the Presidency, intelligence was received of six piratical vessels, of considerable force, under English colours, having made their appearance in the Indian Seas. These vessels, which had been fitted out in the West Indies, took shelter in the ports of Aden, Muscat, and Madagascar, and one, carrying twenty-two guns, captured a valuable trading ship belonging to Madras. This seriously compromised the Company with the Mogul Government, who held them answerable for all depredations committed by their countrymen.

In 1689 war was declared between this country and France, and, in the following February, a French fleet of six sail left for the Indian Seas. On the outward passage it fell in, at Johanna, with the Company's ship 'Herbert,' which, after a most brave defence, blew up, when the majority of the crew perished. It showed no ordinary gallantry, bordering on temerity, for a single ship, armed though the Company's vessels were, to engage a powerful squadron of regular ships of war; such conduct must ever command the admiration of Englishmen, and the Naval history of the Company affords many other instances of a like disregard of odds where the honour of the flag was concerned.

Two years after the capture of the 'Herbert,' on the 11th of October, 1692, another of the Company's ships, the 'Elizabeth,' when within fifty leagues of Bombay, made a gallant and protracted, though unhappily unsuccessful, resistance against a French squadron, consisting of one ship of sixty-six guns, one of sixty, one of forty, and one of twenty guns; the Company were also so unfortunate as to lose a third ship, the 'Berkley

Castle,' which was sunk in the Channel by a French man-of-war, early in 1694, while on her homeward voyage. But these losses, which, coming singly, were not felt so seriously, were dwarfed by the capture, in the following year, off the coast of Galway, by a powerful French fleet, of their homeward bound ships, 'Revolution,' 'Defence,' 'Princess Ann,' and 'Success.' Instead, however, of yielding to despondency, the Company, consisting of about twelve hundred proprietors, bore their loss, as they wrote, "with a true Roman courage," and added £300,000 to their stock, and equipped eight ships for India.

In the year 1695, we have the first notice of the aggressive character assumed by the maritime tribes of Arabs in the Persian Gulf, who, subsequently, caused so much trouble to the cruisers of the Indian Navy, and gave rise to expeditions directed against Ras-ul-Khymah, in 1809 and 1819.

Speaking of these lawless Arabs, Captain Brangwin, one of the Company's officers, gave his opinion "that they would prove as great a plague in India as the Algerines were in Europe," a prediction which was amply verified. The Company's agent at Gombroon described the Arab fleet as consisting of five large ships, carrying one thousand five hundred men, and twelve Arab cruisers; and reported that their depredations were so great that it was supposed the King of Persia would march an army against them; and, he added, in accordance with a request from the Governor of Gombroon, he had obtained the Company's ship 'Nassau,' to assist in the defence of the town. So powerful were these Arabs at this time that they ousted the Portuguese from Mombaza, and, not only pillaged Diu, but, at the close of the 17th century, seized their possessions on the African coast, and founded the state which, until the year 1860, was united with Muscat under the sway of the Imaums or Seyyids.

Surat, about this time, again became the scene of alarm, owing to the advance of the Mahratta troops, within fifty miles of its walls, when the English factory was put into a state of defence. After the retreat of the enemy, the Mogul Governor received news of the capture of several Surat merchant ships, and one, carrying pilgrims, belonging to the Mogul, by an English pirate, called the 'Fanny,' commanded by a notorious rover, named Avory, and carrying forty-six guns, and one hundred and thirty European seamen. This so exasperated the mob of Surat, that the Nawab was compelled to throw into prison the President, Mr. Annesley, and all the English, numbering fifty-three at Surat and ten at Swally, to prevent their being torn to pieces by the infuriated populace.*

* From the earliest times the West Coast of India has been devastated by pirates. According to Pliny, the Roman ships, when visiting these seas, carried a number of archers for protection against these rovers. Ptolemy spoke of their ferocity; and Marco Polo, writing of them in 1269, said, "that with their wives and children they passed all the months of fair weather at sea; that each of

Captain Hamilton describes Mr. Annesley as "a cunning, designing fellow." He says of his dealings with the officers of the Marine:—"The Mogul's subjects have a good many fine large ships that trade all over India. The owners of those ships had a very great regard for the courage, condnct, and art of navigation of the English, above any other European nation in India; and, for those qualifications, the Indian owners procured English officers to go in their ships, and allowed them very handsome salaries and indulgencies. The captains had from their fleets comprised twenty ships, which being ranged at a distance of five miles from each other, made a line of one hundred miles, and that as soon as one descried a merchant ship she made a signal to the rest, so that it was scarcely possible for their victim to escape."—(Pennant, vol. i., quoted by Anderson in his "English in Western India.")

During the seventeenth and eighteenth centuries the cruisers of the Indian Marine were actively employed in the suppression of the native pirates on the West Coast of India, among whom the most formidable were the Sangarians or Sanganians, mentioned by Arrian, whose name Todd derives from Sangam, an "embouchure," because they frequented such places. Hamilton, the author of the "New Account," traces the name to Sangania, a province of Cutch, which has always been notorious for these marauders.

The pirates that now appeared in the Indian Ocean were much more to be dreaded, the ships being large and well-armed, and manned by European crews. Captain Hamilton writes:—"The pirates for many years infested the mouth of the Red Sea, committing frequent robberies and barbarities. Captain Evory was the first that led the way, in Anno 1695; and the pirates finding great booties, purchased with small danger from the traders into the Red Sea, had a project to be masters of the key of that door, so they found the island Prim, which was within gunshot of Babelmandel, to have a good commodious bay for the security of their shipping; upon which consideration they begun to build regular fortifications, and dig for fresh water, and, with much labour, they dug through a hard rock, fifteen fathoms deep, but found none but brakish water; wherefore they desisted, and moved to St. Mary's Island, on the east side of Madagascar, as I observed before, and are since removed, for more security, over to the main island, and there they fortify themselves by marriages into the noble families of that great island, from whence they come into India and cruise in those seas.

"In Anno 1696, they met with a ship from Bombay, commanded by one Sawbridge, who was carrying Arabian horses for Surat. After they took the ship, Sawbridge began to expostulate with them about their way of life. They ordered him to hold his tongue, but he continuing his discourse, they took a sail-needle and twine, sewed his lips together, and so kept him several hours, with his hands tied behind him. At length they unloosed both his hands and lips, and carried him on board their ship; and, after they had plundered Sawbridge's ship, they set her on fire, and burned her and the horses together. Sawbridge and his people were set ashore near Aden, where he died presently after.

"Captain Evory was not so inhuman for the year before he took a large ship belonging to the Mogul, and got a booty of 2,600,000 rupees, which amounted to in sterling money £325,000. He freed the ship and let her go, without torturing the people; but carried a young Mogul lady with him, and some of her female servants, who had been at Mecca." This affair caused the popular *émeute* which resulted in the confinement of Mr. Annesley and his compatriots.

In 1797, pirate ships, flying English colours, plundered and burnt three English vessels, and so bold had they become that one of them attacked the British frigate 'Phœnix,' on board which Sir George Byng, afterwards Viscount Torrington, was serving as lieutenant, which soon sunk her assailant. A large reward was offered for Avory by the Lord Chief Justice of England and the Company, but he succeeded in reaching the Island of Providence in the Bahamas, when he sold his ship and dispersed his crew, five of whom were subsequently apprehended and executed.

£10 to £15 per month, mates from £6 to £9, and the gunners and boatswains had also good salaries, besides the privilege of carrying some goods and merchandise freight free. Mr. Annesley thought those salaries and indulgences were too great for seamen, so he went about to reduce them to about one half, and the other moiety he looked on as his own due by virtue of his post."

Sir John Gayer, who had been appointed Governor of Bombay in May, 1694, on receiving intelligence of the state of affairs at Surat, wrote both to the Mogul and the Governor, protesting the innocence of the Company's agent in regard of the depredations committed by the pirates, and expressing his readiness, on condition of freedom of trade, and the annual payment of four lacs of rupees (£40,000)—the sum annually paid to the Seedee, who appeared unequal to the service—to employ two of the Company's armed ships to convoy the pilgrims to Jiddah, the port of Mecca, thus making a proposal which was actually accepted half a century later, when the Company's senior naval officer acquired the "Tanka," with the title of Admiral of the Mogul's fleet. To this memorial both the Mogul and Governor returned for reply:—"That the English, Dutch, and French should put to sea in search of the thieves," to which the Dutch and French hesitated compliance, while the English expressed their readiness to go on this service, which seemed to abate the animosity felt towards them by the Mogul's officers. It was not until the 27th of June, 1696, that orders were received for the release of President Annesley and the English in confinement at Surat and Broach. But their lives and liberties were again placed in danger on the receipt of intelligence that five pirates, flying English colours, had appeared in the Red Sea, and two more, each mounting fourteen guns, and having crews of one hundred and fifty men, were plundering the country ships, both in the Persian Gulf and Arabian Sea, while yet another was cruising off Tellicherry. As the season advanced the pirates increased in number; three, fitted out at New York, having appeared on the Scinde coast, and made valuable prizes.

These difficulties were increased by the ill-feeling that existed among the small garrison of Bombay, which was reduced by desertions to a point that deprived it of all efficiency; and, still further to aggravate the Company's position, which, indeed, appeared one long struggle against adverse circumstances, the crews of two of their trading ships, the 'Mocha' and 'Josiah,' mutinied in the Eastern islands: and, having murdered their officers, turned pirates. Still, it is gratifying to find that, at this time of doubt and disaster, Sir John Gayer had sufficient confidence in the crews of the ships of the local war Marine at Surat, to repeat his offer of two armed vessels to be annually employed in the service of convoying pilgrims to Mocha, on condition that the Emperor would defray the charges, and give a promise for exclusive trade to the Company. We find that this offer to convoy the pilgrim ships, was accepted by the Mogul, for, on the 20th of March, 1698, three of their armed ships sailed from Surat to Mocha and Jiddah, and convoyed the Mogul fleet in safety back to Surat. During this cruise Captain Kidd, the famous pirate, passed close to them, but escaped to Rajahpore, off which port he plundered a vessel belonging to Bombay; thence, after careening at the Laccadive Islands, he proceeded to Calicut, where he took a vessel, and again made his escape on the appearance of a Company's ship. At Cochin he captured three valuable Dutch prizes, and then retired to St. Mary's, an island off the east coast of Madagascar, where, and at Tullea Harbour, near St. Augustine's Bay, on the west coast of the same island, the pirates had fortified stations,* at which they received stores, supplied from New York and the West Indies. Other pirate craft had taken a Portuguese China ship, and had plundered and sunk the 'Diamond,' an English merchantman, while the 'Mocha' and 'Josiah,' late Company's ships, had taken, or sunk seven or eight sail belonging to Surat.†

In the season of 1697, the Company suffered a considerable pecuniary loss in the capture by the French of the 'Dorothea' and 'Bedford,' outward-bound Indiamen, having on board a captain and eighty soldiers for Bombay. But the treaty, signed at Ryswick, on the 20th September in this year, relieved them of any further anxiety, on the score of losses by capture at sea, though affairs at Surat and Bombay continued in the same precarious state, owing to the probability of civil war on the approaching demise of Aurungzebe, and the oppressions of the native governors.

In 1698 the pirates, grown bold by a long period of prosperity, and the inability of the Company's ships, from their numerical weakness, effectually to extirpate them, had regularly constituted themselves into two squadrons, which swept the Malabar and Coromandel coasts. The Company's ship 'Dorrell' had an indecisive engagement off Malacca with the 'Mocha,' which carried thirty guns, and was manned with a crew of two hundred desperate men. There was also the 'Adventure,' of the same force, commanded by the redoubtable Kidd,‡ and a third, a prize,

---

* The pirates first established themselves on the small island of Perim at the entrance of the Straits of Babelmandeb, which has a more convenient harbour, but having dug through fifteen fathoms of rock without finding water, they abandoned the island for St. Mary's.

† Bruce's "Annals," vol. iii., p. 287.

‡ This noted freebooter, and several others were eventually captured and hanged in chains at Tilbury. Captain Kidd had been sent out in command of the 'Adventurer,' of thirty guns and two hundred men, to attack the pirates in Madagascar, but himself turned rover. Another noted robber was styled by the Deputy-Governor of Bombay, "that grand villain Sivers, commonly called Chivers." He was captured by a Company's ship and taken to Bombay.

lately belonging to Surat, called the 'Quedah Merchant,' both of which were manned principally by crews of Europeans. The two former cruised between Acheen and Malacca; and the latter, mounting thirty guns, together with one ship of fifty-six guns and another of forty guns, cruised along the Malabar coast, and committed great havoc, avoiding, however, an encounter with the Company's armed ships.

Sir John Gayer reported this condition of affairs to the Court, and requested that a squadron of men-of-war should be despatched from England, to be engaged only in abating this nuisance, which not only endangered the Company's ships, but also imperilled their trading privileges, as the Mogul attributed the piracies to the English. This danger was, indeed, soon realised, for, on the 1st of January, 1699, an order came from the Emperor directing that the English, Dutch, and French agents at Surat, should be held responsible for the piracies; and, on the following day, guards were placed over the three factories. Sir John Gayer, on receiving intelligence of the perilous circumstances of the Company's factory and servants at Surat, sailed from Bombay with the Company's ships 'Mary' and 'Thomas,' 'Josiah,' ketch, and 'Benjamin' yacht, and arrived off Swally on the 11th of January. On the following day he gave instructions to President Annesley,* to inform the Governor that he was resolved neither to pay the English proportion of the fourteen lacks of rupees, nor would he give security against the pirates; but, at the same time, intimated he was ready to furnish a convoy to the Mogul ships intended for Mocha, and that the King of England had sent out a fleet of men-of-war† to extirpate the pirates from the Indian seas. This refusal, and the presence of the Company's ships, induced the Governor of Surat to offer to overlook what was passed, on condition of the English giving security to make good all future robberies by the pirates. Sir John Gayer, in reply, proposed to send two of the Company's ships down the Malabar coast, on this service, provided permission should be given to the factory to send the indigo on board the ships; but, in the end, found it desirable to consent, with the French and Dutch, to sign a security bond for payment of the losses sustained by any depredations which the pirates might, in future, commit. And it was fortunate, says Bruce, that the demand was complied with, for, when information reached the Mogul, he reversed an order, which he had just issued, for putting a final embargo on the trade of all the Europeans in his dominions.

* The pusillanimous conduct of Mr. Annesley in agreeing to pay a fine of 30,000 rupees to the Governor, so displeased Sir John Gayer and his council that they superseded him and made Mr. Colt president.

† This was a squadron of the following ships under command of Commodore Warren. The 'Angleses' and 'Harwich,' each of forty-eight guns; the 'Hastings,' thirty-four, and the 'Lizard,' twenty.

It now became expedient to assign distinct stations to the squadrons of the European ships, which were to cruise against the pirates in the Indian seas, but this measure could not be carried out until large presents had been made to the Governor of Surat. The protection of the Red Sea was assigned to the Dutch, who were to pay 70,000 rupees to the Governor, and three Dutch ships were accordingly sent to convoy the Mocha fleet. To the French the Persian Gulf was given as a station, and, in like manner, they were to pay from 25 to 30,000 rupees; and to the English was entrusted the police of what were termed the Southern Indian Seas, with a collateral security, by their brokers, for the performance of this service, and the payment of 30,000 rupees.*

* Bruce's "Annals," vol. iii., pp. 273-275.

CHAPTER III.

1699—1754.

Contentions between the Old and New Companies—Precarious Condition of Bombay—Gallant Conduct of the Company's Seamen at Surat and Bombay—Depredations of the Arab Pirates—Duties of the Indian Marine—Prowess of the Company's Seamen at Carwar—Rise of the Pirate Chief Kanhojee Angria—Expeditions against Angria in 1717 and 1722—Gallant Defence of the 'Morning Star'—Piratical Proceedings of the Angrias—The Mahrattas and the Portuguese—Missions of Captains Gordon and Inchbird of the Marine to the Rajah of Sattara and the Peishwa—Loss, with all hands, of three Ships of the Marine—The Malwan and Cooly Pirates—The Bombay Marine at Tellicherry—Reduction of the Service in 1742, and Increased Depredations of the Pirates—The War with France—Mutiny of the Crew of the 'Bombay'—Increase of the Marine.

IN 1699-1700 serious disputes arose at Surat and in the other ports of the Company, whose charter did not expire until September, 1701, between their agents and those of a newly-formed rival association, styled "The English Company," in contradistinction to the old, or "London Company;" these quarrels were inexplicable to the Native governors, and would have caused the ruin of the English interests in India, had the Portuguese power been capable of effective rivalry. This particularly applied to the unseemly disputes that took place at Surat, in which Commodore Littleton—who, on the death of Commodore Warren, succeeded to the command of the squadron—maintained a strict neutrality, notwithstanding the accusations of breach of duty, and taking bribes, levelled at him by Sir Nicholas Waite, the Agent of the English Company, and the violent proceedings of the same official towards Mr. Colt—appointed President of the London Company in place of Mr. Annesley—for which he pretended he had a warrant, as the King's Consul. Not less intemperate were the proceedings of Sir William Norris, who had been commissioned by the King, as his Ambassador to the Mogul*—the English Company paying the

* Sir William Norris had an audience of the Mogul at his camp at Parnella on the 28th of April, 1701; but, after receiving a firman of the establishment of the English Company's factories at Surat, Masulipatam and Hooghly, and presenting the Emperor with two hundred gold mohurs, negotiations were broken off, owing to his being unable to comply with the demand of the Mogul, that he should keep the seas free from pirates. Accordingly Sir William Norris struck his tents

charges—and both this gentleman and Sir Nicholas Waite bribed the Governor of Surat and his agent to injure the trade of the rival association.* Under orders from the Mogul, Sir John Gayer, who had arrived from Bombay in December, 1700, President Colt, the members of the Surat Court, and others, in all one hundred and nine persons, were, in the February following, kept in duresse in their factory, where, in spite of all remonstrances, they remained for nearly three years, and were only freed on the entreaties of the Surat merchants, who could not send their ships to sea unless they were furnished with recommendatory letters by the President of the London Company. An end was put to this state of hostility between the rival Boards, on the receipt, in December, 1702, of the intelligence of the union of the two Companies.

In a letter written to the Court, in 1702, Sir John Gayer, who, though in confinement within the walls of the factory, continued to be the Company's chief representative, adverted to the weakness of the garrison of Bombay,† and the insolence of the Arabs, who, grown confident by their successes, were only deterred from making attacks on the Company's ships by an impression that they were too strong to become easy prizes;

and returned to Surat on the 5th of November, 1701. He embarked on the 5th of May following, but died on the passage home on the 10th of October, and thus the second mission to the court of the Mogul ended abortively—that of Sir Thomas Roe, for the establishment of commercial relations, being more fortunate.

* It was in 1698 that this rival association made a proposal to Parliament for advancing the sum of £2,000,000 to Government on condition of the subscribers being formed into a new company with exclusive privileges. The original, or London, Company, endeavoured to prevent the appearance of such a formidable rival, by offering Government £700,000, nearly the whole amount of their capital; but such was, at that time, the exigencies of the State, that the larger sum, though at eight per cent. interest, was preferred to the smaller at four. Thus were two Companies formed, the interests of each necessarily clashing with the other. After much rivalry, the two Companies were united by an agreement approved by both Courts on the 27th of April, 1702. But it was not until six years later that a final and cordial adjustment of differences was effected, and they were, by Act of Parliament, perfectly consolidated into one Company, by the title of "The United Company of Merchants, trading to the East Indies." By the same Act, in consequence of a new loan to Government, without interest, their capital was augmented from £2,000,000 to £3,200,000, yielding five per cent. interest, and in 1743 another million was advanced to Government, though the stock of the Company claiming a dividend was not increased to that amount.

† The accounts of the condition of Bombay during the time of Sir John Gayer's administration, show an almost incredible condition of weakness and corruption, due to circumstances mostly beyond his control. In 1697, three years after his succession, we find that owing to the climate, which has since strangely altered for the better, and the licentious mode of living adopted by most Europeans, of seven hundred or eight hundred Europeans residing in the island before Sir John Child's ill-judged " war," not more than sixty were left. Anderson says :—" There were but three civilians left to carry on the Company's business, and it became necessary to close the Courts of Admiralty and Common Law. Not one child in twenty survived the days of infancy." Owing to the lack of funds, the revenue having largely fallen off, Sir John Gayer was compelled to disband three hundred and forty Gentoos and sixty Christians, so that the native troops were reduced to seven soubahdars and four hundred men, while there were only twenty-seven European soldiers!

he also stated that, unless a squadron of six men-of-war, with bomb-vessels, should proceed from England, and act in conjunction with the Dutch, it would be impracticable to keep on terms with the Mogul or the petty princes on the Malabar coast. He requested that if such a fleet was despatched, the instructions to the commander should be distinct and positive, as three of the King's ships which had been sent out, had done nothing to suppress the pirates, and had returned home with cargoes of private goods, on account of Sir Nicholas Waite and others, while the fourth, the 'Harwich,' had been wrecked on the coast of China; the Indian seas, therefore, had been left with no other defence than what the guns of the Company's ships could afford, while the supply of recruits this season had been inadequate to the defence of Bombay.*

Accordingly, in the following season, two ships-of-war, the 'Severn' and 'Scarborough,' were equipped, Captain Richards, formerly in the Company's service, being appointed Commodore, with instructions to cruise between Madagascar and Mocha, and to convoy the Mocha fleet thence to Surat, where he was to consult with Sir John Gayer as to his future plans.

Captain Hamilton, in his "New Account of the East Indies," gives an interesting account of a conflict into which he was drawn against a plundering party of Belooches and Mekranees, while proceeding to Tatta. He says:—"In 1699 a pretty rich caffilla was robbed by a band of four or five thousand villains, the guard, consisting of two hundred and fifty horse, were entirely cut off, and above five hundred of the merchants and carriers, which struck terror on all that had commerce at Tatta. It was my fortune, about four months after, to come to Larribundar, with a cargo from Malabar, worth above £10,000. I could find no Tatta merchants that would meddle with my cargo before it was carried to Tatta; but agreed on the prices of most of the species of my goods, and finding no other remedy but travelling by land, in a caffilla of one thousand five hundred beasts, and as many, or more men and women, besides two hundred horse for our guard. About the middle of January we set out, and after we had marched about sixteen miles, our scouts brought in news of the Ballouches and Mackrans being just before us, in great numbers. I had thirteen of my best firemen with me in the front where my beasts were. We being all mounted on little horses, alighted, and set our beasts on our flank and front, to serve us for a barricadoe, to defend us from sword or target men, and we, at the same time, had room enough to fire over our barricadoe. We were not long in that posture, till the enemy sent a herald on horseback, with his sword brandishing, and when he came within call of us, he threatened, that if we did not instantly surrender at his

* Bruce's "Annals," vol. iii., pp. 439-40.

discretion, we should have no quarters. I had two of my seamen that shot as well with a fuzee as any ever I saw; for I have seen them at sea, for diversion, knock down a single sea-fowl with a single bullet, as they were flying round our ship. I ordered one to knock down the herald, which he instantly did, by a bullet through his head. Another came presently after, with the same threatenings, and met with the same treatment. The next that came I ordered his horse to be shot in the head, to try if we could take his rider, that we might learn somewhat of the enemy's strength. The horse was killed as soon as he appeared, and some of our horse got the rider, and hewed him down, instead of bringing him to us. Our guard of horse continually kept in the rear, but seeing what we had done in the front, took courage, and getting in amongst the bushes, met with some that had a design to attack our flank, and soon defeated them, which put the robbers in such fear, that they betook themselves to flight, and our horse pursuing put many to the sword, so when they returned from the pursuit, we went on in our journey, and travelling four miles, came to a mud wall fort, called Dungbarn, a proper English name for such a fortification. It is built midway between Tatta and Larribundar, to secure the caffilla from being set upon in the night, who all lodge within it, men and beasts promiscuously, which makes it so nasty, that the English appellation is rightly bestowed on it. There are about twenty little cottages built close to it, who breed fowls, goats and sheep, to sell to passengers. And these are all the houses to be seen in the way between Tatta and Larribundar. The news of a victory that I had over three Sanganian pirates at sea, on my voyage from Malabar to Larribundar, had reached Tatta, before the second skirmish by land, so that when I came to Tatta, we were received with acclamations from the populace, and the better sort visited us, with presents of sweetmeats and fruits, ascribing the safe arrival of the caffilla wholly to our courage and conduct."

During the latter years of the 17th, and early portion of the 18th, centuries, so great was the insecurity of the island of Bombay, which was constantly menaced with invasion by the Seedees and Mahrattas, that the Governor was obliged to withdraw seamen from the Company's trading ships to man the little fleet of the Bombay Marine, which now formed the chief security of the island. Indeed, at this time, the safety of the infant settlement was threatened, not only by the Indian Powers, but by the Portuguese, who were obstructing the transport of provisions required by the garrison and inhabitants, and giving secret assistance to the Mahrattas, at the very time when the Mogul's army had taken several of the Hindoo forts, and was besieging Singhur, within five days' march of Bombay. On one occasion a Portuguese ship was firing guns off the harbour of Bombay, when the Commodore, suspecting her to be a pirate, sent his boats to ascertain the real state of the case. The Portuguese commander, seeing the English approach, as if with hostile intent, fired into the boats, when they boarded and captured her, taking the prize into Bombay. Seeing that a mistake had been made, the Commodore restored the vessel to the Portuguese Governor, called the "General of the North," who, however, refused all apology, and threatened to attack the British settlement. An open breach now ensued, the importation of provisions from Salsette was prohibited, and a fleet of fifty "manchuas" was assembled at Mahim, with the view of invasion. The Governor and Commodore were nothing daunted at this fresh peril at a time of great weakness and depression, but made preparations for the defence of Bombay. However, they were relieved from all anxiety by the advent of an unexpected ally. An Arab fleet suddenly appeared, burned all the shipping at Salsette, and landed an armed force, which carried the fort of Versova by assault, and put the garrison to the sword. The Portuguese General now humbly craved assistance, and his people flocked in thousands for protection to Bombay. The Arabs eventually withdrew under apprehension of an attack by the English.* No sooner were these difficulties successfully overcome, and confidence was somewhat restored, than the plague broke out in the island, carried off some hundreds of the natives, and reduced the Europeans to the small number of seventy-six men; this calamity was followed by a storm, which destroyed the produce of the island, and wrecked the greater part of the shipping, by which it was protected.†

In February, 1703, the Mahratta army advanced within two miles of Surat, and, during the following month, burnt the suburbs, and laid siege to the town; thereupon, the Europeans, alarmed for their factories, took up arms for their defence, and, at length, the Mahrattas retired. In this affair the Company's sailors again displayed their discipline and valour, for, we are told, that the writers all refused to serve as sentinels, leaving the whole duty of defence to the sailors. In the latter part of this year, a fresh misunderstanding arose with the Mogul Government, owing to one of the Mocha ships, which had remained at that port after the fleet had sailed with convoy, having been captured by a pirate off Swally Bar. The Nawab, or Native governor, having confined the European agents to their houses, and obliged the brokers of the Dutch and British

* Anderson's "English in Western India." Hamilton says:—"In anno 1694, the Muskat Arabs made a descent on Salset, and committed great depredations in plundering and burning villages and churches, killing the priests, and carried about fourteen hundred captives into irredeemable slavery."

† Bruce's "Annals," vol. iii., pp. 502-3. The pestilence was the same alluded to by Captain Hamilton, as following the departure of the army of Seedee Yakoob in 1690.

Companies to give bills for the sum of £10,000, the estimated value of the ship and cargo, Sir Nicholas Waite, who was now President at Surat of the United Companies, in order to ward off the blow from the English Company's factory, equipped a vessel, and, at the Governor's desire, despatched her on a cruise in search of the pirates; but neither this service, nor the blockade of the river by the Dutch, could induce the Nawab to release the agents, who were confined to their houses, while trade was at a standstill. Meanwhile the Mogul Governor, notwithstanding the demands of Commodore Harland, commanding a squadron of the Queen's men-of-war, refused to release Sir John Gayer, who had now been confined for three years, until his demand for losses, caused by pirates, was satisfied. During this period, the Company's affairs at Bombay were managed by Mr. Burniston, the Deputy-Governor, who, however, died at this crisis. Sir Nicholas Waite, who had proceeded thither and assumed the administration of affairs, acted throughout these proceedings with singular ill-faith and self-seeking, and, to his duplicity, may be largely attributed the continued confinement in which Sir John Gayer was kept, and the dead lock in the Company's affairs, consequent upon the incarceration of that able officer.

The trade at Surat was so completely at a stand, owing to the Governor's refusal to allow goods to be laden, that Sir Nicholas ordered two of the Company's ships to blockade the port, with directions to prevent any of the country vessels putting to sea, and also to detain all such ships having English passes, and take out the English seamen found on board them.* The Dutch had also six ships blockading the river Taptee. In April, 1706, the Mahrattas, having defeated the Mogul army near Ahmedabad, invested the city, but retreated on the 23rd of May, plundering and burning most of the towns and villages between Surat and Broach, upon which they levied contributions. Bombay was also seriously menaced, for, in the previous December, the army of the Mogul was within three days' march of the coast opposite the island, and the trade of the lower Malabar coast, was harassed by Connajee, or Kanhojee, Angria, a Mahratta pirate chief, who now, for the first time, makes his appearance on the stage of Indian history. In this crisis, affairs were still further embarrassed by the decease of Aurungzebe,† in his ninety-third year, which took place on the 20th of February, 1707. This event caused a civil war between the late Emperor's sons, in which Shah Aulum, the eldest, established his ascendancy.

In the same year Sir Nicholas Waite was dismissed the Com-

* Bruce's "Annals," vol. iii., p. 597.
† Aurungzebe commenced to reign on the 12th of May, 1659, his father, Shah Jehan, who lived a prisoner for seven years, having died in the Castle of Agra on the 21st of January, 1666.

pany's service, and Mr. Aislabie was appointed Governor of Bombay, with positive orders to use every effort to obtain the release of Sir John Gayer, which was, at length, effected, after he had languished in confinement for seven years. Mr. Pitt, President of Fort St. George, had reported to the Court in 1706, the departure of the English men-of-war, " without suppressing the pirates, against whom they had been sent to cruise," and also wrote of the audacity of the Arab cruisers from Muscat, which seized every ship they could overpower. During the following year these Arab pirates, emboldened by their success, adopted a more regular system of naval warfare, and, having obtained permission from the King of Pegu to build ships at the ports of his country, spread their fleets over the entire seas surrounding the peninsula of India, causing great losses, especially on the Madras side, while they were so numerous and powerful in the Persian Gulf, that the Shah solicited naval aid from Bombay. "Already," says Bruce, "some of their ships carried from thirty to fifty guns, and they had made descents on several towns on the Malabar coasts, but to obtain plunder and a fixed station, from which they might annoy the trade, or with their collected fleet resist the Mogul or Mahratta fleets, or the more powerful vessels of the European nations. The Mahrattas, on this occasion, equipped a fleet of sixty vessels between Bombay and Goa, which acted not only with the view of repelling the Arab fleets, but as pirates against all defenceless vessels; while Kanhojee Angria, a Mahratta chief, possessed at this time a fleet of considerable force, which had piracy for its only object, and though occupying a port in the Mahratta country, and, therefore, deemed hostile to the Moguls, yet, like all Indian chiefs, he kept his own power distinct, though he acknowledged a kind of political relation with the sovereignty with which his ports were connected."*

Meanwhile the military and naval establishments were kept in a state rendering them wholly unable to cope with their numerous and powerful enemies. Urgent demands were therefore made for military reinforcements, and for "either a supply of seamen, or power to impress them from the ships."

Soon after the occupation of Bombay, a portion of the local force, established at Surat in 1613, was withdrawn for service at Bombay, and, on the formation of that island into the Presidency, it became officially known as the Bombay Marine. An officer was regularly appointed for the year as Admiral, and others were detailed for duty under his orders, the supply being kept up by drafts of officers and men from the ships arriving from Europe. During all these years they had been employed in the suppression of piracy as far as their limited strength permitted, in the protection of Bombay, and also, in conjunction with the

* Bruce's " Annals," vol. iii., pp. 649-50.

squadron stationed at Surat, in convoying the ships trading with the Persian Gulf and Red Sea, and the ports on the Malabar coast; these duties were most arduous and taxed their limited resources to the utmost, but they were fulfilled with ardour and success, and the Service gained the approval and thanks of its masters. During the wars waged by this country with European Powers—the Portuguese (before their separation from Spain) the Dutch and the French—this Marine service had often to struggle against superior maritime forces, but they bore the flag of their country not without credit on many occasions, and earned the respect alike of European rivals and native enemies; indeed, as we have shown, the grants of the early privileges of the Company were mainly won by the prowess of their seamen, who also stoutly defended their factories at Surat against the aggressions of the Mahrattas, when the French *purchased* exemption from their attacks. At the time of the squabbles with rival companies and "interlopers," their ships had been frequently employed in the less congenial task of protecting the trade of the Company from loss, and seizing "interloping" vessels,* and when the depredations committed by the pirates assumed such alarming proportions, as seriously to cripple the Company's trade, and to defy the utmost efforts of a squadron of royal men-of-war to eradicate them, they received King's commissions to seize and destroy these pests of the sea.

Before entering upon a retrospect of the great struggle with the pirate chief Angria, which forms so important a chapter in the " History of the Indian Navy," we will give an account, derived from various sources, of the services of the ships of the Bombay Marine in protecting the Company's factories on the Malabar coast.

That this was no nominal duty we may gather from Hamilton, who was at Bombay at this time, and says in his " New Account of the East Indies :"—" In the year 1715 the Arabian fleet consisted of one ship of seventy-four guns, two of sixty, one of fifty, and eighteen small ships from thirty-two to twelve guns each, and some trankies or rowing vessels from four to eight guns each, with which sea forces they kept all the sea coast in awe, from Cape Comorin to the Red Sea."

The Court of Directors, being dissatisfied with the conduct of the agents in charge of the Southern factories, ordered the Bombay Government to send thither Mr. Stephen Strutt, Deputy-Governor, with the necessary powers.† In his commission, bearing date the 23rd of October, 1715, he is instructed

---

* Orme mentions, that in 1684, one of the Company's ships, on the arrival in Bombay harbour of one of these "interlopers," which attempted intercourse with the shore, fired into her and drove her out of the port.
† General letter, dated the 27th of March, 1714.

to investigate all matters relating to trade at Carwar, Tellicherry, Calicut, and Anjengo; and was also charged with a letter for the Viceroy of Goa, "relating to the ship 'Moonsoon,' taken by a savage (Mahratta) pirate, and retaken by a Portuguese frigate out of the Carwar river, in the year 1706."

Mr. Strutt, with three assistants, embarked on board the 'Catherine,' the 24th of October, under a salute of thirteen guns, returned by all the ships in the harbour, and accompanied by the 'Anne,' commenced a voyage, which, in those days, was sure to be attended with adventure and perils. It is singular to find him, when sailing out of the harbour, noting down the appearance of Kenery, as if it were an island almost unknown, because cautiously avoided by all unarmed vessels frequenting the port, and representing to his Government that it was "two miles in circumference, thirteen miles distance from the mainland, and fourteen from Bombay; that Angria had strongly fortified it, and that it was covered with houses." As he sighted Malwan on the 31st, a grab and galivat made their appearance, "the latter firing both her chase guns very impudently," their object being to cut off and make prize of the defenceless 'Anne,'* but seven shots from the 'Catherine's' guns scared her away. Next day the party were off Carwar,† where they found a Portuguese cruiser, mounting eighteen or twenty guns, and were told that there were two more to the southward, each mounting forty guns, all of these being placed there to keep the coast clear, but, in reality, doing a little piracy on their own account, and fearing to approach either Angria or the pirates of Malwan. Having landed at Carwar and the other factories, Mr. Strutt exhibited his commission, and left certain written interrogatories, which he desired should be answered before his return. At Cochin, which the Dutch had possessed for fifty-two years, he was warmly pressed by the Commodore to go on shore, but declined. Permission, however, having been given to some other Europeans, they visited "the Barron," as he was called, and reported that "he was mighty affable and courteous," although, like many other Dutch officers of distinction, he had been promoted from the ranks.

* "The intent," says the commissioner, "was for the 'Anne,' who being astern, we had lain by before, or they had pusled her, not having any stern ports, and the stern being what these savages annoy others with, and have large guns, are the properest weapons to fight them." "The Malwan pirates," says Grant Duff, "were subjects of the Rajah of Kolapore, but this the Government of Bombay seem not to have known, supposing that they belonged to the Sawunt country." The following is Hamilton's account of these pirates:—"About twelve leagues to the southward of Gheria is an island about two miles in circumference, and fortified with a stone wall round it, called Malwan. It lies about a mile from the mainland, and is governed by an independent rajah, who is also a freebooter, and keeps three or four grabs at sea to rob all whom they can master. And that is all I know of him."

† Carwar, or Sedashighur, is one of the three only good ports on the west coast, the other two being Bombay and Kurrachee.

At Anjengo, the Commissioner dismissed two of the Company's servants, and, on mustering the garrison, found them to consist of a captain and ensign, forty-one Europeans, eighty Topasses and Africans, and a gunner with a small party under his command, their arms being in bad order, and their twenty cannon of all sizes, mounted on carriages of various fashions. Embarking again at Carwar, he steered towards Bombay, and, near Cabo de Rama, generally styled Cape Ramas, seeing three grabs, supposed to be engaged in piracy, with a ship in tow, he gave chase, and fired a broadside at them; but the pirates managed to escape with their prize. At Goa the Viceroy "was mighty courteous, and expressed a mighty desire of a good correspondence with the English;" but he was not so polite as to restore the 'Monsoon,'* which he affirmed had been in the hands of the pirates for thirteen days, and, having been captured by the Portuguese after so long a detention, must be regarded as their lawful prize. At Gheria, Mr. Strutt's boats were suffered to pass without molestation, and he even exchanged civilities with Angria's brother, Angria himself having marched against the Seedee. On the 28th of January, 1717, the 'Catherine' anchored safely in the harbour of Bombay.

We learn from a very curious work, written in 1737, by a Lieutenant Downing, who served in several of the Company's ships-of-war at that time, that, in 1715, when Mr. Charles Boone assumed the Governorship of Bombay,† the island was still in a

* The following is from the records of Government:—"The Merchants' report of the taking of the 'Monsoon,' on the 12th of February, 1706, by the Girrea Savajees.

"This day the 'Aurenzeb' sailed out of Carwar Harbour to Mangalore, at which time the Girrea Savajees, with four grabs and thirty-five galivats (Nillu Purboo, General of the fleet), lay in Bed Cove. She met the 'Monsoon' off Anjidiva, and told Mr. Wilcox, supercargo, the news. That night they kept company together till they came off Collacon. Captain Edwards offered to see him off Cape Raymas, but he said he did not fear them. About midnight Captain Edwards parted company. Early in the morning the Savajees came out of the cove and engaged the 'Monsoon' for three hours, at which time he surrendered. They brought him to the Cove. Next day Mr. Mildmay wrote off to Nillu Purboo, and he delivered up all the Europeans. They said they had very little ammunition on board, having but eighteen shott. After the engagement Mr. Mildmay immediately wrote to the Viceroy this news. The Savajees kept the 'Monsoon' four days in Bed Cove. They went out with a design to carry her to Girrea, but off Goa they had such a strong northerly wind that they could hardly carry sail. At which time there came out from Algrarda one frigate, one grab, one Portuguese merchant, and a fighting munchua. The Savajees put afore the wind, and the Portuguese chased them. They ran the ship ashore in Bed Cove in the night, and left her, having plundered her of four bales of cloth. The Portuguese fired random shotts all that night. Next morning, seeing nobody on board, they lightened her and hauled her off. The Savajees would fain have persuaded the Rajah's people to fire upon the Portuguese, which they refused. The Portuguese the same day carried the 'Monsoon' to Goa. The Savajees had her in possession nine days. That is all the Merchants know of this matter. Carwar, 4th of January, 1714-15."

† In 1715 Bombay—according to the Reverend Richard Cobbe, the chaplain—had a population of sixteen thousand souls; and, as regards its government, Aislabie was the last governor who bore the title of General. He left the Presi-

very unprotected state. He, accordingly, sent to Surat, where he caused to be built, in six months, the 'Britannia,' Captain Weeks commanding, and carrying eighteen guns and one hundred and forty men, and the 'Fame,' Captain Passwater, sixteen guns and one hundred and twenty men. Each of these ships had, in addition to the crew, a company of marines on board. This squadron was now sent on a cruise down the coast; and, after a skirmish or two with Angria's vessels, returned to Bombay, where the force was augmented by two new vessels, one of small size, called the 'Defiance,' Captain Matthews, and the other of twenty-four guns and one hundred and eighty men, called the 'Victory,' commanded by Captain Alexander Hamilton, who was Commodore and Commander-in-chief of all the Company's naval forces at Bombay, or on the coast of India. This squadron, having received a body of troops on board, proceeded in 1718 to Carwar, where the sailors of the Bombay Marine performed good service. Having once been plundered by Mogul troops, the factory, which had been foolishly constructed some distance from the sea, and so "was nothing but a genteel prison," had since been strongly fortified, and to this the inmates now owed their liberty, perhaps their lives, for the Desaee, as the ruler of the State of Sawunt Waree is called, having thrown off his allegiance to the Rajah of Sattara, considered that it was one of his royal privileges to claim all wrecks on the coast as his property, and resented the conduct of Mr. George Taylor, the Agent, who had appropriated to himself the cargo of a ship cast ashore about four miles from the factory.

Commodore Hamilton gives the following interesting account of the operations :—"The Rajah besieged the factory for two months before the season would admit of forces coming to assist them by sea; and when they arrived, the seas run so high on

dency in 1715, and, after a brief interregnum, during which Stephen Strutt, the Deputy Governor, discharged the duties of the executive, was succeeded by Charles Boone, usually styled either President or Governor, who, again, was succeeded in 1720, by William Phipps. The Governor's salary was £300 per annum, the Deputy-Governor, who was also accountant, received £100, and Lawrence Parker, who succeeded Strutt in the office, received £100 as Chief Justice. The third in council had £70, the fourth and fifth, £50 each, the sixth, seventh and eighth, had each £40. Then came "the Minister," as he was called, whose salary was £50 and usually another £50, a "gratuity, if found deserving." A physician and two surgeons received £50 each. Altogether, in 1720, there were forty-six covenanted servants in Bombay—military officers not being then included under that head—whose salaries were paid half-yearly, and amounted to £786 14s. 9d., or Rupees 6293. 3. 7, exchange being at the rate of 2s. 6d. per rupee. There was also a monthly charge of 2,620 rupees made on these gentlemen's account for diet and other allowances, and horses were provided for them at the Company's charge. A separate account was kept for extraordinary disbursements, under which head came the steward's bill of 1,170 rupees, for festivities on New Year's and Christmas Days. There was no restriction on private trade, so that civil and military officers were openly engaged in large mercantile speculations, with the Company's sanction, as may be seen in the extant ledgers, called the "Latty Records."—(*See* "Bombay Quarterly Review," vol. iii.)

the shore, that there was great difficulty in landing in the teeth of an enemy, who had ten times our numbers, so that the first attempt at landing was unsuccessful by our men's neglect and disobedience to the orders they had received, and about fourscore of our bravest fellows were cut off, and some taken prisoners; but, about six weeks after, we had some revenge on the enemy in an engagement on the side of a hill among thick bushes. The enemy, being above our men, began their fire at break of day, to beat our men from a spring of fresh water close to the sea; but our small vessels lying near the shore to cover about four hundred men, that lay to guard the water, fired with so good success, that, in an hour's time, they were obliged to run, and leave near two hundred dead in the woods; and our men pursuing them in their flight, did some execution on them. We were in daily expectation of more forces, and did not offer the enemy battle, because of their numbers and our want of experience, but we harassed the enemies in the night in burning villages, for there was little to plunder; and at sea we took some vessels laden with salt going to the enemy, and three ships of the Rajah coming from Arabia with horses, to the number of one hundred and forty, which created us much trouble to find provender and water for them. However, when our reinforcement came, we could muster, in our fleet, of seamen and soldiers, two thousand two hundred and fifty men. The enemy raised some batteries on the strand to hinder our landing, and we took two of the prizes, and made them shot proof above water, and laid them ashore at high water to batter their batteries, and keep the enemy at a distance with their great shot, till our men were landed and drawn up. Each of our floating batteries were covered with a frigate of twenty or twenty-four guns. When all was ready, we landed one thousand two hundred and fifty men without the least hindrance from the enemy, for they were preparing to flee to the woods; but our fresh-water land officers were so long a drawing up of their men in a confounded hollow square, that the enemy took courage, and, with horse and foot, came running towards our men, firing, and wounding some as they marched in their ranks, which our Commandant seeing, pulled off his red coat and vanished. Some other as valiant captains as he took example and left their posts, and then the soldiers followed, and threw down their arms. We lost in this skirmish about two hundred and fifty, but our floating batteries would not permit the enemy to pursue far, nor durst they stay to gather up our scattered arms, so about eighty sailors went on the field of battle, and brought on board of the Commodore about two hundred stand of arms, most of them loaded. However, the enemy had some loss too, for we found eleven horses dead, and saw many fires along the foot of the hills to burn their dead men in. The Rajah had, by this time, seven thousand men engaged in this war, which expense he began to get tired of, and the loss of his ships and horses was some mortification to him, besides the Sow Rajah* had made an inroad into his northern borders, which made him incline very much towards a peace, and accordingly he sent a Brahman on board to the Commodore of the fleet, to negociate about a peace. The Commodore heard him, and advised him to make his overtures to Mr. Taylor. By the mediation of a Seid, who was a friend to both parties, ten days after the first overture was made, peace was proclaimed on easy terms for both parties."†

We find that, in 1716, the cost of the Marine was £51,700, and it consisted of one ship of thirty-two guns, four grab-ships, mounting between twenty and twenty-eight guns, and twenty grabs and galivats, carrying between five and twelve guns. It was not long before this little force had an opportunity of proving its metal by an encounter with a Maritime Power which had defied the efforts alike of the Portuguese, Dutch, and Mahrattas. This was Kanhojee Angria, who, from being a common seaman in Sevajee's fleet, rose from one post to another, till he was made Admiral of the Mahratta fleet by Rajah Ram. He took part

* The Mahratta Rajah was so denominated by the English.
† At Calicut the tide of English affairs had ebbed, and, in 1714, the Company's agent suffered much personal loss from the failure of an attempt to check the encroachments of the Dutch, who had commenced building a fort on land, which the Zamorin claimed as his own, but which they maintained had been given them by the Rajah of Cochin. The consequence was, that the factors were removed to Tellicherry, and only a Portuguese agent, styled "the linguist,' retained at Calicut. At Tellicherry the Company had obtained, in 1708, the grant of a mud fort which originally belonged to the French, and which, after a few years, the English converted into a solid structure. For twenty years the agent was engaged in hostilities of trifling importance with the principal Nair of the place, and lavished more money upon the fortifications than would have paid for the whole of the investments, and kept up a considerable force of European and Goanese.

The factors of Anjengo, situated seventy-eight miles from Cape Comorin, were, in 1721, horror stricken by one of those calamities which so frequently chequered the lives of Englishmen in India. This was the murder of the Chief and of his council and a numerous suite, by the collectors of the Ranee of Attinga.

In the year 1715, the Emperor Ferokshir,—grandson of Shah Aulum, who died in 1712, after a reign of only five years,—impelled by a feeling of gratitude to Dr. Hamilton, physician to an embassy sent by the Company to his Court, who had cured him of a disgraceful disease, commanded his benefactor to name his own reward; upon which the high-minded and disinterested Hamilton solicited privileges for the Company. This petition, which was delivered to the Emperor in January, 1716, contained among other clauses, " that a fixed sum should be paid at Surat in lieu of all duties," but it was not until January, 1717, just two years after the arrival of the embassy at Delhi, that the concessions were granted. Sir John Gayer had been released after a confinement of seven years, but the Company's servants at Surat had been so greatly oppressed by the Mogul Nawab of Guzerat and his officers, that the factory was actually closed between the years 1712 and 1716, though it was reopened by the terms of this patent, the concession of which was hastened by a well-placed bribe, and the expectation of a possible visit of an English fleet. The history of the small factory at Cambay, like those of Calicut and Anjengo, is also a record of oppression by the Mogul Government, and of depredations by lawless Mahrattas on shore, and the Cooly pirates at sea.

with Sambhajee against Shao, grandson of Sevajee, but was induced by certain concessions to renounce the cause of the former, and release the Peishwa. Kanhojee possessed all the coast from Sawunt Waree to Bombay, but now received, as a bribe for his compliance, ten forts, including Kenery, Kolabah, Severndroog, and Viziadroog, (as the Moguls called it), or Gheriah, and sixteen fortified places of less strength, together with command of the fleet and the recognition of the title of Surkheil. The consequence of this compact was, that the Seedee found himself deprived of some places, the revenues of which he had enjoyed for twenty years; but Ballajee Wishwanath, who commanded Shao's armies, and was now appointed Peishwa, compelled him to submit.* Angria now levied his "Chout," by continuing to plunder ships of all nations that appeared off his coast, but he refrained from molesting the English.

At this time his fleet consisted of ten grabs, mounting from sixteen to thirty guns each, and some of nearly 400 tons, and also fifty galivats, some of 120 tons, and mounting four to ten guns. Animated by a lust for plunder, there now flocked to his standard numerous adventurers, including renegade Christians, mostly Dutch and Portuguese, Arabs, Mussulmen and negroes, a most daring and desperate band. Off the Malabar coast, two ships and four grabs, in Kanhojee's pay, attacked the Company's ship 'President,' when a desperate action ensued. Three of the grabs grappled and attempted to board, and the crew of one actually gained a footing on the 'President's' deck; but their success was short-lived, for they were beaten back with terrible loss. Two of the grabs were sunk, and a third was blown up while lying close alongside the 'President,' so that several of the English crew were scorched, and the ship set on fire in sixteen places. The rest of the enemy's fleet now retreated, and the 'President' was left to refit and enjoy her hardly-won triumph. In this action she lost eleven men killed and thirty-five wounded, but the pirates, whose loss was enormous, learned a lesson as to the necessity of caution in attacking a Company's ship, which they were not slow to take to heart.

In 1717, Angria's cruisers captured the ship 'Success,' sailing under British colours, which so incensed Mr. Boone that he resolved to commence active hostilities against the pirates. "In April, 1717," says Lieutenant Downing, "we got all our fleet together for the siege of the Castle of Gheriah, and, on the 10th, the President reviewed the land forces on shore, and saw all things put in good and sufficient order. We proceeded down the coast, which is not above twelve hours' sail from Bombay, where we, with all our navy, soon arrived, and ran boldly into the harbour, Captain Berlew, Commodore, and arranged a line

* Grant Duff's "History of the Mahrattas," vol. i., pp. 433-436.

from the easternmost part of the fortifications to the outer part of the harbour, keeping all our small galleys and galivats on the off-side under shelter. But they had strong fortifications on both sides, so that we left our strongest ships in the harbour to make a breach in the wall, in order to storm the castle. The rocks were very high and slippery, that one could hardly stand without a staff, and consequently not a place convenient to draw men up in any posture of defence. We endeavoured to get the fire-ship in, but could not, for on the east part of the fort they had a cove or creek, where they had laid up a great part of their fleet, and had a strong boom across the same, so that we could not get among them any otherwise than by throwing our bombs and cohorns very thickly into the garrison, which we did for a considerable time, and were in hopes, after the first and second days' siege, that we should have drove them out of that strong castle; but we soon found that the place was impregnable: for as we kept throwing our shells as fast as we could, in regular time, cooling our chambers before we loaded again, after we had beat down two or three houses in the castle, the shells fell on the rocks in the inside of the castle, and the weight and force of falling would break them without so much as their blowing up, which was supposed to be owing to the fusee of the shell burning too long. As to storming the walls, they were so high, that the scaling ladders would not near reach the top of them." Notwithstanding all their exertions, the commanders had to draw off their forces on the 18th of April, 1717, having, previously, made an attempt to storm with the troops, who were driven back with great loss.

In October, 1718, we find the squadron employed, in conjunction with the troops, in attacking Kenery, now in the occupation of Angria. The first day a continual fire was kept up on both sides from four in the morning till eight at night; the English, however, appear to have been short-handed, as we gather from the notice issued by the Governor, Mr. Boone, the same evening, "that if any would go volunteers for the next day's service, they should be paid on their arrival at Bombay forty rupees, and whosoever should lose a leg or an arm in the said expedition, should have £30 paid by the Company at their arrival in London, and be employed in their service during life." This bait only procured forty men, and the expedition proved unsuccessful; on landing next morning and attempting to carry the strong fortifications by storm, the small British force was driven back with considerable loss. This failure was said to be owing to the treachery of one Rama Kamattee, by whom the garrison were placed on their guard.* This man was brought

* The following letter, said to have been written on this occasion by Rama Kamattee to Angria, is a curious specimen of the style used in addressing the petty princes of India :—
"To the Opulent and Magnificent as the Sun, valorous and victorious, always

to trial on the 24th of March, 1720, on this and other charges of treachery, and, being convicted, was condemned to life-long imprisonment, and confiscation of all his property.

Of this affair, Hamilton says:—" Cundra (Kenery) is fortified by the Sevajee, and is now in the hands of Conhajee Angria. The English have made several attempts to take it, but never could, though in anno 1719, it had certainly been taken, had not a Portuguese traitor, who lay on one quarter of it with some vessels of war to hinder relief coming to it, betrayed his trust, and let some boats pass by in the night with provisions and ammunition, which the island was in great want of. The English landed, and were obliged to retire by some loss they received."

On the Governor's return to Bombay, we find him turning his attention to the construction of a novel class of vessel, for " he gave orders to build a floating castle, or a machine that should be almost cannon-proof." This vessel was flat-floored, and her sides were made of a thickness that was supposed to render her shot-proof; she was fitted to sail with one mast, carrying a topsail, and mounting twelve guns, 48-pounders, and, says Lieutenant Downing, " must have proved of great service to us against any of those castles, which we could approach near enough to cannonade." She does not appear to have fulfilled the expectations formed of her invulnerability, for, in the year following, when in tow of a vessel proceeding on a cruise, she was attacked by pirates, and, to prevent her falling into their hands, was set on fire and sunk.

Angria still continued troublesome, capturing and destroying many vessels trading to Bombay, but, at the same time, losing many of his own through the vigilance of our cruisers.

According to another account, an expedition was conducted against Gheriah in the year 1720, by a Mr. Walter Brown, which is also referred to by Grant Duff, who makes no mention of the attack in 1717, so that it is probable that there is a confusion of dates, and that the expeditions are identical, as the circumstances of the failures in which they resulted, would seem to denote. The author of "A Chapter in the History of Bombay," who derives his information from a contemporary

courageous, the liberal, prudent, and pillar of fortitude, the essence of understanding, the protector of Braminee, defender of the faith, prosperous in all things, honoured of kings, above all councillors, Senor Canhojee Angria, Sarqueel. Ramajee Comatee, your servant writes, with all the veneration and readiness for your service, and with your favour. I remain as always.

"Our General here has resolved in Council to attack and take the fort of Cundry, and thus it is agreed to environ the said fort the 17th day of October, and the armada, powder, and ball, and all other necessaries for war are ready. I therefore write your Honour that you may have the said fort well-furnished. As for the side of Rajaporee, I have spoke to and agreed with Alla Naiq Loucaudee, that they of Rajaporee shall not help either party, thus I have given this notice. I do not write more, only beg that you will retain me in your favour. Dated the 12th of October."

writer,* says of this expedition:—"Mr. Walter Brown was appointed Commander-in-chief, and numerous vessels, with a strong detachment of troops, were mustered. Immediately on entering the river he landed his soldiers, who attacked and put to flight a body of the enemy's troops, while a portion of his fleet ascending, destroyed sixteen vessels, and with the other portion he made a diversion by firing upon the fort. A platoon of Angria's men having come near, the English destroyed half of them; but in doing so, one of their guns burst, and killed four of their own men. Mr. Brown's gain and loss ended here, for hopeless of making any impression upon the fort itself, he withdrew."

The Government of Bombay celebrated this as a victory, and fired salutes; but Angria affirmed it was an inglorious defeat, and, in a taunting letter to the Governor, scoffed at the efforts which the English and Portuguese had made to injure him. He, however, made proposals for peace, but Governor Phipps, in reply, refused to treat until the European prisoners were released.

In April, 1720, four of Angria's grabs, and ten galivats, attacked the English ship 'Charlotte,' and, after a gallant defence, her powder being all consumed, they captured and carried her into Gheriah.

On the succession, in the same year, of Mr. Phipps, as President in Council, hostilities were vigorously prosecuted; but Kanhojee Angria continued to defy the efforts, both of the Portuguese and English, though his ships generally avoided a conflict with the Company's cruisers, and were captured if they risked an action; but they had the protection of the strong forts, which lined the coast, and the cannon of these were of heavy calibre, and were well manned by European, as well as native, gunners.

The Portuguese ill requited the hospitality extended to them in 1694, when the Arab fleets harried and pillaged the coasts of Salsette. Hamilton writes:—"About the year 1720 the priests of Salset disturbed the English at Mahim, animating the people to arms; but a bomb or two thrown into the church at Bandara, had no respect to the priesthood, but sacrilegiously killed one or two, besides some lay brothers, which made them know that war was not their trade. They were also troublesome to the English in anno 1722, but the English surprised a parcel that were about repairing an old fort, contrary to articles of agreement, and killed a score or two, which made the rest take to their heels, and be quiet."

The Bombay Government, incensed at Angria's continued

* A New Account of the East Indies, being the observations and remarks of Captain Alexander Hamilton, who spent his time there from the year 1688 to 1723.—Edinburgh, 1727.

piracies, in 1722 engaged in a joint expedition, with the Portuguese, against the strongly fortified island of Colabah, situated about five miles from Kenery, from which it bears S.S.E., near the shore, at the entrance of a river. The Portuguese furnished the land forces, and there were three ships of the Bombay Marine, commanded by Commodore Matthews, but the attempt failed, owing to the cowardice of the Portuguese; indeed it was said they acted with treachery, having a secret understanding with Angria, from whose depredations they suffered less than other nationalities. The Bombay Marine highly distinguished itself on that occasion, and lost several officers and men. Two years afterwards a powerful Dutch squadron of seven ships, carrying between thirty and fifty guns, and two bomb-vessels, with a body of troops, made an attempt on Angria's stronghold of Viziadroog, but they were repulsed with great loss.

Nor was Angria the only piratical power from whose depredations the English trade suffered, for the Sanganians, whose chief seaport was Beyt, at the entrance of the Gulf of Cutch, also preyed on English commerce. An attempt made by them, in 1717, to capture the Company's ship 'Morning Star,' detailed by Hamilton, led to one of the severest of the naval contests which have been waged on the western coast of India. Ascertaining through their spies that she was on her passage from Gombroon to Surat with a valuable cargo, the pirates waylaid her with two squadrons, consisting of one vessel of nearly 500 tons, three others of between 200 and 300 tons, and four smaller craft, carrying in all about two thousand men. Besides her native crew, only seventeen European fighting men were on board the 'Morning Star,' but they were resolute and prepared to defend themselves to the last. The pirate's largest ship opened the engagement by coming at once to close quarters, and the English commander's thigh was pierced with a lance, but they were then compelled to sheer off. After taking a day to consider a new plan of attack, they threw their two largest vessels on the Englishman's bows, another on his quarter, and closed with the three others, so as to board him from five points. A desperate conflict ensued; seven men of the 'Morning Star' were killed, and as many wounded, she was set on fire in three places, so that her poop and half-deck were burnt through, but, after four hours' close conflict, her crew contrived to disengage her, and, leaving her five enemies so entangled with one another that they could not give chase, she bore away with all speed for Bombay. One of her native seamen and twenty-six native merchants, who had gone from her to the pirates with the hope of dissuading them from their attempt, remained in their hands, and the Sanganians received £600 for their ransom. So dissatisfied, however, were their chiefs with the result of the attempt to capture the small

English ship, that they ordered the officer who commanded their fleet to be put to death.

Madagascar continued to be, as it had been for a century, a stronghold of pirates. In 1720, two of their vessels boldly attacked three ships as they were lying at anchor; two, called the 'Greenwich' and 'Cassandra,' being English, the third belonging to the Ostend Company, who were "interlopers." The 'Greenwich' and the Ostend ship weighed and put to sea, but the 'Cassandra' ran by accident on some rocks. The only piratical vessel which attacked her was of Dutch build, with twenty guns; and she also grounded about twenty yards from the Englishman, so that she lay towards his broadside. In this predicament her decks were swept by the 'Cassandra's' guns, and her crew compelled to seek shelter in the hold, but on her companion coming to her assistance, the English Captain found it necessary to save the lives of himself and crew by taking to the boats. The most remarkable part of this affair was, that he afterwards had the address and courage to visit the pirates, and so gained upon their better feelings by his judicious appeals, that they presented to him their own vessel which he had so severely battered. With this he, and his distressed crew, reached Bombay in September, when their bravery was rewarded by the thanks and liberality of the Governor. Commodore Matthews sailed with his grabs to revenge this and other injuries in 1722, but, says Hamilton, "found they had deserted the island of St. Mary's, leaving behind them some marks of their robberies, for in some places they found pepper a foot thick, lying on the ground in the open air. The Commodore aforesaid went with his squadron over to the main island, but the pirates had carried their ships into rivers and creeks, out of danger of the men-of-war, and to offer to burn them with their boats would be impracticable, since they could have easily distressed the boat's crews out of the woods. The Commodore had some discourse with some of them, but they stood on their guard, ready to defend themselves if any violence had been offered them."*

* Hamilton writes:—"There had been several squadrons of British men-of-war sent to cruise on the pirates, but have had very ill success in finding them out; but one Scot's ship, commanded by one Millar, did the publick more service in destroying them, than all the chargeable squadrons that have been sent out in quest of them; for, with a cargo of strong ale and brandy, which he carried to sell them, in anno 1704, he killed about five hundred of them by carousing, though they took his ship and cargo as a present from him, and his men entered, most of them, into the society of the pirates. It was reported in India, that Commodore Littleton had some of that gang on board the 'Anglesey' at Madagascar, but, for some valuable reasons, he let them go again; and because they found difficulty in cleaning the bottoms of their large ships, he generously assisted them with large blocks and jack-falls for careening them. Whether those reports were true or false, I will not undertake to determine, but I saw a pirate at Bengal, in the French Company's service, that affirmed it. Madagascar is environed with islands and dangerous sholes, both of rocks and sand. St. Mary's,

Captain Hamilton describes the defence, by a handful of Company's seamen, of the British factory at Gombroon in the year 1721, against the attack of four thousand Beloochee horse. He says:—" We heard of their design about ten days before they came, and so we and the Dutch fortified our factories as well as we possibly could, planting little falconets on the top of our walls in swivels, and beating out ports in our walls, to ply great guns, to scour the avenues to our factories. Meanwhile the Persian Governor fired guns every night, to let the enemy know he was a brave fellow; however, they had a mind to see, and on the 15th of December they appeared near the town, on a swift march towards it, which scared the Governor so much, that, though there was a high mud wall between him and them, he got on horseback and fled to a fort on the seashore, leaving a few guns loaded as they were, to the enemy. The Ballowches came first to the west quarters of the town, where our factory stands, and soon made passages through the mud walls. They hewed down all that came in their way, particularly, old people and children, and came in a confused haste to attack our factory, down some lane: but we gave them a warm welcome with our great guns and small shot. They soon found their mistake, and retired in as great haste as they came. Some of their musketeers got into ruined houses, and fired on us; but we being barricaded, they did us little damage, and had our men observed their orders better, we had come off with less. Our firing lasted about three hours, in which time we lost three or four, killed by their own rashness in standing open to the enemy, when they might have done better service under cover of our barricadoes. We had also seven wounded, but none mortally, but one who was a factor, who received a shot in his right hand, which threw him into a fever, of which he died in seven or eight days. The agent being gone to Ispaham some weeks before we had any advice of the Ballowches coming, had carried twenty soldiers along with him for a guard, and left but six in the factory, besides cooks, and a few servants. I saw the factory in danger if they should be attacked, so I reinforced it with thirty-six of my best men, and another small English ship from Bombay, assisted with eight or nine of his, so that when the enemy came, we were about fifty strong. The season being very cold, made our duty hard, for we lay in our arms every night, for ten or twelve nights that the enemy lay in the town. They had a consultation next day after their repulse, how they might make another attack, but none would undertake to

on the east side, is the place where the pirates first chose for their asylum, having a good harbour to secure them from the weather, though in going in there are some difficulties, but hearing that squadrons of English ships were come in quest of them, they removed to the mainland for more security, and there they made themselves free denizens by marriage. And I am of opinion, that it will be no easy matter to dispossess them."

lead their men on, and so the day after consultation, they went to attack the Dutch, who were three times stronger than we, and they met with the same kind reception we gave them; but they had a warehouse within pistol-shot of their factory, with goods to the amount of £20,000 sterling, in it, which the Ballowches broke into and plundered. The Dutch lost twelve men, and had eight or ten wounded, so finding our factories were not to be taken without the danger of much bloodshed, they went plundering the town for eight or nine days, and carried away in money and goods, above £200,000, besides fourteen thousand captives, and as many beasts of carriage, and so went off about five or six miles from the town, which they laid in ashes before they left it. They continued in our neighbourhood, with their plunder, about a month, I suppose till they received new orders how to dispose of themselves."

The failures to coerce Angria tended generally to increase his power. No trading vessels dared to pass down the coast without an escort of ships of war, and the name of this pirate chief was as much dreaded as was ever that of the Algerines in the Mediterranean. Emboldened by his success, Angria now openly attacked English vessels, and, in 1627, captured a richly-laden ship, belonging to the Company, which, together with other prizes, was taken to his fortified harbours. "These," says Grant Duff, "were considered impregnable," and offered from their number and position, peculiar facilities for piratical operations.

Although Kanhojee Angria had, in 1728, made a proposition for a peaceful settlement of disputes, he captured the Company's galley, 'King William,' in the following year, and took Captain McNeale, prisoner. This unfortunate officer, having made a fruitless attempt to escape, was loaded with irons, and so severely beaten that his life was despaired of. Only after many years he was released with some other European prisoners, on paying a ransom of 500 rupees, which, however, were repaid him by Government, in consideration of his severe sufferings. In 1730 a hope was indulged that, by an alliance with the Bhonslays of Sawunt Waree, the common enemy, Angria, might be effectually punished; but this proved visionary, although a treaty was actually made and ratified. Soon after this event, the death of Kanhojee Angria must have occurred.*

Kanhojee left two legitimate sons, between whom his territories were divided. Sukhojee, the elder, obtaining Colaba as his share, and the southern coast falling to Sambhajee, the

* Consultation Book of the Bombay Government, the 10th of February, 1728, 1729, and April, 1735. The Treaty is dated the 12th of January, 1730. Grant Duff surmised that Kanhojee Angria died in 1728, but added in a note, " I am not certain of this date, as I have not observed it in the English Records." Kanhojee is mentioned in the treaty with the Bhonslay, as still alive, and therefore this surmise must be incorrect. Grote also says, in his " Travels in the Indies," " Angria died about 1731, being about sixty."

younger, who resided at Severndroog. The former made friendly advances to the English Government, and, on the 21st of June, 1733, two of his envoys presented themselves before the President in Council, with proposals for peace; but death frustrated his good intentions. Mannajee, one of the three illegitimate sons of the late Kanhojee, having quarrelled with his family, took Colaba by escalade, with the assistance of the Portuguese, and, having put out the eyes of his brother, Yessajee, threw him into prison. Mannajee successfully resisted all Sambhajee's efforts to displace him, and, forming an alliance with Shao, the Mahratta Rajah, or rather with Rajee Rao, the Peishwa, whose power was becoming absolute, he endeavoured to gain the fort of Anjenwil, under the guns of which lay the fleet of the Seedee of Jinjeera.* To prevent such a consummation and check the growth of his power, the Government of Bombay sent Captain McNeale, who had recently gained his liberty, and Lieutenant Inchbird, with the 'Victoria,' 'Bombay,' and 'Princess,' galleys, to the Seedee's assistance; but for some reason, not assigned, they did not sail until the following March; and even then, although their force consisted of two ensigns, four sergeants, four corporals, forty European soldiers, and sixty topasses, with six 9-pounder guns, they were not empowered to take active measures, but merely to consult with the Seedee, and to deliver to him sixty barrels of gunpowder and a hundred muskets. Such lukewarm aid was, as might have been expected, unavailing, and Mannajee Angria, having gained possession of his galivats, was permitted to retain them, on paying 70,000 rupees to Bajee Rao, who also acquired for himself several of the Seedee's forts. Another of Mannajee's conquests caused more anxiety to the Bombay Government than all the rest. Rewaree, on the River Penn, which flows into the harbour of Bombay, became his, and thus he held in his hand a key to the communication of the island with the continent. A passage boat plied regularly between the places, for the convenience of the Brinjaries, who brought merchandise from the interior, and who, it was feared, might, on their return, convey to the pirate chief intelligence of all that was occurring at Bombay.

The growing importance of the English Government was manifested by the flattering letters and proposals which they received in the course of these affairs from Bajee Rao, one of the most sagacious and powerful statesmen of the Mahratta Empire. When besieging Rajapore, he wrote in the name of

---

* See "The First Wars and Treaties of the Western Presidency," in the "Bombay Quarterly Review," to which we are mainly indebted for valuable material relating to the services of the Indian Navy between the years 1726-54. The sources whence this writer drew his materials are, *inter alia*, the Bombay "Consultation Book," and the Diaries of the Company's factors at Surat, Anjengo, Tellicherry, and other factories on the West Coast.

the Rajah of Sattara to the President and Council of Bombay, begging that they would not permit their fleet to interfere with his operations, and, shortly afterwards, he invited them to mediate between himself and the Seedee, sending an envoy of distinction to them, and another to Rajapore, who was met there by Messrs. Lowther and Dickenson. However, much as the English were disposed to be on friendly terms with the powerful Peishwa, they could take no part with him then, because he was in alliance with Angria, their unrelenting foe. Against this pirate chief they at once sent three cruisers, under the command of Captains Lewis, Frampton, and Tolson, who intercepted the enemy as he was sailing from Colaba to Rajapore. As it was never the policy of Mahratta sailors to risk a naval engagement, an exciting chase was the sole result, when the whole of Angria's fleet escaped, with the exception of one large grab which ran ashore in the Bay of Antigheria. In the meanwhile, Messrs. Lowther and Dickenson had arranged with the rival Seedees of Jinjeera a treaty of alliance, afterwards ratified by their Government, according to which both parties bound themselves to act in concert against Angria, and not to treat with him except by mutual consent. They agreed that all prizes taken at sea should be allotted to the English, and to the Seedee all conquests made on land, with the exception of Kenery, which, if taken, should be delivered, with all its guns and stores, to the English, and the fort and district of Colaba, which should be demolished. The contracting parties were to divide equally between themselves the revenues of Colaba, and the English to build a factory or fort at Mhopal, in that district, situated between the rivers Penn and Nagotan.

But the Seedees' prosperous days had passed; their power was on the wane, and of little assistance to the English in combating the more formidable Angrias. So serious were the injuries inflicted by these pirates, and so heavy the expense of fitting out ships to protect trade, that the Company were prevented from making their usual investments, and, in their alarm, even began to anticipate an extinction of their commerce in Western India. Emboldened by success, and looking for support from the Mahratta Rajah of Sattara, the Angrias aspired to bring all the Seedee's territories under their subjection, and possess themselves of every port on the coast between Bombay and Goa. Nor in all probability would their efforts have been fruitless if family dissensions, which so often thwart the best matured designs of Native powers, had not intervened. Mannajee and Sambhajee were still at open feud with each other, and the President and Council resolved to foment their disputes. With that view they sent to Colaba Captain Inchbird, who had become better acquainted with the customs and languages of the natives than all his contemporaries, and was, in consequence, the favourite diplomatist of the day. His instructions were simple; he was directed to assist Mannajee with money and military stores, and "to take all opportunities of spiriting him up to carry on his resentments against his brother."

At the same time naval operations were undertaken, and Commodore Bagwell, with four cruisers, having cruised for a length of time in search of Sambhajee's fleet, of which he only caught occasional glimpses, was rewarded, on the 22nd of December, 1738, by the sight of nine of his grabs and thirteen galivats issuing from the port of Gheriah and creeping timidly along the shore. Disproportioned as his force was in numbers, he at once bore down upon them; but, anxious only to avoid a conflict, they stood into the river of Rajapore, where the gallant and impetuous Commodore beheld them lying at anchor, and in bravado displaying all their flags and pendants. At a loss to account for what he called such "consummate impudence," he conjectured that they must be relying for safety upon a fort, or some hidden dangers of the navigation with which he was unacquainted. After a brief consultation, however, with his captains, he resolved to engage them at close quarters, and made all sail to approach them, his crews giving three hearty cheers. But the enemy's defiance had been only vain show, and, on seeing the English really bearing down upon him, his first aim was to run up the river. The eager Commodore used his utmost efforts to prevent him carrying this into effect. "Before some of them could slip or cut," he wrote, "I was within musquett shott, and did really think I should have been on board one of them." As it was, luck did not declare in his favour; they made off under his heavy broadsides, until he found himself with only four fathoms of water and locked in by the rocks. Ignorant of the navigation, he was compelled to give the signal for returning, but had the satisfaction of hearing afterwards that he had inflicted much damage upon the enemy's fleet and killed his Chief Admiral.

Thus avoiding all encounters with the Company's ships of war, Sambhajee still continued to prey upon their shipping. On the 26th of December, 1735, he inflicted a most severe blow on their trade by attacking, with five of his grabs, the 'Derby,' a large East Indiaman. After a severe engagement, in which all her masts were shot away, he succeeded in making her his prize, and thus procured such a large supply of naval stores that he was enabled to equip his ships as well as any on the coast. The same day on which his ships had fled so disgracefully before the little squadron under Commodore Bagwell, he was much elated by capturing the 'Anne,' one of the Company's grabs, and several smaller vessels with rich cargoes. As though satisfied with his success, he pretended to wish for peace, and, in 1739, made overtures to the English Government; but, as he demanded that they should provide all their trading vessels with his passes, and pay him 2,000,000 rupees annually for the free navigation of the seas, his proposals were at once rejected as absurdly extravagant.

The following January Sambhajee flew at higher game than he had ever before ventured to attack. On the 9th of that month, as the 'Harrington,' 'Pulteney,' 'Ceres,' and 'Halifax,' four Indiamen which had just arrived on the coast from England, were waiting for a convoy, they descried, at sunset, fifteen sail, which they soon made out to be Angria's fleet. Singling out the 'Harrington,' as she was some distance from the rest, the enemy formed their line abreast, according to custom, and firing their bow-guns, bore down upon the Indiaman, which, at first, only replied with her stern chasers; then, finding her weight of metal superior, tacked and delivered three broadsides. After a distant contest of five hours, the pirates sailed away; but, unwilling to lose such a rich prize, appeared again at five the next morning rending the air as they drew near with discordant music. This time the 'Harrington' accepted their invitation at once, and they were proportionately reluctant to engage at close quarters; but at last she came up with three large grabs, including their admiral's, and, shortly after, no fewer than six were within a few yards of her. At noon their admiral's vessel was crippled, and they sheered off, the galivats, which were impelled by oars, taking him in tow, and thus getting to windward where the large English ship could not follow them. Their repulse at that time was most fortunate, as the ammunition on board the 'Harrington' was expended, and her commander could not have continued the fight longer. Knowing that it was his best policy to look his enemy in the face, he lay to for three hours, but they did not venture to renew the engagement.

As for Mannajee Angria, he was a fast and loose friend, or an actual enemy, just as it suited him. Even his friendship was dangerous, and to use a comparison of the Indian moralist, he was "like coal, which when hot burns the hand, and when cold blackens it;" while he professed to be a close ally of the English, his covetous nature could not resist the temptation if one of their unarmed ships happened to be sailing near his quarters. At the very time his envoy was making protestations of friendly sentiments at Bombay, he seized two vessels laden with grain for the island, and, before remonstrance could reach him, two other vessels belonging to the factory of Surat. All complaints and threats he met with excuses and evasions. When, however, he had gone so far as to make English prisoners labour at his public works. such insolence could no longer be tolerated, and, in March 1739, Captain Inchbird, sailing with his little fleet to Caranja, which had just fallen into Mannajee's hands, captured eight of his fighting galivats and thirteen fishing boats. In November, Mannajee took the Island of Elephanta, hoisting his flag there in defiance of the little English garrison stationed in close proximity at Butcher's Island ; and, although he had begun a friendly correspondence, in April, with the English, and showed a disposition to make restitution for past injuries, he detained, in July, four boats which they had sent across the harbour to open communications with the General of the Mahratta Peishwa. As this last insult was offered at a time when a rupture would have been inconvenient, it was overlooked, and a hollow peace was made between him and the English Government. Some time afterwards misfortune changed his disposition, and brought him as a suppliant to Bombay, where he represented that his brother, Sambhajee, having taken Choul, Alibagh, Thull, and Sagurgurh, had laid siege to Colaba, and cut off all the fresh water of the garrison. At his earnest request, Mr. Stephen Law, the Governor, or President, of Bombay, sent a squadron of cruisers, which conveyed a supply of water, forced Sambhajee's fleet to run down to Severndroog, and opened such a heavy cannonade upon his camp as compelled him to remove it from the seaside and throw up entrenchments for its protection. Sambhajee then requested permission of the Commodore to retire to Severndroog, and, on that being refused, he made a disorderly retreat, thoroughly humbled by the English squadron and a co-operating Mahratta force, under the Peishwa's son, Ballajee Bajee Rao, also known at that time under the name, rendered infamous for all time, of Nana Sahib. Mannajee, dismayed at the prospect of the occupation of Colaba by the Mahrattas, hastily patched up a truce with Sambhajee, and the two Angrias, having received a wholesome warning, lived for a time in fraternal concord.*

As there was no hope that Sambhajee would ever cease to be a robber, or that he would honestly observe any treaties he might make with the English, the latter conceived it necessary to their interests to form an alliance with his opponents. The power which, of all others, was every day becoming more formidable, was that of the Mahratta Rajah of Sattara, or rather, of his ambitious minister, the Peishwa. The active and marauding "Sevajees," as the Mahrattas were then called, after their first great leader, now mustered regular armies, with well equipped trains of artillery, and, not content with levying black mail in the open country, were prepared to batter down walls and capture fortresses. For some years they had been engaged in hostilities with the Portuguese, whose possessions near Bombay they coveted, and the heavy reverses which the latter now sustained at their hands, removed the only ally that might

* Grant Duff, vol. i., chap. xvi.

have been of service to the English in the struggle with Angria, which daily became more inevitable.

In 1731 Tanna was threatened by the Mahrattas, and the Government of Bombay, disposed at the time to assist the weaker side, sent three hundred men to garrison it, but, soon afterwards, withdrew their aid and rather countenanced the aggressors. How little the English knew on that occasion of a people who were soon to be the terror of the whole peninsula, may be inferred from the fact that the factory of Surat, when forwarding a dispatch, under date April 20, 1737, to their friends at Bengal, deemed it necessary to explain who the Mahrattas were. "The Portuguese territories adjacent to Bombay," they wrote, "have been suddenly invaded by the Mahrattas, a people subject to the Sow Rajah, who have prosecuted their attempts so successfully as to render even our Honourable Master's island in danger." In 1737 the Mahratta army sat down before Tanna, and, although the Portuguese repulsed two assaults with bravery, the third struck them with a panic, and the place was taken. The English anticipated that they would be the next objects of attack; but, fearing to provoke the invaders by any resolute effort to protect their victims, were satisfied with dispatching fifty men and some ammunition to assist in the defence of Bandora. At the same time they declared their intention of remaining neutral in other respects, and were so inconsistent as not only to apprize the Mahrattas when the Portuguese were making great preparations for the recovery of Tanna, but even to supply the garrison with powder and shot; in consequence of which the expedition failed, and its brave Commander, Don Antonio Frois, was slain. In extenuation of such conduct, the English Governor made the ungenerous excuse that they were but retaliating on the Portuguese for the information which they had communicated, and the supplies they had furnished, to the Seedee when he invaded Bombay.

Soon after Tanna had fallen, Tarrapoor shared its fate. The Mahrattas scaled its walls, and entered sword in hand; but it is recorded that the commandant of the victorious army informed his superior that the garrison "fought with the bravery of Europeans," until they were overwhelmed by numbers. Early in 1739, Chimnajee Appa, the Mahratta general, and brother of the Peishwa, invested Bassein, and having, on the 9th of February, taken possession of Versova, which had been abandoned by the Portuguese, pressed the siege with the greatest eagerness. John Xavier de Pinto, the commandant, endeavoured to appease the enemy by humble messages and an offer of tribute, but nothing short of absolute submission would be accepted. Soon after operations had been commenced in earnest, De Pinto was killed, and was succeeded in his command by De Souza Pereira, who repeatedly wrote to the Government of Bombay stating the condition of the besieged, and joining his entreaties with those of the "General of the North"—as the Governor of Bassein, Diu, Damaun, and Choul, residing at Bassein, was styled—that timely succour might be afforded them. But the English Governor only sent what he called, a "handsome excuse." In the meantime, the siege was carried on with extraordinary vigour, skill, and perseverance; and the Mahrattas sprang twelve or thirteen mines, and made a practicable breach in one of the bastions. Here their troops rushed in many times with unwonted fury, and seemed to have securely established themselves; but they were as often driven back with great slaughter, and hundreds were blown into the air by the explosion of one of their own mines. With singular alacrity the besieged repaired their defences, but, at length, their assailants secured a position on the walls from which they could not be dislodged. Even then the brave Portuguese disputed every inch of ground, until, after a contest of two days, the commandant, seeing that there was no prospect of aid, that eight hundred of his best officers and men were slain, his ammunition exhausted, his surviving troops worn out by continued fighting, enfeebled from want of provisions, and dispirited, held out a white flag and offered to capitulate. Chimnajee Appa rejoiced to possess a city which he had acquired with a loss of no fewer than five thousand men, according to his own admission—of twenty-two thousand, according to reports current at Bombay—offered most favourable terms to his vanquished foe, and, on the 5th of May, the articles of capitulation were signed, and the brave garrison marched out with the honours of war. De Souza Pereira and the remains of his force proceeded to Bombay, where they were well treated and maintained by the Governor, and, at length, on the 29th of September, the remnant of the defenders of Bassein, convoyed by a squadron of ships of the Bombay Marine, sailed and arrived safely at Choul; but then a fresh series of misfortunes commenced. For some reason unexplained they were led by a toilsome march overland, instead of being landed at Goa. Their fatigues, however, were nearly surmounted, and, on the 15th of November, they were within two hours' march of Aguada, where they were sure to find security and repose, when a hostile army was seen approaching. Khem Sawunt, ruler of the state, now known as Sawant Waree, leading three hundred cavalry and five thousand infantry, attacked with fury their enfeebled and disorganised ranks, utterly routed them after a contest of two hours, and slew two hundred men. The English Commodore, being with his fleet at Goa, beheld the broken band of fugitives enter their own territory, and the deep commiseration he felt for them found expression in his official dispatches. He wrote:—" The Portuguese are really in a miserable condition; I can see care and grief in all their faces." As to the brave Pereira, he fell into disgrace at Goa, and took up his residence at the French settlement of Mahé, where, many years afterwards, he was engaged in conducting negotiations between Angria and his new protectors.

Ceasing to struggle with their adverse destiny, the Portuguese prepared to yield their northern possessions, with the exception of Damaun and its little territory. Although no enemy was before the forts of Choul and Mhar, they proposed to abandon both, and offered the former to the English; but the Government of Bombay, in order to prevent its falling into the hands of Sambhajee, proposed to offer it to the Peishwa. Under these circumstances, a way was already paved for a mediation, which the Portuguese now requested the English to undertake. The Mahrattas, on being invited to propose their terms, at first not only demanded the cession of Choul, but also of Damaun, and insisted upon having assigned to them a portion of the customs at Goa, which they proposed to collect by stationing a guard at the fort. Captain Inchbird, of the Bombay Marine, however, having been deputed by the Portuguese, with the consent of the English Government, to treat for them, obtained more favourable terms, and induced their scornful enemies to show some forbearance. On the 14th of October, 1740, articles of peace were signed on behalf of Bajee Rao, the Peishwa, on the one side, and the Viceroy of Goa on the other. The Portuguese engaged to deliver up to the Mahrattas the forts of Choul and Mhar, (at the mouth of the river of the same name) which were to be temporarily occupied by the English, until the Mahrattas should have fulfilled their part of the conditions by withdrawing their forces from Salsette. A brief delay occurred in consequence of the repugnance which the Portuguese priests of Choul felt for any measure by which the possessions of Christians should be delivered to heathens, and they seditiously excited their people to resist the transfer. Their own envoy, perplexed by their obstinacy, admitted that he had discovered in them a malignant spirit, and Inchbird, throwing aside all restraint, exclaimed in disgust, "Sure such unheard of villains and inconsiderate men are hardly to be met with!" However, in November, Choul was delivered by the English to the Mahrattas, and all parties expressed themselves satisfied with the honourable manner in which the conditions of the treaty were fulfilled.

In order that they might feel their way to the supreme authority of the Mahrattas, says a writer already quoted, the Government of Bombay sent Captain William Gordon in May, 1739, to the Rajah of Sattara, with a complimentary letter, giving him secret instructions to concert measures with the enemies of Bajee Rao, the Peishwa, and to use all possible means of undermining that minister's influence. At the same time they agreed it was "expedient to try what effect a cautious and well-managed compliance" might have upon the Peishwa, so they sent also a letter and a present to him by Captain Inchbird. The reports of their proceedings are very different, the one keeping a regular journal, the other only noting down such matters as related to his mission. Captain Gordon entered into details. Leaving Bombay on the 12th of May, he arrived, on the following day, at Rajahpore,* where he was courteously received by the Seedee and furnished with a guide, who accompanied him to Bancoot. On the 15th, as he was sailing up the river Mhar, or Savitri, a Mahratta officer stopped his boat, demanded his passport, and, finding that his mission was not authorised by Bajee Rao, put him under arrest. After a short detention and an examination of his despatches, he was suffered to prosecute his journey, but, on the 19th of May, narrowly escaped being seized by some troops of Sambhajee Angria. The next day he ascended the Ghauts, for the first time in his life.

As Gordon proceeded, he found that the English name was held in honour by the officers of Government, and, wherever he went, met with a polite welcome. The Rajah was not at Sattara, being engaged in the siege of a place called Myrah, at a distance of five days' journey. Thither he hastened, and, on the 8th of June, was received by the Rajah.

Gordon returned to Bombay by Poonah, and traversed the Mahratta territories. The result of his mission was satisfactory. He brought a complimentary letter from the Rajah, and had become convinced that Bajee Rao would not molest Bombay, as he knew how much he was indebted to it for the prosperity of his own territory. The Rajah, Peishwa, and principal chiefs coincided in the opinion that the English ought to be respected. All this information, which must have had a tranquillising effect upon the European population of Bombay, was furnished by Captain Gordon at a cost which, in these days of expensive missions, will raise a smile of contempt on the face of a professional diplomatist; the bill of his expenses amounted to 296 rupees, and he was permitted to retain the presents he had received, which were valued at 240 rupees.†

Of more immediate importance was the mission of Captain Inchbird, of the Bombay Marine, who may be regarded as the first of those distinguished men who have since conferred celebrity on the diplomacy of the English and Mahrattas, the

* Rajahpore, or Rajhpuri, is the capital of the small state of the Seedee, or Hubshee, and is situated on the north side of the river of the same name. Jinjeera, where the Seedee has a palace and fort, and whence he derived his title, is separated from Rajahpore by a shallow and narrow channel. The other island fort is called Kansi.

† Manuscript Copy of Captain Gordon's Journal.

forerunner of Mostyn, Malet, Malcolm, and Elphinstone. His object was to negotiate a treaty, in the name of President Law, with the victorious Mahratta General, Chimnajee Appa, who acted on behalf of the Peishwa, and, for this purpose, he proceeded to Bassein. Even before the negotiations were opened, the Mahratta General, following the established precedents of his country, demanded from the English a pecuniary contribution, but must have been not a little surprised by the firm stand which the envoy most wisely made at the commencement. The outspoken sailor promptly told him that the Honourable Company would never permit their servants to give him money, and would rather see the island of Bombay sunk in the sea than comply with any such request. Under the disappointment of this refusal the Mahrattas began to show their teeth, and complained bitterly that an envoy had been sent from Bombay to the Shao Rajah, at Sattara, before they had been consulted. Inchbird was conscious that they had means of penetrating English secrets which he could not discover, and were aware of Gordon's instructions to undermine the influence of Bajee Rao. His position was embarrassing; but, having extricated himself with singular skill, he succeeded in arranging the terms of a treaty,* dated the 12th of July, 1739, which was ratified at Bombay.

Marked as had been the success of these transactions with the Mahrattas, the feeling of security which they brought to the inhabitants of Bombay, was but transient. Harassing reports were continually current, and, no sooner had the little fleet sailed away from the island with merchant vessels under their convoy, than the Government became painfully sensible how exposed they were to the designs of their unscrupulous allies, particularly if Mannajee Angria should once more prove treacherous and convert his vessels into transports for the Peishwa's plunderers. On the subversion of the Portuguese, only the British remained to cope, single handed, with the Angria; but the Bombay Marine, when the hour for action had struck, proved that it was equal to the task of driving his ships from the sea, and of attacking him in his strongholds on shore. Timid counsels now prevailed at Bombay, and alarming rumours were rife. It was said, upon good authority, that a large force was being mustered at Tanna, and the tone of Mannajee's letters became more insolent. Mischief, it was thought, must

* According to this treaty, the Peishwa conceded to the English free trade in his dominions. The contracting parties mutually engaged that debtors endeavouring to evade their responsibilities, should be either delivered up or compelled to pay all that was due; that runaway slaves should be seized and restored to their masters, and that if the vessels of one power should be driven by stress of weather into the ports of the other, assistance should be rendered them; but such vessels as were wrecked on the coast should be sold, one half the proceeds of sale being paid to the owner, the other half to the Government on whose coast the wreck might be thrown.

be brewing; the alarm spread, and, in a short time, became a panic. Numbers of the inhabitants of Bombay fled, carrying away their valuables, or hiding them underground. It now became a question whether the ships of-war of the Company should be used as convoys, or whether necessity did not require the sacrifice of the trade of Bombay in order that the island itself might be preserved. In this dilemma Government received intelligence of a sad disaster.

On the 9th of November the southern coast was devastated by a frightful storm, in which three of the finest grabs of the Bombay Marine, completely armed and equipped, and commanded by three experienced captains, Rigby, Sandilands, and Nunn, foundered, leaving not a fragment to tell of their fate. Instantly Sambhajee Angria seized the opportunity, and, sallying out, carried away fourteen fishing boats, with eighty-four men, from the mouth of the harbour. Remonstrances were made in vain, and retaliation was for the present out of the question.

At this time the coasts of India swarmed with native pirates, and, in 1733, a Dutch ship turned rover and captured two merchant vessels. The native pirates were called by the English Sevajees, Kempsaunts, Malwans, and Coolies. Under the name of Sevajees were included Mahrattas of all descriptions, but chiefly the subjects of the two Angrias. The word Kempsaunt is a corruption of Khem Sawunt, a name given to several of the Bhonslay family who had been rulers of the Waree State. The first Khem Sawunt with whom the Government of Bombay had any correspondence, was succeeded, in 1709, by his nephew, Phond Sawunt, with whom, in 1730, that Government made a treaty of alliance, offensive and defensive, against Angria; but it does not appear to have been respected for any length of time.* With the Malwans the Government had a

* Memoir of the Sawunt Waree State, by Mr. Courtney and Major J. W. Auld. Of the piratical tribes inhabiting the coast to the northward of Bombay, Hamilton says:—All the country between Diu and Dand point, which is about thirty leagues along shore, admits of no traffick, being inhabited by freebooters, called Warrels, and often associate with the Sanganians in exercising piracies and depredations. They confide much in their numbers, as others do, and strive to board their prizes, and, as soon as they get on board, they throw in showers of stones on the prize's decks, in order to sink them that way if they don't yield; and they have earthen pots, as big as a six-pound Granadoe shell, full of unquenched lime, well sifted, which they throw in also, and the pots breaking, there arises so great a dust, that the defendants can neither see or breathe well. They also use wicks of cotton, dipt in a combustible oyl, and firing the wick, and throwing it into the opposer's ship, it burns violently, and sets fire to the parts that it is thrown on. They have no cities, and their villages are small. The best of them stands about sixty miles to the eastward of Diu, and is called Chance. It is built about a league within the mouth of a river, which has a small island lying athwart it, about two miles into the sea. The island has good springs of fresh water, but no inhabitants. In anno 1716, the English went to burn that village and their pirating vessels, but were unsuccessful in their undertaking. The Warrels occupy all the sea coast as high as Gogo, which lies about twelve leagues within

long dispute on account of their having seized the wreck of an English ship called the 'Anglesea,' but, at length, a treaty of peace was concluded between the East India Company and Sevajee Sunkur Punt, styling himself Governor and Commander-in-chief of Sindeedroog, or Malwan.

The Coolie rovers infested the coast of Guzerat. Their stronghold was Sultanpore on the small river Curla, where they lived under an organized government countenanced by persons high in authority, who, as a return for secret protection, obtained a share in the produce of their depredations. The Government of Bombay having for some time employed paid spies in their country, and ascertained the most favourable time for an expedition, sent against them, in 1734, a small fleet composed of the sloop 'London,' a bombketch and five galivats, under Captain Radford Nunn, who, after a sharp fight, returned in triumph with five of the Coolies' guns and fourteen of their vessels, three of which had cargoes, whilst his own loss included only two Europeans and two natives. The expedition also burnt five vessels, and the Coolies themselves burnt fifty more, rather than that they should fall into the hands of their enemies. Captain Nunn's success, says the writer to whom we are indebted for material in this portion of our work, was most important on account of the moral weight which the English derived from it at a time when they were particularly anxious to have their maritime power acknowledged at Surat, and respected by the natives generally. Six months afterwards two more vessels were taken, and ten burnt. All the prizes were then sold for the small sum of 3,650 rupees, which the Government of Bombay resolved should be divided amongst the captors, but the Court of Directors meanly reversed this order, and claimed a moiety for themselves.

Within six months the pirates took their revenge by employing the same spy system which had been so efficacious against themselves. Acting in collusion with them, the pilot

the Gulf of Cambay. And the coast, from Dand point to Goga, is very dangerous, being thick set with rocks and sandbanks ; and a rapid tide runs amongst them of six or eight miles in an hour, in a channel that is twenty fathoms deep in some places, which causes anchoring to be dangerous also. Goga is a pretty large town, and has had some mud wall fortifications, which still defend them from the insults of their neighbours, the Coulies, who inhabit the north-east side of Guzerat, and are as great thieves by land as their brethren the Warrels and Sanganians are by sea.

The Rev. G. P. Badger, in his notes to his translation of the Arabic "History of the Imaums or Seyyids of Muscat," has hazarded an hypothesis regarding these pirates which is incorrect. Quoting Niebuhr's reference to them in 1764, as " petty people inhabiting the coast," he queries " Malvanes" as Malays, and " Sangerians" as Angrians.—(*See* Note to page 171 of his work.)

Regarding the word Kempsaunt, Hamilton says :—" The Portuguese gave the name of Kema Sancto, or 'Saint Burner,' to a Rajah whom he calls Kempason, who, in the year 1696, ravaged the country about Vingorla, and entering the district of Goa, plundered and burnt all he could lay hands on, not sparing the churches and images."

of the 'Antelope,' a Bombay Marine galivat, which was convoying some richly freighted vessels to Cambay, steered his charges through a wrong channel, where they ran aground, and then, after giving a pre-concerted signal to the Coolies ashore, made his escape by leaping overboard. The 'Antelope' was speedily assailed by a strong force of pirates, and, although gallantly defended for a time, further resistance was rendered hopeless by the explosion of her magazine. Ten Europeans, two Lascars, and two Sepoys perished; and the officer in command and one seaman were the only Europeans that survived.

Tellicherry was at this time the most important settlement of the English under the Presidency of Bombay, Surat even ranking after it in point of expenditure. When war broke out between the Malabarese and Canarese, the English at Tellicherry ranged themselves on the side of the former, and, indeed, became in a little time the principal combatants. Their troops, under Captain Stirling, and a party of seamen of the Bombay Marine, under Captain Nunn, attacked a pagoda, called Cheria Coonay, on Christmas-day, 1738, and, having carried it after a short struggle, succeeded in intercepting the communications of the Canarese army with their fort of Madday. Alarmed lest he should be hemmed in, Ragonath, the Canarese general, after bursting some of his guns, throwing others into wells, and setting fire to his camp, abandoned with precipitation a strong position, and sought refuge under the guns of the fort. Here he entrenched himself, but his troops suffered considerably from the English skirmishers and the fire of their guns, whilst the Malabarese remained inactive spectators of a contest which had originally been undertaken on their behalf. However, as it was thought good policy to conciliate him rather than drive him to despair, he was permitted to enter the fort without being assailed, and Captain Stirling, beating a retreat, closed the campaign. The Chief of Tellicherry afterwards wrote to Ragonath, declaring that if the English forces had not shown singular moderation and forbearance, his whole army would have been destroyed; and, the following April, the Canarese, sensible of their inferiority, made proposals of peace. Thus the first war in which the English of Western India showed any military skill, or contended with field-artillery and what was called a regular army, was brought to a favourable termination, and the officers and seamen of the Bombay Marine added to the laurels they had gained ashore at Surat, Gombroon, Carwar, and other places.

As 1742 was a year of peace, reductions, of which the Government had almost immediate cause to repent, were made both in the marine and military establishments. Officers who had been many years in the Company's service, were harshly dismissed; and, although the local government, feeling the great injustice and impolicy of thus turning adrift faithful servants, deferred the execution of the Court's orders until their victims' remonstrances could be referred home, the delay was only temporary, and the obduracy of their masters left them no alternative. The marine establishment, as reduced, consisted of a superintendent, eight commanders, one of whom was styled commodore, the rank of admiral being abolished, three first-lieutenants, four second-lieutenants, four third officers, and six masters of galivats, besides midshipmen whose number does not appear. The superintendent's salary was £220 per annum, a commander's, from sixty to eighty rupees per mensem; a first-lieutenant's, from thirty-two to forty; a second-lieutenant's, twenty-four; a midshipman's, twelve; a surgeon's, from thirty-one to forty; a gunner's, or boatswain's, twenty-two; a carpenter's, twenty-six; an able seaman's, nine; a native officer's, ten; a marine topass's, six, and a Lascar's, five.

According to the Bombay Diary of 1742-43, the principal ships were the 'Restoration' and the 'Neptune's Prize,' the former being manned by eighty Europeans of all ranks and fifty-one Lascars; the latter by fifty Europeans and thirty-one Lascars. On each of the "prahims" there had usually been thirty Europeans and twenty Lascars; but these numbers were now slightly diminished. According to another MS. authority of respectability, the strength of the Bombay Marine at this time (1742) was as follows:—One ship of forty-four guns, four of twenty-eight guns, four of eighteen guns, six bomb-ketches, and twenty large galivats, employing nearly one hundred officers and from seventeen hundred to two thousand men. Probably this was just before the reduction. As frequent complaints of favouritism were made by the officers, it was resolved that promotion should be regulated according to dates of commissions, and thus the seniority system was introduced into the Service.

An immediate consequence of these reductions was, that the mercantile marine, now larger than ever, suffered serious losses from pirates, and the Company quickly found the error of this policy of misplaced economy. The 'Tiger,' a galivat, when disabled by a waterspout on her passage from Gombroon, was boarded by subjects of the Seedee at Mufdafarbad. Her crew, after a severe conflict in which seven fell, were overpowered, and she was carried away as a prize; but, on a proper representation being made to the Seedee of Jinjeera, whom the Seedee of Mufdafarbad acknowledged as lord paramount, she was restored. Near the port of Surat, Coolie rovers swarmed, and waited for their prey as the ships lying at the bar attempted to discharge their cargoes. The treaty which had been made with Khem Sawunt was, as soon as the Government of Bombay was supposed to be powerless, treated as waste paper; for, notwithstanding its provisions, that chief made prizes of seven vessels valued at eighteen or nineteen thousand rupees. The Malwans seized others valued at ten or eleven thousand rupees. The subjects of the Peishwa showed themselves equally rapacious, and, although their government, when appealed to, promised that the offenders should be punished, it was only on the improbable supposition that they could be discovered and convicted. Even Mannajee Angria, while professing to be a close ally of the British, countenanced his subjects in attacking their vessels, and never hesitated to pick up a stray boat if he could hope to escape detection; yet, on one occasion, he rendered a valuable service in rescuing the 'Salamander,' an English ketch, which had been captured off Colaba by the fleet of Sambhajee Angria. Seven grabs and eight galivats, in the service of the last-mentioned pirate, after fighting for a night and day with the 'Montague' and 'Warwick,' two East Indiamen, carried off five vessels and a Portuguese ketch sailing under their convoy. The merchants of Bombay, driven to despair by the losses they had sustained, held meetings, and unanimously represented to Government that, since the reduction of the Marine, Khem Sawunt and the Malwans, having fitted out small vessels with the express purpose of preying upon their trade, were bringing them to ruin; that, in consequence of the risks they ran, bankers would not advance money on the security of their goods, so that, although the stormy season was over, not a ship had been equipped for the transport of merchandize; and that, unless more cruisers were provided, the trade of the port would be entirely suppressed. These representations led to a small but permanent increase of the Company's Marine.

On the 31st of March, 1744, war was declared between Great Britain and France,* and two French privateers, the 'Apollo,'

* The French now aspired to territorial aggrandisement. As the English had three Presidencies, so also the Isle of France and Pondicherry were each the seat of a French Governor, who had a council under him. The former island was called by the Portuguese Cerne, by the Dutch, who occupied it, Mauritius, after Maurice, Prince of Orange, but the French, when they took possession of it in 1720, styled it the Isle of France. Subordinate to it was the smaller island of Mascarhenas, thenceforth called Bourbon. To the Government of these islands, La Bourdonnais, a brilliant naval officer in the service of the French East India Company, was appointed in 1733, and so indefatigably did he labour for their improvement, that the inhabitants testified their warm gratitude, and the author of "Paul and Virginia" affirms in the preface to his work, that, whatever he has seen in the Isle of France most usefully devised or most ably executed, was the work of La Bourdonnais. The other Government was that of Pondicherry, which the French had obtained and fortified about thirty years before. The city, containing seventy thousand inhabitants, was regularly and beautifully built, and was strongly fortified. Dumas, the Governor, was declared a Nawab of the Empire, and three fine districts were ceded to him. Thus French influence was progressing rapidly even before the advent in 1741 of the ambitious Dupleix, who is ordinarily supposed to have given it the first impulse. Under the Go-

of fifty guns, and the 'Anglesea,' of forty, after cruising, during February and March, 1747, off the Cape of Good Hope, made their appearance near Bombay in August, and having captured the 'Princess Mary,' a ship from Madras, hovered about the coast with a view of intercepting the East Indiamen of the season as they arrived from England. The only protective measure which the Government of Bombay could adopt was to equip for sea three of their ships-of-war, of greatly inferior force, and they also dispatched six fishing boats, to give the alarm to any English vessels approaching the shores of India.

In 1748 a mutiny took place on board the 'Bombay,' one of the finest of the Company's ships, of which we will give an account. It appears that the crew of the 'Anson,' an Indiaman captured by the French off Bombay in August of the preceding year, were drafted into the ships of the Bombay Marine, with their own consent, according to the official account, although they maintained that they were impressed into the service. A large number were placed on board the 'Bombay,' and sent in her on a cruise. As the ship lay at anchor at Rajapore, on the 1st of March, 1748, Samuel Hough, the commander, who was sitting at supper with his chief and second officers, and the surgeon, had his attention suddenly arrested by a disturbance on deck. Immediately the cabin-door was thrown open, and some of the crew rushing in with muskets in their hands, swore that they would blow out their officers' brains if they did not instantly surrender themselves as prisoners. Instead of yielding, Captain Hough made a dash at his assailants, and endeavoured to seize the ringleaders. They retreated, were followed by him and his officers, and one man standing close to him fired a musket at his head. Had he not with his arm struck the barrel upwards, the ball must have passed through his brain; as it was it carried away part of his cap. All the officers then proposed to bar themselves in the steerage, but attempted in vain to close the doors until Hough procured a sword from his own cabin, and with it again rushed upon deck. The mutineers, having now broken open the arm-chest, summoned their officers to lay down their arms, protesting that all they required was their liberty, that opposition to them was useless, as the whole crew were acting in combination, and expressing a hope that they might not be compelled to put their officers to death. Captain Hough, seeing no hope of repressing the mutiny by violence, flung his sword away, and, standing unarmed before the whole body of seamen, asked them, in God's name, why they behaved thus. They

vernment of Pondicherry were the factories, or comptoirs, of Chandernagore in Bengal, Karical on the coast of Coromandel, and Mahé about three or four miles from Tellicherry on the Malabar coast.

told him in reply that they had no complaints to make of their officers; but having been trepanned into the Company's service, they were resolved to have their liberty or die.

He warned them that the consequences would be fatal to them if they persevered in their mutiny; but promised that if they would lay down their arms, they should be sent to England as soon as possible. His address had only the effect of making them more furious. They placed the surgeon and other officers in irons, and ordered their commander to retire abaft the tiller ropes, where he was guarded by ten or twelve men armed with pistols, swords, and blunderbusses. One of their number, named William Brown, was then appointed captain, but soon found how much more difficult it is to organise rebellion at sea than on land. So defective were their arrangements that, unable to weigh anchor, they were obliged to cut the cable; then they found that tide and wind were both against them, and they were drifting on a lee-shore. In haste they let go another anchor, and, for a time, all remained quiet.

Hough, seeing their incompetency to work the ship, supposed that they would now more readily listen to reason, and, with the permission of his guard, walked forward to hold a conference with the principal men. One of them, rushing up to him, presented a blunderbuss at his head, swearing with a fierce oath to shoot him if he uttered another word. Others declared that he and his officers were good men, and should not be hurt if they would only remain silent. Taking advantage of this little current setting in his favour, he desired that the irons should be removed from his officers. With one voice they said, "By God, it was the Captain's desire, and should be complied with." The officers were liberated. All hands came on deck, and the conference was renewed; but some of the older seamen, suspecting a design of returning to port, shouted, "No Bombay! No Bombay!" adding, with horrible oaths, that if they listened to their captain and laid down their arms, they would all be hanged. Fortunately, the mutineers felt their helplessness, and, finding that they could not get the ship to sea, proposed to place the Captain again in command, on condition that the arms and magazine should be left in their possession. At last he contrived to talk with the leaders in private, when, after long hesitation, from fear of their more obstinate and desperate comrades, they were induced to set an example of submission on receiving a guarantee from Hough that they should be paid 2,000 rupees and sent to England in the first ship. All then gathered round their Captain, acknowledged that they had been engaged in a rash undertaking, and expressed their willingness to rely on his promises. In a quarter of an hour, after all the officers had signed an agreement not to take any further notice of the mutiny, the men had laid down their arms and returned to their duty.

Thus, after a duration of seven hours, ended a revolt which threatened to check the naval improvements then in progress, and this happy termination was due to the courage and promptitude of Captain Hough. All the crew of the 'Bombay' were participators, with the exception of some petty officers, but it was remarkable that during the whole time not a man touched a drop of liquor. The Government, without determining whether the promises made by their officers under restraint were binding, felt that it would be inconvenient to punish a whole crew, and, as some captains of men-of-war were anxious to ship men for England, they fulfilled Captain Hough's engagements and permitted the mutineers to escape unhurt. Not so, however, some others. A surgeon named William Wills, having been tried by a court-martial and found guilty of exciting discontent, was taken in a boat alongside each of the four Company's ships then in harbour, and exhibited with a halter round his neck, whilst the particulars of his crime and sentence were read aloud. Four seamen, likewise found guilty, suffered the same punishment, and were also flogged.*

One of the consequences of the war with France, and the representations of the Bombay merchants as to the defenceless state of the trade, was a small increase of the Marine. The enlarged Service, however, only consisted of three ships carrying twenty-eight guns, a grab of twenty guns (from six to twelve-pounders) five ketches, carrying from eight to fourteen guns (from four to six-pounders), eight galivats, and one prahim. Two other ships were alternately employed as guard ships to protect the factory at Gombroon. Each ship or grab had a crew of seventy or fifty Europeans, the ketches thirty or a lesser number, and the galivats a few to work the guns only. To the list of officers were added two commanders, one first-lieutenant, six second-lieutenants, and three third-lieutenants. At the same time, the first attempts were made to improve the religious and moral character of both officers and men, orders being sent from the Court of Directors for the regular performance of Divine service on board all the vessels and a strict prohibition of all gambling, profane swearing, and indecent conversation.† As,

* "Bombay Diary." Letter to the Court, the 23rd of November, 1748.
† Order Book of the Government, August, 1751 :—
"General instructions to the commanders of the Honourable Company's vessels.
"In the first place you are to take care to keep up the service of God on board the vessel you command, according to the Liturgy of the Church of England, that the same may be devoutly and decently performed every Lord's day, and on all other appointed seasons as often as can be done with convenience: and be very strict in observing a good decorum and discipline among your ship's company, severely punishing all profaneness or blasphemies of God's holy name, and

however, it was thought that these reforms would be incomplete until the Bombay Marine should have an official uniform, like a regular naval service, in answer to a petition presented, in 1761, by the officers to the Governor in Council, they were ordered to wear blue frock-coats turned up with yellow, dress-coats and waistcoats of the same colour, and according to a regulated pattern. Large boot-sleeves and facings of gold lace were the fashion for the superior grades, whilst midshipmen and masters of galivats were to rest content with small round cuffs and no facings. With increased numbers, improved discipline, and a regular uniform, the Bombay Marine became a little Navy, although it did not assume that name. The English fleets, with their line-of-battle ships and frigates, floating in the harbour, on various occasions during the next quarter of a century, under the command of Admirals Watson, Cornish, Pocock, and Stevens, threw the Marine into the shade, but, at the same time, taught it emulation and efficiency. On the 25th of March, 1754, the Mutiny Act, as applied to the Company's military* and naval forces in India, received the royal assent after a division in the Lords.

Orme describes the mode of warfare assumed by the pirate-chief, Angria, and the success he had achieved even against European ships of war. He says:—"Eight or ten grabs, and forty or fifty galivats, crowded with men, generally composed Angria's principal fleet destined to attack ships of war, or large merchantmen. The vessel no sooner came in sight of the port or bay, wherever the fleet was lying, than they slipped their cables and put out to sea; if the wind blew, their construction enabled them to sail almost as fast as the wind, and, if it was calm, the galivats, rowing, towed the grabs; when within cannon-shot of the chase, they generally assembled round her stern, and the grabs attacked her at a distance with their bow-guns, firing first only at their masts. As soon as the chase was dismasted, they

on no account permit gaming of any sort." Also "Bombay Diary," the 18th of May, 1756, the 21st of August, 1759, and the 9th and 30th of June, 1761.

* In 1741, according to a writer on the "Rise of the Navy and Army in Bombay," the military establishment was considered as one regiment, consisting of a captain, nine lieutenants, fifteen ensigns, a surgeon, two sergeants-majors, eighty-two sergeants, eighty-two corporals, twenty-six drummers, and three hundred and nineteen European privates, also thirty-one masters—by which term we conceive Indo-Europeans are meant—and nine hundred topasses. They were distributed into seven companies, and their monthly pay amounted to 10,314 rupees.

"There was also a sort of Native Militia composed of seven hundred Sepoys, including Native officers. They were not armed or dressed in any uniform manner, but when enlisted brought the weapons they happened to have, whether swords and targets, bows and arrows, pikes, lances, or matchlocks. They were maintained at a cost of 3,123 rupees per mensem, and were discharged at the pleasure of Government, without pensions, or even donations. These forces were considerably increased after the declaration of war with France, when an artillery company was raised, and the establishment of gunners, gunners' mates, and gun-room crews was abolished. Thus in 1753, the artillery numbered one hundred and seventeen officers and men, and the infantry eight hundred and forty-one.

came nearer and battered her on all sides until she struck ; and if the defence was obstinate, they sent a number of galivats with two or three hundred men in each, who boarded, sword in hand, from all quarters at the same instant. It was now fifty years that this piratical state had rendered itself formidable to the trading ships of all the European nations in India, and the English East India Company had kept up a marine force at the annual expense of £50,000 to protect their own ships, as well as those belonging to the merchants established in their colonies ; for as no vessel could, with prudence, venture to singly pass by Angria's dominions, the trade was convoyed at particular times up and down the sea coasts by the Company's armed vessels. Angria's ships sailed much better than the Bombay fleet, and never fought them longer than they thought proper ; in the meantime, Angria's seldom failed to take such ships as ventured to sail without company along the coast." Besides the 'Derby,' (Indiaman) and 'Ann' (grab), they took a forty-gun ship belonging to the French Company, and, in February, 1754, captured, after a severe action, three Dutch ships of fifty, thirty-six, and eighteen guns, which were sailing together, burning the two largest, and taking the third.*

We have now arrived at a period in the history of the Bombay Marine, when the Service entered upon an extended career of usefulness, and, by the discipline, valour, and skill evinced by its officers and men, vindicated its claim to be regarded as the Navy of India, an honourable title conceded to it many years later by the Sailor King, who felt a sympathy for the small Service whose officers had fairly earned the distinctive appellation by more than two centuries of arduous service.

* Orme's " History of the Military Transactions of the British Nation in Hindostan for the year 1745," vol. i., p. 409, *et seq.*

CHAPTER IV.

1754—59.

Early Career of Commodore James—His Defeat of Angria's Fleet—Expedition against Severndroog—Capture of the Castle—Surrender of Bancoot—Operations against Gheria, and Destruction of the Power of Angria—Subsequent Services of Commodore James; his Retirement and Death—Operations during the War with France—Actions with the French Fleet—Affairs at Surat—Capture of the Town and Castle of Surat—Assumption by the Marine of the Tunkha and Duties as Mogul's Admiral.

THE history of the operations which resulted in the destruction of the power of Angria, "whose forts," says Orme, "were deemed impregnable, as his fleet was, with reason, deemed formidable," is so intimately associated with the name of Commodore (afterwards Sir William) James, that it is necessary we should preface our narrative by a brief sketch of the career of this distinguished officer, who, by his achievements, enhanced, at the same time, his own reputation and that of the Service of which he has ever been regarded as one of the shining lights.

Commodore James was born in the year 1721, near the town of Milford Haven, in Wales. During his earlier years he followed the humble occupation of a ploughboy, which he soon discarded, but we know not whether, in taking this step, he was inspired by a noble ambition to enter some profession in which he might win renown, or that the sight of the sea filled him with a craving for its dangers and excitements, as Dibdin says—

"To leave his poor plough to go ploughing the deep."

Certain it is that young James soon sickened of his work on shore, and, at the age of twelve, took to the sea. He entered himself in the merchant service, but little is known of the early years of his apprenticeship.

In the year 1738 he served under Admiral Lord Hawke in the capacity of ship's boy or servant. A few years after this, Mr. James obtained the command of a ship in the Virginia trade, and set sail from England. At the time we were at war with the Spaniards, and he had the misfortune to be taken prisoner, together with his whole crew, by a man-of-war belonging to that nation. They were carried to Havannah and imprisoned there for a considerable time. At length he and his comrades were released from captivity, and embarked on board a brig which was bound to the colony of South Carolina.

But evil fortune still followed in their footsteps. A few days after leaving Cuba it commenced to blow very heavily. The brig was a crazy old craft, ill adapted to contend against the storms of these latitudes. She began to leak, and as the gale increased in strength, so did the water gain upon her, notwithstanding the efforts of the commander and his men to keep it under. Besides pumping, recourse was had to bailing, but this also was ineffectual. At length Mr. James became convinced that she would not float much longer, and expressed his determination to leave her and take his chance in one of the boats. Seven of the seamen offered to join him in his perilous venture, the remainder preferring to remain on board the brig. Accordingly a small boat was prepared, and stored with a keg of water and a bag of biscuits, and hardly had they got clear of the brig than she suddenly disappeared. The gale continued to blow for some days, though scarcely so heavily as at first; at length it subsided, but, being unprovided with a compass, Mr. James knew not whither to steer, and so for twenty days the boat was driven by the wind where it listed. The supply of fresh water was doled out with the utmost nicety from Mr. James's snuff-box, and the biscuits, which had been rendered almost unfit for food by the salt-water making a clean breach over the boat, were also served out in equal portions. On the twentieth day land was sighted, and, though it proved to be the island of Cuba, any terra firma was joyfully welcome to the tempest-tossed mariners. With great difficulty the party succeeded in affecting a landing on the coast, and, on making inquiries, learned that they were no more than ten miles distant from their old prison; but the starvation and hardships they had undergone had wrought a great change in their estimate of a Spanish dungeon, and, in comparison with the cramped up thwarts of an open boat in a raging sea, they welcomed its squalid wretchedness. Only one out of the party of eight died from the effects of the severe sufferings they had endured; the others indeed lost the use of their limbs for a considerable time, but, ultimately, they all recovered. After a captivity of a few months, the Spaniards released their prisoners, and they returned to England in a British vessel.

Soon after his arrival Mr. James married, and, as an honorable testimony that the obscurity of his origin did not stand in the way of his achieving distinction, any more than it did in the case of Sir Cloudesley Shovel and many other famous English admirals, it may be mentioned that his wife kept a public-house in the now classic region of Wapping, known as the "Red Cow." It is also related of him, as showing his amiable disposition, that as soon as his worldly prospects improved, he journeyed to his native town in Wales and inquired after a young woman with whom he had been brought up as a child, and had interchanged vows of constancy. On learning that she had proved as fickle as himself, he made her some presents he had brought with him and befriended her husband.

In the year 1747 Mr. James entered the Bombay Marine, and he was found to be so enterprising and zealous an officer, that, in 1749, he was promoted to the rank of commander and appointed captain of the 'Guardian' of twenty-eight guns. Having been sent with the 'Bombay' of the same force, and the 'Drake,' bomb-ketch, to convoy a valuable fleet of seventy coasters from Bombay to a point a little to the northward of Goa, he fell in with Angria's fleet of sixteen grabs and galivats, mounting from four to twenty-two guns each, and crowded with men.

The enemy immediately bore up to attack the convoy, of which they expected to make an easy prey; but Captain James quickly formed a line with his three vessels between Angria's fleet and his convoy, to whom he made signal to run southward, and the whole reached Tellicherry in safety. An action now commenced and was vigorously contested for more than two hours, when one of Angria's largest galivats was sunk, and several others much shattered, with heavy loss in killed and wounded. The whole fleet now bore up for Gheria, closely pursued by Captain James's squadron, and suffered much in the retreat; while the loss in the Marine vessels was small.

The squadron returned to Bombay, and the joy caused by this signal defeat of Angria's fleet was very great. Captain James received the thanks of Government and of the merchants, and a short time after, was promoted to the rank of commodore and commander-in-chief of the Bombay Marine. It appears from the records, that he hoisted his broad pennant as such, on board the 'Protector,' of forty-four guns, in the year 1751.

A squadron was also employed at this time at Surat, where the Mogul Emperor's officers were striving one against the other, one party aided by the Dutch, and another by the English. Here the vessels were of much service, as their force gave a great preponderance to the British party. Other ships of the Bombay Marine were employed against the pirates in the Gulf of Cambay and coast of Kattywar, and they captured and destroyed several vessels of these freebooters, affording at the same time ample protection to the trade to the northward of Bombay. A strong squadron, under Commodore James, was kept cruising on the coast of the southern Concan and Canara, and kept in check the piratical craft of Angria, who did not dare again to attack the ships of the Marine. Matters remained in this state until the year 1755.

When Bajee Rao died on the 28th of April, 1740, his son, Ballajee, became Peishwa of the Mahrattas. This prince first saw service in conjunction with the Bombay squadron in 1740, and, says Grant Duff, " he was impressed with a high sense of the English, from their conduct when they relieved Mannajee Angria at Kolabah;" which estimate was, naturally, greatly increased by the military reputation they had achieved in the Carnatic. Ballajee and Mr. Richard Bourchier, the Bombay President, who succeeded to office on the 17th of November, 1750, were mutually desirous of suppressing the depredations of Angria, and settling affairs at Surat, which still continued the chief emporium of Western India, but, owing to the weakness of the Mogul Government, continued to remain in a state of chronic misrule. In the meantime Sambhajee had died, and Mannajee remained in nominal obedience to Ballajee, while his half-brother, Toolajee, who had succeeded to all the territories situated between Bancoot and Sawunt Waree, openly disavowed the authority of the Peishwa, and seized and plundered all ships on the high seas. The Rajah of Kolapoor and the rulers of Sawunt Waree followed a like system, and, says Grant Duff " were indiscriminately termed by the English, Malwans," a name given to them from the Fort of Malwan, or Sindeedroog, which belonged to the Kolapoor Rajah. Though Mr. Bourchier, soon after assuming the reins of office at Bombay, concluded an arrangement with the Mahrattas for the settlement of Surat, the war which broke out between the Peishwa and the Mogul Emperor, subsequent to the murder of Nasir Jung, prevented its being carried into effect. But in 1755 there was a short cessation of hostilities, upon which the Peishwa deputed Ramajee Punt, the Soubehdar of the Concan, to proceed to Bombay and settle a plan of operations for attacking Toolajee Angria.

The Governor and Council resolved to make an attempt, in conjunction with the Mahrattas, to dispossess Toolajee Angria of his strongholds, Severndroog and Viziadroog; and, accordingly, as none of the King's ships were in port, an expedition was organised, consisting solely of vessels belonging to the Bombay Marine. Looking about for a commander, the choice of the Council unanimously fell on Commodore James, who had proved himself to be an officer of energy, capacity, and resource.

On the 22nd of March, of the same year, Commodore James sailed from Bombay with a small squadron, consisting of his flag-ship, the 'Protector,' the 'Bombay,' twenty-eight guns, the 'Swallow,' sixteen guns, and the 'Triumph' and 'Viper,' bomb vessels; and, three days later, was joined by the Mahratta fleet of seven grabs and six galivats, having on board ten thousand soldiers, which had sailed from Choul. So great was the opinion of the strength of Angria's strongholds, that the Commodore received instructions from the Government to the effect that he was not to hazard the loss of any of his ships by attacking the enemy's forts; but he was to blockade their harbours, while the Mahratta army carried on operations by land.

The treaty between the contracting parties consisted of six or seven separate articles. By these the British were to have command of the Marine forces, but mutual approbation was necessary before undertaking any naval operations. The vessels that might be captured from Toolajee Angria, were to be handed over to the Peishwa; Bancoot, with the fort of Himmutgurh, and the sovereignty of the river on which it stands, with five villages, were to be ceded to the English in perpetuity. It appears that the President and Council considered that these stipulations might pledge them more than was prudent, and, therefore, one of the articles stipulated that the British only engaged to guard the sea and prevent Angria's fleet from throwing succours into the northern fort of Severndroog, Anjenwil, and Jyegurh.*

Ramajee Punt, the Mahratta commander-in-chief, landed with his troops about fifteen miles north of Severndroog, in order to march the rest of the way, and the fleet continued its course under the orders of the British commander, who, having learnt on the 28th of March, that Toolajee Angria's fleet was at anchor in the port of Severndroog, made sail thither the same evening, and timed his arrival so as to appear before the place at daylight on the 29th. This he did, as he was apprehensive, from his knowledge of their character, that the enemy, instead of showing fight, would endeavour to make their escape. And so it proved; in sight of the 'Protector,' the whole of Angria's fleet slipped their cables and stood out to sea. As there was but little wind they employed their galivats to tow them out of danger; by this means they managed at first to get ahead of the 'Protector,' but a sea breeze springing up, the frigate, being the fastest of the squadron, gained upon them. On seeing this the enemy stood in-shore, and, as Commodore James had left the rest of his ships a long way astern, he was forced, though very reluctantly, to give up the chase, having inflicted by his fire much loss in men, and damage to their ships. During the day the Mahratta fleet behaved with great pusillanimity. Although their vessels had hitherto sailed better than the English, such was their dread of the power of Angria's seamen, that they all kept in the rear and suffered the British squadron to give chase alone.

The Commodore now stood back towards Severndroog, and, on the 2nd of April, commenced offensive operations against that stronghold, which he decided to reduce first, on account of the approaching monsoon, which would render it inexpedient to

* Grant Duff's "History of the Mahrattas," vol. ii. p. 85.

attack Gheria, or any of the forts south of the three specified in the stipulations.

On his arrival off Severndroog he found that the Mahratta troops had invested three of the forts, but in so pusillanimous a manner were they carrying on the siege, that their batteries were thrown up at a distance of two miles from the works, and even at that range they had taken sedulous care to entrench themselves.

This style of conducting operations did not suit Commodore James, who determined to exceed his instructions rather than expose the English arms to the disgrace of certain failure. He, accordingly, at once detached boats from the squadron to reconnoitre and sound the harbour, and, finding plenty of water for the ketches to run in and bombard the forts, and for the 'Protector' to cannonade, he stood in to within 100 yards of the western face of the great fort, mounting fifty pieces of ordnance, and called " Severndroog," after the island.

The attack was forthwith commenced, and, in the course of the day, he expended eight hundred shot and shell, with considerable effect. At night a deserter arrived with the information that the Governor and many people were killed in the Castle, and that a large number had been wounded. This man further informed Commodore James that it would be impossible to make a breach on the side of the fort he had been bombarding, as the walls, being cut out of the solid rock, were, in that spot, nearly eighteen feet thick, and at least fifty feet high. Accordingly he decided on shifting his station, and, finding that the water to the eastward between the island and the mainland was deep enough to allow the flag-ship and the other vessels to stand in and open fire upon all the remaining forts, three in number, determined upon renewing the attack on the other side. Early on the morning of the 3rd, the 'Protector' was warped in to within half-musket shot of these formidable batteries, one mounting forty-two guns, and the two others twenty-four each, and the action was recommenced with only one foot of water under his ship's bottom at low tide. During the time he was occupied, by means of a spring, in getting the broadside of the 'Protector' to bear upon the enemy, a hot fire was opened upon him by the batteries; but, when in position, he returned the compliment with spirit, bringing one broadside to bear on the north-east bastion of the great fort, and the other on Fort Goa, the largest of those on the mainland. The bastions of Severndroog were, however, so high that the 'Protector' could only point her upper tier of guns at them; but being anchored within 100 yards, the musketry fire from the tops drove the enemy from their guns. His efforts were ably seconded by the 'Swallow' and 'Bombay,' and the bomb vessels; but his cowardly allies, the squadron of Mahratta grabs and galivats, declined to advance within gunshot. The Commodore of the Peishwa's ships was one Naroo Punt, a man who had gained military distinction on land, but who behaved in the most dastardly manner on this occasion. In about four hours the enemy's fire was silenced, and, at noon, a great part of the parapet of the north-east bastion, near to which the 'Protector' lay, and the work itself, were in ruins. About this time a shell exploded and set fire to one of the storehouses, which the Commodore perceiving, he prevented the enemy from interfering with the progress of the flames by pouring in a hot fire of musketry; one of the magazines soon blew up, and thereby the fire was communicated throughout the entire fort. At eleven at night the grand magazine blew up with a tremendous shock. When it was seen that the fort could no longer be held, the garrison abandoned the place and attempted to escape to Fort Goa, but were all intercepted and made prisoners by the English ships. This fort, also, soon after surrendered, and, immediately on the fact being known, the two remaining forts, which were besieged by the Mahratta troops, hung out flags of truce.

Whilst the Mahrattas were marching to take possession of Fort Goa, the Governor, perceiving that the Commodore had not yet occupied Severndroog, got into a boat with some of his most trusty men, and crossed over to the island, hoping to be able to maintain the fort until he should receive assistance from Dabul, which is not far distant. Upon this the 'Protector' renewed her fire upon Severndroog, and the Commodore, finding that the Governor wanted to protract the defence until night, when it was not to be doubted that some boats from Dabul would endeavour to throw reinforcements into the place, landed, under cover of the fire of the ships, half his seamen, who, with great intrepidity, ran up to the gate, and cutting down the sallyport with their axes, forced their way into it; upon this the garrison surrendered. "This," says Orme, "was all the work of one day, in which the spirited resolution of Commodore James destroyed the timorous prejudices which had for twenty years been entertained of the impracticability of reducing any of Angria's fortified harbours."

In the fort were found a quantity of stores belonging to the 'Derby' and three Dutch ships captured in the previous year.

On the 8th of April, the fleet and army proceeded to Bancoot, a fort commanding a river ten miles to the north of Severndroog. This place, terrified by the fate of the latter, surrendered on the first summons, and the Commodore took possession of it in accordance with the terms of the treaty.*

Ramajee Punt was so elated by these successes, that he offered

* The country about Bancoot, being subject to the Seedee, was inhabited by Mahommedans, who supplied Bombay with cattle, which were very difficult to procure in other parts of the coast, as the Hindoo Rajahs worship the cow, and regard the killing of that animal as the greatest of crimes.

Commodore James 200,000 rupees if he would immediately proceed against Dabul and some others of the enemy's forts, a little to the southward of that place. But the south-west monsoon, which, on this coast, sometimes sets in at the end of April, was approaching, and the Commodore, having already exceeded his orders, declined to comply with the request without permission from Bombay; however, in order to obtain it as expeditiously as possible, he sailed thither in the 'Protector,' but found the Governor and Council, notwithstanding the unexpected successes of their arms, still animated by timid counsels, and so solicitous for the fate of one of their bomb-ketches, a heavy flat-bottomed boat, incapable of keeping the sea in tempestuous weather, that they ordered him to bring back the fleet into harbour without delay. On the 11th, according to the terms of the treaty, Commodore James punctually delivered the forts of Severndroog to the Mahrattas, striking the English flag, which he had hitherto caused to be hoisted in them; and, on the 15th, set sail for Bombay, the Mahratta fleet at the same time returning to Choul.

A Royal squadron, under the command of Admiral Watson, arrived in Bombay in the November following, and, the fair season having now returned, the Governor and the Peishwa renewed their intention of attacking Angria, the Admiral readily consenting to assist with the force under his command. It was determined, if practicable, to strike at once at the root of Angria's power by attacking Gheria,* the capital of his dominions, and the principal harbour and arsenal of his Marine force; "but," says Orme, "it was long since any Englishman had seen this place, that, trusting to the report of the Natives, they believed it to be as strong as Gibraltar, and, like that, situated on a mountain inaccessible from the sea."

Commodore James was taken into consultation as to the best means to be adopted to reduce Gheria, and the Governor appointed a Council, consisting of Captain Hough, Superintendent of the Marine, Admiral Watson, and Lieutenant-Colonel Clive, who had just opportunely arrived from England with a strong detachment of troops, to conclude all necessary arrangements and agreements.

* The famous fortress of Gheria is situated on a promontory of rocky land about a mile long and a quarter of a mile broad, lying about a mile from the entrance of a large harbour, which forms the mouth of a river descending from the Balegat mountains. The promontory, on the sides contiguous to the water, is of rock, about fifty feet high, on which are built the fortifications. These are a double wall with round towers, the inward wall rising several feet above the outward. The neck of land by which the promontory joins the continent, is a narrow sand, beyond which, where the ground begins to expand itself, is built a large open town or *pettah*. The river washes the north side of the town, and of the neck of land, where are the docks in which the grabs were built and repaired, and from which they were launched into the river; ten of them, amongst which was that taken from the Company, were now lying in the river, all moored together, almost opposite to the docks.—Orme's " History of India."

Commodore James, though now acting in subordination to Admiral Watson, with that devotion to duty and abnegation of self, which distinguished him through life, offered to make soundings in the harbour of Gheria, and take bearings that might prove of service in the contemplated operations. This he accomplished with complete success. He set sail for Gheria with three of the Company's ships, and, arriving about dusk in the offing, stood in close under the walls; and, in the course of the night, proceeded in a small boat, and carried out his self-imposed mission. He then returned to Bombay.

The following is a copy of the Report addressed by Commodore James to Admiral Watson, dated "December 22, 1755, on board the 'Protector,' off Bombay," describing his reconnaissance of Gheria:—

"Sir,

"I have the honour to inform you that I arrived off Gheria, with the 'Protector,' 'Revenge,' and 'Guardian' under my command, on the morning of the 14th inst., where I saw the enemy's fleet, consisting of three three-mast grabs, eight ketches, and twelve or fourteen galivats in the harbour, rigged and their sails bent, with one three-mast grab having only her lower masts rigged. I stood into seven fathoms water, when I think I was within point-blank shot of the fort, but they did not fire at us. I was exceedingly surprised at finding the place so widely different from what I had heard it represented. I assure you, Sir, it is not to be called high, nor, in my opinion, strong; it is, indeed, a large mass of buildings, and I believe the walls may be thick, but that part of the works which fell under my observation, and which was three-quarters of their circumference, is quite irregular, with round towers and long curtains in the Eastern manner, and which discovers only thirty-two embrasures below, and fifteen above. On the west side of the harbour is a fine flat table-land opposite the fort, and I think within gunshot, but I am sure within distance for bombarding, and from whence a very good diversion might be made, while the principal attack is carried on by the ships, and from a hill to the southward of the fort. The hill is very near to and full as high as the fort, for when we were a considerable distance it hid all the fort except the top of one house and the flagstaff; it is also very plain from our depth of water, that the ships can go near enough for battering, and consequently for throwing shells. There are also three sandy bays under the hill, without any surf to render the landing difficult; the first two are rather too near the fort, but the third is out of their line of fire. The water is deep enough for the ships to cover the descent, and the hill accessible as to make the getting up of cannon, &c., quite easy afterwards. There is a very large town betwixt the fort and this hill, the houses of which are covered with cajans, and which the inhabitants will undoubtedly abandon and destroy upon our landing, and then fly to the fort, as at my attack at Severndroog; in which case, great numbers must be killed by the shells, the place being so crowded and populous that they cannot fall amiss, and many upper buildings must, of course, be knocked down, which will occasion great disorder and confusion. They sent out no boats while I was off the place, and to deceive them, I caused all the sails to be furled a little before dark, and made the signal to anchor, after which I ran out of sight in the night, so that they are ignorant whether I proceeded to the northward or to the southward. Several of the galivats had blue, or green, and white pendants like Portuguese at their mast-heads, and one of them had a white flag with a red cross in the middle, which they hauled down when I drew near. Nothing remarkable has happened during this cruise; the Mahratta fleet was at Severndroog on my going down and coming up. I shall be happy to wait on you to relate further particulars."

Acting upon Commodore James' representations, the Governor and Council of Bombay resolved to prosecute the enterprise with vigour.

On the 7th of February, 1756, the combined military and naval expedition sailed from Bombay. It consisted of eight hundred European soldiers, three hundred topasses, (or Portuguese soldiers), and three hundred sepoys, under the command of the hero known to posterity as Lord Clive; also of the following men-of-war:—His Majesty's ships 'Kent,' seventy guns, flag-ship of Vice-Admiral Watson; 'Cumberland,' sixty-six guns, flag-ship of Rear-Admiral Pocock; 'Tiger,' sixty guns; 'Salisbury,' fifty guns; 'Bridgewater,' twenty guns; and 'Kingfisher,' sixteen guns. The contingent of Company's vessels-of-war consisted of the 'Protector,' forty-four guns, Commodore James; 'Revenge,' twenty-eight guns; 'Bombay,' twenty-eight guns; 'Guardian,' twenty-eight guns; 'Swallow,' sixteen guns; and the 'Drake,' 'Triumph,' 'Warren,' 'Viper,' and 'Despatch,' bomb-vessels, on board of which a company of artillery, under command of Captain Tovey, was embarked. The whole formed a considerable fleet, which was still further reinforced by four grabs and forty galivats of the Mahrattas.

Since the month of November, a body of the Peishwa's troops, under Ramajee Punt and Khundoojee Mankur, had been successfully operating against Toolajee Angria's territories, and the whole of his forts along the coast, to the northward of Gheria, had been reduced.

When the British fleet appeared off his capital, Toolajee was so terrified that he left the town to be defended by his brother, and surrendered himself to Ramajee Punt, to whom he offered a large bribe for his freedom. But the Mahratta General kept him a prisoner, and extorted from him an order, directing his brother to deliver the fortress to him, intending by this step to exclude the English from all participation in the plunder. In order to prevent the accomplishment of this design, Admiral Watson sent a summons to the fort, and, receiving no answer, at once prepared to attack the sea face of the batteries.

Accordingly, on the 12th of February, the British fleet stood in in two divisions, one consisting of the ships of the line and the 'Protector,' to attack the forts, the other, consisting of the smaller vessels, to attack Angria's fleet and dockyards. As they took up their stations along the north side of the works within fifty yards' range, they were exposed to a heavy fire from the batteries, and from the grabs moored in the harbour, to which the guns of the ships and the mortars from the bomb-ketches replied with tremendous effect.

The action soon became general. Between four and five o'clock a shell from one of the ketches fell on board the 'Restoration,' an English ship captured by Angria, when she caught fire, and the flames, speedily communicating to the rest of the ships that lay moored close together, the whole of the piratical fleet was speedily involved in the conflagration. A little later a shell was thrown into the fort setting that on fire also. It now came to Admiral Watson's ears that Toolajee was again scheming to surrender the place to the Mahrattas, with whom he had opened negotiations to that end, and also that the Peishwa's General, notwithstanding that the stipulations of the treaty expressly provided that the occupation was to be a joint one, was not disinclined to entertain the proposals. To avoid the possibility of such a breach of good faith, the Admiral requested Colonel Clive to land the troops, and that officer did so accordingly, and invested Gheria on the land side, so that the Mahrattas could hold no communication with the garrison.*

Ramajee Punt, when he found Colonel Clive had occupied a position between him and the fort, perceived what was intended, and endeavoured to get a few of his men in by any means. With this object he made secret overtures to Captain Buchanan, the officer on picket, offering him a bribe of 80,000 rupees if he would permit him and a party of his men to pass into the fort.

* The point as to the ill-faith of the Peishwa's General has not been clearly established. Captain Grant Duff states that Ramajee Punt intimated on the arrival of Admiral Watson, that he was in treaty for the surrender of Gheria, and promised to come on board his flagship for the purpose of obtaining the sanction of the Commissioners. He did not come at the time specified, but sent a substitute, who was instructed to offer a bribe to Captain Hough, if he would undertake to cause the Admiral to suspend operations. The Admiral was therefore certainly justified in ordering the attack; but on the other hand it appears from the Bombay Records, that a Prize Committee of ten officers, of which Admirals Watson and Pocock, Captain Hough and Colonel Clive were members, had been appointed before they left Bombay harbour, and they had agreed to share the whole prize property in Gheria, without allowing the allies to participate. If the Mahrattas had intelligence of this proceeding, they had an equal right to forestall the English.

This offer was indignantly, and most honourably, in those days
of corruption, rejected by the British officer. To mark their
sense of his conduct, the Bombay Government presented Captain
Buchanan with a gold medal.

On the evening of the 12th of February, the Admiral sent in
a summons under a flag of truce, which was repelled by Toolajee; and, accordingly, on the following day the fleet recommenced
the bombardment with increased spirit. About four o'clock the
enemy hoisted a white flag in token of submission. Admiral
Watson insisted, as a *sine qua non*, that the British troops should
be allowed to march in, and the ensign hoisted on the citadel;
but, as the piratical chief would not accede to these demands,
the bombardment was renewed. At a quarter past five the white
flag was once more hoisted and this time Angria, thoroughly
humbled, surrendered on the terms dictated by his conquerors.
A small detachment of our troops took possession of the chief
work that night, and, on the following morning, the entire force
marched in. In this manner was obtained possession of a
stronghold hitherto considered impregnable, and the result was
achieved with a loss to the squadron of only nineteen men killed
and wounded. Upwards of two hundred cannon, six brass
mortars, and a large quantity of ammunition, together with
eight of our countrymen, and three Dutchmen, were found in
the place, and the specie, amounting to £125,000, was divided
among the English captors, who declared that the Mahrattas
were not entitled to any part of it. The enemy's fleet, which
was destroyed, consisted of one ship of seventy-four guns, two
sixty-gun ships on the stocks, eight grabs mounting from twenty
to thirty guns each, and about sixty galivats. There were thirteen
hundred troops in the fort, and these, together with Angria's family,
were made prisoners. Toolajee, who was captured by the
Mahrattas, was put in irons, and thrown into one of the Peishwa's
forts, where he lingered in a long captivity, and, subsequently,
died at Sholapoor, to which place he had been removed. Six
hundred European and Native troops were left to garrison the
fort, and four of the Company's vessels were stationed in the
harbour as an additional protection. In the beginning of April
the fleet repaired to Bombay, when Admiral Watson, after
refitting his squadron, sailed for Madras.

It is not a very creditable fact, that the Bombay Government
declined for some months to give up Gheria to the Mahrattas,
notwithstanding that it was expressly agreed in the stipulations.
They wished to exchange Bancoot for it, and put forth frivolous
pretexts to excuse their breach of faith. Subsequently the
place was yielded to the Peishwa, in accordance with the terms
of the treaty concluded at Poona on the 2nd of October.*

* The Mahrattas made but an ill use of their newly-acquired stronghold, for we
find a writer, who visited Bombay in 1775, says of them, "Before this period,"

Soon after the fall of Angria, Commodore James, while cruising in the 'Revenge,' twenty-eight guns, fell in with the French ship 'l'Indienne,' bound from the Mauritius. Though she had six more guns, and carried a crew of one-third more men, he engaged her, and, after a short action, captured and carried her into Bombay. A few months later we find Commodore James engaged in an adventure in which his scientific attainments and originality of mind were displayed. He had long supposed that by sailing out of the influence of the southwest monsoon, it was possible for a vessel to reach a latitude where variable gales prevailed, and that by such means a communication might be kept up between the different parts of the Company's settlements on both sides of the Indian Peninsula. He, accordingly, sailed from Bombay in the middle of the

speaking of the capture of Gheria in 1756, " they were not possessed of any maritime force, but at present, having a safe and convenient seaport, with a strong castle to defend it, they pay great attention to their Marine, which has made them as powerful by sea as they have hitherto been considered by land. They are so jealous of this power, that they will not suffer ships of any nation to enter the port of Gheria, excepting such as may be forced in by stress of weather. They make prize of every European ship which they can overcome, and have always continued this practice since they have had this port, excepting with regard to the English, with whom, until the late rupture, they have been at peace many years. The Dutch, French, and Portuguese cannot sail by or near their coast in safety, without being strongly convoyed. A very few months since, five or six merchant ships sailed from Goa, bound for Surat and the isle of Diu, under the convoy of a man-of-war of sixty-four guns, which they attacked with their frigates, and after putting it to flight made prizes of his whole convoy (which were Portuguese), and carried them safely into Gheria." But notwithstanding this success, their strength created no fear in the hearts of the officers of the Bombay Marine, for we find the following reference to them by the same gentleman, who cruised along the Malabar coast on board the 'Revenge,' Commodore Moore, a redoubtable officer of the service, in company with the 'Bombay.' " We were told at Goa that the whole Mahratta fleet were manned, and had sailed from Gheria, and were resolved to attack the 'Revenge' and 'Bombay' grab, with the ships and vessels under their convoy, notwithstanding the limited time of the cessation of arms was not yet expired ; this did not affright the captains, officers, or crews of these ships, who rather wished to have another trial of skill with them, on which account they proposed to sail on the 9th of February. We sailed from the Aquada, and kept sailing up to the northward ; on the 11th we approached near to Gheria. We could not perceive their fleet in that port, or in little Gheria, where we arrived on the 13th. We concluded they were either at sea, or in some harbour to the northward, waiting for us ; our conjectures proved true, for early in the morning of the 16th, we discovered their whole fleet at anchor at the entrance of a port called Cole Arbor (Kolabah), about three leagues to the north of us ; there were so many, so near each other, that we could not count them. We kept on our way, and, as they were to windward, we were in continual expectation of their coming out, and were much surprised they did not. At noon we were so near them as to be able to count their number, which was that of their whole Marine force, consisting of three frigates, five ketches, and ten galivats. We made a tack in shore, which brought us within gunshot. Our Commodore and the fleet then hoisted English colours, and the Mahratta Admiral hoisted his, and a red flag on his main-topmast, when the whole fleet hoisted their ensigns, but none offered to move ; we then tacked off to sea, and kept working to windward till eight in the evening, when we saw the light in Old Woman's Island, and at eight next morning we anchored in the harbour of Bombay, where Commodore Sir Edward Hughes, of the squadron of His Majesty's ships under his command, lay at anchor, the 17th of February, 1776.

monsoon, got into favourable weather to the southward, and arrived on the Coromandel coast, to the surprise of the whole settlement, after a voyage nearly as short, in point of fact, as was ordinarily made during the fine weather of the north-east monsoon. It was at that time a feat unexampled in the navigation of those seas. Pennant, in the first volume of his "History of Hindostan," says that, in effecting the passage, the Commodore crossed the Equator in the meridian of Bombay, and continued his course to the southward as far as the tenth degree of latitude, and then was enabled to go as far to the eastward as the meridian of Atcheen Head, the north-west extremity of Sumatra, whence, with the wind which then prevailed in the Bay of Bengal, he could with ease gain the entrance to the Hooghly, or any part of the Coromandel coast. This track is laid down in Arrowsmith's old map of the world. The voyage thus completed, was of great benefit to the English community on that coast, for Commodore James not only carried the first intelligence of the outbreak of hostilities with France, but at the same time brought five hundred soldiers to the assistance of the Presidency of Fort William. By this timely accession to their strength, Admiral Watson and Colonel Clive were enabled, in March, 1757, to capture Chandernagore from the French, and thus not only struck a heavy blow at their power in the East, but also ruined their trade. In the succeeding September, Commodore James, when in command of the 'Revenge,' was stationed off Pondicherry, in company with H.M.S. 'Triton.' While cruising off here they were chased by a superior squadron of French ships.

In the year 1759, the Commodore returned to England, and having purchased a property at Eltham, called Park Farm, with the proceeds of his share of the booty captured at Gheria, Severndroog, and other places, married a Miss Goddard. Soon after his arrival in England, the Court of Directors presented him with a magnificent gold-hilted sword, on the blade of which was a record of his achievements, but it was not until the 25th of July, 1778, that His Majesty the King graciously rewarded his eminent services with a baronetcy. Commodore James was at once elected to a seat at the Board of Directors, and successively rose to the honourable posts of Deputy-Chairman and Chairman, the latter of which he filled for twenty years. He was also returned to Parliament as Member for West Looe, a Cornish borough, and was conspicuous in the House up to his death, as an advocate of the Company he had served so long in a less peaceful arena. Honours were bestowed freely on Sir William James during the closing years of his life, and he was nominated a Governor of Greenwich Hospital, and elder brother and Deputy Master of the Trinity House. His energies were ever actively employed in extending the greatness and influence of the

Company, and when the King of France assisted the Americans in their struggle for independence, he planned the humiliation of the enemy's power in India, by the capture of Pondicherry, which was indeed carried into effect, though the town was subsequently restored at the peace. The Company were so sensible of his services on this occasion, that they presented him with a handsome service of plate. Owing to the hardships he had endured in early life, and the effects of the unhealthy climates in which he had served, his health began to decline, and, on the very day his daughter was married, the 16th of December, 1783, the year before the passing of Mr. Pitt's India Bill, he was seized with a fit of apoplexy and expired.*

Thus, at the age of sixty-two, passed away this distinguished officer, who not only possessed professional qualities of a high order, but was ever a faithful guardian of the affairs of the Company, whose territorial possessions he had extended. To return to the records of the Bombay Marine.

It would appear that it was usual during the war with France, for some ships of the Bombay Marine to be attached to His Majesty's fleet in the Indian Seas. In the year 1747, Commodore Griffin had arrived from England with a squadron to reinforce the British fleet, which then consisted of eleven ships, the French

---

* His widow, Lady James, erected a monument to the memory of her late husband on the northern brow of Shooter's Hill. It has been thus described:— "Lady James being a woman of considerable taste, resolved to effect her purpose in a manner that could not fail to attract the notice of every traveller who passed into Kent. By way of perpetuating the memory of the capture of Severndroog, the year after the death of its victorious assailant she caused a castellated building to be erected after a design by Mr. Jupp, the summit of which is upwards of 140 feet higher than the cross on the dome of St. Paul's. It consists of three stories, and is surrounded by battlements. The inside is fitted up in an appropriate manner with arms, partisans, shields, javelins, &c., proper to the various nations of the East; and the whole is so contrived as to impress the mind with the belief that it is the identical armoury appertaining to Angria. In the room above this, the naval actions and enterprises of the Commodore are beautifully painted on the ceiling, and from the windows there is a most admirable view of London, the Thames, the shipping, and the adjacent country. This monument of Lady James's affection may be seen on a clear day from many parts of this metropolis, and from the tops of most public buildings. On a tablet over the entrance of the building, which is generally known by the appellation of Lady James's Tower, is the following inscription:—' This building was erected, 1784, by the representative of the late Sir William James, Bart. To commemorate that gallant officer's achievements in the East Indies, during the command of the Company's Marine forces in those seas, and in a particular manner to record the conquest of the Castle of Severndroog, on the coast of Malabar, which fell to his superior valour and able conduct on the 3rd day of April, 1755.'" Sir William James was succeeded in his title and estate by his eldest son, who then became Sir Richard James, and, on his decease, by his remaining son, who also died on the 16th of November, 1792, at the early age of eighteen years, when the Baronetcy became extinct. Lady Rancliffe, the only daughter of Sir William James, died on the 18th of January, 1797, and his widow, Lady James, died soon afterwards. The lineal representative of this gallant sailor is now Sir Richard Levinge, Bart., who has still in his possession the sword of honour voted by the Company to his ancestor, and a magnificent portrait painted by Sir Joshua Reynolds.

having only eight sail at the time on the India Station. Some losses were occasioned by English ships sailing into Madras, not knowing it had been taken by the French, and Commodore Griffin did not consider himself strong enough either to recover that place or to reduce Pondicherry, in which the French had mounted one hundred and eighty pieces of cannon, and had still further strengthened with six additional forts, the whole being held by a garrison of five thousand men.

On the 29th of July, 1748, Admiral Boscawen arrived from England at Fort St. David, with six sail of the line and other ships, when steps were immediately taken for a combined military and naval expedition against Pondicherry. Admiral Boscawen, says Grose, had under his command the largest fleet "ever seen together in the East Indies; for it consisted of nine ships of the line, two frigates, a sloop, and two tenders, besides fourteen of the Company's ships, having three thousand five hundred and eighty sailors on board." The Royal troops consisted of twelve hundred men, eight hundred marines, and eighty artillerymen, and those of the Company, under Major Lawrence, of seven hundred and fifty men, including two hundred "topasses," with seventy artillerymen; the Admiral also landed eleven hundred seamen from the fleet. But the French Governor, M. Dupleix, was able to make a successful defence, and, as the ships could not approach near enough to the works to inflict any damage, the siege was raised, the sailors and heavy guns were re-embarked, and the troops marched for Fort St. David on the 6th of October. Thus terminated this expedition with the loss of seven hundred and fifty-seven soldiers, forty-three artillery, and two hundred and sixty-five seamen. The peace of Aix-la-Chapelle, signed on the 7th of October, put an end to hostilities for a brief space. In the following April occurred a great hurricane, in which Admiral Boscawen's flag-ship, the 'Namur,' seventy-four guns, with seven hundred men foundered, the 'Pembroke,' sixty guns, and 'Apollo,' were both wrecked, with the loss of all hands, and two of the Company's ships were stranded near Cuddalore.

Peace was not long maintained between the two countries, and, on the resumption of hostilities, Admiral Pocock, commanding the Royal fleet on the return to England of Admiral Watson,[*] the victor of Gheria, was joined on the 24th of March, 1758, by Commodore Stevens with reinforcements from England. He accordingly weighed from Madras on the 17th of April with a squadron of nine sail, including the Company's ship 'Protector,'

[*] Admiral Watson, who so ably seconded Clive at Calcutta, died soon after at that city of fever, and a monument was erected to his memory by the East India Company in the Cathedral. George II. created his son, a child aged eight years of age, a Baronet, on account of his father's services, and it may be mentioned as a curious case of longevity, that this gentleman lived to the age of ninety-three, and only died so lately as the 26th of August, 1844.

of forty-four guns, and arrived off Fort St. David on the 29th of April, when he engaged M. d'Aché's fleet, consisting of eleven ships, carrying one hundred and sixty-two more guns, and seventeen hundred more men. An action ensued in which the French were defeated and bore up for Pondicherry. In this battle our casualties were twenty-nine killed and eighty-nine wounded, while the French were said to have lost six hundred killed alone.

Admiral Pocock was not altogether satisfied with the conduct of some of his officers during this action, and he broke the captains of the 'Weymouth' and 'Newcastle.' Having repaired damages at Madras, which once again belonged to the English, and reinforced his fleet with one hundred and twenty convalescent men from hospital, and eighty-four Lascars, Admiral Pocock sailed on the 10th of May, but returned without encountering the enemy. He again sailed with the same ships on the 25th of July, and, on the 3rd of August, encountered M. d'Aché. After a hot action, which lasted two hours, the French Admiral made sail and was pursued until after dark, when he succeeded in escaping into Pondicherry. The British loss was thirty-one killed and one hundred and sixteen wounded, including Commodore Stevens and Captain Martin of the 'Cumberland,' and that of the French, two hundred and fifty-one killed and six hundred and two wounded, including among the latter, the Admiral and his flag-captain.

The French fleet proceeded to Mauritius, where they were joined by two seventy-four's, and one sixty-four gun ship. During this year, the French, under the famous M. Lally, reduced Cuddalore and Fort St. David, and destroyed the fortifications, as they had done at Madras in 1746, but the honour of our arms was retrieved before the close of the year, by a victory achieved by Colonel Forde on the 7th of December, and still more by the successful defence of Madras by Colonels Lawrence and Draper, between the 12th of December, 1758, and the 17th of February, 1759, when the 'Queensborough' frigate, commanded by Captain Kempenfeldt—the same gallant officer who met so tragic an end on board the 'Royal George' at Spithead—and the Company's frigate 'Bombay,' disembarked a timely reinforcement of six hundred men of the 79th Regiment. Thus ended this famous siege, which had been extended over sixty-seven days, the batteries having been open forty-six.

On the 17th of August, 1759, Admiral Pocock sailed from Bombay for the Coromandel coast, to which M. Aché soon after proceeded with a greatly superior fleet. The British Admiral stationed his ships in such a manner as to protect the trade and intercept the enemy. He kept his station off Ceylon until the 3rd of August, when he proceeded off Pondicherry, and thence to Trincomalee for water. Admiral Pocock detached the small frigate 'Revenge,' of the Bombay Marine, which formed one of his fleet, to look out for the enemy off Ceylon, and, on the 2nd of September, she descried fifteen sail standing to the north-east. The 'Revenge' was chased by a French ship-of-the-line, which fired into her, when the British Admiral, notwithstanding the great disparity of force, made the signal for a general chase, but, the wind falling light, he was unable to bring them to a general action. At seven in the evening, Admiral Pocock ordered the 'Revenge' to make sail to the south-east and keep sight of the enemy if possible, and, according to Grose (Vol. II., p. 335), she performed this duty well. At daylight the following morning, the French fleet were about six leagues distant, and Admiral Pocock threw out the signal for a general chase, but, the wind again falling light, was unable to bring the enemy to action, though they formed a line of battle as if desirous of engaging. It being hazy, the English lost sight of the French fleet, when Admiral Pocock again had recourse to the services of the 'Revenge.' She was first sent astern, but, not meeting the enemy, steered ahead, the fleet following in line of battle, with their heads to the northward. On the following morning, the 'Revenge' signalled four sail to the north-east, on which Admiral Pocock made the signal for a general chase. At half-past eleven, the 'Revenge' bore away more to the eastward, and was followed by the squadron; but after continuing the chase until nearly two in the afternoon, and discovering only two ships, with whom he could not come up, the Admiral made the signal for the 'Revenge' to rejoin the squadron. Thence he proceeded to Pondicherry, off which he descried, on the 8th of September, the French fleet to the number of sixteen sail. At four in the afternoon, we are told, "the French squadron appeared to be formed in a line of battle abreast, and steered right down upon the English Admiral, who ordered the 'Revenge' to keep between the two squadrons, and observe their motions during the night."

On the 10th of September the long-expected battle took place between the rival fleets. The French were greatly superior in the number of ships and men, and in weight of metal. Their fleet consisted of eleven sail of the line, carrying seven hundred and twenty-eight guns, and six thousand four hundred men, with two frigates and a storeship, while the English had only nine ships of the line, carrying five hundred and thirty-six guns and four thousand and thirty-five men, besides four frigates, including the Company's ships 'Revenge' and 'Protector.' A severe action commenced about two o'clock and lasted for two hours, seven ships bearing the brunt of the attack of the French fleet, when the latter retired, the English ships, owing to the damage they had received in their spars and rigging, being in no condition to pursue. When night set in, the services of the

'Revenge' were called into requisition to keep between the Admiral and the enemy, and observe the latter's motions, while the British fleet lay-to on the larboard tack, that the disabled ships might repair damages. Some further manœuvring took place on the following day, when the enemy declined a second encounter. Admiral Pocock anchored about three leagues to the southward of Negapatam Roads on the 12th, and, in the evening, sent the 'Revenge' to Madras with letters to the Governor and Council. She returned in a few days, bringing a reply from the Governor, dated "Fort St. George, September 16, 1759," thanking the Admiral and all his officers for their devotion. In this engagement both sides suffered considerably. The French were said to have lost fifteen hundred men killed and wounded; and the English had one hundred and eighty-four in the former category, including those who died of their wounds, and three hundred and eighty-five in the latter. One ship, the 'Newcastle,' lost her captain and had one hundred and twelve men placed *hors de combat*, and the 'Tiger' suffered still more severely, her casualties being one hundred and sixty-eight men. Admiral Pocock, having repaired damages at Madras, proceeded to sea again on the 26th of September, in quest of the enemy, whom he found lying at Pondicherry. The French, however, avoided an action, and the Admiral returned to Madras. On the 17th of October he again sailed, and, on the following day, was joined by four ships-of-the-line from England, under Admiral Cornish, and three Indiamen, with troops on board, under Colonel Eyre Coote. On the 7th of April, 1760, the gallant Admiral sailed from Bombay, for Portsmouth, and, soon after, placed his country under still further obligations to him by the reduction of Havanna.

A succession of heavy blows was given to the French power in India by the capture of Carical and other places, including their great stronghold of Pondicherry, which was besieged by a combined naval and military force under Colonel Coote and Admiral Cornish, and, at length, capitulated on the 15th of January, 1761, when General Lally and his garrison were made prisoners of war. The Navy, including some of the Company's ships, largely participated in this famous siege, and not only blockaded the fort, but landed seamen from the fleet. During the siege a terrible hurricane visited the coast and scattered the blockading squadron under Admiral Stevens, vying, in the losses it occasioned, with the destructive storm of the 2nd of October, 1746, in which the French fleet, then lying at Madras, lost three ships-of-the-line, with twelve hundred men, and also the 'Advice' and 'Mermaid' Company's ships, two of the enemy's prizes, while twenty other vessels of different nationalities foundered at sea; or as that equally terrible tempest of the 13th of April, 1749, already mentioned, when the 'Namur,' seventy-four guns, and other vessels were lost, with all hands. In this storm of January,

1761, His Majesty's ships 'Duke of Aquitain,' 'Sunderland,' 'Newcastle,' and 'Queensborough,' and the Company's ship 'Protector,' which had done such good service as Commodore James's flagship, were driven ashore and lost, and other ships suffered severely, though the arrival of Admiral Cornish with his Division, enabled the Navy to renew the blockade of Pondicherry, which capitulated a few days later.

Peace was concluded between the two countries in 1762, and the 1st of September was observed at Bombay as a day of thanksgiving, when the Governor and Council, accompanied by the principal European and Native inhabitants, repaired to the Green, where the King's proclamation of peace with France and Spain was read and a salute fired.

During these years, so critical for the welfare of the nascent British power in India, the Bombay Marine, besides affording valuable co-operation to the Navy, continued to execute with credit and success their duties as the police of the Eastern seas, for, though Angria's power was most effectually crushed, they had ample employment in keeping in check the piratical vessels hailing from numerous ports in the Concan and Canara coasts, and affording protection and convoy to the trade of the Red Sea, Persian Gulf, and Malabar littoral.

We will now treat briefly of events at Surat, the cradle of the Service, so far as they bear upon its history. The Bombay Presidency, says a writer, had long fixed covetous eyes upon that portion of the revenues of Surat which were allotted to the Seedee for the maintenance of his fleet, in order that he might protect the native trade, and which had received the name of *tunkha*, from the small silver coin originally used for payment during the reign of Ackbar; this *tunkha* was derived from the assignment of the revenues of certain districts, with a portion of the Customs, amounting in all to a yearly sum of about £36,000. Plans for the appropriation of this tribute were now proposed by the Government of Bombay, and, after the details had been fully discussed, an attempt was made to put them into execution. Though still considered hereditary Admirals of the Mogul empire, successive Seedees had been gradually losing their reputation, and when Angria had, in conjunction with the Peishwa, seized their fleet at Rajapore, their flag was no longer respected by the Native powers, or dreaded by the numerous rovers of the coast; indeed they could no longer afford the protection, in consideration of which a portion of the revenues had been assigned to them. Of the sum annually set apart for this duty, only about two lacs reached their treasury, the remainder being intercepted by the Nawab, or Native Governor, of the city, as his perquisite; but so far were they from fulfilling the conditions on which the grant had been originally made to them, that they were themselves at the very time supplicating aid from the Government of Bombay. At that date Angria alone dared to resist the British on the high seas, and even he fled before them unless his force happened on any occasion to be vastly superior. The Company's naval power was acknowledged by all, and they had already established one proof of suzerainty in requiring native vessels from Surat to carry their passes,* and declaring all to be lawful prizes who were without them or those of friendly nations. "Indeed," continues the writer from whom we are quoting, "if superiority, not as regards number of men or ships, or weight of metal, but skill, courage, and other requisites for successful warfare, were alone considered, their claim was irresistible. Negotiations for the transfer of the tunkha and concomitant responsibilities to English hands, were opened in June, 1733, and, at first, were highly encouraging, but it soon appeared that the interests of too many parties were concerned. Besides the Company, the Governor of Surat, and the Seedee, there were the Dutch, who felt that the question was of great importance to them. Forty years before they had endeavoured to obtain the tunkha for themselves, and although they could not apply for it now in their reduced condition, they had regained some of their lost credit by the part which they had taken in the late revolution, and would do their utmost to prevent the most successful of their European rivals from increasing their wealth and influence. Then the Seedee was at the time in close alliance with the English, and it would be dangerous to proceed openly, so as to make him an enemy at a time when the attitude, both of the Mahratta Rajah and Angria, was most threatening. Lastly, there were the interests of Teg Beg Khan, the Mogul Nawab. An attempt was made towards inducing him to forego the lac of rupees which annually found its way into the Treasury, and to pay the whole three lacs fairly to the British."

Mr. Lowther, the chief at Surat, conducted the affair on the part of the President and Council with tact and secrecy. Reports of progress were regularly sent to Bombay, and, for some time, were favourable, but, after lengthy negotiations, the attempt ended in failure, in consequence of the demand made by the Nawab.

A series of disputes, into which the Native Government and factors now were drawn, seems to have had its origin with various classes of native merchants, such as were independent of the English, endeavouring to ruin those whom the English patronised; and the Governor, who, as the factors remarked, was indebted to the English for all he possessed, listened too readily to the malicious stories of informers against them. At length Teg Beg Khan ordered one of the merchants to be arrested, set a guard over the house of another, and extorted a

* A Form of Pass was agreed upon by the President in Council in April, 1734.

sum of 4,600 rupees from the English broker. When waited upon by Mr. Hope and other factors, he released his prisoners; but, instead of refunding the money he had extorted, directed his officers to levy a new tax, called "convoy money," on all English vessels passing up and down the river; and, lastly, he refused all redress when a Parsee servant of the chief had been wantonly and ferociously assaulted by a public servant of the Government. Mr. Lowther, arriving at this juncture with the Company's ship 'Heathcote,' the 'Salamander' bomb-ketch, and the 'Tiger' and 'Shark' galivats, resolved not to land until reparation should be made for the insults he had received, ordered all the English merchants to join him, except two, who were left in charge of the factory, and vigorously prepared to punish the Governor's insolence by laying an embargo upon the trade. Negotiations now ensued, during which the English chief and his friends remained on board their ships at the bar of the river, and refused several invitations to land, peremptorily insisting upon satisfaction for the injuries their dependents had received, and threatening reprisals in case of refusal. Drawing up a formal document, they stated their demands upon the Government in nine articles; of which one was that vessels with English colours, passing up and down the river, should not be molested or required to pay convoy money.

The Native Government had, meanwhile, equipped a fleet which, in their estimation, was more powerful than that of the English, whilst the whole British land force that could be mustered for the defence of a factory situated in the midst of a dense and alien population, and within gunshot of an embattled castle and hostile troops, consisted of twenty-six European soldiers, eight topasses, eighty-four peons, and a few domestic servants. It was natural, under such circumstances, that, relying upon the great superiority of his military strength, and spurred on by his friends, Teg Beg's presumption should know no bounds. In return for Mr. Lowther's nine articles, the Governor submitted to him, on the 8th of February, 1735, an equal number, containing the most unreasonable demands. Immediately after this, however, a little incident must have satisfied him that conciliation would be wiser than vain attempts to overcome his powerful enemies.

At the mouth of the river there was cruising with the professed object of protecting native vessels, what was called "the King's fleet," commanded by a Seedee, and comprising one grab, one smaller ship of war, and four galivats. This naval force soon approached, and, in bravado, sailed round the British blockading squadron, which would have been well pleased to accept this foolish challenge, and settle the difficulties with the Natives there and then. At the request of Mr. Lowther, the officer in command despatched his bomb ketch, with an order that the Seedee should bring his ships to an anchor, and send an officer to wait upon the English representative. As no answer was returned and the defiant attitude continued, the 'Heathcote' saluted her challengers with a broadside, when a short action ensued, which ended in the King's fleet sheering off, and it never again made its appearance during these transactions. Teg Beg and his party now manifested symptoms of concession. The blockade had raised the prices of provisions forty per cent., and the inhabitants attributed their sufferings to the crimes and obstinacy of their rulers, rather than to the measures of the English, whose firmness was at last rewarded as it deserved, by Teg Beg signing all the articles dictated to him. Disputes now arose between the Nawab and the Seedee, who had been deprived of his tunkha, and the latter visited Bombay to solicit the intercession of the President, who, however, asked him to resign at least a portion of the tribute to the English. This led to reprisals on the Surat commerce by the Seedee, until, in August, 1735, the Nawab agreed to pay £24,000 arrears of tunkha, and £15,000 yearly. The Nawab now treated the English factory with insolence, as they had declined to interfere in his dispute with the Seedee, but once more a naval force, consisting of the 'Victoria' frigate, with two smaller vessels, called the 'Princess Caroline' and 'Defiance,' was sent to the bar of the Surat river, and the Government of Bombay showed that they could obtain by compulsion what they still condescended to ask with politeness. But they had no wish to ruin either the Governor or Seedee, and, having overawed them both, were satisfied with an apology for the affronts which had been offered, and a promise that their debt should be discharged by more regular instalments.* Still this settlement was only temporary, and could hardly be otherwise in the unsettled state of affairs consequent on the decay of the central power at Delhi.

The duty of affording protection and convoy to the trade, became very harrassing at Surat, owing to the constant feuds between the Nawab and the Mogul Admiral, and, at times, it became necessary for armed boats to escort the trading vessels up the Taptee, to prevent their being plundered by the villagers on the banks of the river. These people could have been coerced into quietude by the ships of the Marine, but, at this period, such a course would have been detrimental to the trade, which was still very considerable; careful watch and ward was all that could be effected, and this was most effectually performed by the officers and men of the Service. In 1759, however, they had an opportunity of distinguishing themselves, and of performing a service of lasting importance to their masters.

* Surat Diary, 1737-39.

The Bombay Presidency, as we have already mentioned, had long been urgent with the Peishwa to assist them in establishing their trade and privileges at Surat, on a secure footing, and in maintaining peace and order in the city itself. For many years, owing to the constant squabbles and jealousies of the Mogul officers, the city had been in a state of confusion. At one time the Governor and the Mogul Admiral were at open feud, and then at other times there were rivals for the Nawabship, when the Dutch and English factories espoused opposite sides, and fought against each other, though their respective countries were in a state of profound peace. On such occasions, the Northern, or Surat, squadron of the Marine did good service, and maintained the ascendancy of their nationality. At length, disgusted with this state of affairs, so subversive of trade, and finding that he was not likely to obtain the Peishwa's aid, Mr. Ellis, the agent, arranged a plan with the senior naval officer, the execution of which, however, was deferred, owing to orders from the Bombay Government. In 1758, the quarrel between the Nawab, Novas Ali Khan, and the Seedee, came to a climax. In consequence of the decline of the central power, there was no authority to check the pretensions of the latter officer, who had always been accustomed to obey orders emanating from the Emperor and his deputy, receiving the tunkha for his services in protecting the trade. For many years, however, the protector of the trade had become its chief oppressor, and, on some occasions, the Nawab had to make great concessions to appease his powerful subject. Thus matters went on from bad to worse, the Dutch and English agents being unable to keep the peace, if they did not foment the quarrels. When the final rupture took place between these high Mogul officers, the fleet remained faithful to the Admiral, who seized the castle of Surat, thus gaining command of the entire city, and appointed Meer Atchund to the office of Nawab. Fighting and negotiation were tried to oust the recalcitrant Admiral, but in vain, and the Nawab, in his extremity, at length applied to the English agent for assistance. This appeal afforded the long wished for opportunity. Mr. Ellis, who was succeeded, in 1759, by Mr. Spencer, had agreed to afford all the aid at his disposal on certain terms, which were readily acceded to. A treaty, by which the Company gained lasting benefits, was therefore signed, sealed, and delivered, and was afterwards confirmed by the Emperor; and the Bombay Government, to whom the merchants had repeatedly applied for protection from the rapacity and insults of the Seedee and his officers, apprehensive that he might open the gate to the Mahrattas, at length agreed to intervene with an armed force.

An expedition was accordingly fitted out at Bombay, consisting of five of the Company's ships and a body of eight hundred and fifty European troops and fifteen hundred Sepoys. The whole was placed under the command of Commodore Watson, of the Bombay Marine, an officer of remarkable skill and tried ability, under whose orders the officers and men of the Service had upheld the reputation they had earned under Sir William James.

The armament sailed on the 9th of February, 1759, and the troops were landed at Dentilowry, about nine miles from Surat, where they encamped for three days. The first operation was against the "French garden," where the Seedee had placed some of his troops, which were dislodged. A battery was then erected, on which were mounted two 24-pounders and a 13-inch mortar; and, for three days, a heavy fire was maintained against the walls, but without effect. A council of war, composed of military and naval officers, was then convened, at which it was decided that the following plan of operations should be put into execution. "The plan was," says Grose, a contemporary writer and traveller, "that the Company's grab of twenty guns and four bomb-ketches, should warp up the river in the night, and anchor in a line of battle opposite the Seedee's bundar, one of the strongest fortified places they had got. This they did, and a general attack began from the vessels and battery at the appointed time on the 1st of March. The Captain's intentions in this, were to drive the enemy from their batteries, and to facilitate the landing of the infantry at the bundar, whom he had embarked in boats for their transportation. The bomb-ketches made a continual fire until half-past eight, when a signal was made for the boats to put off and land under cover of the vessels. This proved very successful by the prudent conduct and gallant behaviour of Captain Watson, who landed the troops with the loss of only one man. They attacked the Seedee's bundar and soon put his troops to flight, with the loss of Captain Robert Inglish, mortally wounded, Lieutenant Pepperell wounded in the shoulder, and some privates killed and wounded. Having gained this point and getting possession of the town with its fortifications, the next thing to be done was to attack the inner town and castle, for which purpose the 13 and 12-inch mortars were planted on the Seedee's bundar, and began firing as soon as possible at the distance of seven hundred yards from the castle and five hundred from the inner town. About six in the evening the mortars began to play very briskly, and continued their fire until half-past two the next morning, which unusual attack put the castle and town into such a consternation that they never returned a gun."

Negotiations were now opened by the enemy; but the friends of Pharres Khan, the "naib," or deputy of the Nawab, who was very popular with the inhabitants on account of his justice and integrity, now seemed inclined to continue Meer Atchund as governor of the town, on condition that the former should be continued as Naib, which carried the office of chief magistrate. Mr. Spencer, the Company's agent, communicated this resolution to Atchund, who readily agreed to, and executed, a treaty of four points, by the third article of which it was conceded that the Mecca gate of the inner town should be opened, and an attack by the combined forces made against the Seedee, who still continued to hold the castle. The counterpart of this treaty was delivered on the 4th of March to Atchund, who, thereupon, admitted the British force, which marched in with drums beating and colours flying. The Seedee at first appeared determined to defend the castle to the last extremity; but, upon learning that Atchund had joined his troops with the British, he opened negotiations, and, at length, agreed to surrender the fortress, which was of considerable strength, and amply supplied with guns and stores,* on condition of being allowed to march out with his arms and effects.

The fighting during these operations must have been rather brisk, as we find that the losses of the British in killed alone, amounted to one hundred and fifty officers and men. A gratuity of 200,000 rupees (£20,000) was divided among the captors. Some troops and a squadron for the protection of the newly-acquired settlement were left at Surat, and the remainder of the expedition returned to Bombay on the 15th of April.

Certain districts were allotted for the subsistence of the Seedee, though he was for ever deprived of the dignity and emoluments of his high office, which were conferred on the East India Company, together with the revenues and districts allotted for

---

* The Castle is described by Abraham Parsons, who visited Surat in 1776, as "a large and noble quadrangular building, with a circular and capacious bastion at each angle, mounted with three tiers of guns pointing three different ways; the lowest are 36-pounders, the second 24, and the upper tiers 18 and 12-pounders. There are near two hundred cannon mounted on the Castle, besides twenty-four at the saluting battery; the lowest tier are not above six feet from the level of the glacis, or the river at high water, when it washes the Castle walls. There are many guns mounted on the ramparts between each bastion. On one of the bastions is hoisted the British Union flag, and on its opposite, the Mogul's; the English having condescended to accept of being the Mogul's Admiral of Indostan, to please the Natives, hoist his flag on the Castle." Of the town, the same intelligent writer says, "There is a wall and ditch enclosing the city, and another surrounding the suburbs; the distance round the outer wall is computed to be near twelve English miles. In the outer wall are thirteen gates, including three on the banks of the river; in the inner are four gates, so that even the suburbs cannot receive provisions without paying the duty, which is in kind. The whole of the duties are supposed to amount to about forty lacs of rupees; the Mahrattas enjoyed one-third of these duties, and the English think it prudent to continue it to them to keep them quiet, lest they should assist the Nabob in regaining his independence. Here are two principal gates which lead to the Castle, the keys of which are carried to the English chief every night at sunset, when they are locked. They are opened at daybreak in the morning. These gates are guarded by English, the others by the Nabob's officers and soldiers, who send the keys to the English officers. The French, Portuguese, and Dutch have factories here, and the Dutch and Portuguese hoist their respective flags at their factories."

its support. An officer of the Bombay Marine was to hold the official dignity as the Deputy of the Company, and, from 1759 to 1829, a period of seventy years, a captain of the Service was annually appointed to this situation by the Bombay Government. This officer wore the Company's colours at the peak of his flagship, but carried the Mogul's flag at the main. The revenues of the districts and Customs which had been assigned, went to the support of the Surat squadron, which, we find from various records, averaged, between 1759 and 1803, the following vessels:—The Commodore's flagship, a brig or large ketch, eight galivats, mounting from four to eight guns, commanded by lieutenants, and each having about twenty European seamen, the rest of the crew being Natives, and from four to six ketches and brigs employed with convoys during the northeast monsoon.

The Commodore's pay as a captain we find, from a record of 1787-88, was, with an allowance for two servants, 87 rupees per month; while the estimate of his fees for convoy and other perquisites, as assigned the Company by the treaty, amounted to 85,500 rupees for the year! From other papers, we find that the actual receipts in the same year were not less than 97,000 rupees. Besides these money fees, the Commodore had also a tithe on certain articles entering the river, such as grain, poultry, firewood, and many other items which were at times commuted for money, and may be the cause of the difference between the estimated and actual receipts. Thus the post of Mogul's Admiral, which was only tenable for one year, was worth to the incumbent no less than £10,000, a vast sum in those days, when the salary of the Governor of Bombay did not exceed £500, and that of the chief military officer, £250. With trifling modifications, these rules remained in force until 1809 or 1810, when convoy money was reduced, as had been the privilege of private trading in 1798.

However indefensible such rules may appear to us now, they were in harmony with the feelings of the age, and at least the gallant officer who, for one year, enjoyed the dignity and emoluments of the post of Admiral of the Mogul, performed the duties with a thoroughness we are accustomed to expect from British officers, and which earned the commendation of successive Nawabs, who contrasted their energy and skill with the indolence and inefficiency of their predecessors. That this good opinion was borne out by facts, we may readily believe, when we find that, between the years 1759 and 1768, nearly one hundred vessels, belonging to the Cutch, Okamundel, and Kattywar pirates, were captured and destroyed by the Surat squadron.

CHAPTER V.

1759—1790.

Loss of Gombroon—Operations against Hyder Ally's Seaports—Capture of Tannah and Death of Commodore Watson—Commodore Moore's Action with the Shumsher Jung—Desperate Action between the 'Ranger' and Mahratta Fleet—Affairs in the Red Sea and Persian Gulf—Operations against Kharrack—The Bombay Marine at the Siege of Bussorah by the Persians—A Retrospect of the Bombay Marine—Construction of the Dry and Wet Docks at Bombay—Services of the Bombay Marine during the War with France and Hyder Ally.

THE year 1759, rendered memorable as that in which the Company acquired by conquest, in no small measure due to the prowess of their Marine, the oldest of their settlements in India, where they had hitherto only been tolerated as strangers, was also signalized by their ejectment from one of the first factories they had formed in the East, though it had long been of so unprofitable a character as a trading *entrepôt*, owing to the anarchy and confusion of Persian affairs, that the loss scarcely lessened the exultation of the Directors at the intelligence of the acquisition of Surat. This was the capture of Gombroon, or Bunder Abbas, in the Persian Gulf, opposite Ormuz, at which the Company had continued to maintain a factory since the capture of the island in the year 1622.

M. Lally equipped four ships, under Dutch colours, one of which, the 'Condé,' carried sixty-four guns, and another twenty-two, and employed a force of one hundred and fifty European, and two hundred Native, troops, two mortars, and four battering guns, to besiege the small and unfortified English factory. The expedition was entrusted to the command of the Count d'Estaing*—an officer who, later, attained some notoriety as the opponent of Vice-Admiral Byron, in his victory off the island of Grenada, on the 6th of July, 1779—and arrived off Gombroon on the 15th of October, when the ships began to batter the English factory which was gallantly defended by sixteen of the Company's seamen and some Sepoys, under Mr. Douglas, the chief agent.

---

* Count d'Estaing was on parole at this time, having been made prisoner by Colonel Draper in his sally at the siege of Madras, on the 14th of March; but to hide this open breach of the rules of war, M. des Essars and M. Charnoy were appointed nominal commanders.

The French burnt the 'Speedwell' sloop, and at high water hauled in their twenty-two gun ship within four hundred yards of the factory; they also landed their troops and heavy guns, and battered the west face of the building for two hours. About three in the afternoon the French summoned the place to surrender, and Mr. Douglas capitulated, his men being regarded as prisoners of war, with liberty to carry away their personal effects; by one of the articles it was agreed that the twenty-six civilians, found in the place, should be exchanged for Count d'Estaing, who, being on *parole*, was ostensibly proceeding to Europe by way of Bussorah, though, in reality, he conducted the operations. The French, having burnt the factory, and left a quantity of articles as a present to Moollah Ali Khan, the Persian Governor, set sail on the 30th of October, but they certainly derived more profit than honour from this feat of arms, for we are told the account of how they laid regular siege to an almost defenceless factory, was received with surprise and derision by "all military gentlemen in India."

In December, 1760, took place the death, without issue, of Sumbhajee, Rajah of Kolapoor, the last lineal descendant of Sevajee, whom the English also called the Sow Rajah, a name by which the dynasty is generally denominated by Grose and other travellers and writers of that time. After Sumbhajee's death piracy again prevailed to a great extent on this coast. We find it recorded that, in 1765, the Bombay Government sent an expedition, including some ships of the Bombay Marine, which reduced both Malwan* and Rairee, the former belonging to Kolapoor, and the latter to Sawunt Waree.

Early in 1768, the Bombay Government fitted out an expedition, consisting of a squadron of their ships, with four hundred European troops and a large body of Sepoys, to attack Hyder Ally's seaports on the Malabar coast. The enterprise was completely successful. The expedition first made its appearance off Onore, or Honawur, where Hyder Ally, the great ruler of Mysore, familiarly known at this time as Hyder Naick, had begun to prepare a fleet. He had, however, alienated from his interests the captains of his ships by appointing as his admiral Ali Bey, an officer of cavalry, who, of course, was totally ignorant of nautical matters. The consequence was that, when the expedition appeared off Onore, Hyder's fleet, consisting of two ships, two grabs, and ten galivats, sailed and joined the English. Onore, and Fortified Island, at the mouth of the Onore river, were captured, and thence the expedition sailed for Mangalore. The forts were captured with but small loss, and the squadron brought off nine

---

*Malwan is a strong fort on the mainland near Melundy Island or Sindeedroog; the port of Malwan afforded shelter to the pirates who derived their name from the place. About twenty miles to the southward is Raree Point and Fort, the latter situated on a commanding eminence.

vessels of considerable size, besides several of lesser tonnage. The ships of the expedition then returned to Bombay, leaving a small garrison* in the forts.

In 1771 the Bombay Government, in order to exact certain claims on the Nawab of Baroach, or Broach, where they still maintained an agency, sent some troops to enforce their demands, but the expedition failed; in the latter part of the following year, after entering upon some abortive negotiations, a second combined expedition, of which the Bombay Marine supplied the naval portion, was despatched from Bombay, and the city was taken by storm on the 18th of November, 1772, when among those who fell was the gallant and accomplished General David Wedderburn. In the same year the Bombay Government took steps to obtain possession of the islands of Salsette, Kenery, Elephanta, Caranja, and Hog Island, and of the port of Bassein, on which they had long cast an envious eye; indeed, the acquisition of those places had now become almost a necessity for them, in order to prevent any rival maritime power from having access to the spacious and unrivalled harbour of Bombay, already celebrated for its dockyard and other advantages, which conduced to make it the emporium of the trade of the East. Moreover, the expenses of the Bombay establishment far exceeded the receipts, and it was hoped that, by the possession of these places, and the Mahratta share of the revenue of Surat, the balance sheet would show a profit.†

In order to further these wishes, the Company appointed Mr. Henry Mostyn, Resident at the Court of the Peishwa.‡ At this time the Peishwa was at war with the Nizam, and was only too glad to come to terms with the English, and, while near Surat, renewed his overtures to Mr. Gambier, the Company's acting agent, for the assistance of a force to enable him to establish his government at Poona. Accordingly, the President and Council came to a resolution, the original of which is signed by Mr. Hornby and three councillors, one of whom was Commodore Watson, of the Bombay Marine, to assist the Peishwa, Rugonath or Rugoba, with a force of two thousand five hundred men, on condition that he would advance fifteen or twenty lacs of rupees, and, on his being established at Poona,

* In May, Hyder Ally, with his whole army, appeared off Mangalore, and, after a poor defence, the garrison, consisting of forty-one artillerymen, two hundred European infantry, and one thousand two hundred Sepoys, made a hurried embarkation, abandoning their sick and wounded, numbering eighty Europeans and one hundred and eighty Sepoys, and all their guns and stores. Onore and Fortified Island yielded almost without resistance, and Hyder, after recovering all that had been wrested from him in Canara, was able to reascend the Ghauts before the monsoon set in.

† Grant Duff's " History of the Mahrattas," vol. ii., p. 271.

‡ Mahdoo Rao, the Peishwa, died a few days after Mr. Mostyn's arrival, on the very day that Broach was stormed, and was succeeded by Narrain Rao, who again was murdered on the 30th of August, 1773, and gave place to Rugonath Rao, familiarly known in Mahratta history as Rugoba and Dada Sahib.

should cede to the Company, in perpetuity, Salsette, the islands of Kenery, Caranja, Elephanta, and Hog Island, and also Bassein and its dependencies. There were also articles in the treaty regarding the Mahratta share of the revenues of Surat and Broach, and protection from Mahratta inroads. These terms were not agreeable to Rugonath, and it was not until the 6th of March, 1775, that a treaty, consisting of sixteen articles, was concluded between the contracting parties, by which the English agreed to lend the above military force on condition of the payment of one and a half lacs of rupees monthly, with the other cessions and assignments, including the Guicowar's share of the revenue, amounting to £192,500.

Meanwhile, in the previous December, a combined expedition for the reduction of Tannah had been despatched from Bombay, consisting of six hundred and twenty European troops, including artillery, one thousand Sepoys, and two hundred gun lascars, under command of Brigadier-General Robert Gordon, and several vessels and gunboats of the Bombay Marine, under Commodore Watson, the same officer who had commanded the expedition which captured the castle of Surat fifteen years before, and had since added to his reputation by his services on the Malabar coast. So high was the estimate of the ability and professional knowledge of Commodore Watson, entertained by his superiors that, although the situation of Tannah was such as to preclude the employment of the largest vessels of the Company's Marine, "the Governor," says Grant Duff, "expressed a wish that Commodore Watson should superintend the naval part of the enterprise, and have joint authority with General Gordon; and the Commodore, on the General's acquiescence in the arrangement, cheerfully complied." Tannah was, at this time, held by a Mahratta force belonging to the party in possession at Poona, opposed to the Peishwa, and the strong garrison had been recently reinforced by five hundred men. It was sought, at first, to purchase the fort by the offer of a large bribe to the Mahratta officer in charge, who proposed to accept £12,000 for his trust, but the negotiations failed. Meanwhile a powerful Portuguese armament was on its way to India for the avowed purpose of recovering Salsette and Bassein, and, a day after the despatch of the combined military and naval expedition, which was hurried away in order to anticipate them, a portion of the Portuguese fleet anchored at the mouth of Bombay Harbour, and the commander entered a formal protest against the objects of the expedition. The President and Council employed many arguments in justification of their measure, which was, however, an exercise of the law of the strongest, and was only excusable on the *salus populi suprema lex* principle.

A body of seamen from the fleet was landed at Tannah, under Commodore Watson, to co-operate with the soldiers, batteries were opened on the 20th of December, and, on the eighth day, the breach was considered practicable. As it was necessary to fill up the ditch before an advance to storm could be made, an attempt to effect this operation was undertaken on the night of the 27th of December, which, however, was unsuccessful, the column being forced to retire with the loss of one hundred Europeans. On the following evening the assault was delivered, and with complete success; but the troops, exasperated by their losses, put the greater part of the garrison to the sword. "Among those who fell at Tannah," says Grant Duff, "was Commodore John Watson, a brave and experienced officer, who was mortally wounded* on the third day of the siege." To this gallant and lamented officer, to whose memory the Company erected a monument in St. Thomas's Cathedral at Bombay, might be applied the epigram from Tacitus' "Life of Agricola:"—" *Tu vero felix non tantum vitæ claritate, sed etiam opportunitate mortis,*" which may be translated "Thou hast been happy, indeed, not only in the brilliancy of thy life, but even in the occasion of thy death."

Before New Year's Day the whole of the Island of Salsette was reduced, and the Island of Caranja occupied.

While Colonel Keating was engaged in Guzerat in prosecuting the war with the contingent of two thousand five hundred Bombay troops, supplied to enable Rugonath Rao to establish himself at Poona, the Bombay Marine well performed its part, and of many acts of gallantry we will mention one that remains on record. The Mahratta Navy, which was in the interests of the ministers at Poonah, consisted, at the commencement of the war, of six ships—one of forty-six guns, one of thirty-eight, one of thirty-two, and three of twenty-six guns, with five ketches of from twelve to fourteen guns, and twelve galivats having from six to ten guns each. This fleet was met at sea off Gheria, which had been handed over, after its capture, to the Mahrattas, by Commodore John Moore, in the 'Revenge' frigate and 'Bombay' grab, Captain Sheriff, when, notwithstanding the great disparity of force, the Commodore bore down upon the hostile line. The Mahratta fleet, however, avoided an action, and made sail to escape. Having singled out the largest ship, the 'Shumsher Jung,' of forty-six guns, the English vessels gave chase, and, at length, the little grab, being an excellent sailor, brought her to action. The Commodore came up to the assistance of the 'Bombay,' and, after an engagement of three hours, the 'Shumsher Jung' blew up, when the commander and the greater portion of her crew perished, and the ship was totally destroyed.†
A writer who was in Bombay the year following this event, and

---

* His wounds were most painful, but of a rather singular character. A cannon-shot struck the sand near him and drove the particles into his body.

† Grant Duff's "History of the Mahrattas," vol. ii., p. 305. Also "Historical Account of Bombay," and Ives' Voyage.

is likely to be well-informed, says of this action: "The four largest bore down on the two English ships, who waited for them, when a warm engagement commenced; the 'Revenge' engaged their Admiral so closely that their men ran from their quarters. Soon after, by some accident, she took fire and blew up, on which the rest of the fleet betook themselves to flight, and the action being in sight of their principal port, called Gheria, they soon got in under shelter of the castle. Our two ships got their boats out, and saved thirty-four men out of four hundred and twenty, which their Admiral had on board before the engagement began; as many of those that were saved were either burnt or maimed, they were not only humanely treated, but carried to Gheria in boats belonging to our two ships, and there delivered without ransom."

On the 31st May, 1775, the Mahratta war was discontinued, notwithstanding the opposition of the Bombay Government, owing to the dissent of Mr. Warren Hastings, who, as the first Governor-General of all the Company's possessions in India, had assumed the supreme control of affairs on the previous 30th October, and a treaty was signed at Poorundhur, Rugonath being repudiated and offered an asylum at Surat. From hence he proceeded to Tarrapoor, where he requested the Commander of one of the Company's cruisers to give him a passage to Bombay; the commanding officer did not consider himself authorized to refuse the request, and the ex-Peishwa arrived at the Presidency on the 11th of November, where he was received with distinction, and an allowance of 10,000 rupees a month settled upon him.* Passing over intermediate operations, in which the Bombay Marine had no part, we come to the siege of Bassein, which fell to the British arms on the 11th of December, 1779, after a siege of thirteen days; to effect the reduction of this very strong place the north face of which can only be attacked by regular approaches, a large force, with a powerful battering train, had been employed, the European portion embarking in ships of the Bombay Marine, and the Sepoys proceeding by land. Hostilities with the Mahrattas were finally terminated by the treaty of Salbye, which was ratified by the Peishwa, Nana Furnuwees, on the 20th of December, 1782, and formally exchanged on the 24th of February, 1783, the term for restoring the territory conquered since the treaty of Poorundhur, being limited to the 24th of April. Before that date, however, an event occurred which shed lustre on the Bombay Marine, and showed the stern stuff of which its officers and men were made.

The 'Ranger,' a small brig of twelve guns, commanded by

---

* In January, 1779, a British army started from Bombay to place Rugonath at Poonah as Regent, but it was overtaken by disaster, owing to the incompetence of its commanders, Colonels Egerton and Cockburn, and, in retreating from Tullygaum, lost several hundred men.

Lieutenant-Commander Pruen, was proceeding from Bombay to Calicut, for the purpose of conveying some military officers of high rank to the British Army then operating in the Bednore country, among the number being Brigadier-General Norman McLeod,* appointed commander-in-chief in place of General Matthews, Colonel Humberstone, and Major Shaw, when she fell in with the Mahratta fleet, commanded by the Peishwa's Admiral, Anund Rao Dhoolup, who, it appears, was unaware of the conclusion of peace. Though this fleet consisted of two ships, one ketch, all of superior force, and eight galivats, Lieutenant Pruen did not hesitate a moment in engaging them; he might, indeed, have soon satisfied the Mahrattas of their being no longer enemies, but allies, or, at the worst, if compelled to accompany them into the neighbouring port of Gheria, the detention would have been brief, but, sailor-like, his predilection for fighting, and his repugnance to strike his flag without having first vindicated the honour of his country, overcame all scruples and prudential considerations. There were also other reasons for his deciding to fight. He had on board the newly-appointed Commander-in Chief of the British Army, and other officers of distinction belonging to the King's service, and his heart's desire was gratified at this opportunity of showing that a Company's cruiser could fight as stoutly as a King's ship. The little 'Ranger,' accordingly, awaited her antagonists, and the military officers armed for the impending conflict, into which they entered with a spirit not less than that which animated the ship's officers and crew.

A desperate action now ensued. First the large ships plied the little brig with their guns, to which she replied with spirit, and then the galivats were laid alongside, and it was sought to overwhelm the handful of gallant Britons by throwing on her decks as many boarders as could find foot room. But, though the enemy mustered fifteen to one, and the Mahrattas were renowned throughout India as swordsmen, the repeated attempts were met and repulsed with a desperate tenacity of purpose that has never been surpassed in the annals of war. Numbers, however, told in the end, and, at length, the gallant little craft was carried by a united rush of hundreds of men infuriated at the prolonged resistance. On the decks lay Major Shaw dead, and General McLeod, "who," says Grant Duff, "being disabled in one arm, continued to fight until shot through the body, when

* Colonels McLeod and Humberstone, and Major Shaw had previously quitted the army serving in the Bednore country and came up to Bombay in February, in order to prefer charges against General Matthews, who retaliated by a letter, dated the 4th of March, "taxing the whole army, in terms the most severe and unqualified, but altogether general and indiscriminate, with offences of the highest criminality." (See extract of a letter from the President and Select Committee at Bombay, to the Secret Committee of the Court of Directors, dated the 27th of June, 1783, and received overland on the 21st of November.)

he fell, as was supposed, mortally wounded, also Colonel Humberstone* mortally, and three of the other military passengers, desperately wounded." The gallant Pruen was also dangerously wounded, " and," says Mill, "almost every man in the ship was either killed or wounded." The prize was carried into Gheria, but it was a dear-bought one to the enemy. Their loss in killed and wounded was described as immense; one vessel was sunk, and several were seriously damaged. Upon learning of this violation of the treaty, a strong remonstrance was made by the Bombay Government, and the surrender of the Peishwa's districts was suspended; but, upon an apology being made for the outrage, together with the surrender of the vessel, the terms of the pacification were carried out.

The Court of Directors presented Lieutenant Pruen with a valuable sword in token of their appreciation of the devoted gallantry he had displayed, and the Bombay Government gave pecuniary rewards to the survivors of the crew.†

* "He died," says Mill, "in a few days at Gheria, in the twenty-eighth year of his age, and was lamented as an officer of the most exalted promise, a man who nourished his spirit with the contemplation of ancient heroes, and devoted his hours to the study of the most abstruse sciences connected with his profession.

† The President and Select Committee at Bombay, in their letter to the Secret Committee of the Court of Directors, give the following account of this action. After stating that they had ordered General McLeod to succeed General Matthews in the command of the army in the Bednore country, and had directed him, Colonel Humberstone, and Major Shaw, to rejoin the troops, they refer to their having received advices from Mr. Anderson, in a letter dated the 20th of February, of the Mahratta Treaty having arrived from Poonah. They then continue:—

"The peace had been duly proclaimed at Bombay, and every necessary step taken on our part, for the performance of the treaty. The 'Ranger' had sailed on the 5th of April with Colonels McLeod and Humberstone, Major Shaw, and other officers, to join the army. Lieutenant Pruen, commander of the vessel, having been previously apprized of the peace, and furnished with the same orders as had been circulated to all the Marine, not to commit hostilities against the Mahrattas: when, on the 18th of April, we were alarmed by an account that the 'Ranger' had been attacked by the Mahratta fleet on the 8th, three days after leaving Bombay, and after a most desperate resistance of near five hours was obliged to submit to superior force and, with the whole convoy of boats, had been carried into Gheria. We were under great anxiety and uncertainty for a considerable time, regarding the fate of Colonel McLeod, and the other officers, which was not entirely removed till the 23rd of May, when the President received a letter from him dated at Gheria the 5th of that month. In this letter the colonel mentions he had made several unsuccessful attempts to convey advice of his misfortune, and then relates some circumstances of the engagement, referring for a more particular account to Lieutenant Pruen. The account Colonel McLeod gives is, that on the morning of the 8th of April, they found themselves near the Mahratta fleet, belonging to Gheria, which, without speaking or ceremony, attacked the 'Ranger' with great fury. Lieutenant Pruen fought his vessel with the greatest courage. Their defence was desperate, and ceased not till they were almost all killed or wounded. Major Shaw was shot dead, Colonel Humberstone was shot through the lungs. Lieutenant Stuart of the 100th Regiment, was almost cut to pieces on boarding, Lieutenant John Taylor of the Bombay troops was shot through the body, Lieutenant Seton, of the Bombay Artillery, and Lieutenant Pruen, commander of the vessel, were wounded with swords on boarding. In the beginning of the action Colonel McLeod received two wounds in his left hand and shoulder, and a little before it was over a musket-shot passed through

In connection with this action an anecdote is told that is worth relating. It would appear that Lieutenant Pruen was a seaman of what is generally known as "the old school," which, by the way, must be a *very old* school now, as the term has been applied to the naval service, certainly since the days of Benbow, who, probably, was himself contemptuously twitted with new-fangled notions; however this may be, Lieutenant Pruen was a rough and ready seaman, very irritable, and full of prejudices, common enough with a certain class of sailors. Among these he regarded the military, especially when on board ship, as so much " state lumber;" as to his little brig, he considered her the smartest craft that sailed the seas, and he regarded the crew, as indeed they proved themselves, in every way worthy of her. The military officers quickly detected these weak points in the character of the commander, and, having nothing to do, were in the habit

his body, which pierced his lungs and spleen. Lieutenant Pruen's account likewise proves that the Mahrattas began the attack, and that he received a number of shot before he returned a gun. Their force consisted of two large ships, a ketch, and eight galivats, with which the 'Ranger,' carrying only twelve 12-pounders, sustained a close engagement of four hours and a-half, the two ships and the ketch being lashed alongside of the 'Ranger,' in which situation the engagement was continued with musketry only; and the brave defence of the officers and crew prevented the enemy from entering the vessel, till, from the number of killed and wounded, and most of the muskets being rendered unserviceable, the fire of the 'Ranger' was so much reduced, that the commander was under the necessity of striking; and the instant the colours were down the enemy rushed on board and cruelly cut and wounded several of the officers and men, while others jumped overboard to avoid certain death. The same night the 'Ranger' was carried into Gheria, where the Subadar and officers disowning all knowledge of the peace, had refused to release the vessel and officers without orders from Poonah. We are concerned to add that Colonel Humberstone died at Gheria, on the 30th of April, of the wound he received in the action. Colonel McLeod's recovery was long thought impossible, but he is now perfectly restored to health. Lieutenants Stuart, Taylor, Seton, and Pruen are also recovered. The 'Ranger,' with Colonel McLeod and the surviving officers, arrived here on the 29th of May, having been released from Gheria on the 27th in too disabled and despoiled condition to make her way to the southward. Our last letter from Mr. Anderson is dated the 18th of May, upon receipt of the intelligence of the capture of the 'Ranger,' which he immediately communicated to the Mhadajee Scindia, and required him in strong terms to give some explanation with regard to this outrage and the measures he intended to pursue in vindication of his own honour, which was thus brought into question. Scindia declared that none of his late letters from the Minister gave him the least reason to apprehend any sinister intentions of the Mahratta Government, and he assured Mr. Anderson, that he had written in strong terms to the Minister to punish with death the person who committed this act of hostility and to make full restitution of the stores and effects taken, that if they complied with these requisitions he would undertake to reconcile the English Government; but if they refused, they must take the consequences; that for his part, since so enormous an outrage had been committed after the conclusion of the treaty, he must consult and adopt the inclinations of the English. So far from punishing the officer who committed the act of hostility, we are assured by Colonel McLeod that he received from the Minister public marks of approbation and honorary rewards for his conduct. Colonel McLeod was invited to the ceremony held upon this occasion, and some of the officers were actually present when the Subadar exhibited in public durbar, according to the custom of the country, the honorary ornaments which had been sent to him from Poonah."

of playing them off. Thus they frequently asserted that the brig could not fight, or, if she did, that any vessel of equal size would capture her. These sarcastic observations, though made only in joke, sometimes exasperated Pruen to such a pitch that he was only prevented by his position as commander, from taking revenge upon the detractors of his ship and crew; however, the altercations generally ended by his expressing a hope that he might have an opportunity, while they were on board, of showing these "soldier officers" that a Company's cruiser could fight, and that as well as the lordly line-of-battle ships, to which he was referred as "real men-of-war." His wish was gratified, and the military officers, forming the *élite* of the British Army, had the much-desired opportunity; and it is related that, when the desperate action was at its height, and half his men lay weltering in their blood, Captain Pruen coolly turned round to the gentlemen who so bravely bore their part in the fray, and some of whom were already desperately wounded, with the inquiry as to whether the 'Ranger' and her crew could fight?

In 1770 a squadron of ships of the Marine was despatched from Bombay to Mocha, to redress a grievance under which a British subject was labouring, but happily matters were arranged without any bloodshed. In that year the captain of a trading vessel from India was on shore at the British factory at Mocha, when a slave boy, whom he had corrected, ran away and took refuge in an Arab's house, where he was prevailed upon to become a Mahommedan. His master, meeting the boy one day, flogged him, whereupon the mob attacked the factory, and would have sacrificed the English captain but that he managed to effect his escape to his ship. The Governor, having refused to make good the losses he had suffered at the hands of the populace, who had destroyed his effects in the factory, the captain sailed for Bombay, and requested redress from the Government. Two ships of the Bombay Marine were immediately fitted out with every requisite for bombarding the city, and, on their arrival at Mocha, a message was sent to the Governor, apprising him of their mission. The inhabitants were greatly alarmed, and abandoned the forts, which they had been accustomed to consider impregnable, and would have deserted the city had not the Governor prevented it. He thought proper to comply with the demands which were made on behalf of the sufferers, and sent off 4,000 dollars, extorted from the Banian merchants, to the Commodore, who was "happy," says a writer, "to preserve the city from destruction, and to appease the wrath of the British at so cheap a rate."*

We will now give some account of events up the Persian Gulf, where the Company's Marine were engaged on ground that has

* "Series of adventures in the course of a voyage up the Red Sea, on the coasts of Nubia and Egypt, in the year 1777;" by Eyles Irwin, Esq.

been familiar to all officers of the Service since the capture of Ormuz in 1622, and which witnessed almost the last of their services, the Persian war of 1856.

After the death of Nadir Shah, and until the year 1779, when Agha Mahomed Khan, founder of the present Kujjir dynasty, raised himself to the throne, Persia was ruled well and wisely by Kurreem Khan, of the tribe of Zend; throughout his struggle for power he had been supported by the Arab tribes inhabiting the Persian shores of the Gulf, but, later on, some of the petty chiefs became refractory, the most troublesome of these being Meer Mohunna, of Bunder Reeg, a small seaport to the northwest of Bushire—this chief, at once remarkable for his valour and his atrocious wickedness, had, during the course of his career, in order to gratify his cupidity, murdered his parents, brothers, and most of his family. Meer Mohunna now offended the Persian Government, by interrupting the communications between Shiraz and Bushire, which was at this time the principal port in the kingdom, the Company having, in 1762, removed their factory thither from Gombroon, when that place declined and was almost deserted. Being attacked by a Persian force the chief of Bunder Reeg defended his possessions on the continent with the utmost resolution, but, at length, was forced to retire to the island of Corgo,* (Khargú) near Kharrack,† (Khareg). On this small, sandy island he not only supported a numerous body of followers, and defeated all the efforts of Sheikh Nasseer of Bushire to reduce him to obedience, but added to his means by plundering a number of vessels, and, in 1766, succeeded in surprising the Dutch garrison at Kharrack, distant twenty-seven miles from Bushire, from which it is visible on a clear day.

Some notice is here necessary regarding the establishment of the Dutch in Kharrack.

Baron Kniphausen, the Dutch agent at Bussorah, having been fined and imprisoned by the Turkish Governor, proceeded to Batavia and induced his superiors to authorize a plan for aggrandizing the Dutch East India Company. Having received their sanction, he sailed with two ships for the Persian Gulf, and, on securing a grant of the island, took possession of Kharrack, where he erected a small fortification. The Baron then blockaded the Shatt-ul-Arab until the Governor of Bussorah had restored the sums of money he had extorted from him. Under his auspices Kharrack rose rapidly in importance, and became a safe emporium, and, as there is an abundant supply of water, the settlement flourished, and the population rapidly increased from one hundred poor fishermen, as it was when

---

* Corgo is about three miles long by a half a mile broad, and is situated about a mile and a half to the northwards of Kharrack.

† Kharrack is about four miles in length, and may be seen from Bushire Roads in clear weather, the tomb on the highest point being 284 feet high.

Baron Kniphausen took possession of it, until it numbered four thousand souls.* "The Dutch," says a writer in the "Asiatic Journal," (Vol. XXVII., New Series,) "built a regular square fort of four bastions, each of which mounted ten guns. In 1762, Meer Meana, of Bunderick, took two armed galivats, and landing with two hundred men, plundered the island. The Dutch having afforded assistance to the Persians in attacking Meer Meana at Bunderick in which they failed, he retaliated, and in 1766 attacked the Dutch at Kharrack, and compelled them to surrender the island, though they had a garrison of eighty Europeans on the island, who proceeded to Bushire. This island became, under the Dutch, a flourishing settlement, with a population exceeding twelve hundred souls." Abraham Parsons, in his "Travels in Asia and Africa," gives a different version of the capture of the island by the Meer, and says that he first induced the Dutch Governor to visit him at Bunder Reeg, and then forced him, on pain of death, to sign an order directing the commanding officer to surrender. By this acquisition, Meer Mohunna's power was greatly increased, and he became the dread of all neighbouring chiefs. "From this time," says Parsons, "he commenced pirate, fitting out his galivats and other smaller armed vessels as cruisers; they took and plundered vessels of every nation, and he became as great a terror to those who navigated in the Persian Gulf, as the famous Angria had heretofore been in the East Indies." At length, in 1768, Kurreem Khan determined to expel Meer Mohunna. The island of Kharrack was claimed by the Persian Government, and Sheikh Nasseer, of Bushire, was directed to take steps to recover it.

* The above is the account given by Malcolm in his "History of Persia," (vol. ii. p. 82). Ives, in his "Voyage to India," speaks of his visit to Kharrack in 1758, while it was in the possession of Baron Kniphausen, and gives a detailed account of the settlement of the Dutch on the island. Mr. Ives proceeded up the Gulf from Bombay in the Company's cruiser 'Swallow,' Captain Price. Justamond gives the following account of this event :—" Baron Kniphausen managed the Dutch factory with extraordinary success. The English found themselves in imminent danger of losing the superiority they had acquired at this place, as well as in most of the seaports in India. They excited the Turkish Government to suppress a branch of trade that was useful to it, and procured an order for the confiscation of the merchandize and possessions of their rivals. The Dutch factor, who, under the character of a merchant, concealed the statesman, instantly took a resolution worthy of a man of genius. He retired with his dependents, and the broken remains of his fortune, to Kharrack, a small island at the distance of fifteen leagues from the mouth of the river, where he fortified himself in such a manner that, by intercepting the Arabian and Indian vessels bound for the city, he compelled the Government to grant him an indemnification for the losses he had sustained by their behaviour. The fame of his integrity and abilities drew to his island the privateers of the neighbouring ports; the very merchants of Bussorah and the Europeans who traded thither. This new colony found its prosperity increase every day, when it was abandoned by its founder. The successor of this able man did not display the same talents; towards the end of the year 1765, he suffered himself to be dispossessed of his island by the Arabian corsair, Mirmahana."

A large fleet was, accordingly, fitted out and sent against the pirate chief, but so great was the dread in which he was held that they feared to attack him. In this state of affairs, the Sheikh applied to the Company's agent at Bushire, and, as there were two vessels of the Bombay Marine at that port, Captain Price, commanding the 'Swallow,' the senior officer, at once offered to undertake the duty; but his force was utterly inadequate for the object of reducing the island, even if he could have counted upon a loyal co-operation on the part of his faint-hearted allies. On the approach of the combined force to Kharrack, Meer Mohunna's fleet came out to meet them, when an action ensued, from which, however, the Persian fleet took care to keep out of harm's way, and then ran back whence they came, without firing a shot. After some heavy cannonading, the enemy withdrew their fleet under the protection of the fort, and the British vessels remained off the island, where they were joined by the Persian squadron. Captain Price now proposed a joint attack on the fort, which was a well-built work of considerable strength; to this the Persians consented, but, as before, when the firing began, the Bushire fleet were nowhere to be seen. It was useless for two small vessels to contend against the powerful artillery of a strong fort, and, after vainly attempting to make an impression on the walls, Captain Price was forced to retire. It is said that on this occasion, Meer Mohunna fired red-hot shot, which set fire to one of the cruisers, a noteworthy circumstance, as these terrible missiles are generally supposed to have been first employed at the siege of Gibraltar twenty years later.

Shortly after this, a party of nearly forty officers and men from the Company's cruisers landed on the island of Corgo, and, during the night, were attacked by an overpowering force, from Kharrack, under Meer Mohunna, when they were nearly all cut to pieces. As the vessels were now too shorthanded to continue operations, and the Persians, for whose sole benefit they were undertaken, declined to assist, Captain Price quitted his station off the islands and returned to Bombay.*

According to the account of the attack on Kharrack given by Parsons, who says he learned the particulars from some of the Company's officers who were actually engaged, six of the Company's ships and smaller vessels-of-war co-operated with the Persians. He says :—" Although the attack was made by sea,

* The author of the article on Kharrack, in the Asiatic Journal, before quoted, writing of these events, says :—"In 1768 the Persians offered to transfer the island to the Company, if they would. co-operate in effecting its conquest from Meer Meana. They declined the offer, but engaged to assist the Persians in recovering it in the promise of a free and open trade throughout Persia. An attack was made on the island on the 20th of May, but failed from one of the Company's ships taking fire. A renewal of the attack was subsequently abandoned, in consequence of a party from the ships, whilst watering at Corgo, having been surprised by an ambuscade of Meer Meana's, who killed twenty-four and wounded seven of the crew."

with the largest of the English ships against the castle, with that skill and bravery which did them great honour, and by the smaller vessels, which, in conjunction with the Persians, landed at the town, notwithstanding the fire from the eight galivats and the musketry from the town, the attempt was fruitless; the ships suffering so much from the guns of the castle that they were obliged to sheer off to repair the damage; and, although they returned to the attack the next day, it was ineffectual, the castle guns being so much larger than those of the ships, whose heaviest shots were nine and six-pounders." As it is certain that only two of the Company's ships-of-war were engaged in the attack on the castle, it is probable that four of the vessels referred to by this writer were improvised gunboats, or galivats, a class of fighting ships utterly unable to cope with strong fortifications.

From information received from an officer of the Marine captured at Corgo by Meer Mohunna, it appears that there were fifteen hundred fighting men in Kharrack, and about four thousand inhabitants; and that there were also ten Dutchmen who superintended the management of his artillery, and several Armenians. This officer stated "that a force of fifteen hundred Sepoys, and three hundred Europeans, exclusive of a company of artillery, would be required to reduce the island. These must land and make regular approaches. The Meer's forces were fine active men, and in the best order. He had nine galivats; their dimensions were about seventy feet long, twenty-four feet broad, and five feet hold; they sail like the wind, and were kept in the most perfect order."

In the following year, however, according to Malcolm and other reliable authorities, a rebellion of his followers broke out, and Meer Mohunna fled to Bussorah, where he was seized and executed, and his body cast into a field to be devoured by dogs. "The death of this monster," says Malcolm, "diffused universal joy, from the coast of Shiraz to the shores of India, and the inhabitants still pronounce his name with mixed horror and apprehension."

Parsons says that Kurreem Khan, recognizing the inutility of attempting the reduction of the castle by bombardment, owing to the heavy guns mounted on the walls and bastions, resolved to effect its surrender by blockading the island, and starving the garrison out. He, accordingly, sent a large body of troops, with artillery, which were landed on the island in April, 1769, and the place was completely invested. At length Meer Mohunna, seeing that the game was up, embarked on a dark night with a portion of his treasure, and proceeded to Grane, whence he made his way to Bussorah, where he was put to death by order of the Pasha of Bagdad.

Mr. Morley, the Company's Resident at Bushire, endeavoured

to obtain a portion of the Meer's property, as an indemnification for the expenses the Company had incurred in co-operating against him, but the Sheikh refused his demands, when Mr. Morley proceeded to Bussorah, and left the Company's ship 'Revenge' to cruise off the island. Kharrack now re-devolved to the Sovereign of Persia, and Hussein Sultan was appointed Governor, and Admiral of the Gulf, with the title of Hussein Khan.

In 1775 took place the siege of Bussorah,* by the Persian army of fifty thousand men, under the command of Sadoc Khan, brother to Kurreem Khan, Shah of Persia, the Turkish garrison scarcely exceeding fifteen hundred men. At this time a squadron of ships of the Bombay Marine was lying in the river Shatt-ul-Arab, near the creek off the city, consisting of the 'Revenge,' a frigate of twenty-eight guns, 'Eagle,' of sixteen guns, and 'Success,' ketch, of fourteen guns; beside two other ketches of fourteen guns each, built at Bombay for the Pasha of Bagdad. "These ketches are commanded," says Parsons, who had arrived at Bussorah overland from Bagdad, "by an English midshipman in the Company's service, and have on board a few English sailors; the remainder of the crew are Turks. They carry British colours." On the 6th of March, three officers, belonging to the Company's cruisers, engaged on a shooting excursion, were attacked by a large body of armed men, and left for dead; the boat's crew were also stripped and beaten, and their boat taken away. In alliance with the Persians was a piratical prince, whose dominions lay between Bussorah and the Gulf, called by Parsons the "Shaub," who, having pushed up the river during the night with fourteen of his galivats, began, on the 21st of March, to transport across the river, under the protection of the Persian batteries, the heavy guns and equipage of the besieging army. On the following day, the Company's agents quitted their factory in Bussorah, and went on board the 'Eagle' with the treasure and valuables; and, during the afternoon, the 'Success,' accompanied by one of the Pasha's ketches, succeeded in capturing one of the Shaub's galivats, which was burnt, and in damaging others before they reached the Persian camp near a creek some distance from Bussorah. The other ketch belonging to the Pasha, also returned the same evening, the

* Parsons gives a full description of Bussorah at this time. "The mud walls," he says, "are about twelve miles in circuit, and, although not half the enclosed space is built on, yet it is a large city, and before the plague in 1773, was very populous; the population were computed to be upwards of three hundred thousand, and, in September following, only amounted to fifty thousand, the remainder, excepting twenty thousand who fled away, having fallen victims to its fury. At this time they compute the inhabitants to be from eighty thousand to ninety thousand souls. There are four gates and a sallyport, also a deep and broad ditch which is wanting on each side the two principal gates, called Zobeir and Bagdad. There are eight bastions, on each of which are mounted eight brass guns, besides upwards of fifty brass cannon on ships' carriages, mounted round the walls. There is also a battery of twelve brass guns at the Capitan Pasha's quarters, little more than 100 yards below the creek's mouth."

midshipman commanding her having run the gauntlet of the Persian batteries. This young officer had been requested by the Persian General to come on shore, but, apprehending treachery, he sent one of his crew, named Ryley, to personate him, and after this man had landed, the Persian batteries and the galivats* opened fire upon the ketch, which he promptly returned, and in the conflict suffered some loss. Negotiations were now opened by the enemy with the Turkish Governor and the British Agent for the surrender of the city on the payment of twenty lacs of rupees, but the demand was refused.

As fears were entertained that the Persian fleet, which was very considerable, might make an effort to push up the river, the commanding officers of the Company's cruisers made every effort to prevent this junction. The Turkish Pasha placed at their disposal two of his galivats, which were speedily armed with eight guns, and manned with crews of between eighty to a hundred men and officers, drawn from the cruisers. In order to prevent the enemy breaking through, the British naval force set to work to construct a bridge from the large boats employed in the passenger and goods traffic in the creek; no light task considering the great breadth of the river at this point, and the lack of materials. Parsons writes:—"March 24th and 25th. Our Marine officers and men have been very active in placing the anchors, chains, and cables, and bringing the boats to their proper moorings, so as to form the bridge, or rather barricade, as a sufficient number of boats could not be procured, so as to be close enough together to admit planks to be laid from boat to boat, nor, indeed, was it necessary, as every boat's bow was hauled under the chain and there fastened, and at the distance of about sixty feet, another boat, and so on, quite across the river, either under the chain or cables. At the same time one of the boats' anchors and cables was carried out from the bow of each boat, and another from the stern, so as to enable it to resist the tide, whether flood or ebb, without bearing too hard upon the anchors, to which the chain and cables were fastened. Every assistance was given to forwarding the plan, by the Capitan Pasha's men under his command, and our Marine officers never desisted from the work until it was completed that evening, to the satisfaction of every one interested in the preservation of Bussorah. We now flatter ourselves that the Persian army, without further supply of cannon, ammunition, and provisions must now decamp."

On the 6th of April the Persian army took up a position

* Mr. Parsons thus describes one of these galivats, which the 'Eagle' subsequently captured:—"She is eighty-four feet long, twenty-four feet broad, mounts ten carriage guns, 6-pounders, and is built forward like a London wherry and has only one tall mast, which rakes forward, to which is attached a lug sail; she carries twenty-four oars."

extending from about three miles up the river, where the agent had his country house, and at which, since the English factory was closed, the Vice-Consul has resided. On the morning of the 8th of April, sixteen Persian galivats appeared in sight, coming up the river in full sail, to attack the English ships, which, however, did not wait for them. The 'Success' and 'Eagle' slipped their cables, and, with the Pasha's two ketches, set sail to meet them; upon which the Persians "up helm" and made off with the assistance of their sweeps. Their fleet consisted of a small brig of eight guns, called the 'Tiger,'* five galivats of ten guns, and ten others, carrying from six to eight guns each. Mr. Parsons speaks of the good effect produced by the activity of the Marine officers, and says that the Governor, who was going his rounds, accompanied by several of his officers, "seemed well pleased with the behaviour of our little Marine force, and told the Agent that if he would keep the enemy from approaching by water, we had nothing to fear, for that he and his brave fellows would prevent them by land, which the Agent promised to do." Meantime reinforcements of Arabs and Turkish troops from Bagdad arrived, so that "the men on the walls seemed quite cheerful." Before daylight on the 9th of April, the Persians made an attempt to escalade the walls, but were driven back with great slaughter; on the same night they succeeded in setting fire to two of the boats on the Persian side of the bridge of boats, but they only burnt to the water's edge without sinking, so that their object was not attained. The 'Success,' and the two Pasha's galivats moored near that side, opened fire and dispersed the people, also firing into the village, which burned for many hours.

On the following day the English squadron weighed anchor, and worked down the river with the tide and a contrary wind, the Company's Agent being desirous of proceeding to Bushire, and the Commodore of attacking, *en route*, a fleet of twelve

* The 'Tiger' formerly belonged to the Company. In April, 1773, when the plague desolated Bussorah, the Agent and his men quitted the city, and embarked on board the 'Drake' and 'Tiger,' two of the Company's cruisers, with the intention of proceeding to Bombay. Kurreem Khan, Shah of Persia, was on bad terms with them because Mr. Morley, the Agent at Bushire, fearing ill-treatment, had, about five years before, fled on board a Company's cruiser and proceeded to Bombay, which drew all the English trade to the Turkish port of Bussorah. In order to be revenged, the Shah directed some of his galivats to waylay the two cruisers. The 'Tiger' was captured by a surprise, but they feared to attack the 'Drake,' a vessel carrying fourteen guns, on board which was the Agent and several members of the factory. The 'Tiger,' with Messrs. Beaumont and Green on board, was carried to Bunder Reeg, and, by order of the Shah, these two gentlemen were sent to him to Shiraz. They remained here a year, when they were conducted to Bushire. Mr. Green had been permitted to proceed to Bussorah, to which the English Agent had returned to settle his affairs, and was here when the siege broke out. Soon after this the Bombay Government made proposals for the release of the prisoners and the re-establishment of the English factory at Bushire.

galivats and thirteen armed trankies,* of which he had received information on the previous day. " At four," says Mr. Parsons,

* Trankies, though formerly much in use, are not now to be seen in the Persian Gulf; they are impelled by both oars and sails. The following are the species of native craft that navigate the waters of the Gulf. The Batil, a vessel with a long fiddle-headed bow and two masts, which may be distinguished from other craft by the inner part of the stern-post being ornamented with devices cut in the wood. The Batil of the southern part of the Malabar coast is about 50 to 60 feet in length, 16 to 18 feet in breadth, and 8 to 10 feet in depth, and has more of the European form than any of the Indian-built vessels that are met with. The after-part shows the origin to be of Portuguese construction, as it is very similar to that of many of the boats still in use by the people of that country; indeed they are said to be of the same shape as the vessel in which Vasco da Gama sailed to India. They have a deck fore and aft, and are built in a very rough manner, and fastened with nails and bolts. They are equipped with one mast which inclines forward, and a square lug-sail, with one pair of shrouds and a backstay; also a small bowsprit at an angle of about forty-five degrees, with a sort of jib-foresail. The Bagarah of the Persian Gulf is similar to the Batil, with one mast and a small deck-house abaft.

The Baghalah, or Buggalow, is a species of native vessel which it is the fashion to call a "dhow," though dhows are, at the present day, never seen in the Gulf, or indeed, rarely anywhere, only a few being found at Jiddah and some other ports. The baghalah is of great size, sometimes of 200 or 300 tons burden, and carrying several guns—one called the "Duniyah," belonging to the Sultan of Bahrein, had ten. The Persian Gulf baghalahs have two masts raking forward, like those of the batil and bagarah, and a high poop with stern ports, and a long pointed bow. The baghalah is steered with an ordinary tiller, unlike the batil and bagarah which are steered by "yoke lines" leading from a point a little above the water on the outside edge of the rudder,. The baghalah of the Gulf of Cutch is one of the most ancient vessels to be met with. Mr. Edye, formerly Master Shipwright of the Royal Dockyard at Trincomali, describes these vessels minutely in a paper communicated to the Journal of the Royal Asiatic Society. Their extreme length, from stern to taffrail, is about 74 feet, the breadth 25 feet, and the depth in hold 11 feet 6 inches, and they are about 150 tons burthen. The peculiarity of form and extraordinary equipment of these vessels is said to have been the same from the period of Alexander the Great. They are armed with two guns on the after-part, and have their poop-decks with a round stern. Their extreme section is abaft the waist or middle of the vessel : they are very broad in proportion to their length, with a sharp rising floor; the stern is straight, and rakes very little more than the stern-post. These vessels are constructed with timbers and planks, which are nail and trenail fastened in the most rude and unsafe manner possible. The topside above the deck is barricaded with mats on the outside of the timbers, which run up to about eight feet from the deck, and when they have no cargo on board, this barricade is removed. They have only one mast; and a lateen sail, the tack of which goes to the stem head as in all other vessels.

The extraordinary longevity of these native vessels may be gathered from the fact that in 1837, a baghalah, the "Deria Dowlut," or "Wealth of the Seas," which was built at Bownuggur, in the year 1750, was still trading in the Red Sea.

The Arab dhow is a vessel generally of about 150 to 250 tons burthen by measurement, and sometimes larger. It is grab-built, with ten or twelve ports, about 85 feet long from stem to stern, 20 feet 9 inches broad, and 11 feet 6 inches deep. These vessels have a great rise of floor, are calculated for sailing with small cargoes, and are fully prepared, by internal equipment, for defence, with decks, hatchways, ports, poop-deck, &c., like a vessel of war. Many of them are sheathed, on two and a-half inch plank bottoms, with one inch board ; and the preparation of chunam, cocoa-nut oil, and damar (country resin), which is called "galgal," put between the planks and sheathing-board, causes the vessel to be very dry and durable, and prevents the worm from attacking the bottom. This worm is as great an enemy to timber in the water as the white ant is to it on land. On the outside of the sheathing-board there is a coat of chunam or

"the Persian Admiral fired a shot at the 'Eagle' and 'Success.
At half-past four the 'Eagle,' being advanced near to them
returned their fire with a broadside, which was followed by the
'Success.' As soon as we arrived within gunshot—one of our
lieutenants having been burnt on the 26th of March, and
remaining dangerously ill, I acted in his place—the Persians
kept driving through the narrow reach (it was now strong ebb
tide with the wind contrary) continuing to fire at us, which the
'Eagle' and 'Success' returned whenever the guns could be
brought to bear on them, on the different tacks. Presently
after we received a shot through our jib, another through our
ensign, and another through a spare topmast in the booms. The
Pasha's two ketches and galivats could not keep up with us, and
the two former got twice aground. The cannonading on both
sides continued brisk, but we never could get near enough to do
any execution with our musketry. At half-past five we had our
main top-gallant yard arm shot away, much of our rigging cut
and two of our gun ports in the steerage beat in, at which hour
two balls struck and lodged in the ship's starboard side, between
the two after-guns, and were buried in more than half their
diameter. Soon after this the Persians fled, the dull sailer
rowed, being towed by those that sailed best. At six they all
got in close to the Persian shore and anchored in shoal water
we anchored abreast of them as near as our draft of water would
permit, when a furious cannonading commenced at the distance

whitewash, made the same as that between the sheathing and planks, and this coat
is renewed every season they put to sea. These vessels, though often brig-rigged
when formerly used for war purposes by the Joasmi and other piratical tribes
had, generally, only one mast and a lateen sail. The yard is the length of the
vessel, and we have seen a dhow having a spar 100 feet in length : the mast rake
forward, for the purpose of keeping the ponderous weight clear, in raising and
lowering. The tack of the sail is brought to the stem head, and the sheets aft in
the usual way; the haulyards lead to the taffrail, having a pendant and treble
purchase block, which becomes the backstay, to support the mast when the sail is
set; this, with two or three pairs of shrouds, completes the rigging, which is very
simple, the whole being of coir rope. Dhows may be distinguished from baghalah
by a long gallery projecting from the stern, which is their peculiar characteristic

The Pattamars are a class of vessel which may be considered the best sailers in
India, and the most useful as stowing a good cargo. They belong principally
to Bombay merchants, and carry on the whole of the coasting trade to that port
They are grab-built, and the dimensions of the large class are 76 feet 6 inches in
length, 21 feet 6 inches in breadth, 11 feet 9 inches in depth, and about 200 ton
burthen. They are planked, says Mr. Edye, with teak, upon jungle-wood frames
and are really very handsome vessels, being put together in the European
manner, with nails, bolts, &c., and their bottoms are sheathed with inch board
and have the preparation before described. Some of the smaller class of these
vessels of about 60 tons burthen, are sewed together with coir, like other native
boats. The small class have one, and the large class two masts, with the lateen
sail; the foremast raking forward for the purpose of keeping the ponderous yard
clear. The yard is slung at one-third of its length; the tack of the sail is
brought to the stem head through a fixed block, and the sheet hauled aft a
the side as usual. The haulyard is a pendant and treble block from the mast
head aft to midships; thus acting as a backstay for the mast's security, together
with about two pairs of shrouds.

of pistol shot, assisted by our musketry. This was continued until dark, when we both desisted at the same time as if by mutual consent."

At daybreak the following morning (the 12th of April), the Persian fleet was discovered in Harfah Creek, about thirty miles below Bussorah Creek, on the Persian shore; they were quite out of reach and appeared to be aground. At six, the 'Eagle' and 'Success,' followed by the Pasha's galivats and ketches, weighed anchor, and worked down the river, driving before them some Persian galivats coming up the stream. On arriving at the mouth of the Shatt-ul-Arab, the Pasha's two galivats proceeded to Al Koweit—by the English called Grane—a port then dependent on the Turkish Governor of Bussorah. Previous to parting company, all the Turkish and Arab seamen on board the Pasha's two ketches, numbering two hundred and thirty men, were transferred to the galivats, and the former being manned by European seamen from the 'Success' and 'Eagle,' accompanied those ships to Bushire. During the voyage across the head of the Gulf, two trankies were captured by the boats of the two cruisers, and, in the afternoon of the 15th of April, the ships arrived in Bushire Roads, where they found some merchantmen, with the 'Drake,' Company's ship of fourteen guns, flying the Commodore's pennant, and having on board Mr. Robert Garden, a member of the Bombay Council, who had come with despatches from the Governor regarding the establishment of the factory at Bushire, which had been closed for five years, and to demand the release of Messrs. Beaumont and Green, two gentlemen of the Bussorah factory, taken on board the 'Tiger,' a small brig of eight guns, when she was captured by surprise by a fleet of the Shah's galivats.

At this time, Ahmed, the Imaum of Muscat, was fitting out, for the relief of Bussorah,[*] an army of ten thousand men, and his fleet, "which," says Parsons, who passed through Muscat on his way to Bombay, "consisted of thirty-four ships of war, four of forty-four guns each (which were built at Bombay), five frigates, from eighteen to twenty-four guns each; the remainder are ketches and galivats from fourteen to eight guns." This relief came too late, and, after a resistance of eight months, Bussorah fell to the arms of Sadoc Khan, but in the following

[*] Mr. Francis Warden, Member of Council at Bombay, in a memorandum on the "Rise and Progress of the Arab tribes in the Persian Gulf," prepared in August, 1819, states that one of the pretexts set forth by Kurreem Khan, Shah of Persia, for attacking Bussorah, was the granting of aid by the Pasha of Bagdad to the Imaum of Muscat, which prevented him from subduing the Province of Oman. On the death of Kurreem Khan in 1779, Bussorah was reoccupied by the Turks, and from that time may be dated the decline of Persian influence in the Gulf, the contests for superiority between the different petty chiefs involving a condition of anarchy, which, subsequently, required the strong hand of the Indian Government to allay.

year Imaum Ahmed recaptured it, for which the Sultan of Turkey paid him a *kharaj*, or annual subsidy, which was continued up to the time of his grandson, Seyyid Said.

Before commencing the narrative of the part taken by the Bombay Marine in the wars waged with Hyder Ally and his son, Tippoo Sultan, and in the struggle with France, when that fine seaman Sir Edward Hughes met with his match in the Bailly de Suffrein, perhaps the greatest Admiral France has produced, we will briefly recapitulate the condition of the *matériel* of the Service, from the time of its formation up to the year 1776.

When the Company's relations with the Portuguese became more amicable, Mr. Methwold, the President at Surat, in the year 1636, entered into a commercial convention with the Viceroy of Goa, whereby the English were permitted to build four "pinnaces," two at Damaun, and two at Bassein, for the protection of their local trade. Upon the acquisition of Bombay by the Company, the Commissioners appointed by Sir George Oxenden to report upon the island and port, recommended that a dry dock should be built for the purpose of constructing ships of war; and the Court of Directors, in furtherance of this proposal, despatched, in 1670, Mr. Warwick Pett, a naval architect of repute, to construct two vessels for the defence of the island, and to instruct the natives in the art of shipbuilding. Orders were likewise given for two brigantines to be armed for the protection of the Malabar coasting trade.

In 1671 Mr. Aungier, President of the factory at Surat, foreseeing the probability of an attempt by the Dutch, with whom we were at war, to capture the island of Bombay, which, indeed, they made in the following year, and alarmed at the strength of the fleets of the Seedee and other Powers, as compared with his own almost defenceless state, urged the Court of Directors to permit him to build and maintain a respectable naval force. The Court consented to this proposal, so far as to sanction the construction and equipment of two frigates, and three sloops. In 1673, Captain Shaxton had trained one hundred men of his military force, to serve as marines on board the Company's vessels intended for the defence of the island, and Fryer,* who arrived here at this time, speaking of the ships of war then in the harbour, remarks :—" Under the castle, besides innumerable little vessels, as hoys, ketches, and the like, lay three men-of-war, with their top armour out, waste cloths and pennants at every yard-arm ; to wit, the ' Revenge,' twenty-two guns ; the ' Mayboon,' taken from the Dutch, 220 tons ; and

---

* *See* Mr. John Fryer's work styled "A new account of East India and Persia, in eight letters, being nine years' travels, began in 1672, and finished 1681."

the 'Hunter,' fourteen guns." Only five years later succeeded the first of the Company's cold fits of economy, for, in 1678, the Court ordered the sale of all their armed ships, excepting the 'Revenge,' and a few small craft to defend the fisheries of the island. But Mr. Henry Oxenden declined to execute this order, the impolicy of which received, in the following year, a striking illustration, when the Mahrattas occupied Kenery, and the Seedee seized the neighbouring island of Henery, thereby placing Bombay almost in a state of blockade. Indeed, the Bombay Marine, owing to the injudicious reduction, was inadequate for the duties it was called upon to fulfil, which now included the protection of the trade of the Company and of the Mogul in the Indian Ocean and Persian Gulf. Powerful hostile fleets swept these seas, having on board thousands of desperadoes, who sailed under the flag of Sumbhajee, of the Seedee of Jinjeera, and other native semi-independent Powers; while pirates, Native and European, under leaders like Kidd and Avory, became the dread of the Mercantile Marine and of the seaboard of India and the Eastern Islands. We have seen that these latter defied the attempts to extirpate them not only of the Company's Marine, and of the ships of war of Holland and Portugal, but of a powerful Royal Navy squadron* employed in those seas.

The larger vessels for the Company's service continued to be constructed at Surat, and we find that, in 1735, when a ship called the 'Queen,' was built, Mr. Dudley, the master-attendant, was so pleased with the exertions of the Parsee foreman, Lowjee Nusserwanjee by name, that he induced him and a few shipwrights to proceed to Bombay, where a small portion of the site of the present dockyard, then occupied by the principal officers of the Marine, the huts of the Lascars, and the common gaol, was set apart for a building yard.

Constant references are made by old writers to the want of timber for shipbuilding purposes, and so late as 1810, after the first expedition against the Joasmi pirates at Ras-ul-Khymah, Sir John Malcolm suggested that a prohibition should be issued against the exportation of teak, though this proposal had for its object rather the prevention of the construction of a new piratical fleet by that maritime Arab community. On the arrival at Bombay of Lowjee Nusserwanjee, this want of timber led to some delay, but when arrangements were made for secu-

* The captains of these ships were not above engaging in business of a remunerative nature, for we find that three of them returned to England with full cargoes of goods shipped by Sir Nicholas Waite during his popularity with the Nawab of Surat, while the fourth, the 'Harwich,' was wrecked off the coast of China. In 1769, a squadron, under the command of Sir John Lindsay, consisting of the 'Stag,' thirty-two guns, 'Hawk,' sloop, and 'Aurora,' frigate, Captain Lee, having on board as purser, Falconer, the famous sea-poet, sailed from Spithead, but the 'Aurora' foundered with all hands. Sir John Lindsay cruised off the Malabar coast until the arrival of Sir Robert Harland's squadron in 1771.

ring a sufficient supply, he commenced building cruisers for the Company's war Marine, and vessels for the trade of the port.

In consequence of his success, the Superintendent of Marine proposed, in 1754, and the local government sanctioned, a dry dock, which was constructed for the small sum of 12,000 rupees. A few years later, wet docks, sufficiently large for a seventy-gun ship, were commenced, for which Bombay affords exceptional advantages, owing to the rise and fall of the tide being considerable and periodical, the rise at ordinary spring tide being about fourteen feet, and not unfrequently as high as eighteen feet. Mr. Ives, surgeon to Admiral Watson's flag-ship, the 'Kent,' writing of this dock in 1758, on his return from Calcutta in the 'Revenge,' then commanded by Commodore James, says:—' We expected to have found the dock at Bombay capable of receiving a ship of seventy guns, agreeable to the repeated assurances given to Mr. Watson, but we were disappointed in this particular, the hands to carry it on being very scarce. However, Mr. Hough, superintendent of the Company's Marine here, was indefatigable in his endeavours to finish this work of immense labour and the dock is now completed. Commodore (afterwards Admiral) Stevens was here obliged to heave down the 'Elizabeth,' one of the ships of his squadron, to stop a considerable leak, but in the first attempt she had the misfortune to spring her mainmast, by which accident he was detained a longer time than he wished."

Bombay, at this time, possessed every facility for careening and refitting shattered ships, and was largely used by the fleets in effecting repairs after their encounters with the French, or the elements. Speaking of the Bombay Marine in 1754, on the occasion of his first visit to Bombay, at the time of the expedition against Gheria, Mr. Edward Ives* says: "Our East India Company had here one ship of forty guns, one of twenty, one grab of eighteen guns, and several other vessels; more also were building." During Niebuhr's visit to Bombay in 1763, the third basin of the dock was built, and he says that the Bombay Government "maintain eight or ten small ships of war with a number of armed barks," and states that they were much employed in convoying the Company's ships and country vessels from port to port for which service the "natives were obliged to pay very dear." Writing in 1775 of the capabilities of Bombay dockyard, Mr. Abraham Parsons says: "Bombay

* Mr. Ives also gives a description of the fleets of vessels belonging to the Mahrattas and Mannajee Angria, brother to Toolajee, the Chief of Gheria, lying in the harbour. He says:—" Each fleet consisted of about thirty sail, but among Mannajee Angria's there were two ketches which they called grabs." He describes the vessels of these fleets as "not being unlike the tartans of the Mediterranean, only a great deal lower; they carried two guns in their bow, and a vast number of men."

was first so-called by the Dutch, literally in English, Goodbay, which it is in all respects, being so very capacious as to be capable of receiving any number of ships of any size or draft of water, with room sufficient to moor clear of each other in safety. Here is a dockyard, large and well contrived, with all kinds of naval stores deposited in proper warehouses, together with great quantities of timber and planks for repairing and building ships, and forges for making of anchors as well as every kind of smaller smith's work. It boasts such a dry dock as, perhaps, is not to be seen in any part of Europe, either for size or convenient situation. It has three divisions, and three pairs of strong gates, as to be capable of receiving and repairing three ships of the line at the same or at separate times; as the outermost ship can warp out, and another be admitted in her place every spring tide without any interruption of the work doing to the second or innermost ships; or both the outermost and the second ship can go out, and two others be received in their places without hindrance to the workmen employed on the third, or innermost ship. Near the dock is a convenient place to grave several ships at once, which is done as well, and with as great expedition, as in any dock in England. Near the dockyard is a rope walk, which for length, situation, and convenience equals any in England, that in the King's Yard, at Portsmouth, only excepted, and, like that, it has a covering to shelter the workmen from the inclemency of the weather in all seasons. Here are made cables and all sorts of lesser cordage, both for the Royal Navy, the Company's Marine, and the merchant ships, which trade to these ports of India. Besides cordage made of hemp, cables, hawsers, and all kinds of smaller ropes, are made of the external fibres of the cocoa-nut, which they have in such abundance in India, as to make a great article of trade among the natives of this place, and those along the coast between Bombay and Cape Comorin. The yarn made of these fibres is mostly manufactured in the towns and villages on, or near, the sea-coast of Malabar; many vessels belonging to the natives are laden entirely with this yarn, which they always find a quick sale for at Bombay and Surat, let the quantity be ever so great, as it is the only cordage made use of amongst the small trading vessels of the country; large ships use much of it made into cables, hawsers, and smaller ropes; it is called kyah.* Ships built at Bombay are not only as strong, but as handsome, and are as well finished as ships built in any part of Europe; the timber and plank of which they are built, so far exceeds any in Europe for durability, that it is usual for ships to last fifty or sixty years; as a proof of which I am informed

* This kyah, or coir, is still the only description of yarn in use among the coasting-craft on the Malabar coast, being cheaper and equally as strong as hemp or Manilla yarn, though it is more wiry and is not so handy when wet.

that the ship called the 'Bombay,' grab, of twenty-four guns, (the second in size belonging to the Company's Marine) has been built more than sixty years, and is now a good and strong ship. This timber and plank are peculiar to India only; what grows to the south, on the coast of Malabar, is, however, very good, and great quantities of it are brought to Bombay; it is called tick, and will last in a hot climate longer than any wood whatever."

Mr. Parsons speaks as follows of the strength of the Bombay Marine, at the time of his visit:—" The Company's Marine, on the Bombay establishment, are more than twenty in number, the largest of which is the 'Revenge,' mounting twenty-eight guns, twenty of which are 12-pounders; the second is the 'Bombay' grab, the remainder are from sixteen to eight guns; and as there are several little piratical States, both on the north as well as on the south coast of Bombay, the coasting trade could not be carried on in safety without being convoyed by such vessels belonging to the Company. It is usual to see sixty or eighty coasting vessels sailing between Surat and Bombay, convoyed by one or two of these vessels." Mr. Parsons cruised down the Malabar coast with Commodore Moore in the 'Revenge,' in company with the 'Bombay' and the 'Drake,' which lost her Commander, Captain Field, who was drowned while going on board his ship off Onore. His loss," he adds, " is greatly regretted by all who knew him, as he was a young man of excellent character."

In the year 1775, the head builder of Bombay dockyard was Mr. Manackjee Lowjee, one of the famous Parsee firm of ship-builders, of whom, perhaps, the most remarkable was his nephew, Mr. Jamsetjee Bomanjee, who built for the British navy some line-of-battle ships and several frigates which were remarkable for their strength and seaworthy qualities. Some estimate of the durability of the work of these eminent Parsee builders, who were, for more than a century, associated with the Bombay Marine and the Indian Navy, may be gathered from the history of the 'Swallow,' (called after a cruiser of the same name) built by Manackjee Lowjee, and launched at Bombay on the 2nd of April, 1777. After serving in many seas, and in the Indian, Royal and Danish Navies, for a period of more than half-a-century, the 'Swallow' ended her career, not in a ship-breaker's yard, but on a shoal in the Hooghly; she was one of those craft of which the old 'Bombay' grab was, perhaps, as regards longevity, the most remarkable specimen. Briefly, the 'Swallow's' career, from the cradle to the grave, was as follows:—She was first employed as a Company's packet, and made several trips between India and England; was then taken into the Bombay Marine, and, after a short time, returned to the Packet Service, in which she continued for many years.

She was commanded by the following officers:—Captains Bendy, Hall, Penny (while in the Marine), Anderson, Curtis, Clifton, and Luard; and, during the period she was employed as a packet, the following public characters were passengers on board her:—Lord Macartney, when returning to England from his Government of Madras; Lord Cornwallis, on his appointment to India as Governor-General, and on his return from Calcutta; Sir John Shore, on retiring from the office of Governor-General; Mr. Petrie, from the Council at Madras; and various other functionaries of rank. About the year 1800, the 'Swallow," not being required as a packet, was sold to the Danes, fitted in London, and went to Copenhagen, whence she is supposed to have proceeded to the West Indies; but while there, was seized by a British man-of-war for a breach of treaty, and condemned as a prize. She was cut out from her anchorage by a sloop-of-war after a severe action, in which the British ship lost a number of her crew. She was then purchased into the King's service, became the 'Silly' sloop of war, and was latterly commanded by Captain Sheriff; after serving some time in the West Indies, she was, on her passage home, dismasted, and received other damage, in a violent gale of wind. On her return to England, she was sold out of the King's service, and bought by some merchants in London; made three voyages to Bombay, her parent port, as a free-trader, and was lost on the James and Mary shoal in the Hooghly, on the 16th June, 1823.

During the course of the war between France and England, the two countries, not content with carrying on hostilities in Europe and America, also strove for the mastery on the continent of Asia, and very severe, but generally indecisive, engagements were fought at sea, in which we find occasional mention of the Company's ships as participating, though, from their size, they were, necessarily, unable to fight in line of battle.

Early in 1799* the Bombay Government resolved to undertake an expedition against Mahé, the only settlement now remaining to the French on the Malabar coast. Accordingly, a combined military and naval force, the latter drawn from the Bombay Marine, was despatched from Bombay, and, though the place was of considerable strengh, it surrendered on the 19th

* In July of the preceding year, a British squadron, which included a Company's ship, sailed for Madras, under command of Sir Edward Vernon, for the object of blockading Pondicherry, and, on the 10th of August, encountered a superior French squadron, under M. Tronjolly, when a hardly-contested action ensued, which was concluded by the retreat to Pondicherry of the French squadron. On the British proceeding thither, M. Tronjolly withdrew with his ships, when the siege was prosecuted with great vigour, all the Marines and two hundred seamen being landed from the fleet. The French Governor defended the town with resolution, but capitulated the day before the intended assault.

of March without firing a shot. On the 29th of November the fort was blown up and evacuated. During this year, also, a Bombay Marine squadron, consisting of the 'Bombay,' 'Durruck,' 'Eagle,' and 'Manchester,' with some armed pattamars, were actively employed on the coast, the seamen and marines assisting in the operations on shore conducted against Surdan Khan, an officer in the service of Hyder Ally.

In the latter part of 1780, Sir Edward Hughes, while on the West Coast of India, dealt a fatal blow to the rising maritime power of Hyder Ally, against whom we were engaged in a life and death struggle. On the 8th of December, being with his squadron off Mangalore, the principal dockyard and naval arsenal of Hyder Ally, the Admiral saw two ships, a large grab, three ketches, and many small vessels, at anchor in the roads with the Nawab's flag flying on board them. He immediately stood in, and, finding them to be vessels of force, and all armed, anchored as close to them as the depth of water would allow, and ordered the boats of the squadron to destroy them, under cover of the fire of two ships of the Bombay Marine. This service was conducted with the usual spirit and activity of British seamen, and, in two hours, they took and burnt two ships, one of twenty-eight, and the other of twenty-six guns; one ketch of twelve guns was blown up by the enemy at the instant the boats were boarding her; another ketch of ten guns, which cut her cable, and endeavoured to put to sea, was taken, and the third, with the smaller vessels, were forced on shore, the grab only escaping into the harbour, after having thrown everything overboard to lighten her.* For their conduct in this affair the officers and crews of the Company's ships gained the commendation of the Admiral.†

* Vol. I. of Ralfe's " Naval Biography of Great Britain."

† The Indian Government not satisfied with engaging in hostilities against the French and Hyder Ally, undertook operations against Negapatam, the principal Dutch settlement on the Coromandel coast. On the 21st of October, the seamen and marines of the fleet were landed, and, after some hard fighting, during which the Governor made two desperate sallies, he surrendered the fort, the garrison of which numbered over six thousand five hundred men, being considerably more than the besieging army. With Negapatam the whole of the Dutch settlements near the Tanjore coast, fell into the hands of the English, and the fleet, with five hundred troops on board, proceeded to Trincomalee, which was captured on the 11th of January, 1782.

Early in 1781 large naval reinforcements were prepared by the British and French Governments for the prosecution of the war in India. M. de Suffrein, one of the best and bravest Admirals France has produced, left Brest with a powerful squadron, and Commodore Johnstone also sailed for the East, with a convoy of ships, having on board some troops under General Meadows. The two fleets fought a sanguinary action at Praya Bay, in St. Jago, one of the Cape de Verd Islands, in which the English gained the advantage, and after escorting the convoy to the Cape, the Commodore returned to Europe with the greater portion of the ships of war. Some of the transports, with troops, under the command of Colonel Mackenzie, proceeded to Bombay, and thence to Calicut, and General Meadows and Colonel Fullarton, with the chief part of the troops in the men-of-war, sailed in quest of Sir Edward Hughes, and reached Madras on

In the year 1782 the Bombay Marine sustained a great loss in the foundering at sea of one of its finest ships, having on board a picked crew, and commanded by one of the best and most experienced officers in the Service.

In a quaint old work, called "The Oriental Navigator" (2nd Edition, 1801) there appears a notice of the loss, off Bombay, of the frigate 'Revenge,' in one of the gales that are occasionally experienced just before the first break of the south-west monsoon. On the 19th of April, 1782, the 'Revenge,' in company with the 'Royal Adelaide,' sailed for Anjengo, but, experiencing the full fury of the gale, the latter returned to Bombay harbour. The 'Revenge,' commanded by Captain Hardy, described as "an able seaman, and his ship the first in the Bombay Marine," was not seen after the 20th of April, and is supposed to have foundered in the terrific gale then blowing,

the 12th of February, the day following the arrival of the Admiral. Within twenty-four hours De Suffrein arrived off that port, and, after various manœuvres, an indecisive action was fought on the 17th, after which Sir Edward Hughes steered for Trincomalee, and the French Admiral proceeded to Porto Novo, on the coast, where he landed two thousand men to co-operate with an army under command of Tippoo, son of Hyder Ally, which soon after effected the reduction of Cuddalore. The rival fleets soon proceeded to sea again, and, on the 12th of April, a severe action was fought off Trincomalee, in which both fleets suffered severely, but with no decisive result. Of the total casualties, one hundred and thirty-seven killed and four hundred and thirty wounded in the British fleet, the 'Superb,' Sir Edward Hughes' flag-ship, lost no less than fifty-nine of the former and ninety-six of the latter. The loss of the 'Victory' at Trafalgar was only slightly in excess of this, being fifty-seven killed and one hundred and two wounded. A third engagement took place off Negapatam on the 6th of July, and, when victory appeared within the grasp of the British fleet, which sustained a loss of seventy-seven killed and two hundred and thirty-three wounded, a sudden shift of wind enabled De Suffrein to effect his retreat. Undismayed by his losses, the French Admiral refitted his shattered ships, two of which had actually struck their colours in the last action, but hoisted them again upon De Suffrein firing into them, and, by the 1st of August, had to put to sea again, and, being joined by reinforcements from Europe, arrived before Trincomalee on the 25th of August. His great rival did not display equal celerity in refitting his fleet, and, when he sighted that port on the 2nd of September, having left Madras on the 20th of August, it was only to find that the forts had capitulated two days before. The French fleet sailed on the following morning, when the British Admiral, anxious to redeem his laurels, attacked them with resolution, and darkness alone put an end to a desperate conflict of three hours' duration, in which the English gained a decided advantage, though with the loss of fifty-one killed, including two captains, and two hundred and eighty-three wounded. Sir Edward Hughes now returned to Madras, and expressed his determination to proceed to Bombay, notwithstanding the earnest solicitations of the Council, who appealed to him not to leave the coast defenceless. Captain Ritchie, Superintendent of Indian Marine Surveys, offered to conduct the fleet to a safe anchorage at the mouth of the Hooghly during the north-easterly monsoon, the effects of which on his shattered ships, the Admiral greatly dreaded, but Sir Edward was deaf to all expostulations, and sailed for Bombay on the 15th of October. That night a tempest burst over Madras roadstead, and, on the following morning, the whole neighbouring coast was strewed with wrecks of several large ships, and over one hundred small craft. Famine now raged, to which were added the horrors of a pestilence, but the fears of the Madrasees, who daily expected the appearance of the dreaded Bailly de Suffrein, were allayed by the opportune arrival, on the 19th of October, of Sir Richard Bickerton with five sail of the line, and four thousand three hundred European troops.

in which the Royal sloop of war, 'Cuddalore,' and 'Fletcher,' transport, also went down, and the 'Nancy,' transport, and Essex, Indiaman, were dismasted. The same writer says:—
"A part of the mainmast of the 'Revenge,' which had been carried away a little above the deck, was found and brought to Bombay, and, by some particular mark, known by the builder."

The Bombay cruisers were employed at the siege of Tellicherry, and remained there till about the middle of May. The 'Neptune' and 'Royal Admiral,' two of the blockading squadron, then sailed to the northward of the Equator, into the limits of the south-east monsoon, and, after making their westing, steered for Bombay with the south-west moonsoon.

In December, 1782, death removed from this scene of strife, Hyder Ally,* the most formidable enemy the Company had yet encountered in India, though he was not unworthily succeeded by his son, Tippoo Sahib, who had already acquired laurels at the expense of the English by the capture of Cuddalore. Tippoo immediately marched from Paniani, where he was engaged in operations against a small force under Colonel Humberstone, the same brilliant officer who was mortally wounded on board the 'Ranger,' on the 8th of April, 1783, to assume command of the main army, which he joined near Velore about the end of December: here he received a large reinforcement of French troops, with twenty-two guns, and was preparing to offer battle to General Stuart's small army of three thousand Europeans, and eleven thousand five hundred Natives, when he learned of a formidable invasion on the western coast. In the latter part of December, 1782, Colonel Humberstone, after Tippoo's retreat from Paniani, despatched his Sepoys by land to Tellicherry, and his Europeans by sea to Merjee, on the Malabar coast. In the succeeding operations the ships of the Bombay Marine participated, and here a young officer, Mr. (afterwards Sir) John Hayes, destined to add lustre to the annals of the Service, underwent his *baptême de feu*. General Matthews proceeded from Bombay with a strong military and naval force, the latter consisting of ships of the Bombay Marine, under Commodore Emptage, who flew his broad pennant on board the 'Bombay,' twenty-eight guns, and, after capturing the hill fort of Rajamun-

---

* In the "History of Hydur Naik," (as Hyder Ally was called) an original Persian MS. written by Meer Hussein Ally Khan Kirmani, translated by Colonel W. Miles, of the Hon. East Indian Company's service, and published in 1842, in describing the battle of Muhammed Bunder, soon after Sir Eyre Coote's arrival at Madras from Bengal, in 1780, the writer speaks of the great effect of the fire of two ships-of-war. He says:—"Meer Ali Ruza Khan was galloping at the head of his cavalry along the beach, intending by an attack on the troops and followers of the English army to throw them into confusion, when, of a sudden, a shot from a cannon of one of the ships struck him and broke the arm of his valour, and threw him off his horse." The native historian then describes his death, and the defeat and dispersion of Hyder Ally's army.

droog, at the mouth of the river of Merjee, (also called Merjan and Tudree) proceeded against the fort of that name, which soon fell to his arms.

Thence the combined expedition sailed for Onore, a very strong fort situated near the entrance of a salt water river, between Merjee and Hog Island. All the troops that could be spared from the defence of other ports on this extensive coast, were ordered to meet the General at that point, to assist in his intended operations, but, before their arrival, the place was captured. On the 1st of January, 1783, the British batteries, and the guns from the ships, opened on Onore, and, on the 6th, the breach being reported practicable, the fort was stormed. Several of the enemy fell in the first fury of the assault, and the rest, to the number of two thousand, laid down their arms and were set at liberty. Leaving Captain Torriano, the commanding officer of Artillery, in charge of the fort, the Commander-in-Chief embarked on the 15th of January, to join the army which, in conjunction with the squadron, on the following day captured Cundapoor, a place of considerable importance on the Canara coast. Thence proceeding inland, the General, in obedience to orders received from the Bombay Government, ascended the Hussain Ghurry Ghaut, and captured Bednore, the rich capital of this part of the Mysore dependencies, which surrendered through the treachery of the Governor. Most of the minor forts now capitulated, but Ananpore, Mangolore, and some others, still remained in possession of the enemy. The former was taken by storm on the 14th of February, when, it is said, the garrison were put to the sword, but Mangalore held out until the 9th of March, when it also capitulated. During the siege the Bombay squadron did good service, and it is recorded of Mr. Hayes, then only fifteen years of age, that he commanded the launch of the 'Bombay,' and in the most gallant manner cut out from under the batteries two of the enemy's armed vessels.

After this the tide of success ebbed, and the British Army met with considerable reverses. Bednore was recaptured, Merjee and other forts were retaken, and, on the 23rd of May, Mangolore* was invested by a powerful army under Tippoo

* On the 23rd of January, the important city of Mangalore, to which Tippoo had laid siege since the preceding May, with an army estimated at nearly ninety thousand men, was surrendered to him by Colonel Campbell, who, having nobly defended the place with only seven hundred Europeans, and two thousand eight hundred and fifty natives, marched to Tellicherry with the honours of war.

Before the conclusion of peace between the French and English, which, by the withdrawal of the troops of the former, was one of the chief reasons that induced Tippoo to accede to a cessation of hostilities, their respective fleets, under the two great rivals, De Suffrein and Hughes, fought an action on the 20th of June, off Cuddalore, in which the French Admiral escaped defeat only by his able tactics. Hughes retired to Madras, leaving to its fate the British army besieging Cuddalore, which must have encountered defeat owing to the superiority of the combined forces of Bussy and De Suffrein, had not intelligence been received of the conclusion of peace. When we regard the constancy displayed by Sir Edward Hughes

Sahib, who had marched across from the Carnatic. In consequence of complaints against General Matthews for alleged rapacity, and for having violated the rules of civilized warfare, in ordering his troops to give no quarter to the enemy taken in arms at the storm of Onore and Ananpore, he was recalled before these events took place, and it was while General McLeod, accompanied by Colonel Humberstone, Major Shaw, and other officers, was proceeding in the 'Ranger' to the Bednore coast to take up the command-in-chief, that the action with the Mahratta fleet, already detailed, took place.

One of the finest episodes of the war was the defence of Onore,* against an army of ten thousand men, by Captain Torriano, whose force consisted of seven hundred and forty-three officers and men, of whom only forty-two were European soldiers; of the remainder, two hundred and seventy-one were regular Sepoys, and sixty-one were European and Native seamen from the Company's galivat 'Wolfe,' of six guns. With this garrison, assisted by the guns of the 'Wolfe,' which maintained a heavy flanking fire on the enemy, and assisted materially in the defence, Captain Torriano held the place for several months, occasionally receiving some supplies from a Company's cruiser. On the 12th of August, when the 'Wolfe' fired a salute in honour of what is known in the Western Presidency as "cocoa-nut day,"† the enemy were so exasperated at what they regarded as an act of

during these protracted operations, in which he encountered in five general actions, a superior fleet, commanded by perhaps the best admiral France has ever produced, we must award him a high rank among the naval heroes of this country.

* Hyder Ally had always been desirous of rivalling the maritime power, if not of the English, which he recognized to be a hopeless task, at least of the Mahrattas, upon whose strong castle of Gheria with its ports, he must have cast an envious eye. He did his best with Onore and Mangalore, his chief ports, though neither of them were of any extent or value, and at both places he constructed ships. A writer who visited Onore in December, 1775, says of the ships he was constructing at that port:—"Here are two frigates building near the castle; one of thirty-two guns, the other of twenty-four guns. Being desirous to examine their construction, I went in company with two other English gentlemen near to them, without offering to go on board, lest it should give offence. The Governor, being there, overlooking the men at work, observing us walking away, very civilly invited us to go on board and examine them, adding that it would give him great pleasure if we would candidly give our opinions on them. We went on board both of them, and were surprised to find the work so well performed, particularly as they are the first ships of so great a burthen that have been built in Hyder Ally's country. When finished they will be two complete frigates, being very strong and of a fine mould; they have a prow and are what they call "grabs," and one of them is larger than the 'Bombay' grab. Instead of the head or stern fronting the river, their broadsides do; they are built with their sides parallel to the banks. On my asking how they launched them, I was told that when ready, they laid long, straight timbers squared, which reached from the ship's bottom to the water. Then they take away the supports from the side next the river, and the ship resting on those timbers, which are greased, by the force of elephants, first at one end, and then at the other, alternately, is pushed into the river."

† "Cocoa-nut-day" is so called by the English, from the natives of the coast throwing that fruit into the sea, previous to trusting vessels on it after the south-west monsoon which ends towards the latter part of September.

defiance that they opened fire upon her and shot away her mainmast. On the 20th, Captain Torriano, desirous of conveying news of his critical situation, sent off two boats from the 'Wolfe,' one to Mangalore and another to Sedashighur, but both were dashed to pieces on the bar, and the greater part of the crews were drowned.* On the 27th of October, one of the Company's cruisers arrived off the port from Mangalore, having General McLeod on board, who promised to relieve Captain Torriano as soon as he received sufficient reinforcements from Bombay to enable him to force Tippoo to raise the siege. On the 3rd of December, the 'Drake' cruiser, commanded by Captain Penny, and a large galivat, anchored off the port, bearing a letter from the Commander-in-Chief, informing Captain Torriano that he had entered into an agreement with the Nawab for the supply of provisions to the garrison, which were, accordingly, landed from the 'Drake.' Notwithstanding this agreement, the investment of Onore was continued, but, on the conclusion of peace in March, 1784, the fort was surrendered according to the terms, and the garrison embarked in the 'Wolfe,' and other vessels, which took them to Bombay. On landing here on the 18th of April, they mustered two hundred and thirty-eight, being the survivors of seven hundred and forty-three, the remainder having fallen by the sword, but chiefly by disease, aggravated by insufficient food.†

On the 4th of July, 1790, Lord Cornwallis, the Governor-General, signed a treaty with the Nizam, and another with the Mahrattas on the 1st of June, having for its object the punishment of Tippoo, who had captured Travancore by storm, and of whose power all parties to the triple league were in dread. The ships of the Bombay Marine participated in the ensuing operations, while the officers and men were landed to assist in the reduction of some of the forts that fell to the British arms. It was planned that General Meadows, who had been appointed to succeed Mr. Holland as Governor of Madras, with the principal part of the Carnatic army, should occupy the Coimbatore country, and endeavour to penetrate into the heart of Mysore; that General Abercromby, with the Bombay Army, should reduce the territory of Tippoo on the Malabar coast, and, if desirable, effect a junction with Meadows, while Colonel Kelly should guard the passes leading from Mysore into the Carnatic.

* A military writer on the defence of Onore, says :—" It should be recorded as a remarkable instance of attachment to the Service, that some of the lascars cast ashore on the point, were taken prisoners by the enemy and sent to Cundapore in irons; they effected their escape, and four months afterwards, when the garrison was in extreme distress, made their way through the enemy's camp at the imminent hazard of their lives, and returned to the fort."

† For a detailed account of the defence of Onore, see the "Naval and Military Magazine" for 1828. The Commander of the Forces, the Bombay Government and the Court of Directors, acknowledged in handsome terms the constancy and courage of Captain Torriano and his garrison.

Among the Bombay Marine officers who accompanied General Meadows, was Mr. Hayes, who was present with the division under Colonel Stuart at the capture of Palacatcherry, about thirty miles in the rear of the General's head-quarters at Coimbatore. General Abercromby, Governor of Bombay, had not been able to take the field until late in the season, but when he arrived at Tellicherry, he quickly made amends by the rapidity and success of his movements. He appeared off Cannanore with a combined military and naval force, and, after a brief resistance, the place surrendered; thence he proceeded to overrun the country, and, in the space of a few weeks, every place belonging to Tippoo in Malabar was wrested from him, and the whole province placed in possession of the English.* The Bombay Marine participated in the capture of Cannanore, and among the officers present here and at the fall of Carlie, Billeapatam, and other places, was Mr. Hayes. The last event in this war was the siege of Seringapatam, by Lord Cornwallis, who took the field in person, and it was prosecuted with such energy and success that, in March, 1792, Tippoo was glad to purchase peace by the cession of "one-half of the dominion of which he was possessed before the war," including the State of Coorg. England was at this time on the eve of that great struggle with her old enemy, which is known in history as the Revolutionary War, and though the Bombay Marine, from its numerical strength and the size of the ships, did not play an important part in the momentous conflict, yet on the occasions when the Service had opportunities for earning distinction, its officers and men worthily upheld the honour of the British name, and, in no instance, did the Bombay Marine lower its flag except to an enemy of greatly superior force.

* Mill's History, vol. v., p. 356. Also for details of the campaign, see Colonel Wilks' "Historical Sketches," vol. iii.

CHAPTER VI.

1772—1795.

Surveys of Officers of the Bombay Marine—The First Surveying Expedition—Lieutenant Blair's Survey and Administration of the Andaman Islands—Lieutenant McCluer's Surveys in the Persian Gulf and West Coast of India—The Loss of the 'Antelope' on the Pelew Islands and Escape of the Crew—Captain McCluer's Mission to the Pelew Islanders—His Surveys on the New Guinea Coast—Adventures and Death of Captain McCluer—Estimate of his Career and Character—Lieutenant Hayes' Surveys in the Eastern Archipelago.

WE will now turn to another, and more peaceful, arena of service in which the Bombay Marine, or Indian Navy, have earned lasting renown. We speak of the labours of the officers as surveyors, in which capacity they have achieved a reputation that is, perhaps, unrivalled, having regard to the numerical strength of the Service as compared with other navies or scientific services. The Indian Navy may, indeed, be proud of having been the *Alma Mater* of such men as McCluer, Blair, Court, Ross, Lloyd, Maughan, Crawford, Houghton, and, in more recent times, Carless, Haines, Moresby, Elwon, Felix Jones, Grieve, Constable, Taylor (now head of the new Indian Marine Surveying Department), Ward, and a host of other names too numerous to particularize. Among those whose scientific attainments impelled them in favour of research by land, may be mentioned the names of Wood, Ormsby, (whose familiarity with the Arabs has, probably been unsurpassed), Wellsted, Whitelock, Barker, and Wyburd, whose fate remains enshrouded in mystery; also Bowater and Stroyan, who fell victims to the savagery of the tribes among whom they journeyed.

In 1772 was fitted out the first surveying expedition undertaken by officers of the Bombay Marine. It consisted of the 'Fox,' schooner, of about 100 tons, and carrying six guns; the 'Dolphin,' ketch, of a similar armament, but rather smaller, and a pattamar, or native craft. The officers employed in this expedition, destined to be the precursor of many others of a like character, were Lieutenants Robinson (in command) and Porter, and Messrs. Blair and Mascall, midshipmen. These officers explored the coasts of Mekran, Scinde, Kattywar, and a part of that of Persia; also some portion of the coast of Arabia between Muscat and Ras-ul-hadd. The labours of these pioneers were of great benefit to navigation; the survey was minute in some parts, and, when we consider the very inferior instruments with which it was conducted, its correctness is remarkable, and reflects great credit on those officers.*

Between 1777 and 1795, Lieutenant Archibald Blair was actively engaged in making surveys of the Kattywar coast, Salsette, and the Andaman Islands. The official report of the survey of the Andamans, was laid before Lord Cornwallis, Governor-General, in June, 1789, and Dr. Mouatt, head of a mission sent in 1858,† to report upon these islands, says of this report that "not only did it contain a minute and accurate account of the survey conducted under the superintendence of that able officer (Blair), but it was illustrated by a chart, in which the situation of the most remarkable localities was distinctly marked, accompanied with a plan of three harbours, which he had found to be sure places of refuge for the shipping that stress of weather or other causes might drive on the Andaman coasts. The report merited and obtained much praise for the clearness with which it was written, and the intelligible manner in which various operations of the surveying party were described. The chief geographical features of the island were delineated with a fidelity that has secured the approbation of subsequent explorers."

So favourable were the reports of Lieutenant Blair and Colonel Colebrooke, who accompanied him, that the Supreme Government was induced to establish a penal settlement on the Andamans, and, accordingly, a colony, under the charge of Lieutenant Blair, was organized on a site then named Port Cornwallis, near the southern extremity of the great Andaman. This name was subsequently changed to "Old Harbour," and again to Port Blair, in honour of its surveyor, by which it is still known.

The spot chosen for the first colony in Port Cornwallis, or Port Blair, was Mark Island, now called Chatham Island, which was likewise proposed by the expedition of 1858 as the best site for the penal settlement. Captain Blair had taken with him a large staff of artificers from Bengal, as also provisions for six months. His first act was to raise a redoubt, on which he mounted the guns of his ship, the 'Ranger;' and then the

---

* A MS. of this survey was in existence about forty years ago, and is described by one who saw it, as wonderfully accurate, with the exception of the longitudes, as they had no chronometers.

† The combined Report of Dr. Mouatt, Lieutenant (the late commander) Heathcote, I.N., and Dr. Playfair, forming the mission of 1858, was submitted to Government, and was published in 1859, as the twenty-fifth number of the "Selections from the Records of the Government of India." For an account of Blair's Survey of the Andamans, see "Selections from the Records of the Government of India" (Home. No. XXIV.)

colonists, under the superintendence of their able chief, were engaged in clearing away the rank vegetation. While doing so, they were frequently brought into conflict with the natives, who came over from the mainland in considerable numbers, and greatly harassed the working parties by the insidious method of attack they adopted. A convenient watering place for ships was, however, at length cleared, and a reservoir constructed. Sheds were also erected within the redoubt, and the settlers were fully employed in the cultivation of land, which soon began to recompense their labour. On the 19th of December of the same year, Commodore Cornwallis, brother of the Governor-General, with H.M.'s ships 'Ariel' and 'Perseverance,' arrived at the settlement, and the Commodore, in his report to the Government, stated that he found it "fully equal to what it had been represented."

During the three years the penal settlement was established here, Captain Blair occupied his time in completing his surveys, and sailed round the island, when he discovered another larger and more commodious harbour, about two degrees to the northward, and on the eastern shore of the same island, in 43° 28' North lat., and 93° 12' East long. To this place, also called Port Cornwallis, the colony was removed, under orders from India, in 1792, and, in March of the following year, Captain Blair was succeeded in command of the settlement by Major Kyd of the Engineers.*

One of the earliest of the famous race of Indian Marine Surveyors† was Lieutenant John McCluer. The general accuracy

* In consequence of the war with France, the colony was put into a state of defence; large reinforcements were sent, and more guns mounted on the redoubt, to guard against an apprehended attack from the enemy. On the 14th of May, 1794, the Council of the Governor-General reported that the situation of Port Cornwallis was unfavourable to the health of the settlers, and, in the following year, fifty deaths occurred among the native convicts during the rainy season. In February, 1796, accordingly, we find that orders were issued by the Indian Government for the abandonment of this settlement, and the removal of the penal colony, numbering, with guards, seven hundred souls, to the newly-acquired colony of Prince of Wales' Island, as being a more healthy locality.

In the year 1795, Colonel Syme, while on his way to Ava, visited Port Cornwallis, and devoted a chapter to it in his work on the results of the Mission to Ava. After its abandonment in 1796 we hear nothing further from Cornwallis until the year 1824, when the fleet that conveyed Sir Archibald Campbell and his army to Burmah rendezvoused here.

During the course of the researches of the expedition sent to the Andamans in 1858, the Committee examined the site of the settlement formed at Port Cornwallis in 1792, and abandoned in 1796, owing to its unhealthiness, which the Committee ascribed to an extensive bank of mud skirted by belts of mangrove on the south-western extremity of Chatham Island. The remains of the first settlement, now known as Port Blair, were disentangled from the dense brushwood, and the fragments of brickwork were found in good preservation; in accordance with the recommendations of Dr. Mouatt, the convict colony, consisting of Bengal Mutineers, was established at Port Blair in 1858.

† During the latter part of the eighteenth century, between 1770 and 1785, Captain John Ritchie was head of the Marine Survey Department in Calcutta, and, in 1782, he offered to pilot the fleet of Sir Edward Hughes into safe

with which he surveyed a considerable part of the coast of India, entitled his charts, until the surveys of a more recent date, made by officers of the Indian Navy, to a place among the standard works of this description ; and this will be considered the more creditable to his zeal and abilities, when it is known that he was self-taught in this useful branch of science. His first essay in surveying was in the Persian Gulf, in the year 1785. The inaccuracies of the existing charts of this sea, and the deficiency of all authentic information relating to it, attracted his attention whilst employed there in the Company's Service, and he determined, with the limited means he possessed, to make up the defects, and to rescue from darkness the navigation of coasts frequented from the remotest ages of antiquity. It was enough for those ships, which visited the Persian Gulf for the purposes of trade, to guard themselves from the attacks of pirates, who were formidable impediments to the peaceful operations of surveying, and this necessity considered in conjunction with the infant state of the art, sufficiently accounts for this sea being so little known.

The length of time which a minute examination of the coast would have required, was too great, and the obstacles to be overcome too formidable, to admit of its being adopted ; but, as

anchorage at the mouth of the Hooghly during the north-east monsoon, which, however, was declined by the Admiral, who sailed from Madras for the Malabar coast. Captain Ritchie surveyed the coasts of Bengal and the mouths of the Ganges; his work formed part of the material for Major Rennel's map of Hindostan, and many of his charts were engraved by Dalrymple, the eminent hydrographer of the Company, while a MS. volume of his remarks is preserved in the India Office.

This volume is entitled Remarks upon the Coast and Bay of Bengal, the outlets of the Ganges and interjacent rivers, according to the surveys of John Ritchie, hydrographer to the United India Company. Contents.—1. Entrance to the Hooghly and remarks on its pilotage; 2. Rivers eastward to the Megna, Coast Islands; 3. Chittagong and Islands; 4. Tempests to which the head of the bay is subject; 5. Coast of Arracan ; 6. Coast of Ava to Cape Negrais; 7. Andaman Islands; 8. Nicobar Islands. Dalrymple engraved Ritchie's Chart of the Coromandel and Orissa coasts (1771) and others (See Mr. Clement Markham's " Memoir on the Indian Surveys.")

Captain Jervis says, in his " Report on Surveys," speaking of the work done by Captains Ritchie, Blair, and Michael Topping—the latter on the coasts of Arracan, the delta of the Ganges, andon the entire eastern coast thence to Cape Comorin :—" Captain Topping's observations on the currents on the Bay of Bengal, of the 1st of March, 1788, of the 16th of January, and 26th of June, 1792, may probably be found of essential service in future investigations respecting the retreat or advance of the sea on the coast of India, and the exact registration of the tides. His survey of the mouths of the Godavery river and Coringa roads, 18th of September, 1790, and 21st of January, 1791, and his proceedings and report on the Masulipatam Circar, drawn up with a view to ascertain the practicability of applying the waters of the rivers Krishna and Godavery, to the fertilisation of the land, and charts, observations, and levels, communicated 20th of February, 1794, and 2nd of October, 1795, may probably yet induce the Madras Government and authorities at home to reconsider that valuable project." These services led to Captain Topping's appointment as chief surveyor of Madras in 1794, when he drew up a scheme " for the improvement of the geography and navigation of India."

correct positions of the principal projecting points, as well as of the islands lying in the track of vessels, were most essential to the security of navigation, Lieutenant McCluer confined himself to doing this thoroughly. He corrected the best charts he could get, by means of careful observations, and made rough surveys of those harbours of which we were ill-informed.

His survey of the Persian coast is contained in two sheets, that including the south-eastern part of the coast, from the entrance of the Gulf, for a distance of three hundred miles, being on a smaller scale than the other; such as it is, the comparative accuracy of the principal points, rendered it superior to any other then extant, though it has long since been superseded. The other sheet contains the remainder of the coast, with the principal channel of the Shatt-ul-Arab as far up as Bussorah, distant about thirty leagues from the sea; this place, being at that time the chief seat of commerce and communication between India and the Turkish dominions, besides possessing an establishment of the East India Company, was much frequented by their ships. Lieutenant McCluer completed his survey of the north coast, an extent of about five hundred miles, within the space of three years. In the course of his progress he made drawings of various parts of the coast to facilitate the navigation, and wrote useful directions for the same purpose, which latter were used by Captain Horsburgh,* hydrographer to the East India Company, in the early editions of his East Indian Directory.

Lieutenant McCluer made a plan of the Cove of Muscat, whence considerable trade was carried on to China and India, as well as to Bussorah and the various ports in the Gulf. From his surveys, together with those of Captain Wainwright, R.N., in the 'Chiffonne,' the Hon. Captain J. Maude, R.N., in the 'Favourite,' Lieutenant T. Tanner, and other officers of the Marine, a chart of the Persian Gulf was compiled and published by the Admiralty in 1820, though it was superseded by the surveys undertaken in that year. In consequence of the dangerous character of the Arabian coast, owing to the pirates and the prevailing winds, this portion of the Gulf littoral was avoided as much as possible by trading vessels, and nothing was known concerning the navigation of this coast, until many years after this pioneer in the cause of hydrographical research had

---

* The first hydrographer to the Company was Mr. Alexander Dalrymple, who was appointed on the 8th of April, 1779, and in the same capacity to the Admiralty in 1795. He died on the 19th of June, 1808, aged 70, of chagrin caused by his dismissal from the latter post on the 28th of May preceding. Mr. Dalrymple's successor to the post of hydrographer to the Company was Captain Horsburgh, who had served in their ships in the East, and was admirably well fitted for the post. In 1808, Captain Horsburgh published the first edition of his Directory, for which he received a grant of 100 guineas from the Court, and on the 10th of November, 1810, he was appointed hydrographer, and all charts were examined by him up to the date of his death in 1836.

ceased from his labours, when a younger generation of officers of the Bombay Marine took up the arduous task, and completed a more accurate and detailed survey.

The next important survey undertaken by Lieutenant McCluer was that of the Western coast of India. In 1786, says Dalrymple, in his valuable Memoirs, the East India Company ordered the Bombay Government to survey the bank of soundings off Bombay and the entrance to the Gulf of Cambay. There is one paragraph in their instructions which is worth copying; it is as follows:—"Let what is done be done completely, and nothing left undetermined in this space; if any doubt arises, let them repeat their observations in such part, that an implicit confidence may be placed in their work when finished." Lieutenant McCluer had only one assistant (Lieutenant John Proctor) when he began this survey on the 12th of October, 1787, and his vessel, called the 'Experiment,' was too small for sounding in deep water, so that they did not carry the soundings out very far. Ragogee Angria then held possession of Kenery Island and Colaba, Henery Island belonging to the Peishwa. Ragogee had several ships, and, even as late as 1787, plundered every vessel he could lay hands on except those of the English. Besides the 'Experiment,' McCluer had a small pattamar. He says he left the 'Experiment' at Bancoot and went in the pattamar to Zyghur, but the natives would not let him sound and ordered him off. On one occasion he met off Bombay some of the pirates of Severndroog, who, on the same cruise, captured boats and passed Bancoot in triumph whilst he was there. The next day they sent their respects to the British Resident at Bancoot, acquainting him with what had been done, and told him that there were no English letters on board, but that had they found any they would have been happy to have forwarded them. Such was the state of affairs on the western coast of India so late as the last decade of the eighteenth century.

Lieutenant McCluer, assisted by Lieutenant Proctor, and, at a later date, by Lieutenants Ringrove, Skinner, and Wedgeborough, of the Marine, was employed, for some years, on a systematic survey of the West coast of India. He commenced at Bombay, from which point, as a central position, he extended his operations to the southward as far as Cape Comorin, and to the northward, including the Gulf of Cambay, occupying an extent of a thousand miles. The coast was well examined by soundings, and the principal points were determined chronometrically east and west from Bombay. The whole is contained in three sheets. The northern sheet includes the Gulf of Cambay and the coast of India as far south as the parallel of 19° North latitude; the middle sheet extends from thence to Carwar Head; and the southern sheet includes the remaining part of the coast as far as Cape Comorin. The resulting charts* were drawn by Lieutenant Wedgeborough, and many of McCluer's smaller plans were engraved by Dalrymple. McCluer also made one of the earliest plans of Bombay Harbour, assisted by Lieutenant Court, which was afterwards corrected by Dominicetti; and Lieutenant Wedgeborough made a chart of the Laccadive Islands, which were re-surveyed, in 1828, by Captain Moresby. The charts are accompanied by views of coasts, which seems to have been a favourite method of Mr. Dalrymple's and to which Lieutenant McCluer paid great attention ; and we may observe, there can be no doubt of the utility of such information to the navigator, when given with judgment. An extensive table of latitudes and longitudes was drawn up and published, with the notes which Lieutenant McCluer had made in the course of his survey of the coast. These latter appeared in their original state, and were made use of by Captain Horsburgh in his Directory. McCluer was now called away to another service, which may account for the appearance of hastiness and incompleteness in his work.

Captain Jervis, of the Bengal Engineers, who held the post of Surveyor-General of India, speaking of the accuracy of McCluer's work, says in his " Report on Surveys":—" I should not omit to notice the valuable maritime surveys of Captains Huddart and McCluer, aad Lieutenants Ringrove, Wedgeborough and Skinner, on the western coast of India, from 1790 to 1793, which still continue to be good authority to navigators of that coast, and were actually incorporated by Colonel Charles Reynolds,† in his map. At the time they were delivered to the Government, an outcry was raised against their accuracy, which subsequent inquiry has shown to be without a shadow of justice ; and I may mention it as a corroborative proof of the attention and skill which must have been bestowed on the subject by Captain McCluer, that in carrying on a trigonometrical and topographical survey of the coast upwards, with all the helps and improved methods for which our recent acquisition of the country afforded also greater facilities, I found the actual outlines of the coast and exact distances differ very immaterially from those in McCluer's charts, and I had the more favourable opportunity for verifying the fact, as the Superintendent of Marine furnished me with Captain McCluer's original drafts, on a large scale, for the express purpose.‡

* These surveys, with the exception of some roadsteads and detached bits of coast laid down by the late Captain Charles Montriou, and the portion from Beypoor to Comorin, by Captain Selby, remained as laid down by Lieutenant McCluer, until the year 1853, when Lieutenant A. Dundas Taylor, I.N., commenced the work, which he completed in six years.

† This map of Colonel Reynolds was, however, never published.

‡ A writer, reviewing, in 1829, the hydrographical services of Lieutenant McCluer, says of him :—

" When the works of an individual are carefully preserved and consulted as a

It is probable that the world has long since forgotten the circumstances attending the wreck of the Honorable Company's ship 'Antelope,' of fourteen guns, Captain Henry Wilson, off Coorora, one of the Pelew Islands, on the 9th of August, 1783, and the description of the natives given by Mr. G. Keate,* together with the fate of Prince Lee Boo, son of the King, Abba Thulle, who, accompanying the crew of the vessel to England, fell a victim to small-pox on the 27th of December, 1784, at the age of 20, and was interred in Rotherhithe Churchyard, where the Company erected a tomb, with a suitable inscription, to his memory. In Mr. Keate's interesting account of the loss of the 'Antelope,' justice is done to the excellent discipline maintained by Captain Wilson and his officers in the terrible hour when, at midnight, and amid a raging storm, the ship went ashore on an unknown coast, and not less on the following morning, when Captain Wilson proposed that the spirit casks should be staved. Keate says:—" All the sailors, with the utmost unanimity, and with one voice, declared, that however they might suffer from the accustomed recruit of strong liquor, yet, being sensible that having access to it, they might not at all times use it with discretion, they, to their lasting honour as men, gave their full assent to the Captain's proposal, and said, they were ready to go immediately to the ship and stave every vessel of liquor on board; which, on this day, they conscientiously performed; every cask was staved; and so scrupulously did they execute their trust, that there was not a single man amongst them who would take or taste a farewell glass of any liquor. Circumstanced as these poor fellows were, nothing but a long and well-trained discipline, and the real affection they bore their Commander, could have produced the fortitude and steady firmness which they testified on this occasion." On landing, the officers and crew at once set to work and extemporized a dockyard, and commenced the construction of a schooner from the materials of the wreck. Our author says:—" Each determined (unskilled however he might be) to exert his abilities and personal strength to promote and

standard authority by those who survive him, it is a sufficient proof of their excellence, and as much as he himself could desire. Those of Lieutenant McCluer have stood the test of nearly forty years; the considerable addition they formed to the stock of hydrographical information justly entitled their author to the acknowledgments of the maritime world; and at this distance of time we readily bestow our tribute to the memory of a man who has perpetuated his name by his valuable works. His first essay in the Persian Gulf, which alone proceeded from a desire of benefiting navigation, was a fair promise of that zeal which he afterwards displayed in the survey of the coast of Hindostan."

* See "An Account of the Pelew Islands, composed from the journals and communications of Captain Henry Wilson, and some of his officers, who, in August, 1783, were there shipwrecked, in the 'Antelope,' a packet belonging to the Hon. East India Company, by George Keate, Esq., F.R.S," London, 1788. In this work is a plan, with soundings, of the harbour called "Englishman's Harbour," in which they were wrecked, by Captain Wilson.

aid the general plan. Those who were appointed of the carpenter's crew were desired by Captain Wilson to regard Mr. Barker (one of the officers) as their director, and to receive from him such appointments and directions in that department as he should judge most convenient, after he had experienced their separate abilities. Mr. Sharp, the surgeon, and Mr. M. Wilson, were appointed to saw down trees, in which employment the Captain often worked himself. The boatswain, who had formerly served part of an apprenticeship to a blacksmith, now resumed his old avocation, assisted by a mate. The gunner was to see all the arms kept in good order, and occasionally to assist the carpenter's crew. On the 18th of August, it was judged expedient to form a barricade in front of the tents towards the sea; which was done by driving a double row of strong posts, interlaced with branches of trees, to form a thick fence, the space between the two rows of stakes being filled with logs of wood, stones, and sand, to render it as solid as possible. On the inside was raised a foot bank, on which they could stand and fire, in case of being attacked, with an opening left for one of the 6-pounders, which it was intended should be got from the ship the first opportunity, and placed there. They also mounted two swivels (which were large ones) on the stumps of two trees that had been sawed down, in a manner so that they might be pointed in every necessary direction."

On the 4th of November, they set to work felling trees to construct the launching ways, and, on the 9th, that is, in exactly three months time, the officers and crew of the 'Antelope' had completed the schooner, which they christened the 'Oroolang,' after one of the islands; and, when we consider the want of necessary implements and materials, this must be regarded as one of the most extraordinary instances on record of the ingenuity and perseverance for which British sailors are noted. Keate writes:—" The night of the 9th of November proving fine, every hand had sufficient employment in preparing things for launching the vessel; they swept her with a lower-shroud hawser, and carried out an anchor and hawser ahead, and got a runner and tackle purchase upon it; they likewise got a post with wedges set against the stern-post, and everything ready before daylight. The tide ebbed extraordinarily low this night, insomuch that some of them walked dry to the flowerpot island, which had never been done at other time before since their coming to this place; it was low water rather before two o'clock this morning. At daylight they began to try their work, to see if their preparations would answer their wishes, and got the vessel down about six feet; they then stopped till high water, and sent to the King, who, with all his attendants, came to be present at the launch. About seven o'clock our people happily got their vessel afloat, to the general joy of every spectator, all appearing deeply interested in the success of this event. The English gave three loud huzzas at her going off, in which the Natives joined, and shook hands with each other with a cordiality but seldom experienced. The vessel was immediately hauled into a dock that had been dug for her, and safely moored, when all went to breakfast—the King and the rupacks (chiefs) with the Captain, the attendants with the people; this was, indeed, the happiest and most comfortable meal they had eaten since the loss of the 'Antelope.' When breakfast was over, they got out shears, and took in the masts, water-casks, and the two 6-pounders. They now made the King a present of all the other tools they could spare; and took up the ways, on account of the nails, of which they were in want. When the flood tide came in in the afternoon they hauled the vessel into the basin, which was a deep place of four or five fathom water, in the middle of the level sandy flat of the harbour, large enough to hold three vessels of the same magnitude where they could lie afloat at low water. In the night they got on board all their provisions, stores, ammunition, and arms, except such as were intended to be given to Abba Thulle; and renewed their labour in the morning, taking on board their anchors, cables, and other accessories, making bitts, and fitting a rail across the stem of the vessel."

On the same day, the King invested Captain Wilson with " the order of the Bone," constituting him a rupack, or chief, of the first rank. The schooner sailed on the 12th of November, to the regret of all the islanders, having on board Prince Lee Boo, the King's second son, and arrived in Macao in safety on the 30th of November, when they took passage to England in one of the Company's trading ships. During their stay on the island, a portion of the crew, with their arms and some swivel guns, accompanied the King, at his urgent request, on three expeditions against his rebellious subjects in other islands of the group; when their services were decisive in compelling submission. Among the officers of the 'Antelope,' of whom a list is given in Mr. Keate's work, appear the names of two midshipmen, Messrs. John Wedgeborough and Robert White, described as "from Christ's Hospital," who, subsequently, earned distinction as surveyors.

The Court of Directors acknowledged the kind hospitality displayed by the islanders to the crew of the 'Antelope,' between the 9th of August and the 12th of November, by directing the Bombay Government to fit out two ships of the Marine, to proceed to the Pelew Islands for the purpose of carrying presents to the King, and to inform him of the death of his son. Another object of the mission was to make a survey of the Pelew group, with the view of ascertaining whether there was a harbour capable of affording safety and provision to any of the Company's ships which might be disabled through stress of weather in their voyages to or from China. That such might be the case was very desirable, on account of the friendly disposition of the Natives towards the English, and the convenient situation of the islands, though the extensive coral reefs which surround the group, render their approach so dangerous and difficult as to prevent their being much frequented. In obedience to the orders of the Court, the Bombay Marine cruisers 'Panther' and 'Endeavour,' were fitted for the service, and the following officers were appointed to them:—'Panther,' Captain McCluer (also in charge of the expedition), Lieutenants Wedgeborough and White, who, from their scientific attainments and familiarity with the natives of Oroolang, were admirable selections; and Mr. Midshipman Delano. 'Endeavour,' Captain Proctor, Lieutenants Thos. Haswell, Samuel Snook, and Jonathan Mickie.

The ships sailed from Bombay on the 24th of August, 1790, and, soon after parting company, the 'Panther' touched at Anjengo and Madras, and, on the 10th of October, rejoined her consort at Bencoolen, in Sumatra, whence they sailed on the 31st. During the months of November and December they were employed working up the south coast of Java, and visiting many islands and places to the eastward of that island, and experienced much very severe weather, on one occasion the 'Panther' narrowly escaping destruction by lightning. On the 22nd of January, 1791, the ship anchored off one of the Pelew Islands, and the joy of the natives was extreme on recognising Lieutenants Wedgeborough and White. We learn from a journal of the cruise of the ship that a rupack, who came on board, " calling out White, caught him in his arms, and, giving him a most affectionate and ardent squeeze, seemed almost distracted with joy, calling for all his people to come and embrace their friend." Lieutenant Wedgeborough, who landed, received an equally warm reception, and was joined by the King, who came from Oroolang, when, he says, " I had the unspeakable pleasure of once more being embraced by the benevolent Abba Thulle." On their proceeding together to the 'Panther' in the King's canoe, the officer acquainted him of his son's death, upon which, " his countenance, which before bore the most evident marks of joy, became composed and thoughtful; and, after remaining some time silent, he exclaimed ' *Weel, weel, weel a trecoy*' (good, good, very good)." Such confidence in the good faith of his white friends, and touching resignation to the decree of Providence, certainly displayed great magnanimity of character in this " noble savage." On reaching the 'Panther,' Captain McCluer received the King, who embraced him, and was astonished on seeing the cattle and great variety of gifts sent by the Company to him and his people. On the 21st, Captain McCluer landed in state, accompanied by Captain Proctor, Lieutenants Wedgeborough, White, and Haswell, Mr. Nicholson, the surgeon, and escorted by the marines and a party of seamen, " wearing caps with yellow plates, upon which was engraved the Hon. East India Company's crest." They were met by the King and a large concourse of people, and marched with " English colours flying, and a fife and drum playing the Grenadier's March," to a house where the gifts were presented, " the multitude being struck with amazement, and could not utter a word, but frequent *ha's!* of astonishment," while the King "was perfectly at a loss for utterance, or how far to express his gratitude to the English rupacks, as he styled the Hon. Company."

On the 1st of February, the King gave over to Captain McCluer, for the English Government, the island of Amallikala, where the ships were anchored, " saying it should be Englishmen's land," and the same day the British flag was hoisted upon it with all ceremony, and the foundation stone of a fort was laid, to which the name of Fort Abercrombie was given in honour of the Governor of Bombay; the island is described as about " four or five miles in circumference, and has good springs and streams of water, with some excellent small bays." On the following day, Captain McCluer resolved to proceed to Macao in the 'Panther' to forward an account of his proceedings to the Court of Directors by one of the homeward bound China fleet, and directed Captain Proctor, of the 'Endeavour,' during his absence to commence the survey of the island, and to instruct the Natives in the use of the tools of husbandry, and in the cultivation of rice grounds and gardens, for which seeds had been bought in abundance. To effect this systematically, Captain McCluer directed Lieutenant Snook to take charge of the plantations and gardens, Lieutenant Michie to superintend the instruction of the works, and in all fifty men were detailed to assist in the execution of his plans. On the 10th of February, after the King had invested Captain McCluer, and his favourite, Lieutenant White, with the " bone," constituting them "rupacks," the 'Panther' sailed, the ships saluting each other with nine guns, to the amazement of the Natives, who had an especial dread of the cannon.

During the absence of the 'Panther,' a detachment of seamen and marines took part in an expedition against Abba Thulle's enemies, and, writes Captain Proctor, in a marginal note on a copy of Mr. Keate's work on the Pelew Islands, their musketry fire was so effective "that the friends of the English were victorious."

The 'Panther' arrived at Macao on the 2nd of March, and,

on the 20th, the China fleet sailed for England under convoy of H.M.'s ships 'Leopard' and 'Thames,' Captain McCluer taking the opportunity to send his journals to the Court of Directors; on the 26th, he sailed for the Pelew Islands, where he cast anchor on the 10th of June. The King again solicited the assistance of the English against his enemies, in the island of Artingali, which Captain McCluer granted, and Lieutenant Wedgeborough was directed to proceed in command of the party. Accordingly, on the 16th of June, " the long boat left the ship, being completely armed, with one brass 6-pounder, two swivel guns, and a musquetoon, having also ten men with small arms, under the command of Mr. Delano. Lieutenant Wedgeborough went with the King in his canoe, and twenty Sepoys in different canoes, together with Mr. Nicholson, the surgeon." At Ivry, they were joined by two hundred canoes, and proceeded against the enemy, but the sight of the English and the discharge of their fire-arms and rockets created so much terror among the Artingali people that they sued for peace, which was granted, and Abba Thulle, " after this expedition, was acknowledged the superior rupack of all the Pelew Islands."

On the 27th of June, Captain McCluer sailed with his ships " to carry into execution his orders for a survey of the coast of New Guinea, but as he proposed to return, two boys were left behind with the King, and three of the Natives embarked on board the 'Panther.' On the 16th of July, they "sighted land and commenced their survey, on the northern coast of New Guinea, which they continued for the space of two months; during that time their intercourse with the Natives was friendly and kind." Being in want of provisions, they proceeded to Amboyna, where they arrived on the 28th of September, and received great hospitality and kindness from the Dutch people and the Governor, Mr. Van Schilling, who informed them "that they were the only English ships that had visited that island for a century." The 'Panther' and 'Endeavour' sailed from Amboyna on the 10th of October, and resumed the survey of New Guinea on the 24th. On the 26th, nine canoes, full of Natives, came off to the 'Panther,' and Mr. Nicholson, having unadvisedly entered the canoe of a chief from the long-boat, which was towing astern, the savages killed him, and discharged a flight of arrows into the ship, which wounded four of the crew. The guns and small arms now opened fire, and the savages were dispersed with some loss, but Captain McCluer decided with great humanity not to land and burn the town whence the canoes came, as the punishment would involve the innocent with the guilty. "On this unfriendly and savage coast," proceeds the writer of the journal, " they continued until the 21st of December, when, having completed the survey, they stood away for the coast of New Holland, and from thence to the island of Timor, where they were most hospitably received." At Timor, it is recorded "they buried an officer and one of the Pelew passengers." The ship sailed on the 24th of March, 1792, for Bencoolen where they arrived on the 27th of April, another of the Pelew islanders dying on the passage. On the 17th of August they sailed for the Pelew group, stopping *en route* at the Sooloo islands, where they embarked cattle, seed, and grain; on the 20th of January, 1793, they arrived at Pelew, and learned of the death of Abba Thulle.

A few days after their arrival, Captain McCluer despatched the 'Endeavour' to China, where she joined H.M.S. 'Lion,' and the H.C.S. 'Hindostan,' which were in attendance on Earl Macartney, then on an embassy to the court of Pekin, and all connection between the 'Panther' and 'Endeavour' ceased. On the 2nd of February, Captain McCluer, considering that he had fulfilled the objects of his mission, addressed a letter to Lieutenant Wedgeborough, resigning to him the command of the 'Panther,' and expressing his intention of remaining in the islands. Regarding his reasons for this singular step, he says:—"It is nothing but my zeal for my country that prompts me to follow this resolution; and I hope to succeed in the plan I have formed, which may benefit my country and the world in general, by enlightening the minds of the noble islanders. Should I fail in the attempt, it is only the loss of an individual, who assisted to do good to his fellow-creatures." On the following day Captain McCluer, "in the presence of the ship's crew," formally and deliberately resigned his command to Lieutenant Wedgeborough, as their future commander. On the 14th of February, the 'Panther' finally quitted the Pelew Islands, and arrived at Macao on the 7th of March, and, after refitting, sailed on the 22nd of April for Bombay, where she cast anchor on the 17th of August, 1793, after an absence of exactly three years, short of seven days.

Captain McCluer, after a residence of fifteen months, during which he devoted himself to civilising the islanders and ameliorating their condition, embarked in a small six-oared boat of the 'Panther,' which had been left behind at his request, with five Natives, intending to go to Ternate, but when they got to the southward of the islands, meeting with bad weather, he determined to proceed to Macao. This resolution—displaying wonderful hardihood, as the distance is about 1,600 miles, over a stormy sea—he actually carried into execution, and without instruments or charts, and in a small open boat, he reached Macao in safety, after encountering very heavy weather. On the passage, he and his companions subsisted on cocoa-nuts and water, and the hardships were so great that Captain McCluer was confined for a month with fever and ague in the house of his friend, Mr. Van Braam, the chief of the Dutch factory. On recovering his health, he purchased a vessel at Macao, and returned to the Pelew Islands, whence he proceeded with several Natives of both sexes to Bombay. On his way he touched at Bencoolen, where he met the Hon. Company's ship 'Europa,' Captain Applegath, bound for England, and the frigate 'Bombay,' belonging to the Marine, bound to Bombay. By this latter ship he sent some of the Natives to that port, and sailed, in his own little vessel, with the remainder, for Calcutta. But nothing more was ever heard of this gallant seaman, nor of his ill-fated crew, and it is supposed that the craft in which they embarked foundered in the Bay of Bengal.

The women sent to Bombay, being without friends, were for many years charitably maintained by Lieutenant Snook, of the 'Endeavour,' out of his slender resources, the Government being unable to send them back to their friends, as owing to war, they could not spare a ship of the Marine for the purpose. At length, in 1797, Captain Wedgeborough, being on the eve of sailing to England, in command of the 'Princess Royal,' made a representation of these matters, and Captain Wilson, the commander of the 'Antelope' when she was lost, took them in his ship, the 'Warley,' under charge of Lieutenant Snook, from Bombay to Macao; here that officer, whose conduct throughout seems to be characterised by singular charity and forgetfulness of self, purchased a small vessel, at Government expense, and, having fitted her out and provisioned her, sailed on the 4th of March, and, after being forced to return through stress of weather, at length reached the islands in safety. The women were landed with the gifts supplied by Government, and Lieutenant Snook, having embarked some Chinese left on the island by Captain McCluer, returned to Macao, and thence to Bombay. The only other occasion on which a ship of the Bombay Marine visited the Pelew Islands was in March, 1802, when Captain Nathaniel Tucker, commanding the Hon. Company's brig 'Antelope,' of fourteen guns, while on his way from Bombay to China with despatches, touched at the group, when four canoes came off to the ship, in one of which was an English seaman who had escaped from a vessel.

We trust that this episode of Captain McCluer, a forgotten worthy of the Service, may not be deemed one of the least interesting in the History of the Indian Navy.

The following were the results of the labours of Captain McCluer between the years 1790-93. He completed a survey of the Pelew Islands, though on too small a scale to be of much practical benefit to navigators. The survey of the New Guinea coast was attended with what was then regarded as a considerable accession to our knowledge of the hydrography of that almost unknown part of the world. A chart, embracing a space from the Equator to 7° South lat., between the meridians of 130° and 139° East long., contains the tracks of the 'Panther' and 'Endeavour.' The north-west part of New Guinea, with some trifling omissions, contained within these limits and the adjacent islands, are laid down in this chart, but we have no detail of the coast on a larger scale. The name of "McCluer's Inlet," is an abiding reminiscence of the visit of the great hydrographer, and "Assassination Creek," of the unhappy murder of Mr. Nicholson, surgeon of the 'Panther.' Although, as we have already observed, Captain McCluer's hydrographical labours in the Persian Gulf, and on the West coast of India, have long since been superseded by those of his brother officers of a later generation, they were verified, so far as they went, as surprisingly accurate by so competent an authority as Captain Jervis, Surveyor-General of India; and, although his survey of the New Guinea coast may have been superseded, for aught we know, by those of other officers, yet it is not just that his achievements in the then virgin field of marine surveying should be ignored, as has been the fashion by recent writers. We trust, therefore, that this imperfect record of them, gleaned after much research, will place Captain McCluer in his true light before the world, as a Marine Surveyor second only in eminence, and in the extent and value of his labours, to Captain Cook, to whose self-sacrificing character, indeed, his bears a remarkable resemblance.

In 1793 Lieutenant John Hayes was appointed to the command of a surveying expedition, consisting of the vessels 'Duke of Clarence' and 'Duchess,' which were dispatched to explore the coast of Van Dieman's Land. He surveyed this island, now known as Tasmania, the Derwent river, on which Hobart Town now stands, the south-west side of New Caledonia, a *terra incognita*, which, though it was discovered by Captain Cook, who took possession of it in the name of his Sovereign, we have unwisely permitted the French to colonise; also the south-east and north coasts of New Guinea, Gillolo, Batchian, and others of the Molucca islands, Timor, the whole north and south-east face of Java, from Cape Sandano westward, and, having passed through the Straits of Madura, presented the first instance of the progress of a British ship through that intricate channel. During this expedition he adopted such humane and judicious measures in his intercourse with the savage inhabitants of some of the places explored, that not a single life was lost in either side in a quarrel. Unhappily, the results of these complete and protracted surveys, extending over a period of between two and three years, was *nil*, for the ship taking home Lieutenant Hayes' manuscript charts and memoirs, was captured by a French man-of-war, and they were taken to Paris, where we are informed by a relative of his, they were seen by a British officer, soon after the peace, in a public institution. The loss of the results of so much and such lengthened labour and privations was always a source of poignant regret to Lieutenant Hayes.

A pleasant instance of true and disinterested friendship is told in connection with this survey of Lieutenant Hayes. His absence from Bombay was so protracted that, in default of all reports from, or concerning him, the Government came to the conclusion that he and his ships had perished, and, at length, ceased to pay to his wife, the late Lady Hayes, the remittances authorized by her husband, thereby reducing her to great distress. But there was a true friend in Bombay, who, confident that the gallant officer would some day turn up, personally took to the sorrowing lady the monthly remittances as they became due. Mr. F—— lived to see his conviction verified, for the gallant Hayes sailed into Bombay one day, and the Government and his friends—how many were there besides the good Bombay merchant?—regarded him almost as one who had risen from the dead. We need scarcely say that his first act was to repay the good Samaritan who had supported and befriended his wife during the long period of supposed widowhood.

This closes the record of the hydrographical labours of the officers of the Service in the last century, for the outbreak of the Revolutionary War necessitated the employment of all the ships and officers in the life-and-death struggle in which this country was involved with the gigantic power of the Directorate and of Napoleon, and with the Dutch and other allied nations who had possessions in the East.

CHAPTER VII.

1793—1810.

Gallant Action of the 'Vigilant,' Lieutenant Hayes, with Sanganian Pirates—Lieutenant Hayes' Services Ashore and Afloat—Services of the Company's Ships during the Revolutionary War—The Reduction of Ceylon and the Eastern Islands—The 'Bombay' frigate at Coupang—Brilliant Defence of the 'Intrepid'—Reduction of Ternate by Captain Hayes, and Action with Magandanao Pirates—Reorganization of the Bombay Marine—Strength of the Service in 1802—Occupation of Perim—The Expedition to Egypt—Services of the Marine in Sumatra and in the Persian Gulf—Loyalty of the 'Aurora's' Marines—The Reduction of Mauritius—The Services of Lieutenant D. Macdonald.

LIEUTENANT HAYES, after his return to Bombay from the prosecution of his surveys, which ended so disastrously in the capture of all his charts and memoirs, was appointed first lieutenant of the 'Jehangire,' which, in conjunction with the Hon. Company's ships 'Exeter' and 'Brunswick,' sailed from Bombay with the object of intercepting a French Republican squadron, under Commodore Renaud, consisting of the frigates 'Cybèle,' 'Prudente,' and 'Moineau,' which had appeared off Diu and threatened the destruction of that settlement. In 1796, he was actively employed as Commander of the cruiser 'Princess Augusta,' and was soon after selected to carry out a diplomatic mission requiring no less tact than courage. A potentate known as the Hakim of Sonmeanee* had seized a British trading ship, and carried her off to a port in his dominions, and it was to effect her release from that Prince that Lieutenant Hayes set sail from Bombay in the first week of 1797. To enable him to carry out this service, he was furnished with only one small vessel of six guns, called the 'Vigilant.'

On the 13th of January, while crossing the entrance of the Gulf of Cutch, Lieutenant Hayes was attacked by four sail of Sanganian pirates, each more than double the size of the 'Vigilant,' and carrying twice her number of men. A desperate

---

* Sonmeanee, a name derived from two words signifying "neat" and "fishing station," is a small town in Beloochistan, situated on the sea-coast on a bay formed by the projection of Cape Monze on the east. In 328 B.C., Nearchus anchored here with his fleet after leaving the mouth of the Indus, and as the harbour was safe and commodious, he ordered it, says Dr. Vincent in his "Voyage of Nearchus," to be called "the port of Alexander."

action now ensued. The piratical craft boarded one on each quarter and on each bow, and, for some hours, the gallant crew of the 'Vigilant,' animated by the bearing and example of their leader, resisted the overwhelming odds brought against them. In a document I have before me regarding this brilliant feat of arms, one is impressed with the belief that the dauntless and obstinate valour of the British sailor never received a more striking illustration. For three entire hours, the enemy's vessels were lashed alongside the 'Vigilant,' while the pirates made the most desperate efforts to carry the little craft. But the long protracted resistance was at length rewarded with complete success, and the enemy, casting off their lashings, made sail and left the victorious handful of British seamen in the enjoyment of their hardly earned triumph.

At the close of the action Lieutenant Hayes received a ball from a jingall which was pressed against the face, and lost a part of the jawbone and the lower lobe of the right ear. He escaped death by a miracle, for his own musket having flashed in the pan at the critical moment, he was quite at the mercy of his antagonist. The wound was of so serious a nature that his life was despaired of, and his ultimate recovery was a work of time —indeed, he suffered from the effects of the wound to his death, for the upper jaw was completely shattered, and for years pieces of bone were discharged from it, while through life he suffered excessive pain in that part of his face. This, however, was not his last brush with pirates, for, in the following year, Lieutenant Hayes, in an armed boat, boarded and captured two pirate vessels, each carrying one 9-pounder forward and two 18-pounders aft.

While a young officer, he had served under General Matthews in 1782, and under Generals Meadows and Abercrombie in 1790, and he was now again employed, in 1799, on active service ashore against Tippoo Sultan, and was with Colonel Little's detachment till the reduction of Seringapatam by General Harris. On his return to Bombay he was immediately appointed to the command of the 'Alert,' schooner, of fourteen guns, and ordered to proceed to Kenery—which, at that time, was strongly fortified round its circumference, and mounted two hundred pieces of cannon— for the purpose of demanding restitution of some merchant vessels and property carried on shore.

Accordingly Lieutenant Hayes, having brought the 'Alert' close up to the enemy's gateway on the north-east side of the island, which presented the only access to it, landed with part of his crew, and brought off the vessels and property, at the same time causing Angria, a descendant of the celebrated pirate chief of that name, to pay 500 per cent. upon the cargo deficient through plunder.

In 1800 he was in command of the brig 'Fly,' carrying ten

guns and seventy-five men, and was employed in harassing the formidable stronghold of Gheria, which had been surrendered to the Mahrattas, after its capture in 1756, and, with other forts on the coast, had again become a retreat for pirates. Among other places whence they preyed on Indian commerce, was Melundy Island, or Sindeedroog, near Malwan, and Raree,* also known as Yestwuntgurh.

Lieutenant Hayes performed one of those daring feats for which he was distinguished in the Service, at Vingorla, also one of the chief pirate haunts. On appearing before it in the brig 'Fly,' he immediately landed his men, and, capturing the principal battery, dismantled it at noonday, and threw the guns into the sea in the face of the enemy, forcing the chief of the freebooters to restore what British property was in hands, and, for what was deficient to pay the exorbitant interest, the gallant officer had always enforced, 500 per cent. on the value of the articles.

On the outbreak of the Revolutionary War in 1793, measures were immediately taken by the Governments of the three Presidencies for the capture of the French possessions in the East Indies. Chandernagore, Karical, and Mahé were surrendered without resistance, but the strong fort of Pondicherry stood a siege, and only capitulated on the 23rd of August, after heavy losses had been sustained on both sides. During the siege the 'Minerva,' thirty-eight gun frigate, bearing the flag of Rear-Admiral the Hon. W. Cornwallis, assisted by three of the Company's ships, effectually blockaded Pondicherry by sea, and chased away from the coast the French frigate 'Cybèle' and three smaller vessels, supposed to be bringing supplies and reinforcements for the garrison.

The colours captured at Pondicherry were sent to England in the Hon. Company's cruiser 'Scorpion,' but she was captured by a French fleet in January of the following year, when nearing her destination, and the officers and crew were taken to America, whence, after a captivity of six months, they were released and permitted to find their way to England.

Soon after the surrender of Pondicherry, Admiral Cornwallis having quitted the East India station with the whole of his squadron except a twenty-gun ship, the valuable interests of the Company became exposed to the ravages of the enemy, who, besides the 'Cybèle' and the thirty-six gun frigate 'Prudente,' Captain Renaud, and two or three corvettes, possessed some very formidable privateers, which had recently been fitted out in the Isle of France. On the 27th of September, 1793, the Company's outward-bound China ship 'Princess Royal' was captured off

* Raree is a fort on a rocky eminence, about seven miles from the Vingorla river, and situated on the coast near Goa; being a stronghold of the pirates, it was taken by a British force in 1765, but restored in the following year, though it passed into our hands permanently in the year 1818, as did also Gheria, Malwan, and Severndroog.

Anjier Point, in the island of Java, by three French privateers, after a long and gallant resistance.* The Governor-General now despatched a squadron, composed of four or five of the heaviest and best-appointed Company's ships to the China seas, and on the 2nd of January, 1794, a portion of this squadron, consisting of the 'William Pitt,' Captain Mitchell, 'Britannia,' Captain Cheap, and the Bombay Marine cruiser 'Nautilus,' Captain Roper, of fourteen guns, arrived off the eastern entrance of the Straits of Singapore.

On the 13th of January the squadron anchored in Anjier Bay, and, on the 21st, was joined by the Company's ships 'Houghton,' Captain Hudson, and 'Nonsuch,' Captain Canning, when they got under way. Early the next morning, while the 'William Pitt' was examining a detained ship, two strangers were descried in the south-west and chased by a portion of the squadron. The strange ships were two French privateers, the 'Vengeur,' Captain Corosin, mounting thirty-four guns, with a crew of two hundred and fifty men, and the 'Résolu,' Captain Jallineaux, mounting twenty-six guns, with a crew of two hundred and thirty men, both from the Isle of France. The action commenced at eleven, a.m., and in about three-quarters of an hour, both privateers, the 'William Pitt' and 'Houghton' then fast coming up, struck their colours; the 'Vengeur' with the loss of eleven killed and twenty-six wounded, including amongst the latter Captain Corosin, who died after the amputation of his leg.

On the morning of the 25th of January, the British squadron, consisting of the 'Nautilus,' 'Houghton,' 'Nonsuch,' and 'William Pitt,' was lying at anchor to the northward of the Zuften Isles, near Bantam Bay, when they sighted the French frigates 'Prudente' and Cybèle, the late Indiaman 'Princess Royal,' (now named the 'Duguay Trouin') and the fourteen-gun brig 'Vulcan,' the whole under the command of Captain Renaud, of the 'Prudente,' getting under way from off St. Nicholas Point, Java, and also a ship, which proved to be the prize 'Résolu,' trying her utmost to escape from them. At about half-past eight, a.m., the 'Nautilus,' 'William Pitt,' and 'Britannia,' on the near approach of the French squadron, cut their cables and prepared to engage. By this time the shot of the 'Prudente' and 'Cybèle' were passing over the 'Résolu;' the latter, however, continued her course, and ran for protection between the British ships, which now opened their fire upon the enemy. A partial action now ensued, and, after the firing had lasted about eighteen minutes, the French squadron stood away out of gunshot.

As the ships of the British squadron had distributed among

* This ship re-named the 'Duguay Trouin,' was recaptured on the 5th of May, 1794, by the British thirty-six gun frigate 'Orpheus,' Captain Newcome.

them a greater number of French prisoners than the amount of their united crews, and as each ship, from assisting to man the prizes, had scarcely hands enough to work her guns, the squadron bore up for Batavia, to procure a supply of guns and men; Commodore Renaud also made no attempt to renew the action.

On the union of Holland with the French Republic in 1795, England declared war against that country, and the Indian Government prepared an expedition to reduce the island of Ceylon, which did not prove a very arduous task, owing to the disorganised and mutinous state of the Dutch* troops. General Stewart was sent from Madras with a military force, the naval portion of the armament, including the Company's frigate 'Bombay,' thirty-eight guns, Commodore Picket, built at Bombay in 1793, and some smaller vessels of the Marine, being under the command of Rear-Admiral Rainier, who hoisted his broad pennant on board the 'Suffolk,' seventy-four guns. The expedition first attacked Trincomalee, which capitulated on the 26th of August, after a siege of three weeks, just as the British troops were about to storm. After the surrender of some minor places, on the 25th of September General Stewart embarked some troops on board H.M.S. 'Centurion,' fifty guns, and the 'Bombay,' and proceeded to the north side of the island to Jaffnapatam, a strong fort, which was pusillanimously surrendered at the first summons. As the Indian Government now determined to acquire the whole island, considerable reinforcements were sent from the three Presidencies, and, on the 5th of February, 1796, an expedition, consisting of four of the King's ships, and five belonging to the Company, having on board a large body of troops commanded by General Stewart, anchored off Negombo, a fort about twenty-two miles to the northward of Colombo, which capitulated to the squadron, the stores and merchandise, to the value of twenty-five lacs of rupees, falling into the hands of the captors. Meanwhile, the General proceeded to the Dutch capital, Colombo, which was also surrendered without a struggle, although the garrison equalled in numbers the attacking force,† and soon the other Dutch forts in the island followed the example of the capital.

In the latter part of 1797, His Majesty's ship 'Resistance,'‡

* "History of Ceylon," by William Knighton, p. 305.
† The British troops consisted of the 52nd, 73rd, and 77th Regiments, three battalions of Sepoys, and a detachment of Artillery; and the Dutch garrison, of two battalions of Hollanders, the French Regiment of Wurtemburg, with some Native troops. (Knighton, p. 307; Percival, p. 92.)
‡ On the 24th of July, 1798, this fine frigate, by some inexplicable means, blew up in the Straits of Banca, when, with the exception of thirteen seamen, Captain Pakenham, his officers and crew, consisting of two hundred and fifty seamen and thirty marines, together with fourteen Spanish prisoners and some passengers, all perished; of the survivors, only four reached land in safety, after suffering great privations. The 'Resistance,' with a Spanish prize, had put into Balambangan whence they proceeded to Celebes, and arrived in about eighteen days at Limby, near Manado, on that island. The same evening the captain despatched the brig to Amboyna for supplies, when the 'Bombay,' frigate, proceeded to

forty-four guns, Captain Pakenham, and the Company's frigate 'Bombay,' commanded by Lieutenant Henry Frost, anchored off the fort of Coupang, in Timor, the principal settlement of the Dutch who had conquered the island from the Portuguese in 1613. In answer to a summons to surrender Fort Concordia, a strong place having a large garrison, the Dutch Governor* at once gave up the fort, which was occupied by the marines from the ships. Lieutenant Frost, and the surgeon and purser of the 'Resistance,' were appointed Commissioners to receive over the island, and it was settled that they should meet the Dutch delegates at the Council House near the fort. In the meantime, a conspiracy had been formed by some native chiefs, the object of which was to murder the English Commissioners and seize the fort. It was never proved that the Governor was privy to this plot; he denied all knowledge of it, and attributed it to one of his sons, who was married to the daughter of a Malay chief and tacitly acknowledged his participation by absconding when the scheme was providentially frustrated. However this may be, on the day appointed, the British Commissioners, anticipating no treachery, quitted the fort and proceeded to the place of assembly, where they awaited the advent of their Dutch colleagues. There was no suspicion of foul play until, in place of the Commissioners, they only saw the scowling faces of armed Malays; but, at length, Lieutenant Frost apprehending the treachery that was brewing, suddenly quitted the Council House, and the signal for the massacre not having been given, passed through the crowd in safety. He had nearly reached the fort when the attack commenced ; the surgeon was killed, and the purser only escaped with his life through the kindness of an old woman who concealed him. Lieutenant Frost owed his escape to his having taken the precaution to station at the bridge of the fort, a havildar (or native sergeant) and six marines, who behaved with great gallantry. As he neared the bridge the signal was given, and a rush took place, but he just managed to enter the fort. Meantime the pressure at the bridge was tremendous, but the havildar and marines nobly defended it, and kept the crowd at bay until succour arrived, and the fort guns opened fire upon the dense mob, who were

relieve her; meantime Captain Pakenham had sailed for Amboyna, and fell in with the 'Bombay' on the voyage. After refitting at Amboyna, the 'Resistance' sailed to Booroo and Banda, and her last service afloat was the dispersion of several pirate craft in the Straits of Banca, where she met with the terrible catastrophe already mentioned. James places the total loss at three hundred and thirty-two souls.

* This was the governor who had displayed great hospitality towards Captains Bligh and Edwards, and the people that remained of the 'Bounty' and 'Pandora,' for which he received a splendid testimonial from the British Government. He had also been equally hospitable towards Captain McCluer, and the officers and crews of the 'Panther' and 'Endeavour' during their stay there in the early part of 1792.

quickly dispersed with severe loss. In this affair the havildar and two men were killed and the rest wounded; several men of the ships' crews, who were ashore at the bazaar, were also murdered by the infuriated natives.

On the 18th of October, 1798, the Company's cruiser 'Drake,' Captain Bond, sailed from Bombay with presents from the Government to the King of Baba, for his hospitality and humane attention to the crew of the 'Neptune,' which had been cast away on the coast of Madagascar. The 'Drake' arrived at that island towards the end of the month; but as the King of Baba was a few days' journey in the interior, a messenger was despatched with the information, and an officer sent up the river, in a cutter, to meet him. On the 7th of November the King came down and received the presents in the midst of his nobles, with all the pageantry of his court. Like the unsophisticated King of the Pelew Islands, who considered hospitality a solemn duty incumbent on every one, it was a long time before he could be made to understand the object of the expedition, nor could he then conceal his surprise that the Company should have thought it necessary to send him remuneration for succouring those in distress. More than once he inquired of Captain Bond "whether among the number of those who had shared his protection he had a relation or friend." Upon receiving an answer in the negative, he unaffectedly replied, "Then wherefore have you come so far, and taken so much trouble." At length he was made sensible that the English owned themselves indebted to his hospitality, and, in the presents which had been delivered, had acknowledged the obligation. The officers of the 'Drake' remarked as two singular customs, that his sable Majesty used as his throne the knees of his wives, who bent one knee upon the earth to support themselves, and that when he mounted and descended the sides of the ship, on proceeding to inspect the 'Drake,' he always made use of the back of one of his chiefs.

In the year 1800, the Hon. Company's frigate 'Cornwallis,' of fifty-six guns, commanded by Captain Isaac Gonsalez Richardson, having convoyed some of the Company's trading ships to England, sailed from the Downs with a return fleet bound to India. The services performed by the ships and officers of the Bombay Marine during the momentous period of the history of this country, embraced between the years 1800 and 1814, were most praiseworthy, and the small cruisers did not shun a conflict with the heavily-armed privateers which quitted the ports of France and the Mauritius in great numbers in order to prey upon British commerce in Indian waters. While the trade was protected against pirates, who received severe chastisement when they attempted to resist, the French privateers were severely handled when they encountered the Company's cruisers, though they generally managed to escape, owing to the inferior sailing qualities of the Bombay ships.

Conspicuous among these actions was that fought by the Company's snow,* 'Intrepid,' Captain Hall. On the 22nd of November, 1800, the 'Intrepid,' carrying ten guns (6-pounders), fell in off Muscat with a French privateer of twelve guns (9 and 12-pounder carronades), when a desperate action took place at less than pistol-shot range. Between 9.30, when the first shot was fired, and 11.45 a.m., the enemy, well aware of his vast superiority in men—the 'Intrepid,' being, as was usual with the Company's cruisers, underhanded—made two attempts to run her on board and throw an overpowering force on the brig's decks. With consummate skill and coolness Captain Hall manœuvred his ship so as to baffle his adversary, while he maintained a well-directed fire from his guns. Shortly before eleven the gallant officer received a mortal wound, but the action was continued by his First-Lieutenant, Mr. Thomas Smee, who was inspired by the indomitable resolution of his commander. The men stood to their guns with equal spirit, though latterly the action was fought within half pistol-shot, and on each occasion that the privateersmen tried to board over the stern, they repelled them with great slaughter. At length the enemy found that they had met their match, and a little before twelve, the Frenchman made all sail away. The 'Intrepid' was too much cut up aloft to give chase, but in half an hour her officers and crew having, with commendable smartness, refitted her rigging, bent new sails, and rove new braces which had been shot away, she was under a press of canvas in pursuit. The enemy, however, owing to her superior sailing qualities, escaped. The 'Intrepid' lost her captain, who died on the 30th November, and five men killed, and both her lieutenants, Messrs. Smee and Best, Mr. Harriott, midshipman, the boatswain, and nineteen men wounded.

The crew with which this action was fought consisted of only forty Europeans, two-thirds of whom were Marine Society's boys from the 'Warspite,' and about the same number of Sepoys and Lascars. When we consider the loss among the officers and the numerical weakness of the crew, we maintain that few actions more honourable to those concerned, are recorded even in the annals of the British Navy, whose every page is illumined with deeds of gallantry such as the world has not seen equalled since the days of Greece and Rome. That the 'Intrepid' was so manœuvred as to prevent the enemy from carrying their intention of boarding into effect, and that the

* A snow only differs from a brig in having the boom-mainsail hooped to a trysail mast, a spar which is unknown in a brig, but which is carried in a snow close to the mainmast.

guns were worked with such effect by raw lads and natives, who are perilous stuff to fight naval actions with, speaks more for the skill, seamanship and courage of the officers of the ship than could any words of eulogy on our part. Not less honour and credit are due to the gallant boys of the Marine Society, which, for nearly three-quarters of a century, supplied the Service with a never-failing supply of smart young lads, possessed of all the pluck and seamanlike qualities characteristic of the Anglo-Saxon race.

And yet we hear nothing of any rewards or honours being meted out to the officers, whose devotion was displayed by the circumstance that they were all wounded, while their painstaking care in training into good gunners such unpromising material, was evinced by the successful resistance they made to a vessel of such superior force; so little, indeed, was thought, or, perhaps, known, of this deed of valour on the part of the small and uninfluential Bombay Marine, that James, in his exhaustive and complete record of the services of our sailors during the Great War, makes no mention of this brilliant defence of their ship by the officers and men of the 'Intrepid.' Sad to relate, the sea soon after swallowed up both the cruiser and the survivors of the action of the 22nd of November.

Soon after her return to Bombay, the 'Intrepid,' under the command of Captain George Roper, the successor to her late commander, Hall, was despatched, in company with another cruiser, the 'Comet,' Lieutenant William Henry, to the China seas, to learn the fate of the Company's ship 'Talbot,' which was supposed to have been wrecked, but the same darkness that shrouded the fate of the ship in quest of which they were sent, has settled over the fate of these two cruisers. From the day they sailed out of Bombay Harbour they were never heard of again.

> "And though no stone may tell
> Their name, their work, their glory,
> They rest in hearts that loved them well,
> They grace Britannia's story."

Among the officers lost in these ships were—'Intrepid,' Captain G. Roper, Lieutenants Stephen Best, William Nicholson, and William Henry Taylor. 'Comet,' Lieutenant W. Henry and Acting-Lieutenants Charles Baker and Isaac Richardson.

In 1801 the Indian Government despatched the 'Swift,' twenty guns, commanded by Captain Hayes, and the 'Star,' brig, under Lieutenant Scott, to co-operate in the attack on the Dutch possessions in the Moluccas, or Spice Islands. Admiral Rainier left these two vessels to blockade the island of Ternate,*

---

* Ternate, the northernmost of a chain of islands adjoining the west coast of Gilolo, was formerly the seat of sovereignty over all the adjacent Molucca Islands,

HISTORY OF THE INDIAN NAVY. 211

but this monotonous duty did not suit a man of the ardent temperament of Captain Hayes, who found a congenial colleague in Lieutenant Scott. At the head of only forty-five seamen, with escalading ladders, he advanced against Fort Tabooka, Ternate, under the fire of its guns and the cross-fire of two field-pieces and six hundred Natives, 600 yards distance on the right flank. The assaulting column, together with the rest of the advance division, under Colonel Burr, commanding the troops, was forced to retreat, with the loss of one-third of their number. Nothing daunted by this reverse, he engaged Fort Orange and four batteries, on Ternate, on the 11th of May, within pistol-shot range, for two hours and a-half, but after a severe action was obliged to haul off; a second time, on the 16th of May, the 'Swift' and 'Star' were carried within pistol-shot range of the batteries, and sustained the concentrated fire of more than thirty pieces of heavy ordnance. At length Lieutenant Hayes' temerity was rewarded with success; the forts were silenced and stormed, and, soon after, on the 21st of June, 1801, the whole island surrendered to Colonel Burr, who had invested the town and works on the land side.*

The 'Swift' lost in this service twelve killed and wounded, and the 'Star' ten; that the casualties were comparatively so few, considering the brilliancy of the service, is owing to the fact that the gunners in the forts were unable to depress their

including Tidore, Batchian, Motir, and Machian; the King of Ternate extended his rule over seventeen or eighteen islands, and maintained a considerable naval force. The Portuguese first visited these islands in 1510, but on their expulsion by the Dutch in 1607, the native princes were interdicted from having any intercourse with them. The Dutch erected in Ternate three forts called Orange, Holland, and Williamstadt.

* The following extract from a despatch of the Company's Resident at Amboyna, which was communicated by the Court of Directors to Lord Hobart, Secretary of State, gives a brief account of the capture of Ternate. "The Dutch Governor made a most resolute resistance, having defended the place with uncommon firmness for fifty-two days, though I am sorry to add, at the expense of the poor inhabitants, who perished from famine, from ten to twenty a day, from our strong blockade by sea and land. During this excellent disposition of our military and marine forces, the latter under the command of that gallant officer, Captain Hayes, the armed supplies for the enemy were intercepted through his vigilance, which certainly contributed in a high degree to the ultimate success of the enterprise. The value of the captured property taken by the squadron amounts to a lac and 50,000 dollars, (equal to £20,000). The difficulties the Honourable Company's forces by sea and land had to encounter in this arduous service, and the spirit and intrepidity which they manifested during a siege of nearly two months, do them infinite credit, and have seldom or ever been exceeded in this part of the globe. The accounts we have received of the strength of Fort Orange and its numerous detached batteries, proved exceedingly erroneous, insomuch that Colonel Burr declares the place to be extremely strong by nature, and most exceedingly improved by art, with a powerful garrison, and so well provided with arms and ammunition, as to throw difficulties in the way of our force, which were as distressing as unexpected; they, however, persevered and kept their ground with so much bravery and resolution, as to compel the enemy to surrender their different strongholds one after the other, until the principal fort and town were so completely blockaded by sea and land, and so reduced by famine as to make them sue for conditions, which, I understand, are very satisfactory."

P 2

guns sufficiently to sweep their decks, and thus it happened that while the hull escaped with few shot holes, the spars and rigging of the two little ships were much cut up. During the rigorous blockade of Ternate, an American ship, with supplies from Batavia, attempting to force an entrance, was captured by the 'Swift,' and amongst the cargo on board were hams, cheese, wines, and spirits, for the Governor, Mr. Cranstone. Captain Hayes, with chivalrous feeling, forwarded these luxuries under a flag of truce, to the Governor, but the equally high-spirited Dutchman returned all the packages with the reply, "that he could do well without them, preferring to share the rations of the garrison to such luxuries."

A sloop of war of sixteen guns, launched at Bombay during the year, received the name of 'Ternate,' in honour of this achievement of an officer of the Service.

Subsequently to this gallant service, the crew of the 'Swift' was attacked with a malignant fever from which Captain Hayes nearly lost his life; and many officers and men, engaged in this expedition, fell victims to the epidemic. Hearing of the depredations of a fleet of Magindanao pirates, Captain Hayes, notwithstanding the shattered state of his own health, and the short-handedness of his crew, owing to the ravages of disease, on the 1st of August sought out the fleet, consisting of forty sail, and attacked them single-handed, though he might, without dishonour, have declined to encounter so superior a force, as an act of temerity. After a severe action, in which the 'Swift' was, at times, in great peril, owing to the determined efforts of the pirates to board, he beat them off with immense loss; nor did the 'Swift' escape unscathed, her casualties being three men killed, and five, including her commander, wounded. By this action he saved the Company's settlement in the Celebes which had been threatened by these marauders.

The following account of this brilliant action, is from the pages of the "Annual Register" of 1803:—"By a letter officially received this day, (3rd February) from Bombay, it appears that, on the 29th of July last, Captain Hayes, of the Company's ship-of-war 'Swift,' received a requisition from the Resident at Amboyna, to proceed to the relief of an outpost, named Amoorang, then closely infested by the Magindanao pirates; their fleet consisted of forty large proas, from which one thousand two hundred men had been landed, with twelve pieces of brass ordnance, of 8 and 6-pounders. On the 1st of August, at half-past five p.m., the 'Swift' came up with the piratical fleet, and instantly opened a cannonade upon them, which continued to half-past nine. Besides the annoyance of the enemy, Captain Hayes' attention was imperiously called to the critical situation of his own vessel, which was surrounded by islands, and upon a dangerous reef; to this circumstance were the vessels which escaped destruction indebted for their safety. The 'Swift,' however, captured two; one she passed over, and cut in two; seventeen others were run ashore, and about six hundred of the enemy are supposed to have perished during the conflict. The Company's settlements upon the Celebes, as well as granaries completely stored, have thus been protected from the most serious depredations, by the dispersion of these daring pirates, who had overrun the whole of the Sangir islands, reduced the capital, Tairom, to ashes, and carried thence two hundred female captives, besides males, many of whom perished on the occasion of this attack; one only of the former was saved by the 'Swift,' and one of the pirates from the wreck of the proa which had been run down. Each of the enemy's vessels carried from sixty to eighty men, one 6 or 8-pounder brass gun forward, besides many smaller ones, with muskets, lances, &c."

The Company's ships 'Bombay,' 'Swift,' and 'Star,' also did good service at the island of Celebes, particularly at the reduction of Manado and Gonong Tella, and Lieutenant Court, first of the 'Bombay,' was appointed to the command of Fort Amsterdam, which he held for nine months " under the most critical circumstances." Subsequently, in reward for his distinguished services, he was appointed Resident at Manado and commandant of all the troops in Celebes, by Mr. Farquhar, the newly-appointed Governor of the Moluccas, a post he held with conspicuous success until, in terms of the peace, our conquests in the Moluccas were restored to the Dutch.

Some of the vessels of the Bombay Marine continued to be employed at the Moluccas, until these islands were given up to the Dutch, and, during the interval, they had several encounters with the pirates, which swarmed in those seas. At this time there were generally two vessels employed at Pulo Penang, or Prince of Wales' Island, and two in the Bay of Bengal under the orders of the Supreme Government, protecting the trade from the depredations of French privateers.

On the 1st of August, 1798, (the day on which Nelson won his memorable victory of the Nile) the Court of Directors issued an order revising the Marine Regulations, and conferring on the officers relative rank with their military Service, as well as a retiring pension. The pay of the officers was fixed at the rate it continued to remain for the succeeding thirty years, when the Service finally assumed its last phase as the Indian Navy; they were also prohibited from trading, a privilege which had been allowed up to that time, and, in fact, the Bombay Marine was created a regular Naval Service for war purposes only. A Superintendent was appointed, but the office was vested, for some inscrutable reason, in a civilian; and the two senior officers of the Service were appointed Master-Attendant and Commodore at Bombay. These three officers, with the two captains next in seniority, were formed into a Marine Board for conducting the Civil Branch, including the dockyard and financial details of the Service; and the executive, under the supervision of the Government of Bombay, was vested in the Superintendent, who, at a later date, was assisted by a senior captain of the Service selected by himself. The appointment of Superintendent was retained in their own hands by the Court of Directors, and Mr. Philip Dundas, brother, we believe, of the first Lord Melville, was the first incumbent of the post. Relative rank, as follows, was given to the officers of the Service by these Regulations:—The Commodore to rank with a Colonel in the Army. Captains of the larger vessels of twenty-eight guns and upwards, or senior captains, to rank with Lieutenant-Colonels in the Army. Junior Captains with Majors. First Lieutenants to rank with Captains in the Army. Second Lieutenants with Lieutenants in the Army. The Superintendent of the Marine, in consideration of the importance of his office, to be next to the Members in Council. The Master-Attendant next to the Superintendent, and to sit above the Commodore.

The duties of the Service were distinctly defined under the following heads:—1. The protection of the trade. 2. Suppression of piracy and general duties as vessels of war. 3. Convoying transports, and carrying troops if necessary. 4. The prosecution of Maritime surveys in the East. There was also another duty performed by the Marine, of considerable importance to the shipping of Bombay. Immediately before the south-west monsoon, an experienced officer, with a proper establishment of boats, was stationed at Worli, and another at Mahim,* in whose charge was included Versovah, whose duty it was to render aid to vessels fetching to the northward of the port of Bombay. This duty was performed by the Marine, with signal success, up to about the year 1816, when it was discontinued.

At this time, also, various improvements were made in the internal economy of the Marine, and some fine vessels were built. But the Service laboured throughout its career under great disadvantages in securing a suitable supply of seamen, and at the period of which we write it lay in the power of the commanders of King's ships to draft men out of the Company's cruisers, though this power was later taken away from them. Except in war-time, there was great difficulty in procuring suitable hands for the ships, and, in later times, when the

* Mahim Bay, at the south extremity of the island of Salsette, is formed by Worli, the north-west point of the island of Bombay, on the south, and Bandra, or Bandora, Point on the north, the latter about six miles from Malabar Point and nine from Bombay light-house. Since the construction of the Mahim and Sion Causeway, Mahim Bay is much filled up, and now only affords a refuge for fishing boats. Versovah is an island about twelve miles north of Malabar Point.

Indian Navy was armed with all the privileges of a Naval Service, the complements of the vessels of war, so far as regarded the able-bodied seamen, were maintained at their necessary strength by drafts from the jails. Often has the writer brought off to his ship from Aden prison a batch of seamen, who had the option of confinement in the "chowkee," or service on board one of the Honourable Company's ships, and we can aver that oftentimes the best men were these so-called "jail-birds," who, though amenable to discipline under the terrors of martial law, were too high-spirited to submit to the brutality of a certain class of merchant skippers, who subject their crews to worse treatment than any costermonger dare inflict on his donkey in England.

Notwithstanding all the disadvantages under which the Bombay Marine laboured at the time of which we are writing, and the paucity of the ships, it continued to perform good service to the State; the pirates were kept in check throughout the Eastern seas, protection was afforded to the Indian coasting trade, which in those days was of considerable value, maritime surveys were prosecuted with vigour and success, and lastly, many officers of the Service, travelling out of the sphere of their regular duties, performed honourable service with the troops engaged in the great struggle which we prosecuted during the eighteenth century with the Mahrattas, and the Mysore Princes, Hyder Ally and Tippoo Sultaun.

In the year 1802, the following were the ships of the Bombay Marine:—The frigates 'Cornwallis,' of fifty-six guns—built at Bombay, in 1800, and named after the Governor-General—and 'Bombay,' thirty-eight. The sloops-of-war 'Mornington,' twenty-two, launched at Bombay in 1800, and named after the then Governor-General; Teignmouth, sixteen, built in 1799, and named after Sir John Shore; and 'Ternate,' sixteen, built in 1801. The fourteen gun brigs 'Antelope' and 'Fly,' added to the Service in 1793. The snows 'Drake,' eighteen (1787); 'Panther,' fourteen (1778); 'Viper,' fourteen; 'Princess Augusta,' fourteen (1768); 'Princess Royal,' fourteen (1768); 'Comet,' ten (1798); and 'Intrepid,' ten (1780). The ketches 'Queen,' fourteen; and 'Rodney,' fourteen. Besides these vessels,* there were prizes and others purchased into the Service, for special, or temporary, uses, such as the 'Swift,' 'Star,' 'Les Frères Unis,' 'Alert,' 'Assaye,' and others; and there were also some small craft and pattamars, armed with guns.

The *personnel* of the Bombay Marine at this time was composed of the Superintendent, Mr. Philip Dundas, the Master-

* The armament of some of these ships differs from that given in the narrative, which may be accounted for by the circumstance that ships-of-war, though pierced for a certain number of guns, frequently carried more or less. Thus when the old carronades fell into disuse, fewer, but heavier and more serviceable, guns were employed.

Attendant, Captain Robert Anderson, the Commodore, Captain James Sutherland, thirteen Captains, thirty-three First-Lieutenants, twenty-one Second-Lieutenants, and thirty-seven Volunteers.*

The Master-Attendant, who took rank and precedence immediately after the Superintendent, received 25,000 rupees per annum, considerably more than £2,500 at the current rate

* The following is a copy of the official printed list of the officers of the Bombay Marine on the 1st of January, 1802, which fell into the hands of an officer of the Service about thirty years ago, in the bazaar at Bussorah, having, doubtless, belonged to the chief of the Company's factory then established in that city. It will, probably, be considered of interest not only by the Service, but by those readers who have followed with interest the varied services of many of the officers whose names appear in it.

Captains.

Names and Stations.	Dates of Commissions.
Charles John Bond—Member of the Marine Board	Nov. 15, 1786
Walter Borlase—Member of the Marine Board	Dec. 18, 1787
Thomas Hardie—'Marquis Cornwallis'	May 9, 1793
Emanuel Margoty—'Bombay'	„ 9, „
Isaac Gonsalves Richardson—On shore	„ 9, „
Samuel Speak—On shore	June 26, „
Robert Billamore—Returning to Europe	„ 27, „
Nathaniel Tucker—'Antelope'	„ 28, „
Edward Stepheson—Commodore at Surat	Aug. 21, „
Thomas Turner—'Fly'	June 21, 1799
Thomas Skinner—'Teignmouth'	Dec. 1, 1800
William Maughan—In Europe	Aug. 8, „
Thomas Dobinson—'Ternate'	„ 2, 1801

First-Lieutenants.

George Roper—'Intrepid'	Nov. 9, 1792
John Hayes—Eastward	„ 9, „
Edward Lowes—'Panther'	„ 9, „
Charles Keys—On shore	Jan. 19, 1793
Thomas Hawkswell—'Princess Royal'	May 9, „
Levi Philips—Assistant to the Superintendent, Judge Advocate, and Secretary to the Marine Board	„ 9, „
Thomas Dade Beaty—'Viper'	July 30, „
John Wales—In Europe	„ 31, „
John Proctor—In Europe	Aug. 1, „
Henry Frost—'Mornington'	„ 7, „
William Manwaring—At Amboyna	„ 7, „
Robert Budden—'Drake'	„ 7, „
John Wedgebrough—Absent with leave	„ 21, „
Samuel Snook—1st Assistant to the Master-Attendant	Feb. 12, 1798
Thomas Bennett—On shore	„ 12, „
James Jeakes—'Alert'	„ 12, „
John Lawrence—Red Sea	„ 12, „
Jonathan Mickie—Assistant to the Marine Storekeeper	„ 12, „
George Barnes—Boat-Master at Surat	„ 12, „
Charles Gilmour—'Princess Augusta'	„ 21, „
Philip Bewicke—Proceeding to Europe	„ 21, „
Charles Court—At Mannado	„ 21, „
John Walter Hamilton—'Mornington'	„ 21, „
Robert Scott—To the Eastward	„ 21, „
William Hewitson—'Bombay'	„ 21, „
Thomas Smee—'Marquis Cornwallis'	Aug. 8, 1800
John Sexton—'Mornington'	„ 8, „

of exchange, exclusive of some fees of which we have not the particulars; and the pay of the Commodore was 24,000 rupees

First-Lieutenants.—(Continued.)

Names and Stations.	Dates of Commissions.
John Alexander Ramsay—In Europe	Aug. 8, 1800
Edmund Smyth—'Antelope'	,, 8, ,,
Richard Bird—On shore	,, 2, 1801
William Nesbitt—2nd Assistant to the Master-Attendant	,, 2, ,,

Second-Lieutenants.

Names and Stations.	Dates of Commissions.
William Henry—'Comet'	April 27, 1797
Charles Saunders—Sick quarters	Feb. 12, 1798
Duncan Davidson Conyers—'Bombay'	,, 12, ,,
Robert Deane—At Banda	,, 12, ,,
Richard Bennett—'Panther'	,, 12, ,,
Charles Sealy—'Marquis Cornwallis'	,, 12, ,,
John Ackenby—'Teignmouth'	June 21, 1799
Joshua Allen—'Bombay'	,, 21, ,,
James Watson—'Viper'	,, 21, ,,
John Pruin—'Marquis Cornwallis'	,, 21, ,,
John Stanney—In Europe	,, 21, ,,
Richard Morgan—'Mornington'	,, 21, ,,
Stephen Best—'Intrepid'	,, 21, ,,
Jacob Maughan—'Ternate'	Aug. 8, 1800
William Nicholson—'Intrepid'	,, 8, ,,
William Eatwell—'Rodney'	,, 8, ,,
William P. Foley—In Europe	,, 8, ,,
George Walker—'Panther'	,, 8, ,,
William Henry Taylor—'Intrepid'	,, 8, ,,
Charles H. Salter—'Antelope'	,, 8, ,,
George Rowling—To the Eastward	,, 8, ,,

Volunteers.

Names and Stations.	Dates of Appointments.
Henry Davidson—'Princess Royal'	—
William Douglas	—
William Blythe	—
David D. Murray	—
Francis Salmond	—
Andrew Brown	—
Daniel Ross—'Amboyna'	—
George J. Hepburne—'Marquis Cornwallis'	—
William Thomas Graham—'Bombay'	—
George Henderson—'Amboyna'	April 20, 1796
Edward Lowther—In Europe	May 12, ,,
James Watkins—'Princess Augusta'	,, 11, ,,
William Bruce—On shore	—
Charles Gowan—'Teignmouth'	April 13, ,,
John Russell—'Queen'	—
Nathaniel Gilmore—'Fly'	Jan, 27, 1795
Charles Baker—'Comet'	June 3, ,,
Thomas Harriott—'Marquis Cornwallis'	Mar. 31, 1797
Horace Ange—'Mornington'	—
Isaac Richardson—'Comet'	April 21, ,,
George H. Hanrey—'Antelope'	,, 26, ,,
Thomas Blast	Dec. 28, ,,
John Hall—'Viper'	Jan. 20, 1798
William Milne—'Marquis Cornwallis'	,, 11, ,,
William Maxfield—'Alert'	,, 16, ,,
Charles Lord—'Fly'	—

per annum. Some years later the title of junior captain as a substantive rank, was created, and the numbers of the superior grades stood at eight senior and eight junior captains; the lieutenants' list remained at the same strength, while the number of the rank of midshipmen or volunteers, fluctuated with the will of Government and the exigencies of the Service.

Mr. P. Dundas occupied the office of Superintendent for three or four years with considerable credit to himself and benefit to the Bombay Marine, and, at the end of that time, was removed to another office; his loss was regretted by the officers of the Service, whose honour and welfare he had ever studied, while mindful of the interests of Government. He was succeeded by Captain William Taylor Money, who proved himself an equally efficient head of the Service entrusted to his care, and united the regards of his employers with the good-will and loyalty of his subordinates.

To assist in thwarting Napoleon in his schemes on Egypt, which, however, Nelson and Abercromby did most effectually in their victories of the Nile in 1798 and Alexandria in 1801, the British Government despatched, in 1799, a naval force from England to cruise in the Red Sea.

At the same time, orders were sent to the Bombay Government to secure and fortify the island of Perim, which is the first notice we have of the intention, subsequently carried into effect, of Great Britain seeking to command the waters of the Red Sea, by the same means she has so successfully employed in the Mediterranean; thus, in her hands, in course of time Aden and Perim have become almost as important strategic points as Gibraltar and Malta, and are scarcely less essential to the protection of the highway to her Eastern possessions. Mention has already been made of Perim, in the Straits of Babelmandeb, as the island which the European pirates, under Avory and Kidd, first occupied, but which, owing to the want of water, for which they made extensive borings, they were obliged to evacuate for other ports in Madagascar. Acting under instructions, the Bombay Government, in April,

Volunteers.—(Continued.)

Names and Stations.	Dates of Appointments.
George Furghall—'Rodney'	Mar. 15, 1798
Thomas Dyke Ballantyne—'Marquis Cornwallis'	Sept. 5, ,,
John Mack—Inspector at Surat	Feb. 22, 1799
David Ross—'Bombay'	Mar. 6, ,,
Philip Maughan—'Ternate'	—
David McDonald—'Mornington'	—
Henry Hardy	Feb. 27, 1801
William Arrow—'Teignmouth'	—
Frederick Faithfull—'Bombay'	Feb. 3, 1801
John Spier Young—'Fly'	—
David Jones—'Teignmouth'	—

1799, despatched some of their ships with three hundred European and Native troops, exclusive of followers, under the command of Colonel (afterwards General Sir) John Murray, who was appointed Political Commissioner for the Red Sea; and on the 3rd of May, Perim, not being claimed by any Government, was formally taken possession of by the East India Company.

The island only remained in the occupation of the English until the 1st of September following, when it was evacuated, owing to the want of water, the troops being withdrawn to Aden, whose chief, Ahmed, offered them an asylum. Colonel Murray remained at this stronghold, destined at no distant date to pass under the sway of his country, until the following March, when he brought his troops back to Bombay.

Acting in co-operation with the military and naval expedition to Egypt of 1801, under Sir Ralph Abercromby and Lord Keith, on the 21st of April in that year, a small squadron of vessels, under Rear-Admiral John Blankett, in the 'Leopard,' fifty guns, landed at Suez a portion of the 86th Regiment and other troops which, after taking possession of the town, previously evacuated by the French, marched on the 6th of June to Cairo, under command of Colonel Lloyd of the 86th Regiment. On the 15th of June, the 'Leopard' and other vessels anchored at Cosseir, where a squadron, under command of Captain Sir Home Riggs Popham, of the 'Romney,' fifty guns, had been engaged since the 8th of the the month in landing the second division of General Baird's army, which had been despatched from India, the first division, under Colonel Murray, having arrived and disembarked in the preceding month. Several vessels of the Bombay Marine participated in this expedition, and assisted in transporting General Baird's force from Bombay to Cosseir. The total of the force consisted of five thousand two hundred and twenty-six soldiers, and included a division of one thousand two hundred men from the Cape, and two regiments and some artillery from the Bombay Presidency. General Baird marched across the Desert *viâ* Kenneh on the Nile, to Cairo, which, however, had been surrendered by General Belliard to General Hutchinson on the 27th of June, several days before his arrival; the capitulation of General Menou and his entire army of eight thousand men at Alexandria, on the 2nd of September, caused the final ruin of the cause of France in Egypt. The officers and crew of the Bombay Marine engaged in this expedition received the Egypt medal.

In 1800, at the request of the Court of Directors, Sir Home Popham, commanding H.M.S. 'Romney,' had been despatched from England on a double mission to the Red Sea, having for its object the revival of the trade in coffee, as well as the conveyance of troops to Egypt. Sir Home proceeded in company with the 'Leopard' to Mocha, where Admiral Blankett died on the 14th of July, and to Calcutta, whence he returned in 1802 to the former city as Envoy from the Governor-General, Lord Wellesley, but the mission he despatched to the Imaum of Sanaa to conclude a treaty, ended abortively.

The cessation of hostilities, arising from the peace of Amiens, the news of which was brought to India by Mr. P. Maughan, of the Bombay Marine, was only employed, by Napoleon to strengthen his hands for continuing the war, and, at length, he threw off the mask, and publicly expressed his animosity towards this country in a memorable interview with Lord Whitworth, the British Ambassador. On the 16th of May, 1803, our Ministry declared war, which raged without intermission until Napoleon's abdication in 1814. On the reception of the news of the outbreak of hostilities, the Indian Government despatched the 'Bombay,' frigate, thirty-eight guns, bearing the broad pennant of Commodore John Hayes,* the

* The following is a copy of the Commission from the Governor-General and Council, under which Captain Hayes acted, and it is of interest as indicating the very full powers conferred on such officers of the Bombay Marine, as commanded the confidence of the supreme authorities in India:—

"Commodore's Commission.

"To John Hayes, Esq., Captain in the Bombay Marine.

"Greeting—

"Whereas, open hostilities have taken place between our Sovereign Lord the King, and the French and Batavian Republics, and whereas, we, the said United Company are duly authorized and empowered, by virtue of divers Charters in that behalf, given and granted unto us by the predecessors of our said Sovereign Lord, King of Great Britain, France, and Ireland, to raise and maintain forces and armies, both by sea and land, and to appoint such and so many Generals, Commanders, and other officers as we shall think fit for the purpose of encountering and resisting by force of arms all and every, the enemy and enemies of our said Sovereign Lord the King and ourselves, and the said enemies and every of them, their ships' armour, ammunition, and other goods, to invade and destroy in such manner as in and by the said Charters is provided, mentioned, and contained. Now we, the said United Company, in consideration of the premises, and reposing especial trust and confidence in your good conduct, loyalty, and courage, do by these presents, and under and by virtue of the Royal Charter aforesaid, and all other powers in us vested, constitute and appoint you, John Hayes, Esq., Captain in the Bombay Marine, to be, during the hostilities aforesaid, and during our pleasure, and the pleasure of our Governor-General in Council, Commodore of all the ships and vessels employed in our Naval and Bengal Marine service, for and under our Presidency of Fort William in Bengal, and of all our regular, extra, and freighted ships whatsoever, wheresoever you shall fall in with them, and to take the command of the same as Commodore with the same authority as belongs to the office of Commodore in the Naval Service of our said Lord the King, and in the same manner as used in the said service, and to be Captain of the Bombay ships of war to be employed in our said Naval and Marine Service, against the said French and Batavian Republics, and all other nations and people, against whom you may and shall be lawfully commanded to act during such hostilities, either by proclamation issued by our Governor-General in Council or by orders from our said Governor-General in Council specially to you directed. You are therefore duly to command, exercise, and keep in good order and discipline, all commissioned officers, warrant officers, seamen, and others subordinate to you, according to such authority, rules, powers, and provisions, as, in and by the said Charters, are mentioned and contained, and as legally may be done, and we do hereby command them to obey you conformably thereto as their Captain, in which station you are to observe and follow all such orders and directions as you shall

'Mornington,' twenty-two guns, 'Teignmouth,' sixteen guns, and other vessels, to the eastward, to protect the trade in the Bay of Bengal, and in adjacent waters, one vessel being also stationed, under the orders of Mr. R. T. Farquhar, Lieutenant-Governor of Penang, or Prince of Wales' Island, which the Company had acquired by purchase from the King of Queda in 1785.

During the period Commodore Hayes held the chief naval command in these seas, he asserted the right of his Honourable masters on the coast of Sumatra, by recapturing the fort of Muckee, and recovering the remaining part of the ordnance and stores taken from the Company's agents by the treachery of the Malay inhabitants. After cannonading, for three days, the three batteries the enemy opposed to him, he landed at the head of two divisions of seamen, selected by him from the crews of the Honourable Company's ships 'Bombay' and 'Castlereagh,' and, after a sharp conflict, took possession of the works, which, together with other batteries in the interior, he caused to be dismantled and destroyed. On these occasions, sixty-seven pieces of ordnance and other valuable stores fell into his hands, and were, together with the property that he recovered, sent to Mr. Ewer, the Government Commissioner at Bencoolen, in Sumatra, then in the possession of the British, but exchanged with the Dutch Government for Malacca, in the year 1824.

During the period Commodore Hayes commanded the Bengal squadron, it is a fact that has been recorded as an evidence of his energy and public spirit, that no British merchant ships suffered by capture within the limits of his cruise or authority; and yet his striking qualifications as an able naval commander, greatly militated against his acquiring the pecuniary emoluments which, in those days, were regarded as one of the great incentives to exertion in the East. As we have mentioned, it was the custom for the senior officers of the Bombay Marine to receive the advantages accruing from convoying for a certain number of voyages the merchant ships that traded to Mocha and Bussorah, and also to hold in annual rotation the lucrative post of Commodore at Surat, a situation

receive from time to time from us, our Governor-General in Council for the time being, in pursuance of the trust hereby reposed in you; and we do by these presents authorize and empower you, John Hayes, Esq., by force of arms or otherwise, to apprehend, seize, and take the ships and goods belonging to the said French and Batavian Republics, and all and every their subjects and people, being enemies of our said Lord the King, and of ourselves, pursuant to the powers and within the limits in the said Charter for that purpose mentioned and prescribed, and to bring the same to such port as shall be most convenient, in order to have the same legally adjudged and condemned as prizes.

"In witness whereof our Governor-General in Council has hereunto set our Common Seal.

(Signed) "WELLESLEY,
"BARLOW,
"UDNEY."

which usually enabled Marine officers to retire with an ample fortune. To none of these good things of office did the gallant Commodore succeed; when, therefore, he took his departure on furlough to England in 1806, he was a poor man, though, doubtless, it was a poverty honourable to him as a patriot and a seaman, for in times when the hands of many public servants in both the Military and Civil services were not withheld from the receipt of bribes, it was honourable for an officer who had filled such responsible posts to show his to the world, undefiled from the pollution of aught save his bare pay.

In 1807, while in England, he was, as a special reward for his services, appointed Deputy Master-Attendant at Bengal, and was designated to succeed as Master-Attendant on the death or resignation of the incumbent, without in any way prejudicing his rank, standing, or pay, in the Bombay Marine.

Captain Hayes returned to India in November, 1808, and, from that date, acted as Deputy Master-Attendant and Secretary to the Marine Board until the 15th of April following, when he was appointed Master-Attendant and a member of the Marine Board. While holding this double appointment, he proved himself a thorough man of business, and evinced, in the most practical manner, his desire to effect a saving in the hitherto somewhat reckless system of expenditure in the Marine Department. By dint of careful supervision, he saved the Government, during the first six years he held the office of Master-Attendant, seven and a-half lacs of rupees, or £75,000; still further, by his attention to the economical management of the interests confided to his charge, it appears from official statements that by employing in various services, foreign to the original purpose of their construction, certain vessels under his control, and thereby avoiding the expense of hiring private ships for those services, he effected a saving of not less than three lacs of rupees (£30,000). He also improved the Pilot Establishment. Such were some of the beneficial results accruing to the Government through the exertions of this meritorious officer.

In 1803, the Company's fourteen-gun brig 'Fly,'[*] Lieutenant

---

[*] This small cruiser had been before employed carrying despatches to and from the Indian Government, for we find that Lord Nelson, immediately after the battle of the Nile, deputed one of his officers with letters to the Governor of Bombay reporting his brilliant victory. The bearer of these despatches proceeded viâ Aleppo and Bagdad, where the Turkish Pasha received him with great consideration, and embarked at Bussorah on board the 'Fly' for Bombay. The Company continued to retain a Resident at Bussorah during the first quarter of the present century, long after their trade had ceased to be of any consequence; but this functionary was of service in forwarding despatches, representing British interests, and promoting the trade between the port and merchant vessels carrying the English pass and colours. The establishment, which was kept up at a cost of £5,000 per annum, was located in the finest house in the city, and vied in the splendour of its surroundings with the *entourage* of the Mutesillim, or Governor, himself. Later on, the post of Resident was suppressed, for there no longer remained any excuse for its maintenance, the despatches when forwarded overland

Mainwaring, was captured off the island of Kenn (Kais) in the Persian Gulf, by the French privateer 'La Fortune,' thirty-eight guns, commanded by the famous Captain Surcouff. Before the enemy boarded his ship, the Captain of the little cruiser ran her into shoal water near that island, and sunk the Government despatches and some treasure with which he was charged, in about two and a-half fathoms of water, taking marks for the recovery of them, if possible, at some future time.

The narrative of the adventures of the crew of the 'Fly,' as given by Buckingham in his "Travels," is of romantic interest, and very characteristic of those times. The passengers and crew were taken to Bushire, where lay some other vessels captured by the French privateer. They, and some other prisoners collected there, were set at liberty, except the commander, Lieutenant Mainwaring, and his officers, Lieutenants Arthur and Maillard, who were taken to the Mauritius, probably with a view to effect an exchange. A number of those who were left behind, purchased by subscription a country dhow at Bushire, and fitted her out with necessaries for her voyage to Bombay. On their passage down the Gulf, as they thought it would be practicable to recover the Government packet and treasure off Kenn,* they repaired to that island, and were successful, after much exertion, in recovering the former, which, being in their estimation of the first importance, as the despatches were from England to Bombay, they sailed with them on their way thither without loss of time.

Near the mouth of the Gulf, between Cape Mussundom and the island called the Great Tomb, they were captured by a fleet of Joasmi pirates, and, after some resistance, in which several were wounded, were taken into their chief port, Ras-ul-Khymah. Here they were detained in the hope of ransom, and, during their stay, were shown to the people of the town as curiosities, no white men having been before seen there. When these unfortunate Englishmen had remained for several months in the possession of the Arabs, and there appeared no hope of their ransom, it was determined to put them to death. Luckily the poor captives bethought themselves of the treasure, and com-

---

being mostly sent in Company's cruisers viâ Cosseir, on the Red Sea, and Cairo. The Company, however, continued to retain an agent at Marghill, on the banks of the Shatt-ul-Arab, about four miles from Bussorah, and this officer, who also held the post of British Vice-Consul, was placed under the authority of the Political Resident and Consul-General at Bagdad.

* Kenn, called also Kais or Keys, is the Kisi of Marco Polo, and the Kataia of Arrian. "At Kataia," he says, "ends the province of Karmania, along the coast of which they had sailed 3,700 stadia." Between two or three miles to the westward of Mashi Point are the ruins of the ancient Mahommedan town of Hariri (Kis) extending for three-quarters of a mile along the shore, which was the great emporium of the India and China trade in the twelfth century, before Ormuz rose into importance. Its site is now marked by mounds, with tottering masses of masonry.

municated to the chief the fact of a quantity having been sunk near the island of Kenn, and of their knowing the exact spot, by bearings on shore. They offered, therefore, to purchase their own liberty by a recovery of this treasure for their captors, and a bargain was solemnly struck to the mutual satisfaction of both parties. They soon sailed for the spot, accompanied by divers accustomed to that occupation on the pearl banks of Bahrein, who, on anchoring at the precise points of bearings taken, commenced their labours. The first divers who went down were so successful that all the crew followed in their turn, so that the vessel was at one time almost entirely abandoned as she lay at anchor. As the Arab crew were also busily occupied in their golden harvest, the moment appeared favourable to escape; and the still captive Englishmen were already at their stations to overpower the few on board, cut the cable, and make sail, when their motions were either seen or suspected, and the scheme was thus frustrated. They were now given their liberty as promised, and were landed on the island of Kenn, where, however, no means offered for their immediate escape. The pirates having, at the same time, themselves landed on the island, commenced a general massacre of the inhabitants, in which their released prisoners, fearing they might be included, fled for shelter to clefts and hiding-places in the rocks. During their refuge here they lived on such food as chance threw in their way, going out under cover of the night to steal a goat and drag it to their haunts. When the pirates had, at length, completed their work of blood, and either murdered or driven off every former inhabitant of the island, they quitted it with the treasure which they had thus collected from the sea and shore.

The Englishmen now ventured to come out of their hiding-places, but had no means for effecting their escape, until good fortune, in a moment of despair, threw in their way the wreck of a boat which was still capable of repair; in searching about the now deserted village, other materials were found, and also sufficient planks and logs of wood for the construction of a raft. These were both completed in a few days, and the party embarked for the Persian shore. The boat was lost in the attempt to cross the channel and all on board perished, but the raft, with the remainder of the party, reached land in safety. As the packet of Government despatches had been found only to contain papers, which the Arabs neither understood nor valued, it had constantly remained in the possession of the unfortunate sufferers, who contrived to guard it with almost religious zeal.

On gaining the mainland, they set out on foot for Bushire, following the line of coast for the sake of the villages and water; in this they are said to have suffered incredible hardships and privations of every kind. No one knew the language of the country, which was a *terra incognita* to them; they were almost destitute of clothes and money, and were constantly subjected to plunder and imposition. The Indian sailors, Sepoys, and servants, of whom a few were still remaining when they set out, had all dropped off, and the Europeans, one after another, were also abandoned on the road. The packet being light, was still, however, carried by turns, and preserved through all obstacles and difficulties, and with it they reached, at length, the island of Busheab, to which they crossed over in a boat from the main. Here they were detained, and money was even demanded of them by the sheikh, for his protection, or permission to land on the island. Finding entreaty would not prevail with this inhospitable chief, and rendered desperate by their accumulated miseries, they threatened the vengeance of the British Government, if they were not instantly furnished by him with a boat for the conveyance of themselves and the despatches in their charge to Bushire. This had the desired effect, the boat was provided and the party embarked. One of the number expired in the act of being conveyed from the shore, several others died on the voyage itself, and one on their arrival at Bushire; leaving, out of all their numerous party, two survivors, a Mr. Yowl and Pennel, an English seaman. These ultimately reached Bombay with the packet, for the preservation of which they were thought to be adequately rewarded after their almost unexampled sufferings, by a mere letter of thanks from the Government.

The Bombay Government, on hearing of the loss of the 'Fly,' determined to try and effect the capture of the French privateer, 'La Fortune,' and selected Lieutenant Court, an officer distinguished alike for his gallantry, his scientific acquirements, which he displayed in the survey of the Red Sea, and his political talents, as evinced by him when Resident in Celebes. Lieutenant Court, then in command of the cruiser 'Princess Augusta,' was actively engaged in blockading Severndroog, now again the haunt of pirates, but returned to Bombay, and, shifting his pennant to the 'Ternate,' of sixteen guns, was about to sail for the Persian Gulf to seek for an enemy carrying double his armament of guns and men, when intelligence arrived of her capture by H.M.'s frigate 'Concorde.'

Not long after the loss of the 'Fly,' the 'Viper,' of fourteen guns, was also captured by a French ship of greatly superior force, and about the same time a severe action was fought between the 'Teignmouth,' sixteen guns, commanded by Lieutenant Hewitson, and a French privateer of the same force. The fire of the enemy had for some time ceased, and the 'Teignmouth' was about to take possession, when an explosion of powder took place on board the cruiser, by which several men were killed; upon this the privateer made sail, and, though Lieutenant Hewitson gave chase, he could not overtake her.

The 'Teignmouth' lost eight men killed, and a large number wounded, including Lieutenant Arrow, father of the late Sir Frederick Arrow, Deputy-Master of the Trinity House, and Lieutenant Hewett, of the Madras Army, who lost an arm.

In 1805, the Company's frigates, 'Cornwallis,' fifty-six, and 'Bombay,' thirty-eight, were made over to the Royal Navy, and the following vessels were built in Bombay for the Service:—1805, 'Prince of Wales,' sloop-of-war, fourteen guns. 1806, 'Mercury,' sloop-of-war, fourteen guns; 'Nautilus,' brig, fourteen guns, and 'Sylph,' schooner, eight guns. 1807, 'Benares,' sloop-of-war, fourteen guns. 1809, 'Aurora,' sloop-of-war, fourteen guns, and ten-gun brig 'Vestal.' 1810, ten-gun brigs, 'Ariel,' 'Psyche' and 'Thetis.'

The harbour or bay of St. Paul's, in the Isle of Bourbon, having long been the rendezvous of French cruisers on the Indian station, and afforded shelter to the valuable prizes made by the enemy, Commodore Josias Rowley, of the sixty-four-gun ship 'Raisonable,' the senior officer of the British squadron cruising off the Isles of France and Bourbon, concerted with Colonel Henry S. Keating, commanding the troops at the adjacent small island of Rodriguez, recently taken possession of by the British, a plan for capturing the batteries and shipping at St. Paul. This was carried into effect on the 21st of September, 1809, by a combined military and naval force, including the Bombay Marine cruiser 'Wasp,' Lieutenant Watkins.'*

* On the 16th September, 1809, says James, a detachment of three hundred and sixty-eight officers and men embarked at Fort Duncan, in the island of Rodriguez, on board the thirty-six-gun frigate, 'Néréide,' Captain Robert Corbet, eighteen-gun sloop 'Otter,' Captain Willoughby, and the Hon. Company's cruiser, 'Wasp,' Lieutenant Watkins; and on the evening of the 18th joined, off Port Louis, in the Isle of France, the rest of the squadron, consisting of the 'Raisonable,' thirty-six-gun frigate 'Sirius,' Captain Pym, and thirty-eight-gun frigate, 'Boadicea,' Captain Hatley. On the 19th a force of six hundred and four soldiers, sailors, and marines, was put on board the 'Néréide,' when the squadron stood towards Bourbon, and, early on the following morning, arrived off the east end of the island. On approaching the Bay of St. Paul, the 'Néréide,' to prevent suspicion, preceded the other ships, and, at daybreak on the 21st, having anchored close to the beach, the frigate disembarked the troops without causing any alarm, about seven miles from St. Paul. The troops and marines, commanded by Colonel Keating, and the detachment of seamen by Captain Willoughby, immediately commenced a forced march, with the view of crossing the causeways that extend over the lake, before the French could discover their approach. This important object the British fully accomplished, nor had the French time to form in any force until after Colonel Keating and his party had passed the strongest position. By seven a.m. the troops were in possession of the first and second batteries, and, immediately, Captain Willoughby, with his detachment of seamen, turned the guns of those batteries upon the shipping, from whose fire, which was chiefly grape, and within pistol-shot of the shore, the force had suffered much. A detachment now marched and took quiet possession of the third battery, having previously defeated the islanders in a skirmish. The enemy having been reinforced from the hills, and by a party of one hundred and ten soldiers from the French frigate 'Caroline,' the guns of the first and second batteries were spiked, and the seamen sent to man the third battery, which soon opened its fire upon the 'Caroline' and her

As to the means employed by the French, in Mauritius and Bourbon, to obtain crews for their prizes, James, the naval historian, says:—" There could have been no difficulty in manning the 'Caroline,' as the 'Cannonière' and 'Sémillante,' on their departure for Europe as merchant ships, had left behind the principal part of their crews. There was, also, we regret to have to state, another source whence the French at the Isle of France derived a supply both of sailors and soldiers, but chiefly of the latter. When any prisoners were brought in, every art was made use of to inveigle them into the French service. As the bulk of the prisoners consisted of detachments of soldiers taken out of the Indiamen, and as the majority of these were Irish Catholics, an assurance that France had not yet abandoned her intentions of conquering Ireland and restoring the Catholic religion, was generally found a successful expedient, especially when accompanied with threats of the most rigid confinement in case of refusal. Other deserters, no doubt, had not the excuse of the poor Hibernian to make. Nor were soldiers on this occasion the only traitors; between twenty and thirty of the late 'Laurel's'[*] crew entered with the enemy they had so resolutely fought."[†] In marked contrast to this was the conduct of the Sepoy marines of the Company's cruiser 'Aurora,' fourteen guns, Lieutenant Watkins, captured off Mauritius by the French frigates 'Iphigenia' and 'Astrée.'

On the capture of the 'Aurora' she was taken into Port Louis, when every inducement was held out to the marines to

consorts. The fourth and fifth batteries shared the fate of the others, and by 8.30, a.m., the town batteries, magazines, eight field-pieces, one hundred and seventeen new and heavy guns of different calibres, and all the public stores, with several prisoners, were in the possession of Colonel Keating and his small force. In the meantime the British squadron, having stood into the bay, had opened a heavy fire on the French frigate, two captured Indiamen, and other armed vessels in her company, as well as upon some batteries, and then having brought to an anchor in the road, close off the town of St. Paul, began taking measures to secure the 'Caroline' and the rest of the French ships, all of which had cut their cables and were drifting on shore. The seamen of the squadron, however, soon succeeded in heaving the ships off, without any material injury. "Thus was effected," says James, "in the course of a few hours, by a British force of inconsiderable amount, the capture of the only safe anchorage at Isle Bourbon, together with its strong defences and shipping, and that with a total loss of fifteen killed, fifty-eight wounded, and three missing." The captured ships were the 'Caroline,' French frigate, 'Grappler,' fourteen-gun brig, the Company's late trading ships, 'Streatham' and 'Europe,' and five or six smaller vessels. By evening the demolition of the different gun and mortar batteries and of the magazines was complete, and the whole of the troops, marines, and seamen returned on board their ships.

On the 23rd, at daybreak, they were all in the boats, ready again to land, when terms for the delivery of all public property in the town were drawn up and agreed to. General Des Brusleys having shot himself, through chagrin, as alleged, at the success of the British, a prolongation of the armistice was granted for five days. On the 28th the truce expired, and the British force immediately began shipping the provisions, ordnance stores, and small remainder of the cargoes of the captured Indiamen. This done, Commodore Rowley made sail from the Bay of St. Paul.

* The 'Laurel' was a British frigate captured by the French.
† James' "Naval History," Vol. v.

abjure their allegiance, and join the French, but all solicitations were without effect. A new system was then tried, which will ever reflect dishonour on General Decaen. Everything short of torture that could be devised was put in practice; the Sepoys were forced to perform dirty work and to endure hardships and want of provisions. Each morning also they were brought out and shown the captured Bengal and Madras Sepoys, in French uniforms, enjoying luxuries, but all was without effect; persuasion was again tried in vain, for the Marines answered by abusing the traitors, who had forgotten their military oath, and deserted their colours, and such an effect had their noble example upon these men, that, at length, overcome with shame, a large body of them threw down their arms and quitted the ranks. After this unexpected event, the Bombay marines were confined on board the hulks and in cells, enduring every hardship until they were released by the capture of the island in the following year. On the return of the 'Aurora' to Bombay, the whole of the preceding details were brought to the notice of Government, when every man had a handsome medal presented to him having on one side an inscription, in the native language, detailing their noble conduct, and, on the reverse, the same in English. Each man received promotion of one step, and was noted for further advancement, and other privileges were conferred, while a Government Order was published paying a high and just compliment to their fidelity, and stated the rewards granted to them. This order, moreover, was read at the head of every Native regiment in the Bombay army, and explained to the men. These faithful fellows were Concanny Purwarries, and there can be no doubt that the loyalty they exhibited against every allurement and threat, was, in no small measure, due to the good treatment they received at the hands of the officers of the 'Aurora.'

During the year 1809, Isle Bourbon, which had been abandoned after its conquest in the previous September, and Isle-de-la Passe, a rocky islet about four miles from Grand Port, in Mauritius, were captured by the British squadron under Commodore Rowley; but the effect of these successes was neutralized by the loss of four British frigates, the 'Néréide,' 'Iphigenia,' 'Magicienne,' and 'Sirius,' though Captain Willoughby, of the 'Néréide,' still further increased his reputation for unsurpassed gallantry by his brilliant defence of his ship, when ninety-two men were killed and one hundred and thirty-eight wounded. These disasters, though they were redeemed by the stubborn valour shown by the officers and crews of the vanquished frigates, were yet almost unexampled in our annals, and their effect was still further increased by the loss of Isle de la Passe, which the Captain of the 'Iphigenia' was forced to surrender with his frigate, and by the capture of the 'Africaine,' thirty-eight gun frigate, Captain Corbet, by the French frigates 'Astrée' and the late prize 'Iphigenia.' In this desperate action the 'Africaine' lost her captain, mortally wounded, forty-nine officers and men killed and one hundred and fourteen wounded. Not long after the surrender, the British frigate 'Boadicea,' Commodore Rowley, arrived on the scene of action, and recaptured the 'Africaine,' whose three masts had gone over the side, and the two French ships declined to fight a second action, but returned to Port Louis. On the 17th of September, the 'Ceylon,' classed as a thirty-two gun frigate, but carrying forty guns and two hundred and forty-five men, commanded by Captain Gordon, and having on board General Abercromby and staff, was captured by the French ships 'Vénus,' forty-four guns, and three hundred and eighty men, and 'Victor,' sixteen, after a protracted and gallant resistance. Once more Commodore Rowley was enabled, on the afternoon of the same day, to prevent the French from carrying off their prize, and also forced the 'Vénus' to strike her colours after a brief engagement, while her consort, the 'Otter,' eighteen guns, took in tow the recaptured frigate 'Ceylon,' which was none other than the old 'Bombay,' of thirty-eight guns, formerly belonging to the Bombay Marine, which has so frequently figured in our narrative.

The Indian Government had long seen the necessity of wresting the island of Mauritius from the French, who made it the *point d'appui* for their depredations on British commerce in the Eastern seas;* here their ships of war and privateers found a safe asylum, whence, after refitting, they proceeded to sea again and swept the waters of the Indian Ocean between the Cape and Malacca. Hitherto they had preyed upon the Company's commerce, though, generally, not without having to fight for their prizes, but now grown more bold, and well handled by officers like Duperré, Hamelin, Bouvet, and others, they encountered British frigates of equal force. Accordingly, preparations were made at the Cape and at Bombay, for the reduction of the island and the retrieval of these disasters. An army of 10,000 men was dispatched from India under the command of General (afterwards Sir John) Abercromby, and the following ships of the Company's Marine, which had shortly before returned from an expedition against the Joasmi pirates in the Persian Gulf, were directed to proceed from Bombay :— The 'Malabar,' twenty guns ; 'Benares,' fourteen ; and the ten-gun brigs, 'Thetis,' 'Ariel,' and 'Vestal.'

By the 21st November, 1810, all the different divisions of the expedition, except that expected from the Cape of Good Hope, had assembled at the island of Rodriguez, and as, on account of the lateness of the season, it was considered un-

* In the year 1807 alone the loss to Calcutta shipping by capture was said to have exceeded £300,000.

advisable to wait for the arrival of the Cape division, the expedition, the naval portion* of which was under the command of Vice-Admiral Bertie, set sail for Mauritius on the following morning, and arrived in sight of the island on the 28th. On the 29th the men-of-war and transports, numbering in all nearly seventy sail, anchored in Grand Baie, situated about twelve miles from Port Louis, and, in the course of the same day, the army, with its artillery, stores, and ammunition, the several detachments of marines serving in the squadron, and a large body of seamen, under the orders of Captain Montagu, disembarked without opposition or casualty. On the morning of the 30th there was slight skirmishing with the enemy, and, on the 1st and 2nd of December, an affair, rather more serious, took place between the British main body and a French corps, which had taken up a strong position to check the invaders. The French, however, were soon overpowered by numbers, with the loss of their guns, and several men killed and wounded. The loss on the part of the British, including that sustained on the 30th, amounted to twenty-eight officers and men killed, ninety-four wounded, and forty-five missing. Immediately after the termination of this action, General Decaen, the French Governor, proposed terms of capitulation, and, on the following morning, the 3rd December, the articles were signed, and ratifications exchanged, by which the island was surrendered to Great Britain. The garrison of the Isle of France—henceforth known as Mauritius, the name formerly given to it by the Dutch—consisted of only one thousand three hundred regular troops, though there were upwards of ten thousand militiamen, who were, however, almost useless. Two hundred and nine pieces of heavy ordnance were captured, together with ample stores of ammunition and every other requisite for service. In Port Louis were five French frigates, 'Bellone,' 'Minerve,' 'Manche,' 'Astrée,' and (late British) 'Iphigénie,' the 'Victor' corvette, brig 'Entreprenant,' and Honourable Company's cruiser 'Aurora;' also the 'Charlton,' 'Ceylon,' and 'United Kingdom,' captured Indiamen, and twenty-four French merchant ships and brigs. From that day, Mauritius has remained one of the most valuable dependencies of the British Crown.

* The following were the British ships of war attached to the expedition, including a portion that blockaded Port Louis :—Seventy-four-gun ship 'Illustrious,' Captain Broughton; forty-four-gun frigate 'Cornwallis,' Captain Caulfield; thirty-eight-gun frigates 'Africaine, (Vice-Admiral Bertie) Captain Gordon; 'Boadicea,' Captain Rowley; 'Nisus,' Captain Beaver; 'Clorinde,' Captain Briggs; 'Menelaus,' Captain Parker; 'Néréide,' Captain Henderson; thirty-six-gun frigates 'Phœbe,' Captain Hillyar; 'Doris,' Captain Lye; thirty-two-gun frigates 'Cornelia,' Captain Edgell; 'Psyche,' Captain Edgcumbe; 'Ceylon,' Captain Tomkinson; sloops, 'Hesper,' Captain Paterson; 'Eclipse,' Captain Lynne; 'Hecate,' Captain Rennie; 'Actæon,' Captain Viscount Neville; gun-brig 'Staunch,' Lieutenant Craig; Government ship 'Emma,' Captain Street, and a large fleet of transports.

The Bombay Marine, under the command of that able and energetic officer, Captain R. Deane, of the 'Malabar,' co-operated with zeal and efficiency in the operations ending in the surrender of the island, and Admiral Bertie made honourable mention of the commanders, officers, and crews, in a separate letter of thanks. But, nevertheless, strange as it may seem, the Admiral made no reference in his despatches to the Service, so that the future historian could not even gather from these records that any vessel of the Bombay Marine participated in the expedition; and, indeed, the effect of this omission is apparent in the pages of James, the naval historian of the Revolutionary War, who particularizes the names of "gun-brigs," and "Government vessels," but makes no allusion to the well-equipped squadron of Company's ships, which, having shortly before returned from completing their task of breaking up a notorious nest of pirates in the Persian Gulf, for which they had received the cordial thanks of the Bombay Government and the hearty acknowledgments of the senior naval officer, Commodore Wainwright of the British Navy, were despatched to participate in the reduction of the Island of Mauritius.

A good idea of the gallant service performed by the Bombay Marine, during the Revolutionary War, will be gathered from some extracts which we will make from a work, published by a late officer of the Service, entitled "A Narrative of the Early Life and Services of Captain D. Macdonald, Indian Navy." Captain D. Macdonald, brother of Sir John Kinneir Macdonald, sometime British Envoy to the Persian Court, went out to India to join the Service in 1799, in the 'Scaleby Castle,' and, after a long passage, during which a malignant fever carried off no less than one hundred and eighty seamen and soldiers of the 34th Regiment, arrived at Bombay in the summer of 1800. On recovering his health, which had suffered severely from the fever, he was appointed to the sloop-of-war 'Mornington,' fitting out under the command of Captain Richardson, for the especial service of the Supreme Government, then administered by Lord Mornington, afterwards Marquis Wellesley. She had been recently launched and equipped, and, says Mr. Macdonald, " in those days of naval architecture, was considered by all competent authorities, a beautiful specimen of her class; her armament consisted of twenty 32-pounders and four long 18-pounders."

The 'Mornington' sailed from Bombay about the end of September, with despatches for Vice-Admiral Rainier, the Naval Commander-in-chief in India, and, having *en route* landed, at Tellicherry, General Carnac, an octogenarian warrior who had borne a conspicuous part in the wars of Clive and Warren Hastings, and looked into Trincomalee, proceeded to Madras. The Admiral having left Madras Roads, his despatches were handed over to Captain, (afterwards Admiral Sir) Pulteney Malcolm, of H.M's. ship 'Suffolk,' and the 'Mornington' was directed to afford convoy to three country ships returning to Calcutta, in whose company she encountered one of those severe tempests which not infrequently occur in the Indian Ocean, about the breaking up of the south-west monsoon. The 'Mornington' was totally dismasted, and reduced to the extremity of peril. Captain Macdonald gives a vivid picture of the terrific hurricane and the narrow escape she had from foundering. The ship, however, succeeded in reaching Calcutta under jury masts, and her commander was succeeded by Captain Frost, an officer of rare judgment and enterprise, whose gallantry at Coupang has already been related. At Calcutta a fleet of merchant ships, arrived from England to load with rice in that year of scarcity, was lying at anchor, and the 'Mornington,' having taken her pick of seamen from these ships, who were disgusted at the ill-treatment they had received, proceeded to sea well manned and found. Mr. Macdonald says that her usual cruising-ground was in the upper part of the Bay of Bengal and Sandheads, and, when once the south-west monsoon had fairly set in, it was customary to run down to the eastward, as far as the entrance to the China Seas, taking care to be back in Atcheen roads by September, in readiness to resume her station as soon as the season would permit, which was generally towards the early part or middle of October.

Returning about this time in 1801, with a Danish Indiaman, which the 'Mornington' had captured in the Bay of Bengal, richly laden with spices and an assorted cargo, besides a large remittance in gold dust from Batavia, they fell in with one of the enemy's cruisers off Ganjam, in chase of a small English ship under a press of sail. It was late in the afternoon, and in the midst of a heavy squall of wind and rain, that the 'Mornington' came so unexpectedly to the rescue, and but for her opportune arrival upon the scene the capture of the chase was inevitable, as the Frenchman was overhauling her "hand-over-fist." On the subsidence of the squall, the latter discovering the 'Mornington' so close to his lee-beam, went about under all the canvas he could spread, whilst the merchantman bore up and joined the cruiser. Captain Frost lost sight of the enemy owing to the darkness of the night, but succeeded in saving from his fangs one of the Honorable Company's packets, 'Georgiana,' Captain Leigh, bearing despatches from England for the Governor-General, and having on board, in charge of them, the Hon. H. Wellesley, afterwards Lord Cowley, who was proceeding to join his noble brother at Calcutta. It was shortly afterwards ascertained that the enemy's ship was 'La Confiance,' M. Surcouff, the same officer who captured the 'Kent,' Indiaman, after a sanguinary conflict, and committed the most brutal and cruel excesses on the unfortunate passengers and crew of that ship, and who later captured the fourteen-gun brig 'Fly.'

The years 1800-2 were singularly propitious for the privateers, among the most successful of which were ' La Confiance,' already mentioned, and 'l'Eugénie,' the former pierced for twenty-six but carrying twenty-two guns, and two hundred and fifty men, and the latter, commanded by M. Constance, carrying eighteen guns and one hundred and eighteen officers and men ; the very superior sailing qualities of ' l'Eugénie,' made her particularly mischievous, while her bold commander cruised within the limits of the pilot's water. Such audacity drew from the underwriters repeated applications to Government, who, in their turn, were exceedingly anxious that her career should be arrested, and the attention of all the commanders of the ships-of-war on the station, was directed to effect its speedy consummation. The 'l'Eugénie' was a large American schooner, expressly built for privateering, and of extraordinary swiftness. Captain Frost was greatly annoyed at her having escaped him, and determined by disguising his ship, to allay all suspicion of his warlike character, and bring her to action. With this design, a false poop, to resemble that of a country ship, was hastily constructed, the painting changed, patches of old dirty canvas were put into the topsails and courses, and every other expedient adopted to render complete this " scene of excellent dissembling."

A few days sufficed for the transformation of the smart little man-of-war, and Captain Frost had just dropped into the track she probably would be watching, when, early one morning, the look out from the mast-head descried a sail far on the lee-beam, having chosen, as was rightly conjectured, the station off the Swash, for intercepting the outward-bound. From the peculiarity of her rig, then uncommon in those seas, there could be no doubt of her identity, and pursuing his course as if wishing to avoid her, the captain of the ' Mornington' had soon the satisfaction of perceiving that the trick had succeeded, for the enemy tacked, and continued to make short boards until her whole hull appeared above the horizon ; now the closer inspection of the 'Mornington' presented no alarming appearance, but only strengthened the delusion, whilst Captain Frost kept steadily on a wind, with the sails lifting, in order to favour her approach. By sunset the enemy had fetched into his wake, and was pressing on in anticipation of a rich and easy prize. As the night fell the ' Mornington' shortened sail, and by eight o'clock ' l'Eugénie' ranged silently under her lee-quarter, hauled her fore-sheet to windward, then hailed in good English, asking the ship's name, and desiring them to heave to, that a boat might be sent on board, to which request an assent was promptly given. Seeing the ship pay off, however, they almost immediately became aware of the fatal snare into which they had been drawn, and, bearing up also at the same moment, discharged a volley of grape and musketry into the 'Mornington,' by which the running gear was cut up, and one seaman mortally wounded. Having his ship now before the wind, Captain Frost's chief aim was to dismantle the enemy aloft, lest by any possibility she might cross him on either tack, and once more getting to windward, elude capture. In this endeavour he, happily, succeeded, and, after an exciting pursuit of three hours, during which the enemy threw overboard boats, guns, spars, and even the caboose, to facilitate their escape, the 'Mornington' came alongside again, when the second captain hailed from the companion-ladder begging her to cease firing, as they had surrendered; in the act of speaking a shot struck the trumpet from his hand, carrying with it a great portion of the poor fellow's nose. As all hands had fled below from this shower of shot, there was no one on deck to let run the throat and peak halyards, but in a few minutes this was done, and the French ship was a prize to the 'Mornington.' On taking possession she was found to be greatly crippled, and her sails so cut, that she could not be brought to the wind. As was expected, she proved to be 'l'Eugénie,' carrying eighteen guns and one hundred and eighteen men, and had made only one prize since the 'Mornington' had last met her.

Nothing could exceed the joy and satisfaction expressed by the merchants and underwriters of Calcutta, at her capture, and the Government purchased her into the service, named her the 'Alert,' and gave the command to Lieutenant Hamilton, then senior lieutenant of the 'Mornington.'

About the beginning of 1802, before tidings of the cessation of hostilities ordered on the preceding 12th of October, preparatory to the conclusion of the peace of Amiens, reached India, the Government were apprized of a frigate and corvette watering at one of the Mergui islands, upon which Captain Frost was directed to proceed off Cape Negrais, where he joined H.M S. 'Sybille,' Captain (afterwards Sir) Charles Adam, cruising between the island of Cheduba and that promontory. Captain Macdonald says:—"After a fruitless search in the quarter the enemy were reported, we turned the ship's head over more to Cape Negrais, and early on the following morning found ourselves in company with a stranger. She was discovered about the end of the middle watch, laying to, and must have sighted us about the same time, for as we wore to speak her, she got instantly under a cloud of canvas, and when the day broke we were in full chase of this long, low, black, and roguish-looking ship, whose masts hanging angularly over her stern, plainly denoted her nation and calling. The land breeze continuing to freshen as the sun mounted upwards, gave us a decided superiority over her, and enabled Captain Frost, by hanging on her lee-beam, to prevent her escape before the wind, which they were prepared to attempt, having all her studding-sail booms rigged out, and which, as we afterwards ascertained, was her best point of sailing. The 'Sybille' followed close in her wake, and by eight o'clock we arrived within gunshot, when, finding little or no chance in flight, her commander bore up, exchanged a few broadsides with us, and surrendered. She was not 'La Confiance,' as we had hoped, but 'l'Hirondelle,' M. le Même, pierced for twenty 12-pounders, with one hundred and sixty men, her first cruise out, and had made but few captures. The 'Sybille' accompanied her into port, whilst we remained in search of her consort, who, it was imagined, was still hovering in that latitude."

Mr. Midshipman Macdonald was promoted to an acting-lieutenancy on board the prize 'Alert,' and proceeded in her on a demonstration against Macao, where the fleet of men-of-war and transports lay for some months inactive off Lintin, exposed to bad weather. The 'Alert' then returned to Calcutta and Bombay, and was soon after sold out of the Service. Lieutenant Macdonald describes her as a beautiful craft, of extraordinary sailing qualities, with heavy spars and a mainmast that plumbed the taffrail.

He then joined the 'Antelope,' and after serving in her some months in the Red Sea and Persian Gulf, returned to Bombay, whence he was despatched to Broach, in charge of two gunboats, to serve in the 'Nerbudda,' under the orders of Sir John Murray. "Soon afterwards," he says, " I was appointed senior lieutenant of the 'Teignmouth,' one of the largest class brigs recently introduced into the Service, and commanded by Captain Wales, a gentleman of rare professional attainments. I continued with him for a period of nearly two years, chiefly on my former station off the Sandheads, under the orders of Commodore Hayes, in the 'Bombay' of thirty-eight guns, with a complement of three hundred and forty as fine fellows as had ever been got together, to whom the protection of the Sandheads was confided."

In July, 1805, the 'Teignmouth,' was sent to England with the treaty which brought to a close the Mahratta war and Lord Wellesley's brilliant Indian administration. It was not until the second week of November that she arrived at Plymouth, and, after a brief stay, returned with despatches for Sir Edward Pellew, at Madras, and Sir Thomas Troubridge at Penang, the admirals respectively in command of the Indian and Eastern Archipelago stations. Having delivered the despatches—that to Sir T. Troubridge conferring on him the command at the Cape, in proceeding to assume which that noble seaman perished in the 'Blenheim,' seventy-four guns, with all hands—the 'Teignmouth' sailed for Calcutta, and thence proceeded to Bombay, convoying two ships, by what is called the Southern Passage.

Here Lieutenant Macdonald received command of the 'Lively,' a small schooner of eight guns and forty men, and, in the latter part of 1807, on receipt of intelligence from Colonel Schuyler, Political Agent at Goa, that a Surat ship, captured by two French corvettes, had put into Goa to refit, he was removed for the occasion into the 'Mosquito,' pattamar, carrying seven 12-pounders, and a party of artillerymen, in addition to her crew, and sent with H.M's. brig 'Diana,' Commander Kempthorne, to lie in the offing and capture her on leaving that port. Here they watched the prize for three months, but she at length escaped, owing to the 'Diana' having hugged the weather-shore too much, and the pattamar not being fleet enough to cut off her retreat in the double-reef topsail breeze she chose for the attempt. Lieutenant Macdonald now resumed command of the 'Lively,' and, in October, 1808, proceeded in company with two armed pattamars, to the northward to watch the piratical ports of Beyt and Poshetra, at the mouth of the Gulf of Cutch.

Lieutenant Macdonald instituted so vigorous a blockade of the port of Poshetra and the neighbouring island of Beyt, that the chief gave in his submission, though the hydra head of piracy was raised again as soon as the little squadron was withdrawn to Bombay. While off the Guzerat coast, Lieutenant Macdonald encountered, with his little schooner, four piratical dhows of the Joasmi Arabs, of whom a detailed account will be given in a later chapter, and for his gallantry received the thanks of the Bombay Government.

On his return to Bombay he proceeded to take charge of the flotilla co-operating with the army in Travancore, and on the fall of Trivandrum, which terminated this war, carried General Stewart to Colombo. Early in 1810, a new brig, the 'Ariel,' of ten guns, was launched in Bombay and Lieutenant Macdonald received the command.* He sailed in July for Madras, whence he was sent by Sir George Barlow, with despatches, to Lord Minto at Calcutta, and, in October, sailed with Mr. (afterwards Sir) Stamford Raffles, to Penang and Malacca. Under that able governor, Lieutenant Macdonald was employed in important missions to the Sultan of Palimbang, and other native chiefs, and so meritorious were his services that Lord Minto, the Governor-General, conferred on him a captain's commission as a special reward.

* Lieutenant Macdonald was fortunate in leaving three ships which met with tragic fates after his connection with them had ceased. The 'Lively' was blown up and his successor killed; the 'Sylph' was captured by a strong piratical force, and nearly every soul was murdered; and the 'Ariel' foundered, and eighty-two out of eighty-five souls were drowned.

CHAPTER VIII.

1811—1816.

Services of the Marine at the Reduction of the Island of Java and its Dependencies—The Expeditions to Palimbang and Samarang—Gallantry of Lieutenant Deane in the Sambas River—Expedition against the Rajahs of Sambas and Boni—Services of Lieutenant Deane—Gallant conduct of the Marine at Macassar—Rescue of the crew of H.M.S. 'Alceste,' by the 'Ternate.'

SCARCELY had the ships of the Hon. Company's Marine, employed at the reduction of Mauritius in 1810, returned to Bombay, than they were engaged in another, and still more important enterprise.

In 1811, Lord Minto, Governor-General of India, decided upon undertaking the conquest of the Island of Java, then in possession of the Dutch, who, however, owing to Napoleon's successes, had become his allies rather by compulsion than from choice, and, accordingly, a powerful combined military and naval expedition was fitted out, to which all three Presidencies provided a contingent. His lordship proceeded to Madras, whence the major part of the troops was drawn, in the Hon. Company's ship 'Mornington,' Captain Robert Deane, to superintend the arrangements of the naval and military chiefs, whilst Sir George Hewitt and Commodore Hayes conducted the fitting out and embarkation of the Bengal Division. The Royal Navy, when all the ships were assembled, was represented by a powerful fleet,* consisting of three ships of the line, one forty-four-gun frigate, the 'Akbar,' (formerly the Bombay Marine frigate 'Corn-

---

* The following were the ships of the Royal fleet on the 9th of August, when all were assembled under command of Rear-Admiral the Hon. Robert Stopford :—'Scipion,' seventy-four, Rear-Admiral Hon. Robert Stopford, Captain Robinson; 'Illustrious,' seventy-four, Commodore Broughton, Captain Festing; 'Minden,' seventy-four, Captain Hoare; 'Lion,' sixty-four, Captain Heathcote; 'Akbar,' forty-four, Captain Drury. Thirty-eight-gun frigates, 'Nisus,' Captain Beaver; 'Présidente,' Captain Warren; 'Hussar,' Captain Crawford; 'Phaeton,' Captain Fleetwood Pellew. Thirty-six-gun frigates, 'Leda,' Captain Sayer; 'Caroline,' Captain Cole; 'Modeste,' Captain Hon. George Elliot; 'Phœbe,' Captain Hillyar; 'Bucephalus,' Captain Pelley; 'Doris,' Captain Lye. Thirty-two-gun frigates, 'Psyche,' Captain Edgcombe; 'Sir Francis Drake,' Captain Harris. Sloops of war, 'Procris,' Captain Maunsell; 'Barracouta,' Captain Owen; 'Hesper,' Captain Reynolds; 'Harpy,' Captain Bain; 'Hecate,' Captain Peachey; 'Dasher,' Captain Kelly; 'Samarang,' Captain Drury.

wallis,') four frigates of thirty-eight guns, six of thirty-six guns, two of thirty-two guns, and seven sloops of war. The Bombay Marine likewise supplied a division of eight ships, under the command of that veteran seaman, Commodore John Hayes, who resigned his post as Master-Attendant at Calcutta in order to place his services at the disposal of the Governor General, under whose immediate auspices the expedition was fitted out. Commodore Hayes hoisted his broad pennant on board the 'Malabar,' twenty guns, Commander Maxfield, as a first-class Commodore, and he had under his command, the 'Mornington,' twenty-two, Captain Robert Deane; the 'Aurora,' fourteen, Commander Watkins; 'Nautilus,' fourteen, Commander Walker; 'Vestal,' ten, Commander Hall; 'Ariel,' ten, Commander Macdonald; 'Thetis,' ten, Lieutenant Phillips; and 'Psyche,' ten, Lieutenant Tanner. There were also fifty-seven transports and several gunboats, making a total of nearly one hundred sail.

On the 18th of April, 1811, the first division of the troops, commanded by Colonel Robert Rollo Gillespie,* sailed from Madras Roads, and, on the 18th May, anchored in the harbour of Penang, or Prince of Wales' Island, the first rendezvous. Three days later the second division of the Army, under command of Major-General Frederick Wetherall, also arrived, having quitted Madras six days later. On the 24th the entire expedition sailed from Penang, and, on the 1st of June, arrived at Malacca, the second rendezvous, where the Bengal troops had preceded them five or six weeks. Lord Minto, who had taken great personal interest in the preparation of this expedition, had also arrived in the 'Modeste' frigate, Lieutenant-General Sir Samuel Achmuty, the Commander-in-chief of Madras, in command of the expeditionary army, in the 'Akbar,' and Commodore Broughton, senior naval officer, in the 'Illustrious,' seventy-four guns. On the 11th of June, the fleet, leaving behind twelve hundred sick, sailed with the army, numbering ten thousand seven hundred effective men, of whom five thousand were Europeans; and, passing through the Straits of Malacca, arrived on the 3rd of July at the High Islands, which was the third rendezvous. On the 10th the fleet quitted the High Islands, and, in ten days, reached Point Sambur,† at the extremity of the south-west coast of Borneo, forming the fourth and last rendezvous. Sir Samuel Achmuty, having assembled the whole expedition here on the 26th of July, sailed on the following day for Java. On the 30th the fleet reached

* This gallant soldier fell on the 31st of October, 1814, while leading a storming party in a second abortive attempt to carry the fortress of Kalunga, in Nepaul.

† According to James, the naval historian, the fleet arrived at, and sailed from Port Sambur on the 20th and 21st of July respectively; but we have preferred to rely for our dates in the "Memoir of the Conquest of Java" by that careful and able military historian, Major William Thorn, who was Deputy Quartermaster-General to the Expeditionary army.

Bumpkin Island near Indramay river on the Java coast, and here they remained until the 2nd of August, in expectation of being joined by some frigates with intelligence. The expedition then set sail, and, the same day, were joined by the ship having on board Colonel Mackenzie, who had reconnoitred the whole coast and reported that the most eligible spot for the disembarkation of the army was the village of Chillingching, distant about ten miles from Batavia. The fleet, therefore, which had brought to in the afternoon, again got under weigh, and every preparation was completed for effecting the disembarkation without delay. On the evening of the 3rd, the fleet made Cape Carawang, and, early on the following morning, ran in for the mouth of the Marandi river. Here the ships anchored during the interval between the land and sea breezes, and, on the latter setting in, again got under weigh, and having reached Chillingching about two p.m. on Sunday the 4th of August, the signal was immediately made for the troops to land.

On the 31st of July, while Commodore Hayes, with the 'Malabar' and 'Mornington,' was proceeding through the Straits of Gaspar, he fell in with two large Chinese junks bound from Batavia to Amoy. By the orders of Council, Batavia being in a state of blockade, they were good prizes, and were, in fact, laden with Dutch property valued at £600,000 sterling. The junks were captured by the cruisers, and Captains Deane and Maxfield proposed to send them to Prince of Wales' Island for condemnation, but Commodore Hayes declined to adopt this course for reasons set forth in the following letter, which he addressed to the commanders of the 'Malabar' and 'Mornington':—

"Hon. Company's Ship-of-war 'Malabar,' at sea, July 31, 1811,
"Lat. 50° 41'S. Long., 106° 46' E.

"Gentlemen,—As the Government of China seeks every pretext to embarrass the Hon. Company's commercial transactions at Canton, I am induced to believe the captured junks taken possession of by your respected ships under your immediate command, may be made a plea to interrupt the important trade in that quarter, which is now not only considered of vital interest to them, but to the State generally. I feel myself imperiously called upon to prevent any occurrence which may be productive of such destructive effects; I am, therefore, impelled to direct you to withdraw the prize masters and crews from the junks in question, and to command you to permit them to proceed towards their original destination. In thus exercising my authority, perhaps exceeding its legal bounds, I am not insensible of the great sacrifice which must be made by enforcing the foregoing commands; but I trust we alike feel we have the honour to serve the most liberal masters in the world, and I congratulate myself upon the conviction that the officers to whom these commands are addressed, know how to appreciate the acquisition of wealth when placed in competition with the interests of their employers and of their country.

"I am, gentlemen, your faithful servant,

"(Signed)   JOHN HAYES, Commodore of all the Hon. Company's ships and vessels, Java Expedition.

"To Captains R. Deane and W. Maxfield, Commanding the Hon. Company's Ships-of-war 'Mornington' and 'Malabar.'"

Such disinterestedness is as rare as it is noble, but it was of a piece with the conduct of Commodore Hayes throughout his long and brilliant career; and it is with feelings of pride we place on record this act of a man whose name has shed undying lustre on the Service of which he was so distinguished an ornament.

The army had been divided, while at Malacca, into four brigades, and so complete had been the arrangements that the whole force was landed that evening without accident or loss. The 'Leda' frigate, Captain Sayer, an able and intelligent officer, protected the disembarkation to the left, whilst on the right were stationed the squadron of Company's cruisers under Commodore Hayes, and several small gunboats. The advance, under Colonel Gillespie, pushed inland, to a small village in order to gain possession of the road to Cornelis, and to protect the landing of the remainder of the army, which took place without opposition from the enemy, who had left this part of the coast unguarded, as General Jansens, the newly-appointed Governor-General of Java, regarded the natural obstacles as sufficient to deter its being selected for the descent. During the night a skirmish took place between the outposts and a patrol of the enemy's cavalry, but no serious obstacle was offered to the advance of the British army upon Batavia, the capital. On the 6th the 'Leda,' the sloops, and the Company's cruisers, proceeded off the entrance of the river Anjole, while the advance occupied a new position about six miles from the capital. Encouraged by the inactivity of the enemy, Sir Samuel Achmuty pushed forward the infantry of the advance, and, during the night of the 7th, crossed the Anjole on a bridge of boats, constructed by the squadron under the orders of Captain Sayer. On the following morning the Commander-in-chief sent in his aides-de-camp to summon the town, and they returned with the head-magistrate, who was deputed on the part of the burghers to crave the protection of the British. The town having surrendered at discretion, the ships of war fired a Royal salute, and, in the evening, Colonel Gillespie entered with the greater part of the advance and took formal possession of the place. On the 9th Rear-Admiral the Hon. Robert Stopford joined the expedition in his flag-ship, the 'Scipion,' and assumed command of the fleet.

The night of the occupation of Batavia was not suffered to pass without an effort to retrieve his fortune on the part of General Jansens, who had taken post at Weltervreeden, not more than three miles distant. The attack was, however, repulsed, and, on the morning of the 10th of August, the army advanced on the enemy. An action now took place between the advance, under Colonel Gillespie, and the French advanced division, under General Jumel, which resulted in the defeat of the latter, and the occupation of Weltervreeden with its arsenal containing three hundred guns; in this affair the British loss was seventeen killed and seventy-five wounded. General Jansens, who had served with distinction in the French Army, now removed to Cornelis, described by Thorn as "an entrenched camp, defended by two rivers with a number of redoubts and batteries; the circumference of these fortified lines comprised nearly five miles, defended by two hundred and eighty pieces of cannon." A battering train was landed from the ships, the reserve joined the army from Chillingching, and the bridge was removed from the Anjole river, the communications beyond that point being abandoned. The materials for a siege having been collected,* the British Army broke ground on the night of the 20th of August, within 600 yards of the enemy's works. The batteries being nearly completed on the night of the 21st, twenty 18-pounders and nine howitzers and mortars were brought up from the ships, and mounted early on the following morning. To assist in working these batteries a body of five hundred seamen was landed from the fleet, under the command of Captain Sayer, and also a strong detachment of marines. The Dutch made a sortie at daybreak on the 22nd, but, being driven back, opened a heavy fire from forty guns, which caused considerable loss to the working parties of soldiers and seamen. During this day the casualties were ninety-six of all ranks, including six officers killed and mortally wounded.

There was a lull on the following day, and, on the 24th, the British batteries opened with a salute, which was returned in the most spirited manner, and a severe cannonade continued during the greater part of the day. Before evening, the superiority of our fire was made manifest; the nearest redoubts of the enemy were silenced, and many of their guns dismounted. The British batteries had hitherto been worked by a company of the Royal Artillery, two companies of the Bengal Artillery, and five hundred seamen from the fleet; but, owing to the casualties and the fatigue incidental to the duty in very sultry weather, it

* Speaking of the work performed at this time, Commander Macdonald, who was present, says in his " Narrative :"—" Both the officers and crews of the Hon. Company's ships of war were almost incessantly employed, day and night, under Commodore Hayes, in this arduous and most laborious duty, and in conveying the guns to the landing-place, whence they were conducted to the batteries."

was found necessary, during the night of the 24th, to send to the batteries* every available man from the regiments.

The Commander-in-chief having resolved to storm the enemy's works, Colonel Gillespie was selected to lead the principal attack. The troops moved off soon after midnight on the 26th of August, and, guided by a deserter, made a long detour of many miles, coming upon the enemy unexpectedly. A desperate struggle ensued, but the redoubts were stormed at the point of the bayonet, under a tremendous fire of grape and musketry. Meantime the remainder of the army, under the Commander-in-chief and General Wetherall, joined by a strong detachment of seamen under Captain Sayer, threatened the enemy's lines in front at the point where our batteries were placed, and the diversion had the required effect in drawing off the fire of a large body of troops from the main attack. The enemy now fled at all points, and were hotly pursued by the Dragoons, led by that brilliant soldier, Colonel Gillespie, and all the available troops joined in the pursuit, including the Naval Brigade; the whole road for ten miles was lined with the *débris* of a beaten army, and upwards of six thousand prisoners were captured, including two generals and nearly all the superior officers and heads of Departments. Thus fell the fortified works of Cornelis, with its two hundred and eighty pieces of cannon, and, before night, an army of thirteen thousand regular troops, including a regiment of Voltigeurs, newly arrived from France, was either dispersed, taken, or destroyed. In achieving this great success our loss was heavy, and fell principally on the columns engaged in the principal attack, of whom five hundred and twenty-six, including forty-eight officers, were killed or wounded. It is recorded of Commodore Hayes, that on learning the intention of the Commander-in-chief to storm Cornelis, with characteristic zeal and gallantry, he offered his services to lead in person the assault with one hundred picked seamen. Sir Samuel Achmuty, in reply, stated that there were too many military competitors for that honour to permit his granting the request, but, otherwise, he would have been very happy to avail himself of his services.

General Jansens, accompanied by General Jumel, commanding the forces, fled to Buitenzorg, which he intended to fortify and hold against the British; but he was driven thence

---

* The following was the distribution of the Artillerymen and seamen at the batteries:—No. 1 Battery, twelve iron 18-pounders. Royal Artillery, thirty-six; Bengal Artillery, thirty-six; seamen, ninety-six; Madras Lascars, eighteen; Bengal Lascars, eighteen. No. 2 Battery, eight iron 18-pounders. Royal Artillery, eighteen; Bengal Artillery, thirty; seamen, sixty-four; Lascars, twenty-four. No. 3 Battery, 8-inch howitzers. Bengal Artillery, eighteen; seamen, eighteen; Lascars, twelve. No. 4 Battery, 8-inch mortars. Royal Artillery, nineteen; seamen, twenty-four; Lascars, sixteen. No. 5 Battery, two howitzers. Bengal Native Artillerymen, twelve; seamen, twenty. Total men to work the guns, four hundred and seventy-nine.

by the British cavalry, who found in the batteries forty-three pieces of cannon. " The total loss sustained by the army between the 10th and the 26th of August, amounted," says Thorn, " to fifteen officers and one hundred and twenty-eight European and Native soldiers killed; and six hundred and eighty-four were wounded." According to the same authority, between the 4th and 26th of August, the loss of the seamen and marines employed on shore, was fifteen killed, and six officers and forty-nine men wounded.

General Jansens, having fled to the eastward, the Commander-in-chief, on the 31st of August, despatched some frigates to Cheribon, a place of considerable importance from its commanding situation; and the fort, through which General Jansens had passed only two days before, was surrendered at the first summons. The enemy's force, now numbering fifty officers, two hundred Europeans, and five hundred Native troops, who had followed General Jansens by the eastern route, finding themselves cut off by the capitulation of Cheribon, surrendered at discretion, and were sent back to Buitenzorg as prisoners of war. Carang Sambong, a place about thirty-five miles in the interior, was garrisoned by a detachment of seamen and marines on the 6th of September; the forts of Taggal, between Cheribon and Samarang, and of Samanap on the island of Madura, were captured by the Navy, and Captain Harris, of the frigate 'Sir Francis Drake,' defeated a desperate attempt which was made to recapture the latter place.

As Sir Samuel Achmuty found from intercepted letters that General Jansens intended to make a stand at Samarang, 350 miles from Batavia, he hastily proceeded thither on the 9th of September, and was joined the same evening, by Admiral Stopford with a portion of the fleet. On his arrival before that place, where the French General had taken up a position, the British Commander-in-chief made fresh proposals to him to surrender the island, and put an end to a further useless effusion of blood, but the Governor-General refused to treat. While waiting the arrival of a sufficient number of troops to attack Samarang, the Admiral despatched the armed boats of the squadron to cut out some vessels which flanked the approaches of the town, which was successfully accomplished.

General Jansens evacuated the town on the 12th, and took up a fortified position, mounted with thirty pieces of cannon, within a few miles of the place, which the Commander-in-chief resolved to attack. This operation was undertaken by Colonel Gibbs with a small force, the main portion of the British Army, owing to a mistake, having sailed to Zedayo, but nothing could withstand the headlong valour of the troops, who carried the position with a rush. This was the last effort of General Jansens, who fled to the fort of Salatiga, and, finding himself wholly deserted by his men, the same night sent a messenger offering to treat for a capitulation with Lord Minto, the Governor-General, who was then at Batavia. This was refused by Sir Samuel Achmuty, and, ultimately, after some difficulty as to terms, General Jansens, on the 18th of September, signed a treaty surrendering Java and all its dependencies, together with all his troops. On the same day that this capitulation of Onarang was concluded, the Admiral arrived at Zedayo, and, on the 22nd, news having arrived of the treaty, Sourabaya was surrendered without opposition. Subsequently Macasssar, Timor, and all other dependencies of the Dutch Government at Batavia, were occupied by the British forces, and thus successfully terminated a brief but glorious campaign.

On the conclusion of hostilities, medals were awarded to the senior officers of the force and those commanding regiments and ships, but eventually every soldier and seaman engaged in the Expedition, including the Bombay Marine, was awarded a medal.

During the course of these operations, the officers and men of the Marine performed their duty to the satisfaction of their superiors, including Lord Minto, who himself witnessed their zeal and good conduct. In a letter to Commodore Hayes, dated the 2nd of May, 1812, the Governor-General in Council conveyed to the "captains, officers, and men composing the squadron of the Marine employed under your orders, the expression of his Lordship's high approbation and applause." Also in a despatch to the Court of Directors, Lord Minto, while in Java, wrote on the 5th of October, 1811, as follows:—"I cannot conclude this despatch without indulging myself in the satisfaction of bearing testimony to the zeal and good conduct displayed by Commodore Hayes, and the captains, officers, petty officers, and men of the Marine employed in this important expedition." Unhappily Commodore Broughton was actuated by petty feelings of jealousy, and sought to degrade the officers of the Marine, who held regular commissions and ranked with their brethren of the sister Service. Commodore Hayes was not the sort of a man to sit still under a sense of injury, and hence an ill feeling was engendered between the Royal Navy and Company's Marine. Lord Minto, to whom Commodore Hayes appealed, supported him, and it was hoped that, on the arrival of Rear-Admiral Stopford from the Cape of Good Hope, matters would work more smoothly, but it was not so. It is a thankless task to revive such disputes, but justice to the Service should induce us to place on record that while Admiral Stopford thanked the officers and men of the Bombay Marine serving under his orders, he copied Admiral Bertie in studiously omitting in his despatches all mention of the Hon. Company's vessels, so that from this source it is impossible to gather where and when the cruisers were engaged; and yet they were fairly entitled to a share of such credit as was gained by the naval portion of the Expedition, though, indeed, the chief honours were reaped by the Army, the Navy having afforded to them but small opportunities for achieving distinction. On another point, also, the Service was treated with injustice, for which no explanation or reparation was offered. By order of the Court of Directors, captains in the Bombay Marine were entitled to share in the distribution of prize money as majors in the army, but by order of the Prince Regent in the distribution of prize money gained at Mauritius and in the Java Expedition, the captains of the Marine shared with lieutenants of the Royal Navy, and thus Captain Deane was robbed of several thousand pounds of hard-earned money, as appears in his Memorial presented to the Court of Directors.

In marked contrast to the treatment received by the Service at the hands of the Naval Commanders-in-chief at the reduction of Mauritius and Java, was the approbation expressed by Commodore Sir Josias Rowley. second in command on the former occasion, and by Commodore Sayer at Java during the period some of the cruisers were under his command. Both these fine seamen, like others before and since, recognized the zeal and enterprise exhibited by the officers and crews of the Hon. Company's ships, and gave generous expression to their approval.

Java, of which Mr. (afterward Sir) Stamford Raffles was the first lieutenant-governor, continued in a very unsettled state after its reduction by the British, necessitating the retention of a considerable garrison, which was placed under the command of Colonel Gillespie, and of a portion of the fleet, including some of the Hon. Company's cruisers, whose services were, soon afterwards, called into requisition, to punish Sultan Bedr-oo-deen, of Palimbang,* in the island of Sumatra, who had massacred the peaceful European and Native residents belonging to the Dutch factory at that place, which, being dependent on Java, had passed under British protection.

Accordingly, to punish this act of perfidy, an Expedition was fitted out at Batavia, and sailed on the 20th of March, 1812, under the command of Colonel Gillespie. The Expedition consisted of three companies of H.M. 59th Regiment, five companies of H.M. 89th Regiment; detachments of Madras Horse Artillery, dismounted Hussars, Bengal Artillery, Sepoys of the 5th and 6th Battalions, and some Amboynese. The squadron consisted of H.M. ships 'Phœnix,' Captain Bowen, senior officer; 'Cornelia,' Captain Owen; and

---

* Palimbang, styled in the Malay Historical Records, "the City of Safety," is situated about sixty miles from the mouth of a river of the same name, and had at this time a population of from twenty to thirty thousand Malays and three hundred Arabs.

'Procris,' Captain Freeman. The Hon. Company's cruisers 'Teignmouth,' Captain Hewitson, and 'Mercury,' Captain Conyers. The gunboats 'Wellington,' and 'Young Barracouta,' and four transports, which also embarked some guns and a considerable quantity of military stores for the new settlement on the island of Banca, opposite the mouth of the Palimbang river.

On the 3rd of April the fleet reached Nanka Island, where they remained a week at anchor. Tents were pitched on shore, and all the artificers were employed in the completion of the boats intended for the passage of the Palimbang river, by constructing platforms for the field-pieces and coverings to shelter the troops from the heat of the sun and the ill effects of the night air. A severe gale on the night of the 9th of April, occasioned the loss of several of these boats, and damaged many others, but, nevertheless, as further delay was impossible, the fleet got under weigh on the following day, and, at noon on the 15th, came to an anchor opposite the west channel of Palimbang river. The two succeeding days were employed in getting the 'Procris,' 'Teignmouth,' 'Mercury,' and the gunboats 'Young Barracouta' and 'Wellington,' over the bar; and, on the evening of the 17th, the greater part of the troops were removed from the frigates and transports and placed on board these smaller vessels, whose lighter draught enabled them to proceed up the river. A violent storm, which came on during the night, considerably damaged the boats and destroyed the coverings for the men, made with so much labour and difficulty; the four serviceable flat-bottomed boats which alone were capable of affording any kind of shelter to the men, were appropriated to the field artillery and such troops as could be accommodated in them.

A number of armed proas having been seen at the mouth of the river, a party of seamen and thirty soldiers was sent up in boats, but, on their approach, the enemy fled, and the village of Soosang was found to be deserted. The remaining troops proceeded on board their respective ships, on the evening of the 18th, after which the squadron got under weigh, and were carried ten miles up the stream by the flood tide, and, towards midnight, came to an anchor. The utmost care was necessary in proceeding up the river to coerce the Sultan of Palimbang, as not only was resistance expected at the batteries established at Borang, but the employment of fire-rafts on the stream as it narrowed higher up, formed an element of danger. The most careful watch was kept by a division of look-out boats, astern of which were three divisions, consisting of light boats, gun launches, and flat boats with field pieces; then came the squadron, consisting of the 'Procris,' 'Teignmouth,' and 'Mercury,' with the two gunboats escorting the flats and other

boats with the troops.* Little progress was made on the 19th of
April, owing to the continuance of the ebb tide until four in the
afternoon, and some of the vessels, while under weigh, got
entangled among the branches of the trees and shrubs, which it
was necessary to cut away. On the following day an envoy
arrived from the Sultan, requesting to be informed what were
the intentions of the British Commander in advancing towards
his master's capital with so large a force, to whom Colonel
Gillespie replied that he would, in person, acquaint the Sultan
with the nature of the propositions of the British Government,
of which he was the bearer. Little progress was made on the
20th and 21st of April, owing to the flood tide being slacker
the further they went up the river, and, on the latter day, two
messengers arrived in quick succession with letters from the
Sultan, professing friendship for the English, to which Colonel
Gillespie replied, expressing his intention to be in Palimbang in
two days. At sunrise on the 22nd, the batteries at Borang
appeared in sight, but, owing to the grounding of the 'Procris,'
the flotilla came to an anchor about five miles from them.
During the course of the day the defences were reconnoitred,
when it was found that the passage of the river was further
disputed by a large Arab ship with guns, and a number of
armed proas and floating batteries, which were moored across
the stream *en echellon* so as to rake the line of advance, whilst

* The following were the directions and orders of sailing, issued by the commanders of the Expedition:—"When the signal is made to anchor it will be accompanied with a red pendant over. If the squadron are to anchor in a line with the same pendant under. If a line abreast, or athwart the river, the division of light boats under Lieutenant Monday, will always anchor in line abreast, about half a mile ahead of the leader of the line of battle. The other boats will anchor in their stations. The gunboats, flats, and launches rather ahead of the leader of the line, and on each bow.

"The line of battle abreast will be formed by the division of light boats in advance, anchored in a line abreast. The gunboats, flats, and launches in the next line. 'Mercury,' 'Wellington,' 'Procris,' 'Young Barracouta,' and 'Teignmouth.' In this order, if it should become necessary to bring the broadsides of the ships to bear up the river, the signal will be made for the boats first and second line, to retire through the intervals of the third line, and form in the rear, in two lines as before. The light boats are to keep a strict look out and have the fire graplings and dogs constantly ready. The look out boats of the light division are never to be more than one mile from the headmost ships or vessel of the squadron, unless otherwise directed by signal; and no boat whatever, except the Commander of the Forces be in her, to pass ahead of the headmost look-out boat without permission. The boats of the light division are never to lose sight of the squadron, even though the winding of the river should enable them to do so without exceeding their prescribed distance. On the approach of armed boats of the natives, the look-out boats are to retreat in silence and good order to the body of their division, which is also to fall back to the 'Procris,' where they will receive further orders, and no boats are, on any account, to fire a shot, or attempt a dash, though the circumstances be ever so favourable; nor, in short, commit any act of hostility without orders. The squadron are to observe and obey the signals of the 'Barracouta,' where the Commander of the Forces is embarked. The 'Barracouta' wears a Union Jack while the Commander of the Forces remains on board." Here follow various signals for forming the line of battle according to circumstances.

the three batteries, which appeared to be fully manned and mounted with a large number of cannon, swept the channel; numerous fire-rafts were also placed on the front and flank of the batteries, which were further protected against the approach of the boats, by piles driven into the river, and by strong palisades in the rear and flanks.

At this time another messenger arrived from the Sultan, expressing his readiness to receive the British Commander, and requesting him to visit the capital without his troops; Colonel Gillespie replied by a demand for an unmolested passage up the river, to which the envoy assented, at the same time offering to give up possession of the batteries and the armed ship. When, however, several boats proceeded to inspect the works, they were met by emissaries from the batteries, requesting them to retire, while the armed proas prepared to resist an advance, and the shouting and excitement exhibited by the enemy in the batteries, denoted no signs of submission.

Upon this Colonel Gillespie, the same night, sent an officer to Borang, to demand a decisive answer as to whether or no the batteries would be surrendered, and he himself followed close after at the head of a strong detachment of troops, supported by the gun launches and field artillery in the flat-bottomed boats. On their arrival at daybreak before the works, the garrison betook themselves to flight, and the place was immediately occupied by the British. One hundred and two guns were captured, which were found to be all ready loaded and primed. A portion of the troops was accommodated on board the Arab ship, and the remainder were quartered in huts and those floating batteries which had coverings. Thus, without resistance, was captured this Malay stronghold, situated about forty miles from the coast, which might have caused serious loss had it been properly defended; it was found to be built on artificial ground, entirely surrounded by water, and fenced, on the flanks and rear, by strong stockades, with many wooden piles in front extending nearly 200 feet into the river.

In the evening the troops were re-embarked, and the flotilla proceeded; fires appeared in all directions, and several fire-rafts, fitted with combustibles, came blazing down the river, but they were towed to the bank by graplings, and Malays employed setting fire to them, were dispersed by the boats' guns. On the following morning, Colonel Gillespie learnt that the Sultan had fled from Palimbang and that rapine and murder were rampant within the city, the Sultan's adherents meditating a wholesale massacre of the wealthy Chinese and other inhabitants. Upon hearing this intelligence, Colonel Gillespie resolved to push on to prevent these excesses, and, accordingly, proceeded towards Palimbang, accompanied by some British naval and military officers, a few seamen in a gig and barge, and a guard of only seventeen picked grenadiers of the 59th Regiment, in canoes, leaving directions that more soldiers should follow. It was an adventurous undertaking, but the British commander was a man utterly destitute of any feeling of personal fear, and the cool hardihood displayed by the small band of Britons in threading the streets of a large city, amid crowds of murderous Malays armed with the deadly creese, appeared to disarm the multitude, who were seen to clutch their weapons, but offered no opposition as the party pushed through the mob to the palace. The town was burning in several places, and the streets and buildings, particularly the palace, bore the appearance of a place that had just been carried by assault. Colonel Gillespie, whose life was attempted by an assassin as he passed through the streets by torchlight, closed the palace gates, and placed all his available men on guard until the arrival of a strong party of the advance relieved the garrison from all danger. By this almost unexampled act of daring, a formidable position, mounting in the forts and batteries no less than two hundred and forty-two pieces of cannon,* was seized, the author of a cruel massacre of British subjects was driven from his throne and deposed, and the majesty of the British name vindicated.

At noon of the 28th of April, the Union Jack was hoisted under a Royal salute, and, on the following day, Colonel Gillespie received a brother of the Sultan, whom he determined to place on the throne. Visits were exchanged between the British Commander and this prince, who was saluted by nineteen guns from the 'Mercury,' and, on his entering the public hall of audience, with a similar number from the shore batteries. On the 5th of May a treaty was ratified with the new Sultan, and he was installed on the *musnud* on the 14th, with the title, Sultan Ratu Ahmed Nazir-oo-deen, under circumstances of great pomp, Colonel Gillespie himself taking him by the hand and seating him on the throne, in front of which passed all the European officers and principal Natives, the former saluting the new sovereign and the latter kissing his hands, knees, or feet, according to their rank; salutes were fired by the ships-of-war in the river, which were also gaily dressed in flags, to the delight and astonishment of the Natives. On the 16th Colonel Gillespie and a large party of officers supped with the Sultan, whom, as chief among the Malay princes, he treated with especial consideration, and, on the

* Of the iron and brass guns found in these works, the latter were chiefly Dutch, though some of them appear, by the inscriptions on them, to have been of native manufacture. One of the largest of these, a 42-pounder, sent to H.R.H. the Prince Regent in the name of the captors, bore the following inscription in Arabic:—"Made by Sultan Ratoo Ahmed NajMuddin, in the city of Palimbang, the abode of Safety, in the year 1183." This date corresponds to A.D. 1769.

following day, the troops having embarked, the latter took possession of the palace.

Sultan Nazir-oo-deen ceded to the British Government the island of Banca, which was formally taken possession of by Colonel Gillespie on the 20th of May, and named Duke of York's Island, though it is now again known by its old native name.*

Colonel Gillespie reported in most favourable terms of the conduct of the officers and men of the 'Teignmouth' and 'Mercury,' and Mr. Raffles spoke of them as follows in General Orders, dated the 27th of May, 1812:—"Colonel Gillespie is also requested to inform the Honourable Company's cruisers, that the Lieutenant-Governor will have much pleasure in communicating to the Supreme Government, the favourable sentiments which are entertained of the conduct of this branch of the Naval Service."†

* Banca soon ceased to be held by a British force, owing to the great mortality that prevailed among the garrison. The ruins of Fort Nugent, so called in honour of the Commander-in-chief in India, a few miles from Minto, the capital, are, however, still discernible amid the brushwood; and at this point the transport 'Transit,' having on board seven hundred troops for China, including three hundred men of the 90th Regiment, with Captain (now Sir Garnet) Wolseley, was wrecked in the summer of 1857. Banca was surrendered to the Dutch by the terms of the treaty, making over to them Java and its dependencies, and, in December, 1816, the island was delivered over to a Commissioner appointed by the Netherlands Government.

† The subsequent expeditions of the Dutch against Palimbang, and the defeats they sustained, showed that the success attained by the small British force under Colonel Gillespie, was due entirely to the skill of the Commander and the discipline and gallantry of the men. On the departure of Colonel Gillespie a military force was left to secure the tranquillity of Palimbang. The old Sultan Bedr-oo-deen remained in the interior until 1814, when, by an unfortunate and extraordinary act of the British officer in charge, he was again brought down to Palimbang, and temporarily placed on the throne, on paying the sum of 200,000 dollars as a fine. The arrangement was disavowed and annulled by Mr. Raffles, who, in August, 1814, sent a commission to Palimbang to inquire into the affair, including among its members, Captain Macdonald, of the 'Aurora,' and Nazir-oo-deen was again placed on the throne, and the money returned to the old Sultan. The treaty which stipulated the restoration of Java to Holland, included also the transfer of the island of Banca, which had never been in possession of the Dutch, but had been ceded by the old Sultan to Great Britain, in consideration of the expenses incurred in the expedition. The Dutch claimed to stand on their former footing at Palimbang, by virtue of their ancient treaties with that State, but both Sultans protested against their return on any terms; and Naziroo-deen, who had been raised by us, and whose authority had long been undisputed, urged in the strongest manner that we should not desert him. For the sake of peace, our Government contented themselves with a protest, which it is said the First Commissioner, Elhout, put in his pocket with a contemptuous smile; and Palimbang being thus left to its fate, the Dutch soon turned their attention to make the most of it. The treasures of the old Sultan were very inviting to the Dutch, who have ever been sordid in their Colonial relations, and their Commissioner at Banca opened a negotiation with the deposed Sultan, giving hopes that in consideration of certain payments of cash and other sacrifices, he might again expect to be reinstated. These negotiations were not so secretly conducted as to escape the knowledge of the reigning Sultan, who, becoming aware of the danger, and being perfectly unprepared for resistance, dispatched an embassy across the country to our Government at Bencoolen, declaring the

From Palimbang the troops of the Expedition, with the exception of the necessary garrison for Fort Nugent, in Banca, predicament in which he stood, and earnestly praying for protection and support on the grounds that to the British authority he was indebted for his elevation, which had been for years acquiesced in by the people of Palimbang, that he considered the treaty still binding, and that he was willing to make such further arrangements with us as would secure him a positive right to our exclusive protection under the impending danger. In reply to this appeal, Captain Salmond, of the Bombay Marine, Master-Attendant at Bencoolen, was sent overland to Palimbang. On his arrival, he went immediately to the Sultan, and, having effected the object of his mission, had retired to rest when, in the darkness of night, a force from the Dutch garrison surrounded the palace, and, having seized him, sent him a prisoner to Batavia. The next act of the Dutch Commissioner was to send Sultan Nazir-oo-deen as a close prisoner to Batavia; his property was also seized and publicly sold in order that, according to the expression of the Dutch Commissioner, "not a trace should be left of his former existence." A treaty was concluded with Sultan Bedr-oo-deen, who found himself once more at the head of affairs in Palimbang, stripped, however, of his treasure, and burthened with a heavy debt. The conduct of the Dutch authorities was marked with various instances of oppressive violence; and the Commissioner accused the Sultan of participating in the alleged hostility of the people. He was, accordingly, peremptorily ordered to pay the residue of his debt to the Dutch Government, and to surrender his sons, as hostages for his good behaviour. In spite of his protestations of innocence, the Dutch Commissioner ordered a party of soldiers to proceed into the palace, and secure the person of the Sultan and his family. The attempt roused the opposition of the populace, and after three days' hard fighting, the remnant of the Dutch force, which originally consisted of five hundred well-appointed soldiers, was obliged to fly to their ships leaving behind their followers, who were indiscriminately murdered. The Sultan now set seriously about providing for the defence of the place. He caused the guns of H.M.'s ship 'Alceste,' wrecked in 1817, to be weighed from the wreck, and planted in favourable and commanding situations; the navigation of the river was intercepted, and the whole resources of the country were put in requisition to meet the impending danger. On the arrival of the Commissioner at Batavia, with the account of the disaster at Palimbang, orders were immediately issued for the equipment of a military force, which consisted of one thousand five hundred men from Batavia, and the same number from the Samarang division, under the command of Colonel Bischoff, whose brother had fallen in the late conflict. The unfortunate Sultan-Nazir-oo-deen was dragged from his confinement for the purpose of proceeding with the Expedition, in the hope that his presence might distract the measures or weaken the efforts of the Palimbang people. The Expedition, which included a seventy-four-gun ship, and a frigate, cast anchor at the mouth of the Palimbang river on the 9th of October, 1820, and proceeded up the river on the following day; but on the 21st of October, the Dutch were beaten back with severe loss, stated by advices from Batavia to have amounted to two hundred and fifty men and six officers killed and wounded. This loss was experienced at an island, the batteries of which riddled the 'Wilhelmina' frigate, which received one hundred and eighty shot. The Expedition returned to Batavia, and Admial Wolterbeck, Commanding-in-Chief, compared the defences of the island to a second Gibraltar.

A second and more powerful expedition, including five thousand Europeans, was sent against Palimbang, and, having succeeded in forcing the works on the river, the Sultan Bedr-oo-deen, on the 26th of June, 1821, surrendered himself, and was succeeded by his brother; the Dutch losses were seventy-three killed and two hundred and thirty-seven wounded.

Owing to their want of energy, the Dutch had suffered the pirates in these waters to make so much head that they attacked their ships and settlements, and the Malays landed at Banca, and drove the troops there into the fort. On the 8th of June, 1821, the Dutch armed ship 'Samarang,' mounting six guns, and amply supplied with swivels and muskets, was attacked by a proa on the north coast of Java, and lost thirteen killed and wounded in defending herself.

sailed, on the 22nd of May, for Samarang, in order to coerce the Sultan of Mataram who aimed at subverting the British or Dutch Government in Java. Colonel Gillespie, after quitting Fort Nugent, first proceeded in the schooner 'Wellington' to Batavia, whence, accompanied by Mr. Raffles, he hurried overland to join his little force. On the 17th of June they arrived before Djoecarta, as the Craton, or residence, of the Sultan was called, but the squadron, which had gone round by the island of Banca, was nearly a month in making the passage. The Craton was about three miles in circumference, surrounded by a broad wet ditch, and defended with a high rampart and bastions, mounting nearly one hundred guns; the interior was strengthened by other defences, and the whole was held by seventeen thousand men. Some skirmishing occurred before the place, in which several troopers of the 22nd Dragoons were killed and wounded, and, on the 19th, when the King's and Company's ships had arrived with all the troops, a heavy fire was opened on the Craton from an old Dutch fort, about 800 yards distant. Colonel Gillespie, with his usual daring, resolved to attempt the capture of the works by a *coup de main*, and, accordingly, two hours before dawn on the 20th of June, a strong column—consisting of detachments of H.M. 14th, 59th, and 78th Regiments, led by Colonel Watson of the 14th, supported by other columns under Colonels McLeod of the 59th Regiment, and Dewar, of the 3rd Bengal Volunteer Battalion—succeeded in effecting an entrance, and this fortified palace was carried by assault after some severe fighting. The British loss in this brilliant feat of arms, numbered twenty-three killed and seventy-six wounded, including Colonel Gillespie and eight officers, but the success was complete, and the large number of dead lying in the works, in which ninety-two guns were captured, attested the severity of the conflict. The Commander-in-chief in India issued a General Order, dated 30th of September, congratulating the troops on the brilliant successes they had achieved in Palimbang and at the storm of the Craton of the Sultan of Mataram.

Major Mears, of the Madras Army, who was left in charge of Fort Nugent with a small garrison, a few months after the departure of Colonel Gillespie, undertook, in concert with the 'Aurora,' Captain Macdonald, an expedition against the ex-Sultan of Palimbang, who, with a large body of his followers, was stockaded in one of the many islands at the confluence of the rivers, a few miles above Palimbang, whence he threatened that city and intercepted supplies. Accordingly, two hundred men were embarked in the 'Aurora,' the boats of which proceeded up the river. In the attack on the stockade, which was carried in the most gallant style by the soldiers and sailors, there were several casualties, including the gallant Major Mears, who died of his wounds.

In 1813, an expedition, in which the Bombay Marine participated, was undertaken against Pangeran Annam, the Sultan of Sambas,* a town situated about forty miles up the river of

* Since the Dutch abandoned Sambas, about fifty years before, three Sultans had reigned on the *musnud*. Mr. J. Hunt, in a Report, communicated, in 1812, to Sir Stamford Raffles, gives some interesting accounts of the pirate races of Borneo at that date. When Magellan visited it in 1520, the island was called by the natives Pulo Kalamantan, the name Borneo being applied only to the capital at that time a rich and populous city ; hence the Portuguese navigator, concluding that the whole island belonged to this prince, gave it the name of Borneo, which the natives pronounce *Bruni*, meaning courageous. Like other places, as Ternate, Malacca, Acheen, and Bantam, the population and wealth of Borneo rapidly decreased, and from having, at the time of its discovery, according to Pigofetta, the companion of Magellan, twenty-five thousand houses, the city only numbered three thousand inhabitants in 1809 ; a result entirely due to the decay of commerce, caused by the depredations of the pirates who swarmed in those waters. To the Portuguese conquerors succeeded the Dutch, and when the English captured the city, they found the Soloo Rajah in prison, and released him on the stipulation that the whole north portion of Borneo, ceded to him by the Rajah of Borneo Proper, should be transferred to the Company ; these terms were signed and delivered to the Company's representative, Mr. A. Dalrymple, in 1763. Among other places occupied by the Portuguese was Sambas, from which they were driven by the Dutch in 1690, but the latter evacuated this place and established themselves at Pontiana in 1786 ; they built a fortified wall round the palace and factory, but were compelled to withdraw from it when the war broke out with the English in 1796. The Hon. Company's ships had for a lengthened period traded with the ports of Borneo prior to the year 1760 (Vide Hardy's Shipping Register), and established a factory at the city of Borneo ; twice also they attempted to establish themselves on the unhealthy island of Balambangan, lying north of Borneo, near Maludu, and, in 1775, the Company's ship 'Bridgwater' was sent to Pasir for a similar purpose ; but these attempts at settlement were chiefly frustrated by the sordid jealousy of the Dutch, who instigated the Soloos and other savages to cut off the British settlers at Balambangan and Pulo Condore, and brought disgrace on themselves by their massacres at Amboyna, Banda, and Bantam. In 1804, Mr. Farquhar recommended the reoccupation of Balambangan, to which Lord Wellesley assented. The 'Mornington,' Captain W. J. Hamilton, having Mr. Farquhar on board, accompanied by several storeships and transports, set sail from the Hooghly, but a few weeks served to dispel the illusions by which he had been beguiled, and the settlement was finally abandoned.

"In 1774," says Forrest, in his Voyage to New Guinea, "the British were expelled from their infant settlement of Balambangan by an insurrection of the Soloos, who murdered the garrison and plundered the factory. Five years before this the Sambas pirates massacred Captain Sadler with his boat's crew off Mompava, and made off with a large quantity of gold dust, though they did not succeed in capturing his ship."

The pirates of Borneo Proper committed a base act of treachery in 1788. The Sultan invited Captain Dixon to come up to the town with his ship, the 'May' of Calcutta ; the captain accepted the invitation, and while he and his crew were at dinner, the Sultan and his people fell upon them, murdered the captain, three officers, and ten Europeans, retained the lascars as slaves, plundered the cargo, and burnt the ship.

In 1800, Captain Pavin and a boat's crew were murdered in the palace of the Sultan of Soloo whilst the Commander was taking a cup of chocolate. In 1810, the Soloos plundered the wreck of the ship 'Harrier,' and carried off several of the crew, who were at this time retained as slaves at Bayagan Soloo. Among other great princes with whom the Company's ships were brought into contact, were the Sultan of Matan, an independent Rajah, who was formerly styled Sultan of Sukadana, once the most celebrated city in Borneo, but which was burnt down by the Dutch.

In the year 1812, the principal piratical ports in Borneo were :—Sambas, the

the same name in the island of Borneo. This prince, who was one of the principal chieftains of Borneo, had, for a long period, been guilty of various acts of piracy, so that it was very unsafe for trading vessels to venture near any part of the extensive coasts of this great island, particularly of the north-west portion; here armed proas were continually on the watch, both in Sambas and the Borneo river, and the Dyak pirates not only plundered the vessels, but put the crews to death under circumstances of horrible barbarity.

In 1804, the brother of the Rajah of Sambas, a desperado as brave as he was cruel, captured the ship 'Calcutta,' and murdered all the crew. On hearing of this catastrophe, the Lieutenant-Governor of Prince of Wales' Island and its dependencies, Mr. (afterwards Sir) Thomas Farquhar, who, up to the conclusion of the peace of Amiens, had been British Resident at Amboyna and Chief of the Moluccas, directed Lieutenant Robert Deane, of the Bombay Marine, commanding 'Les Frères Unis,' of sixteen guns, under the orders of the Penang Government, to proceed through the Straits of Malacca to the west coast of Borneo, where he was to cruise in search of the 'Calcutta,' which he was informed was "strongly manned and armed." The Lieutenant-Governor says in his letter of instructions, dated the 20th of March, 1805:—"It is of the utmost importance that this freebooter should be seized; and you will, therefore, use your utmost endeavours to apprehend him by visiting all the haunts and ports along the coasts of Borneo. If you meet the 'Calcutta' at sea, there can be no doubt of your being able to make an easy capture of her. Should she be in port, you will endeavour by some well-concerted plan to cut her out, for which purpose, principally, you have been provided with a strong detachment of marines. So soon as this service is performed, you will be pleased to return to this port through the Straits of Banca, where you are to gain every information in your power respecting the enemy, particularly their naval force in Batavia, or in the Eastern seas. In the prosecution of the foregoing orders, you are to make every possible search after, and destroy, all piratical boats that may be infesting the Straits of Malacca,. providing this can be done without deviating from the main object of these instructions." Lieutenant Deane did not find the 'Calcutta' at sea, but receiving information that she was in the Sambas River, proceeded thither, accompanied by the armed ship 'Belisarius,' Mr. Lynch, with the intention of attacking the pirate chief. He soon found the 'Calcutta,' which had taken up a strong position, supported by

most important; Borneo Proper and Tampasuk, where there were four hundred proas, both places being under the Rajah of Borneo Proper; the Pasir pirates; the Soloo pirates; the Illano, or pirates in the isle of Magindanao, on whom Captain Hayes had inflicted a severe defeat some years before. There were also the smaller ports of Lingin, Rhio, and Billiton.

six gunboats, with two armed junks, the total force of guns being fifty-eight. Having made his dispositions, Lieutenant Deane, without any hesitation, attacked the 'Calcutta,' and, after a smart action of forty minutes' duration, succeeded in capturing her, the junks and two gunboats, and sinking two others, while among the killed was the pirate chief, who had commanded in person. In consequence of this success, the trade to Malacca and Prince of Wales' island, which had for a long time been stopped, was again opened. The Lieutenant-Governor, in his despatch to the Governor-General, dated 12th of June, enclosing a copy of Lieutenant Deane's despatch, speaks of this gallant officer and his spirited conduct on this occasion, in the following terms:—"I have already had the honour of detailing to his Excellency the mode in which the 'Calcutta' was manned and armed, and the great injury that the Eastern trade had sustained from the piratical freebooter who commanded her. I happy to inform you that this man, the brother of the Rajah of Sambas, was killed in the action. The difficulties of access to the 'Calcutta,' stationed in a strong position, and supported by two large China junks several miles up the river Sambas, contribute greatly to the honour of this achievement, and reflect great credit on Lieutenant Deane's abilities, valour, and perseverance. Lieutenant Deane has served under my orders for nearly five years, during which period of time I have invariably experienced in him every qualification of a valuable officer, and a series of conduct that has uniformly entitled him to my highest approbation. I therefore take the liberty of recommending Lieutenant Deane to the most favourable notice of his Excellency in Council." Captain Money, the Superintendent of the Bombay Marine, in thanking Lieutenant Deane, under date 1st of September, took the opportunity of expressing his approval of the gallantry of his three officers, Lieutenants Wheatel and J. Philips, and Mr. Midshipman Lord.

The lesson these pirates had received from Lieutenant Deane was soon forgotten, and, in 1806, we find that the pirates of Borneo Proper murdered the entire crew of the merchantman 'Commerce,' and shared the plunder with the Sambas people. Further outrages were committed in the succeeding years, and, in 1812, Pangeran Annam, of Sambas, captured the Portuguese ship 'Coromandel,' from Calcutta, and also nine seamen of H.M.S. 'Hecate,' who were all either brutally murdered, or retained as slaves after being hamstrung or otherwise maimed. In these depredations the Sambas Rajah was much assisted by the Tampasuk pirates, under the Rajah of Borneo Proper, who could command ten large well-equipped war proas. The naval force that Pangeran Annam could muster in the event of hostilities, consisted, at this time, says Captain Macdonald, "of from ten to twelve proas, carrying from seventy to eighty men all expert rowers, having two long guns in the bow, under cover of a strong, slanting bulwark, and a ship he had taken belonging to the Portuguese at Macao, carrying fourteen 6-pounders with a motley crew of all nations." There was also a brig, besides the ten proas from his allies of Borneo Proper. The population of Sambas amounted to twelve thousand Malays and Dyaks, and thirty thousand Chinese. So great was the terror created by this prince not only among traders, but in the breasts of the Sultans of neighbouring States, that the Sultan of Pontiana* applied to Java for a British garrison, which was granted.

In consequence of these hostile acts, the Lieutenant-Governor of Java, in 1812, despatched up the Sambas H.M. ships 'Procris,' 'Barracouta,' and 'Phœnix,' Captain Bowen, senior officer, with some gunboats, and one hundred men of the 78th Highlanders; but the 'Barracouta' was unable to force the river defences, and the batteries opened so heavy a fire that she was compelled to retreat, having suffered some loss. This failure so affected the gallant Captain Bowen, who was also borne down by fever, that he died soon after his return to Batavia. After this, the Hon. Company's cruiser 'Aurora' and some gunboats, maintained a blockade of the river, until a sufficient force could be sent to punish the Sultan of Sambas for his numerous aggressions, and vindicate the honour of the British flag; while so employed the 'Aurora' recaptured some valuable junks taken by these people, and chased into the river the ship 'Coromandel.' The Sultan, apprised of the intentions of the British, made every preparation for defence, and removed all his valuable property and booty into the interior. In June, 1813, a second expedition was ordered to proceed to the Sambas, and consisted of the following ships and troops. H.M. frigates 'Leda,' Captain G. Sayer, (Senior Naval Officer); 'Hussar,' Captain Hon. G. Elliot; 'Malacca,' Captain D. Mackay; and 'Volage,' Captain Leslie; the eighteen-gun sloops, 'Hecate,' Commander Drury, and 'Procris,' Commander Norton. The Hon. Company's ships 'Malabar,' twenty, Captain R. Deane; 'Teignmouth,' sixteen, Captain Sealy; 'Aurora,' fourteen, Commander Macdonald, and five gunboats. There was also the transport 'Troubridge' and Indiaman 'Princess Charlotte of Wales,' having on board

---

* The Sultan of Pontiana was almost the only prince in this part of Borneo who lived by commerce. The city is situated at the junction of the Matan and Landa rivers, some fifteen miles from the sea. A point about two-thirds of the way up the river, was strongly fortified; and the Sultan's palace, surrounded by the stone wall built by the Dutch, was strengthened by a battery of eleven guns. The population of Pontiana was about seven thousand souls, and the King's revenue 40,000 dollars. A few Chinese and Siamese junks traded with the place, and the naval force consisted of two small ships, two brigs, fifty proas, and about one thousand men. The Sultan had also a second port at Mompava, about sixteen miles to the northward of Pontiana, and of the same extent and population.

the troops, consisting of the 14th Regiment, Colonel Watson, who commanded the force, a company each from the Bengal Artillery and the Company's European Regiment, and the 3rd Bengal Volunteer Battalion. The men-of-war rendezvoused off the Sambas river, which had been blockaded since January, 1813, by the 'Teignmouth' and 'Aurora,' assisted by some gunboats, and a small body of European and Native troops under Captain Morris of the Bengal Army, who also acted as chief Political officer.* For the effective manner in which they had main-

* Captain Macdonald was at Rembang, in Java, fitting the 'Aurora' with a new main-mast when he received the summons to blockade the Sambas river, and made the passage in less than fifteen days, against strong north-westerly gales. He says: —"On the evening of the 4th of February, 1813, very soon after our arrival off the river Sambas, we discovered a large junk, which, in endeavouring to enter, had taken the ground; as it appeared possible to cut her out, I determined to make the attempt before high water would enable her to get fairly within the bar, which is upwards of a mile in width. Accordingly, having got the ship as near to her as we could guess, under cover of a dark and rainy night we manned and armed the boats, and as the day began to dawn, pushed off, keeping the ship as near as possible to support them. Elated with his previous success, the Pangeran, as I fully expected, had, with a strong party from the shore, joined her during the night, intending to preserve her from her impending fate; but so quiet and noiseless had been our approach, and so unexpected our proximity, that we were close at hand ere he had time to do more than arouse from his slumber and spring into the sampang, which, laying ready manned alongside, soon carried him beyond our reach, his people following with the utmost precipitation in the boats that brought them from the shore; had we been a few moments earlier, or the night less dark and drizzling, so as to have admitted our seeing our true position, nothing could have saved that individual himself from our grasp; as it was, we got possession of the vessel, and with the aid of the land wind, dragged her through the mud and down to Pontiana, where she was placed under the care of the Sultan. The succeeding month was also a propitious one for us, having on the third of March intercepted another of his vessels, laden with various kinds of supplies, including a quantity of powder and shot, which his agents had procured from the Rajah of Borneo Proper; suspecting that we had gone to one of the neighbouring islands to replenish our wood and water, they took advantage of that temporary absence to seek admission, but unluckily for their interest, selected the very day we so unexpectedly returned; she came skimming down along shore, with a fine breeze and smooth sea, and had nearly accomplished her object as we arrived; fortunately for us it was near the hour for high water, and being by this time somewhat better acquainted with the channel, we pushed on into little more than our own depth, crossed her, thereby compelling her to bear up, and assisted by the evening breeze, brought her into blue water, and soon saw her also under custody of the Prince of Pontiana, who expressed much gratification at the confidence reposed in his people. She was of great bulk, and navigated by a renegade Portuguese, who had been mate or steersman in one of the ships which the Pangeran cut off, and with whom he took service, engaging for a stipulated sum, to carry this vessel to and from the coast of China, and bringing back the annual supplies for the Chinese population of Montrada and Lauduck; exclusive of her crew there were on board upwards of two hundred emigrants of all denominations and kinds, seeking employment in these mining districts, and the loss of the various materials with which she was loaded greatly distressed the general, but particularly the Chinese population. Here (at Pontiana) I found the long expected detachment had just arrived from Batavia, under the command of Captain Morris, of the Bengal Army, who accompanied me back to Sambas and set about immediately hutting the troops under the high promontory which bounds the northern entrance to the river. Two fast sampangs of light and easy draft, each capable of containing a dozen or more small-arm men, besides the rowers, were procured and placed at his disposal, and one of the gunboats anchored in

tained this blockade under the most discouraging conditions, the captains of the cruisers received the thanks of the Lieutenant-Governor. After touching at Pontiana to procure boats to ascend the river and other necessaries, the expedition arrived, on the 22nd of June, off the mouth of the Sambas, where there is a considerable mud flat, extending a distance of four or five miles out to sea, but without a regular bar. Vessels drawing 13 feet may get over it at high-water springs, but at ordinary high tides there is only 11 feet, with 9 feet at the ebb. Twelve miles above the bar the river branches into two parts; the broad, or northern, branch is called the Borneo river, and the other, leading to Sambas, known as the Landa river, is extremely serpentine, deep to the very bushes on both sides, and quite clear of natural obstructions up to the town, except near Siminis Creek, about ten miles below the fort, where a reef of rocks runs out into the stream. About five or six leagues up the Landa branch, and about thirteen from the sea, stands the town and palace of Sambas, on the confluence of that river with the Salako. On the right bank of the former, and about a league below the town, was a strong fort, having two tiers of guns, built of two rows of large piles, the interstices being filled with mud and stone. A boom was constructed across the river, one-eighth of a mile below this fort; and, on the opposite bank, was a second powerful fort, having a cross fire with the other battery, while in the rear of both were redoubts, the whole commanding a reach of the river one mile and a half in extent. The land makes an elbow at this point, which obliged the 'Barracouta' to haul athwart the river to get her broadside to bear; and it was while thus engaged, after having made an ineffectual attempt to burst through the boom, which was placed originally across the stream, that she drew upon herself the fire of the heavy batteries, and experienced considerable loss. The river also at this point is very narrow and winding, rendering it difficult to proceed under sail.

On arriving at the mouth of the river, the frigates remained outside the mud flat or bar, but the sloops and cruisers tried to run over it. The 'Aurora,' not drawing more than eleven feet, managed to do so, but the 'Hecate,' 'Procris,' 'Malabar,' and 'Teignmouth,' after running in a squall, stuck fast about the middle; the mud being soft, anchors were laid out, and, by incessant labour, in four days they were hove through and entered the river. The disembarkation of the troops, consisting of about seven hundred or eight hundred Europeans and six hundred Sepoys, commenced on the 23rd June, the day after the arrival of the ships, and, by the 25th, the whole of them, together with the

the fair way, in communication (by signal) with us, the more effectually to prevent any egress by the channels farther southward, all the other branches being carefully watched from without."

ordnance and stores, were trans-shipped into the gunboats and Malay craft from Pontiana, which now commenced the ascent. The squadron proceeded up the river, and, to co-operate with the troops, all the available boats were hoisted out, fully armed and manned with five hundred seamen and marines, under command of Captain the Hon. George Elliot.

Previous to the advance, Colonel Watson despatched a letter to the Sultan, requiring him to surrender the defences of Sambas, but, as he had already withdrawn into the interior, no answer was received. On the night of the 26th, the fleet anchored off the mouth of the Landa river; and from hence the commander detached two strong parties, each accompanied by a detachment of seamen and marines, to attack the forts and town in rear, while, with the remainder of the force, he proceeded up the river, and, on the night of the 27th, anchored below and beyond range of the batteries. A third column, under Captain Watson of the 14th, consisting of detachments of the 14th, artillery, and seamen, was landed at three a.m. on the following morning, to attack these works, and, after surmounting many obstacles, carried by assault the two principal batteries and three redoubts in their rear, although resolutely defended. A battery and five redoubts on the opposite side of the river were then evacuated by the enemy. On the commencement of the firing, Colonel Watson pushed up the river with a party kept as a reserve to second whichever column began the attack. He says in his despatch:—" The front battery fired at the boats advancing, although Captain Watson was at that time in its rear, endeavouring to force an entrance. It is difficult to ascertain the loss of the enemy, as many were killed endeavouring to escape in boats and across the boom. From the best information I can obtain it amounts to about one hundred and fifty men, including a brother of the Sultan's, the eldest son of Pangeran Annam, and twelve others. Pangeran Annam made his escape in a small quick sailing boat." In the meantime one of the other columns, under Captain Brooke of the 3rd Bengal Volunteer Battalion, had some sharp fighting, while the boats of the squadron, acting in co-operation, pulled for the boom, over which they were dragged by the crews, who then cut adrift the boom under a heavy fire from the batteries. The loss incurred was seven killed and fifty-nine wounded, including four officers,* which, as Colonel Watson said in his despatch, " was less than might have been expected considering the number and difficulty of access to the batteries." In these works, thirty-one brass, and thirty-six iron, guns, of various calibres, were captured,

* Captain Macdonald says:—" Here I received a contusion on the left arm, which, not noticed at the time, caused me many years afterwards much pain, and, ultimately, to retire from the Service.

together with six thousand round shot and twenty-six barrels of gunpowder.

The town of Sambas was occupied without further opposition, but little booty was obtained, though the 'Coromandel' and the entire fleet fell into the hands of the victors. Though the loss in action was not considerable, the climate made dreadful havoc. A large number of the 14th Regiment died from fever, and the ships of war also suffered to a similar extent. The 'Malabar' and 'Aurora' lost many men, but the 'Teignmouth,' which remained after the others had left for Java, was the greatest sufferer. Out of a crew of seventy-five Europeans she lost two-thirds, the natives on board suffering in an equal proportion, and, at one time, she had only one officer and eight or ten men fit for duty.

So fatal were the effects of this Expedition on the officers of the Bombay Marine, owing chiefly to the long-continued exposure on boat duty during the blockade of the coast and in the operations up the Sambas river, that, out of twenty-two officers in the three Company's ships, within a few years of their return to Bombay, only two remained in the Service, the rest having died or invalided. As in all wars in tropical climates, the exposure to the torrid heat of the noon-day sun, followed by the malaria of the midnight dews, and the pestilential exhalations of the swamps, laid the seeds of disease which, if not immediately followed by fatal consequences to the sufferer, in many instances embittered the remaining years of his life. Happily in these days, Sanitary Science and the thoughtful care bestowed on the comfort and health of our soldiers and sailors, have relieved military operations undertaken even in the most unhealthy climates, of a large percentage of loss.

Not long after the return of the naval and military forces to Java, another Expedition was directed against Rajah Boni of Macassar, in Celebes, who was constantly guilty of acts of hostility towards the British in these islands. In April, 1814, a combined military and naval force was fitted out at Java, under Major-General (afterwards Sir Miles) Nightingall, in which were employed the Company's ships 'Malabar,' 'Teignmouth,' 'Aurora,' and some gunboats, under the senior officer, Captain Deane of the 'Malabar.' The Expedition, having arrived at Macassar, prepared, on the morning of the 7th of June, to attack the Rajah, as that chieftain declined to make the reparation demanded of him, and refused to surrender the "somdang," or regalia, of Goa,* which he had forcibly seized. The ships having battered the defences of the town, at daybreak all the barriers were carried

* The Rajah of Goa was formerly the most powerful chief in Celebes, but the Rajah of Boni, having become the principal ally of the Dutch, was by them raised to the supremacy of the island. In the year 1780, a force of Buggis or Buggese, as the inhabitants of Celebes are called, in the employment of the Rajah of Goa, showed great courage in an attack on the Dutch fort of Rotterdam at Macassar, but they were beaten off with considerable loss.

in succession by the troops under Colonel McLeod, though not without some loss, and, within an hour of the commencement of the attack, the town and palace were in possession of the British. The Rajah had effected his escape during the night, but in his residence, which was committed to the flames, were found five guns, a large quantity of gunpowder, and arms of all description. The strength of the enemy was three thousand men, and their loss in killed and wounded was very considerable. The Rajah was deposed from the *musnud* of Boni, and it was considered that, by the arrangements made by General Nightingall, the tranquillity of this fine island was assured; the sequel, however, proved that this expectation was ill-founded. The 'Aurora' immediately afterwards sailed for Calcutta with one of the chiefs, and the general staff of the army, including Mr. Crawford, Resident of Samarang, author of the "History of the Archipelago." Soon after Commander Macdonald was made Collector-General of Customs and Land Revenues in Java, and Magistrate of the city of Batavia, as a reward for his services, but was obliged, at the end of two years, to return to England, owing to the wound received at Sambas, and, in 1820, he retired from the Service.

Among those who also left the Service, owing to the effects of exposure and hard work, was the gallant captain of the 'Malabar,' whose services deserve a brief record.

Captain Robert Deane entered the Bombay Marine in November, 1791, and was employed as midshipman on board the Hon. Company's cruiser 'Morning Star' until October, 1792, when he was placed in command of the armed pattamar 'Deriah Dowlut,' to cruise on the Malabar coast against pirates, and prevent the smuggling of pepper. In July, 1793, he was appointed Acting-Lieutenant on board the Hon. Company's cruiser 'Scorpion,' and, on her capture by a French fleet, in the following January, while proceeding to England with the colours captured at Pondicherry, was taken to America; by this event he lost the whole of his money and property, for which he never received compensation. Lieutenant Deane was released and returned to England in 1794; and, in May of the following year, sailed for India. He served as a volunteer at the capture of the Cape of Good Hope; and, on his arrival at Bombay, on the 1st of January, 1796, was employed as Acting-Lieutenant on board the Hon. Company's schooner 'Alert' until October, 1797, when he was appointed Second-Lieutenant of the Hon. Company's ship 'Swift,' in which he also served as First-Lieutenant and Commander. In June 1799, while in command of the 'Swift,' he was ordered by Mr. R. T. Farquhar, Resident at the Moluccas, to cruise round Ceram, after two country ships, reported to be smuggling spices on that coast; while thus engaged he fell in with the 'Venus,' country ship, which had sailed from Amboyna to Banda with a cargo of Government rice, and had run ashore on a shoal to the north of Ceram, where she was deserted by her crew. With characteristic energy Lieutenant Deane succeeded, after six days' hard labour, in getting the ship off, and brought her to Amboyna. In July, 1800, he proceeded in the 'Swift,' accompanied by the Hon. Company's brig 'Antelope,' and a country ship, to carry live stock to the garrison at Banda, where there was, at that time, a great mortality for want of fresh provisions. On the passage a heavy gale of wind came on, which dismasted the 'Antelope,' and obliged her, and also the country-ship, to bear away for Amboyna, but, although the 'Swift' was making four feet of water an hour, and it was with difficulty that she could be kept free with two pumps, Lieutenant Deane, knowing the distressed condition of the Island, proceeded at great risk, and landed three months' fresh provisions, which was the means of saving the lives of many of the troops.

In August, 1800, Mr. Farquhar appointed him Master-Attendant at Banda, but active service was more to his liking, and, in the following year, he resigned the appointment, and joined the 'Swift,' then commanded by that brilliant seaman, Captain John Hayes. As First-Lieutenant he served in the 'Swift' when she was engaged against the batteries of Ternate within pistol shot for two hours and a half, on the 11th and 16th of May, 1801. When the 'Swift' was off the Island of Ternate, Colonel Burr, commanding the troops, declared it impossible for him to keep possession of Fort Kaio Maru, unless some assistance was rendered by the squadron, then under Captain Hayes, upon which Lieutenant Deane volunteered and proceeded on shore with twenty-five seamen, and kept possession of the fort two days and two nights under a heavy fire from a hill battery. He also participated in Captain Hayes' brilliant action with forty sail of Magindanao pirates in August, when seventeen vessels were destroyed. Lieutenant Deane commanded the 'Antelope' until April, 1803, when that ship proceeded to Bombay to refit. On leaving Amboyna, Colonel J. Oliver, commanding the troops at the Moluccas, wrote as follows, under date 4th of April, 1803:—" I beg leave to express to you my thanks for the zeal, alacrity, and judgment which has at all times distinguished your conduct while under my command. I earnestly hope that this public testimony of my approbation may be of use to you in future, and I sincerely wish you health and success through life." At Malacca, where the 'Antelope' touched on her way to Bombay, Lieutenant Deane joined the 'Mornington' as First-Lieutenant; and, in May, 1804, was appointed to command the 'Wasp' schooner. In October following, at the particular request of Mr. Farquhar, now Lieutenant-Governor of Prince of Wales' Island, he was allowed by the Bombay Government to take command of 'Les Frères Unis,' of sixteen guns, under the

Penang Government, in which vessel he performed the exploit already detailed in treating of the events of that year.

In January, 1806, Captain Deane returned to Bombay, and was appointed to the command of the Hon. Company's ship 'Mercury,' which was employed in the conveyance of despatches and protection of convoys, to the Persian Gulf and Red Sea, where he succeeded in recovering two dhows laden with very valuable merchandize from Surat, which had been seized by the Sheikh of Hodeida, and carried into that port, where every means was adopted, by dismantling them, taking away the rudders, and guarding the craft with a strong force, to prevent their being retaken; notwithstanding which, Captain Deane succeeded in cutting them out, and delivered them up to the merchant owners of Mocha, free of all expense, for which he received the approbation of Captain Money, the Superintendent of Marine, and the thanks of the Governor of Bombay. In 1809 he was transferred to the command of the 'Benares,' and, in the following year, proceeded in the 'Malabar,' as senior officer of the Bombay Marine, on the Expedition against Mauritius. On the reduction of that island, he was ordered with despatches to Calcutta, where he was specially selected for the command of the Hon. Company's ship 'Mornington,' which conveyed the Governor-General, Lord Minto, to Madras; and from thence proceeded, under his lordship's immediate orders, on the Expedition against Java. For his conduct during that expedition he received the thanks, not only of Commodore Hayes, but the special acknowledgments of the Governor-General. On the fall of Java, Captain Deane conveyed Mr. Archibald Seton to Prince of Wales' Island, to take charge of the Government,* and proceeding thence to Calcutta, he was transferred to the command of the 'Malabar,' and sailed with despatches for Java. When passing Saugor, the 'Malabar' was boarded by an officer from the Indiaman, 'Princess Charlotte of Wales,' conveying troops to Java, who informed him that the crew of the ship were in a state of mutiny, and that the commanding officer had been obliged to send back to Calcutta fifty-one men of the Bengal Artillery; knowing that they were much wanted at Java, Captain Deane immediately made sail after the vessel conveying them to shore, and brought her to after firing several shots,

---

* On quitting Prince of Wales' Island, Mr. Seton addressed the following letter to Captain Deane:—" A period of twelvemonths has just expired since I first had the pleasure of being introduced to your personal acquaintance, during which time various circumstances have occurred by which I have been enabled to estimate its value, and I can truly say I estimate it highly, and that I hardly know, after the experience of two voyages, which to admire most, your gentlemanly kindness as a host, your humane and considerate attention to your ship's company, or your vigilance, professional intelligence, and spirit as a navigator, exploring your way through a passage extremely intricate, and as yet but imperfectly known. Accept my sincerest thanks for your kindness, and my warmest wishes for your health, happiness, and prosperity."

and, on the following morning, took the Artillerymen on board the 'Malabar,' and conveyed them to Batavia, for which he received the thanks of Sir Stamford Raffles, the Lieutenant-Governor of Java.* In his letter of the 12th of April, 1813, conveying his thanks, the Lieutenant-Governor instructed Captain Deane " to proceed to the eastern ports of this island, for the purpose of receiving under your charge some gunboats, and proceeding to Pontiana therewith, under instructions which will be separately communicated to you." This had reference to the Sambas Expedition, already detailed, on the conclusion of which Captain Deane participated in the expedition undertaken against Rajah Boni of Macassar; but, at length, even his iron constitution broke down under the long-continued strain of service in these Eastern Islands, extending, with only the intermission of service in the Persian Gulf and Red Sea, from 1798 to 1814. In November of the latter year Captain Deane returned to Calcutta, and was ordered to proceed immediately to England by the Medical Board. He now found that his health was irremediably broken, and thus, after twenty-three years as arduous service as any man could well have experienced, he was compelled to retire on the pension of his rank, not having amassed any private means, as with an utter absence of self-seeking, he had ever sacrificed his own interests with the view of promoting those of the Company.†

* The following is a copy of the letter of the Secretary to Government, under date the 12th of April, 1813 :—" I am directed to acknowledge the receipt of your letter of the 9th instant, reporting your arrival at this port, with a detachment of Artillery on board your ship. The Hon. the Lieutenant-Governor in Council, entirely approves of your having received this detachment on board the 'Malabar,' and desires me to convey to you the thanks of this Government for your zealous attention to the public service on this occasion."

† While in England, Captain Deane received from Captain Money, the late Superintendent of the Bombay Marine, and Sir Stamford Raffles, late Lieutenant-Governor of Java, the two men, perhaps, better qualified than any others from long and intimate service relations, to form a correct estimate of his character and services, letters from which we will make the following extracts :—Captain Money writes under date the 14th of June, 1817 :—" When I succeeded to the office of Superintendent of Marine, my predecessor left, for my guidance, his opinion of the character of the officers of the corps, and to your name were annexed these words : 'He is the complete officer and gentleman ;' and so perfectly did I find you answer to this description, that I invariably selected you, when within my command, for the execution of every service that particularly required the exercise of such qualifications. I ever found you prompt to obey ; you never started a difficulty ; and I never was disappointed. In short, I always considered you a valuable servant of the Company, and an honour to the Service to which you belonged." Sir Stamford Raffles says in his letter, dated the 8th of August, 1817 :—" I have known you long, and for the period of five years, in which your services were principally employed in immediate connection with my authority, I have had repeated occasions to return you the thanks of Government for your zeal, alacrity, and perseverance in the public service. I can testify that the ever to be lamented Earl of Minto, while Governor-General of India, entertained the highest opinion of your character, and was forward to express his warm approbation of your conduct while engaged in the Java Expedition ; and for myself, that while you acted under the orders of the Java Government, as Senior Officer of the Marine on that station, not only was your

In 1815, the Hon. Company's brig 'Psyche,' Lieutenant J. Faithful, was stationed at Prince of Wales' Island, but did not long remain there, being succeeded by the 'Ariel,' Lieutenant D. Jones, which cruised about the Straits. In May, of this year, a party of men from the 'Teignmouth' was actively engaged in an attack on a fortified village dependent on the dethroned Rajah of Boni. Lieutenant T. C. Jackson, Assistant-Resident of Macassar, embarked in the 'Teignmouth' with a party of sixty European soldiers and thirty Natives, and proceeding to Langa, to the north of Macassar, whose inhabitants had been committing acts of piracy, landed with his small force and a party of sailors on the 12th of May. After some smart skirmishing, the detachment drove the enemy back, and attempted to storm the village, which was strongly stockaded. In this they were unsuccessful, and Lieutenant Jackson fell mortally wounded into the arms of two sailors, who formed part of the advance. At a later period the village of Langa and of Soopa, about eighty miles from Macassar, made their submission.

The year 1816 was an active one for the squadron of the Hon. Company's cruisers engaged in maintaining the peace among these Eastern islands. The 'Thetis' and 'Ariel' were stationed at Penang and in the Straits of Malacca, and found active employment protecting the trade against the depredations of the pirates which swarmed in all the waters to the east of the Bay of Bengal. The 'Malabar,' Lieutenant Hepburn, and some vessels employed in the survey, were engaged carrying troops from Java and the other islands in the occupation of the British, to Calcutta, on account of the Nepaul War, in which the gallant Gillespie had fallen, and which was not brought to a conclusion until the genius of Sir David Ochterlony triumphed over all difficulties.

The fourteen-gun brigs 'Nautilus,' Lieutenant C. Boyce, and 'Antelope,' Lieutenant J. Hall, were stationed off the British settlements at Java and Banda, and, on one occasion, the 'Antelope' fell in with and destroyed a fleet of pirate proas off the latter island. The 'Benares,' Captain Eatwell, 'Teignmouth,' Captain Sealy, and 'Ternate,' Captain Davidson, with some gunboats, were stationed at Macassar in the island of Celebes, and were of much assistance to the small British garrison quartered in Fort Rotterdam, an old Dutch fortress of considerable

conduct uniformly approved, but the Government often found it difficult to express itself in terms sufficiently strong, of your gallantry and zeal. For preserving harmony with H.M.'s squadron on that station, and uniting with it whenever necessary; for making personal sacrifices at all times, when the public service demanded expedition, and for a readiness and activity to forward the public service, and the interests of the Honourable Company, I feel that, in my late capacity as Lieutenant-Governor of Java, I was under great obligations to you; and I am confident that you will find from your Hon. Employers, every liberal consideration which your length of service and distinguished conduct entitle you to expect."

strength. These three ships performed some gallant service at Macassar during the year 1816.

On the 5th of April the boats of the 'Ternate,' Captain Davidson, attacked and drove ashore off the Tenette River, two large war proas, each mounting four guns and full of men; in this affair Lieutenant John Charlton Kinchant, a very promising young officer, was killed. In June the crews of the 'Teignmouth' and 'Benares' had an opportunity of earning distinction of which they did not fail to avail themselves. Our old enemy, the Rajah of Boni, had become aggressive and had taken up a post about eight miles from Macassar, at the entrance of Baliangan Pass, which led to a hill, where they had entrenched themselves in fifteen strong redoubts—called "bentengs"* in this part of the world—flanked on both sides by nearly precipitous rocks, containing caverns which were used as magazines or for shelter from artillery fire. As it could not be borne that a native chief should thus, as it were, blockade a British port and the capital of the island of Celebes, Major D. H. Dalton, the Political Resident and Commandant, resolved to dislodge him. At his request, on the 7th of June, Captain W. Eatwell, of the 'Benares,' senior naval officer, landed a body of seventy seamen and forty-five marines from the 'Teignmouth' and 'Benares,' to co-operate with the military force. The 'Benares' was left as guard ship at Macassar, all the disposable troops having been withdrawn from the fort, the 'Teignmouth' was stationed off Maros River, and the 'Ternate' off Tinoritty to deter the chief from reinforcing the enemy near Maros. Major Dalton's force consisted, in addition to the Naval Brigade, of a small detachment of Bengal Artillery, three hundred and forty men of the Hon. Company's European Regiment and the 4th Bengal Volunteer Battalion. A portion of the seamen were attached to the guns, which consisted of two 18-pounders, two howitzers, and one 6-pounder, and the marines were incorporated with the troops. The attack commenced at daylight on the 8th of June, and continued, under the heat of a tropical sun, until four in the afternoon. "At that hour," says the writer of a published account in the "Asiatic Journal," "the enemy, after a most desperate resistance, was driven with great loss from the whole of his entrenchments. Our loss on this occasion is very considerable, being seventy-four killed and

---

* Bentengs are breastworks of turf, about five feet in height, and tunnelled with numerous bamboo pipes, through which the defenders shoot, the bamboos being so arranged that the fire shall take effect upon the legs and lower part of the body of the enemy, and so effectually place him *hors de combat*. The approaches to the "benteng" are further strewn with *bambu doeri*, a thorny species of bamboo, as the name implies, the stems of which are so tortuous and thickly interlaced as to defy even large shot and shell. These earthworks are placed in a series, one behind the other, so that if the most advanced one is in danger of capture, the defenders leave it, and take shelter behind the succeeding one, and so on.

wounded. The conduct of every officer and man landed from the cruisers has been most exemplary. The exertions of Lieutenant Guy, Mr. Munday, master's mate, and Mr. Moresby, midshipman, attached to the guns, are highly spoken of. The detachment of marines from the 'Benares' particularly distinguished themselves. The enemy's force was estimated at two thousand. The Commander-in-chief of Boni's forces, with two other chiefs, was killed, and their loss is computed at five hundred men killed and wounded."

From other sources we learn that the fighting was severe throughout the day, and the Commandant, thinking he should be unable to carry the redoubts, was about to bivouac for the night, when one of them was captured by a rush of the seamen; upon this a general attack took place, and the whole were carried in a very short time. The success was complete, and the royal flag of Boni was found by the side of the dead chieftain. Major Dalton acknowledged the services of Captain Eatwell and Lieutenant Guy, who, he says, showed "their usual zeal and alacrity, and ably assisted on the occasion." In this action eleven men were killed and sixty-three wounded, of whom eight died, the total number of casualties being identical with those in the memorable battle of Plassey, where Lord Clive founded our Indian Empire. Captain Eatwell had a narrow escape of his life during a hand-to-hand mêlée, and was only saved from the creese of a Malay by one of his men who ran his pike through him.*

* The following is Major Dalton's Report to the Lieutenant-Governor of Java, detailing the operations by which the strong works, or "bentongs," at the Baliangan Pass, were carried by his small force:—" On the 7th of June, in the afternoon, we moved to our advanced post, two miles distant from the enemy's position; this intrenchment was very strong and planned with great skill, forming a chain of redoubts, which described an area of a circle with salient and entering angles to an extended line of about six hundred paces, flanked on both sides by rocks, which are high, nearly perpendicular, and containing caverns which answered us places of refuge against our fire; one of the caverns in a principal redoubt served as a magazine, and there was a fort or casement capable of containing about a thousand men. This redoubt, with the one on its right, formed the key of the position, being within the distance of a few hundred yards of the point, where, in going through the pass the defile is very narrow. For attack, the troops were formed into two columns, and a reserve, commanded by Captain Wood and Lieutenant Davison, of the Bengal European Regiment; a detachment, with a small howitzer, under the command of Captain Rawlins, 4th Battalion, was sent to the enemy's left to endeavour to turn his position, and another party, under Lieutenant Watson, European Regiment, was sent to his right, to drive them from the straggling rocks, and at all events, to push him into the range of fire of our battery. The battery ceased a little after six in the morning, and although extremely well served the positions appeared to be too extensive and well constructed to receive from our guns any quick or decided impression; the enemy was supposed to be about two thousand strong, he had not any large guns, but muskets and swivels in abundance. The attack on the enemy's left, after the most spirited and persevering exertions, was checked by obstacles which were not to be surmounted. That on his right had obtained some partial success, and which I endeavoured, with a reinforcement, immediately to improve; it was led on with promptitude and effect by Lieutenant Ashe, assisted by Lieutenant Goding. We now completely succeeded in turning the position of the enemy,

On the 8th of June, 1816, the 'Teignmouth' lost her entire detachment of marines, numbering one non-commissioned officer and seventeen privates. On that day, they had been placed in charge of two proas which had been detained, when it is supposed the Malay crews, taking advantage of a dark and stormy night, cut the cables, and, having overpowered the Sepoys, managed to make their escape; whether the Sepoys were murdered or drowned was never known, as nothing was ever heard of them or the proas. The marines of the 'Benares' performed good service during the period of their service in the Eastern islands, and it is only just that we should chronicle their faithful and courageous conduct both on shore and afloat. Originally numbering twenty-eight non-commissioned officers and privates, they returned to Bombay in 1817, at the end of the commission, reduced to a strength of only eleven, and there was not one of the survivors but could show scars of from one to three or four wounds. The Naick, or native corporal, who returned in command, was promoted to be a native commissioned officer, as also was the drummer, who had discarded his instrument for the bayonet. These men belonged to the old Bombay Marine Battalion, and, like the marines of the 'Aurora,' who distinguished themselves at Mauritius by their fidelity, were natives of the Concan.

Whilst hostilities were in progress against the Rajah of Boni, it became a matter of great importance to prevent his receiving supplies of military stores from his agents at Penang and Malacca. To prevent this, Captain Eatwell placed two smart midshipmen, Messrs. William Denton and Duff, in charge of two gunboats, to cruise in the track of the proas from the Straits of Malacca, while the ships took up the stations most likely to conduce to the attainment of the object in view; the cruisers' boats also, under the command of Lieutenant Guy, an able and zealous officer, were stationed at various islands, and were suc-

and obtaining the command of the pass from whence he withdrew his supplies; but at the moment of this success, the officers of the party were unfortunately wounded, the men were drawn off and screened from the fire of the redoubts, but at the same time enabled to keep a fire on them. We got a 6-pounder up, which fired occasionally; the battery continued to play, but the enemy still appeared resolute, nor did he waver till about four in the afternoon. It was instantly perceived, the assault in the most intrepid manner followed, and the two principal redoubts were in a few seconds in our possession.

"The enemy's chieftain, Datoo Cheeta, resisted to the last, and is reported to have been killed in the assault; the royal flag of Boni was found by his side. After carrying the principal redoubts we experienced no further resistance; the enemy fled in many directions, and in a close intricate country, was immediately concealed from our view. The loss of the enemy was considerable. I have sincerely to lament that our loss in men is severe; but when the nature of the attack is considered, and the obstinate defence made by the enemy, our loss in numbers may be deemed perhaps moderate. For the present achievement I am entirely indebted to the cordial assistance of the officers and men in the performance of my duty, and the determined bravery with which they completed its intent."

cessful in intercepting several of these vessels. Many deeds of daring were achieved by these ships' boats, which lost two men killed and several severely wounded, while employed on this duty.

Mr. Denton also performed good service in his gunboat. One day, while cruising off the bay of Boloo Comba, in the island of Celebes, he fell in with a large proa, but as, owing to a dead calm, his little craft could not close with the enemy, he pushed off with two small boats. Before the second boat could get alongside Mr. Denton boarded the enemy, but the odds were too great, and he was repulsed with the loss of two men, himself and the remainder of the boats' crew being hurled overboard. He was picked up by the second boat, and, as a light breeze had sprung up, proceeded to the gunboat and made sail towards the proa. A second time he tried to carry the enemy by boarding, but failed, owing to their numerical superiority. He now ran the proa close on board at the bow, and himself having lashed her bowsprit to his taffrail, steered for Boloo Comba, engaging her the whole time. At length, when five miles from that place, the proa sunk from the effects of the gunboat's shot, and, out of her crew of seventy desperadoes, only eleven survived. This vessel was proved to be laden with gunpowder, and, had she succeeded in entering the port of the Rajah of Boni, would have enabled him to continue his resistance to the British.

These operations closed the services of the Bombay Marine in the Eastern islands, for, in pursuance of a convention concluded between the British and Netherlands Governments, the former agreed to deliver up to the Dutch the island of Java and its dependencies.* The 'Nautilus' brought instructions to the Lieutenant-Governor arranging for the transfer, which took place, with appropriate ceremonies and under the usual salutes, on the 19th of August, 1816. Before that date the troops and civil and military authorities at Batavia, were embarked in eight transports, and the ships of the Bombay Marine† returned to Bombay after a lengthened, eventful, and distinguished service, during which they had taken part in five important Expeditions; namely, the conquest of Java, and the minor operations directed against Palimbang, Samarang, Sambas, and Boni, besides much harassing service in keeping the police of the seas. How well they had performed this duty, may be gathered from the great

---

* Of all our conquests from the Dutch, the Cape of Good Hope was alone retained, and their settlement of Cochin was exchanged for the island of Banca, which had been acquired by a deed of cession from the Rajah of Palimbang. By the treaty of 1814 with France, most of the colonies and factories taken from her during the war were restored, except the island of Mauritius.

† While employed under the Bengal Government, the officers received a high rate of extra pay, which was also made in *sicca* rupees, a coin of greater value than the old Bombay rupee.

increase in piracy that took place directly after the cruisers had quitted the station, and the columns of the Indian papers of that day are filled with accounts of the depredations and atrocities committed by the piratical proas which swarmed around the coasts of Borneo, Java, and Celebes, the Dutch ships of war displaying a surprising lack of energy and enterprise in checking the growing evil.

Perhaps the last services one or two of the cruisers of the Bombay Marine were enabled to render on this station, were calculated to be of a more pleasing character in the retrospect, than any war service could be; we refer to those connected with the saving of life, which the seaman, in the evening of life, when "fighting his battles o'er again," and recounting to his children the oft told tale of battle, fire, and wreck, will recall with a proud consciousness that not all his energies were expended in depriving as many of his country's enemies of life, as the opportunities at his disposal enabled him to compass.

In September, 1816, when the British troops were being withdrawn from Java, four hundred men of the 78th Highlanders embarked for Calcutta on board the 'Princess Charlotte' transport, but the ship, running upon a sunken rock, the day after her departure, was, with great difficulty, navigated back to Batavia Roads. Here the troops were transferred to the 'Francis and Charlotte,' a vessel of 700 tons, which sailed for Calcutta on the 29th of September. On the 5th of November, the ship with the ill-fated Highlanders on board, ran on one of the sunken reefs surrounding the island of Preparis, which lay about twelve miles on the larboard quarter. The boats could only hold one-fifth of the souls, which, including soldiers, women, children, and the crew, numbered upwards of five hundred and forty. A great portion of these were landed on the island, and a ship, the 'Prince Blucher,' bearing in sight, took on board the remainder, who had been exposed on a rock near the wreck for five days; owing to the tempestuous weather that now set in, the captain of the 'Prince Blucher' deemed it prudent to proceed to Calcutta, where he arrived in nine days. Lord Hastings, the Governor-General, immediately despatched two of the Company's cruisers to proceed to the island and bring off the remainder of the shipwrecked people, amounting to one hundred and fifty men, who were found on the thirty-sixth day after the wreck, in a state of deplorable weakness. They had been subsisting on shell-fish, but latterly, none had been procurable, and they were in too exhausted a condition to search for them at low-water. Several of them died after being taken on board the cruisers, and the sudden change from total privation to plenty, proved fatal to many more.

A few months later, another of the Hon. Company's ships was of service to the cause of humanity, by rescuing the crew of H.M.'s frigate 'Alceste,' of forty-six guns, commanded by Captain Maxwell. The 'Alceste' had sailed on the 9th of January, 1817, from Manilla for England, with Lord Amherst and suite, then returning from the embassy to China; within nine days of her departure, while making for the Straits of Gaspar, the frigate struck with a tremendous crash on a reef of sunken rocks, and, in a few minutes, the water filled the hold and flowed over the orlop-deck. The Ambassador and his suite were immediately landed on the island of Pulo Leat, about four miles distant, and, before night, all the crew joined them. As it was now found that the island was destitute of food, every effort was made to recover as much as possible from the wreck, and, during the next few days, they succeeded in collecting several casks of flour and some arms, which were of almost equal importance to them in their unfortunate situation, as a large number of Malay pirate proas had made their appearance, and not only took possession of the wreck, but threatened to attack the breast-work enclosing a circular position, within which Captain Maxwell had retired with his crew. Meantime, Lord Amherst, with the other members of his embassy, forty-seven in all, had proceeded in a large cutter to Batavia, in order to procure assistance, and it arrived not a day too soon. On the morning of the 3rd of March, the Hon. Company's cruiser 'Ternate,' of sixteen guns, hove in sight, and, advancing on the pirates, quickly dispersed them with her broadsides; before nightfall all the officers and crew of H.M.S. 'Alceste' were safely on board the little cruiser. Captain Maxwell who, throughout these trying circumstances, had exhibited the gallantry and self-denying example which are the most cherished characteristics of the British officer, and who was well seconded in his efforts to maintain discipline by his crew, said, during the course of his examination at the court-martial convened to try him for the loss of his ship, "Having seen all my companions in distress fairly embarked, I felt, in walking off to the boat, that my heart was lifted up with gratitude to a kind Providence who had watched over us." And he had cause for thankfulness, as appears from the following account of the proceedings of the day preceding the arrival of the 'Ternate,' which reads like a page out of Marryat's novel, 'Masterman Ready:'—" At dawn on Sunday, the 3rd of March, the whole horde of savages advanced to the island, yelling and firing their pieces, and beating their gongs, and they anchored within a cable's length of the shore. Some further attempts were made at a parley, and a negotiation for assistance, but without any feeling of sincerity on the part of the Malays. Their force kept continually increasing, and in the course of the day no less than fifty proas and boats had arrived, with at least five hundred men on board. Their object was evidently to slaughter the Europeans for the sake of plunder, and as they hourly grew stronger, they were less careful to conceal their intentions. That evening, Captain Maxwell assembled his men, and informing them that he was hourly expecting an attack from the pirates, made a spirited appeal to them, and promised them victory. His address was received with three hearty cheers, which resounded far and wide, and produced an evident effect on the savages, who mistook the hurrahs for a war-cry, and stood on the defensive. The night passed without any attack, but the morning discovered the enemy strengthened by the arrival of ten more vessels, with a hundred additional men. The position of the English grew momentarily more critical, and they began to ponder which alternative they should accept, that of dashing at the pirates, and, at the risk of being butchered themselves, getting possession of their boats; or that of standing on their defence until their scanty provisions were exhausted, or assistance arrived from Java. While they were yet undecided which course to adopt, one of the officers climbed a tall tree, and reported something like a sail at a great distance. A look-out was immediately sent up with a glass, and sweeping the horizon, soon announced a vessel standing towards the island under all sail. At this news, the anxieties of the shipwrecked crew vanished at once, and gave place to a joy as general as unbounded, and from many a heart sincere thanks were returned to the Almighty for their happy deliverance. The vessel approaching proved to be the 'Ternate,' despatched by Lord Amherst to their assistance. The horde of pirates made a precipitate flight at her appearance, amidst a volley from the now rescued crew. All were embarked on board her, and arrived in safety at Batavia, where the Ambassador himself received them hospitably, and had them comfortably provided for."

CHAPTER IX.

1811—1820.

Operations against the Pirates of Kattywar and Cutch—The 'Malabar,' Captain Maxfield, in Burmah—Expeditions against Malwan and Dwarka—Gallant Services of Lieutenant Grant in Kattywar—Action between the 'Nautilus' and 'Peacock'—Services of the Bombay Marine during the Mahratta War—Shipbuilding in Bombay Dockyard—Operations at Mocha.

BETWEEN the years 1811-16, owing to the absence of a large portion of the cruisers of the Bombay Marine in the Eastern Islands, the duties fell very heavily on the small force disposable at head-quarters, who had thus scarcely any rest in port, but were hurried from one sphere of duty to another. The pirates on the coast of the southern Concan, Kattywar,* and Cutch, were in consequence very troublesome and daring, and the squadron of small craft, schooners and armed pattamars, were actively and successfully employed against them; the only remaining available cruiser was employed in protecting the Red Sea trade.

The pirates established at Beyt, had, from time immemorial, been very daring in their depredations. In 1803, a small, but well-appointed, squadron, consisting of H.M's. ship 'Fox,' and Honourable Company's brigs 'Ternate' and 'Teignmouth,' was despatched by the Bombay Government to beat up their quarters, and, after a bombardment of two or three days without

* The Guzerat Peninsula is now known by the name of Kattywar, from the tribe of Kattees, who inhabit the central division or province of the ten into which the Peninsula is divided; of these ten divisions eight belong to Rajpoots of diverse tribes, and one alone, Soruth, to the Mahommedan dynasty of Joonughur. The proper name of the peninsula is, however, Soorashtra, so called by the Greeks, from Soo (Good) and Rashtra (country); it is sacred in Hindoo eyes from its having been the scene of Krishna's exploits and death, and vast numbers of pilgrims crowd from all parts of India to its shrines, the most famous of which was the Temple of Somnauth, desecrated by the Mohammedan conqueror, Mahmoud of Ghuznee, and rendered historical in modern times by Lord Ellenborough's famous "proclamation of the gates." The first to establish order in Kattywar was Colonel Walker, Resident at Baroda, who, in 1805, checked the incursions of the Mahratta hosts who levied *chout* by certain regular payments. Full details of the Guzerat Peninsula may be found in No. 37 of the Bombay Government Records, in which are also the Reports of Captain (now Sir George Le Grand) Jacob, who places the population of Kattywar at 1,147,000 in 1842. The entire length of the coast-line of Kattywar from Beyt Island to Diu Head is one hundred and sixty miles.

any salutary effect, a division of seamen and marines was landed, but could penetrate no further than the *pettah*, which, as at Broach and other Mahratta towns, lay under cover of the guns and musketry fire of the garrison. Several men fell in the attempt to assault this strong fortress, but, though unsuccessful, their blood was not shed in vain, as after they had retired, a great portion of the pirates took alarm and evacuated the island of Beyt. These now established themselves in the ruins of the ancient temple of Somnauth which they fortified, and continued to molest the traders in the Gulf of Cambay, until driven out by a second expedition in which the above ships participated. The pirates soon again became troublesome, and, in 1808, Lieutenant Macdonald was employed blockading the ports of Beyt and Poshetra, with the schooner 'Lively' and two armed pattamars, and succeeded in forcing the piratical chiefs to give in their submission. But no sooner were the blockading vessels withdrawn than the people of the seaboard of the Guzerat peninsula returned to their nefarious calling.

At length, at the close of 1811, an expedition was sent to Kattywar, under the command of Colonel Lionel Smith, of H.M's. 65th Regiment, with which a squadron of cruisers cooperated, Captain Sealy being senior naval officer. The squadron consisted of the 'Benares,' fourteen guns; 'Prince of Wales,' fourteen guns; Zephyr' and 'Sylph,' schooners, of eight guns, and four armed pattamars. As was customary in those days, an officer of the Marine was appointed boat-master to the force, whose special duty it was to superintend the arrangements connected with the transports and boats, and see that they were well found and in good order. As the 'Benares' and 'Prince of Wales' were too large for service in the shallow waters of the Kattywar coast, they were withdrawn, and Lieutenants Blast and Hardy remained with their schooners 'Zephyr' and 'Sylph,' and four pattamars, each armed with six 12-pounder carronades. Very efficient service the little squadron performed, and Mr. Midshipman Grant,* who had been appointed acting-lieutenant of the 'Rodney,' the pennant vessel of Commodore James Jeakes, commanding on the Surat station, particularly distinguished himself.

A merchant ship proceeding from Bombay to Surat having been plundered by pirates, when an officer of the Bombay European Regiment, who was a passenger on board her, was

* This meritorious officer, who entered the Service in 1810, died in September, 1874, at the age of eighty-one. He had already gained the approval of Sir John Malcolm, for while midshipman of the Hon. Company's sloop-of-war 'Mercury' at Bussorah, he was selected to command an Arab ship taken up by the Political Resident to carry the British Envoy's suite to Bombay, the Resident having applied to Captain Conyers for an officer to perform this duty. His knowledge of navigation and seamanship was displayed by his bringing the ship in safety to Bombay, when General Malcolm recommended him to the Government of Bombay for promotion.

severely wounded, Mr. Grant was directed to take command of the Company's armed pattamar 'Bhowany,' carrying six 12-pounder carronades, and proceed after the pirate. In the latter part of December, 1811, while cruising in search of her, he fell in with the 'Zephyr,' Lieutenant Blast, who directed him to proceed in company to Kori or Lukput River, in Cutch, where, according to intelligence, some piratical craft had taken shelter. Lieutenant Blast stationed the 'Deria Dowlut,' pattamar, on the opposite side of the river to stop the passage of all boats and vessels to or from Lukput Bunder; the 'Dart' gunboat he stationed at the inner entrance abreast of the Cotaseer Creek, where the pirates were said to have taken up a position; and the 'Bhowany,' with Mr. Midshipman Kinchant in command, was placed at the outer entrance of the creek to prevent their escape in that direction. Mr. Grant having volunteered to cut the three pirate vessels out, proceeded with all the boats of the small squadron up the creek, where they had taken up a strong position under shelter of the guns of Fort Nuranseer. The affair was completely successful. Mr. Grant pulled up the creek, disregarding a heavy fire that was opened on him from the baghalas, which were boarded and carried in gallant style. Lieutenants Blast and Hardy, and the other officers and men of the squadron engaged on the Scinde coast in the suppression of piracy, received the thanks of the Government of Bombay, and Mr. Grant, who received command of the gunboat 'Dart,' was honoured by a special letter of thanks from the Marine Office, under date the 24th of January, 1812.

In February, 1812, Colonel Smith attacked the fort of Nowanugger, when the officers and men of the Bombay Marine afforded valuable co-operation, and earned the thanks of the military commander. In April of this year, Acting-Lieutenant Grant again displayed his zeal and activity by capturing, with the 'Dart' and 'Deria Dowlut,' after a smart action, a large piratical vessel, having on board the notorious leaders Rajah Nackwah and his father, Vesey Nackwah; for this service he again received the thanks of Government.

At the close of 1811, and beginning of the following year, the 'Benares' and 'Ternate' were employed in the Persian Gulf, and one ship was engaged in convoying the Red Sea traders; in the Bay of Bengal some vessels were stationed at Chittagong and Teck Naaf.

In December, 1811, intelligence arrived at Calcutta of the sudden irruption into the territory of Chittagong of a large Burmese force, which spread considerable alarm along the whole line of our frontier, and induced the political agent, Mr. Pechell, to apply for immediate succour. A battalion of troops was instantly warned for service, and one wing, with ammunition and a large supply of treasure, embarked on board the

'Aurora,' fourteen guns, Captain Macdonald, then refitting at the Calcutta dockyard, with which he started in a very crowded state, towing the launch, and accompanied by the 'Phœnix,' 'Thetis,' and 'Vestal,' with the rest of the regiment, amounting in all to nine hundred men. On the sixth day he arrived at Chittagong, when the troops were no sooner disembarked, than the insolent Mughs retreated within their own boundary.

Our political relations with the Burmese Empire had become gradually more unsatisfactory in proportion to the aversion evinced by the British authorities to engage in an expensive war. This state of affairs dated from Colonel Syme's second mission in 1803, when a plot, believed to have the concurrence of the King of Burmah was concocted, for the forcible seizure of the Envoy's person while *en route* to Amurapura, together with the captain of the 'Mornington,' who had taken up his residence at Rangoon, and to whom in the dead of night the project was disclosed by an American, in the service of that government, who also furnished him with a canoe in time to effect his escape to the ship. By this officer's prompt and decisive measures on the following morning, in demanding hostages for the Envoy's safety, and assuming a position to enforce these demands in event of denial, this treacherous scheme was effectually defeated; though the Mission failed of producing any cordial or permanent results.

The British territory, bordering on the kingdom of Arracan, was frequently disturbed by predatory excursions, for which it was impossible to obtain the slightest redress; and, in 1811, Captain Canning, aide-de-camp to the Governor-General, was despatched in the 'Malabar,' Captain Maxfield, as diplomatic agent to the Court of this capricious potentate. The Burmese Government was ripe for aggression, and the Viceroy of Rangoon received orders from Ava, which were published in the streets, to send the Envoy, as well as the commander of the cruiser, up to the capital in irons. An attempt, indeed, was made to carry the order into effect, for when the Envoy was returning with his escort and followers to the 'Malabar,' two war boats, out of about twenty that were in motion round the cruiser, tried to seize one of the 'Malabar's' cutters. But Captain Maxfield was a man of prompt action, and he ordered the guns to be pointed at the two war boats, but not to fire, as the Envoy was still in the cutter and might be sacrificed. Captain Canning reached the cruiser in safety, when a message was immediately sent to the Viceroy, complaining of the outrage, and demanding instant reparation by the delivery of the commanders of the war-boats in irons, on board the 'Malabar,' and the disavowal of the act of aggression; the Viceroy was allowed half-an-hour to decide, at the expiration of which time, he was informed, the 'Malabar' would, in the event of refusal, attack the town. In response to this imperative summons the commanders of the war-boats were sent off handcuffed, and the Viceroy made the required atonement for the outrage.

During the year 1812, the western squadron was reinforced by the 'Mornington' twenty-two guns, and 'Thetis' and 'Ariel,' ten-gun brigs, from Bengal, they being relieved by the 'Teignmouth,' sixteen guns, and 'Antelope,' fourteen guns, which had been employed in China; the former vessel and the 'Malabar' and 'Aurora' proceeded early in the following year to Java, and participated in the expedition against the Rajah of Sambas, where, as already mentioned, the 'Teignmouth' lost more than two-thirds of her crew.

Towards the end of 1812, a small military force, under the command of Colonel Lionel Smith, assisted by the Hon. Company's cruiser 'Prince of Wales,' fourteen guns, and a squadron of small craft, proceeded against a nest of pirates who had long established themselves at Malwan,* on the Malabar coast, rendering navigation unsafe for trading vessels unless under convoy, and compelling the Bombay Government to retain a cruiser to blockade the coast. The expedition was completely successful, and the pirates were so thoroughly rooted

* Malwan had for centuries been the haunt of pirates. The port of Malwan is situated between the fort of that name and Melundy island, or Sindeedroog, and lies between Gheriah and Vingorla. Malwan and three other ports had formerly belonged to the Rajah of Kolapoor, while between them and the Portuguese territory of Goa, lay the small principality of Waree, ruled by the Bhonsla family. The late Duke of Wellington, then Major-General Wellesley, apprehensive of the safety of the single Company's cruiser employed to blockade the coast of Malwan, a fear not shared by the officers of the Bombay Marine engaged in that service, wrote in 1804 that he regarded "the blockade of the Rajah's ports by a Company's cruiser as always inconvenient and expensive," and recommended the adoption of a treaty on their paying compensation for the country vessels plundered. Again, writing to Colonel Sir William Clarke, commanding the 84th Regiment at Goa, he remarks that "nothing can be more scandalous than the system of piracy which has long been carried on on the coast of Malabar; and I am convinced that the measure which I have proposed to the Rajah is an expedient which will answer the purpose expected from it, only for a time. I indeed doubt much whether the Rajah of Kolapoor or the Bhonslah have the power, supposing them to have the inclination, to prevent piracy; and that object is, in my opinion, to be affected only by severe instantaneous punishments of pirates on their own coasts, and in sight of their own people; and if it should still be persisted in, by sending strong armaments within all the creeks and rivers, with orders to destroy boats, vessels, the fortifications which protect them, and even the habitations of the pirates."

The capture of the fortresses of Newtee and Rairee, during the Mahratta War in 1818, by a force under Sir William Keir Grant, in which the Bombay Marine participated, finally put an end to the depredations of these restless people. At this time only the principality of Sawunt Waree, a strip of territory forty miles in length by twenty-five in breadth, remained between the Southern Concan and the Portuguese district of Goa, and its ruler, called Phund Sawunt, gave trouble in 1844, though the reigning prince in 1857, was faithful. The family was known by the title of Desaee, and the dynasty was also called Bhonsla in the eighteenth century. He is now a petty chief, entitled to a salute of nine guns.

out that they have never again been able to make head there.

In 1813, Mr. Grant, now First-Lieutenant of the 'Prince of Wales,' again distinguished himself by cutting out, with a party of seamen and marines from his ship, a pirate vessel that had taken shelter in the Ranpeer River, Scinde. In consequence of his meritorious services, Captain Carnac (afterwards Sir James Rivett Carnac, Governor of Bombay) Political Resident at Baroda, strongly recommended him to Government, and Lieutenant Grant was appointed to the command of the Guicowar's naval force, which was no sinecure in those days, as the Joasmi pirates were at the height of their power, and their well-armed and manned dhows, sailing in squadrons, swept the Arabian Gulf and the coasts of India, almost as far south as Bombay. Within a year of his appointment Lieutenant Grant, when on a cruise, recaptured off Damaun, a ship under English colours that had just been seized by a large pirate vessel, which he drove off. In 1815, during the course of the military operations in Kattywar, Lieutenant Grant landed with his men and took command of the artillery at the siege of the fort of Kundorna. The Guicowar lost upwards of one thousand five hundred men killed and wounded during the investment of this important fortress, and Lieutenant Grant effected the breach in a short time by the accuracy of the fire of the guns which he himself served. For this service he received the thanks of Government, and the Political Agent at Kattywar, writing on the 8th of July, 1815, from the camp, bore testimony to the "indefatigable zeal" he displayed, and added, "the professional exactness and skill with which the shots were thrown, and the general effect of the ordnance, were such as frequently to call for the marked commendation and applause of the superior officers, as well as the troops in general of this force."

In the same year Lieutenant Grant was convoying twenty-four trading vessels with two armed pattamars, when a fleet of Joasmi pirates hove in sight and began to attack the convoy; a sharp action now ensued, and Lieutenant Grant succeeded in beating the enemy off. He also captured a pirate vessel out of Cutch, which had been harassing the trade along the Kattywar coast, and a little later in this year (1815) captured, off Porebunder,[*] a pirate vessel commanded by the notorious chief, Hussein Nurreadah, who had, for a long time, preyed on the trade of the Gulf of Cambay. For these services he received

---

[*] Porebunder, on the Kattywar coast, in the district of Jetwar or Burda, is a place of considerable commercial importance, and the town, which is within the fort, is surrounded by walls one and a half miles in circumference. The Rajpoot Rana of Porebunder is subordinate to the Guicowar of Baroda, to whom he pays tribute, as well as to the British Government, to whom a portion of the customs' dues was ceded in 1809 for the maintenance of a small military force. Fifteen miles from Porebunder is Novee Bunder, the capital of the district, a place of commercial note.

the thanks of the Guicowar, who presented him with a sword and a palankin, in which to go to Court on state occasions, and conferred on him the rank of captain in his service—honours and gifts the bestowal of which were approved by the Government of Bombay in Council, and by the Court of Directors. Further to enable him to support the eight bearers necessary to carry the palanquin when attending at Court, the Guicowar granted him the village of Velun, near Diu Head.*

In 1815, in consequence of the continued depredations of the piratical tribes of Cutch against neighbouring States in alliance with the Company, the Governor of Bombay ordered a squadron of cruisers, under Captain Blast, including the 'Vestal,' Lieutenant James Watkins, and 'Sylph,' Lieutenant James Arthur, to be despatched to blockade the coasts, and issued a proclamation to that effect. He also directed the despatch of a body of troops, composed of H.M. 17th Dragoons and 65th Regiment, the Hon. Company's European Regiment, and three companies of Native Artillery, under the command of Colonel East. After a brief siege, a detachment, under Colonel Barclay, captured Anjar, about two miles from Bhooj, the capital of Cutch, while the main column proceeded to Okhamundel,† where the squadron, under Captain Grant,

* The following is a copy of the letter of the Guicowar, dated 23rd October, 1817, conferring these honours :—

"Anund Rao Guicowar Sena Khaskyl Shumsheer Bahadur writes his compliments.

"The distinguished valour and courage which you displayed whilst in company with Vitell Row Dewanjee Soobah of Kattywar, Marluckgury, have been duly brought to the notice of this Government by the above-named officer, as also by Captain James Rivett Carnac, Resident. From this we are sensible of your being interested in the welfare of this Government. Likewise the gallant conduct, discipline, and military knowledge which you evinced whilst in command of the Artillery at the siege and capture of the Fort of Kundorna, and other various meritorious services rendered by you; as also your exertions, valour, perseverance on a late occasion, while in command of the Sirkar pattamars, in saving numerous merchant vessels, and capturing two of the vessels belonging to the pirates, have all been brought to the notice of this Government. This Government, therefore, entertain the highest opinion of your ability and merits.

"The Government is also much gratified to learn your conciliatory conduct in preserving the friendship and attachment of their servants and subjects in general.

"The Government therefore grants you as a mark and token of its approbation of the various meritorious services which you have, from time to time, rendered, the rank of Captain, with a suitable uniform and sword. In order to enable you to accompany the Soobah on his journeys, and to travel by land, a palanqueen is granted to you by the Sirka, in which you are to ride.

"What more can be said?"

† Okhamundel is derived from two words, *okha*, Punjabi for "bad," and *mendel*, a term applied to any district or division. The inhabitants of the peninsula are called Wadhel Rajpoots and Waghers, and the latter have ever been a notorious race of pirates, who have resisted all authority and given rise to numerous expeditions on the part both of Native rulers and the British Government. Of the entire length of the Kattywar coast, one hundred and sixty miles, the northern portion, thirty miles, forms Okhamundel, and is almost severed from the main by the Runn of Cutch, a mud flat submerged in the rainy season. The

afforded valuable co-operation. In February, 1816, operations were commenced in the peninsula, by the reduction of the fortified post of Dhengee, which was captured by storm after a siege of three days; thence the column marched to Dwarka, famed for its temples dedicated to Krishna, but just as the batteries and ships, the latter under Captain Blast, were about to open fire on the place it surrendered at discretion. The Expedition now proceeded to the island of Beyt, but the chief, considering resistance hopeless, sent in his submission. The 5th Regiment Native Infantry was left to garrison the captured places, and the remainder of the troops proceeded to Nowanuggur, the Jam's capital, and Joonughur, a strong fort on the southern coast of Kattywar. The squadron remained some time longer on the coast, until the peninsula of Okhamundel was delivered over to the Guicowar. Between the years 1818-19 a squadron was kept cruising off the coasts of Scinde and Cutch, under command of Lieutenant Tanner, in the 'Antelope,' who had considerable success in destroying several pirate vessels.

In 1820 the garrison maintained in Okhamundel by the Guicowar, was so insufficient for the purpose of keeping the restless Waghers in order, that they rose upon the troops whom they overpowered, when they obtained possession of the province. To retrieve the loss, in November of that year, a British force was despatched against Dwarka, under command of Colonel the Hon. Leicester Stanhope; and, on the 26th of November, the place was taken by escalade, with the loss of four killed and twenty-eight wounded. The 'Nautilus,' of fourteen guns, commanded by Lieutenant Middleton, participated in this Expedition, and her officers and crew were honourably mentioned in Colonel Stanhope's despatch. A column has been erected at Dwarka to commemorate its capture, a little to the west of the great temple* and close to the edge of the cliffs.

In the latter part of the year 1817, Captain Grant received the thanks of the Bombay Government for fitting out, with extraordinary promptitude, a corvette of sixteen guns, belonging to the Governor of Diu, and a brig, which he armed with the guns and men of his own gunboats, in order to cruise against some Joasmi pirate vessels, which were infesting the Kattywar and Cutch coasts; none of the Company's cruisers were at the time on the station, and his zealous exertions were rewarded with success, until he fell in with the 'Teignmouth' and

next twenty-two miles from the Runn at Mudhi to Miani, form part of Halar, the territory of the Jam of Nowanuggur; the southern ten miles, like Okhamundel, is also under the Guicowar. From Mul Dwarka to Seel Bunder, forty-five miles, belongs to the Nawab of Joonughur, and from Mahadeopore to Miani owns the sway of the Rana of Porebunder.

* This temple, which is built of stone, and is whitewashed, stands at an elevation of 168 feet above the sea level; it is a prominent object, being visible in clear weather a distance of seventeen or eighteen miles.

'Aurora,' in company with which the corvette continued the cruise. While thus engaged he was instrumental in saving treasure amounting to sixty bags of dollars, and the greater part of the cargo of a vessel, formerly known as the 'Princess Royal,' belonging to some of the principal merchants of Surat, which had been wrecked on the Kattywar coast; for this act, the merchants, upwards of twenty in number, and the underwriters, presented him with a letter of thanks, and he received from the Governor in Council, a despatch conveying his "high approval" for his meritorious conduct, and his humanity in preserving the crew from the hands of the "lawless soldiery" of the Government of Joonughur, who had appropriated the whole of the valuable cargo, besides forty-two bags of dollars and silver, in recovering which, says the Political Agent, "Captain Grant, who had returned to the coast for the express object of procuring restitution, was subjected to personal insult and danger."

In 1820, by an unexpected event, the active career of Captain Grant was temporarily brought to a sudden termination, and though he served in India some years after this event, his constitution had received so rude a shock by the cruel ill-treatment to which he was subjected, that he never recovered his health, and was ultimately forced to quit the Service, and retire upon a pension. Captain Grant had been so successful in his vigorous measures for the extirpation of piracy on the coast of Kattywar, that the Guicowar considered it unnecessary to maintain a naval establishment. He, accordingly, received orders to proceed inland from his station, Velun Bunder, near Diu Head, to Amrellie Fort, to deliver over charge of his vessels to the Guicowar's Sersooba or Dewan. While proceeding on this journey with an escort of four mounted men, he was waylaid by a *baha-wuttia** band of thirty-five horsemen, commanded by a noted Kattee outlaw chief, one Bawawalla, and, after a brief struggle, in which his servant was killed, and his moonshee and two of his small escort were wounded, the party were overpowered. Captain Grant was personally unable to make any effectual resistance, as he only carried a riding whip, and was carried away to endure a confinement of nearly three months in the most pestilential jungles of the Kattywar peninsula.†

* Baha-wuttia means literally "out of country," and the outlaws, who were thus termed, were the most cruel of the human race, and not only ravaged the country and robbed all degrees of the community, but did not scruple to maim or murder even those who offered no resistance.

† His sufferings were such that most men would have succumbed to them, but he was gifted with an iron frame and indomitable resolution, and survived more than half a century; in April, 1871, at the request of General Sir George Le Grand Jacob—who had filled the post of Political Agent at Kattywar, between the years 1839-43—he supplied him with the following "Narrative of his Captivity," which appears in that officer's work, entitled "Western India:"—" On first coming up, Bawawalla said that he wanted to consult me about his affairs, and on this pretext got me to dismount; my people being rendered helpless, I

His release was effected through the agency of the British Political officer, but his constitution received so severe a shock from the cruel treatment to which he had been subjected during

> was forced to remount my horse and gallop off with the gang, who took me into a large jungle called the Geer, where I was kept prisoner on the top of a mountain for two months and seventeen days. During the whole of this time, two armed men with swords drawn, kept guard over me. I laid amongst the rocks, drenched with rain night and day, with the exception of two nights, when the gang forced me to accompany them, and we stopped in a friendly village. In this expedition I was occasionally allowed to ride, but always surrounded by a strong band, that made all attempt at escape impossible. In one village, where the people favoured Bawawalla, the women took my part, and upbraided him and his men for my cruel treatment. Towards unfriendly villages the custom of the gang was to ride up to the gates and chop off the heads of little boys at play, and then go off rejoicing and laughing at their cursed exploits. When they returned to the encampment, after a day's murdering foray, the young Kattees used to boast how many men they had killed, and one day I heard the old fellows questioning them rather particularly, whether or not they were sure they had killed their victims. 'Yes,' they said; 'they had seen their spears through them, and were certain they were dead.' 'Ah!' remarked an old Kattee, 'a human being is worse to kill than any other animal; never be sure they are dead till you see the body on one side of the road and the head on the other.'
>
> "At times the chief, Bawawalla, in a state of stupor from opium, would come and sit by my side, and holding his dagger over me, ask how many stabs it would take to kill me. I said I thought one would do, and I hoped he would put me out of my misery. 'I suppose you think,' he would answer, 'that I won't kill you; I have killed as many human beings as ever fisherman killed fish, and I should think nothing of putting an end to you; but I shall keep you awhile yet, till I see if your Government will get me back my property, if so I will let you off.'
>
> "When not out plundering, the gang slept most of the day. At night the halter of each horse was tied to its master's arm; when the animals heard voices they tugged, and the men were up in an instant. Their meals consisted of bajree cakes with chillies and milk, when it could be got. I used to have the same. Once or twice my servant was allowed to come to me, and brought the rare treat of some curry and a bottle of claret from Captain Ballantine. The wine Bawawalla seized on at once, thinking it was daroo or spirits, but on tasting the liquor, he changed his mind, and spitting it out declared it was poison, sent no doubt on purpose to kill him. By the way of test I was ordered to drink it, which I did with very great pleasure, and finding me none the worse, he gave up his idea of poison. Among his people there were two young men who showed some feeling for me. One of these was shot in a pillaging raid, shortly before my release. They used to try and cheer me up by telling me I should be set free. Occasionally, when opportunity offered, they would inform me how many people they had killed, and the method they pursued when rich travellers refused to pay the sum demanded. This was to tie the poor wretches by their legs to a beam across a well, with their heads touching the water, and then to saw away at the rope until the tortured victims agreed to their demands, then the Kattees would haul them up, get from them a hoondee, or bill on some agent, and keep them prisoners till this was paid.
>
> "Sometimes they told me of their master's intention to murder me, which was not pleasant. He and his men had many disputes about me, just as his hopes or fears of the consequence of my imprisonment prevailed. I can never forget one stormy night they were all sitting round a great fire, and I lay behind them. Lions and wild beasts roared around us, but did not prevent me overhearing a debate upon the subject of what should be done with me. The men complained that they had been two months in the jungle on my account, their families were in the villages, very badly off for food, and that they would stay no longer. Their chief replied, 'Let us kill him, and flee to some other part of the country.' To this they objected, that the English would send troops and take their families

his confinement, that he was unable to enter on active duty until 1822, when, on Captain Mack, of the Marine, being drowned while piloting the Hon. Company's ship 'Buckinghamshire' out of Bombay, owing to the heavy sea capsizing his boat, he was promoted First-Assistant in the Master Attendant's Department. He signalized the first year of his return to active employ by a gallant exploit, and, in the words of the Superintendent of the Bombay Marine to the Governor of Bombay, "had the good fortune, off Surat Bar, by great energy and risk, in heavy blowing weather, to save the lives of a detachment of His Majesty's 4th Dragoons while under his convoy, for which he received the thanks of Colonel Dalbiac* and the marked approbation of Government."

prisoners, and ill-use them. So in the end it was agreed to keep me for the present.

"My release was effected at last through our Political Agent, Captain Ballantine, who prevailed on the Nawab of Joonughur to use his influence to get another Kattee, who had forcibly taken Bawawalla's Pergunna, or district, to restore it to him, and Bawawalla thus having gained his object, set me free. My sufferings during confinement were almost beyond endurance, and I used to pray in the evening that I might never see another morning. I had my boots on my feet for the first month, not being able to get them off from the constant wet until I was reduced by sickness. Severe fever with ague, and inflammation of the liver came on, and with exposure to the open air drove me delirious, so that when let go I was found wandering in the fields at night covered with vermin from head to foot. I shall never forget the heavenly sensation of the hot bath and clean clothes I got in the tent of the Nawab of Joonughur's Dewan. The fever and ague then contracted continued on me for five years, and the ill effects still remain, my head being at times greatly troubled with giddiness, and I have severe fits of ague; my memory is also much affected, but I can never forget the foregoing incidents, though it is now upwards of fifty years since they occurred."

* The following is an extract from a letter addressed to Captain Grant by Colonel Dalbiac, commanding the 4th Dragoons, afterwards General Sir Charles Dalbiac, Inspector-General of Cavalry, dated 29th May, 1822, and written at "Arras while on the march to Khairah:"—

"I felt confident throughout that the detachment would receive every assistance which could possibly be derived from skill and exertion. Such, according to Lieutenant Coney's Report, has indeed proved to be the case, for it is to your aid chiefly that I must ascribe the preservation of this valuable detachment. Allow me then to express the sincere obligation which I shall ever consider myself under for the important service rendered to this part of the Regiment under my command, which I have requested Mr. Meriton to communicate in a particular manner to his Excellency the Commander-in-Chief."

Captain Grant had already distinguished himself as a philanthropist, and Captain James McMurdo, Political Agent at Kattywar, sent a correspondence to the *Bombay Gazette*, which appeared in that paper on the 26th of January, 1820, describing the noble work he had done among the poor inhabitants of Kowrinar, when they had been stricken with the plague. Of this correspondence we will only insert the two following letters. The Ser Soobah of Kattywar writes:—

"As a river of sweet water brings relief to the world, so have you extended your favours by the wisdom of your actions. We are in friendship one. The Supreme who keeps the globe without visible support, who has spread the heavens like a tent, is always in our remembrance. Since you have left us we have never forgot you, and we daily expect news of you. In the meantime, we have received from the inhabitants of Kowrinar reports of the assistance you were to them when they were attacked by the Mirgee (*cholera morbus*): for this

In 1815 occurred a circumstance which, at the same time, stamps with honour the name of a gallant officer of the Bombay Marine, and with ignominy that of his opponent, a Captain in the Navy of the United States, with which nation this country had been at war during the previous three years. On the 30th of June, 1815, the Hon. Company's cruiser 'Nautilus,' of fourteen guns, commanded by Lieutenant Boyce, while off Anjier

reason we have sent you this with our thanks, as well as those of the inhabitants, whose report is enclosed. You have saved them; they are pleased; and in seeing them happy, we are ourselves most happy. What can we say more?"

The second letter, which is signed by one hundred of the Native inhabitants of the afflicted district, and is addressed to Captain Grant, "the Protector of the Poor," is in the following terms:—

"From the bankers, traders, and other inhabitants of this place, this is our Report. The trouble you took when we were attacked by the pestilence, in administering to the poor of this place, not only medicine, but relief of all kinds from your own resources, by which means you not only saved a great many persons from death, but as if inspired by heaven, treated them with all manner of kindness. How much can we thank you for these favours. Out of seven hundred persons who were seized with this distemper, seventy-five only died, and of those fifteen or twenty only died after the remedy had been applied, and twenty-five others died before any assistance was given; in the other thirty it appeared to have been too long delayed; but six hundred and twenty-five persons were, by the favour of heaven and your exertions, rescued (called again to life.) For all this, what can we give you but thanks and prayers to God for your prosperity and long life; the reward is with Him, and our thanks that he permitted so valuable a person to reside amongst us; it is indeed fortunate. From far and near they came unto you, and were relieved; pray God that it may be returned tenfold. And as long as you remain with us, we look up to you for protection, for if it had not been for you we should have had no assistance. Believe this, we pray, and continue your kindness towards us."

As assistant to the Master-Attendant at Surat, Captain Grant received the thanks of Government for saving the Hon. Company's ship 'Duke of York,' off the entrance of the harbour during the south-west monsoon. Likewise he received the thanks of the merchants for saving from destruction on the south-west prong, the ship 'Milford,' of Bombay. Captain Grant continued in the Master-Attendant's office until 1828, when he was appointed Senior Naval Officer on the Surat station.

In bringing his services to the notice of the Bombay Government, Captain Crawford, Superintendent of the Marine, says, under date of the 19th of March, 1833:—"This officer always displayed great courage, talent, and energy, for which he invariably received the warmest approbation of his immediate superiors in the Civil, Military, and Naval Services; even recently the Hon. the Court of Directors, in their despatch in the Public Department, under date of the 24th of August, 1831, especially notices the exertions of Captain Grant and Commander Cogan, in securing pirates and recovering plundered property." In 1833 he proceeded to England on sick leave, and in 1836, when his health had been restored, the Court of Directors appointed him to the command of the new steam sloop 'Berenice.' This vessel he took to Bombay in the year 1837, she being the second ship (the 'Atalanta' having sailed a few months before) that was propelled by steam the whole voyage round the Cape of Good Hope from England to India. Soon after Captain Grant's arrival in Bombay, in June, 1837, his health failed, and he was again obliged to return to England, where he arrived in the beginning of 1838, after which he resigned the Service, having served twenty-three years in India, and altogether in the Service twenty-eight years. He soon after succeeded to the Senior Pension list of £800 per annum, which the gallant old officer enjoyed for a period of thirty-six years."

in the Straits of Sunda, with despatches for the Supreme Government at Calcutta, sighted a vessel, which proved to be the United States sloop-of-war 'Peacock,' commanded by Captain Warrington, the same ship which, on the 29th of April, 1814, had captured H.M.'s brig 'Epervier,' Captain Wales, of eighteen guns, and one hundred and seventeen men. The following is an exact account of their respective armaments: 'Peacock,' a full-rigged ship of 539 tons, and carrying twenty 32-pounder carronades, and two long 18-pounders, total twenty-two guns, with a crew of one hundred and eighty-five, or, as some said, two hundred and twenty men; 'Nautilus,' a brig of 180 tons, carrying ten 18-pounder carronades and four long 9-pounders, and, being much under-handed, having a crew of only thirty-nine European officers and seamen, and forty marines and Lascars,* the total on board, including some European invalid soldiers, being about one hundred. We cannot do better than give the account of the action that ensued between the 'Nautilus' and 'Peacock,' in the words of Lieutenant Boyce—a gallant young officer who had served under Captain Eatwell as First-Lieutenant of the 'Benares' while that ship was employed under the Bengal Government—in his official despatch, addressed to the Secretary of the Company's Marine Board:—

"Sir,—I beg leave to acquaint you, for the information of the Board, that the wounds received on the 30th of June last, in a short but smart action with an American sloop of war, off Anjier, in the Straits of Sunda, have hitherto prevented my transmitting an official report of the circumstances attending that melancholy affair. I am happy to state that my health is now tolerably re-established; and I think myself particularly fortunate, considering the nature of the wounds, that the honour of addressing you on this subject has been reserved for my pen, although, no doubt, public rumour has, ere this, put you in possession of most of the facts which I now do myself the honour to state, and request that you will do me the favour to submit them to the Honourable Board. On the 30th of June last, being off Anjier, in the Straits of Sunda, on my passage to Bengal, in charge of public despatches from the Java Government, about four p.m., a strange sail hove in sight, standing with a fair wind to the north-eastward; and as the Hon. Company's cruiser 'Nautilus,' under my command, was working to the south-westward, the two vessels approached each other rapidly. When the stranger was distant about three miles, I observed that she had British colours hoisted, and

* As was customary with such of the Company's cruisers as could not make up their complements with European seamen, Lascars were shipped in the 'Nautilus' to make up the required number. As the difficulties of recruiting seamen for the Service decreased, owing to the great number of merchant ships that arrived in Bombay Harbour from England, the crews of the Company's cruisers were latterly entirely composed of European seamen.

knowing that universal peace had been restored to Great Britain, I despatched a boat in charge of my master, Mr. Bartlett, to obtain intelligence, which reached the stranger nearly at the same time as the Master-Attendant's from the shore; and I observed with my spying-glass, that the officers had no sooner got up the ship's side than the crews were forcibly taken out and both boats made fast astern. I prepared for action, and the stranger at once opened her tier of ports, and bore down towards us. To prevent her crossing our hawse I tacked, then shortened sail, hove to, and soon afterwards hailed the stranger, 'What ship is that?' To which I received no reply until repeated four times, and then merely 'halloo!' About this period the English blue ensign was hauled down, and American colours hoisted. I then asked, 'Am I to consider you in the light of a friend or an enemy?' The reply was, 'An enemy.' I then informed the American captain that peace had been ratified between Great Britain and the United States of America; also, that I had the proclamation on board, and hoped that a due consideration of this would induce him to spare bloodshed. I was then commanded, in a very loud and peremptory manner, to 'haul down my colours,' which was immediately repeated still louder, and with the addition of 'instantly;' to which I replied, 'I shall do no such thing.' The American then opened his fire upon us, by which two men were killed at the gun near me, and I received a grape shot, in a slanting direction, through the upper part of the thigh. A short but brisk action ensued, and observing some casualties, my First-Lieutenant, Mr. Robert Mayston, and several others, wounded, and being myself disabled by a 32-pound shot, which shattered my right knee joint, and splintered my thigh bone; also considering the great disparity of force, I deemed it my duty, although I must confess that it was with no small degree of reluctance, to strike the British colours to the American. Her first-lieutenant, about dusk, took possession of us. She proved to be the United States sloop-of-war 'Peacock,' Captain Warrington, carrying twenty 32-pounder carronades, and two long 18-pounders. Her crew is said to consist of two hundred and twenty men. Both anchored for the night about six miles off Anjier, and in the morning I was permitted to be taken on shore, as well as the rest of the wounded, in compliance with my request to that effect. About two p.m. on the day following the action, the Hon. Company's cruiser 'Nautilus' was restored, and Captain Warrington addressed a letter to Mr. Macgregor, Master-Attendant at Anjier, stating, that in consequence of the information received from him, and the several different sources from which he had heard that a peace had been concluded between the United States and Great Britain, he felt himself bound to desist from hostilities, and regretted that his reasonable command had not been complied with by the commander of the 'Nautilus' brig the preceding afternoon. On the 4th of July the 'Nautilus' sailed for Batavia, where she arrived the day following, and was sent from thence to Rembang, on the coast of Java, in the temporary charge of Acting-Lieutenant Barnes, who was ordered on board from the Hon. Company's cruiser 'Malabar,' by Captain Hepburn, to receive such repairs as the damages she had sustained required. In the meantime I remained, on account of my wounds, at Anjier, where I was most handsomely received and accommodated by the kindness of Colonel Yule, Resident, and attended by Mr. Harvey Thompson, surgeon of the district. On the 14th of July it was deemed necessary to amputate my right leg. I submitted to the operation, and it was accordingly taken off above the knee. On the 20th following, I was removed to the residence of Colonel Yule, at Ceram, and there I remained, experiencing every mark of hospitality and the most unlimited attention, until the return of the 'Nautilus' from Rembang; at which period, finding my health tolerably restored, I rejoined her on the 23rd instant. I beg leave to subjoin a list of the killed and wounded on board the Hon. Company's cruiser 'Nautilus' on the 30th of last June; and in having to lament the loss of so many, I regret that a fairer opportunity for their exertions was not afforded them and myself, with a vessel of more equal force.

(Here follows a list of killed and wounded.)

"What loss the American may have sustained I am not able to say. If report is to be relied on, they had four or five men wounded, and their bow gun dismounted. The damage the 'Nautilus' received in the action was considerable, both in her hull and rigging. The bends on the starboard side, the side engaged, were shivered from aft to the fore-chains, and the bulwarks, from the chess-tree aft, much torn. The launch and cutter were both perforated with shot, the lower masts and tiller slightly wounded with grape, and the boom mainsail shot through in many places. Two guns were disabled by the enemy's shot, and the sheet anchor completely so, by the loss of its iron stock, ring, and fluke. Four 32-pound shot that were found last have been picked out of her, one was under the counter, very nearly level with the water. A great number of small arms and gunner's stores were thrown overboard by the Americans, on their taking possession, to clear the deck. The packets, I am happy to say, remain untouched, but almost everything below was ransacked. It now only remains for me to do that justice to the conduct of the officers and crew of the 'Nautilus,' on the 30th of last June, which they so well deserve, by declaring my admiration of their firmness, and thus publicly expressing my satisfaction at their conduct throughout. The two Sepoys and native servant with amputated limbs, have, I understand, recovered, and been sent by Captain Eatwell, of the

Hon. Company's cruiser 'Benares,' to Calcutta, in the Hon. Company's cruiser 'Antelope.' Lieutenant Mayston's wound was once healed, but has broken out afresh; he is however now, I am happy to say, on the road to recovery. My own cure has been greatly impeded by two unfortunate fistulas in the stump, which have caused me to suffer much. The rest of the wounded are all well. I beg to subscribe myself, with the utmost respect,
"Sir, your most obedient servant,
CHARLES BOYCE, Commander.
"H. C. cruiser 'Nautilus,' the 24th of September, 1815.
"John Lowe, Esq., Secretary to the Marine Board."

The above despatch was written by the gallant captain of the 'Nautilus' more than three months after his spirited action with the 'Peacock,' his recovery during the interval appearing at times hopeless; it is a manly and modest despatch, and we will contrast it with the following extract from the official letter of his opponent, dated 11th November, 1815, which breathes throughout the consciousness of criminality :—

"As it is probable you will hereafter see or hear some other account of a *rencontre* which took place between the 'Peacock' and the East India Company's brig 'Nautilus,' on the 30th of June last, in the Straits of Sunda, I take the liberty of making known to you the particulars. In the afternoon of that day, when abreast of Anjier, as we closed with this brig, which appeared evidently to be a vessel of war, and completely prepared for action, her commander hailed, and asked if I knew there was a peace. I replied in the negative, directing him at the same time to haul his colours down, if it were the case, in token of it, adding that, if he did not, I should fire into her. This being refused, one of the forward guns was fired at her, which was immediately returned by a broadside from the brig; our broadside was then discharged, and his colours were struck, after having six Lascars killed and seven or eight wounded. As we had not the most distant idea of peace, and the vessel was but a short distance from the fort of Anjier, I considered his assertion, coupled with his arrangements for action, a *finesse* on his part to amuse us, till he could place himself under the protection of the fort. A few minutes before coming in contact with the brig, two boats containing the Master-Attendant at Anjier and an officer of the army came on board, and as we were in momentary expectation of firing, they were, with their men, passed below. No questions in consequence were put to them; and they, very improperly, omitted to mention that peace existed. The next day, after receiving such intelligence as they had to communicate on the subject (part of which was official) I gave up the vessel, first stopping her shot holes and putting the rigging in order. I am aware that I may be blamed for ceasing hostilities without more authentic evidence that peace had been concluded; but, I trust, when our distance from home, with the little chance we had of receiving such evidence, are taken into consideration, I shall not be thought to have decided prematurely."

This is a sorry attempt to escape the just reprobation which Captain Warrington's conscience warned him would be visited upon his conduct by every right-feeling and brave officer of either the British or American Services. James, in his "History of the Naval Occurrences of the War between the United States and Great Britain," completely demolishes the sophistries by which Captain Warrington sought to excuse his cowardly attack upon a vessel of such inferior force :—" The British and American accounts of this rencontre," he says, " differ materially as to one fact; the knowledge of Captain Warrington, at the time he approached the 'Nautilus' with a hostile intention, that peace had been signed between Great Britain and the United States. We will, in the first instance, suppose the American officer to have been unacquainted with the circumstance, till, as he admits, he was hailed and asked if he knew of it by the 'Nautilus's' commander. After that, would not a humane man, would not a brave officer, have deferred firing till he had ascertained the fact? But Captain Warrington says: —" I considered the assertion, coupled with his arrangements for action, a finesse on his part to amuse us, till he could place himself under the protection of the fort.' It was, then, an 'assertion,' as Lieutenant Boyce states; happy inconsistency! and a most important assertion too, concluding with 'I have Mr. Madison's proclamation on board.' Had not the 'Nautilus' 'shortened sail' and 'hove to?' Did that appear as if her commander wished to place himself under the protection of the fort? and that fort, instead of being at 'a short distance,' was five miles off. Was it not time for Lieutenant Boyce to make 'arrangements for action' when he saw a ship like the 'Peacock' bearing down upon him, with ports ready opened? Let us suppose for a moment that, just as the American commander was listening to the hail from the 'Nautilus,' she became suddenly transformed into H.M. ship 'Volage,'* Captain Warrington would then have promptly hailed in turn with the best speaking trumpet in the ship: thanked Captain Drury for his politeness; and been the first to urge the folly not to say wickedness, of wounding and killing each other, while any doubt existed about peace having been signed. But it was a vessel he could almost hoist on board the 'Peacock;' he therefore called out, 'Haul down your colours instantly.' This reasonable demand, Lieutenant Boyce very properly considered, as an imperious and insulting mandate, and fully alive to the dignity

* The 'Volage,' carrying thirty-three guns, and a complement of one hundred and seventy-one men, was, at this time, cruising in the East Indies.

of the British flag, and to the honour of the Service of which he was so distinguished an ornament, prepared to cope with a ship whose immense superiority, as she overshadowed his little barque, gave him nothing to expect short of a speedy annihilation. Then, says Captain Warrington, 'one of the forward guns were fired at her, which was immediately returned by a broadside from the brig; our broadside was then discharged, and his colours were struck, after having six Lascars killed and seven or eight wounded.' The Master of the 'Nautilus,' Mr. Joseph Bartlett, was on board the 'Peacock' during the action, and swore positively* 'that two or three broadsides were fired,' and

* The following is the correspondence and evidence referred to by James in his strictures on Captain Warrington's conduct:—

"The Bench of magistrates of Batavia, having appointed a commission, consisting of the Magistrate, Mr. Turr, and the Magistrate and Acting Bailiff, Mr. Cassa, these two gentlemen, on Friday morning, the 7th of July, 1815, proceeded on board of the 'Nautilus,' then lying in Batavia Roads, and received the following voluntary deposition of Mr. Bartlett, Master of the cruiser, and now Acting-Commanding officer. That in the afternoon, about four o'clock, of the 30th of June, the cruiser 'Nautilus' was working out to proceed on her passage, when a strange sail was seen, and he was ordered by the Captain, C. Boyce, to proceed with the boat and see what ship it was. That on his arrival on board, he was instantly ordered by the Commander of the vessel to go below, not being allowed to ask any questions; that a short time after he heard say, 'Strike your colours, or I will sink you' and then, that orders were given to fire the bow gun into the cruiser 'Nautilus,' which did not bear, when a second gun was fired. That further, two or three broadsides were fired, when he heard that the 'Nautilus' struck her colours; and after this two heavy guns and some musketry were fired into the 'Nautilus.'"

Extract from evidence of Mr. McGregor, in reply to interrogations by the Magistrate, Mr. Turr:

"Question.—Did you communicate to the officers of the enemy's ship before the action between her and the Hon. Company's cruiser 'Nautilus' took place, that peace had been concluded between Great Britain and the United States, and ratified by both parties? Answer.—I did; I communicated to the First-Lieutenant, on his informing me that I was a prisoner of war; but I scarce said it, when the Captain came forward and ordered me to be taken below. I communicated the above also to the purser of the ship, in the ward-room. Question.—What time had you been on board before the commencement of the said action? Rather more than a quarter of an hour. Had any reply been made by any of the officers of the American sloop-of-war on your communication? Answer.—Yes. Question.—By whom? Answer.—The Purser. Question.—What was the reply? Answer.—I do not know how we can avoid a little brush; and the purser ordered me to go out of the way into the side cabin."

The following was the Report addressed by Mr. R. B. Macgregor, Master-Attendant at Anjier, to Lieutenant-Colonel Yule, Resident at Bantam, dated the 1st of July, 1815.

"I have the honour to report for your information, that I was this afternoon released, as a prisoner of war, from the United States sloop-of-war 'Peacock,' Captain Warrington, in consequence of the intelligence forwarded to him by me, which he deemed perfectly satisfactory, that peace had been ratified between the United States and Great Britain at Washington by Mr. Madison, on the 18th February, 1815. Enclosed, I have the honour to transmit a copy of a letter from Captain Warrington, acquainting me that he would desist from hostilities."

The following is the Enclosure referred to:—

"From Captain Warrington to Mr. Macgregor, Master-Attendant at Anjier.
July 1st, 1815.

"Sir,—In consequence of the information received from you, and the several

that the American continued his fire, even after the flag, and, as it appears, until the pendant of the 'Nautilus' was hauled down. Nineteen of the crew have deposed to the same effect. Captain Warrington's object in framing this falsehood was evidently to show what execution had been done by his one broadside.

"From the first gun fired some of the 'Nautilus' men were killed; and Lieutenant Boyce was dangerously wounded, a grape shot measuring two inches and one third in diameter, entering at the outside of his hip and passing out close under the backbone. This severe wound did not, however, disable him. In a few minutes a 32-pound shot struck obliquely on his right knee, shattering the joint, splintering the leg-bone downwards, and the thigh-bone a great way upwards! This, as may be supposed, laid him prostrate on the deck. The first, and only Lieutenant, received a mortal wound, the Master, who would have been the next officer, was on board the 'Peacock.' It was then, and not till then, that the gallant Boyce, lying bleeding on the deck, ordered the 'Nautilus's' colours to be struck. Of the 'six Lascars killed,' two were European invalids, and one a seaman, of the 'seven or eight (Lascars) wounded,' two were seamen; and was Lieutenant Mayston a 'Lascar?' was Lieutenant Boyce a 'Lascar?' That Captain Warrington well knew he was uttering a falsehood, is clear; because the 'Peacock's' surgeon had, at Lieutenant Boyce's request, attended the 'Nautilus's' wounded; and his official return would certainly have noticed a distinction so evident, as that of Native or European. The 'Nautilus's' First-Lieutenant, Mr. Mayston, languished till the 3rd of December, a period of five months, when mortification of his wound carried him off. About a fortnight after the action, Lieutenant Boyce suffered amputation very near to his hip, on account of the length and complication of the fracture. The pain and danger of the operation was augmented by the proximity of the grape-shot wound. His life was subsequently despaired of, but after a long course of hopes and fears to his numerous friends, this brave and amiable young man (or what Captain Warrington has left of him) still survives. The damage and loss of the 'Peacock,' as stated in Lieutenant Boyce's letter, was as much as, from the shortness of the action, and the immense disparity between the two vessels, could reasonably be expected. Of course the American Captain, who had escaped unhurt, the moment he was informed of the casualties on board his prize, either visited or sent a condoling

different sources from which I have heard that a peace had been concluded between the United States and Great Britain, I feel myself bound to desist from hostilities, and regret that my reasonable demand had not been complied with by the Commander of the 'Nautilus' brig yesterday afternoon.

"Respectfully, your obedient servant,
"L. WARRINGTON, Captain U.S. Navy,
"Commanding the U.S. sloop-of-war 'Peacock.'"

message to her so dreadfully mangled commander? Reader! he did neither. Captain Warrington, in the words of the poor sufferer, in his memorial to the Court of Directors, proved himself totally destitute of fellow feeling and commiseration; for during the time he retained possession of the 'Nautilus,' (which was till two o'clock the next afternoon) he was not once moved to make a commonplace enquiry after the memorialist, in his then deplorable condition."*

* James examines at length the discrepancies in the statements of the British and American officers, and we will give an extract from his acute analysis. " It now becomes necessary to consider the facts attending this action, or more particularly the commencement of it by Captain Warrington, as they arise out of the statements of the British officers, who had gone on board the 'Peacock,' and remained in her during, and long after, the engagement. Captain Warrington admits that the Master-Attendant at Anjier came on board a few minutes before coming into contact with the brig. Mr. Macgregor, upon his oath, says, 'Rather more than a quarter of an hour.' The portion of credit due to any assertion of Captain Warrington may be measured by the concealment and falsehood so conspicuous in his account of the 'Epervier's' action. Nothing appears in Captain Warrington's letters about the arrival on board the 'Peacock' of the 'Nautilus's' master, Mr. Bartlett, and who was the 'officer of the army,' that came in the second boat? Cornet White, a passenger on board the 'Nautilus,' who was requested to accompany Mr. Bartlett in the gig to obtain information. Captain Warrington had his reasons, no doubt, for concealing, in his official despatch, that he had any of the 'Nautilus's' officers or crew on board his vessel. Scarcely had Mr. Bartlett stepped upon the deck, than, without being allowed to ask a question, he was hurried below. Happily Mr. Macgregor met with rather better success. The instant he arrived on board, he communicated to the 'Peacock's' first-lieutenant, the most authentic information of peace having been concluded between Great Britain and America, grounded on no less authority than Mr. Madison's proclamation; which Mr. Macgregor had himself received from an American ship, passing the Straits on her way to China. What effect had this communication? Captain Warrington, whom the single word 'Peace' ought to have made pause, before he proceeded to spill the blood of his fellow-creatures, ordered Mr. Macgregor 'to be taken below.' Had the Master-Attendant no opportunity of communicating his important intelligence to any other of the 'Peacock's' officers? In his way below, Mr. Macgregor met the purser, who was in superintendence of the magazine, and repeated to him what he had told his first-lieutenant. The purser jocosely said: "I do not see how we can avoid a little brush.' Almost immediately afterwards, Macgregor (according to Lieutenant Boyce's memorial) heard orders given to return the ammunition into the magazine; which showed an evident relinquishment of the intention to attack the 'Nautilus.' But, while the orders were executing, they were countermanded, and all hostile preparations resumed. It was then that Mr. Macgregor was desired to retire into one of the side cabins: and very soon afterwards the firing commenced. Captain Warrington, in his letter to Mr. Macgregor, says, 'In consequence of the information received from you, and the several different sources from which I have heard that a peace has been concluded, &c.' Here it would appear as if Captain Warrington had received information of the peace from other parties than those in the two boats, which, he admits, came on board just previous to the action. But the official letter says: 'The next day, after receiving such intelligence as they (the Master-Attendant and officers of the Army) had to communicate on the subject (part of which was official), I gave up the vessel, &c.' This proves that the source of all Captain Warrington's information on the subject arose out of the communications of those very persons who, as he says, 'were, with their men, passed below.' But Captain Warrington, as the purser said, wanted to have a little brush with the British brig. He saw at once what a diminutive vessel she was, and accordingly ordered his men to fire into her."

The naval historian, after commenting at length on Captain Warrington's conduct, which he stigmatizes as it justly deserves, adds:—"The Governor-General of India, the Lieutenant-Governor of Java, and the different heads of departments throughout the British dominions in the East, also the King's Navy, and the King's Army, serving there, have all been unanimous in bestowing the tribute of praise upon the noble behaviour of Lieutenant Boyce."

It was indeed a terrible alternative that was placed before him, when the demand came from over the water that he was to strike his flag or be sunk there and then; the time for consideration afforded him was but short, but it was long enough for the gallant officer, who did not hesitate a moment as to the course he should pursue. Urged by a sense of the duty he owed to the flag of his country, a duty paramount to all considerations based on the absolute certainty of defeat, perhaps of annihilation, from the guns of a ship three times his size, and under whose fire his little craft lay almost defenceless, the Commander of the 'Nautilus' replied to the insolent demand of the American by an equally haughty refusal. After the requirements of honour and duty had been satisfied, Boyce hauled down his flag, himself severely, and his first-lieutenant mortally, wounded, and his only other officer—for at this time the 'Nautilus' was as shorthanded in officers as in European seamen— a prisoner on board the 'Peacock.' The determination of Captain Warrington to have "a brush with the brig," was shown by the remark of the purser, who, as well as the other officers was doubtless aware of the intentions of his captain. Though a Court of Inquiry, held on the conduct of Captain Warrington by the officers of his own Service, acquitted him of all blame, and American papers vied with each other in extolling the "hero," whose capture of the little brig conferred considerable "glory" on the Yankee Navy, yet his unseemly haste to shed blood, when it could be done with comparative impunity, will ever brand his name with ignominy among brave and right thinking men of both countries. The Governor-General of India in Council said of him:—"He contemplates Captain Warrington's proceeding as destitute of any possible extenuation;" and Commodore Hayes, who, on his return from Java, had resumed his office of Master-Attendant at Calcutta, described Captain Warrington in his despatch, as "the ruffian who has alike dishonoured himself and disgraced the Columbian Eagle."

It would appear that the Captain and officers of the 'Peacock,' in seeking to enhance the "glory" of their victory over the 'Nautilus,' magnified her size according to the invariable custom of American officers in describing the British ships they captured, which were, indeed, in every instance of inferior force. In 1833, however, the same 'Peacock' visited Aden when the 'Nautilus' lay there, and her officers and those of the American man-of-war 'Boxer,' could scarcely be induced to believe that the little Company's cruiser was the same vessel that had been captured by Captain Warrington, as "they had always understood her to be a vessel of nearly the same size as the 'Peacock.'" The clearing up of this point did not flatter their national vanity. Commander Boyce, the victim of American rowdyism, was compelled to retire from the Service in 1817, in consequence of his wounds, and, though now in his ninety-second year, is, as he lately informed us, still in the possession of his health and faculties, and in the enjoyment of a pension voted sixty years ago by the Congress of the United States, who have thus had to pay pretty heavily for this particular item of "glory."

During the Mahratta War of 1817-18, some of the Company's cruisers, stationed at Fort Victoria, near Severndroog, had the good fortune to be actively engaged, and acquitted themselves so well as to earn the frequent and hearty commendations of the Bombay Government, and the military officers under whose orders they served. The vessels engaged were the 'Prince of Wales,' Lieutenant Dominicetti, 'Thetis,' Lieutenant Arthur, 'Sylph,' Lieutenant Robson, and some small craft; and the officers and crews, who were landed to assist the troops, bore a conspicuous part in the capture of the forts on the coasts of the Concan. A detachment was employed at the surrender of the forts of Severndroog on the 4th of December, 1817, and the Governor in Council, in General Orders of the 20th of December, expressed his high sense of the gallantry of the seamen and marines. The escalading party consisted of only thirty seamen, led by Lieutenant Dominicetti, and fifty sepoys, under the command of Captain Campbell, of the 9th Regiment. The General Order states that, though opposed by very superior numbers, the energy of this small force succeeded in surmounting every obstacle, escalading and taking in open day the Fort of Kundah, notwithstanding the heavy fire of the enemy. This gallant and successful enterprise so completely intimidated the enemy, that the two other forts of Goa and Gunjeera were abandoned during the night.

Shortly afterwards the troops on this station were increased by the newly raised 1st Battalion of the 10th Native Infantry, commanded by Lieutenant-Colonel M. Kennedy, who, with a small force, including a naval brigade of seamen, under their own officers, and the marines from the Company's cruisers and pattamars, under the command of Captain Farquharson, reduced the strong forts of Madunghur, Ramghur, Paulghur, Russulghur, Anjenweel, and other strongholds, with the territories dependent thereon. The following were the General Orders by the

Right Hon. the Governor in Council, published upon the several occasions :—

"Bombay Castle, 9th March, 1818.

"The reduction of the Fort of Madunghur was announced in General Orders, of the 20th ultimo, but having since received a detailed report from Lieutenant-Colonel Kennedy, of his operations against that Fort and Jambah, the Right Honourable the Governor in Council takes occasion, in publishing to the Army, the Detachment Orders issued by Lieutenant-Colonel Kennedy, again to express his cordial approbation of the conduct of those engaged.

Detachment Orders by Lieutenant-Colonel Kennedy.

"Fort, 15th February, 1818.

"Lieutenant-Colonel Kennedy has the highest satisfaction in congratulating the troops under his command on the brilliant success of this morning.

"To Captain Farquharson, Lieutenants Dominicetti and Cogan, of the Marine, to the seamen, native officers and soldiers, volunteers for the storming party, Lieut.-Colonel Kennedy offers his most sincere acknowledgments for the intrepid and gallant manner in which they assaulted the triple stockades in front of the communication gateway, and carried by escalade the two Forts of Madunghur and Jambah. For the excellent plan of attack laid down in yesterday's Orders, and so gallantly carried into execution this morning, Lieutenant-Colonel Kennedy is indebted to Captain Farquharson, who proposed and principally arranged it. Neither can the Lieutenant-Colonel pass over unnoticed the excellent conduct of Lieutenant Waddington, who converted successfully into real attack what at first was intended only to be feint.

"To Lieutenant Dominicetti and Ensign Dashwood, for their highly zealous exertions in erecting the battery, Lieutenant-Colonel Kennedy's best thanks are due.

"The precision of the fire from the battery, where Ensign Dashwood and Captain Robson, of the Marines, served, and of the guns placed under charge of Captain Taylor and Lieutenant Cogan, greatly contributed to the success of the enterprise, whilst the manner in which the feint, under Captain Taylor's directions was conducted, does every credit to Jemadar Sonmeter, 1st Battalion 11th Regiment,* the Native officer leading it on.

"Lieutenant-Colonel Kennedy assures the whole of the officers, military and marine, that no part of each individual's merit shall pass unnoticed in his report to the Commander-in-chief."

To this Order was appended the following by the Governor in Council :—

* This was the Bombay Marine Battalion.

"Bombay, Tuesday, March 17th, 1818.

"The great exertions of the troops in constructing a battery on the summit of the hill, and giving up their tents, carpets, and cumlees for making sandbags, evince in a particular manner the zeal of all, and merit the highest commendation.

"The manner in which the enterprise was planned and so ably and spiritedly conducted by a detachment, not exceeding half the number of the garrison, is highly creditable to Lieutenant-Colonel Kennedy, and all the officers and men of the Honourable Company's military and marine services employed, and it is gratifying to observe that during these operations, the success of which so much depended on the united exertions of the two branches of the Service, the most perfect cordiality has existed."

Again the same high authority issued the following General Orders :—

"Bombay Castle, 10th March, 1818.

"The Right Hon. the Governor in Council has great satisfaction in publishing the following detachment orders issued by Lieutenant-Colonel Kennedy, on taking the forts of Ramghur and Paulghur, and to express his approbation of the conduct of the Lieutenant-Colonel and of the officers and men engaged on the occasion.

"Paulghur, 4th March, 1818.

"The commanding officer begs to return his best thanks to the officers and men of the detachment he has the honour to command, for their cool, steady, and gallant conduct in the attack and escalade of the forts of Ramghur and Paulghur this morning. The difficulties the detachment had to encounter in climbing a hill of such an abrupt ascent under a heavy fire from two forts, where they were necessitated to assist themselves up by the bushes and rocks that lay in their way, reflect the highest credit on every individual engaged in this hazardous enterprise. The commanding officer cannot refrain from particularizing the names of Captain Farquharson (who was the first man who mounted the wall), Lieutenants Cogan and Seymour, than whom none could have behaved with greater zeal and gallantry during the arduous service they were engaged in this morning."

By General Orders of the 25th of March, 8th of June, and 19th of June, the Governor in Council announced the reduction, by the troops in the Concan, of the forts of Russulghur, Gunga, Byramghur, Bowunghur, Jyghur, and Wijeyghur; also of the town of Sunghumseen, and fort of Rutnaghurry, at all of which the seamen and marines of the squadron were present.

About the same time a detachment of seamen and marines landed at Malwan, and were employed for some time under Lieutenant-Colonel Imlach, C.B. This officer's force was too small to enable him to attack the fort of Seedghur, near Malwan, but in March, a portion of H.M. 89th Regiment, bound by sea for Bancoot, was obliged by adverse winds to put into Malwan. Colonel Imlach directed their immediate disembarkation, and with the combined force, renewed the designs he had formerly been compelled to abandon. On the 15th of March he moved to Seedghur, and, on the following day, opened fire from a battery, which, by noon, produced so great an effect that the garrison evacuated the fort by the opposite side. On the 28th he proceeded to Bhugwuntghur, and, having driven in the enemy's outposts, that place was likewise abandoned. Its fall was followed by that of Deoghur, which was evacuated, and by the capitulation of Compta and Acheera, so that the British force was placed in full occupation of the province of Salsee.* The last important service of the Bombay Marine in this quarter, was the dislodgment of the enemy from a position on the banks of the Dewghur river. The following was the order published by the Bombay Government referring to this service:—

"Bombay Castle, 14th May, 1818.

"The Right Hon. the Governor in Council has much satisfaction in announcing his approbation of the gallant conduct of the detachment under Brevet Captain Hughes, assisted by Captains Robson and Dominicetti,† and a party of the seamen and marines belonging to the Hon. Company's cruisers, 'Prince of Wales' and 'Sylph,' on the occasion of an attack made on the advanced posts of the enemy on the banks of the Dewghur river, when the enemy was surprised with the loss of above twenty-five killed and wounded and nine prisoners."

The Governor-General was pleased to order three months full batta as gratuity to be issued to the troops and seamen employed on service in the Concan.

Among matters of interest connected with the Bombay Marine, other than its war services, may be mentioned the launch at Bombay, on the 28th of December, 1818, from the

---

* "Memoir of the Operations of the British Army in India, during the Mahratta Campaign of 1817, 1818, and 1819." By Lieutenant-Colonel Valentine Blacker, C.B. The military results of the brief Mahratta War, which forms the most salient feature in the eventful administration of Lord Moira, better known as the Marquis of Hastings, may be summed up in a few words. Between November, 1817, and June, 1818, twenty actions were fought in the field, and one hundred and twenty forts, many scarcely accessible, some deemed impregnable, fell by surrender, siege, or storm, the distance between the most northern and most southern of these forts being not less than seven hundred miles. The forces engaged on either side cannot well be compared for want of accurate knowledge. Colonel Blacker, in his "Memoir of the Operations," has estimated the aggregate strength of the Mahratta armies at two hundred and seventeen thousand, while the British forces in the field, including the auxiliary and irregular troops, amounted to one hundred and sixteen thousand, of whom only thirteen thousand were Europeans.

† This young officer, distinguished both for his enterprise and scientific attainments, was lost to the Service by death early in 1824.

Upper Duncan Dock, built in the year 1810, by Captain W. Cowper of the Bombay Engineers, and so called after the Governor, General Duncan, of the 'Malabar,' seventy-four guns, a teak-built ship constructed by the venerable builder, Jamsetjee Bomanjee; and soon after, the keel of another line-of-battle ship, to be called the 'Ganges,' rated at eighty-four guns, but pierced to carry ninety-two, and of 2,289 tons, was laid by that disguished naval architect. On the following 10th of February, a new fifty-six-gun ship, for the service of the Imaum of Muscat, was floated out of the old middle dock, and received her name of 'Shah Allum' at the hands of Mr. Meriton, the Superintendent of Marine, who employed a copious effusion of rosewater and attar, instead of wine, as the christening liquid, the use of the latter being contrary to Mahommedan usage. Again, on the 5th of September in this year, a third ship, a thirty-eight gun frigate, called the 'Seringapatam,' was floated out of the dock and added to the strength of the British Navy; and within the next few years, besides the 'Ganges,' eighty-four guns, the following ships were constructed for the Royal Service —'Asia,' eighty-four guns, (which noble line-of-battle ship bore the flag of Sir Edward Codrington at the Battle of Navarino); the 'Bombay,' eighty-four guns; the 'Manilla,' forty-six guns; and the 'Madagascar,' forty-six guns.* Soon after this a ship was also built for the Bombay Marine, by the Parsee naval architect, Mr. Jamsetjee Bomanjee. This was a small thirty-two gun frigate, which, on being floated from the Upper Bombay Dock, on the 2nd of May, 1821, received the name of

* Of the strength and superiority of the Bombay-built ships, an unimpeachable witness, the First-Lieutenant of one of them, the 'Salsette' frigate, bears testimony in the following letter to the builder, Mr. Jamsetjee Bomanjee. This officer came to Bombay in 1819 as Captain of the merchant ship 'Stakesby,' when he wrote to the Parsee builder requesting him " to accept of the accompanying clock as a small mark of esteem, and kind of remembrancer that under Divine Providence, his professional abilities were the happy means of preserving Mr. Henderson and the rest of the crew of H.M.S. 'Salsette' from what appeared to the human eye unavoidable destruction; that ship, with five other small vessels of war, and twelve valuable merchantmen under their convoy, being beset by the ice in the Baltic Sea in the winter of 1808-9, and she alone escaped shipwreck." In accepting this present, and the gratifying letter which accompanied it, Mr. Jamsetjee said in the course of his reply, dated on the following day (the 15th of June, 1819) :—"The 'Salsette,' (first named the 'Pitt') was, as you are aware, *our first efforts in frigate building* for the Navy, and you will forgive me when I say that the praise I received on that occasion was, in a great measure, owing to the very seamanlike style of the 'Pitt's' equipment, under your superintendence as First-Lieutenant in charge of her. I had heard a rumour of the 'Salsette's' escape while frozen in the Baltic; but to have this rumour confirmed by an officer in His Majesty's Service who had first contributed to her *début* as a man-of-war, and who had, subsequently, under Providence, witnessed the strength of her hull, in withstanding a danger that overwhelmed so many vessels in company, is more gratifying to me than I can find words to express." The 'Ganges,' eighty-four, was launched on the 10th of November, 1821, on which occasion the Governor, Mr. Mountstuart Elphinstone, stood sponsor, her designer and constructor, the venerable Jamsetjee Bomanjee, having died a few months before the launch of this noble ship.

'Hastings,' in honour of the Governor-General, and passed into the harbour under a Royal salute from the battery.

The following table of precedence* in India, was fixed by the warrant of the Prince Regent, dated the 31st of May, 1814:— "The Governor-General; the Vice-President and Deputy-Governor of Fort William; the Governor of Madras; the Governor of Bombay; the Governor of Prince of Wales' Island; the Chief Justice of Calcutta; Chief Justice of Madras; the Lord Bishop of Calcutta; the Members of the Supreme Council; the Members of Council, Madras; the Members of Council, Bombay; the Puisne Judges of Calcutta; the Puisne Judges of Madras; the Recorder of Bombay; the Recorder of Prince of Wales' Island; the Commander-in-chief of H.M.'s Naval Forces; General and Flag-officers above the rank of Major-General; Superintendent of Marine, Bombay; Major-Generals and Rear-Admirals; Captain of the Fleet, as Junior Rear-Admiral; Brigadier-Generals, Commodores with broad pennants, and First Captain to the Naval Commander-in-Chief; Colonels, Post-Captains of three years, and Commodores Hon. Company's Marine; Hon. Company's Advocates-General of Bengal, Madras, and Bombay; Senior Merchants, the Archdeacons of Bengal, Madras, and Bombay, Lieutenant-Colonels, Post-Captains under three years, and Senior Captains Hon. Company's Marine; Junior Merchants, Majors, Masters and Commanders, Members of the Medical Board, Commanders of regular Indiamen, and Junior Captains Hon. Company's Marine; Commanders Hon. Company's Marine; Factors, Captains in the Army, Lieutenants in the Navy, Surgeons, Chaplains, Lieutenants Hon. Company's Marine, Commanders of extra Indiamen and Packets; Writers, Lieutenants in the Army, Second Lieutenants Hon. Company's Marine, Assistant Surgeons and Veterinary Surgeons; Second Lieutenants in the Army; Lieutenants Fire-workers, Ensigns and Cornets; Adjutants and Quartermasters not holding superior commissions; Midshipmen of the Navy, Cadets and Volunteers, Hon. Company's (Bombay) Marine.

In 1820 the Bombay Marine were actively engaged at Mocha. It was a period of fifty years since they were last employed on a mission to this seaport, which, on that occasion, resulted in the Commodore obtaining the satisfaction he was sent by the Bombay Government to demand, without the necessity of firing a shot. On this second visit, which was due to the following circumstance, affairs were not settled so amicably. In the month of July, 1817, says Captain R. L. Playfair, in his valuable "History of Arabia Felix or Yemen," a dispute arose between Lieutenant Dominicetti of the Bombay Marine, commanding the Hon. Company's cruiser 'Prince of Wales,' then

* In this table of precedence, which we have copied from the Bengal Almanack of 1820, there is no mention of the Commanders-in-Chief of the three Presidencies.

at Mocha, and the nacoda, or captain of a vessel under charter to the Company, which resulted in an Arab being detained for a short time at the British Factory. This man was released on a requisition from the Dowlah, or Governor, but no sooner had he left the building than the yard and factory were filled with three or four hundred soldiers, who rushed upon the small guard of marines from the 'Prince of Wales,' dragged them into the street, and beat them in a most inhuman manner; they also seized the captain of a merchant vessel then at the factory, and subjected him to a like ignominious treatment. Lieutenant Dominicetti, who was at this time confined to bed with a severe fever, was attacked by the soldiery, who beat him with sticks and the butt ends of their muskets until he was rendered insensible, and finally dragged him naked and half dead, to the Governor's house. Here every species of insult and contumely which could be devised, was heaped upon him; he was spat upon by the infuriated mob, who saluted him with every term of abuse which the Arabic language could supply, and was eventually imprisoned, while the Residency was ransacked and pillaged.

The Bombay Government of course instituted an inquiry into the conduct of the Governor of Mocha. Considerable delay attended the investigation of the charges, and it was not until the end of November, 1819, that the ultimatum of the Government of Bombay was sent to the Imaum of Sanaa. This required that His Highness should inflict a suitable punishment on the late Dowlah of Mocha, who had been dismissed from office, in presence of the Company's representative; that pecuniary satisfaction should be made for the acts committed within the Residency; and that several British seamen, who had deserted, should be given up.

The Governor-General of India, who expressed regret that steps had not been taken at an earlier period to obtain reparation, authorized the despatch of a squadron to Mocha, to enforce the reclamations of the Bombay Government, and directed that, in addition to the demand for the punishment of the Dowlah, and an indemnity for losses sustained, means should be adopted to secure, for the future, the observance of respect to the British Resident, and a clear understanding of the terms on which the factory was to continue; for this purpose certain terms* were

---

* The terms of this treaty were as follows :—

(1). That the Resident should have a guard of the same strength as at Bussorah and Bagdad, to ensure his respectability.

(2). That all servants of the factory should enjoy British protection, and be amenable only to the jurisdiction of the Resident.

(3). That all Indian merchants should be under the protection of the British flag, and all differences amongst themselves be settled by the Resident, or in the event of any of the Imaum's subjects being concerned in the disputes, by an agent on the part of the local government and the Resident conjointly.

(4). That the Resident should be exempt from all degrading compliances; that he should have liberty to ride on horseback when and wherever he pleased, and

to be obtained from the Imaum of Sanaa and embodied in a treaty. Captain Bruce, the Resident at Bushire, formerly an officer in the Marine, who was appointed agent for the Government of Bombay in conducting these negotiations, sailed for Mocha on the 23rd of August, 1820, and, on his arrival, made known to the authorities the demands of the British Government, but declined to land until an officer had arrived from Sanaa to make the required apology. From the intercourse which passed between Captain Bruce and the Dowlah's agents, every expectation was entertained of a favourable result; and a letter was addressed by the Dowlah to the Imaum, enclosing the ultimatum of the Bombay Government, and expressing a hope that its demands would be complied with. But the authorities at Mocha, notwithstanding their pacific professions, were mounting guns on the different towers, and the militia were ordered in from the several villages; to give time for the arrival of these levies the Dowlah made a request, with which Captain Bruce complied, that a few more days than had been first fixed, might be allowed for the arrival of the answer from Sanaa. On the 24th of October Captain Bruce received the Imaum's reply, conveying friendly assurances, stating that a person would be sent to communicate with him, and requesting that he would land at Mocha; private letters from Sanaa were also to the effect that the Imaum was highly displeased with his Minister for having allowed matters to proceed to so great a length.

On the arrival of the Imaum's deputy, Futteh Hoosain, who gave an assurance that all demands would be acceded to, Captain Bruce proceeded on shore, accompanied by the Dowlah's brother and a party of merchants. The result proved entirely unsatisfactory, as Futteh Hoosain said he had no authority to bring Haji Futteh, the offending Governor, to Mocha, but that he was authorised to accompany Captain Bruce to Sanaa, where that Dowlah would be brought. Captain Bruce replied that, until the apology had been made at the British Residency, he could not proceed to Sanaa, and as, after protracted discussions, it was evident that they were only attempting to evade the demand, he determined to proceed on board ship,

have free ingress and egress at all the gates of Mocha, amongst others, that of Sheikh Shaduli, from which Europeans had been excluded for some years past, on account of the pretended sanctity it derived from the tomb of that saint being in an adjoining mosque.

(5). That the rate of export duty on British trade be reduced from $3\frac{1}{2}$ to $2\frac{1}{4}$ per cent., which was the same as the French had paid since they bombarded Mocha, nearly a century previously.

(6). A piece of ground to be allotted for a cemetery, and no British subject to be insulted on account of his religion.

(7). The British Resident to have free permission to proceed to Sanaa, to communicate with the Imaum, whenever he might deem it necessary; the Dowlah of Mocha, on those occasions, furnishing an escort.

acquainting the local authorities of his fixed determination not to land again till the Dowlah was forthcoming. Captain Bruce warned all the vessels in the roads, that the port was blockaded, and that if any of them remained on the arrival of the squadron, they would be destroyed. The Expedition arrived on the 2nd of December from Bombay, after a passage of fourteen days. It consisted of H.M.S. 'Topaze,' Captain J. R. Lumley, Senior Naval Officer; the Hon. Company's cruisers 'Benares,' Commander Faithful, and 'Antelope,' Lieutenant Robson; 'Thames,' mortar-vessel, Lieutenant Elwon; storeship 'Ernaad,' Lieutenant Jones. On board the mortar-vessel was embarked a detachment of the Bombay Artillery, under Lieutenant William Jacob of that corps.

Captain Lumley, on being informed of Captain Bruce's proceedings, immediately resolved to bombard the place. A previous messenger had been received from the Dowlah, requesting a further reference to Sanaa, which was refused; and, during the course of the day, a flag of truce came off with a message to the effect that, if hostile operations were delayed for eighteen days, the British demands would either be complied with or the place would be evacuated. An hour and a-half was allowed by the Commodore for the authorities to send off hostages, who should remain on board for three days, to allow time for the production and punishment of Haji Futteh. No reply having been received within the time specified, the vessels were ordered to open fire.

The operations commenced on the 4th of December, by a general cannonading and bombardment by the cruisers and mortar vessels, which had been warped up to the South Fort, the 'Topaze' meanwhile firing on the town. The South Fort being silenced, the cruisers and mortar vessels took up a fresh position against the North Fort, a detached work near the town. At length the fort appearing to be silenced and abandoned, although no practicable breach had been made, boats were sent to take possession of and destroy it. The assaulting party consisted of all the seamen who could be spared, together with a party of artillerymen and marines. On their being about to land, it was discovered that the garrison, if they had abandoned the fort, had now reoccupied it, for a large body issued thence and rushed down to the beach to prevent the landing; they were, however, beaten back with loss, but, before the assaulting party could reach the fort, the Arabs had shut the gate, which being in a very narrow passage, could not be blown open by the 3-pounder brass gun brought for that purpose.

The enemy bravely contested the ground, and, when driven in, threw down 32-pound shot and quicklime on the heads of the assailants, which blinded their eyes, while their fire proved more destructive. After vainly attempting for a quarter of an hour to force an entrance, the retreat was reluctantly ordered, and with difficulty effected, many having to swim to the boats, which were found to be riddled with bullets. The storming party sustained a loss of eight killed and twenty-four wounded, the detachments from the 'Topaze' and 'Benares' being the chief sufferers. The ships reopened their fire on the return of the shore party.

On the following morning another flag of truce was received, which was followed by two hostages, who conveyed an assurance from the Dowlah that, in fourteen days, the demands should be complied with. This term of grace was conceded, but, on its expiration, a deputation of merchants came on board, praying for a further prolongation, in consequence of the approach of the Bedouins, who, they expected, would enter and plunder Mocha in the confusion; as two of the deputation engaged to go to Zebeed, and bring in Haji Futteh, two additional days were granted, on condition that, before the date of the expiry of the truce, a notification should be received that the ex-Dowlah was on the road.

The unsuccessful attack on the North Fort, however, had led the Dowlah and his people to suppose that their fortifications were impregnable, and they, accordingly, delayed their submission. The truce of fourteen days was, under various pretences, extended to twenty, during which preparations were making on both sides for a renewal of hostilities. British prestige having suffered by the repulse experienced in the attack on the North Fort, it was decided to direct the first efforts to destroying the work. Accordingly, the 'Benares' and 'Antelope,' each equipped with two additional long 18-pounders and an 8-inch mortar, and the 'Thames,' with her two long 18-pounders and 13-inch mortar, were hauled in under the north side of the fort, at a distance of less than 600 and 400 yards respectively; while the 'Topaze' took up a position about 800 yards to the westward of the fort, her draught of water not allowing a nearer approach. Finding that no dependence could be placed on the faith of the authorities, the flag of truce was hauled down on the morning of the 26th of December, and, at seven a.m., the squadron recommenced the attack on the North Fort, called " Taire,"* or the " Impregnable," a strong work of ten guns.

* After the capture of "Taire," the Green Flag of the Prophet was found in the ruins, and a poem by one of the defenders, of which the following is a translation :—" It happened on a certain day that five English ships of war came here to fight a battle with the warriors of this fort; their guns could do but little against true believers, for we fought that day—and who would not fight under our gallant commander—we fought the battle of the Imaum, under the holy banner of our Prophet like the sons of Thunder. They came to land, but we soon put them to flight; we drove them to their boats, and many there were of them who bit the dust, who left their bodies at the Ahmoody Gate festering in the sun, a prey to the dogs. Thus we Sons of Thunder fight and conquer; let them

Upwards of four thousand 18, 24, and 32-pound shot had been vainly expended in endeavouring to effect a breach in the sun-dried brick, or mud, walls of which the whole of the defences were constructed, as the projectiles either passed through or buried themselves, without cracking the walls. Mining was out of the question, for there were neither tools nor implements, and all hope of making a breach by the ordinary methods failed. It was then proposed by Lieutenant Jacob, to effect a breach by firing spherical case loaded with powder only,* fired, with reduced charges, point blank from the 18 pounders. This was done, and, in less than four hours, an excellent practicable breach was formed; a strong party was now landed from the ships, and, by two p.m., the fort was taken possession of and blown up, the guns were spiked, and the barracks burnt.

On the 27th of December, the 'Topaze' moved up abreast of the town, and the two cruisers commenced warping up to the right, on the north side of the Abdouroof, or the "Protector," a fort of nine guns, with a citadel, and somewhat stronger than "Taire." The work of warping was very heavy, owing to its blowing a gale of wind. The firing was intermittent on both sides, and the boats of the squadron were much annoyed by a galling fire of matchlocks, while employed laying out warps for hauling the cruisers and the bomb-ketch close into position under this fort. On the following day, the violence of the wind almost stopped the progress of the laborious duty of warping into position, and, at the urgent solicitation of the Imaum's Vakeel, a truce was granted for one day. On the 30th of December, at six a.m., the two cruisers and bomb-ketch, having taken up their stations in the coil of the bight, on the north side of the fort, at a distance of 500 and 350 yards respectively, and the frigate in her draught, opposite the town, a general bombardment was opened. "The effect of our fire," says a correspondent, in a letter which appeared in the 'Bombay Gazette' of the 21st of March, "was again equal to our most sanguine expectations; in a few hours we had the satisfaction of seeing this strong fort crumbled to the dust; like the former one, the shot and shells from the cruisers tumbled it down piecemeal. By nine o'clock the citadel was breached and the work unten-

come again, we will make them bite the dust, we will show them that we can fight and conquer still, or lay down our lives under the Holy Banner."

* It has generally been stated that common shell was used on this occasion, but this would appear to be incorrect from the following letter addressed to us by Captain Campbell, I.N.:—"It was William Jacob's idea about firing *spherical case*, loaded with *powder only*, at the Mocha forts, for he told me of it himself, and I carried out the idea in Burmah against the teak stockades, and it answered admirably. It was not common shell, but spherical case, or shrapnel, with the lead balls all shaken out and filled with powder, and fired with a reduced charge. Of course it needed much care not to burst them in or at the muzzle of the gun."

able; the garrison, about four hundred in number, were driven out, and, not being able to run the gauntlet across the isthmus, were compelled to decamp towards the south-east point, and swim across to the main, by which many were drowned. At ten a.m., possession was taken, and the British Union displayed on the flagstaff; the guns were then spiked and thrown down, and five mines were sprung, which, with the assistance of a rope, completed the destruction of this stronghold; and the "Protector," so formidable at sunrise, was before noon a confused mass of rubbish." While exploding one of the mines, Lieutenant John H. Wilson of the 'Benares' and one seaman were seriously burnt.*

* The following account is from an officer who was present throughout the operations:—"No sooner had we anchored, but the signal was displayed on board H.M.'s ship 'Topaze,' to 'prepare for battle' and 'to take up proper positions for bombarding the North Fort.' The frigate moved into 20 feet water; the 'Antelope' and 'Benares' were laying within her, in little more than their draught, at the distance of about 600 or 700 yards from the North Fort, and the Thames mortar boat was placed close in shore, opposite the town, between the two forts; and everything was ready for opening a heavy fire on the following morning, and expectation was high as to the effect it would produce. At eight a.m. on the 4th of December, the business was begun by a broadside from the frigate, and followed by the same from the two cruisers. The fire was at first smartly returned by the enemy from all the cannon in their five batteries, but with little effect, and shortly after began to slacken. The effect of our guns was good, considering the distance; for in the course of an hour the north battery was silenced, and a party of Arabs, who were stationed therein (finding our fire particularly directed to that part of the defences), quitted their post, and made a precipitate retreat across the isthmus, towards the Mecca gate of the town. The fight had now become a chase, and I observed one of them knocked down by a cannon shot, which overtook him in the race. The North Fort was now thought to be entirely abandoned by the enemy, and the 'Antelope' made a telegraphic signal to that effect. In the meantime the 'Thames' mortar-boat threw her 13-inch shell into the town, to the great dismay and consternation of the terrified inhabitants, who had never believed things would be brought to such a pass. At ten a.m. the 'Antelope' got under weigh, and worked up in a beautiful style (under double-reefed topsails and courses), to attack the South Fort, but in tacking under the lee of this fort, her keel touched, and, missing stays, she lay aground at the distance of 500 yards, but in an excellent position for cannonading it. The fort immediately opened its guns on the 'Antelope,' but was soon silenced by the superior fire of that cruiser, whose precision and execution was particularly noticed. The frigate had still continued a heavy and well-directed cannonade on the north battery, and the shot which missed it passed over into the town; the effect was considerable and manifest, yet it was to be regretted that her draught of water prevented her getting close enough to make a practicable breach. By noon the 'Benares' had also got up to the southward, and taken up a position for supporting the 'Antelope,' and covering the bomb vessel from the fire of the centre battery, when a flag of truce came off and a general truce was displayed by the squadron. The 'Topaze' now made telegraph signal; 'Great many killed on shore; they want eight days' truce; I have given them one hour and a-half.' At two p.m., finding our proposals not answered, the firing was recommenced on the North Fort by the frigate, and on the town by the two cruisers and the mortar boat, and was continued during the afternoon. At a quarter past two p.m. the boats of the squadron, manned and armed with a party of marines and artillery under the command of Lieutenants Moriarty, Wright, and Atkinson, of the 'Topaze,' Lieutenants Wilson and McDowall, of the 'Benares' and 'Antelope,' and Lieutenant Jacob of the Artillery, having been assembled round the frigate by signal, pushed off with the view of taking

VOL. I. X

During the night the bomb-ketch continued to throw shells into the town, and, on the following day, the bombardment was partially resumed; but the destruction of the South Fort was decisive in bringing to terms the Imaum's Vakeel, Meer Futteh Ullah, now appointed Dowlah, who, on the morning of the 2nd of January, came off to wait on Captain Bruce, a concession hitherto unheard of. Having afforded Captain Bruce the strongest assurances of a full concession of all demands, that officer landed on the 4th, accompanied by the captains of the ships of war, and rode to the house of Futteh Ullah, who received him with the utmost consideration; the late Dowlah was present at this interview, but placed on a seat at some distance from

possession of the North Fort. They effected a landing about half-past two o'clock under cover of the guns of the 'Topaze;' but, on getting to the fort, the door was barricaded; and the party having no means of escalading the wall, and being unable to force the gateway, the assailants were reluctantly compelled to retreat to their boats, under a galling fire from the matchlocks of the Arabs, and with a heavy loss in killed and wounded. Although foiled in their object, no words can do justice to the merits of the party employed on this enterprise; the coolness and determined spirit of gallantry which actuated every individual was never more conspicuous than on this trying occasion. Both officers and men were observed going round and about every side of the fort, seeking in vain for a hole to creep through, or in any way to gain access to the area of the work; while many were falling by a murderous fire from the matchlocks of the enemy, who, unseen and in security, took deliberate aim at their victims through loop-holes in the walls, and by hurling shot, stones, and quicklime on their heads from above. This is one of the melancholy instances which occasionally occur on expeditions of this nature; and while we regret the loss of those brave men who fell in this affair, no blame can be attached to any party. That experienced and gallant officer who commanded the force, Captain Lumley, had doubtless very strong reason to believe that the fort was abandoned, and, from the circumstance of no men having been seen in it, and not a gun having been fired from it since nine o'clock, it was but reasonable to conclude so, and in his zeal for the acquisition of an important object of the expedition, namely, the destruction of the North Fort, he directed it to be taken possession of as the best means of terminating hostilities, and securing British interests by a speedy acquiescence with our reasonable and just demands. The shells from the bomb-ketch were thrown into the town with admirable effect during the night, and (at 1,200 yards range) penetrated the flat roofs of the houses and through two floors, and exploded in the lower apartments, destroying whole families. The explosion of some shells in the early part of the night caused two extensive conflagrations in the town, which destroyed the prison and Governor's stables, &c. The attack of the North Fort recommenced on the morning of the 26th of December, at a few minutes after six. Our fire was returned by the enemy from the North and South Forts, Bunda, Five Gun, and North Gate Batteries, and kept up throughout the day. By ten, the North Fort having been rendered untenable, was abandoned, and by noon it was occupied by a detachment of Marines, Bombay Artillery, and Sepoys, landed under the command of Lieutenant W. Moriarty, and by three the guns were spiked, their carriages destroyed, and three mines sprung, which completely destroyed it. In consequence of the state of the weather, the operations against the South Fort did not commence till the 29th. The 'Benares' and 'Antelope' cruisers, and 'Thames' bomb vessel, were warped close to the South Fort; the depth of water not admitting of the 'Topaze' being also warped near enough, her fire was directed in keeping the town batteries in check. By half-past ten in the morning of the 30th, the South Fort was taken possession of, and demolished in the same manner as the North one. On the following day the enemy opened a cannonade partially; but our object having been fully accomplished, our squadron shifted beyond the reach of the fire."

the Meer. During the day he was put into close confinement, with a guard over him, and, by an express order from the Imaum, his property was seized and confiscated for having transmitted false accounts of the real state of affairs. In the evening, Futteh Ullah returned Captain Bruce's visit on board the 'Ernaad.'

Saturday, the 6th of January, 1821, having been fixed for Haji Futteh's affording public atonement for the wrongs he had committed, on that day, Meer Futteh Ullah, accompanied by his Council, a number of other functionaries and the principal merchants, brought the offender to Captain Bruce's house, where were assembled Captain Lumley, the commanders of the Company's cruisers, and a large party of officers. The Meer, leading Haji Futteh by the hand, formally announced to Captain Bruce that he had brought him, by the Imaum's order, to be delivered up for punishment, in any way he thought proper; that His Highness deeply regretted what had occurred, which had been entirely without his authority, and that he trusted, therefore, that this public acknowledgment would be considered sufficient atonement. He then delivered Haji Futteh into Captain Bruce's hands, when that officer replied that sufficient reparation had been offered, and Haji Futteh was freely forgiven, an act of generosity which deeply affected the late Dowlah, who, for some time, in vain attempted to give utterance to his gratitude. On the following day, Captain Bruce and the Naval commanders, accompanied by a high official on the part of the Dowlah, rode through the Shaduli gate, hitherto undesecrated by the foot of an unbeliever, after which the Dowlah issued a proclamation, which was repeated for three successive days, announcing that no one was to presume to offer molestation or insult to any person belonging to the English, in the streets or the different gates of the town, which were to be for their free use, the same as to themselves, and that any one transgressing this proclamation would be severely punished.

On the 14th, Meer Futteh Ullah delivered to Captain Bruce a firman, which had been issued by the Imaum, reducing the duties to $2\frac{1}{4}$ per cent.; and, in the course of the following day, copies of the treaty, which had been sent to Sanaa, were returned, duly signed and sealed by the Imaum and the members of his Council.* All the demands of the Bombay Government were now amply fulfilled, and the British factory was placed on that honourable footing which it should ever have occupied.

Lieutenant Robson,† commanding the Hon. Company's cruiser 'Antelope,' was left in charge of affairs as British Resident,

* Bombay Book of Treaties, p. 672.
† This gallant officer, who had gone through great personal fatigue, suffered so much in health, that he expired at Mocha on the 15th of August, 1821, two days before the arrival of his late ship the 'Antelope,' with the new British Resident, Captain Hutchinson.

with a guard of thirty Sepoys. "Thus," says Captain Playfair, "through the entire success of this Expedition, the national character was honourably redeemed from that stain which the natives of Arabia admitted it had received, and were surprised we had so long tolerated; and important advantages were obtained and secured by treaty."* While serving on this Expedition, Lieutenant Thomas Tanner, of the Marine, made a survey of the fort and batteries of Mocha, which forms one of the plates† in Major Straith's "Treatise on Fortification," the text book for the scientific services.

On the conclusion of the arduous operations at Mocha, Captain Lumley issued the following order:—

"H.M.S. 'Topaze,' off Mocha, Dec. 21, 1820.

"The gallant and spirited conduct displayed by the captains and commanders, and all the officers and seamen, artillery and sepoys, of the Company's cruisers, under my orders, during the late arduous attack and destruction of the forts of Mocha, having met my warmest approbation, I take the present opportunity of conveying my high sense of their very meritorious services on that occasion; and I am to request that the respective captains

* This treaty had not long been concluded, when a disposition appeared on the part of the Imaum to evade its provisions. The first instance occurred in considering whether Indian merchants, trading to Mocha under the protection of the British flag, shared equally with the English merchants in the benefit of the reduction of duty to 2¼ per cent. As, however, the terms of the treaty were ambiguous, and afforded good grounds for disputing the right to insist on this privilege, the point was waived. Early in the following year, it was observed that another, and much more serious, oversight occurred in the treaty, namely, that the stipulation which provided that the dependents of the factory should be entirely under British protection and control was omitted in the Arabic counterpart. This circumstance was made known to the Imaum, but he declined to rectify it; upon which he was given to understand, that, if attempts were made to seize or punish any person, of whatever nation, who might be in the Resident's exclusive employ, the latter was immediately to withdraw from Mocha, pending such steps as the Government of India might deem it necessary to pursue.

† This plate is numbered 4 in the Fourth Edition of Major Straith's work, and consists of plans, numbered 144, 145, and 146. "The two forts," says Straith, "stood on two prongs, which, abutting into the sea, completely defend the harbour and sea front of the town of Mocha. Each of these two forts mounted a heavy battery of iron guns, with casemated embrasures, and both forts were well within range and support of several heavy batteries on the sea front of Mocha." Speaking of the first unsuccessful assaults of the North Fort, the same authority says:—"Even had the assaulting party been provided with scaling ladders, it would have been almost certain destruction, for they would have been exposed, in the interior area, to a concentrated loop-holed fire from three sides of the quadrangle; and even if the lower entrance into the casemated barrack-rooms had been forced, the upper apartments would have secured a safe retreat, from which a deadly fire would have been poured down on the heads of the assailants, the trap-doored staircase being a removable ladder. The plans and sections of these forts are given in figures 145, 146, as showing the sorts of defences to be expected in offensive operations in these quarters of the globe, and the hopelessness of attacking them without the effective assistance of artillery." We learn from General Sir George Le Grand Jacob, brother of Lieut. W. Jacob, that the latter was blown into the air by a mine sprung in the breach, and that he was so seriously hurt that, for some days, his life was despaired of.

will signify the same to them respectively, and to assure them that I shall not fail to represent their gallant behaviour to the Hon. Company's Government accordingly. I have also to return my warmest thanks to Lieutenant Jacob, of the Artillery, for the great precision with which the shells were thrown by him into the town and forts of Mocha; as also to Lieutenant Tanner, of the Hon. Company's Marine, who so willingly offered his services, and who proved particularly useful, and whose behaviour was highly meritorious, during the late arduous attack above-mentioned.

"(Signed) G. R. LUMLEY,
"Captain and Senior Officer.
"To the respective Captains and Commanders of
 the Hon. Company's cruisers 'Benares,'
 'Antelope,' 'Ernaad,' and 'Thames.'

The Governor of Bombay in Council gave formal expression to his satisfaction, in an Order, dated March 31, 1821, in which was published the following extract from Captain Lumley's despatches relating to the services of the Bombay Marine:—

"The good conduct evinced by the officers, seamen, and Sepoys, of the Hon. Company's vessels, merit the fullest praise; the ready obedience to all my orders, even the frequent anticipation of them (produced by a sense of what the immediate exigencies of the Service required), marked particularly the zeal of Lieutenants Faithful and Robson, and the position in which they always placed their vessels, denoted as strongly their ability as officers. I have to express my satisfaction with Lieutenant Jones, commanding the 'Ernaad,' and Second-Lieutenant Elwon of the 'Thames,' Lieutenant Tanner, passenger in the 'Antelope,' very handsomely volunteered his services where he might be useful."

The Captain of the 'Topaze,' than whom the British Navy did not possess a more gallant or meritorious officer, died on the 23rd of July, 1821, in a great measure owing to excessive exertion and exposure during the operations at Mocha. He was buried at Penang on the 28th of July, greatly mourned by all who knew him, and not less by his country, in whose service he had lost an arm and had suffered other wounds. Lieutenant Faithful also died on the 22nd of April, 1823, and as Lieutenant Robson expired on the 15th of August, 1821, from the over-fatigue he had undergone, death soon removed the three principal actors in the capture of the Mocha forts.

CHAPTER X.

1797—1820.

The Joasmi Pirates; their origin and early history—Attack on the 'Viper'—Their Defeat of the Imaum of Muscat, and Aggressions on the British Flag—The Treaty of 1806—Attack on the 'Fury'—Capture of the 'Minerva' and 'Sylph'—Their Repulse by the 'Nautilus'—The Expedition of 1809; Capture of Ras-ul-Khymah, Luft, and Shinaz—Recognition by Commodore Wainwright and the Bombay Government of the gallantry of the Marine—Renewed Depredations of the Joasmi Pirates—Action between the 'Aurora' and a Joasmi squadron—The Abortive Demonstration before Ras-ul-Khymah in 1816—Repulse of a Piratical Fleet by the 'Antelope,' and other actions with the Joasmis—The Expedition of 1819; Siege and Capture of Ras-ul-Khymah and Zayah—Complimentary Orders on the Services of the Marine—Final Pacification of the Joasmis, and Signature of the Treaty of the 8th of January, 1820.

THE Persian Gulf, as a field for the services of the Bombay Marine, came prominently into notice during the early years of the nineteenth century, and, for two decades, it became a scene of active strife, until, at length, the piratical tribes who infested its waters, were finally humbled, and the flag of England became as paramount throughout every creek and inlet of the Persian Gulf as in Bombay Harbour itself.

We first hear of the maritime Arab tribes, of whom the Joasmi were the most bold, coming into actual conflict with the ships of the Bombay Marine in the year 1797, and, subsequent to that date, many passages of arms took place between the small British cruisers and the heavily-manned craft that flew the flag of Abd-ul-Wahab, the great reformer of the religion of the Koran, whose followers, called Wahabees, carried fire and sword throughout the peninsula of Arabia. The Joasmi* occupied that part of the Arabian coast, extending from Khor-es-Shem, or Elphinstone's Inlet, near Ras Mussendom (or Masandim) to Abu Thubee, a low sandy coast line running in a south-west

---

* There were also three smaller tribes of Arabs on the coast between Ras-ul-Khymah and the island of Bahrein, called the Mahama or Owaimir, Beni Yas, whose capital is Abu Thubee or Abu Zhabi, and Menasir. Though they seldom committed acts of piracy on the high seas, these Arabs would seize any vessel that approached their coast, and in 1834, the Beni Yas attempted a daring act of piracy, which met with condign punishment.

direction for about 150 miles. The towns on this coast, which was generally designated by navigators, " the Pirate Coast," are all built near the entrance of a Khor, or salt-water inlet, and the maritime robbers, established here from a very remote period, not only made themselves dreaded by their neighbours, but defied the efforts to subdue them of the Portuguese, (who nominally claimed the whole coast of Oman until expelled by the Arabs), and extended their depredations along the southern coast of Arabia, and even to the shores of India and the Red Sea. Their chief towns were Sharjah, or Shargah, the residence of Sultan Sugger, the noted Joasmi chief, and Ras-ul-Khymah,* formerly called Julfa, a large town built on a long sandy peninsula, or spit, projecting into the sea, and enclosing a deep narrow bay protected by a bar, over which, at spring tides, there is scarcely 11 feet of water, although at these periods there is a rise of 6 feet above the usual level. Vessels drawing 14 feet cannot approach within two and a half miles, though gunboats drawing 3 feet may advance within pistol-shot of the beach and point-blank range of the town.

The "pirate coast" was called by the Persians Julfarah, after the chief town, and Es-sirr by the Arabs. "In the time of Mahomed," says Morier, in his "Travels in Persia," "there existed a predatory tribe, whose chief is described in the Koran, according to Ebn Haukal, as 'the King, who forcibly seized every sound ship.'" In the early part of the seventeenth century, Julfa was occupied by the Persians, who had captured Ormuz in 1622, and by the Portuguese, each having a separate fort and garrison there. The powerful Omanee chief, Nasir-bin-Murshid, first attacked the Portuguese, who still held Sohar, Muskat, and other places on the Oman coast; at his death in 1649, he was succeeded by his cousin, Sultan-bin-Seif, who, by treachery, captured Muskat, and some of his vessels attacked and killed the crews of two Portuguese men-of war, which continued to hover about the coast. Fired with this success, the "Imaum," for such was the religious title assumed by this dynasty, "about the year 1670," according to Hamilton, attacked

* Ras-ul-Khymah, the chief town of the Joasmi, at this time contained about one thousand houses, and probably still possesses some four or five thousand inhabitants. The town is chiefly constructed of stone houses, with some square buildings forming the Sheikh's residence, of greater elevation than the rest. On one corner of the highest building is a dome, which is about sixty feet above the level of the sea; and on another high building to the left flies the Joasmi flag, red with narrow white border. A great many boats and baghalahs belong to this port, which has long since recovered from the effect of the Expeditions of 1809 and 1819, the teachings of which, however, have happily created a permanent and salutary impression of the power of the British Government. From hence to Shargah, the largest town of the Joasmis, having a population now of between eight and ten thousand inhabitants, the coast is generally low, and thinly planted with date trees, and full of shallow creeks, well calculated to afford protection to the peculiarly constructed boats of the pirate tribes. Other ports are Ramse or Rams, Boo Haille, and the ports of the Beni Yas.

Diu and Damaun, Portuguese possessions in India, and sacked the churches. His son, Seif, in 1698, drove the Portuguese from Mombaza, Pemba, and Kilwa, and added these possessions to Oman; this prince had a formidable Navy, one of the ships carrying eighty guns. So powerful had the Omanees become that, as we have mentioned during the course of this narrative, the trade of the English East India Company was greatly endangered, and one of their agents in Persia—who had all, indeed, successively insisted on the necessity of sending an armed force to destroy them—declared that "they were likely to become as great a plague to India, as the Algerines were in Europe." Some of the ships owned by these "pirates," as Morier calls them, had from thirty to fifty guns; and one of their fleets, consisting of five ships, carried between them fifteen hundred men.

Niebuhr makes no mention of Ras-ul-Khymah, under that name, but there appears an account of the origin of the word in a curious work,* which formerly was in the library of the famous Orientalist and traveller, Sir W. Ouseley, written by an European officer of the household of the late Seyyid (or Syud) Said of Muscat. He says of Ras-ul-Khymah:—" Their founder, Joasmi, pitched his tent on a point of land a little elevated above the sea shore, which being very conspicuous to all other ships passing by, the sailors called the place Ras-el-Keima, which in Arabic signifies 'the point of the tent,' and in process of time a town being built, the original name was transferred to it." During the latter part of the eighteenth century, the arms of Mohammed-ibn-Abdul-Wahab,† whose name signifies "Bestower of Blessings," subdued the whole of Nedjed and the country between Derreyah, the capital, and the Gulf; and "before he died," says Palgrave, " he saw his authority acknowledged from the shores of the Persian Gulf to the frontiers of Mecca." For three years these fierce pirates held out against the Moslem reformer, but, at length they gave in their adhesion to the new tenets, and, after the manner of proselytes, enforced its behests upon all disbelievers with fiery zeal. For a, long time the Joasmis only attacked the crews of native trading vessels, and, according to their invariable custom on such occasions, gave the crews the option of forthwith conforming to their religion or

---

* "History of the Seyd Said, Sultan of Muscat, with an account of the Wahabees, by Sheik Mansur, an Italian, who was physician to the Sultan, and commanded his forces against the Joasmis."

† For further particulars regarding the history, government, and religion of the Wahabees, I would refer the reader to Burckhardt's " Notes on the Bedouins and Wahabees." According to Palgrave's " Central and Eastern Arabia," the following was the succession of Wahabee chiefs:—Saood, the founder of the dynasty; Abd-ul-Aziz, his son and successor; Saood II. the disciple of the founder; Abd-ul-Aziz, his son, who was assassinated about 1803; Abdullah, a younger son, beheaded at Constantinople; Toorkee, son of Abdullah, assassinated in 1834; and Faisul, son of Toorkee.

suffering a cruel death. But they waxed bolder as years passed by and they grew in strength.*

Since the capture of Ormuz, the Company had retained two or three of their ships of war in the Persian Gulf for the protection of their commercial interests at Gombroon and the agencies at Bushire and Bussorah, with which places, particularly the latter, a considerable trade was carried on. The officers of the Bombay Marine were enjoined not to interfere with the piratical acts of the Arab tribes of the Persian Gulf, but only to act in self-defence, which encouraged the Joasmis—who, like all Easterns, construed non-intervention into an avowal of weakness—to commit an act of treachery which brought its own punishment. In the year 1797, the first capture of a British vessel was made by the Joasmis. The 'Bassein,' snow, carrying public despatches, was seized on the 18th of May off Rams on the Joasmi coast, by a fleet of dhows, and carried into Ras-ul-Khymah, but was released after a detention of two days. In the following October, the pirates, encouraged by the impunity they had enjoyed, made their first attack upon a Company's cruiser, but the reception they met with was not encouraging.

The Hon. Company's brig 'Viper,' of fourteen guns, was lying in Bushire Roads, where were also some Joasmi dhows, under the command of Sheikh Saleh, nephew to the Joasmi chief, who was then at war with the Imaum of Musqat. As their object was to intercept the Sooree Arabs who were at Bussorah, no fear of any hostile movement on the part of these vessels existed in the mind of the Captain of the 'Viper,' who proceeded on shore to the house of the British Political Resident. This gentleman, lulled by the protestations of friendship of Sheikh Saleh, unwisely gave an order to the Captain of the 'Viper,' to supply the dhows with powder and shot, ostensibly to attack the Sooree Arabs; and no sooner had they secured enough for their purpose, than they weighed anchor as if for a cruise. It was about eight o'clock in the morning, and the crew of the Company's cruiser were having their breakfast on deck. Suddenly two of the dhows, which were passing under the 'Viper's' stern, opened fire with round shot upon the little craft. The officers, who were below rushed upon deck. Lieutenant Carruthers, the senior, called the men to quarters, and none too soon, for the dhows, crammed full of men, bore down on the little man-of-war, intending to capture her by boarding. The crew of the 'Viper' cut the cable and made sail on the ship, while the guns were cast loose, and soon opened a well-

* Mr. J. Warden, Member of Council at Bombay, says in a paper on the Joasmis that Oman Hussain-ben-Ali was invested by the Wahabees with the fullest authority, which enabled him to compel the heads of the Joasmis residing at Shargah and Ras-ul-Khymah, to cruise in conjunction with vessels from Rams in the service of the Wahabees, against all ships, without exception, appearing in the Gulf.

directed fire on their treacherous assailants. The superior seamanship of the Englishmen told in their favour, and, by dint of smart manœuvring, Lieutenant Carruthers succeeded, not only in preventing the enemy from carrying into execution their intention to board, when their numerical superiority must have given them the victory, but beat the dhows off, and ended the conflict by chasing them out to sea. Unfortunately this gallant young officer was killed towards the latter part of the action. He had been previously wounded by a musket-ball in the loins, but refused to leave the deck, and was soon after shot through the forehead. Mr. Salter, the senior midshipman, who took command on the death of his superior, fought the ship with determined bravery, and the great loss she incurred, thirty-two out of a total crew of sixty-five, testified to the severity of the action.*

Notwithstanding the glaring nature of this outrage, which cost many gallant men their lives, no hostilities were ordered by the Bombay Government, but the Joasmis had received so severe a lesson that many years elapsed before a second attempt was made to attack a British vessel of war. The Company's Resident at Bushire wrote to the Joasmi chief demanding explanations as to the treacherous attack on the 'Viper' and the capture of the 'Bassein,' but his remonstrances were met on the part of Sheikh Suggur by professions of regard for the English, contending in respect to the attack on the 'Viper,' that the cruiser had fired first on the dhows. He stated that Sheikh Saleh left Ras-ul-Khymah, and, having separated himself from the tribe, proceeded to the Persian shore, where he established himself among the Beni Khalid Arabs, marrying a woman of that tribe, which was one of a villainous character; that since the commencement of hostilities between the Joasmis and people of Oman, Sheikh Saleh had acted independently of Ras-ul-Khymah, committing depredations according to his inclination; that the Joasmis had no disputes with the English, and considered the people of Oman† alone as their enemies.

---

* According to Mr. Warden, in his Memoir of the "Rise and Progress of the Arab Tribes in the Persian Gulf," already referred to, this affair, and also the attack on the 'Bassein' snow, "was supposed to have been by Arabs, in the interest of the deposed Prince of Oman, the elder brother of Syud Sultan." Mr. Warden states that it was not until 1804, which was two years after the Wahabees had reduced to obedience the Joasmis, that the latter commenced their piratical depredations. It is certain that the Wahabee element has exercised only a baneful influence in Persian Gulf politics.

† These hostilities arose in consequence of the unsettled state of the Muscat Government on the death of Syud (or Seyyid) Ahmed, and the usurpation of Seyyid Sultan. The latter had involved himself in serious disputes with the Arabs of the Gulf, which brought on a war with some of the tribes, who had united against him; and the Bombay Government conceived that the acts of aggression experienced by British vessels, had been from Arabs in the interest of the deposed Prince of Oman. At the close of the year 1798, the Imaum of Muscat was threatening Bussorah, on account of some claims against the Pasha of Bagdad.

It was not until early in the present century that the Joasmis may be said to have engaged in piratical depredations as their recognised occupation, for up to the close of 1804, with the exception of the attack on the 'Bassein,' snow, and 'Viper,' cruiser, they manifested every respect for the British flag. The influence of the Wahabees* having been introduced over the " pirate coast," and the Government of Muscat, on the death of Seyyid Sultan, having also temporarily fallen under the control of that power, the characters of the different tribes in the Gulf underwent a material change, and the attention of the British Government was directed to check the spirit of piracy which, at this period, began to display itself.†

In 1803, a remarkable man appeared upon the scene, in the person of Sultan Bin Suggur, Chief of the Joasmis. In that year he succeeded to the Sheikdom of the tribe upon the death of his father, Suggur, who had assumed the chief authority in 1777, upon the retirement of his father, Rashid Bin Muttur. Sultan Bin Suggur had three brothers and seven sons, and was in many respects a remarkable man; he lived to a great age, and his noble presence and patriarchal appearance were familiar to the officers of the Indian Navy, with whom, notwithstanding the losses and defeats his tribes had sustained at their hands, he and his sons, the eldest of whom was appointed Governor of Shargah in 1838, remained on terms of friendship. The other *dramatis personæ* in Persian Gulf politics, at this time, were Shakboot,‡ Sheikh of the Beni Yas, whose head-quarters were at Abu Thubee, who had been supreme since 1793-94; and Abdoola Bin Ahmed and Suliman Bin Ahmed, joint rulers of Bahrein, (literally "the Two Seas") then held by the el-Uttûb, or Uttoobee Arabs, who, with the assistance of the

In order to enable him the more effectually to execute his hostile intentions Seyyid Said negotiated a peace with his formidable enemies, the Joasmis, through the interposition of the British Resident at Bussorah.

* The Joasmis must have been kept in check by the progress of the Wahabees, who had by the month of May, 1802, reduced to nominal submission the whole coast from Bussora to Dibba, which included their territory. They appear, however, towards the close of 1804, to have been in alliance with the Uttobees of Bahrein, since it was in an engagement with these two tribes that Seyyid Sultan, the Imaum, lost his life.

† See " Historical Sketch of the Joasmi Tribe of Arabs from the Year 1747 to the Year 1819. Prepared by Mr. Francis Warden, Member of Council at Bombay." Also a continuation of the same, from the year 1819 to the close of the year 1831, by Lieutenant S. Hennell; and from 1832 to July, 1844, by Lieutenant A. B. Kemball; and from the latter period to the close of the year 1853, by Lieutenant H. F. Disbrowe, successive Assistants to the Resident in the Persian Gulf. ("Bombay Government Records," No. 24, 1856.)

‡ He was deposed in 1816 by his son, Mahomed, who was, in his turn, dispossessed two years later by his brother, Tahnoon, through the assistance of the Imaum of Muscat. In 1833 Tahnoon was killed by his younger half-brother, Khaleefa Bin Shakboot, who was assisted by his own brother, Sultan. This brother and the father continued to reside at Abu Thubee, but had no share in the government.

Wahabees,* early in 1801, retook the island from the Imaum of Muscat, who had expelled them only a few months before.

In 1804, Seyyid Sultan met his death at the hands of the Wahabee pirates off Linjah, while on his return from Bussorah, to which he had proceeded to receive the annual gratuity, awarded by the Sultan of Turkey to the successor of the Imaum Ahmed, who, in the year 1756, raised the siege of that city, then beleaguered by the Persians. The following were the circumstances under which Seyyid Sultan died at the hands of his traditional foe. He left his frigate, the 'Jinjawar,' off Linjah, and embarked in a tender, called 'El-Badry,' in order to proceed through the Clarence Straits to Gombroon. About midnight of the 19th of November, 1804, according to the Arabic historian, whose work is translated by the Rev. G. P. Badger, he was hailed by three boats from Ras-ul-Khymah, and it was agreed that they should fight at daylight. The Seyyid disdaining to flee, commenced the conflict at dawn, and was almost victorious when a musket-ball struck him in the mouth and he expired on the spot. Upon this the enemy overpowered the crew, but spared their lives.† During his rule, Seyyid Sultan's brother, Imaum Said, being still alive, he never assumed the title of Imaum, which, as Palgrave remarks, "is unused in Oman itself, and belongs to European and not to Arab nomenclature." Since the time of Said, son of the Imaum Ahmed, who founded the dynasty in 1741, the rulers of Oman have never adopted the title of Imaum, but are uniformly designated "Seyyid," or lord. Said, the last of the race who adopted the religious title of Imaum, or chief priest, died during the regency of his nephew, Seyyid Said, between 1811-21, but the latter never laid claim to the title, and he and his successors always retained the appellation of Seyyid, in preference to the religious prefix, though the English knew him as the Imaum.

On Seyyid Sultan's death his two sons, Salim and Said, ruled conjointly, and ultimately, on the death of Salim in 1821, the younger brother, Said, became supreme, and for fifty years ruled Oman with prudence and firmness, while he showed his

* The Wahabee chief, Saood the Second, the first patron, and the successful defender and propagator of the new doctrine, died about 1800, and his son, Abdul-Asiz, at once turned his arms against Kateef, Bahrein, and the Kingdom of Oman.

† Fraser, in his narrative of a Journey into Khorassan, says, " While proceeding with his fleet to the island of Kishm, and thence to Khameer, to visit the great sulphur mines, which he received from Persia, he left his ships, five in number, becalmed between Polior and the Tombs, and got into a boat to proceed alone, when, night coming on, he was attacked by five Joasmi boats, which happened to be crossing from the Arabian side to celebrate a wedding at Linga. The contest was severe, but ended in the murder of the Imaum and his whole party, and it was the more distressing, as his own ships were near enough to see the flashes of the guns, though being becalmed they could have rendered no assistance, had they even known the danger of their chief."

sagacity in maintaining a close alliance with the British Government.

In the year 1805, two English merchant brigs, the 'Shannon' and 'Trimmer,' belonging to Mr. Mannesty, the Company's Resident at Bussorah, while on the voyage from Bombay to that place, were attacked near the islands of Polior and Kenn, (Kais) by several Joasmi pirate boats, and, after a slight resistance on the part of the 'Shannon' only, were captured, and the native part of the crew of each put to the sword. The captain of the 'Shannon' had his arm struck off as he had been seen to fire a musket, but the European seamen were landed and permitted to disperse.

The vessels were armed, one of them with twenty guns, and, being manned with Arab crews, were sent from Ras-ul-Khymah to cruise in the Gulf, where they committed many successful piracies on maritime trade.

The Bombay Government had been so ill-advised as to place the lives of their officers and men absolutely at the discretion of these pirates by issuing an order signed by the President in Council, directing all the commanders of the ships of the Bombay Marine on no consideration to attack these blood-thirsty rovers, and threatening to visit with displeasure any officers who might molest them. In the same year that they attacked the merchant brigs, 'Shannon' and 'Trimmer,' the Joasmis, encouraged by impunity, surrounded the Hon. Company's cruiser, 'Mornington,' twenty-two guns, with a large fleet of forty sail, and attempted to capture her. An action ensued, and the 'Mornington' drove off her assailants with great loss.

Though enraged at the attack upon the two merchant brigs, the Government did not appear to be very anxious on the score of the safety of their own ships of war, whose captain's hands they had tied by orders not to take the initiative even in self-defence, but to wait until they were fired upon, instructions which resulted soon after in a sad catastrophe. "The Governor of that period," says the traveller, J. S. Buckingham, "from ignorance of the character of this people, could never be persuaded that they were the aggressors, and constantly upraided the officers with having, in some way, provoked the attacks of which they complained—continuing still to insist on the observance of the orders, in not firing on these vessels until they had first been fired at by them." In consequence of the attack upon the two brigs, the Company's ships were directed to operate against the Joasmis in conjunction with the Imaum's Government; the combined forces accordingly proceeded, in the year 1806, to the island of Kishm, where they blockaded the Joasmi fleet, which was reduced to such distress that they sued for peace. Captain David Seton, the British

Political Agent, agreed to grant them a truce until the pleasure of his Government should be known, and a treaty was concluded at Bunder Abbas, dated the 6th of February, 1806, by which they agreed to give up the 'Trimmer,' the 'Shannon' having been previously restored completely stripped, and to " respect the flag and property of the Hon. East India Company and their subjects," and " to assist and protect" any English vessels touching on their coast. Captain Seton represented to his Government that " the whole bulk of the Joasmis were desirous of returning to their former mercantile pursuits," but he had suffered himself to be cajoled by these wolves in sheeps' clothing. Piracy was bred in the bone among these restless, truculent Arabs, and the fleets of large and heavily-armed dhows moored in the harbours-of Shargah and Ras-ul-Khymah, were not destined for the peaceful pursuits of pearl-fishing on the Bahrein coast, but for deeds of rapine and blood.

For a brief period the Joasmis continued true to the provisions of the treaty of 1806, so far as regarded the British ships cruising in the Gulf; but it is probable that this temporary abstention from acts of piracy on the British flag, was induced only by a fear of the consequences, as we find that during the year 1807, owing to the exigencies of European politics, there was a powerful squadron of ships of war in the Persian Gulf. Urged on by the intrigues of General Sebastiani, special envoy of Napoleon, then in the very height of his power, the Turkish Government, in December, 1806, declared war against Russia, with which Power we made common cause, though indeed the Czar Alexander had forestalled the Porte by invading what are now known as the Danubian Principalities. Sir John Duckworth was despatched by Lord Collingwood in February, 1807, to coerce the Sultan, and that admiral actually forced the Dardanelles, and arrived within eight hours of Constantinople, when, being hampered by the action of the British Minister, precious time was lost, the defences of the city were strengthened, and Duckworth was forced to retire without accomplishing anything. In order to assist in bringing Turkey to her senses through her Asiatic possessions, a squadron was despatched to the Persian Gulf from Bombay, consisting of H.M.S. 'Fox,' Captain Hon. A. Cochrane, and eight of the Company's cruisers. The 'Fox' took the Persian Ambassador up the Gulf, and proceeded to Al-Koweit, or Grane,* whence she soon afterwards returned to Madras, the Turkish Governor disclaiming the acts of his Government. The squadron of

* Al Koweit—for the English name Grane is a corruption, and is utterly unknown to the Arabs of the Gulf, says Captain Constable in his " Persian Gulf Pilot "—is, perhaps, the best port in the Gulf, and contains a population of some twenty-five thousand souls of the Uttobee tribe, while it numbers one hundred and thirty trading vessels, between thirty and three hundred tons.

cruisers remained in the Persian Gulf for a year, and hence there was a brief cessation to the course of piracy on the part of the Joasmi. In the month of April, 1808, after the return of the squadron to Bombay, the Joasmi dhows from Rams, Shargah, and other places on the coast, sent out to cruise without the permission of their lawful chief, Sheikh Sultan Bin Suggur, whose sole possession at this time was Ras-ul-Khymah, made their first appearance on the coast to the northward of Bombay, and Captain Seton reported that the acts of piracy " can only be considered as a general one at the instigation of the Wahabees." While off the Guzerat coast, in command of the schooner 'Lively,' Lieutenant Macdonald fought a gallant action with four piratical dhows, each larger and carrying more men than his own little craft. He says :—" Calling the small pattamar close under our lee, we stood on till within half gun shot, when the two largest being most in shore, luffed up, whilst the others passed on to leeward, with the obvious intention of hemming us between them; to avoid so unpleasant a dilemma we went about, and crossing the two weathermost, brought our carronades and musketry so effectually into play, as to drive the fellows who were ranged along the gunwales, for boarding, instantly under cover; meantime, the leaders, by inattention, or attempting to wear, became entangled, and thrown into the utmost confusion, whilst we plyed them with grape and canister till they separated, and went off before the wind. So smooth and motionless, and so near were we all this while, that it was impossible to miss half so good a mark; almost every shot told in passing to windward; and as they slid onwards, we saw men suspended over the side of the one nearest to us, with whom we had been principally occupied. As the firing ceased, we could hear them shouting " Shoof, shoof,"—that is " fly, fly "—to their companions to seaward, and as long as the wind lasted they stood off shore, in close communication as before; and when afterwards becalmed, their mainsails were lowered down, and their boats passed to and fro till the sea breeze came in, when they made their way down the coast, and we saw no more of each other until the subsequent detention of three of their number in Surat Roads, where they had ventured under the guise of honest traders. They were, however, detected by the Commodore's boat's crew visiting and discovering several wounded men concealed under an awning, which created a strong presumption that all was not as it should be, and led to their seizure and being sent to Bombay for examination; Mr. Secretary Goodwin, of the Public Department, and Captain Court, Secretary in the Naval Department, investigated the case, and, though fully satisfied of their identity and guilt, the Government, in consideration of their long detention, set them free again to exercise their calling on some hapless coaster." The natural result of this feeble paltering with maritime brigandage was the encouragement of the pirates, who, during the year 1808 captured twenty native vessels, which so elated them that they despatched a fleet of fifty sail towards Cutch and Scinde.

At length they flew at higher game, and attacked the Honourable Company's cruiser 'Fury,' of six guns, commanded by Lieutenant Gowan, when carrying despatches from Bussorah to Bombay; but the gallant officers and men of the little cruiser beat off their assailants with heavy loss. "The attack," says Buckingham, "was made by several boats in company and during a short calm; but the resistance made was determined and effectual, and the boats were made to sheer off with the loss of a great number of men. On the arrival of the 'Fury' at Bombay, the commander waited on the Governor in the usual way; but on reporting the affair of the battle, instead of being applauded for his spirited resistance, and his preservation of the despatches under his charge, he received a severe reprimand from the Governor himself in person, for disobeying the orders given, and daring to molest the *innocent and unoffending* Arabs of these seas."

During the latter part of the year 1808, they attacked the ship 'Minerva,' belonging to Mr. Mannesty, on her voyage from Bombay to Bussorah. The attack was made by several dhows, which, watching a favourable opportunity, threw on board a large body of men, and the crew of the 'Minerva' were, of course, quickly overpowered. The ship was first purified with water and perfumes, and then the wretched captives were bound and brought forward singly to the gangway, where one of the pirates cut their throats, with the exclamation Mahommedans use in slaying cattle, " Allah Ackbar " *(God is Great)*, regarding this terrible deed of blood as a propitiatory sacrifice to the Deity.* The captain was said to have been cut up into fragments, which were thrown overboard; the mate and carpenter were alone spared, probably to make use of their services, and an Armenian lady, wife of Lieutenant Taylor, then at Bushire, was carried captive, but, in accordance with Arab custom, no indignity was offered to her, and she was ransomed a few months later by Mr. Bruce, Political Agent at Bushire. The ship was taken to Ras-ul-Khymah, where twenty guns were mounted on her, and she was sent to cruise in the Gulf.

On the 20th of October, only a few weeks after this, they mastered the Honourable Company's cruiser 'Sylph,' a small schooner of only 78 tons, and mounting eight guns, the commander's hands being tied by the instructions of his Govern-

* " Travels in Arabia," by Lieutenant J. R. Welsted, I.N., F.R.S.

ment until it was too late to offer any effectual resistance. The 'Sylph' formed one of a squadron carrying the Mission, under Sir Harford Jones, to the Court of the Shah of Persia, when, on being separated from the rest of the ships, a fleet of dhows was seen bearing down on her. Lieutenant W. C. Graham, her commander, was alive to the peril of his position, but he could take no steps to keep them at bay, as they committed no openly hostile act; they only steered for him, and he had received peremptory orders, any infringement of which would involve dismissal, on no account to fire on the Arab craft until they first opened fire upon him. These orders placed a small cruiser absolutely at their mercy, for the Joasmi did not care to engage in a gunnery duel with British seamen, even with long odds in their favour; their tactics consisted in running on board an enemy and throwing some hundreds of desperate men, armed to the teeth, on to the deck of a vessel, thus bearing down all resistance. This method of fighting was well known to the officers of the Indian Navy, and the crews were specially trained to repel boarders should a calm, or the loss of any top-hamper, as masts or spars, place their small vessels at the mercy of an overwhelming force of the enemy.*

The dhows quickly approached, and ran alongside with their large overhanging prows, which form a peculiar feature of this class of vessel, towering above the little cruiser's waist. From this vantage ground a crowd of men poured volleys of huge stones upon the heads of the unfortunate officers and crew, who were powerless to do more than return a feeble musketry fire. It was too late now to use the guns, or make any effectual resistance, and, in another instant, the decks of the 'Sylph' were swarming with a host of desperadoes, who, with the name of the Prophet on their lips, and a thirst for Christian blood in their hearts, quickly bore down all resistance, and commenced a wholesale massacre. Lieutenant Graham fell, covered with wounds,† down the fore hatchway, where one or two of the crew who had been hurled below, dragged him into a storeroom, of which they barricaded the door from within by a crowbar; his chief officer, Acting-Lieutenant Denton, who had served

---

* The writer who, as a midshipman, was for a lengthened period senior executive officer of a small brig-of-war, can recall the drill of "forming Lion's mouth," as it was called, which was specially practised by the crews of small cruisers, to repel boarders. The enemy was supposed to be boarding, forward or aft, as the case might be, and at the word "Form Lion's mouth," a couple of the small 6-pounder howitzers were wheeled across the deck at the other end of the ship, with all hands armed with cutlasses in rear of them. At the order the guns were fired (supposed to be with grape) at the enemy, and then a rush was made at the foe, staggered by this unexpected discharge.

† Lieutenant Graham, who subsequently held a shore appointment at Bombay, survived for half a century the terrible wounds he received on this occasion on the head and shoulders.

as a midshipman on board the 'Colossus' at Trafalgar, only survived the wound he had received on that great day to be butchered by these murderous fanatics; and, in a few minutes, almost the entire crew had perished, fighting desperately. The Joasmis now made sail on the schooner, and were bearing her off in triumph to their own ports, when an unexpected event snatched the prize from their hands, and resulted in the rescue of Lieutenant Graham, and the remnant of his men, from the cruel fate that would have awaited them on their being dragged forth from their secret hiding-place. This event was none other than the appearance of His Majesty's thirty-six gun frigate, 'Néréide,' Commodore Corbett, forming part of the squadron, which now hove in sight, and, perceiving the 'Sylph' in company with the dhows, divined what had occurred and made sail in pursuit. On nearing the prize, the Joasmis quitted her, and took to their dhows, to which the Commodore gave chase, but without success, as owing to their superior sailing, they were enabled to effect their escape: it was thought at the time that the 'Néréide' had sunk one of the dhows by a broadside, but this was subsequently found to be a mistake.

The Government, in sending to the Persian Gulf wretched little craft, like the 'Sylph,' of eighty tons, not one-third the size of the ordinary Joasmi war dhows, which, moreover, cruised in squadrons, carrying among them hundreds of men, positively invited the loss of their ships, and, still worse, of the crews; but then the Government only suffered in prestige, while their gallant seamen paid the penalty with their lives.

Only three days after this affair the Joasmi pirates attempted to capture the Company's brig 'Nautilus,' fourteen guns, in a similar manner, but met with a warm reception at the hands of the Commander, Lieutenant Bennett. "The 'Nautilus,'" says Buckingham, who acquired his information from those engaged in the Persian Gulf at the time, " was proceeding up the Gulf with despatches, and in passing the island of Anjar, on the south side of Kishm, near the Persian shore, was attacked by a squadron of pirates, consisting of a baghalah, a dhow, and two trankies; the two former mounting great guns, the others having oars as well as sails, and all being full of armed men. The attack was made in the most skilful and regular manner, the two larger vessels bearing down on the starboard bow, and the smaller ones on the quarter. As Lieutenant Bennett had received the same positive orders as his brother officers, not to commence an attack until fired on, he reserved his guns until they were so close to him that their dancing and brandishing of spears, the attitude with which they menace death, could be distinctly seen, and their songs and war shouts heard. The bow gun was then fired across their hawse as a signal for them to desist, and the British colours were displayed. This being disregarded, it was followed by a second shot, which had no more effect. A moment's consultation was then held by the officers, when it was thought a want of regard for their own safety to use further forbearance, and a broadside was instantly discharged among them all.

"An action now commenced between the 'Nautilus' and the two largest of the boats, mounting cannon, and continued for nearly an hour; the trankies lying on their oars during the contest to await its result, and seize the first favourable moment to board. As the superiority on the part of the cruiser became more decidedly apparent, these latter, however, fled, and were soon followed by the others, the whole of whom the 'Nautilus' pursued, and fired on during the chase as long as her shot would tell."

Among the killed in this action was the boatswain, and among the wounded, Lieutenant Thomas Tanner,* who survived to a great age, and, in the year 1859, was elected Mayor of Exeter, his native town.

These repeated aggressions of the Joasmi, coupled with an insolent demand from the Chief of Ras-ul-Khymah, whose harbour was the principal resort of the larger craft, for the payment of tribute by the Bombay Government, in order that their merchant ships might be permitted to traverse the waters of the Gulf unmolested, at length opened the eyes of the Governor of Bombay and Court of Directors as to the fatal impolicy, and, indeed, absurdity, of the instructions enjoined upon their naval officers. The public voice called for the punishment of the piratical horde which had heaped insults and injuries on the English name, and when the blood-red Joasmi flag was seen flaunting itself on the coasts of Cutch and Scinde, and twenty craft were captured in Indian waters, the authorities awoke to a sense of shame and bethought them it was high time to make a hostile move if British trade was not to be driven out of the Persian Gulf. These counsels were quickened by the aggressions of the Wahabees, who had established a preponderance throughout Oman, so that the Imaum was virtually dependent upon them, while, in another direction, their armies appeared

---

* Lieutenant Tanner was a gallant and meritorious officer, and had already done good service to his country. He entered the Royal Navy in March, 1801, on board the 'Fisgard' frigate, under command of the late Sir Byam Martin, Admiral of the Fleet, and assisted in blockading the combined French and Spanish fleets in the port of Brest; he was also employed against the enemy on the coasts of France and Spain, and in cutting out from under the batteries at Corunna the twenty-gun ship 'Neptune,' a gunboat, and some merchantmen. After the peace of Amiens, in 1802, Mr. Tanner was transferred to the Bombay Marine, and served under Commodore Hayes and other officers, on the coast of India and among the Eastern islands of Borneo and the Moluccas, before proceeding to the Persian Gulf, where, and at Mocha in 1820, he saw much service.

before the walls of Bussorah; and, though they received a temporary check at Linjah and Charrack,* whence the Persians from Lar compelled them to retire to Bassadore, on the island of Kishm, their fleet of twenty-two vessels attacked and defeated that of Mahommed Nubhee Khan, Governor of Bushire, at Khor Hassan,† where they captured six ships.

In 1809, Sultan Bin Suggur, the legitimate Joasmi chief, having been invited to Dereeyah, the Wahabee capital, was treacherously detained by Saood; but, having contrived to escape, he found his way to Yemen, embarked at Mocha, and, proceeding to Muscat, threw himself on the protection of the Imaum, to whom he disclaimed all complicity in the attack on the 'Sylph,' and confessed his desire to conform to Captain Seton's treaty of February, 1806.

The Wahabee chief, Saood, having appointed Hussein Bin Ali, cousin of Bin Suggur and Joasmi Sheikh of Rams, a port near Ras-ul-Khymah, his vice-regent over the pirate coast, nominated Wahabee officers throughout the country. Bin Ali was vested with authority to compel the Joasmi chiefs at Linjah and Ras-ul-Khymah to send their vessels to sea in conjunction with those from Rams, and to cruise in the service of the Wahabee Sheikh against all vessels, without exception, appearing in the Gulf, reserving one-fifth as his share of the plunder, the remainder being divided among the captors.‡ This organised system of piracy created such a terror among all the maritime Arab tribes of the Persian Gulf, that they obeyed without reserve the mandates of the terrible Saood rather than incur the vengeance that awaited all who thwarted his will.

According to a well-authenticated calculation, the Joasmi fleet consisted of sixty-three large vessels, and eight hundred and thirteen of smaller size; and this truly formidable armada was manned by nineteen thousand men. This force was increasing, and, in the month following the capture of the 'Minerva,' a fleet of seventy sail, with crews averaging between

---

* Linjah is one of the most flourishing towns on the Persian coast, near the island of Kishm; and Charrack, opposite the small island of Kais (Kenn) is a small Joasmi port, near to which is Charrack Hill, having an elevation of 5,000 feet, and forming a conspicuous feature in the landscape. The hill is said to be the Mount Ochus of the ancients, and the town was once occupied by the Danes, who formed a settlement here.

† Khor Hassan is a town distant three leagues south-west from Ras Reccan, the extreme point of the tongue of land which, projecting to the north, forms on its west side the Gulf of Bahrein. Khor Hassan was the chief town of the famous pirate chief, Rahmah Bin Jaubir, who, in 1826, fought a desperate action with an Uttoobee baghalah of greater size, and finding that he had no chance of success, set fire to his magazine and blew up himself, his vessel, and crew. Such were the desperate freebooters with whom the cruisers of the Bombay Marine had to contend. They gave no quarter, and were astonished at receiving it.

‡ "Historical sketch of the Joasmi," by Mr. F. Warden.

eighty and two hundred men, was cruising about the Gulf and threatening Bushire.

The Bombay Government, having determined to relieve the Imaum* from the power of the Wahabees, and, at the same time, to suppress the Joasmi pirates, organised an Expedition which proceeded to the Persian Gulf in 1809. The instructions, dated the 7th of September, directed to Captain Seton, in political charge of the Expedition, were drawn up with a degree of caution and forbearance towards the Wahabees†, which appeared to denote an intention to truckle to them, and which resulted in rendering nugatory the fruits of the Expedition, notwithstanding that it was notorious that the Joasmi chiefs and people were acting under Wahabee compulsion in engaging in piratical depredations.

The naval portion of the Expedition assembled at Bombay, under command of Commodore John Wainwright, consisted of H.M.'s ships 'Chiffonne,' thirty-six guns, and 'Caroline,' thirty-six guns; the Company's cruisers, 'Mornington,' twenty-two guns; 'Ternate,' sixteen guns; 'Aurora,' fourteen guns; 'Mercury, fourteen guns; 'Nautilus,' fourteen guns; 'Prince of Wales,' fourteen guns; 'Vestal,' ten guns; 'Ariel,' ten

---

* The first treaty on record entered into by the Imaum of Muscat with the Indian Government, was, according to the Rev. G. P. Badger, that dated the 12th of August, 1798. Its object was to secure his alliance against the suspected designs of the French and the commercial rivalry of the Dutch in that quarter, and to obtain his sanction for the establishment of a British factory and garrison at Gombroon, or Bunder Abbas. The second, which is dated 18th of January, 1800, and signed on the part of the Company by Sir John Malcolm, Envoy to Persia, provides for the reception of a British Political Resident at Muscat. In these documents, Seyyid Sultân is styled "Imaum."

† Captain Seton was instructed that "all operations by land were to be avoided otherwise than might be momentarily necessary for the more effectual destruction of the pirate vessels in their harbours; and in any case Captain Seton was to be careful to make it known in due time to the Wahabee and the officers of his Government, that it was our sincere wish to continue, at all times, on terms of friendship with him and with the other States of Arabia, (which were all in subjection to the Wahabees), desiring only to provide for the security of the general commerce of the seas, and of the Gulf of Persia in particular, so long and so unjustifiably interrupted by the Joasmis, in breach, also, of a positive treaty concluded with their chief in 1806; the motives and objects of our interposition, involving no views of aggrandisement on our part, but being altogether limited to the repression of maritime depredations (such as is equally condemned by the professors of every religion). and the just support of our ally, the Imaum of Muscat, cannot reasonably give offence to any other State or Government."

"The British Government," says Morier, in his 'Travels to Persia,' "knowing the intimate connection of the Joasmi pirates with the Wahabees, proceeded in the suppression of the evil with 'cautious judgment;' and when, by the extension of these outrages to themselves they were driven to vindicate the honour of their flag, and to extirpate their enemies, they regarded all the ports, which had not actually committed depredations on the British, as still neutral, and endeavoured to confine their warfare to reprisals for specific acts of violence, rather than to commit themselves generally against the Wahabees, by attacking other piratical tribes of that alliance who had not violated the commerce of England."

guns; 'Fury,' eight guns; and 'Stromboli,' bomb-ketch. The troops, who were embarked on board four large transports, consisted of Her Majesty's 65th Regiment, flank companies of Her Majesty's 47th Regiment, a detachment of the Bombay Artillery, and about one thousand Sepoys, the whole being under the command of Colonel Lionel Smith, of the 65th Regiment.

The fleet sailed from Bombay in September, and it had not quitted the harbour twenty-four hours before an accident occurred, involving loss of life. The 'Stromboli,' bomb-ketch, was in tow astern of the 'Mornington,' when suddenly her bottom fell out and she foundered, carrying with her Lieutenant Taylor, of the Bombay Marine, Lieutenant Sealy, of the Bombay Artillery, and the greater portion of her crew. The despatch of this vessel, laden with a heavy cargo of ordnance and shot and shell, on such a mission, was due to the most culpable carelessness. It appears that a long period anterior to this she had been condemned as unfit for service, and, for three years, lay moored, as a floating battery, off the entrance of Tannah River, as is called the strait which separates the island of Salsette from the mainland. From thence she had been removed to Bombay Harbour and moored off a sunken rock, whence she was taken on the strength of the squadron and fitted out to cross the stormy Arabian Sea, and carry the heaviest and least buoyant cargo that a ship can be freighted with.

After a long passage the Expedition reached Muscat, where it remained some days to refresh and arrange the future plans. The Imaum, on whose behalf the Expedition had been, in a great measure, undertaken, regarded the project of an attack on Ras-ul-Khymah with so small a force as ill-advised, but the British officers and men were sanguine of success. The fleet at length sailed for Ras-ul-Khymah, and the desperate resistance they encountered did not belie the Joasmi reputation for courage and resource.

The ships arrived off that town on the afternoon of the 11th November, but, in consequence of the shallowness of the water, the frigates were not able to approach within four miles; the Company's cruisers, however, owing to their smaller draught, anchored as near as two miles.* Early in the day, a small Joasmi squadron, consisting of the full-rigged ship 'Minerva,' carrying twenty guns, and four dhows, were on the point of proceeding on a cruise, but seeing the hostile armada, they immediately 'up helm' and made for their harbour. Owing to its being low water the 'Minerva' was unable to get in, but ran aground under a small fort about a mile south of the town, where, being attacked by the smaller vessels and gunboats, her crew were driven out of her, and she

---

* See Report of Captain Wainwright to Rear-Admiral W. O. B. Drury, Commander-in-Chief of Her Majesty's ships, dated "H.M.S. 'la Chiffonne,' off Ras-ul-Khymah, November 14, 1809."

was taken possession of; but the heavy fire of musketry which was opened from the shore, obliged the captors to abandon her, after setting her on fire. In this preliminary affair, Lieutenant Allen, commanding the 'Prince of Wales,' gained great praise. This officer ran alongside the 'Minerva' as she lay under protection of the guns of the fort, but unfortunately grounding, his ship became exposed to a heavy and destructive fire. Lieutenant Allen managed to bring some guns to bear on the enemy, and returned their fire so effectually as to drive them out of the fort. In this affair the 'Prince of Wales' had two men killed, and many, including Mr. J. Brown, boatswain, wounded. The squadron now anchored abreast of the town, and preparations were made for the attack, and for landing the troops when some impression had been made upon the works.

"The warm defence made from the shore, and the well-directed fire kept up to prevent the 'Minerva' being got off, began to show us," says an eye-witness, "that we had to deal with an enemy on whom we had not set sufficient value; added to which, it being now discovered that the frigates could not get within three miles of the town, owing to the shallowness of the water, and having lost our only bomb vessel, the prospect was far from cheering."

The only means for cannonading or bombarding with any effect, were thus confined to the smaller cruisers, supported by the gunboats, and such an attack was accordingly made on the 12th, but, notwithstanding a heavy fire of shot and shell maintained, says Captain Wainwright, "with considerable effect for three hours," the inhabitants, from the numerous batteries and entrenchments thrown up in front of the town, kept up a cool and well-directed fire, which did considerable mischief. The narrow, low peninsula on which Ras-ul-Khymah stands, is about three-fourths of a mile in length, and the breadth of the isthmus does not exceed one-fourth of a mile; across the latter was a high wall flanked by four towers, and along the sea front were the batteries and entrenchments before alluded to, evidently thrown up under the direction of some European. The harbour is formed by this peninsula and the mainland opposite, and is about half a mile broad; but nearly the whole of the piratical fleet was hauled up along the inner side of the town. The number of armed men in the place was about five thousand, but it was known that a much greater force could be drawn to their assistance, in the course of two or three days, from the adjacent ports. Towards the outer end of the harbour, the houses were so extremely close that landing appeared impracticable; also the wall across the isthmus opposed great obstacles to landing at the south end of the town, while the strong garrison and the numerous nomad population, rendered it undesirable for the small British force to undertake regular siege operations.

The commanders were not to be dismayed, however, by appearances, but ordered the boats to be prepared to receive the troops at two in the morning of the 13th. The main body, consisting of H.M.'s 65th Regiment, and flank companies of the 47th, with detachments of marines and native troops, rendezvoused alongside one of the cruisers stationed off the south end of the town, while two gunboats and the ships' boats, with a few troops, pulled in towards the mouth of the harbour. The latter, as the first dawn of day appeared, commenced a most furious fire on the north end of the town, which impressed the enemy with the idea that they were trying to force their way into the harbour. Their whole attention was consequently drawn to that point, and a heavy fire of musketry was opened by them, which was the signal for the main body of the British troops to land at the other end of the town and push directly for the wall.

The enemy too late perceived the rapid advance of this body in the boats, and, the fire then opened from their towers and buildings not appearing to check its progress, boldly came down to the beach to dispute the landing, sword in hand. The troops had been ordered to form under the rise of the beach, which would secure them, in some degree, from the enemy's fire; but, before this could be done, and when little more than one company had landed, a desperate attack was threatened on their left. The good conduct and steadiness of the gunboats, which had been appointed to flank the landing, was here most conspicuous, for, steadily reserving their fire of grape to the last moment, the enemy, when nearly in contact with our troops, received a most severe check, which gave time for the formation of the advanced guard of the British; these, in their turn, made a desperate and successful charge, and the first rays of the sun which darted over the lofty mountains forming the background to this scene of strife, lit up the cross of St. George floating on the towers of Ras-ul-Khymah, thus proclaiming that the hour of retribution, though long delayed, had at length struck.

The British forces burned with ardour to advance into the heart of the town; but their commanders, before undismayed by sinister appearances, now showed equal prudence in not giving way to too much elation at the improved prospects of success. Instead of immediately following up the blow and hastily entering a town defended by a well-armed population, they took possession of the land wall and its towers, and of a few of the buildings in the vicinity, in the meantime landing and bringing up their field pieces, ammunition, and scaling ladders. The circumstance of most of the houses being flat-roofed, and furnished with numerous loopholes for musketry, made this measure more advisable. When prepared to advance into the town, an attack was commenced on some of the most commanding buildings, by effecting lodgments in the adjacent ones, supported by the fire of field-pieces, and the cross fire of the gunboats, but, formidable as this nature of attack appeared, the obstinate defence showed that progress by this mode would be most tedious. In Ras-ul-Khymah, as in most Eastern towns, the huts of the poor are intermingled with the houses of the rich, presenting a most motley appeararance, the former being constructed with kajan, (the small branches of the date tree closely interwoven), and the latter of large whitish bricks, which, at a little distance, have the appearance of good stone. Most of the larger houses now became separate fortifications, but this circumstance was turned to their destruction; for, by setting fire to the huts, and the wind blowing along the town from the point at which the landing was effected, the houses became enveloped in flames, and the Joasmis were gradually smoked out of their positions. The most obstinate and gallant resistance was made, however, by the defenders of some of these buildings. In one instance, a large house was defended even after the British had scaled the roof and had dropped several hand grenades into it, through holes worked with their bayonets, when at last its defenders rushed out and made a gallant, though vain, attempt to cut their way through the troops that surrounded it.

It was two in the afternoon before the British troops had worked their way to the centre of the town, where was situated the palace of the Sheikh or Governor. It was expected that a desperate effort would have been made here by the enemy to rally, but, finding the compact order of the British not to be shaken, and the fire of their artillery most destructive, they were soon dislodged from it. The height of this building, and of its tower, gave such a command over its neighbourhood, that the enemy found any further steady resistance vain; they still, however, defended the north end of the town, while the inhabitants effected their escape across the harbour in boats, which it was not the wish of the commanders to prevent.

By four o'clock the seamen of the squadron had set fire to upwards of fifty vessels, thirty of them being very large war dhows;[*] the guns of some of these were loaded, and many of the dhows, and of the houses, had depôts of gunpowder, the explosion of which, with the general conflagration in the town and harbour, added to the scene of desolation and misery attendant on a town taken by assault, and presented a striking picture. Ras-ul-Khymah was found to contain goods of very considerable value, and, to judge from appearances, so complete had been the confidence of the enemy in themselves, that

[*] Captain Wainwright's despatch of the 14th of November, 1809

nothing seemed to have been removed into the interior, many warehouses being found filled with valuable goods, which were now set on fire and consumed. All these valuables might with ease have been embarked on board the captured vessels, which was suggested at the time, but the commanders acted on the principle that the British forces had come to inflict vengeance, and not acquire gain. No looting was permitted, and the only articles taken off to the ships were a little treasure and a few jewels, which had been found in some buildings stormed by our troops,* and which the individual captors were permitted to retain. The town was now set on fire with its contents, and the flames quickly reduced all to ashes. The British loss was trifling, considering the resistance encountered, while at least three hundred of the Joasmis were slain in defending their houses with the desperate tenacity characteristic of the race. Commodore Wainwright expressed his thanks to the captains, officers, and men of the following cruisers, which participated in these operations:—'Mornington,' Captain Jeakes; 'Aurora,' Lieutenant Conyers; 'Nautilus,' Lieutenant Watkins; 'Prince of Wales,' Lieutenant Allen; 'Fury,' Lieutenant Davidson; 'Ariel,' Lieutenant Salter; and 'Vestal,' Lieutenant Phillips.

The punishment thus meted out was condign and terrible, but the deterrent effects were, in a great measure, neutralised by Colonel Smith hastily re-embarking the troops on the morning of the 14th, on receipt of a report that a large body of Arabs was nearing the city from the interior. This hurried exit reassured the Joasmis, who, far from giving way to depression at the sight of their smouldering hearths, a weakness unknown to this fierce race, again opened fire upon the troops. The embarkation, says a writer already quoted, took place at daylight in the morning, and, while the fleet remained at anchor, during the whole of the day parties continued to assemble on the shore displaying their colours, brandishing their swords and spears, and discharging their muskets from all points; so that the conquest was scarcely as complete as could have been wished, since no formal act of submission had yet been shown. The officers of the Expedition are themselves said to have regretted that their work was to be abandoned so prematurely; but whether the report of the reinforcements expected from the interior, or the temporizing and lukewarm instructions of the Bombay Government, guided the measures of the leaders in their retreat, is not accurately known.

From Ras-ul-Khymah the Expedition proceeded to Linjah, a flourishing port of the Joasmis, on the Persian coast, near the island of Kishm, and probably containing at that time nearly

---

* Milburn, in his "Oriental Commerce," says, "Considerable plunder was taken in the town. One soldier is said to have had fourteen hundred gold Mohurs."

ten thousand inhabitants. From this place the people fled into the mountains on the approach of the squadron, taking all their moveables with them. On the 17th of November Linjah was occupied without resistance, and burned to the ground, and the vessels, amounting to twenty, nine of them being large war dhows, were destroyed. H.M.'s ship 'Caroline,' with the transports and the greater portion of the troops, was now sent for supplies to Burka (or Birkeh), a large town on the Batnah coast, about thirty-eight miles to the west of Muscat. Other ships were detached on separate services, such as blockading passages and examining Kongoon and three other Joasmi ports, where, however, no vessels were found. Commodore Wainwright despatched the 'Ternate' and 'Nautilus' to the eastward of Kishm, to prevent the escape of the Luft pirates, while he entered the channel between that island and the main at the western end; but, having got the 'Chiffonne' aground, owing to his ignorance of the navigation and the intricacy of the channel, he determined to proceed to Luft by the eastern passage, and left the 'Vestal' to guard the west end of Kishm.

On the 24th of November the 'Ternate' and 'Nautilus' joined him, and, having procured pilots at the town of Kishm, he sailed for Luft with his flag-ship, and the 'Mornington,' 'Ternate,' 'Nautilus,' and 'Fury,' and the 'Mary,' transport, with five hundred troops, chiefly British. The squadron arrived at noon of the 26th off the town of Luft, a Joasmi port on the north side of the island of Kishm. The channel being narrow and difficult of approach, the 'Ternate,' 'Nautilus,' and 'Fury' were warped into their stations, and a summons was sent on shore, as the people had not abandoned the town, but had taken post in a large and strong castle, having many batteries and redoubts. After twenty-four hours had been expended in fruitless negotiation with the chief, Moolla Hussein, the three cruisers being in their stations, the troops, preceded by the gunboats, were landed under Colonel Smith about two o'clock on the 27th of November. While forming on the beach, a slight skirmish took place with such of the armed men as were flying for shelter to the castle. The troops then advanced towards the fortress, which is described as having walls fourteen feet thick, pierced with loop-holes, and only one entrance through a small gate well cased with iron bars and bolts. It was intended to have blown this gate open with a howitzer, and then to have taken the place by storm; but, on reaching it, while the ranks opened, and the men sought to surround the castle and seek for some other entrance at the same time, they were picked off so rapidly and unexpectedly from the loop-holes above, that a general retreat took place, the howitzer was abandoned even before it had been fired, and the troops sought shelter by lying down behind the ridges of sand and little hillocks immediately underneath the castle walls. An Irish officer, jumping up from his hiding place, and calling on some of his comrades to follow him in an attempt to rescue the howitzer, was immediately killed, and some others, who only raised their heads to look around them, were picked off by the musketry from above. The whole of the troops were accordingly ordered to keep under shelter until the darkness of the night favoured their retreat to the beach, whence they re-embarked after sunset, without molestation.

"Meantime," says Commodore Wainwright in his despatch of the 7th of December, "the gunboats and the 'Fury,' which being of light draught, had been towed within musket shot of the fort, kept up a ruinous fire which very much shattered the strong fort by sunset." A message was then conveyed to Moolla Hussain in the castle, summoning him for a second time to submit, and fixing until two a.m. for the period of evacuation, when, in the event of non-compliance, it was threatened that the squadron should bombard the castle from a nearer anchorage, and no quarter be afterwards shown. With the dawn of morning, all eyes were directed to the fortress, when, to the surprise of the whole Expedition, a man was seen waving the Union Jack on the summit of its walls. This gallant action was performed by an officer of the Bombay Marine, Lieutenant Hall, who had commanded the 'Stromboli,' bomb vessel, at the time of her sinking, but had saved himself by swimming, and now commanded the 'Fury, which was one of the vessels nearest to the shore. "During the night," says Buckingham, "he had gone on shore alone, taking an Union Jack in his hand, and advanced singly to the castle gate. The fortress had already been abandoned by the greater number of the inhabitants, but some few still remained there. These, however, fled at the approach of an individual, either from deeming all further resistance unavailing, or from supposing, probably, that no one would come singly, but as a herald to others immediately following for his support. Be this as it may, the castle was entirely abandoned, and the British flag waved on its walls by this daring officer, to the surprise and admiration of the whole fleet." The town and fortifications, together with eleven dhows, were then taken possession of, and the latter were burnt. As Luft had been taken by the Joasmis from the Imaum of Muscat, it was delivered over, together with property to the value of £20,000 belonging to the Imaum, to Sheikh Dewish, head of a tribe of Arabs friendly to His Highness. The loss in this affair was very heavy, the squadron having twenty-seven killed and wounded, including Mr. Hay, Midshipman of the 'Mornington,' Mr. James W. Guy, Midshipman of the 'Ternate,' and Mr. T. Smith, boatswain of the 'Nautilus.'*

* *See* Captain Wainwright's despatch dated Burka Road, 7th December.

The squadron now proceeded to Moghu,* and also visited Sharjah, Jezirat-el-Hamrah,† and Rams, three small towns on the opposite coast, near Ras-ul-Khymah, where nothing was effected beyond the destruction of such vessels as were found at each of them, this, as it would seem, being the extent of the orders of the Bombay Government to the leaders of the Expedition. When the bottom of the Gulf had been thus swept round, the Expedition returned to Burka Roads, where they rejoined the remainder of the force, including the 'Caroline' frigate, and remained some days at this rendezvous in order that the British commander might concert fresh measures with Seyyid Said. His Highness, who, in the first instance, considered as desperate the attack on Ras-ul-Khymah with so small a force, warmly expressed his great satisfaction at the success of his gallant allies, and his gratitude for the benefit he had derived, particularly by the capture of Luft and its surrender to him; he now proposed to accompany the Expedition with a large force to attack Shinas‡ and Khor Fukaun, which had been taken from him by the Joasmis.

On their arrival at Shinas on the 31st of December, says Buckingham, a summons to surrender was sent to the Wahabee chief, Ibn Abdool Uzzeer,§ the favourite general of Saood, to which he

---

* Moghu or Moghunah, is situated in the bay between Ras Bostonah and Ras Yarid on the Persian shore. Until the acquisition of Bassadore on the north-west extremity of the island of Kishm, Moghu was the station for the Indian Navy squadron. In "Nearchus' Voyage" (Gronov. edition) Moghu is called Sidodone. Ras Yarid is called by Niebuhr, Ras-el-Jerd, or "Baldhead." Many other places in the Persian Gulf are rendered classical by the allusions to them in the "Voyage of Nearchus," B.C. 328. To the West of Kongoon is Uhm-Kheilah, called by sailors, Cape Berdistan (or Verdistan) the "Place of Cold." Ormuz, mentioned by Arrian (p. 352) is called Organa, Gerun, and Gyrina by Strabo. Minab, or Minaw, from Mina-aub (blue water) is called Anamis by Nearchus. Neoptana, in Karmania, is the country of the Ichthyophagi, which terminates at Cape Jask (Bardis) Arrian, p. 344. Other places outside the Gulf, identified as having been visited by Alexander's Admiral, are Cape Gwadel, or Ras Noo, which he describes, Gwadel Bay, called Mosarna, and Ashtola island, which he calls Carmine. The stadium of Nearchus, it should be noted, is 18·7 to the nautical mile. Koh Mubarek, near Cape Jask, means the "Blessed Mount," and is called by Marcian, the "Round Mount of Semiramis" (Geogr. Minores, p. 21). It is not mentioned by Arrian.

† This place is a town and fort ten miles from Ras-ul-Khymah, built on an island in an inlet. The fort has five or six towers, one a high square structure, with two rows of windows. Rams, consisting of a port and small town, stands six miles north-east of Ras-ul-Khymah.

‡ Shinas is a considerable town, with a strong fort, twenty-seven miles to the north-west of Sohar on the Batnah (or the "Inner") coast, which extends from Muscat to Khor Kelbeh. Khor Fukaun, on this coast, is in a sandy bay, and is a place of no importance.

§ The native Omanee historian, whose account is translated by Dr. G. P. Badger, makes no mention of this General, but says that the Governor of the Castle, one Mohamed-bin-Ahmed, on the commencement of the bombardment, proceeded to procure assistance from Muttak-el-Mutairy, the Wahabee general, but was unable to break through the investing force. After the departure of the British, he says, Muttak fell upon the army of the Imaum, and put them to flight, Seyyid Said escaping with difficulty.

replied by a prompt refusal; upon which a bombardment was opened from the ships and boats, but without producing much effect. On the following morning the whole of the troops were landed, and a regular encampment formed on the shore, with a battery, completed on the evening of the 2nd of January, 1810, and other necessary siege works. A heavy bombardment was opened from the ships of war and battery, throughout the night of the 2nd, during which about four thousand shot and shell were discharged against the fortress, to which the people had fled for refuge after burning down the town. Early in the morning of the 3rd, Colonel Smith wishing, like a brave soldier, to spare so gallant a foe, again sent a summons to the chief, who replied that death was preferable to surrender, and so well was he seconded by his men, that when the towers and other works were crumbling round them under the terrible fire of the British squadron and battery, they hurled back upon the assailants the grenades and fire balls before they could burst, and even thrust their spears up through the fragments of the ruins in which they themselves remained buried. Twice during the bombardment had Colonel Smith ceased firing in order to spare an unavailing effusion of blood, and it was only, when the breach of the main work was reported practicable, and the troops were on the point of storming, that the survivors, on being assured of protection from the fury of the troops of our ally, the Imaum of Muscat, surrendered to the British commander. The loss in killed and wounded sustained by the enemy was said to exceed one thousand. The fort was given up to the Imaum's troops, but it was so much shattered that His Highness did not think it prudent to keep possession of it.

Seyyid Said expressed some hesitation as to the policy of attacking Khor Fukaun, from an apprehension of experiencing a similar obstinate resistance to that encountered at Shinas, which would only render the fort untenable; all intention of attacking it was, therefore, abandoned, as it had no British interests connected with it, there being no pirate vessels belonging to that port. The troops of the Expedition, accordingly, returned to Bombay, but the frigates and cruisers repaired from Muscat to the Gulf, where they remained several months before they finally dispersed.* Notwithstanding this severe chastisement, the

* On the return of the Expedition to Bombay, the general expectation of some reward for these services became so well known to Captain Wainwright and Colonel Smith, that they felt it their duty to represent it to the Government of India. There were three grounds for such an expectation; first, nearly the whole of the vessels destroyed were vessels of war, and ready for sea, which entitled the captors to the allowance usually called head money; secondly, the Expedition were entitled to the property recaptured, and formerly belonging to the Imaum of Muscat, as lawful prize, but from the services that sovereign had rendered the East India Company, by supplying the Expedition with wood and water, and boats for landing the troops, the commanders thought themselves justified in giving it up on the part of the Company; and lastly, the circumstance

snake was scotched, not killed, and, before another decade, a second Expedition was demanded finally to root out this powerful race of pirates.

The commanders were unable to form a treaty with Ras-ul-Khymah, Sheikh Sultan Bin Suggur, the legitimate chief, having been seized by the Wahabees, and his Government completely overthrown; independently of which, no treaty could be binding on the Joasmis, without the direct authority and participation of Saood,* on whose will they were entirely dependent. Such, however, had been the impression created by the success of the operations against the principal pirate ports, that the commanders succeeded in their demands for the destruction of all the dhows and large boats of the petty chieftains from Rams to Abu Haile, on the Arabian side, as well as at Moghu on the coast of Persia. The chief of Charrack, not having any dhows or large boats, was admonished to refrain from giving encouragement or protection to pirates in future. A similar message was sent to the chief of Nikiloo,† with a demand, at the request of the Imaum, for the release of Sheikh Jubara of Congoon‡. It was not deemed material to insist on the destruction of trankies and small boats—a measure that would have been hard on the poorest of the inhabitants, and created an odium against the British name, which did not generally exist, as many

of the valuable property at Ras-ul-Khymah having been destroyed from political motives, and the great personal risk to which every individual had been exposed, in fighting against an enemy from whom no quarter was to have been expected, had any reverse taken place. The answer returned to this application was, that there was no precedent for such a proceeding; so neither officers nor men received any honorary or pecuniary reward.

* A communication was opened with Saood advising him to prohibit the piracies of his dependents, and in answer, the Wahabee chief observed:—"The cause of the hostilities carrying on between me and the members of the faith, is their having turned away from the Book of the Creator, and refused to submit to their own prophet Mahomet. It is not, therefore, those of another sect against whom I wage war, nor do I interfere in their hostile operations, nor assist them against any one; whilst under the power of the Almighty, I have risen superior to all my enemies. . . . Under these circumstances, I have deemed it necessary to advise you that I shall not approach your shores, and have interdicted the followers of the Mahomedan faith and their vessels from offering any molestation to your vessels; any of your merchants, therefore, who may appear in, or wish to come to my ports, will be in security; and any person on my part who may repair to you, ought in like manner to be in safety." He concludes the letter with a contemptuous reference to the Joasmis whom the English had just conquered, "Be not, therefore, elated with the conflagration of a few vessels, for they are of no estimation in my opinion, in that of their owners, or of their country. In truth then war is bitter; and a fool only engages in it, as a poet has said."

† Nikiloo is a town on the Persian coast, opposite to Shitwar Islet at the eastern end of Shaikh Shuaib.

‡ Congoon, or Konkun, on the same coast, has a good anchorage, and behind the town are some hills, one of remarkable appearance being called Barn Hill. Congoon was the name used in the Persian Gulf up to the time when, by the adoption of the new Hunterian system of orthography, the name became transmogrified into Konkun, to the unbounded bewilderment of the "ancient mariner," as in numerous other instances of proper names in the Persian Gulf.

of the small villages on both sides of the Gulf, had been compelled to join in piratical pursuits. As the Uttoobees of Bahrein had never committed any depredations against British trade, even at times when the Joasmis were enriching themselves by their frequent capture of our vessels, the commanders abstained from attacking Khor Hassan.

On his arrival at Bombay, Commodore Wainwright, both in General Orders and in a report to Government, expressed in the warmest terms his approval of the discipline, efficiency, and enterprise displayed by the Bombay Marine during the period they were under his command. The Government of the day highly appreciated this testimony, and, in consideration of the good services rendered by the officers, created a new grade, by appointing eight Lieutenants to be Commanders, a rank hitherto unknown in the Service. By this increase the strength of the Marine now stood thus :—One commodore, one master-attendant (the senior captain), eight senior and eight junior captains, eight commanders, twenty-six first and twenty-four second-lieutenants, and forty-eight midshipmen.

From tho Persian Gulf a portion of the Service proceeded to take part in the Expedition against Mauritius, and thence, in the following year to Java, where they earned fresh distinction. In the Eastern Islands they were actively employed between the years 1811-16 in the various expeditions against pirates and Native States, already detailed, and only returned to Bombay to participate in the final operations against the Joasmis.

It was the prevalent opinion at Bombay, founded on the results of this Expedition, that the Joasmis had been rendered quite incapable of committing any further depredations by sea. The Resident at Bussorah confirmed this view, but added :— "Such was the revengeful and vindictive spirit of the Wahabee tribe, and of the inhabitants on the Arabian side of the Gulf, under the jurisdiction and authority of Sheikh Saood, that they will attempt to wreak their vengeance on any defenceless British vessels which they may meet." Accordingly, as their country produced no timber suitable for ship or boat-building, Mr. Mannesty recommended a prohibition being imposed on the exportation of timber from the ports of India either to those of the Red Sea or the Persian Gulf, even including Muscat, from which place the pirates would contrive to procure it. But, though this course was strongly approved by Sir John Malcolm, it was not adopted by the Bombay Government. The lesson of 1809, though severe, did not create an abiding impression, although one would have thought that the Joasmi pirates had learnt that honesty was not only the best policy, but that pearl-fishing during the season, with the monotonous and uneventful life of trading, was on the whole more profitable, as the large returns of piracy were swallowed up by such wholesale acts of vengeance and confiscation as the destruction of their fleets and conflagration of their towns with their accumulated plunder.

The 'Benares' and 'Prince of Wales' cruised in the Gulf in 1811, when the British flag was respected, but, on their return to Bombay in November, the Joasmis recommenced their depredations. In the beginning of 1812, and in the following year, they destroyed several large dhows and baghalahs belonging to the ports of Bussorah and Congoon; boats navigating under British colours did not escape depredations, while others were detained at Porebunder, and prevented from prosecuting their mercantile pursuits. In 1813 the Imaum prepared an expedition against the port of Ras-ul-Khymah, for the purpose of reinstating in his Government Sheikh Sultan Bin Suggur, who, as already mentioned, had been treacherously confined by Saood, but succeeded in effecting his escape. As Bin Suggur promised that if the Imaum would restore him to his hereditary possessions, he would ever consider himself his vassal and would abstain from committing piracies, his Highness requested Mr. Bruce, the British agent at Bushire, at that time on a visit to Muscat, to accompany him to witness the treaty which he proposed entering into with Sultan Bin Suggur, and for the purpose also of negotiating a separate treaty to the same effect with the Joasmi chief on the part of the British Government. As the renewal of the treaty entered into by Bin Suggur with Captain Seton in 1806, was deemed essential for restraining the piratical acts of his subjects, Mr. Bruce was instructed to adopt the necessary measures, and to contract similar engagements with the other chieftains in the Gulf.

The Imaum's expedition failed, but a second one, equipped in 1814, for a similar purpose, terminated in a peace concluded between the Imaum and the Joasmis, by which Sheikh Sultan Bin Suggur was established at Sharjah. Later on, in consequence of piratical depredations, remonstrances were transmitted by Mr Bruce to the chief of the Wahabees at Dereeyah, and to his vice-gerent at Ras-ul-Khymah, Hussein-bin-Rahmah, who stated in reply that he was not aware that any vessels bearing the British pass and colours had been captured by the Joasmis, but that if it should prove to be the case, such property as might be forthcoming would be restored, and that in future he would issue instructions to his tribe not to molest any ship or vessel under British colours. On the 2nd of October, a Wukeel, or envoy, arrived at Bushire with letters from the Wahabee Chief* and Hussein-bin-Rahmah; the former disapproving of

---

* Great reverses fell upon the Wahabee cause at this time. In 1813 Abdullah, son of Saood, was driven out of the Hedjaz by Ibrahim Pasha, adopted son of Mehemet Ali, Pasha of Egypt, and, in the following year, occurred the death of Saood. Five years later Abdullah, who succeeded his father, was taken prisoner and executed at Constantinople, and the Wahabee capital, Dereeyah, was destroyed. Before the end of 1824, Toorkee, son of Abdullah, who had been

the conduct of the Joasmi chief and of his tribe, and binding himself to compel him to deliver up such goods as could be proved to have been captured, while the latter again denied having taken any British property. The Wukeel was authorised to enter into an engagement with Mr. Bruce, who, accordingly, deemed it advisable to propose a few preliminary articles of agreement with the envoy, renouncing all claims and passing an act of oblivion on the past, on the conditions specified in the engagement. The Joasmi chief having expressed his intention to depute an agent to Bombay, Mr. Bruce was induced to conclude the preliminary agreement in question. But it was no better than waste paper, for in August, 1814, some vessels, bearing the British pass and colours, were captured off Porebunder. Mr. Bruce, on receipt of orders to remonstrate against this act, despatched a dhow to Ras-ul-Khymah, with letters to Hussein Bin Rahmah and his Wukeel, who had entered into the preliminary engagement above specified, and with one also to Sultan Bin Suggur at Linjah, but, to his astonishment, the Nakhoda returned in a few days in a most wretched plight, and stated that he had been robbed by the chief of Linjah, and that the Ras-ul-Khymah Sheikh had seized his boat. This flagrant breach of faith was speedily followed by the capture of a baghalah belonging to the Imaum of Muscat, whilst at anchor in the roads of Moghu, whose people were privy to this depredation, and had, in fact, given information of the baghalah being there. Besides the seizure of this vessel, which was laden with horses for the remount of the 17th Dragoons, and with sulphur on account of British subjects, six others were captured off the Scinde coast.

The success that attended the subsequent cruises undertaken by the Joasmis, added so much to their strength that it induced most of the other ports on the same coast, from Cape Nabend to the southward, to follow the same system. The Sheikh of Charrack, in particular, was encouraged to form a connection with Ras-ul-Khymah, and Abdoolla Bin Ahmed of Bahrein openly avowed his determination to adopt piracy, as the surest mode of acquiring wealth and strength. Thus the Arab tribes of the Persian Gulf once more embarked on a course of flagrant and open breach of the law of nations.

In 1815 a vessel belonging to Bombay, sailing under a British pass and colours, was captured off Muscat, the greater part of her crew put to death, and a ransom exacted for the release of the remainder. About this time a Joasmi fleet, consisting of a ship and twenty-five baghalahs and batils, while cruising at the entrance to the Gulf, fell in with the Imaum, who was on the

taken prisoner by Ibrahim Pasha in 1819, but had effected his escape, succeeded in recapturing Riadh, the new capital near Dereeyah, and partially restored the ascendancy of the Wahabees.

look-out for them with a squadron, consisting of the 'Caroline,' frigate, with two other ships and a number of smaller vessels. A smart action ensued off Cape Keriat, during which the Joasmis attempted to board the Imaum's ship, and had actually got possession of the forecastle, when they were dislodged by the guns from the poop being fired forward, loaded with grape. The Imaum's other vessels having fallen astern, he was obliged to bear up and run into Muscat. His Highness wrote to the Governor of Bombay requesting the assistance of some of their ships, and, early in 1816, renewed operations against the Joasmis, but, beyond an ineffectual blockade of Ras-ul-Khymah for four months, he was unable to do anything against them; nor, in the opinion of Mr. Bruce, was he capable of effecting anything without British support, for which he would have gladly ceded any of the ports or islands in the Gulf that were subject to him.*

Encouraged by the seeming impunity they enjoyed, the Joasmi pirates attacked, on the 6th of January, 1816, off Dwarka, the Hon. Company's armed pattamar, 'Deriah Dowlut,' having a crew of native officers and men, which was proceeding to Porebunder. On the pattamar showing the Company's colours, the pirate, a large baghalah, fired a shot at her, and a smart action ensued, which was kept up with great briskness until two more piratical vessels appeared, which convinced the syrang that the only chance of escape lay in flight; all sail was therefore made upon the pattamar. A running fire continued for three

* On the 15th of June, 1816, Mr. Bruce reported that the Imaum had proceeded with a large force to reduce the Uttoobee and Joasmi Arabs to his allegiance, having been joined by the Asseloo and Congoon Arabs, and three vessels from Bushire despatched to his assistance by orders of the Governor of Shiraz. With this armament the Imaum proceeded to Bahrein, and landed the troops on the island of Arad, which is separated from Bahrein by a narrow channel for boats, and commenced the attack with some prospect of success, but ultimately experienced a signal defeat with great loss, two of his principal Sirdars being amongst the killed.

Mr. Bruce, who had quitted Bahrein a few days before the Imaum arrived, wrote to His Highness to dissuade him from the attack, as he knew that many of the Imaum's troops were secretly in the interests of the Uttoobees, and offered his mediation to settle his differences with the tribe, but received no reply to the proposal. The Imaum, after this defeat, proceeded to Congoon with the whole of his fleet, for the purpose of taking on board a reinforcement of troops, consisting of one thousand musketeers and four hundred irregular cavalry, which the Prince of Shiraz had engaged to furnish on certain conditions: but the expedition was abandoned, the Imaum having discovered that the Government of Persia was actuated by motives of treachery, and contemplated his seizure and that of some of his chiefs.

In the month of May, 1817, Rahmah bin Jaubir, a chief in the Wahabee interest, who was at war with the Uttoobees, proceeded to Muscat, with the view of prevailing on the Imaum to make another attack on Bahrein, but His Highness was too much occupied in his own territories to undertake it, having met with a repulse from a Joasmi force that marched against Khor Fukaun, which surrendered to these freebooters. Thus matters stood at Muscat at the time of the second and decisive expedition of the Bombay Government against the Joasmi pirates.

z 2

hours, when the syrang received a severe wound and was carried below; in about an hour after, the tindal, who had assumed the command, was killed by a shot in the stomach; the three baghalahs had by this time closed, and, instantly boarding, by force of numbers overpowered the brave little crew of the 'Deriah Dowlut.' Some jumped overboard, and others into the hold, and out of a crew of thirty-three, seventeen were murdered, eight were carried prisoners to Ras-ul-Khymah, and the remainder, being wounded, were landed on the coast and proceeded to Bombay. The 'Deriah Dowlut' only mounted two 12-pounder and three 2-pounder iron guns, while the pirate vessels carried each six 9-pounders, and had crews of from one hundred to two hundred men, armed with swords, spears, and creeses. But their next venture was not equally successful.

In this same month of January, they attempted to cut off a large baghalah laden with treasure, in tow of the 'Aurora,' fourteen guns, Captain Jeakes, upon which the cruiser wore round and fired into them. After a smart action, during which Captain Jeakes exhibited seamanlike skill of a high order, in manœuvring his ship so as to prevent the pirates from capturing his convoy, the enemy were beaten off and made sail. In this affair the Joasmi fleet consisted of about fifteen dhows and trankies, and the fire of the 'Aurora' was so sustained and accurate that she sank many of them, the remainder making their escape under cover of night.

Captain Richard Kinchant, who was Acting-Lieutenant on board the 'Aurora,' writes to us of this action: " At Bushire we received orders from the Political Resident of the Persian Gulf, Captain Bruce, formerly of the Bombay Marine, to convoy to Muscat, on our way to Bombay, a large baghalah containing a considerable amount of treasure for the Imaum of Muscat. On our passage down the Gulf, one evening a little before sunset, we fell in without about fifteen dhows and trankies, and they looked to me like a forest of masts ahead with all sails down. We looked well to the baghalah astern, in tow of us, knowing that their object in laying in wait for us was to cut her off. The 'Aurora' stood on her course with a light nor'-wester, steering right through the fleet, and as we approached we gave them both broadsides, shotted with grape or canister, which told well. During the action that ensued we sank many and disabled others. We had to pay great attention to our convoy to prevent their cutting her tow-rope, and some of the smaller craft, pulling twenty oars, ventured near at times for that purpose. Captain Jeakes directed me to superintend the management of the baghalah, so I was on the poop of the 'Aurora' the whole time, and had no very easy task in keeping so towering a vessel close to the 'Aurora' without great risk, and small shot came fast and thick among us on the poop. We continued to pepper them with grape and canister, and if we could only have had two hours more daylight, we should have given a better account of them. At dusk, the chief of Ras-ul-Khymah, who was in command, burnt a blue light and stood over to the Arabian coast with the remainder of his fleet. Captain Jeakes thanked me on the quarter-deck for my management of the baghalah, which would have been a great prize to them. On our arrival at Muscat, the Imaum presented Captain Jeakes with a valuable sword and Arab horse, which became a great favourite with the sailors."

Soon after this action the Joasmis chased and fired at the American ship 'Persia;' they also attacked the 'Macaulay,' and overhauled a French schooner bound from Mauritius to Bussorah, sailing under convoy of a ship of that nation, and, in broad daylight, took out of her much treasure, coolly informing the captain on his remonstrating, that had the crew been English all their throats would certainly have been cut. So great was now the dread entertained of the Joasmis that Mr. Bruce could not obtain a vessel to convey to Ras-ul-Khymah a letter of remonstrance to the chief in regard to these depredations. A few weeks later several other captures took place, including a ship, name unknown, under English colours, from Pulo Penang, which was taken by five dhows full of pirates, who murdered all the crew and passengers.* In the same year four ships sailing from the port of Surat bound to Mocha, under British colours, were taken in the Arabian Gulf by a Joasmi squadron under their Admiral, Ameer Ibrahim, and the crews were almost all murdered. The loss of property was estimated at over ten lacs of rupees, and many other captures were made of vessels sailing under our protection, attended by similar acts of atrocity. Nevertheless the retaliatory measures of the Government were limited to remonstrances—for it will scarcely be credited that the commanders of the cruisers were instructed not "to sink, burn, or destroy" the piratical craft whenever met with, but to avoid firing on them until their hostile intent was made apparent—and to the disposal of the cruisers for the

* A Bombay letter, speaking of the Joasmi method of capturing ships, says :— "It depends solely in boarding; with the best mode of effecting which they are acquainted, and for which purpose they approach the stern of the vessels, and if not opposed by guns in that quarter, and by boarding nets, they board and overpower the vessels by numbers of men. The best precautions, therefore, which can be used by our merchant vessels, are stern chasers loaded with grape-shot, boarding nets and musketry, which, in addition to its own charge, should receive two or three pistol balls over the ball-cartridge. These merciless freebooters, we understand, inquired with a savage anxiety, if there were any Europeans on board the 'Deriah Dowlut,' whom they would immediately have massacred; and the manner in which they murdered the crew of that vessel, was by placing the necks of the unfortunate men over the gunnel of their vessel, whom they required to repeat the leading verse of the Koran, and as soon as they came to the part which differed from the tenets of the Wahabee sect, it was the signal for execution, and the head was instantly severed from the body."

protection of the trade, until the exigencies of the public service in other quarters should admit of an expedition being detached against the pirates. Surprise has been expressed by contemporary writers that the Joasmis, whose fleets were supposed to have been destroyed in their ports during the 1809 Expedition, should have so quickly recovered the effects of their losses as to cover the seas with their ships; but this apparently unaccountable circumstance is explained by the fact that owing to the Persian Gulf having never been surveyed—a task accomplished by the officers of the Indian Navy a few years later—certainly one half of the Joasmi ships had been secreted in the various inlets and backwaters, which abound in the pirate coast, probably to a greater extent than on any coast-line of similar extent in the world. Country ships and merchantmen generally were now forced to sail under convoy of ships of war, and the services of two or three of H.M.'s ships, in addition to those of the Company that were available, were called into requisition.

The Bombay Government always appeared to regard with equanimity the attacks of the pirates upon their small cruisers, but, as in 1808, when the merchant ship 'Minerva' was captured, they vigorously resented the seizure of the four Surat ships. After much delay, owing to the majority of the ships of the Bombay Marine being employed in the Eastern Islands, a small squadron was assembled at Bombay for despatch to the Persian Gulf, consisting of H.M.'s sloop 'Challenger,' eighteen guns, Captain Bridges, and the Company's cruisers, 'Mercury,' fourteen guns, and 'Vestal,' ten guns. By these a despatch was forwarded to the Resident at Bushire, instructing him to demand from the chief at Ras-ul-Khymah, the restitution of the Surat ships and cargoes. The squadron left Bombay in the early part of September, 1816, and, after a long voyage, in which the 'Mercury' lost her mainmast, the 'Challenger' reached Bushire in November, and the other vessels a few days afterwards. In the meantime, the 'Ariel,' which had touched at Bushire on her way down from Bussorah, had been despatched to Ras-ul-Khymah with a letter from Mr. Bruce, inquiring into the circumstances of the captures alluded to, and reproaching the Joasmis for a breach of faith in their departure from their agreement to respect the British flag. To this they replied by a flat denial of the charge of having captured English vessels hailing from Surat, coupled with the remark, that, if even they had seized the vessels in question, they would not thereby have departed from the terms of the treaty, and that they would respect the sect of Christians and their property, but none other; that they did not consider any part of Western India as ours except Bombay and Mangalore; and that if we interfered in favour of the Hindoos and other unbelievers of India, we might take all India and Muscat too, when nothing would be left for them to plunder. This was plain speaking indeed, and to such diplomatic utterances only the sword could give any adequate reply. On the 18th of November, the 'Ariel' having returned to Bushire, the squadron of four ships sailed thence, with Mr. Bruce and Mr. Taylor on board, and arrived before Ras-ul-Khymah on the 26th of November.

At daylight on the following morning, a boat was sent from the 'Challenger' to take on shore Mr. Taylor and an Arab interpreter, as bearers of a letter from Mr. Bruce, stating the firm conviction of the British Government, that the capture of vessels flying the English flag was committed with a knowledge of their nationality, and insisting upon the immediate restoration of the plundered property, amounting to about twelve lacs of rupees. A demand was also made in this communication that the commander of the piratical squadron, Ameer Ibrahim, should be delivered up for punishment, and that two of the sons of the chiefs should be placed in the hands of the Bombay Government as hostages for their future conduct. A refusal to comply with all or any of these requisitions, would be considered as a defiance of British power, and therefore noon was fixed for the return of a definitive answer, by which the future movements of the squadron would be regulated.

The bearers of this letter soon returned and reported that they were denied admittance within the gates of the town, upon which Captain Bridges proceeded on shore, and was conducted through the town to the presence of the pirate chief, who was attended by about fifty armed followers. An eye-witness, Mr. Buckingham, says:—"The chief Hussein-bin-Rahmah was a small man, apparently about forty years of age, with an expression of cunning in his look, and something particularly sarcastic in his smile. One of his eyes had been wounded, but his other features were good, and his teeth beautifully white and regular, his complexion very dark, and his beard scanty and chiefly confined to his chin. He was dressed in the usual Arab garments, and a Cashmere shawl turban, and a scarlet benish of the Persian form, to distinguish him from his followers. These were habited in the plainest garments, with long shirts and keffeas, or handkerchiefs, thrown loosely over the head; and most of them, as well as their leader, wore large swords of the old Norman form, with long straight blades of great breadth, and large cross handles, perfectly plain short spears were also borne by some, with circular shields of tough hide ornamented with knobs of metal and gilding. They are thought to have at present about sixty large vessels from their own port, manned with crews of from eighty to three hundred men. Forty other craft of a smaller size may be counted among their auxiliaries, from the ports of Sharjah and Rams, on the Arabian coast. Charrack and

Linjah, on the Persian coast, and Luft, on the inside of the island of Kishmah, are subject to their authority. Their force, if concentrated, would thus amount to at least one hundred vessels, with perhaps four hundred pieces of cannon, and about eight thousand fighting men, well armed with muskets, swords, and spears. No circumstances are ever likely to bring these, however, all together; but on an invasion of their chief town, at Ras-ul-Khymah, they could certainly command a large reinforcement of Wahabees from the desert within ten or fifteen days notice. The cannon and musketry of these pirates are chiefly procured from the vessels which they capture; but their swords, shields, spears, and ammunition are mostly brought from Persia."

On returning to the 'Challenger,' Captain Bridges waited until the hour of noon had passed, when a gun was fired, the topsails sheeted home, and the signal made to prepare to weigh anchor, though it was intended to allow another hour of grace for the answer from the shore. In the meantime a boat arrived with deputies from the chief, bringing a reply, in which he stated the impossibility of restoring either the property demanded, since that had long since been divided and consumed, or paying the amount of its value in money, as this was more than their whole present wealth; he also peremptorily refused to deliver up Ameer Ibrahim, who was his kinsman and near friend, denying that this chief was guilty of anything which deserved punishment in capturing, with the vessels under his command, the persons and property of idolators and strangers to the true God. The Wahabee chief offered to send deputies to Bombay to treat on the affair, and it was added, that as all things were of God, and deliberation might possibly accord better with his councils than hasty determination, he requested a delay until noon of the following day, in order that he might know what Divine wisdom had decreed should take place between them.

The letter of instruction from the Government of Bombay had ordered that, on the refusal of the Joasmi chief to comply with the requisitions therein stated, the squadron was to quit the place, after signifying to him that he might expect the displeasure of the British Government. As, however, it was determined to allow him until the following noon to deliberate, the squadron remained at anchor, until the wind having freshened at sunset from the north-west, and a heavy swell setting into the bay, it was deemed imprudent to continue at anchor there during the night. The ships, therefore, weighed in company and stood out to sea, the wind increasing to a gale towards midnight.

The squadron lay at the anchorage off the island of Anjar, on the opposite coast, during the whole of the night of the 28th, until the strength of the north-west gale having abated, it weighed anchor soon after sunrise, and stood across the gulf towards Ras-ul-Khymah, where they anchored at two p.m. On the following day a letter was sent to the chief signifying the cause of their hurried departure, and granting him until the following noon to prepare his final answer to the original requistions.

At about noon on the 1st of December, a boat appeared, bringing some messengers from Hussein-bin-Rahmah with an answer as unsatisfactory as his former replies. The signal was now made to weigh, and the squadron bore down nearly in line, under easy sail, and with the wind right aft, or on shore; the 'Mercury' being on the starboard hand, the 'Challenger' next in order in the centre, the 'Vestal' following in the same line, and the 'Ariel' completing the division. A large fleet of small boats was seen standing in from Cape Mussundom, and escaped by keeping close along-shore and passing over the bar, thus getting into the creek, or backwater, behind the town. The squadron continued to stand on in a right line towards the four anchored dhows, gradually shoaling to two and a half fathoms, when stream anchors were dropped under-foot, with springs on the cables, so that each vessel lay with her broadside on to the shore. A fire was now opened from the ships in succession, the 'Vestal' discharging the first gun upon the four dhows anchored close in shore, which were full of Arabs brandishing their weapons in the air, their whole number probably exceeding six hundred men; but owing to the great distance the fire was not very effective. The 'Challenger,' having a draught of fourteen feet, could not approach within a mile of the beach, but, at the risk of grounding, the 'Vestal' and 'Ariel' dropped to within six inches of their own draught of water, and under the 'Mercury' there was less than a foot. These ships now re-opened their fire, which they maintained with much spirit. The shot from the dhows fell short, but two of the forts, after some time past in preparation, at length opened with some effect, and one shot carried away the 'Vestal's' fore-shrouds in its passage, and then dropped under the weather-bow. The Arab colours were displayed on all the forts, crowds of armed men were assembled on the beach, bearing large banners on poles, and dancing around them with their arms, as if rallying around a sacred standard, so that there was no sign of submission. Seeing that all the efforts of the ships were unavailing, Captain Bridges signalled to cease firing, and, about four o'clock, the squadron weighed and stood out to sea.

On the following day the ships separated, the 'Mercury' and 'Ariel' proceeding to Sharjah, Linjah, and Charrack, for negotiations similar to those entered into at Ras-ul-Khymah; the 'Vestal' to Bombay, where she arrived on the 16th of

December; and the 'Challenger' to Muscat to give information of hostilities, and afford protection to vessels bound upward from thence, as besides five heavy armed baghalahs blocking the entrance to the Bussorah River, the Joasmis had fifteen sail cruising between Ras-ul-Had* and Cape Jask on the Persian shore.

In October, 1817, some piratical craft landed their crews at Busheab Island,† in the Persian Gulf, and burnt and plundered the villages on the island, carrying off the cattle and killing a large number of the inhabitants. Before the close of the year, also, they entered the harbour of Asseloo, and took five large baghalahs valued at £30,000, and murdered the crews. So great was the fear of these pirates, inspired by their sanguinary acts of cruelty, that a panic seized the inhabitants of Bushire, who were with great difficulty restrained from entirely deserting the city. The Joasmi chief, apprehending an attack by the Turkish troops, sent a force to build a fort at Bassadore, on the western extremity of the island of Kishm, which had formerly been occupied by the Portuguese, who built fortifications and reservoirs, and which became during the forty years preceding its abolition, the head-quarters of the Indian Naval squadron in the Persian Gulf. What may be described as a reign of terror ensued upon the sea, and merchant vessels feared to leave any port without the escort of a ship of war, for the pirates had become so bloodthirsty by long impunity that, not satisfied with plundering ships, they massacred the crews. A shocking instance of this occurred on the Okhamundel coast, when some piratical craft boarded a pilgrim vessel having eighty souls on board, of whom forty were ruthlessly butchered, and the remainder, after being hacked about with a wanton barbarity, were permitted—with the exception of some women—to sink in the ship, which was scuttled; however, the poor wretches managed to keep the craft afloat, and navigated her into Beyt, where they were duly cared for by the English agent, but few of the survivors recovered from their wounds.

The Joasmis, grown bold by these successes, enlarged the sphere of their depredations, and once more appeared off the coast of India. In the latter part of 1818, two native vessels laden with cotton, were captured in their passage from Guzerat to Bombay, off the Island of Diu; and an Arab vessel, called the 'Mustapha,' having English colours and officers, was captured about sixty or seventy miles to the northward of Bombay. This success was not due to remissness on the part

---

* The name Ras-ul-Had, which is the extreme east point of Arabia, signifies in Persian and Arabic, a " boundary or limit."

† Busheab Island, called Sheikh Shuaib, and Jezirat-es-Sheikh by the Arabs, is situated to the northward and eastward of Kenn, and is thirteen and a half miles in length.

of the men-of-war, either of the King or Company, engaged in keeping the police of the seas, as they were few in number, and could not be ubiquitous. From the 26th of October, 1818, to January in the following year, the Company's cruisers, 'Thetis' and 'Psyche,' met the Joasmis on the high seas no less than seventeen times, sailing in divisions of from two to ten vessels, and were constantly driving them from port to port, frequently getting within range of them, but these dhows had so much the advantage in sailing over the cruisers, that the latter were rarely able to sink any of them.

In December, 1818, the Joasmi fleet, numbering fourteen sail, were returning to the Gulf from their cruising station off the Cutch and Kattywar coasts, when they were intercepted by the 'Thetis' and 'Psyche,' off Ashtola* Island, on the Beloochistan coast, proceeding to the westward in three divisions. H.M.S. 'Eden,' Captain Loch, was also, at this time, proceeding to the Gulf, when she fell in with the two Company's cruisers, chasing this fleet off Gwetter Bay, in which the pirates took shelter. The British ships remained outside, and Captain Loch, contrary to the advice of the commanders of the two brigs, opened negotiations with the chiefs of the hostile fleet. Time was to be given them until morning, but when daylight broke the birds had flown; the Joasmis, taking advantage of the darkness of the night, had weighed, and, standing round the bottom of the bay, which is three leagues deep and five wide at the entrance, passed out at the opposite end to where the British ships were anchored. Captain Loch had only his obstinacy to thank for this failure, as the commmanders of the Company's cruisers, having a lengthened experience of the duplicity and cunning of these Joasmis, had warned him that they would certainly play him false. A little later the Hon. Company's brig-of-war, 'Antelope,' fourteen guns, fought a spirited action with the Joasmis, upon whom she inflicted great loss.

At daybreak on the 21st of December, 1818, the 'Antelope,' Lieutenant Tanner, descried a fleet, consisting of a full-rigged ship, five large baghalahs, one dhow, and two of the largest-sized batils. The men were sent to their quarters, and the 'Antelope, stood for the fleet, upon which four of the baghalahs, the dhow, and the batils, hauled in shore towards the Island of Kishm. Directly after a boat left the side of the ship and brought intelligence to the 'Antelope' that she was the 'Rahomany,' a ship of war belong to the Imaum of Muscat, and that she and the remaining baghalah had maintained a running fight for nearly two days with the pirates, and that, as their

* Ashtola, called also Haptalah and Sungadeep, is an island off the Beloochistan coast, about 4,500 yards long and 1,200 broad. Nearchus, who anchored off this island, calls it Carmine.

ammunition was almost expended, their capture would have been certain had not the 'Antelope' come to their assistance. Sail was immediately made in chase, and, on nearing the pirates, a shot was fired from a brass 3-pounder boat's gun, on the forecastle of the cruiser, to try the range; upon this challenge, the pirates opened fire on the brig, and a hot action ensued. On closing the Kishm shore, the pirate vessels wore and stood across the 'Antelope's' bows, upon which she tacked to engage them at close quarters. Her fire told with terrible effect as she neared them, and a batil was observed, after speaking one of the baghalahs, to proceed to the others with a message, upon which the whole squadron bore up and steered for the 'Antelope's' main chains. It was an anxious moment for the gallant crew of the little brig, as it was evident that the pirates, in desperation, intended to try their favourite manœuvre of boarding with an overwhelming mass of men. But the officers and men were equal to the emergency, and worked their guns with such cool precision that, though within half a cable's length, the enemy hauled off, having sustained very heavy loss. Soon after they made a second attempt to board, but were again heavily dosed with grape, upon which they bore up for Ras-ul-Khymah.

The 'Antelope' gave chase, but, after a pursuit of five and a half hours, the wind being light, they escaped, two of their baghalahs being in a shattered condition. The pirates afterwards acknowledged to a loss of one hundred and seventeen men, which principally arose during their attempts to board. The relative force of the parties to this encounter, was as follows :— The 'Antelope,' twelve 18-pounder carronades and two brass 12-pounders, with a crew, all told, of seventy-one Europeans and thirty-seven natives. One of the baghalahs, which was considerably larger than the brig, carried eight guns and two hundred and fifty men; a second had six guns and two hundred men; the dhow had four guns and one hundred and twenty men; the two smaller baghalahs each carried two and three guns and one hundred men; and the two batils had each three guns and one hundred and fifty men; thus making a total of twenty-nine guns and one thousand and seventy men, and it was subsequently ascertained that their object in carrying such large crews, was to form a settlement in Kishm so as to command both sides of the Gulf. Thus the 'Antelope' frustrated this intention, and rescued one of the ships and a baghalah belonging to our ally, the Imaum of Muscat.

On Christmas morning, 1818, H.M.S. 'Eden' and the Hon. Company's cruiser 'Psyche,' fell in with two trankies, and, giving chase, compelled them to drop a captured boat they had in tow, but the trankies succeeded in effecting their escape. During the whole of the same day the 'Thetis' continued in chase of seven Joasmi sail, baghalahs and trankies, but all of them escaped under cover of the darkness of the night. On the following day she saw and chased four more sail, but they also eluded her, owing to their superior sailing qualities. The 'Eden' had been directed to proceed to Bahrein in company with some of the Company's cruisers, to make inquiries regarding some European females said to be in captivity at Ras-ul-Khymah; and, on the 10th and 11th of January, 1819, fell in with eight Joasmi sail off the islands of Kishm and Anjar, (called also Angaum,) when two baghalahs were sunk, and the six smaller craft, being trankies, managed to effect their escape. Shortly before her arrival at Manamah, the chief port of Bahrein,* H.M.S. 'Conway' had proceeded thither, and found

* Manamah, situated on the north-east extremity of the island, is a large town, probably containing not less than twenty-five thousand inhabitants. Separated from it by a narrow strait scarcely a mile across, and so shallow that at low tide a man can wade across is the island of Maharag, having a large town of the same name, containing the country houses of the wealthy inhabitants of Manamah. On a neighbouring headland stands a large square fort of imposing appearance, and provided with guns. At the western extremity of Manamah is a large mass of white buildings, the residence of the Sheikh. Bahrein possesses more than one hundred and forty trading vessels, besides four hundred pearl boats, each having from ten to twenty men. The island is mentioned in ancient geography under the names of Tyrus (by Arrian) and Aradus, from which, says tradition, the Phœnicians of the Mediterranean coast emigrated to the two small islands forming the sites of the cities of Tyrus and Aradus. Bahrein receives its name from the sea springs, and Pliny mentions springs of fresh water under the sea which are still found there. In the sixteenth century Bahrein was taken by the combined arms of Portugal and Persia, and Antonio Corréa, the admiral of the former, who proceeded from Ormuz to attack the native king, added the title of Bahrein to his name. The Portuguese historian relates how, stung by the exactions of their Christian oppressors, who "even forced from them their wives and daughters, the inhabitants of Ormuz and its dependencies formed a conspiracy against the Portuguese, and broke out into an open insurrection against them suddenly at Ormuz, Bahrein, Muscat, Kuriat, and Sohar, all in one night, by previous concert, and by a private order from their king. The attack was so sudden and well concerted that above one hundred and twenty of the Portuguese were slain on that night."

Early in the eighteenth century Bahrein was captured by Sultan-bin-Seif, Imaum of Muscat, and about the year 1770, was tributary to Sheikh Nansur-ul-Muskoor of Bushire, the most powerful Arab chieftain on the Persian coast. The Uttoobees, an Arab tribe, seized on Bahrein A.D. 1784, and held the island until 1800, when Seyyid Sultan, ruler of Muscat, seized Bahrein and left his son, a boy of eleven or twelve, as governor. The Uttoobees regained possession of the island within twelve months, but were conquered in 1807-8 by the Wahabees, who sent fifteen chiefs as hostages to their capital at Dereyah. One of these, called Abdool Rahman escaped, and joining Seyyid Said, the new ruler of Muscat, induced him to send an expedition, which succeeded in dispossessing the Wahabees of the island. Abdool Rahman was appointed Governor, but he treacherously threw off his allegiance and placed himself under the protection of the Wahabees, to whom he agreed to pay tribute. Again in 1816 the Imaum attempted the reconquest of the island, but was repulsed with great loss, Ahmed, one of his two brothers, being slain. In 1820, the Uttoobees, alarmed at the hostile preparations made by the ruler of Muscat, offered terms of peace, including an annual tribute equal to about £6,000, and the usual custom dues on all merchandise carried up the Gulf. At this time the Imaum's territories included, besides his hereditary possessions in Oman, the islands of Kishm and Ormuz, and he rented from Persia,

lying at that place seventeen Joasmi sail, having on board five or six thousand men, returning from El Kateef,* where they had arrived too late to aid the Wahabee chief against Ibrahim Pasha. Captain Barnard, as in duty bound, respected the neutrality of the port—though it was notorious that the pirates disposed of a large proportion of their plunder in Bahrein—and accordingly sailed from thence in order to allow the Joasmi armament to quit the island. This they did, and some of their ships, proceeding across to the Persian coast, continued their depredations.

On her arrival in the Gulf, the 'Eden,' under instructions from the Bombay Government, accompanied by the 'Conway,' and the Hon. Company's cruisers, 'Benares,' 'Mercury,' and 'Antelope,' proceeded to Bahrein in February, 1819, and, after some negotiations, the Sheikh succeeded in convincing Captain Loch that the report regarding the European females was incorrect, and at the same time entered into an agreement to abstain from receiving captured British property in his territory, though of course, *suo more*, he paid no heed to his engagements directly the British squadron had sailed. At Captain Loch's request the Sheikh communicated with Hussein-bin-Rahmah, the Ras-ul-Khymah chief, offering, on the part of the British Government, the release of a number of Joasmi prisoners in exchange for native women captured by the pirates, and eventually the proposal was agreed to, and seventeen poor creatures were restored to liberty. Before quitting Bahrein, Captain Loch again committed a mistake, owing to his perversity and ignorance of Persian Gulf politics, in which he was too proud to take advice from the commanders of the Company's cruisers. The British Native agent at Bahrein informed him there were some Joasmi vessels in the southern anchorage, which the Sheikh and his Ministers strenuously denied, declaring them to be belong to the Beni Yas tribe, whose chief port is Abu Thubi. But the senior officer, though warned of the mistake he was about to commit, sent the boats of the squadron, under cover of the 'Antelope,' to cut them out; a stout

Gombroon, or Bunder Abbas, and its dependencies, a tract of about ninety miles. His commerce was considerable, and, in 1820, he had five ships, including the 'Shah Alum' of fifty-six guns and the 'Caroline,' thirty-six guns; also two large baghalahs and four batils, his private property, besides being able to command all the vessels of his subjects.

* El Kateef town is on the west side of the bay of the same name, on the mainland, near the island of Bahrein. The bay is large and unsafe for ships. The town holds a prominent place in old histories and voyages of the Persian Gulf, particularly during the Portuguese tenure of Ormuz. For a detailed account of the Portuguese operations against El Kateef and Bahrein, see Manuel de Faria y Sousa's "Portuguese Discovery and Conquest of Asia," in Vol. vi. of Kerr's "Collection of Voyages and Travels." The conquest of those places was undertaken in the same year that Camoens, the immortal author of the "Lusiad," sailed for India to advance by the sword the fortune which had been so little promoted by his pen.

resistance was offered, but the dhows were boarded and carried off, though in attempting to get them out they were wrecked. The Bahrein chief made a great clamour about this violation of his neutrality, and the Abu Thubi Sheikh, whose property the vessels really were, made a demand for restitution upon the Bombay Government, which considered itself bound to pay the damages, and also, we believe, blood money for the men killed.

The Bombay Government, having at length resolved to take decisive measures for extinguishing piracy in the Persian Gulf, assembled a powerful armament at Bombay. The troops, which numbered three thousand and sixty-nine fighting men, of whom one thousand six hundred and forty-five were Europeans and one thousand four hundred and twenty-four Sepoys, were placed under the command of Major-General Sir William Grant Keir,* and consisted of one company of artillery, H.M.'s 47th and 65th Regiments, 1st Battalion 2nd Regiment Native Infantry, the flank companies of the 1st Battalion 3rd Native Infantry and the Marine Battalion, and half a company of pioneers. The following were the ships of war, some of which were in the Persian Gulf:—H.M.S. 'Liverpool,' fifty guns, Captain F. A. Collier, C.B., who arrived on the 25th of September from Mauritius, to assume naval command of the Expedition; and H.M. ships 'Eden,' twenty-six guns, Captain Loch, and 'Curlew,' eighteen guns, Captain Walpole—the latter brig, which arrived only a few days before from the Persian Gulf, having been attacked on her way down by fifteen large Joasmi boats, which she succeeded in driving off after five hours' fighting, during which she sank three and captured seven. The Company's ships were:—the 'Teignmouth,' sixteen guns, Captain Hall, (senior officer); 'Benares,' sixteen guns, Commander Arthur; 'Aurora,' fourteen guns, Commander Maillard; 'Nautilus,' fourteen guns, Lieutenant Faithful; 'Ariel,' ten guns, Lieutenant Greenway; and 'Vestal' ten guns, Lieutenant Watson. Besides these cruisers, which actually participated in the ensuing operations, the Hon. Company's ships 'Ternate,' sixteen guns, 'Mercury,' fourteen guns, and 'Psyche,' ten guns, were engaged cruising about the Gulf, and, during the month of November, the former was sent to Bushire to bring Mr. Bruce to Ras-ul-Khymah to confer with the General, who was invested with supreme political authority.

The first division of troops, consisting of the artillery and

* The divisional staff consisted of Major E. G. Stannus, Assistant Adjutant-General; Captain D. Wilson, Assistant Quartermaster-General; and Captain G. F. Sadleir, of the 47th Regiment, Interpreter. The force originally intended for embarkation, included the flank companies of the 2nd Battalion 4th Native Infantry, half a company of Pioneers, and one company of Artillery Lascars, which were countermanded, owing to the Governor-General having received a communication from the piratical chiefs offering to give up hostages.

two British regiments, embarked on board the transports* on the 30th of October, amid the cheers and good wishes of the people of Bombay, who crowded on the beach and landing-stages to bid them God speed; and, on the following day, the embarkation of the Native troops took place, under a similar popular ovation. The two following days were occupied in making arrangements for taking up other vessels as store and hospital ships, as it was found that in case of sickness the transports would be rather crowded; and, on Wednesday, the 3rd of November, Sir W. Grant Keir having embarked on board the 'Liverpool,' the first division of the fleet proceeded to sea, under convoy of the 'Liverpool,' 'Curlew,' and 'Aurora.' The remaining part of the Expedition sailed a few days later for the Persian Gulf. It was about time that some such active steps should be taken to extirpate the audacious horde of pirates, for by accounts published in the "Bombay Gazette" of October the 27th, it appears that the pirate fleet, cruising off the coasts of Kattywar and Cutch, consisted " of sixty-four vessels, having on board a crew of seven thousand men;" and the "Bombay Courier" of October the 23rd, mentions that "thirty-five sail of Joasmi have proceeded on a cruise off the coasts of Mekran and Scinde."

The fleet proceeded to the rendezvous at Kishm, while the 'Liverpool' sailed to Muscat, which she reached on the 13th of November, and, on the 17th, the military and naval chiefs had an interview with the Imaum, who promised to co-operate with four thousand men and three vessels of war. As it was a matter of importance that a reconnaissance should be made of the defences of Ras-ul-Khymah, Sir W. Grant Keir proceeded thither, on the 25th of December, in the 'Liverpool,' leaving the convoy to water at Kishm, and, the same day, met the Hon. Company's cruiser 'Benares,' having on board Dr. Jukes, who had been sent on in advance of the Expedition on a special mission to arrange for the Imaum's co-operation, and a commissariat officer, who was to make arrangements for the provisioning of the large force on their arrival at Kishm. Sir W. Grant Keir communicated with Dr. Jukes, and learnt from him that the letter† of the Governor of Bombay to the Prince of Shiraz, had been forwarded from Bunder Abbas direct to Shiraz on the 16th of November, and that a duplicate had been

* The following were the transports for the troops and ordnance stores:—
'Hannah,' 'Ann,' 'Jessy,' 'Orpheus,' 'Jemima,' 'Glenelg,' 'Bombay Castle,' 'Pascoa,' 'Diana,' 'Ernaad,' 'Faiz Remaun,' 'Angelica,' 'Carron,' 'Cornwall,' 'Francis Warden,' 'Conde de Rio Pardo,' 'Orient,' and 'Upton Castle.'

† This letter from the Governor, the Right Hon. Sir Evan Nepean, was explanatory of the objects of the British Government in equipping so large a military and naval force for service in the Gulf, and requested the co-operation of the Persian Government in the operations about to be undertaken against Linjah, Moghu, Charrack, and other points on the Persian coast which had completely identified themselves with the Joasmis.

transmitted by the Hon. Company's cruiser 'Teignmouth' on the 4th of the same month, to Mr. Bruce, the Political Resident at Bushire, also to be forwarded to Shiraz. As it was desirable that Ras-ul-Khymah should be blockaded, Captain Collier ordered the 'Benares' to accompany him to assist in the operation, and, on the same day, the two ships arrived off the place. The military commander, accompanied by his staff and the commanding engineer, reconnoitred the town during the 26th and 27th November, and, after careful consideration, arrived at the conclusion that the troops now at Kishm would be sufficient for the reduction of Ras-ul-Khymah, without waiting for the arrival from Bombay of the four remaining transports. The 'Benares' was, accordingly, despatched to summon the fleet, and, upon its arrival on the 2nd of December, immediate arrangements were made for disembarking the troops and camp followers from the transports. During the afternoon the remaining four transports from Bombay came in sight; on the same day the Imaum arrived with two frigates and about six hundred men, considerably less than he had promised, but his zeal appeared unabated, and his co-operation was of no little value.

On the following day the disembarkation was conducted, under cover of the gunboats and armed launches of the squadron, with surprising celerity and good order, considering the great distance the ships were obliged to anchor from the town, and the lack of a sufficiency of means for transporting so large a force with all the guns, supplies, and stores necessary for siege operations. The landing was effected under the superintendence of Captain Loch, assisted by Lieutenant Moffat, R.N., and Lieutenants Edward Seawright and George Barnes Brucks, of the Company's Marine, who had been appointed agents for transports before leaving Bombay. Captain Collier reported to Government of these officers as follows:—"Lieutenants Seawright and Brucks, agents for transports, deserve the highest commendation; their duties have been arduous and harassing. Nothing could exceed the zeal of these officers, and I truly feel confident that they will meet that reward they are so truly deserving of. In short, any praise I can bestow will fall far short of what they deserve." The troops were landed by the ships' boats about two miles from the town, under protection of the armed launches of the squadron, the large boats belonging to the Imaum being of great service, while his people worked with energy in bringing up the guns and ammunition to the batteries. That little resistance was encountered in landing, was due, in a great measure, to the valuable diversion caused by the 'Aurora' and 'Nautilus,' which brought up near the mouth of the creek and opened a heavy fire in that direction; for their services on this occasion the officers and men of these vessels received the hearty commendations of the senior naval officer, who was one of those rare disinterested characters who are animated by no feelings of petty jealousy, but can recognize zeal and ability when manifested in other officers than those of their own service. "The conduct of Captain Maillard of the 'Aurora," he says, " who anchored close to the town with this ship and the 'Nautilus,' is truly meritorious; the well-directed fire he kept up does his officers and men great credit."

To assist in the siege operations a body of five hundred seamen was landed from H.M's and the Hon. Company's ships, and was placed under command of Lieutenant Campbell, First of the 'Liverpool,' an officer who displayed in no common degree the qualities of energy and resource for which the British Navy is so pre-eminently distinguished. During the arduous work in the batteries, the contingent from the Company's cruisers, serving on shore with their officers, vied with their brethren of the Royal Service in the ardour and zeal with which they worked the guns.

Some account of the defences of Ras-ul-Khymah at this time, derived from an officer of the Bombay Marine who was present, will properly preface a narrative of the operations which resulted in its capture and final abasement from its position as the capital of as powerful and warlike a race of pirates as any in the East. "The town was walled in along the sea face, across the end nearest the point, and also across the south-west face, the walls, which were well built, being about nine feet high and two feet thick. At intervals were round towers about twenty feet high, the lower half of solid masonry, and a small store or guard-room between this portion and the roof which was surrounded by a parapet with loopholes for guns instead of embrasures. The side next the creek was open, but had a number of guns planted along it. To the southward of the town was a square fort, or ghuny, in which were mounted some small guns. On the island of Mahara, opposite the town, was also a strong tower, and there were several more in the date groves. The number of men in the town at the time of the arrival of the Expedition is said to have amounted to near seven thousand, but, from various enquiries I have made since, I do not think it exceeded at any time four thousand. These consisted of the Joasmis, Taal, Shahine, and Motarish tribes, and there were also about one thousand mercenaries who had been in the Mahratta service. A very large portion of the property of the place was removed, on the arrival of the Expedition, to the date groves; most of the women and children were also sent there, and the chief Hassan Bin Rahma, with his brother Ibrahim, prepared for the defence."

The following narrative of the operations before Ras-ul-Khymah, embracing a few circumstantial details, is from an officer of the Royal Army who was present:—"The batteries of the town bore directly on the entrance of the port—the harbour was full of shipping—the main land on the opposite coast appeared picturesque and verdant, with innumerable date trees, and the mountains of Arabia reared their dim, hazy outline in the background. The place of our encampment and soil of the tongue of land was parched, sandy, and herbless. Two thousand of the Imaum's troops joined us; they had forced the passes in the hills, deemed impregnable, and brought in some prisoners.

"Parties of seamen were landed to assist in the erection of the batteries. Smart skirmishing took place during the 4th; the rifle company of the 65th advanced within twenty yards of the largest fort and reconnoitred. The gunboats particularly distinguished themselves by their activity.

"The first line of trenches having been made by means of sandbags, an advanced battery opened on the place at the distance of three hundred yards. A mortar battery to the right was served very effectively. There was a gun from one of the enemy's batteries which enfiladed the trenches, whilst we could get none of our artillery to bear on it. It did considerable execution among the men. Major Molesworth of the 47th mounted the parapet of the trench, to reconnoitre more minutely, and in an instant fell back in the trench, his head blown to atoms. At length, however, we succeeded in silencing the piece. The ships of war having approached nearer the town, in conjunction with our batteries, opened a most vigorous fire on the morning of the 5th. Shells were thrown with evident effect. The gunboats contributed as before their powerful assistance. Towards the close of the day's work a Joasmi spy was brought in prisoner; he informed us that the enemy had suffered great loss, nearly ninety killed, besides wounded. The Sheikh's brother had lost his leg by a cannon-shot.

"The duties of the seamen in the trenches were severe and unremitting. Whilst the soldiers were relieved every four hours, the sailors remained frequently twenty-four hours, without any rest or respite. Jack grumbled a good deal at this unfair distribution, though he did not work the less strenuously. It was not a little vexatious to be saluted with a " good night " by several parties in succession as they quitted the trenches, with the prospect of comparative comfort in the camp, whilst the poor fellows left behind had to pass the time as they best could. The firing from the ships and batteries still continued on the 6th, that of the Arabs was very faint, and they evidently did not possess much ammunition, as large stone shot came hailing in upon us, but often wide of the mark. As soon as a discharge was made from our guns, the Arabs were seen leaping out of the embrasures to pick up the round shot, which they immediately returned. The walls and towers did not exhibit any very decided traces of the efficiency of this day's cannonade. The firing had terminated for the day, the men had been relieved, silence reigned in the batteries, the night was very dark, and the picket, as usual, on the alert. About one, a dark object, like a large black dog, was seen creeping along on all fours, several similar objects following. The advanced pickets were instantly cut down ; all was hurry, shout, and bustle. The trenches were filling with a large party of Arabs, engaged in a close contest with our men, who were speared and stabbed in a twinkling. Already the Arabs had succeded in dragging away a howitzer in triumph. The alarm spread like wildfire through the trenches. A part of the 65th Foot, under Major Warren, instantly advanced in double quick time, attacked the assailants, drove them out of the trenches, and recaptured the howitzer. A desperate conflict ensued ; the Arabs fought like furies, but they were soon bayoneted ; nearly all of them, ninety in number, were found lying in the trenches. They had divested themselves of their upper garments to facilitate their onset, and if we mistake not, their bodies seemed anointed with oil.

"It being found that our 12 and 18-pounders produced but a slight impression on the walls and towers, while the enemy availed themselves of our own shot to annoy us greatly, as they fitted exactly the calibre of their guns, it was resolved that several 24-pounders should be erected as a breaching battery. Two 24-pounders were accordingly landed, with considerable exertion, from the 'Liverpool,' and had to be dragged a long way through heavy deep sand. The battery was erected nearer the town, and a party of seamen and marines, under the command of Lieutenant Mills, was landed to work the guns. Lieutenant Campbell, of the 'Liverpool,' commanded the whole of the seamen on shore. The 24-pounders opened on the 8th with marked effect, and the walls and towers appeared to shake and totter under the force of the shot. The enemy tried to make use of our cannon-balls, but found that they were too bulky for their guns, and were therefore under the necessity of having recourse to their own stone and grape shot.*

* Here the gallant officer interpolates the following amusing anecdote, so peculiarly characteristic of "Jack Ashore :"—"Towards the afternoon of the 8th, and during the hottest of the cannonade, a bullock and a white cock were descried close under the wall of the town, exposed to the showers of shot from our batteries, from which they remained unharmed. The attention of several of the men was called to these objects, 'What a fine mess they would make !' shouted one of the sailors, with an expletive to which we would rather not give currency. 'Bill, I say, you bear a hand with me in towing them things out.' Over the trenches both of them vaulted, and scampered away at a slapping pace towards the ramparts, heedless of the balls plunging around them. We slackened our fire as speedily as possible ; the men in the trenches cheering and exulting in the boldness of the enterprise. The Arabs crowded on the walls, firing their matchlocks with steady aim at the two fellows as one of the sailors coolly drove the animal towards us, whilst the other, after a sharp chase, captured the cock.

"Before nightfall, repeated flags of truce were despatched from the town, but to these no attention was given, and darkness put an end to the firing. The cannonade was recommenced at an early hour the next morning, and as the progress of the breach became hourly more apparent and practicable, the necessary arrangements were made to assault the works. On receiving the announcement, great satisfaction was expressed by the force, for though a severe struggle was expected, success was deemed certain, and much plunder was anticipated. About one hundred seamen were assembled in the trenches, and these, with the gallant 47th, and the grenadier and flank companies of the other regiments, composed the storming party. On a signal being given, the whole rushed from the trenches in sight of the enemy, and advanced rapidly towards the breach, which was soon mounted, and the place entered. No one disputed the entrance, not an Arab was even visible in the town, from which they were observed running at their utmost speed towards the hills. The disappointment of the men was excessive, and the result of their search over the town for an enemy ended in the unearthing of four decrepid hags, whom the gallant Arabs did not deem worth removing. Still more disgusted were our fellows at finding that plunder there was none. Towards the close of the siege, the garrison had been employed in secretly removing all their effects out of the place; bullocks and goats only were left, and these Jack was seen driving, in herds of five, ten, and twenty, down to the beach, each man jealous of any interference with his flock, and conveying as many of the goats on board as he could stow away. The Union Flag was immediately hoisted in place of the blood red flag of the pirates, and orders were issued to dismantle the whole fortification and raze the place. The walls of the several gooharries and towers were five and a half feet thick, and so strong and well built as to render them impregnable to all, except European artillery. Our total loss in this tedious siege was one officer and four men killed, and three officers and forty-nine men wounded. The loss experienced by the enemy was very great, being at least three hundred killed and seven hundred wounded; and sixty-two guns were captured in the place. Hassan Bin Rahma, Chief of Ras-ul-Khymah, with nearly one thousand followers, surrendered himself prisoner. He stated that during the siege, while he was holding a council, a shell from our

They returned to the trenches, loudly huzzaed by their comrades; 'We've got the ——, my lads! and now for prime beef steaks to you all.' The neck of the cock was wrung, and the bullock's throat cut, and the body cut up into large pieces, which the men cooked in the trenches and devoured with keen appetite, amidst many an applauding joke and praise of their brave conduct. The officer, whose duty it was to reprimand the men for this breach of discipline, could hardly control his risible faculties, or assume a grave look or stern demeanour."

batteries burst into the room, and instantly exploding, killed and wounded about one hundred of his fighting men, and created infinite consternation throughout the garrison."

Of the sortie on the night of the 6th of December, an officer of the Bombay Marine, already quoted, says:—" About 80 or 100 yards to the right of the howitzer battery was the backwater, and the Arabs left the town at low-water about half-past eight p.m., and by crouching down and keeping silent, got in the rear, and made a rush on the battery without being perceived. The surprise was complete, and had they continued the attack along the trenches, our loss would have been severe, but having gained the battery, they commenced dragging away the howitzer, which they removed more than 100 yards; Ibrahim, brother of the chief, and a number of the Arabs, were wounded in the battery. This was the only sortie made, and from what I have learnt since from Hassan Bin Rahma, the Sheikh, its failure quite dispirited the defenders, who, up to this time, had entertained hopes of being able to hold the fort; for the Arabs have no idea of protracted operations, and concluded that if we did not succeed in a few days we should retire. The following day the seamen's battery opened, and the day after the breach was practicable."

He continues, "Very little property was found, but about eighty vessels of various sizes, from 250 to 40 tons, fell into the hands of the captors. I have since learned that about forty of the better class of boats had been secreted at places then unknown, and the only property of value not removed from the town was the chief's, the most valuable and portable of which was buried. His reason for this was, so he assured me, the fear that if he had sent away his property his people would not have remained to fight. The number of guns mounted in the town was about seventy or eighty, many of which were, however, unserviceable, owing to the vents being half an inch in diameter and all honey-combed; there were two or three brass guns, one a 24-pounder. During the siege the seamen had their full share in the duties, more particularly those of a laborious character connected with the guns. Though the loss was not large, scarce a man of the rifle company of the 65th escaped a scratch of some sort, but they never reported themselves wounded unless quite disabled. On this occasion the Marine had full justice done to them by the General and by their immediate commander, Sir F. A. Collier, who, both in his despatch to the Admiral and to the Government, bore testimony to their zeal and ability, and thanked many of the officers by name in General Orders."*

---

* The following is Sir William Grant Keir's despatch to the address of the Adjutant-General of the Army, describing the operations after the completion of the landing:—" The troops were formed across the isthmus connecting the

In his second despatch of the 3rd of January, 1820, Sir W. G. Keir estimated the loss of the enemy " as little less than a

peninsula, on which the town is situated, with the neighbouring country, and the whole of the day was occupied in getting tents on shore to shelter the men from the rain, landing engineers' tools, sand bags, &c., and making arrangements preparatory to commencing our approaches the next day. On the morning of the 4th the light troops were ordered in advance, supported by the pickets, to dislodge the enemy from a bank within 900 yards of the outer fort, which was expected to afford good cover for the men, and to serve as a depot for stores previous to the erection of the batteries. The whole of the light companies of the force, under command of Captain Backhouse of His Majesty's 47th Regiment, accordingly moved forward, and drove the Arabs with great gallantry from a date grove, and over the bank above described, close under the walls of the fort, followed by the pickets under Major Molesworth, who took post at the sandbank, whilst the European light troops were skirmishing in front. The enemy kept up a sharp fire of musketry and cannon during these movements; and I regret to add that Major Molesworth, a gallant and zealous officer, was killed by a cannon shot at the head of the pickets; Lieutenant Stepney, of the 65th, was wounded on this occasion. The troops, however, maintained their position during the day, and in the night effected a lodgment within three hundred yards of the southernmost tower, and erected a battery for four guns, together with a mortar battery on the right and a trench of communication for the protection of the covering party. The weather having become rather unfavourable for the disembarkation of the stores required for the siege, it was with considerable difficulty that this primary object was effected; but every obstacle was surmounted by the zeal and indefatigable exertions of the Navy, and on the morning of the 6th we were enabled to open three 18-pounders on the fort; a couple of howitzers and six-pounders were also placed in the battery on the right, which played on the defences of the towers, and nearly silenced the enemy's fire. The 'Liverpool,' during these operations, warped in as close to the shore as her draught of water would permit, and opened her guns on the town, which must have created considerable alarm in the garrison, but she was unfortunately at too great a distance to produce any decided effect. The enemy, who during the whole of our progress, exhibited a considerable degree of resolution in withstanding, and ingenuity in counteracting an attack, sallied forth at eight o'clock this evening along the whole front of our intrenchments, crept close up to the mortar battery without being perceived, and entered it over the parapet, after spearing the advanced sentries. The party which occupied it was obliged to retire, but being immediately reinforced, charged the assailants, who were driven out of the battery with considerable loss. The attack on the left was repelled instantaneously by the spirited resistance of the covering party under Major Warren, who distinguished himself much on this occasion by his coolness and gallantry. The enemy repeated his attack towards morning, but was vigorously repulsed. During the 7th, every exertion was made to land and bring up the remaining guns and mortars, which was accomplished during the night, after incessant labours, by the sailors, assisted by working parties from the troops, and those of his Highness the Imaum, who cheerfully volunteered their services. They were immediately placed in battery, together with two 24-pounders, which were landed from the 'Liverpool,' and in the morning the whole of our ordnance opened on the fort, and fired with scarcely any intermission till sunset, when the breach on the curtain was reported nearly practicable, and the towers almost untenable. Immediate arrangements were made for the assault, and the troops ordered to move down to the trenches at daybreak the next morning. The bombardment continued during the night, and the batteries having recommenced the fire before daylight, completed the breaches by eight o'clock. The accompanying orders will explain to his Excellency the disposition of attack, as well as the measures taken to guard against the possibility of a failure, in the event of the enemy defending himself as desperately as might have been expected from his previous defence. These precautions, however, were unnecessary; the party moved forward about eight o'clock and entered the fort without firing a shot; and it soon appeared that the enemy had evacuated the place. The town was

thousand," and adds, "the Sheikh himself has acknowledged that four hundred fighting men of his own tribe were either killed or wounded, which would appear to establish a much higher proportion, but the most authentic accounts agree in fixing it nearly at the number I have stated." The British loss in achieving this great success was only five killed, including Major Molesworth, and fifty-two wounded, of whom three were officers.

Sir William Grant Keir, both in his General Orders of the 9th of December and his despatch to the Bombay Government of the 10th of December, pays a just tribute of thanks to Commodore Collier and the naval part of the Expedition, specifying the officers and men of the Bombay Marine. The Commodore, also, in his letter from Ras-ul-Khymah, to the address of the Secretary to the Bombay Government, reports of the Service:—"To Captain Hall, the senior officer of Marine, and the officers and crews of the Hon. Company's cruisers, every praise is due for their unremitting exertions, both on shore and afloat." The efficient little squadron of the Bombay Marine also received the meed of praise from Lieutenant-General Sir Charles Colville, G.C.B., Commander-in-Chief at Bombay, in his letter to the Hon. Mountstuart Elphinstone—who had succeeded Sir Evan Napean as Governor of Bombay, on the 1st of November in this year—enclosing the despatch of the commander of the Expedition.

After the capture of Ras-ul-Khymah, the 'Curlew,' 'Aurora,' and 'Nautilus' were despatched to blockade Rams, six miles north-east of that place, where there were some pirate vessels and a fort. The town was found to have been abandoned, but its inhabitants were supposed to have taken shelter in the hill fort of Zayah, situated at the head of a creek about two miles from the sea coast. This place was held by over four hundred men under a former Wakeel of the famous Wahabee chief, one

taken possession of and found almost entirely deserted, only eighteen or twenty men and a few women remaining in their houses. Upon the whole, it appears evident, considering the spirited behaviour of the enemy at the commencement of the siege, that their sudden resolution to evacuate the place was occasioned by the overwhelming fire of the Artillery, of which they could have formed no previous idea, and which the ample means placed at my disposal, enabled me to bring against the town. Our loss, I am happy to say, is much less than could have been expected from the length of the siege, and the obstinacy with which the enemy disputed our approaches. I have had no means of ascertaining theirs, but it must have been severe. I beg that you will assure His Excellency that I feel entirely satisfied with the conduct of the troops; their gallantry has been exceeded only by their patience and cheerfulness under every species of privation and fatigue, and the peculiarity of this service has called forth a full display of these qualities which are equally creditable to the soldier as the most intrepid acts of bravery. By the orders which I do myself the honour to enclose, His Excellency will be enabled to estimate the services performed by Captain Collier and the naval part of the expedition; and I can only add, that the acknowledgments expressed are scarcely adequate to the assistance I have received from them."

Sheikh Hussein Bin Ali, whom it was necessary to subdue as from his talents and lawless habits, as well as from the strength and advantageous situation of his fort, he was likely to seek to revive the piratical system at the first favourable opportunity. The squadron proceeded thither with a large detachment[*] of troops, under Major Warren, commanding the 65th Regiment, but the General, on his arrival, discovering that the fortifications were more formidable than had been represented, ordered up a reinforcement of the 47th and the flank companies of the first battalion of the 3rd N.I., to complete the close investment of the place, and Commodore Collier also landed two 24-pounders from the 'Liverpool,' which were placed in battery with the other artillery, by the sailors of the squadron, who won great commendation by their cheerful alacrity.

The service that ensued, though short, was arduous in the extreme, owing to the difficulties of transporting the guns and stores for a siege, and the resolute defence made by the enemy. One officer, Ensign Mathieson of the 65th, was killed during the desultory fire that took place between the 18th and 22nd of December, when the investment of the fort was completed. At half-past eight that morning fire was opened from the batteries, one to breach the fort on the north-east side, and the second to destroy the defences of the Sheikh's house in the town to the westward, and such was the precision of the practice, that, in two hours, a practicable breach was effected, and the column told off for the assault were about to advance, when a white flag was displayed. Hussein Bin Ali's followers, if not the Joasmi chief himself, had recognised the futility of further resistance, and, after some little delay, marched out to the number of three hundred and ninety-eight fighting men, the women and children being at the same time collected together in a place of security. At half-past one, p.m., the British flag was hoisted on the hill fort and at the Sheikh's house, and, soon after, the whole of the prisoners were taken on board the squadron, and were brought to Ras-ul-Khymah, where they were landed. The loss of the British force was one officer and three men killed, and sixteen men wounded, one of whom died. A detachment of seamen participated in these operations, under the command of Captain Walpole of the 'Curlew,' and the indefatigable and gallant First Lieutenant of the 'Liverpool' commanded in the 24-pounder battery. Major Warren pays a handsome encomium to the zeal and ability displayed by these and the other officers and men of the Naval Brigade, which enabled them to "overcome the difficulties attending the landing of the supplies and stores, particularly the guns, which,

---

[*] Thirty Artillerymen, with two brass 12-pounders, two 8-inch mortars, and four field-pieces; H.M. 65th Regiment, and the flank companies of the 1st Battalion 2nd Regiment N.I.

after being brought up a narrow, intricate, and shallow creek, a distance of upwards of three miles, had to be dragged through a muddy swamp, and afterwards over a considerable space of rocky and intersected ground, before they could be placed in the batteries."* He continues, "Nor can I conclude this report without feeling that it is due to Lieutenant Brucks, the Agent of Transports, to bring to your notice his laborious exertions in the particular line of his duties, during the embarkation and subsequent landing of the troops on the 18th inst., on which occasion the officers and men belonging to the cruisers and transports, had all to endure a day of most severe labour and privation." The Commander of the Expedition, in his Field Orders to the Army, dated "Ras-ul-Khymah, 25th of December, 1819," says of the services of the Naval Brigade:—"The Major-General feels at a loss to express in adequate terms his obligations to the Navy, but the value of their services will be estimated when he declares that the enterprise must have failed without their assistance." The column, after destroying the fortifications, returned to the camp before Ras-ul-Khymah on the 26th of December.

On receipt of the intelligence of the fall of the pirate stronghold, whence the Joasmi fleets had issued to prey upon the commerce of all countries, the Governor of Bombay issued a General Order, dated the 28th of December, announcing the success of the British arms, in which he speaks as follows of the services of the Bombay Marine:—"The conduct of Captain Hall, and of Lieutenants Maillard, Arthur, Faithful, Greenway and Watson, in command of cruisers, and of Lieutenants

---

* The military officer whose description of the capture of Ras-ul-Kymah we have already given, says of the operations at Zayah:—"A strong fort on a neighbouring hill, called Zaire, still held out. The duty undertaken by the seamen was most arduous in this case; two 24-pounders were dragged by the poor fellows for a space of two miles over rough and swampy ground. After batteries had been erected, a brisk cannonade was kept up against the fort, and shells were thrown without intermission. The firing was unremitting and tremendous. The fort was deemed quite impregnable by the natives, but they had soon speedy reason for entertaining a mortifying belief to the contrary; they accordingly manifested a wish to capitulate. The General offered unconditional surrender; which, after half-an-hour's deliberation, was acceded to. Sheikh Hussein Bin Ali, the Chief, was sent prisoner on board one of the transports. He was the most active and the most cruel of the pirates, about thirty years of age, handsome in person, mild in demeanour, but with a look of sullen, tiger-like ferocity lurking in his restless eye.

"On our return to Ras-ul-Kymah, we found the place totally in ruins; the forts and towers having been blown up by the indefatigable soldiers and seamen employed on that duty. A strong work was in a state of forwardness for such of our troops as it might be deemed requisite and expedient to leave behind for the entire prevention of future piracies, and a check upon the Arabs in their attempts to rebuild their forts and strongholds.

"On the 3rd of January we quitted the coast and proceeded to the different harbours in the vicinity, in order to capture and destroy all the piratical vessels and small craft. This operation was carried into complete effect, and it is hoped has succeeded effectually in destroying the roots and nipping the branches of piracy for a long period to come."

Seawright and Brucks, and the officers and men of the Hon. Company's Marine, employed on this service, have been spoken of in terms of high commendation by the Major-General, and also by Commodore Collier, whose established reputation and experience of the qualifications that distinguish the Naval profession, renders his testimony to the character of the Bombay Marine of peculiar value in the estimation of the Governor in Council." The Governor-General in Council, in publishing the despatches of the military and naval chiefs, on the 21st of January, 1820, issued a General Order, concurring in the praise bestowed by the Bombay Government, and, on the 21st of March, 1820, on the return of the Expedition to Bombay, the Governor in Council issued a General Order highly eulogising the services of all arms, and expresssing the thanks of his Government.*

The fleet were now employed visiting all the Joasmi ports on the coast, and destroying their war-vessels and blowing up their forts; thus Jezirat-ul-Hamra, Ejman, Amulgavine, Shargah,† and several other places, were visited and reduced to a condition of impotence, but no resistance was encountered anywhere.

On the 8th of January, 1820, a General Treaty of Peace was concluded at Ras-ul-Khymah between Major-General Sir William Grant Keir, on the part of the British Government, and nearly all the chiefs of the maritime tribes of Arabs in the Persian Gulf, by whom it was subsequently signed at different times and places. The sole purpose and scope of this treaty was the entire suppression of piracy, and the adoption of such

* By an order, dated Bombay Castle, 17th of February, 1827, the military and naval forces engaged in the operations against the Joasmis in 1819, were informed that the Court of Directors, by despatch dated the 12th of April, 1826, directed that, "in addition to the prize property realised by agents," the "full valuation of all boats captured and destroyed by the forces," including the moiety legally accruing to the Company, together with interest at six per cent. per annum from the 30th of September, 1820, making a sum of 266,625 rupees, should be paid to the captors. "John Company," though mercantile in his condition, was assuredly, on some points, more lordly than his "Imperial" successors, and such liberal conduct offers a striking contrast to the view, perhaps legally admissible, entertained by the India Office on the Banda and Kirwee prize case, which has given rise to so much protracted and expensive litigation.

† Sharjah, in Persian, or Shargah, as the Arabs call it, the most important town on the coast, contains a population of about ten thousand. Five miles to the north-east is Aymaun or Ejman, a small place of about one thousand two hundred inhabitants, who during the season send nearly one hundred boats to the pearl fisheries. Amulgavine, or Amalgawein, stands about twelve miles to the north-east of Ejman; the old town was deserted after its destruction in this year, and the people now reside at Libini, a thriving place having some one thousand five hundred souls, and sending seventy or eighty boats to the fisheries. Jezirat-el-Hamra is a fort and town ten miles south-west by west from Ras-ul-Khymah, built on an island formed by a khor or inlet. The pirate coast was supposed to end at Debaye, a town of the Beni Yas tribe, having about one thousand two hundred inhabitants, distant seven miles from Shargah. From Debaye to Abu Thubi, the capital of the Beni Yas, the coast stretches in a south-west direction a distance of sixty-seven miles.

measures of precaution and general co-operation as seemed best adapted to attain the object in view;* but it is an interesting,

> * The following is a translation of the general Treaty of peace with the Arab tribes of the Persian Gulf, dated the 8th of January, 1820:—
> "In the name of God, the merciful, the compassionate! Praise be to God, who hath ordained peace to be a blessing to his creatures! There is established a lasting peace between the British Government and the Arab tribes, who are parties to this contract, on the following conditions:—
> "Art. 1. There shall be a cessation of plunder and piracy by land and sea, on the part of the Arabs who are parties to this contract for ever.
> "Art. 2. If any individual of the people of the Arabs contracting shall attack any that pass by land or sea, of any nation whatever, in the way of plunder and piracy, and not of acknowledged war, he shall be accounted an enemy of all mankind, and shall be held to have forfeited both life and goods; and acknowledged war is that which is proclaimed, avowed, and ordered by Government, and the killing of men and taking of goods without proclamation, avowal, and the order of Government, plunder and piracy.
> "Art. 3. The friendly (literally the pacificated) Arabs shall carry, by land and sea, a red flag, with or without letters in it, at their option; and this shall be in a border of white, the breadth of the white in the border being equal to the breadth of the red, as represented in the margin, the whole forming the flag known in the British Navy by the title of 'White pierced Red;' and this shall be the flag of the friendly Arabs, and they shall use it, and no other.
> "Art. 4. The pacificated tribes shall all of them continue in their former relations, with the exception that they shall be at peace with the British Government, and shall not fight with each other; and the flag shall be a symbol of this only, and of nothing further.
> "Art. 5. The vessels of the friendly Arabs shall all of them have in their possession a paper ('Register') signed with the signatures of their chief, in which shall be the name of the vessel, its length, breadth, and how many karahs it holds; and they shall also have in their possession another writing ('Port Clearance'), signed with the signature of the Chief, in which shall be the name of the owner, the name of the Nakhooda, the number of men, the number of arms, from whence sailed, at what time, and to what port bound; and if a British or other vessel meets them, they shall produce the register and the clearance.
> "Art. 6. The friendly Arabs, if they choose, shall send an envoy to the British Residency in the Persian Gulf, with the necessary accompaniments, and he shall remain there for the transaction of their business with the Residency; and the British Government, if it chooses, shall send an envoy to them also in like manner, and the envoy shall add his signature to the signature of the Chief, in the paper ('Register') of their vessels, which contains the length of the vessel, its breadth, and tonnage; the signature of the envoy to be renewed every year. Also all such envoys shall be at the expense of their own party.
> "Art. 7. If any tribe or others shall not desist from plunder and piracy, the friendly Arabs shall act against them according to their ability and circumstances; and an arrangement for this purpose shall take place between the friendly Arabs and the British, at the time when such piracy shall occur.
> "Art. 8. The putting men to death after they have given up their arms is an act of piracy, and not of acknowledged war; and if any tribe shall put to death any persons, either Mahomedans or others, after they have given up their arms, such tribe shall be held to have broken the peace, and the friendly Arabs shall act against them, in conjunction with the British, and, God willing, the war against them shall not cease until the surrender of those who performed the act, and of those who ordered it.
> "Art. 9. The carrying off of slaves (men, women, and children) from the coast of Africa or elsewhere, and the transporting them in vessels, is plunder and piracy; and the friendly Arabs shall do nothing of this nature.
> "Art. 10. The vessels of the friendly Arabs, bearing their flag above described, shall enter into all the British ports, and into the ports of the allies of the British, so far as they shall be able to effect it, and they shall buy and sell

and we believe, little-known fact, that by Article 9 of the Treaty, the slave trade was abolished in the Persian Gulf. This was due to the interposition of Captain T. Perronet Thompson.

A separate treaty was concluded the same day with Hussein Bin Rahmah, the Joasmi chief of Ras-ul-Khymah, stipulating the release of all Indian prisoners, the occupation of the towns of Ras-ul-Khymah and Mahara, and the surrender of all his vessels, with the exception of the boats employed in the pearl-fisheries off the Bahrein banks. A similar treaty was likewise entered into with Sultan Bin Suggur of Shargah and the other Sheikhs, for the "surrender of the towns, guns, and vessels which are in Shargah, Ejman, Amulgavine, and their dependencies," with the exception of the fishing boats, stipulating, however, that "the General will not allow the troops to enter the towns to lay them waste." Separate treaties were also entered into with the Beni Yas Sheikhs of Debaye and Abu Thubi, the latter a powerful chief named Shakhboot, and the chiefs of Bahrein, Sheikhs Soleiman Bin Ahmed and Abdoola Bin Ahmed.

In February the fleet, consisting of seven men-of-war and fourteen transports, proceeded across the Gulf to the island of Kenn to water, and here the Expeditionary force was broken up. Early in March the first division of transports, with detachments of artillery and H.M.'s 47th and 65th Regiments, arrived at Bombay under convoy of the Hon. Company's cruiser 'Ternate,' and, ten days later, the remaining five transports arrived under convoy of the Hon. Company's cruiser 'Mercury.'

therein; and if any shall attack them, the British Government shall take notice of it.

"Art. 11. These conditions aforesaid shall be common to all tribes and persons who shall hereafter adhere thereto, in the same manner as to those who adhere to them at the time present.

"Issued at Ras-ul-Khymah in triplicate at mid-day on Saturday, the 8th of January, 1820, and signed by the contracting parties at the place and times under written. Signed at Ras-ul-Khymah, at the time of issue, by

"W. GRANT KEIR, Major-General.

"HUSSAN BIN RAHMAH, Sheikh of Hatt and Faleia, formerly of Khymah.

"RAZID BIN AHMED, Sheikh of Jeizerat-ul-Humrah."

The treaty was also signed on the 11th of January by Shakboot, Sheikh of Abu Thubi: and on the 15th of January by Hussein Bin Ali, Sheikh of Zayah. Also by the uncle of the Sheikh of Dobaye, a minor, on the 28th of January; and by Sheikhs Suleiman Bin Ahmed, and Abdoolla Bin Ahmed of the house of Khalifa, Sheikhs of Bahrein; and on the 15th of March, by Rashid Bin Humeed, chief of Ejman, and Abdoolla Bin Rashid, Chief of Amulgavine.

The only piratical chief of consequence who refused to sign the General Treaty was Rahmah Bin Jaubir, Chief of Khor Hassan, near Bahrein, who pleaded that he was subordinate to the Persian Government; which plea was admitted on the Governor of Bushire becoming responsible for his conduct. This was the same veteran desperado, who, in 1826, characteristically ended his life by setting fire to the magazine of his ship and blowing up himself and crew.

The 'Liverpool,' with Sir W. Grant Keir on board, after visiting Bushire, quitted the Persian Gulf for Bombay on the 24th of March, the General having left to garrison Ras-ul-Khymah, a force, consisting of twenty artillerymen, the 1st Battalion 2nd Regiment N.I., two companies of the Marine Battalion, and the flank companies of the 1st Battalion of the 3rd N.I., the whole being placed under the command of Captain T. Perronet Thompson, of Her Majesty's 17th Dragoons, who, being an excellent Arabic scholar, had rendered great service to the General as interpreter, at the time of the signature of the Treaties, to the translation of which his name is appended. In the following April, the Bombay Government sent orders to Captain Thompson to remove the detachment to Deristan,* after dismantling the sea defences, and to give up the town to Sultan Bin Suggur, the legitimate chief of Ras-ul-Khymah, whose power was soon so greatly in the ascendant, that, in 1824, all the Joasmi ports appear to have acknowledged his supremacy.† On a communication, however, being made to the chief, he positively refused to take possession if the works were destroyed; a reference was consequently made to Bombay, when final orders were issued to carry out the original instructions. This was accordingly done, and the town was finally abandoned by the British garrison on the 18th of July, 1820.

* Deristan is a large bay in Kishm, to the north-west of the island of Angaum or Henjam.

† In the commencement of 1823, Sultan Bin Suggur began the erection of a fort at Shargah, but was informed by the Political Resident that he must suspend the work until the instructions of the Government could be received. An application from the inhabitants of Ras-ul-Khymah, says Lieutenant Hennell, for permission to erect a wall across the isthmus, was likewise referred to the Government, which intimated, in its reply, that it was not intended to prevent the erection of forts or buildings on the Arabian coast, as the treaty concluded by Sir W. G. Keir did not appear to authorise any such interference. About this time the Sheikh of Rams was deposed through the influence of Sultan Bin Suggur and all the Joasmi chiefs, and in the following year Rashid Bin Humeed of Ejman, who had declared to the Resident that he would never submit to the authority of the Chief of Shargah, acknowledged his supremacy. In 1859, fifty-six years after succeeding his father, Sheikh Suggur, he was still living at the age of 103 years, the patriarch of the Joasmi, and his stately bearing and venerable appearance were well known to the officers of the Indian Navy, with whom the old Chief was ever on the best of terms.

CHAPTER XI.

1820—1824.

Loss of the 'Ariel'—Repulse of a British force by the Beni-boo-Ali Arabs—Historical Sketch of the Bombay Marine Battalion—Success of the Second Expedition against the Beni-boo-Ali—Changes in the Uniform of the Bombay Marine.

THE Expedition against the Joasmi pirates in 1819, closed with a terrible catastrophe to one of the ships of the Bombay Marine, which was more fatal in its effects than the entire British loss sustained throughout the preceding operations. The Hon. Company's cruiser 'Ariel,' was a brig of 160 tons, carrying ten 12-pounder carronades, and, at this time, a crew all told, of eighty-three souls; her officers were Lieutenants W. C. Greenway and Duff, two midshipmen, Messrs. D'Arcy and Chitty, Mr. Garraway, gunner, and Mr. Johnstone, boatswain. After taking part in the siege of Ras-ul-Khymah, where her commander, who was a most energetic officer and able seaman, received much praise from Commodore Collier, the 'Ariel' was directed to proceed to Bussorah with despatches, and it was in returning thence to Bushire that she foundered. The brig left Bussorah on the 12th of March, 1820, and, during the night of the 17th, when the accident occurred, the deck then being in charge of the gunner, a most careful and experienced officer, was supposed to be about twenty miles from the island of Kharrack. The 'Ariel' was beating against a south-easter under double-reefed topsails, when the gunner, apprehending from the threatening appearance of the sky in the north-west quarter,* a sudden shift

---

* The prevailing wind in the Persian Gulf is the north-wester, called by the Natives "Shemal," which blows about nine months in the year in the northern half of the Gulf. It blows almost incessantly during June and part of July, when it is called the "Burra," or Great Shemal; the general duration is three days, though it sometimes lasts seven, and the worst shemals often last only one day. This wind blows down the Gulf, changing its direction with the trend of the coast. In the northern part of the Gulf the air during the shemal is generally loaded with dust from the deserts of Mesopotamia, which shrouds the land so that often the white surf on the beach is the first sign of danger. In the Shatt-ul-Arab, during the continuance of a shemal, the dust is so dense that neither bank of the river is visible, and vessels, rigging, and decks, are covered with fine

of wind, reported to the captain that a squall was approaching. Lieutenant Greenway, who was at the time ill in his cot, gave directions that all was to be made snug aloft. All hands were immediately turned up on deck, the courses were hauled up and the topsails lowered on the cap. This was scarcely accomplished when a tremendous squall struck the little craft; taking her right aft, it hurried her into and through the opposing sea caused by the north-easterly gale, and in a moment, before any warning could be given, the 'Ariel' was buried beneath the waters and went down head foremost.

Of the entire crew of eighty-three souls only five were saved, Mr. Joseph Glen, the surgeon, Mr. Johnstone, boatswain, Brown, a seaman, Wall, a boy, and the native cook. The following is an extract from a letter by Dr. Glen,[*] describing the escape of the survivors:—"I was in bed, but luckily awake. I turned out on hearing the wind, and as our berth opened into the main hatchway, I went out and stood between decks to see what was the matter. As I looked up the vessel heeled, the water came rushing over the larboard gunwale, the launch went over the side, and at the same time I heard a crash above me, which must have been the mainmast. At this time I heard a horrid shriek, and found myself below water. All this must have taken place in less than a minute and a half from the first coming on of the squall. On coming to the surface I found myself among pieces of boards, and heard a few men around. I, however, felt myself irresistibly pulled below the water, and went to the depth of three or four fathoms. It was the vortex formed by the sinking vessel. On reaching the surface a second time, and swimming a little, I saw a canoe bottom upwards, to which I made, and got upon it. Hearing some people in the water near me, for it was quite dark and rainy, I called out, and was joined by six or seven of my unfortunate companions. All else was now quiet, except the tossing of the waves, and the piercing cries of a little boy, who was at some distance, but to whom we could give no assistance. In a few minutes he sunk, and we were left, the remainder of eighty-three persons, who but a few minutes before had no idea of danger. The squall was now over, but a heavy sea continuing, made the canoe roll over and over, which always threw us to some distance in the water, and exhausted us very much. After tumbling about in this way for some time, three or four men could stand it no

sand which fills the eyes and mouth. The air is generally very clear and cloudless, but during the winter the shemal, as in the above instance, is often accompanied by a storm of thunder and lightning; a heavy swell from the north-west is often a precursor of a shemal, and should be taken as a warning.

[*] Dr., now Physician-General, Glen still survives, and has published a pamphlet describing his experiences during the day and night he was in the canoe, which was the property of the officers who used it when duck-shooting up the Shatt-ul-Arab.

longer, and dropped off. There were now four of us only remaining of eighty-three persons, who composed the ship's company, and expecting every moment to share the same fate. However, we at last contrived to right the canoe, and kept her on her keel, although full of water, by placing a few small spars that we found floating about, across the gunwale, which prevented her rolling. We fastened these the best way we could with strips of shirts and handkerchiefs, and sat upon them. We also saw the high land about Bushire, but that was far off. At this time we were joined by two other men, who had kept near us on a spar until our little raft should be ready. One of these poor fellows died before we reached the shore. Sitting upon this swamped boat naked, and every sea coming over us, we continued to drift towards the island, and about two p.m., we got within a mile or two of the beach, and expected in half-an-hour more to land. At this time, to our great distress, I discovered that the tide began to set us off again, and to drift us round the island. As we were evidently leaving the shore fast, it was proposed to swim ashore, but on making the experiment we found ourselves so weak, and the distance so great, that we were glad to put about, and it was with great difficulty some of us reached the canoe. Luckily the current soon changed and sent us back again, and a little after sunset we were cast upon a reef of rocks, over which we swam and waded till we got upon dry land. After walking two or three hours along the beach, we arrived at the town, and were immediately taken to the Sheikh. He gave us a room in his house, and supplied us with what clothes and provisions he had, for the island is very poor. We remained there three days, and during that time received every attention and kindness we could expect. On the 22nd of March, the Sheikh gave us a boat, in which we arrived at Bushire the same evening, and of course were supplied with everything. We left Bushire on the 28th. For several days after our unfortunate wreck I was laid up, swollen with the sun and salt-water, and from having been cut a good deal with the rocks on landing, but otherwise I have been in good health."

The 'Ariel' was a deep-waisted, chest-like brig, of a class common in the Royal Navy at the close of the Revolutionary War, which from the frequency of their foundering, were known as "coffins" or "deaths," and were employed up to so recent a date as the year 1839, in carrying the Government mails across the Atlantic, when they fully maintained their unenviable characteristic of foundering or capsizing in a stormy sea. It was found, on subsequent inquiry, that the 'Ariel' had been condemned as unseaworthy before Mr. Meriton, the Superintendent, sent her on her last cruise. On her arrival at Muscat the mainmast was found to be so rotten from step to cap that it was a wonder it had not saved the crew the trouble of hoisting out by going over the side; it was replaced by a crooked spar presented by the Imaum, which was a few feet shorter than the foremast. However, no spars or other appliances could have saved the 'Ariel,' which foundered, like other brigs of the so-called "coffin" class, owing to her build, though this did not exonerate the Superintendent who sent her on a cruise in an unseaworthy condition.

After the reduction of the Joasmi ports in 1820, a strong squadron of the Marine vessels was stationed at Ras-ul-Khymah, to enforce the fulfilment of the stipulations of the treaty, and maintain a surveillance of the coasts; and the brig 'Psyche' was moored in the creek above the town, so as to sweep the approaches with her guns in the event of any attack upon the garrison. In May 1820, Captain Thompson, the Commandant and Political Resident, expecting an attack by the Arabs, a body of two hundred seamen, under the command of Lieutenant Tanner, was landed nightly from the cruisers, and every one was much harassed. At length, as already mentioned, in July Ras-ul-Khymah was evacuated in favour of Deristan, in the island of Kishm, and the officers and seamen were employed assisting in the demolition of the fortifications and embarkation of the guns and stores, when, owing to the intense heat, many valuable lives were lost.* The garrison embarked on board the cruisers on the 11th of July, under the light of a grand conflagration of the last of the Joasmi craft and the woodwork and "cadjans" of the houses, and proceeded to the opposite coast. Owing to calms, which prolonged the passage to three days, the water ran short, and the men, when landed, were sick and worn out; according to one account, fully one-third of both services were laid up with fevers, but they soon recovered at Deristan, which was found to be a fairly healthy station.

Complications soon, however, arose with the Beni-boo-Ali, a tribe of Arabs, which, owing to military mismanagement,

* Among those who died from the effects of exposure and over-fatigue, was a young officer of singular promise and possessing many accomplishments. This was Mr. Albert Waterworth, midshipman of the Hon. Company's cruiser 'Antelope,' who, after an illness of nine days, contracted at Ras-ul-Khymah, where he had been for some weeks past actively employed with a party of seamen on shore, died at Deristan on the 23rd of July, of inflammatory fever, at the age of eighteen. The following tribute to the worth of this young officer, written by his commander, Lieutenant Tanner, appeared in the Bombay papers:—" With considerable talent and a good education, this lamented young officer possessed many eminent virtues; he was distinguished by an active and enterprising character, sound principles, and an amiable disposition, with mild and engaging manners, that secured to him the respect and regard of all who knew him. This tribute of regard to the memory of departed worth, cut off in the flower of youth, is offered by his commander, who sincerely feels, and will long deplore, the great loss which his own ship and the Service at large has sustained by the melancholy event. His mortal remains were attended to the grave by the officers and seamen of the squadron with every mark of respect."

brought about a great disaster. Government having heard of some irregular proceedings on the part of the people of Ul Ushkara, a small place on the sea-coast, near Ras-ul-Had, belonging to the Beni-boo-Ali* Arabs, Captain Thompson was directed to proceed against them in the event of the conduct complained of being piratical. The 'Mercury,' fourteen guns, was accordingly despatched to Ul Ushkara, to convey a letter to the chiefs of the Beni-boo-Ali, and, on arriving off the place, sent a boat with her pilot, a man of some consideration, who had been engaged at Muscat. Owing to the surf being high, this man swam ashore with the letter, but, on landing, was cut to pieces; upon seeing this outrage the boat's crew opened fire, and killed several of the natives. On the return of the 'Mercury,' Captain Thompson immediately determined to take hostile measures against the Arabs for this act of treachery, and, by his orders, a force, consisting of six companies of Sepoys from the 1st Battalion 2nd Native Infantry and Marine Battalion, with a party of artillerymen and eight guns, was embarked on board the following ships of war:—H.M.S 'Curlew,' and the Hon. Company's cruisers 'Ternate,' 'Prince of Wales,' 'Mercury,' and 'Psyche.' The Expedition sailed for Muscat, orders having been left for the 'Teignmouth' to join them on her arrival at Deristan.

Muscat was reached on the 11th of October, and quitted on the 22nd, after a plan of operations had been arranged with the Imaum Seyyid Said, by which it was agreed that, as the landing at Ul Ushkara was nearly impracticable, and could not be supported by his Highness' contingent of two thousand men, the Expedition should proceed by sea to Sohar, where they were to be joined by the Imaum's troops. A party of about one hundred seamen was landed to accompany the force, but owing to some differences between Captain Thompson and Commander Price Blackwood, of the 'Curlew,' Senior Naval Officer, which, looking to the causes of the disaster that ensued, may be said to have mainly contributed to it, the military commander declined the aid of the seamen, who were re-embarked. On the 1st of November, the detachment marched from Sohar, accompanied by the Imaum's contingent, commanded by that Prince in person, and taking with them two 6-pounders, two howitzers, and two iron 18-pounders, together with nine hundred camels and other draught cattle. After a fatiguing march, the combined force arrived, on the 8th of November, at a town of the Imaum's, called Belad Beni-boo-Hussein, within three miles of Belad Beni-boo-Ali, the capital of the tribe, to

---

* The Beni-boo-Ali, a fierce and turbulent race, resided in Jaalan, a province belonging to the Imaum, whose authority they had thrown off in June of this year. Forster, in his learned work, "The Geography of Arabia," supposes them to be identical with the Blenlai, a tribe mentioned by Pliny.

which they had retreated after setting fire to Ul Ushkara and fourteen of their boats. Captain Thompson having formed an entrenched camp, a demand was forthwith sent for the surrender of their fortifications and town, together with the persons who had murdered the messenger at Ul Ushkara. The summons was despatched in the name of the Imaum, but conveyed an intimation from the Political Agent, that the British had entered upon a course of hostility in order to punish the tribe for having committed acts of piracy by sea, and that, though they acted in concert, this cause was quite distinct from the reasons which had induced his Highness to proceed against them. In answer to this summons, the Beni-boo-Ali agreed to comply with the proposed conditions, except the one stipulating for the surrender of their arms. Unhappily, when everything that could be reasonably expected from a brave and warlike tribe of Bedouins, had been conceded, Captain Thompson refused to waive the imposition of a demand, compliance with which was synonymous with disgrace.

Accordingly, the combined force, exclusive of a guard left to defend the entrenched camp, consisting of the four light guns with a detachment of artillerymen, three hundred and eighty Sepoys, and two thousand of the Imaum's troops, moved, on the following morning, towards the enemy's town, which was situated with its rear resting on a deep date grove, round which it was necessary to defile in order to reach the assailable front, which faced the sandy plain, and was protected by ditches. On arriving within sight of the town, the light company of the 1st Battalion 2nd N.I., which had headed the column, opened fire and began to fall back, according to orders, and, soon after, the enemy, said to number nine hundred men, appeared in motion on some elevated ground, with the apparent design of turning the right flank. Captain Thompson immediately directed the troops to form column of sections to the right, in order to present a new front to the enemy, and then to charge bayonets. Some hesitation appears to have been displayed by the Sepoys in obeying this last order, and, as the only remaining course, they were directed to fire; but the enemy, nothing daunted, continued to press forward, broadsword in hand, and fell upon their wavering ranks with yells, when instantly a terrible scene of confusion and slaughter ensued. In vain the officers, with the devotion rarely absent among English gentlemen, strove by word and example to rally the panic-stricken Sepoys, who broke, and, throwing themselves on the Imaum's troops in the rear, infected them with the same spirit of fear. There was a general flight of the broken remnants of the force, closely pursued by the enemy, and they only found shelter within the entrenched camp at Beni-boo-Hussein. In this affair, two hundred and seventy men were killed, together with six out of the eight officers engaged, exclusive of Captain Thompson and a Lieutenant Bothwell, who was carried off by some Arabs, but died about two months after, from fever brought on by fatigue and suffering. The Arabs gave no qnarter to the wounded, and even dragged out of his palanquin the surgeon, who was sick, and butchered him on the spot. The Imaum displayed great personal courage, and was shot through the hand while endeavouring to save an artilleryman.*

During the night the enemy made an attack upon the entrenched camp, which was repulsed, but Captain Thompson and his Highness, finding it could not be held, retreated with the remnant of the force and those of the Imaum's followers that remained, upon Muscat, which was reached on the 17th of November.† During the defence of the entrenched camp Mr. Fallon, Assistant-Surgeon of the 'Prince of Wales,' doing duty with the troops, afforded much assistance in rallying and collecting the dispirited Sepoys; and, as Captain Thompson says, "the Imaum, during the whole of these circumstances, displayed an admirable character, and though wounded, persisted in remaining with the detachment, and causing it to be supplied with provisions, camels, shoes, and every assistance his country could afford." Captain Thompson sent the 'Prince of Wales' to Bombay with his official despatch, and returned to Deristan with the remnant of his force, about four hundred and sixty men, of whom more than half were camp followers. Shortly after the return of this detachment, the 2nd Battalion 12th N.I. arrived to relieve them, but so great were the fears entertained at Deristan of an attack, that the 'Teignmouth' proceeded over to the Arabian coast to prevent the despatch of a hostile expedition, but she found all quiet; before her return all the squadron were employed in transporting the troops to the town of Kishm,‡ in the island of that name, though there was no occasion for the alarm that had prompted this step.

During the Expedition against the Beni-boo-Ali, the detachment of the Marine Battalion, consisting of two companies,

* The Imaum received a magnificent sword from the Governor-General in July, 1821, for his gallant and loyal conduct.

† Captain Thompsom's despatch to Government, dated the 18th of November, 1820.

‡ The troops were not actually stationed in the town, but on the summit of a precipitous rocky hill, near the shore and about a mile to the north-west of the town of Kishm, forming a very strong position. Lieutenant Brucks says that a thermometer was hung to a tent rope, and the mercury rose to 160°, when the instrument burst. During the eighteen months they remained here, five or six officers and a large proportion of the men died from the intense heat. (*Vide* "Memoir on the Persian Gulf," by Brucks, in the "Government Records," No. 24, 1856, page 607.) The cause of the intense heat in this camp was the prevailing wind, or shemal, which blows along the island of Kishm, or from west-south-west, so that the breeze reached them heated by blowing along sixty miles (the length of the island) of hot desert land and heated rocks.

suffered heavily, having lost one European and four native officers, and eighty-four non-commissioned officers and men killed, only twenty men having survived.

The present would appear a favourable opportunity for giving a brief sketch of the services, up to this date, of the Bombay Marine Battalion, now known as the 21st Regiment of Bombay Native Infantry, as extracted from Government General Orders and other published Records.

The Marine Battalion was raised in 1777, up to which date the duties of Marines were performed by Sepoys from the land forces. In the present century, when ships of the Indian Navy were sent away from the Presidency on war service, the Sepoy Marines were sometimes removed, and their places supplied by drafts of Europeans from the Bombay Artillery, as during the China War of 1840, and the second Burmese War of 1852; but almost the entire achievements of the Marine Battalion were gained afloat in the Hon. Company's ships of war with no European officers but those of the Indian Navy, so that the survivors of the latter Service have cause to view with especial satisfaction the honour paid to the regiment by H.R.H. the Prince of Wales, during his recent visit to India, in presenting them with new colours, and they will contemplate with pride the promise made on that occasion by the future King of England, that these colours shall adorn the walls of Marlborough House, and eventually—though distant may be that day—of Windsor Castle.

The Bombay Marine Battalion was raised by order of Government, under date the 3rd of January, 1777, as follows:—

"The Honourable the President and Council have been pleased to order that five hundred Sepoys shall be raised as a corps for the service of the Marine, and the same encouragement given to them as to the other Sepoys in the establishment. This corps to consist of five companies, and each company to consist of one subadar, two jemadars, one European sergeant, six havildars, six naiques, one fifer, two drummers, and eighty-five privates. They have also been pleased to appoint Captain James Jameson to the command of this corps, and Lieutenant William Hudson adjutant; also to add a black commandant, a European sergeant, a black adjutant (to be one of the jemadars), a black doctor, a fife-major (one of the fifers), a drum-major (one of the drummers), a head sub-assistant apothecary, and two other sub-assistants."

The battalion was not deemed effective until late in the year 1777, when it was reviewed and directed to assume the peculiar duties for which it was formed. The following Order was published:—

"17th November, 1777.

" General Orders.—The commanding officer, being entirely satisfied with the appearance and behaviour of the Marine Battalion at the review this morning, thinks proper to signify the same in public orders, and desires the commandant to thank the inferior officers in his name for their diligence and attention.

" As that Battalion is intended to perform all marine duties, one havildar, one naique, and eight Sepoys of that corps are immediately to relieve the like number now on board the 'Betsy' schooner; they are also, on Thursday morning next, to relieve all the detatchments from on board the other galivats and vessels in the service of the Hon. Company now lying in the harbour of Bombay, with the like number."

By the foregoing Order the Battalion entered on the performance of its Marine duties, but its strength not being found adequate, it was augmented to an establishment of eight companies by an order of Government, under date the 9th of January, 1778, as follows:—

"The Honourable the President and Council, finding the Marine Battalion of Sepoys insufficient in number to the duties required from it, have been pleased to order that it be augmented as soon as possible to eight companies, which are to consist of one hundred private men each, with the same number of black officers as are at present allowed to each company, and no increase of European officers."

While the Bombay Marine was actively employed in the year 1779, against Surdan Khan, an officer in the service of Hyder Ally, the detachments of the battalion from on board the several vessels, 'Durruck,' 'Eagle,' 'Manchester,' and 'Bombay,' and the pattamars, then on the coast, were landed at Tellicherry, and, under the command of Captain Jameson, directed to join the British force. In the actions that ensued on this service many officers and men were killed and wounded. These detachments were afterwards employed on board their respective vessels in preventing the retreat of merchants, with goods down the creek of Calicut, during the time the British troops were besieging that fort.

In consequence of the great demand for men for Marine duties, in 1785 Government ordered drafts from the 1st, 3rd, 4th, and 5th Battalions to complete the complement of the corps. In 1788, the Marine Battalion consisted of eight companies, each company of one subadar, two jemadars, five havildars, five naiques, two drummers and fifers, one waterman, and one hundred Sepoys. In November of this year, when the distinctions for the Native corps were selected by the Commander-in-Chief, the battalion feather was ordered to be black, with blue "angricks," (*sic* in original), and another badge was added.

In 1791 the companies of the battalion were ordered to be augmented by an addition of one havildar, one naique, and seventeen Sepoys. At this period Government allowed a bounty of three rupees to each recruit on approval by the Deputy Adjutant-General. The battalion furnished this year a portion of non-commissioned officers and men for the newly-raised Local Battalion at Surat, where, and at Bancoot, the corps was recruited.

When the regulations for modelling the Army, transmitted to India by the Court of Directors, were published, under date the 24th of May, 1796, the corps was directed, by orders of the Governor in Council, to be commanded by a major, and to have a similar number of inferior officers as the other battalions of Native Infantry; it was formed into ten companies, and one major, four captains, eight lieutenants, and an adjutant were posted to it.

Early in 1797, the detachment of the battalion serving on board the 'Vigilant,' of six guns, under Lieutenant Hayes, was distinguished by the approbation of Government, as published to the Army, under date the 31st of July, in the following terms :—" The Board fully concur with the Commander-in-Chief in the justice and expediency of noticing the gallant conduct of the detachment from the Marine Battalion, in the late action on board the 'Vigilant.' With regard to the Native officers and Sepoys, the Commander-in-Chief is requested to cause the havildar to be promoted to jemadar, the two naiques to be havildars, and two of the Sepoys to be selected for naiques, with the gratuity to the party of one month's pay"

The Commander-in-Chief noticed in General Orders, under date the 21st of January, 1798, the conduct of a detachment of the battalion that had served on board the 'Viper,' fourteen guns, in the following flattering terms :—" The firmness and bravery evinced by the detachment of the Marine Battalion on duty on the 'Viper,' during the last trip up the Gulf of Persia, in defending the vessel when attacked under circumstances of peculiar difficulty, are considered by Government as highly meritorious, and the Commander-in-Chief has particular pleasure in conveying these sentiments to the detachment. The Board, ever happy to have it in their power to encourage fidelity and bravery by a due notice thereof, have been pleased to direct that the notification of the high sense that they entertain of such meritorious conduct, be accompaned by a gratuity of one month's full pay to the aforesaid Marine detachment, and by a present of a silver chain and badge of the value of one hundred rupees to Sheikh Gunny, havildar, who commanded the party. The badge to be engraved with the figure of a ship with a viper's head, and inscribed with the words 'The reward of fidelity and valour.'"*

By an Order, dated the 7th of September, 1808, the Governor in Council directed that the Havildar, Sheikh Ebram, should be promoted as a reward for his gallant conduct whilst in command of a detachment on board the 'Fury,' eight guns, Lieutenant Gowan, when attacked by pirates in the Persian Gulf; and, by an Order of the 4th of February, 1809, all the widows of men of the Marine Battalion who were killed on board the 'Sylph,' were pensioned from the date of their husbands' decease.

In 1809 a detail of the Marine Corps, under Captain Egan, formed part of the force employed against the Joasmi pirates, and Colonel Lionel Smith, commanding the troops, praised them for the manner in which his orders were carried into effect. Government were also pleased to express their approbation of the services of the detachment, by orders dated the 11th of March, 1810.

The same year the following Order, prescribing the duties of the Sepoys on ship-board, was promulgated by Government:—

"Bombay Castle, April 28th, 1810.

"The Honourable the Governor in Council has been pleased to order the following regulation to be framed for the government and conduct of the Marine Sepoys, serving on board the Hon. Company's cruisers, with the view of defining their duties, so as to prevent the recurrence of complaints between the two branches of the Marine service.

"The Sepoys are to assist in working the ship below, in hauling up and paying down cables, in hoisting in and out of boats, water and provisions, and in manning the tackle-falls on all occasions. 2nd. They are to draw and hand along water for the purpose of washing the ship, and are personally to clean out their own berths. 3rd. They are not to wash their clothes but upon days specifically approved by the regulation of the ship. 4th. They are not to be compelled to go aloft, to scrub

* In March, 1803, the following was announced in Government Orders:—
"There being a vacancy in the Marine Battalion, resolved that Havildar Sheikh Abdul Rayman be promoted to the rank of Jemadar, vice Soolaman Israil, removed to the 6th Regiment. Government being happy at the opportunity of distinguishing such meritorious military conduct as evinced by Sheikh Abdool Rayman in the action with the piratical galivats on the 27th of January last, when under the command of Sergeant Evans, date of promotion, February 26th, 1803.

"By the officer Commanding-in-Chief. Government acknowledging the gallantry and good conduct of the Marine Battalion that served under Sergeant Evans, has in their liberality been pleased to order, that each of the non-commissioned officers and privates shall receive two months' pay as a gratuity. Lieutenant-Colonel Williamson will be pleased to indent for the amount and to present the reward to the detachment in such public manner as he may judge proper to promote zeal and emulation in the corps."

the decks, or perform any menial office. 5th. In case of misconduct a non-commissioned officer to be confined, and (if the havildar) a naique, or (if the naique) a private is to be selected to perform his duty till he can be tried, or upon due sense of his misconduct, it shall be deemed proper to release him. 6th. In no case is a non-commissioned officer to be struck, or to have corporal punishment. 7th. Privates are, for crimes of a serious nature, to be confined, till they can be brought to trial, but for offences of less importance, when absent from the Presidency and the support of discipline requires immediate punishment, they are to be punished with a "rattan," according to the degree of the offence, by the drummer or fifer, in presence of the detachment to whom the cause of the punishment is to be clearly explained, or for misconduct not demanding corporal punishment, they may have allotted to them the task of picking oakum or knotting yarns while their comrades are relieved from duty."

After the reduction of Mauritius the following honourable testimony to the fidelity of a detachment of the corps, was published by Government on the 3rd of April, 1811, to which reference has already been made. "The Hon. the Governor in Council having received official information from the Commander of the 'Aurora' cruiser, that the late Government of the Isle of France, and its officers, had endeavoured to prevail upon a detachment of the Marine Battalion, embarked on board that vessel, to enter the French service after her capture by the French frigates 'Astrea' and 'Iphigenia,' on the 21st of September last, and that various ineffectual means, as well of persuasion as of a coercive nature, had been resorted to, to induce the Sepoys to swerve from their allegiance to the Hon. Company, deemed it proper to cause the circumstance of these transactions to be thoroughly investigated.

"The Board of Officers appointed for this purpose having closed their proceedings, the Governor in Council has sincere satisfaction in announcing that the result of the inquiry has afforded another distinguished proof of the fidelity and attachment of the Native Army of this establishment, under circumstances of a very trying nature. It appears that in addition to repeated offers of encouragement, and failing in that, to the infliction of severe and even cruel treatment, to induce and compel the detachment generally to betray their duty to the Hon. Company, Sheikh Boodle in particular, upon refusing to enter the French service, was thrice severely wounded in the arm and once on the head, the effects of which (it is apprehended) have incapacitated this faithful soldier from the performance of further duty.

"The conduct of the detachment, though not unprecedented by various examples of similar attachment in the Native troops of this establishment, being accordingly considered as highly worthy of a marked testimony of public approbation, the Governor in Council is for this purpose, pleased to direct that a silver badge, with a suitable inscription, be presented to each man of the party as enumerated in the following list." (Here follows the list of promotions and the names of the seventeen faithful Marines.) The badges were accordingly presented to the men on general parade by the Adjutant-General of the Army, on the 3rd of September, 1811, the Commander-in-Chief complimenting the detachment in handsome terms in the orders of the day.*

An havildar of the Marine Battalion having greatly distinguished himself while employed in the 'Dart,' pattamar, against the piratical vessels in the Gulf of Cutch, the Governor in Council, by an Order, dated the 25th of March, 1812, promoted him to the rank of jemadar in the 2nd Battalion 7th Regiment Native Infantry.

A detachment of the corps serving on board the 'Benares,' cruiser, was employed with other troops and seamen at Macassar on the 8th of June, 1816. The Orders published on the 28th of August, speak handsomely of their conduct. A havildar and two privates were killed, and a naique and three privates wounded. The same detachment having for a time been transferred to the 'Nautilus' cruiser whilst to the eastward, distinguished themselves in the action with the 'Peacock,' and Lieutenant Boyce spoke of them in the highest terms. A detachment from the Marine Battalion, under the orders of Captain William Morrison, of the 9th Regiment, was employed in the reduction of the Forts of Severndroog, which surrendered on the 4th of December, 1817, and the complimentary General Orders of the Governor in Council have already been referred to.

On the 23rd of January, 1818, the following Order directing the Marine Battalion to be formed into a regular regiment of the Line, was issued to the Army :—

"Bombay Castle, Jan. 21, 1818.

"His Excellency the most noble the Governor-General in Council having been pleased to direct the formation of the Marine Battalion into a Regular regiment of the Line, the Right Hon. the Governor in Council, in giving effect to his Lordship's

* The conduct of the detachment which served on board the 'Aurora,' in refusing to enter the French service, as before specified in the General Orders of Government, is thus noticed in the Honourable Court's letter of June 6, 1812, published to the Army December 15th, 1812 :—

Para. 151.—" The conduct of the Native Marines in refusing to enter the French service under the circumstances described, is highly creditable to their fidelity, and well deserving the rewards which you have bestowed upon them.

Para. 152.—" We desire that you will cause these sentiments of approbation to be officially communicated to them, as well as our sanction of the rewards being conferred upon them."

Orders, is pleased to direct that the augmentation shall bear date the 1st of January, 1818, that day having been fixed upon in commemoration of the heroic conduct of the 1st Battalion 1st Regiment of Native Infantry of this establishment, in the memorable action of Corrygaum, when it bravely and successfully defended itself against an attack of the Peishwa's army. The Marine Battalion is accordingly formed into a regiment and denominated the 11th Regiment Native Infantry."

The following General Order was published by the Commander-in-Chief:—

"The 11th Regiment Native Infantry is to wear dark green facings, gold epaulettes and yellow buttons. The 1st Battalion will continue the anchor as a device placed under the number of the regiment, and the 2nd Battalion will be distinguished only by the numerical number XI."

In order to reinforce the small detachment employed against Severndroog, an additional detail, under Captain Francis Farquharson, had been sent off, with artillery, but arrived too late to be employed in that service, the place having surrendered the day before they reached the harbour of Severndroog. Shortly afterwards a small force, including fifty men of the 1st, or Marine Battalion, 11th Regiment, under Lieutenant Capon, with the details from the corps serving as marines in the cruisers and pattamars employed in that quarter, under Captain Farquharson, assisted in reducing the strong forts of the Concan, where they displayed a gallantry which repeatedly called forth the thanks of the Governor in Council.

Towards the close of September, 1819, a force being under orders to proceed to the Persian Gulf, for the purpose of reducing the piratical States, a detachment from the Marine Battalion, consisting of two captains, four lieutenants, four Native officers, ten havildars, and one hundred and eighty rank and file, was ordered to form part of the Expedition. Whilst the Expedition was occupied in the reduction of Ras-ul-Khymah, the men of the battalion serving on board the cruisers, were landed, and, with their comrades on shore, formed into a Provisional battalion under the command of Captain Deschamps. A native officer of the battalion, Subahdar Sheikh Nathoo was appointed aide-de-camp to Major-General Sir W. Grant Keir. On the conclusion of this service, two companies remained to form part of the garrison of Ras-ul-Khymah, and participated in the ill-fated expedition against the Beni-boo-Ali Arabs in November, 1820. On this occasion Lieutenant Short, one subahdar, three jemadars, one colour-havildar, nine havildars, three naiques, three drummers, and sixty-eight privates were killed, and only twenty privates survived to return to Kishm.

In a future chapter we will continue the records of the Marine Battalion from this date.

HISTORY OF THE INDIAN NAVY.

As soon as news of the disastrous expedition against the Beniboo-Ali reached the Bombay Government, they took immediate steps to retrieve the tarnished lustre of the British arms, and restore our influence in the Persian Gulf, but at the same time they recalled Captain Thompson,* and expressed their disapproval of his proceedings.

A strong British force,† under Major-General Lionel Smith, C.B.—the same officer who commanded the troops in the Expedition against Ras-ul-Khymah in 1809, and Malwan in 1812—was embarked at Bombay on board fifteen transports and ten baghalahs, having a tonnage in the aggregate of 10,402 tons, and the following cruisers of the Company's Marine acted in co-operation :—'Teignmouth,' Captain Hardy, senior naval officer ; 'Prince of Wales,' Commander Stout ; 'Psyche,' Lieutenant Dominicetti ; and ' Vestal,' Lieutenant Robinson.

The Expedition sailed from Bombay on the 11th of January, 1821, and arrived off Sohar on the 27th, when the disembarkation

---

* Captain Thomas Perronet Thompson, who died in 1869, in the eighty-sixth year of his age, was a noted man, and is better known as General Thompson, the prolific author of pamphlets and articles on Political Economy and Free Trade, and a Member of Parliament. Though a Dissenter, he went to Cambridge, where he became Seventh Wrangler; but in his twentieth year he quitted college and entered the Navy, serving as midshipman on board the ' Iris,' flagship of Admiral Gambier. The Navy not being to his liking, he entered the Army as second-lieutenant in the Rifle Corps. He served in that wild and unsuccessful expedition undertaken by Sir Home Popham and General Beresford against Buenos Ayres, and was taken prisoner there when the force capitulated. At the age of twenty-five he was appointed Governor of Sierra Leone, but owing to his zeal for negro emancipation, which formed through life a prominent feature in his political creed, he got into collision with the residents, and was recalled at the end of two years. He took part in the campaign in the south of France in 1814, but missed Waterloo owing to his regiment, the 17th Dragoons, having been sent to Bombay. His knowledge of Arabic procured him the post of interpreter to Sir W. G. Keir in 1819, and, as we have already mentioned, it was owing to his pertinacity that he managed to persuade both parties to insert Article 9 in the Treaty of the 8th of January, 1820, by which the slave trade was declared piracy, the first time such a declaration was ever made in a formal treaty between two Powers. In 1821 General Thompson returned to England, and soon after retired from military life. He now became a Radical reformer, and conduced by his writings in the " Westminster Review " to the abolition of the Corn Laws, and his " Corn-Law Catechism," published in 1827, ten years before the existence of the Anti-Corn Law League, was a memorable production in its day. In 1835 he was returned for Hull in the Radical interest, but he finally retired from Parliament in 1859, ten years before his death.

† Europeans.—H.M.'s 65th Regiment, the Bombay European Regiment. First troop of the Brigade of Bombay Horse Artillery, 5th Company of the 2nd Battalion Bombay Foot Artillery.

Natives.—1st Battalion 7th Regiment (afterwards 13th) Native Infantry; 1st Battalion 2nd Regiment (afterwards 3rd) Native Infantry ; flank companies of the 2nd Battalion 2nd Regiment (afterwards 4th) Native Infantry ; 1st Battalion 3rd Regiment (afterwards 5th) Native Infantry ; 1st Battalion 4th Regiment (afterwards 7th) Native Infantry ; 2nd Battalion 9th Regiment (afterwards 18th) Native Infantry ; 3rd Company Pioneer Battalion. Total, one hundred and seventeen officers, one thousand two hundred and sixty-three European soldiers, one thousand six hundred and eighty-six Sepoys, and one thousand six hundred and eleven camp followers. Grand total, four thousand six hundred and seventy-seven.

took place. Owing to a want of caution on the part of the General, the Expedition was within an ace of suffering a severe reverse before it started on the march to the interior, the Beni-boo-Ali Arabs have delivered a "chupao," or night attack, which was nearly proving successful. The British camp had been pitched about one and a-half miles from the beach, while the General, with his staff and the Bombay European Regiment, took up their quarters near the shore; the Arabs, seeing their advantage, determined to make a descent upon the General's camp, and either kill or capture the entire party. Accordingly three hundred of them made a flank march of fifty miles on the night of the 10th of February, and attacked the sleeping camp before their presence in the neighbourhood had even been discovered; but they miscalculated on their strength, and were repulsed, after some sharp fighting, in which the British lost one officer, Captain Parr, and sixteen men killed, and three officers, including Colonel Cox, the Brigadier, and twenty-three men wounded. Some of the wounded soldiers lost their arms by a single stroke from an Arab sabre, but the enemy did not succeed in escaping without loss, eleven of their number being killed and twelve wounded; among the latter was their chief, who was captured. After this experience of the character of the men with whom he had to deal, the General removed his quarters to the main camp.

A sufficiency of camels and draft cattle having been procured from the Imaum, and every preparation made, the division marched for the interior, accompanied by sixty seamen from the cruisers, under the command of Lieutenants Robinson and Dominicetti, and the remainder of the ill-fated detachment of the Marine Battalion, and, on the 2nd of March, 1821, arrived before the capital of the tribe. With a bravery worthy a better fate, the gallant Bedouins, disdaining the protection of breastworks or other defences, advanced on the open plain to give battle to their white foes. A short but desperate struggle ensued. The Beni-boo-Ali thought to repeat their former tactics, and, filling the air with their war-cry, charged down upon the serried ranks of bayonets with broadsword and target. With a desperate valour that astonished the veteran officers who had been engaged throughout the Mahratta War, and disregarding the showers of grape from the 12-pounders, they strove with their swords to find the weak points in that line from which a storm of lead poured destruction into their ranks, and, with the fanaticism of a religion that taught them that death at the hands of the enemies of their faith was a sure passport to the bliss of Paradise, they threw themselves on the bayonets of the soldiery, and with reckless impetuosity tried to break through the death-dealing squares. But all in vain was a gallantry that has never been surpassed in the annals of war.

Of less than one thousand warriors, five hundred were left on the field dead or wounded, and two hundred and thirty-six were made prisoners, of whom ninety-six were wounded. The main attack was directed on the right brigade, consisting of four hundred men of H.M.'s 65th Regiment, and three hundred of the 1st Battalion 7th Native Infantry, under Colonel Warren of the former regiment, and of the total loss of twenty-nine killed and one hundred and seventy-three wounded, the 65th lost four killed and thirty-eight wounded, and the 7th Native Infantry twenty-two killed and one hundred and twenty-six wounded. After the repulse of the main attack the fort was cannonaded and surrendered, and so ended this little war. The British column blew up the works and defences, the Imaum's soldiers cut down the date-groves and turned away the water-courses, and then, having made a desert of what was once a smiling oasis, inhabited by brave men, the avenging troops marched back to Sohar, whence the British division embarked for India.

The Bombay Marine* squadron employed in this Expedition, received the thanks of the Governor of Bombay in Council, and while every officer and man participated in the great fatigues incidental to landing and transporting the *matériel* of a small army in the field, a detachment were fortunate enough to share in the dangers and glories, such as they were, of the action of the 2nd of March. These were deemed sufficiently great to cause the Bombay Government, by a General Order, dated the 11th of February, 1831, ten years after the service, to permit the Company's troops engaged in the Expedition to bear on their colours and appointments the word "Beni-boo-Ali;" and H.M.'s 65th Regiment* also bear the word "Arabia"

* The only officer of the old Bombay Marine surviving in this year (1877) who took part in the operations against Beni-boo-Ali, is Captain Richard Kinchant, who was first-lieutenant of the 'Prince of Wales,' and had charge of the first division of transports. This old officer is also the sole survivor of those who took part in the Mahratta War of 1817-18, where, as second-lieutenant of the 'Thetis,' he was engaged at the capture of Severndroog, Gheriah, and Malwan, on the Malabar Coast; he also participated in the operations before Ras-ul-Khymah and Zayah, where, as he says in a letter to us, "we slept on the bare sand, with a rock for a pillow, and for a canopy the heavens above us."

† This was the last service performed by this distinguished regiment in India, where since its arrival on the 7th May, 1803, it had seen much arduous work. After participating in the operations against the Mahrattas, including the unsuccessful siege of the Great Jaut fortress of Bhurtpore by Lord Lake's army in 1805, the regiment arrived at Bombay in 1809, when the command was assumed by Lieutenant-Colonel Lionel Smith; from this date until its return to England, it was constantly employed on service with the Bombay Marine. The 65th was first engaged in the Expedition of 1809 against the Joasmis, and on its return landed at Bombay on the 21st February, 1810. On the 16th September following, it sailed from Bombay in company with the 84th, and took part in the reduction of the Island of Mauritius, which it quitted for Bombay on the 3rd of January, 1811. After a few weeks passed in Ceylon, the regiment landed at Bombay on the 21st of April, and participated in the expedition, under command of its colonel, against the chief of Nowanuggur in Kattywar. On the fall of this place on the 22nd of February, 1812, when the Bombay Marine acted in co-

to commemorate their signal services at Ras-ul-Khymah and in the action of the 2nd of March, 1821.

General Smith, in his Divisional Orders issued the day after the capture of the enemy's works, mentioned the naval detachment employed at the front in the following complimentary terms :—" Lieutenant Robinson, of the Hon. Company's Marine, and the volunteer seamen from the fleet at Sohar, rendered the division great service, and underwent the most trying labour and fatigue in dragging heavy guns. Major-General Smith requests Lieutenant Robinson will accept and communicate his best thanks, and he will express to Government how much he is indebted to that officer for his useful exertions."

Among those desperately wounded and taken prisoners was the chief, Mahomed bin Ali, who, with one hundred and fifty males, the remnant of the tribe, was sent to Bombay. Here they were detained for two years, but, in 1823, the Court of Directors sent out instructions to Mr. Mountstuart Elphinstone, then Governor of Bombay, to use his influence with the Imaum of Muscat to procure the restoration of the remnant of the Beni-boo-Ali tribe to their native place. After some correspondence, owing to a reluctance on the part of his Highness to have back such restless neighbours, even though they were powerless, the Imaum consented, and the survivors returned to their desolated homes. In the following year, the chief having represented to the British Political Resident the distressed condition to which his people were reduced, owing to the destruction of their date-groves and water-courses, the Bombay Government presented the tribe with a sum of 2,500 German dollars to enable them to recover somewhat of their former prosperity. It speaks well for the generosity of these Arabs that when Lieutenant Wellsted, I.N., the eminent tra-

---

operation, the regiment returned to Bombay, where it landed on the 23rd of April. On the 22nd of November, 1814, it embarked for service in Guzerat, and on the 11th of June, 1815, marched from Baroda and formed part of Colonel East's column in the operations against the Kattywar rebels, which ended with the capture of Beyt and Dwarka. The 65th arrived at Bombay on the 20th of May, 1816, and after serving against the Mahrattas, under Major Warren, in February, 1818, proceeded to Cutch, when after some active service it returned to Bombay on the 15th of April. Then followed the second expedition against Ras-ul-Khymah, and on the 8th of March, 1820, the regiment once more took up its quarters at Colabah in Bombay. After only a brief repose of two months, a detachment of the regiment proceeded, in May, 1820, once more to Cutch, where it was employed under Colonel the Hon. L. Stanhope in the brilliant assault of Dwarka. The detachment arrived at Bombay on the last day of the year, and on the 6th of January following sailed with the expedition organised under command of its old colonel, now Major-General L. Smith, C.B., to chastise the Beni-boo-Ali. This was its last service in India, and on the 19th of August, 1822, after an absence of nearly twenty-two years from England, the regiment had proceeded to Bombay from the Cape of Good Hope, the gallant 65th sailed from Bombay for the last time. General Sir Lionel Smith was appointed Governor and Commander-in-Chief at Mauritius, and died there about 1840, when he was succeeded by the late Sir William Gomm.

veller, visited them in 1835, they received him with open arms, and treated him most hospitably; they also conversed with him freely on the subject of their defeat, but, while entertaining no animosity against us, inveighed bitterly against the Imaum.* Altogether the retrospect of this Beni-boo-Ali *imbroglio* is not one on which we can look back with unmixed satisfaction, and while the murder of the pilot called for punishment which would have been sufficiently inflicted by the surrender of his murderers, a condition agreed to by the chief, there is reason to believe that the first Expedition was prosecuted by Captain Thompson as a concession to the interests of the Imaum of Muscat, not warranted by his instructions from the Bombay Government.

On the conclusion of this service the 'Prince of Wales' sailed for the Persian Gulf, and her first lieutenant, Mr. R. Kinchant, was placed in command of the 'Vestal,' ten-gun brig. He signalized his first command by attacking off the town of Biddah, on the Arabian Coast, opposite El Kateef, four trankies, full of armed men, which had been disturbing the peace of the Gulf. Lieutenant Kinchant attacked and sunk these trankies by his fire, for which service he received the thanks of the Bombay Government, and the captain of a ship of the Royal Navy then in the Gulf, informed him that had he been in the King's service he would have received promotion. In 1826 Lieutenant Kinchant received command of the 'Nautilus,' and so valuable were his services during the succeeding four years, in maintaining order and keeping down piracy in the Persian Gulf, that his Highness the Imaum of Muscat presented him with a valuable sword.

During the month of August, 1821, H.M.S. 'Liverpool,' fifty guns, visited the Persian Gulf on her return from China, and lost in a few days, from the effects of the great heat, Lieutenants Fenwick, Girardot and Bell, Surgeon Alexander, her assistant-surgeon, and five men. Mr. James B. Fraser, author of "Travels in Khorassan," who was at Bushire on the 19th of August, when the 'Liverpool' arrived at that port, says, speaking of the sufferings caused by the intense heat:—"For some time the lower deck of the ship resembled a slaughterhouse from the number of persons constantly undergoing the operation of venesection in every part of it."†

---

* For this hatred they had good cause, as Khadim-bin-Ali, brother of the chief taken to Bombay, died of his wounds on the way to Muscat, and eighty of the captives carried thither by the Imaum were confined in the eastern tower, where, says the native historian, "they died of starvation."

† It has been variously stated by writers of that day that the loss on board the 'Liverpool' was thirty or fifty men, and we, having mentioned the lesser number in a work of travel, entitled "The Land of the Sun," published in 1870, the late Captain John Wheatley, R.N.—who was good enough to inform us that he had perused the book with much pleasure—wrote the following letter correcting the erroneous statement. Captain Wheatley, then mate of the 'Liverpool,'

At this time a change was made in the uniform of the Bombay Marine. Hitherto the senior and junior captains and commanders had worn buff lapells and gold lace on their full-dress coats, and lieutenants buff lapells only; but, as a recognition for the good service rendered during the past few years in the Eastern Islands, at Mocha, and in the Persian Gulf, the following Orders were issued by the Bombay Government relative to the wearing of uniform by the officers of the Service:—

"Minute of Council, 24th of May, 1820. The Hon. the Governor in Council, considering it proper that the officers of the Hon. Company's Marine on this establishment should be placed, in respect to uniform, on a level with those of all other military services under this Government, has been pleased to direct that the commodore, the senior and junior captains, the commanders, and the first and second lieutenants, shall wear epaulettes, according to their respective ranks, distinguished as follows:—

"Commodore.—Two gold epaulettes, with a silver lion and two stars on each.

"Senior Captains.—Two gold epaulettes, with a silver lion and one star on each.

"Junior Captains.—Two gold epaulettes, with a silver lion only on each.

"Commanders.—Two gold epaulettes, plain.

"First-Lieutenants.—One gold epaulette, plain, on the right shoulder.

"Second-Lieutenants.—One gold epaulette, plain, on the left shoulder.

"It is further directed, that the undress of all officers (with the exception of the commodore) be without lace; and that the

participated in the operations against the Joasmi pirates of 1819-20, and died on the 19th of October, 1875:—" I hope you will not be annoyed at my stating that you have been misinformed as to the deaths on board of H.M.'s ship 'Liverpool,' in the Persian Gulf in 1821, as related in your book, the 'Land of the Sun.' The third-lieutenant, Girardot, having died late in the day, after having had the forenoon watch, orders were left for the officer of the morning watch to bury him as soon as he could see to read. A little before eight a.m. this officer, G. Bell, called me over (I was mate of the watch), and asked me why the cook had not brought the dinner aft. I answered that it was not yet eight o'clock; he replied that it was so hot he thought it was near noon. In about ten minutes time he called me over again and repeated the question. Seeing that he was not well, I prevailed on him to go below, saying that I would report eight o'clock to the captain, and sent for the midshipman to call the surgeon. He died in about an hour, as did the first-lieutenant, who had been unwell since the ship left China in the early part of the year. A day or two afterwards we lost the surgeon and assistant-surgeon, but only five men, and one of these fell, or rather was supposed to have fallen asleep, and fallen overboard from the main deck bow-part, where he was last seen seeking to cool himself. Excepting the officer of the watch, two look-out men, the quartermaster and man at the wheel, the crew were kept below, and all hands turned up to perform any operation. On arriving at Bushire we obtained a surgeon from a Company's cruiser."

undress of the commodore be distinguished by two rows of broad gold lace on the collar only; and that the full dress of all the officers do remain as it now is, with the addition of the epaulettes of their ranks respectively.

"This arrangement is to have effect from the 4th of the ensuing month of June."

The above remained the uniform of the Service until after the China War of 1840-42, when fresh regulations relative to the dress of the various grades were issued, under date 25th of April, 1843. Finally, by a Standing Order of the 28th of July, 1852, lieutenants and pursers were allowed two epaulettes as in the Royal Navy, and additions were made to the uniform of captains and commanders, and the various other ranks.

The year 1822 was a period of rest for the Bombay Marine, none of the cruisers, almost for the first time during the last thirty years, being engaged in warlike operations. One or two vessels were employed at Penang, and found some occupation in hunting up the pirates, who were still very active and aggressive; some cruisers were employed in the Red Sea, others on the coast of India on various duties, and five sail found full and constant work in the Persian Gulf, where they were engaged in cruising on the Arabian coast to watch the Joasmis and other pirate tribes. The military force* stationed at Kishm, under command of Colonel Kennett, suffered so severely from the intense heat, owing to the camp being on a rocky hill exposed to the heated prevailing wind, or *shemal*, that, in February, 1822, the troops were removed thence by the Company's cruisers to Sallack, on the south coast, eight and a half miles south-west of Deristan, and, later, to Bassadore†

---

* The troops in the island of Kishm consisted of Artillery, the Bombay European Regiment, 2nd Battalion 12th Regiment N.I., and Pioneers.

† Bassadore, which has the advantage of an excellent harbour, is situated at the point forming the north-west extremity of Kishm; a short distance within the point stand the ruins of the once flourishing Portuguese town of Bassadore. A survey of the port was made by Lieutenant J. H. Grubb, commanding the Hon. Company's brig 'Ternate,' which the Bombay Government caused to be published as "Directions for entering Bassadore Island," under date "Bombay Castle, 21st January, 1823;" and some years later, a "Report on Bassadore, with a Plan of the Roads," by Mr. Midshipman H. H. Hewett, was published. Lieutenant Grubb died soon after completing this survey, and at the same place, Moghu Bay, and on the same day (the 18th of June, 1823), Lieutenant R. Reynolds expired, both being young and accomplished officers. At the time of the abolition of the Indian Navy, the service buildings at Bassadore consisted of a hospital for invalid seamen, a store-house containing ships' stores, a cooper's shed, a forge, and a house for the small guard of the Marine Battalion stationed here. There were also three water reservoirs, a small bazaar for the supply of stores for the ship's companies, the house of Kadadah, the Persian merchant who catered for the officers of the squadron, and a small village inhabited by camp followers, some not of the most reputable kind. There were two or three houses belonging to officers, including the commodore's residence, where was a flagstaff for the display of the Union Jack, and, finally, a depot for a few hundred tons of coal brought from Bombay for the use of Hon. Company's ships of war.

on the same island, which continued to be the headquarters of the Indian Navy squadron up to the date of its abolition.

In 1823 the military force hitherto retained in the Gulf since the Expedition to Ras-ul-Khymah, was removed to Bombay, and the Bombay Marine squadron was left alone to fulfil the police duties of this inland sea. The year 1824 found the Service employed in a new sphere of active duty, but before treating of the part taken in the Burmese War by the Bombay Marine, we will detail the services of its officers in the more peaceful domain of Maritime Survey.

Though the preceding chapters, detailing the operations of the Hon. Company's Marine between the years 1793-1821, is a record of continuous service against the French, the Dutch, the pirates of the Eastern Archipelago and of the Persian Gulf, and other enemies of the Company by land as well as by sea, a record which, considering the strength of the Service, it cannot be gain-said was both varied and brilliant, yet the Bombay Marine did not neglect those scientific achievements with which the name and history of the Indian Navy will ever be identified. The small squadron of Company's cruisers were hurried, almost without intermission, from one field of active service to another; from the capture of Ras-ul-Khymah to Mauritius, thence to Java and the Eastern Islands, then back to the Persian Gulf and the Red Sea; but yet, amid the toils and dangers of active service, a small band of officers was constantly employed in surveying, and extending our knowledge of, the Eastern seas between Japan and the Cape of Good Hope.

CHAPTER XII.

1804—1828.

Proposed Survey of the Red Sea—Lord Valentia and Captain Keys—Resumption of the Survey by Lieutenants Court and Maxfield—Survey of the China Seas by Lieutenants Ross, Maughan, and Crawford—Services of Lieutenant Court, first Marine Surveyor-General in Bengal—Surveys by Lieutenant Maxfield—Examination of the East Coast of Africa by Captain Smee and Lieutenant Hardy—Death of Captain Court and Appointment of Captain Ross as Surveyor-General in Bengal—His Resignation and Appointment of Captain Lloyd—Surveys by Lieutenants Dominicetti and Collinson—Survey of the Persian Gulf by Lieutenants Maughan, Guy, Brucks, Haines, and other officers.

SINCE the cessation of all surveys in the year 1795, when Lieutenant Hayes returned from his voyage in the Eastern Archipelago, the ships of the Bombay Marine were fully occupied against France and her allies; but on the conclusion of the peace of Amiens, which proved so short and hollow, the surveys were resumed, and, notwithstanding the risk encountered by the officers of the Service, in prosecuting their researches, risks of no imaginary description, as some of them were captured while so engaged, and languished for a length of time in French dungeons, such was the ardour inspiring these gallant votaries of science, that no sooner were they released than they resumed their labours, while others of their brother officers eagerly volunteered their services for the dangerous but honourable task of benefiting mankind by mapping out the unknown seas of the Eastern hemisphere.

The only chart in existence of the Red Sea was drawn by Lieutenant Robert White, of the Marine, who, in the year 1795, when in command of the Hon. Company's cruiser 'Panther,' proceeded to Suez, making a cursory examination of its shores. In the year 1802-3, Lord Valentia,[*] while travelling in the East, was a guest of Lord Wellesley's at Calcutta, and proposed to his lordship to embark in one of the Company's cruisers on a voyage to the Red Sea, "for the

[*] "Voyages and Travels to India, Ceylon, the Red Sea, Abyssinia, and Egypt, in 1802-6, by George, Viscount Valentia." 3 vols. (London, 1809.)

purpose," as he says, "of investigating the Eastern shore of Africa, and making inquiries into the present state of Abyssinia, and the neighbouring countries." The Governor-General consenting, Lord Valentia, accompanied by his secretary, Mr. Salt, proceeded to Mangalore, where the 'Antelope,' carrying fourteen guns and a crew of eighty-seven men, was awaiting him. The brig was commanded by Captain Keys, who, his lordship says, was told "to consider himself as under my command," which, we may observe, must have been galling to an experienced officer who found an amateur civilian traveller placed over him on board his own ship. That the arrangement did not answer, was not surprising, and the fault can scarcely be entirely attributed to Captain Keys, of whom his lordship says, that "his manners were perfectly gentlemanly." The other officers were Lieutenants Hall and Maxfield, Mr. Hurst midshipman, and Dr. Maghie. The 'Antelope' sailed on the 13th of March 1804, from Mangalore for Aden and Mocha, where differences first arose between Captain Keys and his noble passenger. Thence the 'Antelope' proceeded to Dhalac, on the opposite coast, where, upon Lord Valentia sending Mr. Salt to request the use of a boat for the purpose of surveying, Captain Keys told him that he was commander of the ship, adding that his lordship appeared to be actuated by an intention "to take to himself the credit of discoveries and observations made by him and his officers." From Dhalac the 'Antelope' proceeded to Massowah, of which Lieutenant Maxfield made a survey. On the 8th of June, writes Lord Valentia, "I wrote officially to Captain Keys, informing him of my intention to go to Suakin, but that if the winds should prove too strong, I might probably go only as far as Ageeg, and then proceed for Jidda." It is not surprising that this peremptory style of correspondence was displeasing to Captain Keys, who, in his reply, notified that the 'Antelope' "must leave the Red Sea by the middle of August, in order to save her passage for the season." Then ensued a further heated correspondence, in which Lord Valentia accused Captain Keys of disobeying the Governor-General's orders, and that officer disclaimed any such intention. The 'Antelope' quitted Massowah on the 19th of June, and, on the same day, anchored in Antelope Bay, near Valentia Island, and, writes Lord Valentia condescendingly, "as the Captain wished Lieutenant Maxfield to survey it, I consented to stay for two days for that purpose." But the heat was so extreme that Mr. Maxfield fell ill, "when," writes the noble author, "I determined to depart the next day." He adds, "A great quantity of biscuit was this day condemned and thrown overboard. I heard that the salt provisions were in an equally bad state, and that there was only a small quantity of spirits on board; it was therefore fortunate we did not continue our voyage."

On the 24th of June the 'Antelope' arrived at Mocha, and, on the 7th of July, Lord Valentia having, as he says, "resigned his nominal command," proceeded on board H.M.S. 'Fox,' Captain Vashon, and, on the 9th, the 'Antelope' sailed for Bombay, taking Mr. Salt with official letters from Lord Valentia for the Governor, Mr. Duncan, and the Governor-General, preferring charges against Captain Keys.

The Captain of the 'Antelope' was placed under arrest* on his arrival at Bombay, and, on the 4th of December, 1804, Lord Valentia, who had returned to Bombay in the 'Fox,' again sailed for the Red Sea, in the Hon. Company's cruiser 'Panther,' commanded by Lieutenant Charles Court, appointed, as his lordship observes, " in consequence of the very high character which he bore as a seaman and a man of science." The 'Panther' had for a tender the 'Assaye,' a small schooner captured from the French, and purchased into the Marine, to the command of which Lieutenant Maxfield was appointed. The other officers were, Acting-Lieutenants Hardy, Crawford, and Hurst, and Mr. Criddle, Midshipman, all excellent observers. Lieutenant Court was of a more compliant nature than Captain Keys, and no hitch occurred to mar the success of the expedition. On the 19th of December they reached Mocha, and, on the 27th, Lieutenant Maxfield sailed for Massowah On the 2nd of January, 1805, the 'Panther' proceeded to Dhalac, Lord Valentia noting that he was " extremely surprised to find how incorrectly the Aroe Islands were laid down in Sir Home Popham's chart of the Red Sea," adding that "Captain Court expressed his surprise that Mr. Maxfield had been able to lay the places down so accurately in his chart,"—referring to the former voyage of the 'Antelope.' On the 6th of January Lieutenant Court landed at Dhalac, for the purpose of surveying the island, accompanied by Mr. Criddle, Midshipman, and also by Captain Rudland, of the Bombay Army, and Mr. Salt. The survey was completed by the 14th, and, on the following day, the 'Panther' proceeded to Massowah, where the 'Assaye' lay at anchor. On the 21st of January the ships sailed, and, on the 28th and 29th, Lieutenants Court and Maxfield were engaged on the survey of Port Mornington, (of which, and of Dhalac and Valentia Islands, and environs, there are charts in Vol. ii. of his lordship's work) the bay in which they were anchored being named Panther Bay. The survey of the coast and adjacent islands, was continued; the 'Panther' at one time running on a rock, whence she was only warped off after the guns, stores, and top hamper had been removed into a dhow, the

* Captain Keys was not long in disgrace, however, and, for many years, held the post of Master-Attendant at Bombay, and Member of the Marine Board.

officers and men displaying great smartness and discipline. On the 11th of February they arrived at Suakin, of which Lieutenant Court made a survey, and, on the 26th they sailed to Lent Bay, Sheikh Baroud, and Daroor, where the 'Panther' would have been lost but for Lieutenant Court's presence of mind in cutting her two cables, when the ship wore clear off the rocks, "though without an inch to spare." Thence, after visiting other points on the coast, the ships returned to Massowah, and on the 27th of March, anchored in Mocha Roads.

The 'Assaye' was now condemned as unseaworthy, as " the whole of her iron works were totally decayed, her timbers deficient in number, and, together with her bows and upper works, very bad, her bottom worm-eaten and rotten, and not a bolt to be discovered in her." Lord Valentia adds, " It is really astonishing how Mr. Sutherland and the Committee of Survey at Bombay, could have reported her fit for the service of the Marine, since she could not have been in a much worse state when she entered the Red Sea." But she was, doubtless, considered good enough for the duties of the survey, and for the safety of the scientific officers who would be attached to her. The 'Assaye' was broken up, and, on the 2nd of April, Lieutenant Maxfield and his crew were turned over to the 'Alert,' a merchant ship just restored by the authorities at Macullah, who had seized her. On the 8th of April the Hon. Company's cruiser 'Princess Augusta,' Lieutenant Bennett, arrived from Bombay, for the purpose of recovering the 'Alert,' and brought a new commander from the owners for that ship. Lieutenant Maxfield having lost his command, was ordered to return to Bombay with despatches, and, says Lord Valentia, "rough drafts of any discoveries which Captain Court had paid me the highly flattering compliment of dedicating to me."* He was accompanied by Acting-Lieutenant Hurst of the 'Panther,' who exchanged with Mr. Midshipman Denton of the 'Princess Augusta,' of whom Lord Valentia reports that "he turned out a fine manly lad, who had been educated at Eton."† The 'Princess Augusta,' accompanied by the 'Alert,' now sailed for Macullah to settle matters regarding the seizure of the latter ship and murder of her crew; and the 'Panther,' Lord Valentia remaining on shore, proceeded to the Straits of Babelmandeb, whence she returned on the 1st of June, her captain, says his lordship, "having completed his survey, and discovered more errors in Sir Home Popham's chart." After affairs at Macullah were settled amicably, the 'Alert' proceeded to Bombay on the 27th of May,

---

* The 'Princess Augusta' was one of three cruisers built in the same year at Bombay, the others being the 'Queen' and 'Princess Royal.'

† A brother of this officer, when Lieutenant of the Hon. Company's cruiser 'Sylph,' of eight guns, commanded by Lieutenant Graham, was killed in action against the Joasmi pirates in the Persian Gulf, on the 20th of October, 1808.

and the 'Princess Augusta' returned to Mocha where she cast anchor on the 15th of June. Important despatches having arrived from Suez for India on the 18th, the cruiser again sailed for Bombay on the 21st of June. On the same day the 'Panther' sailed for Massowah, taking with her Mr. Salt, accompanied by Captain Rudland, a Mr. Carter,* Pearce, a seaman, and seven attendants, who proceeded on an exploring mission into Abyssinia.

The 'Panther' arrived at Massowah on the 28th of June, and, on the 20th of July, the travellers started from Arkeeko on their journey; the cruiser, on the following day, returned to Mocha, where she cast anchor on the 16th of August. On the 10th of September the 'Panther' sailed to continue the survey of the opposite coast, and, on her return to Mocha, in the latter part of the month, the ship's company were instrumental in saving the town from being burnt down. On the 4th of November, embarking Lord Valentia, Lieutenant Court sailed again for Massowah, which was reached on the 7th of November, when Mr. Salt and his party came on board, having only that day arrived, after successfully accomplishing the journey to Antalo, the capital of the Rus, or ruler, of Tigre, of which an account may be found in Lord Valentia's work. The 'Panther' sailed on the 14th of November, but, after a narrow escape from destruction, when she lost four anchors, was forced to return to Massowah; here the cutter's crew, under Mr. Denton, got into a collision with the natives, and the long boat, armed with wall-pieces, under Lieutenant Crawford, was sent to their assistance. There was a brisk exchange of firing, in which the guns of the 'Panther' took part. On the 28th she sailed for Port Mornington, and thence proceeded to Jiddah, where she arrived on the 9th of December. Having received anchors, and provisions and water, of which he was in much need, Lieutenant Court sailed on the 2nd of January, 1806, for Suez, where he arrived on the 26th of January. On the 9th of February Lord Valentia finally quitted the 'Panther,' and, with many regrets, his lordship bid adieu to Lieutenant Court, "whom," he says, "I could not but love and esteem, and the other officers whose conduct had been certainly meritorious, and towards me uniformly kind and attentive. It was a pain-

* This gentleman soon after took the situation of supercargo on board the American ship 'Essex,' and was murdered with all the Europeans by some pirates, the instigator of the deed, one Seid Mohammed Akil, who had fortified the island of Camaran near Loheia, scuttling the ship after he had taken out the treasure, amounting to 120,000 dollars. The cruisers 'Mornington' and 'Ternate' were sent from Bombay to seize him, and drive him and his allies, the French, from Camaran, but he had timely intelligence of their destination, and quitted the island demolishing the defensive works. Pearce, on the other hand, did well, and rose to place and power in Abyssinia. He wrote, on the 28th of February, 1816, to Captain Court, an account of his position and prospects.

ful moment to us all. The lads cheered me as we quitted the vessel." Lord Valentia proceeded to England, and the 'Panther' returned to Bombay.

A large space of coast-line, and many islands were visited for the first time by the 'Panther' and 'Assaye,' and their positions were laid down, the names of those concerned in the survey being identified with some of the discoveries, as Court's Passage, Valentia Island, Annesley Bay (his lordship's family name), Antelope Bay, Panther Bay, Assaye Bay; also Port Mornington and Wellesley Islands, after the Governor-General, and Duncan Islands, in honour of the Governor of Bombay. The results of the survey made by Lieutenants Court and Maxfield, in the 'Panther' and 'Assaye,' were embodied in a chart, in two sheets, which may be found in Lord Valentia's work, and, considering the short time actually employed in the survey, and the miserably inadequate means at their disposal, the soundings and positions laid down show the result of a careful and comprehensive examination most creditable to those concerned. Lieutenant Maxfield, for his chart of Massowah and neighbouring coast, received a grant of 600 rupees from the Government, and his two assistants, Lieutenant Crawford and Acting-Lieutenant Hurst, were each awarded 200 rupees. In this chart of the Red Sea by Lieutenants Court and Maxfield, are laid down, not only the course of the 'Panther' and 'Assaye,' but the track of the Hon. Company's cruiser 'Swallow' in 1776, of the 'Venus' in 1787, and of the 'Panther' in 1795, under Lieutenant R. White, when Mr. Court was second lieutenant of that ship.

Even more important than this survey of the Red Sea, which was not of a sufficiently detailed character to fulfil the requirements of the navigator, was the admirable survey of the China Seas made by the officers of the Marine.

In 1806, Lieutenant Daniel Ross, accompanied by Lieutenant Philip Maughan,* proceeded in the 'Antelope' to China for the purpose of surveying those seas, and ascertaining the fate of two cruisers of the Service, the 'Intrepid,' Captain Roper, and 'Comet,' Captain Henry, which, as the reader will remember, had been despatched to inquire after the Hon. Company's ship 'Talbot,' but themselves were never heard of, though it is supposed they were lost on the fatal Paracels.

Lieutenants Ross and Maughan commenced their arduous task with the coasts east and west of Macao, from Tienpak westward, to the Lema Islands eastward, the various islands

* Lieutenant Philip Maughan—there were three officers of the name of Maughan in the Service, William, Jacob, and Philip—had already done good service as a Surveyor, for in 1804 he had made a chart of the Gulf of Cutch, for which the Government awarded him 1,000 rupees "as an encouragement to others to emulate his praiseworthy conduct."

and channels being minutely examined. These portions, with separate surveys of the Paracels Islands and shoals, and the coast of Palawan, were sent home and published by the Court.* A considerable delay then occurred, owing to the 'Antelope' having been captured by the French, and Lieutenants Ross and Maughan being conveyed as prisoners to Batavia. On their release and return to India, Captain Ross received charge of a second Expedition for the survey of the China seas, which was commenced in 1812, and Captains Maughan and Crawford subsequently joined him. About this period Lieutenant Houghton was first employed as draughtsman on this service. From that time forward, the survey was continued with all despatch by these officers, in two cruisers; the south-eastern part of the China Sea occupying one season; the Natuna, Anamba, and Tumbelan islands, with their channels, and parts of the coast of Borneo, the Straits of Gaspar and Carimata, and neighbouring rocks, other two seasons. Then they surveyed a portion of the coast of China, from the Great Lema to Namoa islands, with parts of the Pescadores and the island of Formosa, and made a cursory examination of the Bashee islands and channels. A slight survey of the southern and eastern coasts of Hainan was also made, and several of the harbours were very carefully examined. The same was done with the coast of Cochin China, for the purpose of testing the accuracy of the charts made by M. Dyot, an intelligent French officer in the service of the king of that country.

In 1818 and 1819, Captain Ross and his coadjutors were employed on the survey of the entrance to the Straits of Malacca, and the north and south sands within. The party on this duty assisted in forming the new settlement of Singapore,† under Sir Stamford Raffles, and constructed minute charts of the harbour and the adjacent coasts and islands. Connected with the general survey, the officers were engaged in various detached duties. On one occasion the two surveying vessels were ordered to accompany the ships of Lord Amherst's Embassy to the Gulf of Pecheli, when they proceeded to the mouth of the Peiho river. On their return, the officers, when detached from the other ships of the Embassy, visited and made separate surveys of parts of the coast, and two or three

---

* There were also published "Directions to accompany the Chart of the South Coast of China, by Daniel Ross and Philip Maughan, Lieutenants of the Bombay Marine." Printed by order of the Directors of the East India Company. (London, 1808.)

† Singapore owed its establishment as a free port to the suggestion of the enlightened Sir Stamford Raffles, then Governor of Bencoolen, who found a ready response from the Marquis of Hastings. "You found it," said the Singapore residents in an address to the Governor-General on his leaving India in 1823, "less than four years ago, a village of two hundred Malayan fishermen, and it is now a colony of one thousand industrious inhabitants collected from every quarter."

harbours of the province of Shantung. During the progress of these surveys, many discoveries were made of the highest importance to the navigation of those seas, and points and positions of objects fixed with accuracy, which had long been desiderata from the extreme want of correctness in all former charts.

In 1820 the surveys of the China seas were closed, and the vessels returned to Bombay. The work was not only of an arduous character, but great tact and caution were necessary, for fear of giving umbrage to the Chinese Government. The operations, when conducted near the shore, were closely watched, and at many of the harbours, particularly Amoy, Chinese warboats cruised about or anchored near the ships; the same jealousy was also exhibited off Formosa and Corea; hence the surveyor's exertions were frequently cramped, as they had received strict injunctions to avoid giving offence.

Captain Ross' charts, which were published, as they were completed, by the Court of Directors, were incorporated into a general chart by Captain Horsburgh. Though made more than half a century ago, with inferior instruments, and at a time when the science of marine surveying was in its infancy, these surveys have stood the test of revision in our day, and Admiral Sir Richard Collinson—than whom a more competent authority does not exist—expressed to us the surprise he experienced at their accuracy when going over the same ground during the China War. Captain Ross' health was so much shattered by exposure during the fourteen years over which the survey lasted, that he was only just enabled to complete the work, for which he received a grant of £1,500 from the Court of Directors.*

In 1809, the Court of Directors established a Marine Survey Department in Bengal, and Captain Wales, of the Marine, was appointed the first Surveyor-General. He was an officer of rare professional and scientific attainments. His father, Mr. John Wales, accompanied the great circumnavigator, Captain Cook, in the capacity of astronomer, in his first and second voyages, and was afterwards elected Master of Christ's Hospital; from him the son imbibed that taste for astronomy which gained him a considerable reputation in India, while his acquirements in the sister science of marine surveying, were the means of raising him to his present eminence. But Captain Wales did not long survive his appointment, and died in the following year, when he was succeeded by Captain Charles

* We find in the Records of the India Office that at a Special General Court of Proprietors of the East India Company, held on the 4th of April, 1821, confirmation was given to the Resolution of the General Court of the preceding 21st of March, approving the Resolution of the Court of Directors of the 17th of January, in which this grant of £1,500 was made to Captain Daniel Ross for his surveys.

Court, who held the office with conspicuous success for a period of eleven years. That the Service should contain on its rolls at one time such eminent men as Wales, Court, Ross, Crawford, Maughan, Houghton, and others we have mentioned, is certainly a noteworthy circumstance.

Mr. W. T. Money, Superintendant of the Bombay Marine —afterwards a Director of the Company—spoke as follows of the character and services of this distinguished officer, when introducing him to the Court of Directors on the 15th of July, 1809 :—" Upon this occasion, Hon. Sir, I have to discharge a very pleasing part of my duty in bringing to your notice the services and merits of a very respectable officer. Lieutenant Court, after acquiring a knowledge of his profession in the East Indian Service, was appointed to the Hon. Company's Marine in the year 1790, and served as second lieutenant of the 'Panther,' on a cursory survey of the Red Sea, under Lieutenant White; and in the same station on board the ' Bombay' frigate, Commodore Picket, he was actively engaged in the reduction of Colombo and its dependencies. As first lieutenant of the same ship he gallantly served at the reduction of Monado, in Celebes, and was appointed to the command of Fort Amsterdam, which he held for nine months, under the most critical circumstances, in a hostile country. In reward of his distinguished merits in this trying situation, he was appointed Resident at Monado, and commandant of all the British troops in Celebes.

" During the period of his command in this important post, which he held for seven years, he completely succeeded in conciliating the vast population of that valuable island, and attaching all ranks to the British Government; having, by the personal influence which his wise conduct had acquired for him, accomplished a treaty with all the chiefs, by which very considerable advantages were secured to the Hon. Company, and many barbarous customs, which tended to render a people, naturally mild and inoffensive, cruel and vindictive, were solemnly abandoned. Had peace not restored to the Dutch their possessions to the eastward, Monado would have been rendered, by Mr. Court's prosperous administration, a valuable acquisition to the East India Company.

" Upon the restoration of the Moluccas, Lieutenant Court returned to the active duties of his profession ; and in command of the ' Princess Augusta,' with a small squadron, he blockaded Severndroog, where he captured thirty-six vessels, seven of the largest of which he cut out from under the guns of the fort, and obtained restitution of a dhow laden with Company's coffee to a considerable amount.

" From this station he was recalled and selected to command the Hon. Company's ship ' Ternate,' in pursuit of ' La Fortune,' which had recently captured the 'Fly,' but upon his arrival at Bombay, he found that the enemy was a prize to H.M.S. 'Concorde.' Lieutenant Court was then, at particular request, appointed to command the 'Panther,' and proceeded with Lord Valentia to the Red Sea, where he prosecuted a tedious, an arduous, and a difficult survey of the Abyssinian coast, with great credit to himself and perfect satisfaction to his lordship.

"Soon after his return to Bombay in 1807, he was selected to be my assistant, and from his attention, assiduity, and ability, I have derived such valuable aid in the discharge of my public duties, that I part from Mr. Court's services with the utmost regret, and shall ever hold them in thankful remembrance."

Beside the survey of the China Seas, two vessels, under the command of Captain Maxfield—the same officer who had done such good service in the 'Antelope,' and in command of the 'Assaye,' tender to the 'Panther,' under Lieutenant Court, between the years 1803-6—were employed surveying the Bay of Bengal and searching for various shoals. His chart of the coast from Saugor Point to Lighthouse Point, at the mouth of the Hooghly, from a survey executed in 1816, was in use until it was superseded by Captain R. Lloyd's work in 1841. In 1821 Captain Court sent Captain Maxfield in the 'Henry Meriton,' to investigate the capabilities of an anchorage inside the Armagon, or Armogham shoal, north of Madras, Lat. 14° 1′ N. Long. 80° 10′ E., in consequence of a report by the Commander-in-Chief in Indian waters, Admiral Sir H. Blackwood, that H.M.S. 'Leander' had found safe anchorage there for four days during the monsoon. Captain Maxfield, who made a chart of the shoals of Pulicat and Armagon, spoke favourably of the anchorage inside the latter, since known as Blackwood's Harbour. He observes in his report, which was published by order of the Madras Government, on the 19th of July, 1822, that, "it offers many public advantages, and from its vicinity to Madras, promises security to shipping trading to that place, which is no where else to be found on the coast of Coromandel."

In 1810 Captain Horsburgh was appointed Hydrographer to the Company, in succession to Mr. A. Dalrymple, who had died two years before. Captain Horsburgh* had brought out the

* Captain Horsburgh held the office of Hydrographer up to the time of his death in 1836. The following fourteen charts, compiled by Horsburgh, were published by the Company, viz. :—1. North Atlantic Ocean. 2. South Atlantic Ocean. 3. Part of the Indian Ocean. 4. East Peninsula of India. 5. West Coast of Sumatra. 6. Straits of Rhio and Durian. 7. Straits of Banca and Gaspar. 8. Carimata Passage. 9. Strait of Sunda. 10. China Sea (two sheets.) 11. Canton River. 12. East Coast of China. 13. Eastern passage to China (three sheets.) 14. Tracks through Pitt Passage and Dampier Strait (1793).

first edition of his famous "East Indian Directory," a work compiled to a great extent from the surveys of the officers of the Marine, in the year 1808. Nine years later appeared the second edition, and from that time up to the year 1873, three other editions were published. In the latter year Commander A. Dundas Taylor, of the Indian Navy, an officer second to none in the service as a scientific surveyor, produced the first part of his "India Directory," and though, as he modestly states on his title page, he only claims for his book that it is "founded" upon Captain Horsburgh's work, it has, in point of fact, been entirely rewritten.

On the 2nd of January, 1811, the 'Ternate,' Captain T. Smee, and 'Sylph,' Lieutenant Hardy, sailed from Bombay on a mission to examine the African coast as far south as Zanzibar, and gather information relative to that state, and adjacent countries. Having convoyed two merchant vessels, bound for Mocha, as far as Socotra, they parted company on the 12th of January, and, passing Cape Guardafui, continued examining the coast line of Africa, and leaving the Juba River, (or Rio dos Fuegos of old navigators) on the 9th of February, anchored at Patta (in lat. 2° 9′ S. long. 41° 2′ E.) when Captain Smee and Lieutenant Hardy paid a visit to the ruler, Sultan Hammed, to whom they presented the gifts and letters from Mr. Duncan, the Governor of Bombay. This chief, however, was very unfriendly, and the British officers, after a detention of a whole day, thought themselves fortunate in being permitted to return to their ships in safety. The natives along this coast are very treacherous, and on the last occasion on which a British ship of war had visited them, in February, 1799, when the 'Leopard,' flagship of Admiral Blankett, and the 'Dœdalus' were proceeding on a voyage to the Red Sea, Lieutenant Mears and several men were entrapped and killed at the Juba River.* On the 23rd of February, the 'Ternate' and 'Sylph' anchored at Zanzibar, when the captains paid a visit to the Hakim, or Viceroy, of the Imaum of Muscat; while at Zanzibar the ships fired royal salutes in honour of the capture of Mauritius, an event, which Captain Smee records, was displeasing to the Hakim, whose attitude was unkindly towards the British. It was not until the 7th of April that the Governor returned Captain Smee's visit, when both the ships dressed and saluted. On the 9th the 'Ternate' proceeded to Mocha, where she arrived on the 26th of April, but the 'Sylph' remained behind to protect the Surat merchants from the extortionate demands of the Hakim, who expressed his determination to compel them to pay 3,500 crowns as the tribute exacted by the Imaum, although they had already paid the customary port dues. This the 'Sylph' prevented, and ultimately convoyed the trading

* See Memoir by Captain Bisset, of the 'Leopard,' published by Dalrymple.

ships to Bombay.* In addition to exploring the East African Coast the officers of the Mission made a brief vocabulary of the Soowalie, Soomalie, and Galla dialects, and collected much information relative to the political and commercial state of Zanzibar and the adjacent portions of the continent.

Captain Court died at Calcutta on the 9th of September, 1821, universally regretted,† and was interred with the military honours due to his rank, the Hon. Company's surveying ship, 'Henry Meriton,' firing minute guns, and a large detachment of H.M.'s 87th Regiment, under the command of Colonel Shaw, C.B., escorting the remains to the grave. He was succeeded in the office of Marine Surveyor-General of India by Captain Daniel Ross, F.R.S.—a man possessing attainments as a marine surveyor far in advance of his time—with Captain John Crawford of the Marine, who had been engaged in the Red Sea survey under Captain Court, as his chief assistant. Captain Ross, who was called the "Father of the Indian Surveys," introduced, among his subordinates, the scientific methods which he had employed with such good results in the China Seas. Captain Ross had many difficulties to combat, and between the years 1824-26, the Burmese War caused the interruption of the surveys,‡ when the surveying ship 'Research,' Captain John Crawford—with Messrs. C. B. Richardson and C. Montriou, of the Marine, as his officers—was fitted with ten guns, and participated in the military operations, when Mr. Rogers, the second officer, was killed in action. However, during a portion of these years, Captain Ross was enabled to

* For details of this voyage see "Observations During a Voyage of Research on the East Coast of Africa from Cape Guardafui south to the island of Zanzibar, in the Hon. Company's cruisers 'Ternate,' Captain T. Smee and 'Sylph,' schooner, Lieutenant Hardy. (Vol. vi. of "Transactions of Bombay Geographical Society, p. 23-61.)

† The "Calcutta Journal" of that date paid the following tribute to the worth of Captain Court:—" In the year 1813, he had the misfortune to lose his wife, one of the daughters of Sir George Holroyd, whom he had married in 1809 while in England, a young lady whose personal attractions were only surpassed by her unassuming virtues and superior mental attainments; from that period to the termination of his own earthly career, he shrunk from the world's observation, and never regained the wonted serenity of his mind nor the vigour of his faculties. The severity of his premature loss confirmed that disposition to retirement which was congenial to the natural modesty of his mild and unassuming character; and although he possessed, in the resources of his cultivated and accomplished understanding, and in the amiable virtues of his heart, most of those qualities which contribute to adorn the intercourse of private life, or which are conducive to distinction in a more extensive sphere of action, he nevertheless passed the remainder of his life in a seclusion, which, if it withdrew him from public observation, was yet favourable to the cultivation of those characteristic endowments which he chiefly valued, and the benign and gentle influence of which has left an indelible impression on the memory of his surviving friends."

‡ The following is a return of the cost of the Bengal Marine Surveys from 1821 to 1824. 1821-22.—Annual expense of survey vessels 'Nearchus,' 'Minto,' 'Sophia,' and 'Henry Meriton,' Rs. 1,19,055. 1823-24.—Annual expense of survey vessels 'Research' and 'Investigator,' Rs. 59,379.

employ his own ship, the 'Investigator,' also fitted as a man-of-war, in the survey of the Mergui Archipelago, and the 'Research,'* when she was not employed in the military operations. In 1825-26 Captain Crawford surveyed part of the Coast of Arracan in the Hon. Company's armed brigs 'Sophia' and 'Freak,'† and in February, 1827, he hired the brig 'William,' of 150 tons, and continued in her the survey of the Arracan coast. Lord William Bentinck, on his accession to power in 1828, inaugurated a reign of retrenchment, and, unhappily, his lordship extended his economies to the Marine Survey Department, which was ordered to be broken up; the 'Freak' was sold, and the 'Investigator' declared to be unseaworthy on account of the ravages of the white ants. " Stout old Daniel Ross," says Markham, "was urgent and importunate in advocating a resumption of the good work; and, in 1830, he again had two brigs, the 'Flora' and 'Sophia,' in the Mergui Archipelago, under his assistant, Lieutenant Lloyd, while he himself examined the coast of Arracan.‡ Captain Ross did his work with great care and regard for scientific accuracy, and it

* On January 23, 1827, the 'Research' proceeded under Captain Dillon, in search of the French Navigator, La Perouse. Captain Dillon asserted, in a letter to the Calcutta papers, that in May, 1826, while proceeding from Valparaiso to Pondicherry, he found some articles belonging to La Perouse at Tucopia, one of the Malicolo Islands, part of the new Hebrides group. Commodore Hayes wrote a letter to the Calcutta papers, approving Captain Dillon's theory and advocating the despatch of the 'Research.' In this letter the Commodore mentions several geographical facts connected with this portion of the Pacific, which he examined in 1793-95, and in particular states that he ascertained that the Louisiade group forms no part of the mainland of New Guinea. The 'Research' first proceeded to Tasmania and Sydney, and thence to Malicolo, where Captain Dillon succeeded in procuring certain articles said to be relics of the great navigator. From thence he proceeded to New Zealand and Sydney, where his arrival in January, 1828, created an extraordinary sensation. According to the "Sydney Gazette," the "'Research' was daily thronged with visitors," and the articles exhibited "strike conviction into the mind of the most sceptical, and satisfy all of their undoubted identity." Captain Dillon was credited "with the utmost praise for coolness, intrepidity, and skill" in navigating his ship. With these relics Captain Dillon proceeded to Calcutta, and thence made his way to England and France. The French Monarch, considering that he had proved his title to the reward promised by the Decree of the 28th of February, 1798, by an Ordinance dated the 22nd of February, 1829, conferred on Captain Dillon the dignity of Knight of the Legion of Honour, and besides granted him an indemnity of 10,000 francs and an annual pension of 4.000 francs, while the Company renounced all claims to participate in these rewards.
† See "Remarks on the Coast of Ava from Thaygin, or Pagoda Point, to the Calventuras ; to accompany the Survey carried on in the Hon. Company's armed brigs 'Sophia' and 'Freak,' by order of Commodore Hayes, commanding the flotilla, Coast of Arracan." By Captain John Crawford, Bombay Marine, Calcutta, the 6th of October, 1826.
Captain Daniel Ross, the Marine Surveyor-General, in a Notification, dated Fort William, March 29, 1827, reports "having surveyed the Martaban river from the West Point of Palo Gaun, round its northern extremity, past Moulmein, down as far as Long Island."
‡ Captain Ross' MS. Sailing Directions for the Mergui Archipelago survived the general destruction of Records, and are still preserved in the Geographical Department of the India Office.

VOL. I.   D D

was all on a trigonometrical basis. He measured bases on shore by running a ten-foot rod along a cord stretched tight between the extreme points, and kept in position by stakes, the direction being verified by a telescope. When work on shore was impracticable, recourse was had to measurement by sound. The vessels were anchored when the weather was calm, and the time was taken between the flash and report of a gun, on the assumption that sound travels 1,140 feet per second. All angles were taken with a sextant, and the triangulation was verified by frequent astronomical observations. In Ross' time the Government of India used to strike off a few copies of his charts at Calcutta by lithography, and send the originals to the India House for engraving and publication." The Company published Captain Ross' charts of "Chittagong to Arracan River," and "Arracan River to Foul Island."

In November, 1833, Captain Ross resigned his appointment, and retired to Bombay, where he was appointed Master Attendant, and, in 1838, succeeded Sir Charles Malcolm, Superintendent of the Indian Navy, in the office of President of the Bombay Geographical Society. He was succeeded in the post of Marine Surveyor-General by his Assistant, Commander Robert Lloyd,* who had served under him for ten years. He held the office until 1840, when it was abolished, and during that period did much and useful work. One of the great clogs to the usefulness of the department arose from its being placed under the control of a Marine Board, composed of civilians who knew little more of the necessities of the survey and of the means by which the duties could be accomplished, than the green-covered table round which their meetings were held.

Lieutenant Dominicetti, who was employed on a survey of the coasts of the Southern Concan, wrote a valuable report, dated the 9th of June, 1819, an extract from which, relating to the ports of Viziadroog and Zyghur, was published by order of the Governor in Council. At this time Lieutenant Robert Moresby was engaged on a survey of the Madagascar Archipelago, which was published by the Court of Directors in 1822. Lieutenant W. S. Collinson, in the Company's cruiser 'Prince of Wales,' with Lieutenants J. C. Hawkins and R. Moresby as his assistants, was engaged in surveying to the eastward, and, under date "'Prince of Wales,' the 31st of October, 1822," he published his "Directions for passing through the north-east entrance of the straits of Singapore from the Straits of Dryon." While thus engaged the Supreme Government directed him to proceed to the Nicobars, in order to search and rescue the survivors of

---

* This veteran officer still survives, the last of the school of surveyors of which McCluer, Court, Ross, and Crawford, were distinguished exemplars; and who were the predecessors of the school of Haines, Carless, Moresby, and Elwon, and of the still later band of hydrographers.

the crew of the ship 'Futtel Mine,' which was stated to have been lost some months before on the island of Nancowrie in that group. Accordingly, in December, Lieutenant Collinson sailed from Prince of Wales' Island, and in his report, dated the 15th of January, 1823, states that he first searched the Great Nicobar, when he learned from the natives that a ship had been lost on the south-west side, about two or three years previous, but that the survivors had been removed from the island a few months before by a brig with a European crew. He then visited the islands of Little Nicobar, Nancowrie, Carmorta, and Bampoka, the inhabitants of which he describes as "mild and inoffensive," but he discovered no trace of the missing ship or crew.

In 1820, on the conclusion of the Expedition against the Joasmi pirates, a systematic survey of the Persian Gulf was undertaken under orders of the Bombay Government, which rightly considered that a thorough knowledge of every creek and backwater of the pirate coast, was absolutely essential to enable the Company's cruisers to follow or ferret out the Arab craft, whose familiarity with the coast enabled them to elude pursuit. Nearchus was probably one of the first Europeans to traverse the waters of the Gulf, of which Benjamin of Tudela speaks in 1292; but it was not until the visit of the illustrious Niebuhr in 1764, that any attempt was made to construct a chart. As far as it goes, this chart is described by Lieutenant J. R. Wellsted, I.N., in his "City of the Caliphs," as of "extraordinary accuracy." Of the labours of Lieutenant McCluer, of the Bombay Marine, we have already spoken; he wrote a memoir as well as made a chart of the little traversed waters of this inland sea, and, at a later period, surveys of portions of the Gulf were made by some officers of the Service.

In March, 1811, when the 'Benares' and 'Prince of Wales' were sent to cruise in the Persian Gulf, an officer was put on board the 'Benares' specially to survey such places as the cruising duties would permit; these vessels returned to Bombay in November of the same year, and of necessity, the scientific results achieved were of that elementary order known as a "flying survey."

In November, 1817, Lieutenant Tanner visited the ports of Bahrein and the pearl banks of that island, for his memoir and surveys of which he received the thanks of Government, and they were published in Horsburgh's Directory. To the credit of this talented and energetic officer it may also here be mentioned that he established the first regular code of signals used in the Bombay Marine, for which Government highly commended him.

Though it was not until 1820 that the survey of the Persian Gulf commenced, it appears that the Court of Directors had issued instructions directing its prosecution so far back as the latter part of 1815; the disturbed state of the Gulf, however, rendered hopeless the task of examining its shores. The survey was, in the first instance, entrusted to Captain Philip Maughan, a veteran hydrographer, who had been the chief assistant of Captain Ross throughout his arduous and lengthened survey of the China Seas between 1806-20. Captain Maughan entered the Bombay Marine in the year 1798 as a midshipman. He saw much service when a young officer, and received a ball in the leg, which he carried to the grave at his death in November, 1865, at the advanced age of eighty-two years. In consequence of this wound Mr. Maughan proceeded to England, but returned to Bombay overland, being, perhaps, one of the first to proceed by this route. He brought to India the news of the peace of Amiens in 1802, making the voyage from Suez to Bombay in a native craft. In 1820 Captain Maughan proceeded to the Gulf in command of the 'Discovery,' a ship of 289 tons and fourteen guns, with Lieutenant J. M. Guy, as assistant surveyor, in the 'Psyche,' ten-gun brig, of 180 tons. Operations were commenced at Cape Mussendom, the design being to examine the western, or Arabian, shore, which had been little frequented by merchant ships, owing to its being the haunt of pirates from time immemorial, and only occasionally visited by vessels of war, who avoided the dangers incidental to traversing one of the most difficult coasts in the world. In November, 1821, Captain Maughan was forced through ill-health to give up the survey, when Lieutenant Guy succeeded to the command. At this time we find that the following were the officers attached to the two surveying vessels, and, if we add to these the names of Lieutenants W. Denton, S. B. Haines, J. R. Wellsted, H. B. Lynch, J. P. Sanders, Henry A. Ormsby, F. D. W. Winn, C. E. B. Mitchell, R. Ethersey, G. B. Kempthorne, and H. Pinching, who were employed at various times in one or other of the two ships, certainly we have not often seen a greater combination of special talent than the list displays :—

'Discovery.'—Lieutenant John Michael Guy, Commanding; Lieutenant Robert Cogan, First-Lieutenant; Lieutenant W. E. Rogers, Second-Lieutenant; Lieutenant W. L. Clement, Third-Lieutenant; Lieutenant John Houghton, Draughtsman; Mr. J. Anderson, Assistant-Surgeon; Mr. E. B. Squire, Midshipman; Mr. Thomas Mullion, Midshipman; Mr. H. H. Whitelock, Midshipman.

'Psyche.'—Lieutenant George Barnes Brucks, Commanding; Lieutenant W. Lowe, First-Lieutenant; Lieutenant J. H. Rowband, Second-Lieutenant; Lieutenant Thomas E. Rogers, Third-Lieutenant; Mr. W. Spry, Assistant-Surgeon; Mr.

George Pilcher, Midshipman; Mr. Charles Boyè, Midshipman; Mr. George Peters, Midshipman. The task, notwithstanding that the officers suffered much from fever, was now pushed on with all despatch, being only obstructed by the necessity for the small cruisers to proceed in search of water and supplies; and, early in 1822, Lieutenant Guy forwarded to Government an interesting report of the so-called Pirate Coast. The difficulty of surveying this tract was much increased by the coast-line being, in many places, almost invisible from the ship's anchorage, with scarcely an object for many miles that could be employed as a station. Lieutenant Guy discovered twenty-seven islands and islets, and the last group he explored, consisted of nine, on which there were some three or four hundred inhabitants, who had quitted the town of El Biddah, in 1821, when their houses had been burned by the Hon. Company's brig 'Vestal,' in consequence of their piratical doings.

On the 11th of February, 1823, Lieutenant Guy was obliged to proceed to the Presidency owing to his health having failed, and Lieutenant Brucks succeeded to the command. The MS. of the portion of the survey completed by Lieutenant Guy, is preserved in the Geographical Department of the India Office, and was the work of Lieutenant Houghton,* who executed it at the request of his commander. Horsburgh, the hydrographer to the Company, entertained the highest opinion of the talents of this latter officer, and always expressed great admiration for the beautiful execution and artistic finish of his charts. Lieutenant Guy was also greatly indebted to Lieutenants Cogan, Haines, Whitelock, and W. E. Rogers, the latter of whom, on the retirement of Lieutenants Guy and Cogan, succeeded to the command of the 'Discovery.'

Lieutenant Brucks prosecuted the survey with great vigour, and, in April, 1825, the whole western coast of the Persian Gulf having been surveyed, the 'Psyche' returned to Bombay, and was sold out of the Service in July. Early in the following year Lieutenant Brucks resumed operations, and examined the head of the Gulf, thence proceeding down the coast of Persia. " In order to form some idea of the difficulties encountered in these operations," says a contemporary writer, " as well as the energy and perseverance of the gentlemen employed, it may be observed that, in the course of a fortnight, in spite of all the obstacles they met with from the extensive sand-flats, running sometimes nearly eight miles off shore, through which the officers and men had to wade middle deep, they were enabled to

---

* Lieutenant C. G. Constable refers to the accuracy and finish of this talented officer's work, in his paper read before the Bombay Geographical Society on the 21st of February, 1856. Captain Houghton died in London on the 19th of May, 1874.

complete a distance of seventy-nine miles." Lieutenant Brucks pushed on his operations with unabated vigour, and, having subjected the whole of the Persian littoral within the Gulf, together with the several islands, banks, and shoals, to a careful examination, completed the survey in the April of 1828.

The survey of the entrance to the Gulf was resumed in October, and pushed on with great zeal and success until the following February, when Lieutenant Brucks, having completed the examination of the coast as far as Guadel, at length succumbed to the lengthened hard work and exposure. Proceeding to Muscat he made over charge of the 'Benares' to Lieutenant S. B. Haines, who, assisted by Lieutenant Pinching, and other officers, prosecuted a minute survey of the Mekran and Guadel coasts. Up to this time the whole shore from Mandavee to Kurrachee had been practically unsurveyed, while from this point to Cape Guadel, the coast of Mekran had been but slightly laid down by Lieutenant Maskal, and from thence to the entrance of the Persian Gulf only flying surveys had been made until Brucks and Haines, and their coadjutors, undertook the task. In April, 1829, this latter talented officer visited Kurrachee, and make a rough survey of the harbour, though the native authorities, with a just premonition that such a step would be the prelude to its occupation by the insatiable lords of more than half of India, showed the greatest reluctance to permit the examination. In May, 1829, the 'Benares' returned to Bombay.

Lieutenant Brucks was not a scientific observer of the calibre of Ross, Lloyd, and others of the Service, but his deficiencies were amply made up by the acquirements of a singularly able band of assistants. The survey of the Persian Gulf occupied nearly nine years, and, in 1829, when it was completed, only one of the officers who had joined the 'Discovery' and 'Psyche' at its commencement—Brucks himself, who attained the rank of Commander on the 24th of March, 1829—was so fortunate as to retain his health, and just as all was nearly complete, he also broke down and was obliged to take two years' leave.*

The following detailed account of the work done during the last eighteen months of the survey, is derived from the journal of one of the officers :—The 'Discovery' left Bassadore and com-

* The following were the resultant charts :—Entrance to the Gulf of Persia, Lieutenant Brucks, 1828. Coast of Arabia from Ras Goberhinde to Ras Soaste, Lieutenant Brucks, 1828. Gulf of Persia, Commander Brucks, 1830. Persian Gulf (Arabian side) from Cape Mussendom to the Euphrates. Island and harbour of Bahrein, Lieutenant Brucks, 1825. Anchorage of El Katiff, Lieutenant Brucks. Entrances to the rivers at the head of the Persian Gulf, Lieutenants Brucks and Haines. Coast of Persia, from Ras Tuloop to Bushire, 1826. Bushire Roads, 1826. Coast of Persia from Bushire to Bassadore, Lieutenants Brucks and Haines. Clarence Straits, Commander Brucks. Coast of Persia and Beloochistan from Koe Mubarrack to Kurrachee, 1823.

menced to survey the Channel called Clarence Strait, on the 6th of December, 1827 ; arrived at Bunder Abbas, on the 9th of January, 1828. Then surveyed Ormuz and Larrack, and on the 30th of January commenced the survey of the south coast of Kishm Island, at Kishm Point. Anchored in Angar Sound on the 3rd of February, 1828 ; arrived at Bassadore on the 17th of February, after which went to Kishm, where they obtained a pilot for the Arabian coast east of Mussendom. They then sailed across and commenced to survey at Ras Goberindee on the 25th of February, 1828. The 'Discovery' was towed between Lima Island and the main by her boats, and here they experienced strong tides. On the 13th and 14th they were at anchor in the little cove of Dooal Huffar; the breeze was fresh from north-west to south-west, with hard puffs, and at eight a.m., on the 15th of March, they weighed and made sail across the cove, but, owing to a sudden shift of wind when in stays, she was nearly driven against the rocks, and dropped an anchor and laid out a long warp. The rocks at this time were seen covered with men, when before, as long as the ship was safe, no one was visible. That afternoon they anchored off the town of Dibbah, Fort S., 43° W., 11 fathoms sand ; at night a fresh gale set in from south-west, water quite smooth. On the 20th of March, the 'Discovery' anchored in Khore Fakaun in 6¼ fathoms. Here they filled up their water, and the crew washed their clothes on shore. On the 25th of March they were off Khore Culbah. The 'Inspector,' schooner, had joined them at Dibbah, so that she assisted in the survey of this part. On the 6th of April anchored in Muttrah Bay, and surveyed that and Muscat Cove. On the 20th of April, 1828, left Muscat for Bombay.

The 'Discovery' was sold out of the service in May, 1828, and on the 11th of August following, the 'Benares' sailed for the Persian Gulf with the following officers : Lieutenant S. B. Haines, in command ; Lieutenants H. N. Pinching, F. D. W. Winn, Henry Ormsby; Master, Thacker,* and Midshipmen Charles Parbury,† James Young, C. D. Campbell, and G. B. Kempthorne. The 'Benares' made the "direct" passage to Bassadore in twenty days, the weather being very stormy, and discharging some stores she had brought for the squadron, proceeded to Bahrein to demand return of the cargo of a native vessel under British colours, which had been plundered by the Sheikh and his people. The 'Benares' carried her armament of fourteen guns, and full complement of men, and was as ready to fight as to survey. It was not, therefore, until Lieutenant Haines had warped his little ship into the harbour, and threatened immediate hostilities that restitution was made, and the

* Died from the effects of climate.
† Proceeded to England on sick leave and died from the effects of climate.

'Benares' returned to Bombay with a costly cargo of spices. In October, Commander Brucks rejoined the 'Benares,' with Lieutenant Haines as Assistant-Surveyor, and Mr. Midshipman H. A. M. Drought joined the ship. On the 8th of that month the 'Benares' sailed from Bombay to resume the survey of the Gulf. She went to Bushire, and from that place sailed for the pearl banks off Bahrein. On the 19th of November the survey was commenced, according to the journal, at Jez-el-Suffie, whence they went to Sherarow, anchored at Guffoy, and sailed to Arlat, Arzennie, Dalmy, and other places; returned to Bassadore on the 3rd of December, sighting Seir Aboneid and Bomosa on the way. Left on the 18th of December to survey off Bassadore, and after three days surveying on the flat, sailed to survey the Mekran coast. Began due east of Ormuz on the 6th of January, 1829. On the 19th of January, anchored near a shoal to survey it, in 6 fathoms, Koe Mubarrack rock bearing N. 45° W. On the 22nd of January engaged surveying Jask Bay. On the 8th of February broke off the survey at Charbar, and sailed to Muscat, when Lieutenant Brucks left, being sick. Lieutenant Haines resumed the survey at Charbar, on the 20th of February, and surveyed to Kurrachee, which the 'Benares' left on the 12th of April, and returned west to Guadel Bay, whence she sailed on the 30th of April for Bombay.

Several papers of great value and interest, descriptive of the Persian Gulf, were contributed by officers of the Service. Lieutenant Brucks wrote a "Memoir Descriptive of the Navigation of the Persian Gulf."* Lieutenant Kempthorne supplied to the Journals of the Royal and Bombay Geographical Societies, articles on the "Identification of Places Visited by Nearchus' Fleet;" on "The Ancient Commerce of the Persian Gulf;" and on "A Visit to the Ruins of Tahrie,"† near Congoon. Lieutenant H. H. Whitelock, of the 'Discovery,' wrote "An Account of the Arabs of the Pirate Coast," and an admirable paper, entitled "Descriptive Sketch of the Islands and Coast at the entrance of the Persian Gulf."‡

On the cessation of the monsoon, in October, 1829, the 'Benares' was again employed on a survey not less important than that of the Persian Gulf, and equally admirable and accurate in its execution; we refer to that of the Red Sea. Of the officers who had served under Brucks and Haines, only Pinching, Winn, Young, and Campbell, were engaged in this arduous task, under the command of Captain Thomas Elwon.

* Bombay Selections, No. 24, pp. 527-634.
† Royal Geographical Society's Journal, Vol. V., p. 263. Transactions of the Bombay Geographical Society, Vol. I., p. 294, and Vol XIII., p. 125.
‡ Royal Geographical Society's Journal, Vol. VIII., p. 170. Bombay Geographical Society's Transactions, Vol. I., p. 113. In the latter volume, pages 32-54, may also be found Lieutenant Whitelock's paper on the Pirate Coast.

A detailed account of this survey will be given in another chapter.

On the 4th of February, 1828, Commander Moresby sailed from Bombay in the cruiser 'Thetis,' to commence the survey of the Laccadive Islands,* but no detailed account of the operations was afforded, though the Court published a chart. The examination was not executed with the minuteness with which, seven years later, the same highly scientific officer conducted the survey of the Maldive group, which, with his work in the Red Sea, will remain a monument to his industry and skill.

* Laccadive is a corruption of the Sanskrit words, "Luksha Dwipa," or "one hundred thousand islands;" and was given them at a time when being little known, they were supposed to be much more numerous than they are now ascertained to be. They were discovered by Vasco da Gama, and subsequently came under the rule of the Ranee of Cannanore, by whom they were ceded to Tippoo Sultan, and now nominally form part of the British province of Canara.

CHAPTER XIII.

THE BURMESE WAR. 1824—1826.

The Bombay Marine in Burmah—The 'Mercury' at Negrais—Capture of Rangoon—Defence of Kemmendine—Actions up the Irrawaddy of the 8th of July and 4th of August, 1824—Capture of Tavoy and Mergui—Repulse of the Burmese on the 5th of September by the Flotilla—Capture of Martaban—Gallant attack by two Cutters of the Hon. Company's ship 'Hastings '—Operations by Captain Barnes at Ramree on the 17th and 18th of July, and 15th and 16th of October, 1824—Unsuccessful Attack on Ramree on the 3rd of February, 1825—Repulse of the Burmese by the Hon. Company's brig 'Vestal,' Lieutenant Guy—Commodore Hayes in Arracan—The Attack on Chamballa—Capture of Arracan—Occupation of Ramree and Sandoway—Gallant Conduct of Lieutenant Greer—Repulse of the Enemy at Kemmendine in November and December, 1824—Expedition to Tantabain—Capture of Bassein—Advance up the Irrawaddy—Repulse at, and subsequent Capture of, Donabew—Occupation of Prome—Actions of 1st, 3rd, and 5th of December, 1825—Occupation of Meaday—General Order of Sir James Brisbane—Capture of Mellown—Action at Pagahm Mew—Conclusion of Peace—General Order by the Governor-General—Votes of Thanks by the Court of Directors and the Houses of Parliament—Honours for the Bombay Marine.

IN 1824, war broke out between the Indian Government and the King of Burmah, and a squadron of the Bombay Marine, of which four vessels and the surveying ships 'Psyche' and 'Discovery,' remained on the Persian Gulf station, was employed throughout the operations, which were unusually arduous and protracted.

Early in 1824, orders were given for the equipment of a military force of from eight thousand to nine thousand* men,

* The troops embarked from Bengal in April, 1824, were :—H.M's. 13th and 38th Regiments. Detachment of 2nd Battalion 20th (afterwards 40th) N.I. Artillery, with four 18-pounders, four 6-pounders, four 5½-inch howitzers, and four 8-inch mortars, and the usual detail of Engineers and Staff Services. Total, two thousand and eighty-nine Europeans, or, three thousand two hundred and thirty-one men in all, embarked in seventeen transports. The Madras Division consisted of H.M's. 41st Regiment; the Madras European Regiment; 1st Battalion 3rd, 2nd Battalion 7th, 2nd Battalion 8th, 1st Battalion 9th, and 2nd Battalion 10th Regiments of Native Infantry. Artillery, with four 18-pounders, six 12-pounders, six 6-pounders, six howitzers, and four mortars, also details of Engineers and Staff Corps. Total, one thousand nine hundred and eighty-eight Europeans, four thousand five hundred and thirty-eight Sepoys, making, with camp followers, eight thousand seven hundred and seventy-eight men, embarked in twenty-three transports. The army in Burmah was reinforced four times during the war, and it appears that up to the 1st of May, 1825, there were landed a total of two thousand five hundred and eighty five Bengal troops, which was drawn from the Presidencies of Calcutta and Madras, and placed respectively, under Brigadier-Generals McCreagh and McBean, the Commander-in-Chief being Brigadier-General Sir Archibald Campbell, one of Wellington's Peninsular veterans. The men-of-war that participated in the operations were:—H.M.'s ships 'Liffey,' fifty guns, Commodore Charles Grant, C.B., naval Commander-in-Chief in India, who was at this time at Bombay fitting out the 'Asia,' eighty-four guns, built for the British Navy by Nowrojee Jamsetjee, son of the late Jamsetjee Bomanjee, and floated out of dock on the 17th of January, 1824; 'Slaney,' twenty guns, Commander C. Mitchell; 'Larne,' twenty guns, Commander Frederick Marryat (the famous novelist); and 'Sophie,' eighteen-gun brig, Commander G. F. Ryves. The Hon. Company's ships 'Hastings,' thirty-two guns, Captain Barnes; 'Teignmouth,' sixteen guns, Captain Hardy; 'Mercury,' fourteen guns, Captain Goodridge; 'Thetis,' ten guns, Commander Middleton; 'Prince of Wales,' fourteen guns, Lieutenant Collinson; and 'Jessy,' brig, fitted out at Penang and commanded by Captain Poynton. The 'Hastings' was a twenty four-gun frigate, pierced for thirty-two guns, and commissioned for the first time, and had on board a detachment of eighty men of the Bombay Artillery, under Captain Russell and Lieutenants Law and Stamford, to assist in working the guns, and thirty men of the Bombay European Regiment, under Lieutenant Bell, who acted as Marines.

There were also employed on the Arracan coast, the Hon. Company's ships 'Ternate,' Lieutenant Macdonald; 'Vestal,' Lieutenant J. W. Guy; and 'Research,' Captain Crawford. In addition to these regular ships of war, there were the Hon. Company's gun-brigs and schooners, 'Goldfinch,' 'Robert Spankie,' 'Eliza,' 'Emma,' 'Phœnix,' 'Sophia,' 'Kitty,' 'Phæton,' 'Narcissa,' 'Hebe,' 'Mary,' 'Sulkea Packet,' 'Active,' 'Tiger,' 'Swift,' 'Gunga Saugor,' 'Tom Tough,' and 'Powerful,' which were all armed with two twelve-pounder carronades and four swivels. There was also a flotilla of twenty row

including three hundred and sixty European Artillerymen, eighty-six of the Rocket troop, and three hundred and fifty-three Cavalry of the Governor-General's Body-Guard. The Madras Division up to the same date, received reinforcements, including H.M's. 47th and 89th Regiments, and some Regiments of Native Infantry, which brought the total of troops from that Presidency engaged during the war, to twelve thousand seven hundred and seventy-six combatants. There were numerous changes in the Staff during the war. Brigadier-General McCreagh commanded the Bengal Division, with Brigadier M. Shawe, C.B., 87th Regiment, second in command; Major Evans and Colonel Elrington commanded the Brigades, and Colonel G. Pollock (the late Field Marshal Sir G. Pollock) the Artillery. The Madras Division was commanded by Brigadier-Generals McBean (left in August, 1824,) Fraser (left in October, 1824,) and Willoughby Cotton, from January, 1825, to the conclusion of peace. The Brigadiers were Colonels Mallet, Smelt, Brodie, H. F. Smith, C.B., and Henry Godwin, and Colonel Hopkinson commanded the Artillery.

boats, each carrying one eighteen-pounder carronade in the bow, and the steam vessel 'Diana.'*

The Expedition rendezvoused at Port Cornwallis in the Andaman Islands, and, on the 5th of May, the fleet sailed for Rangoon, the General detaching a part of his force,† under Brigadier-General McCreagh, C.B., with H.M.S. 'Slaney' and the Hon. Company's transport 'Ernaad,' against the island of Cheduba, which was captured on the 19th of May, after some spirited fighting. Sir A. Campbell also sent on the same day against the island of Negrais, another detachment,‡ under Major Wahab, with the Hon. Company's ship 'Mercury,' Captain Goodridge. On the evening of the 11th, the 'Mercury' and transports anchored off Pagoda Point, near Negrais, and, getting under weigh the following morning, brought to off the middle of that island at noon. Parties of troops were landed the same evening, and the British flag hoisted without opposition. As a supply of provisions was necessary for the troops destined to garrison the island, on the 16th of May the 'Mercury' crossed over to the mainland with a detachment of troops under Major Wahab, and sailing up the Bassein river nearly ten miles, disembarked the troops at a village on an island, the inhabitants of which were given to understand that provisions were required and would be paid for. On the following evening, a large number of people, with war-boats, collected opposite the island about five miles distant, and as their intentions appeared hostile, and they had thrown up a stockade, six companies were brought over from the island and proceeded to the attack. About 4.30 the 'Mercury' anchored off the stockade and opened fire, and soon the breastwork, which was held by seven hundred men, was carried with a loss of only two killed and four wounded. Twenty-eight boats were captured, some of

---

* The Hon. Company's steamer 'Diana' was undoubtedly the first vessel propelled by paddles that floated to the eastward of the Cape of Good Hope. She was launched on the 12th of July, 1823, at Kyd's Dock, Kidderpore, and the Calcutta "John Bull," in announcing the event, added, with prophetic foresight, "She sits well on the water, and is a great ornament to the river. We hail her as the harbinger of future vessels of her kind who will waft us to our native shores with speed and pleasure." Up to the time of her purchase by the Bengal Government, shortly before the Burmese War, she was managed by Mr. Anderson, the Engineer, who, like most of those who originate improvements, derived little personal advantage. The 'Diana' was eminently useful on the Irrawaddy, and it is a remarkable fact that up to March, 1831, when she came to Calcutta for repairs, the little steamer had run for eight years with only such occasional repairs to her engines as her engineers could give. The 'Diana' was not a seagoing ship, but her continued passages, at a period subsequent to the war, from port to port on the Tenasserim Coast during the south-west monsoon, proved her to be seaworthy. The gun-brigs and row-boats referred to above, which also carried lug-sails, were manned by natives with Europeans in charge.

† Detachment of H.M's. 13th Light Infantry, and seven companies 20th Regiment Native Infantry, in two transports.

‡ 17th Madras Native Infantry, and Detachment of Madras Artillery, in two transports.

great size, all of which Captain Goodridge destroyed, together with a large quantity of muskets and other arms, and fourteen guns were taken on board the 'Mercury.'

Sir Archibald Campbell, meanwhile, proceeded to Rangoon* with the main part of the Expedition. The mouth of the river was reached on the 10th, and, on the following morning, the fleet of ships-of-war and transports, led by the 'Liffey,' sailed up the river, and, in a few hours, arrived off the city. Commodore Grant anchored his frigate opposite a landing place, called the King's Wharf, where was a battery of from twelve to sixteen guns. The infatuated Burmese defenders of this work, had the temerity to open fire on the 'Liffey,' which, however, effectually silenced them by a broadside. The troops were soon landed, and, in twenty minutes, the town was in possession of the British commander; thus, bloodlessly as far as the British were concerned, fell Rangoon, in which were captured seventy guns, eighteen carronades, and twelve smaller pieces of ordnance.

On the 15th of May, the Hon. Company's ships 'Hastings' and 'Teignmouth' arrived, and, a few days later, the former was sent to Cheduba to relieve H.M.S. 'Slaney,' which proceeded to Calcutta, and was not engaged in any of the subsequent operations of the war. Nothing of moment occurred during the remainder of the month, except some fighting on May the 16th, at Kemmendine, about three miles above Rangoon, and an affair, on the 28th, at Johazong, about nine or ten miles from the British lines, where the Commander-in-Chief was in personal command; in both these actions the stockades were carried with the utmost gallantry, and the Burmese received a lesson of what they might expect if they stood to receive a charge of British bayonets. In the Commander-in-Chief's returns of the casualties between the 21st and 31st of May, the only seamen killed was a man of the 'Teignmouth,' who is specified as having been "killed whilst sounding."

As it was found that a ship of the class of the 'Liffey'† could not proceed up the river, she left Rangoon on the 31st of May, when Commander Marryat assumed command of the squadron

* Rangoon is situated about twenty-eight miles from the sea, on the northern bank of a main branch of the great Irrawaddy river; the city at this time extended for about nine hundred yards along the bank, with a width of about six hundred or seven hundred yards at its widest part. The centre of the town was protected by palisades ten or twelve feet high, strengthened internally by earth.

† The 'Liffey' proceeded to Penang, where Commodore Grant, C.B., died on the 25th of July following. Shortly after this, H.M's. ship 'Sophie' was sent to Calcutta for provisions, and Captain Marryat being temporarily laid up with illness, was removed to the lines near the Great Pagoda. The mortality and sickness during this first Burmese War, was far in excess of that encountered by the Expedition of 1852.

until the appointment of a successor. About this time the 'Mercury' returned from Negrais with the detachment of troops, as it was found impracticable to establish a post on that island. The south-west monsoon had now set in, and it became impossible for the troops to proceed up the river, as owing to the disappearance of the inhabitants from Rangoon, there was great difficulty in providing and equipping a flotilla or procuring a sufficiency of rowers; the desolate state of the country also obliged the Expedition to draw its supplies from India.

On the 2nd of June, the Commander-in-Chief received information that the enemy had assembled in great force, and were stockading themselves at Kemmendine, with the intention of attacking the British lines. He, therefore, ordered two strong reconnoitring columns from the Madras Division, to move, on the following morning, upon two roads leading from the great Dagon Pagoda to the village of Kemmendine, and himself proceeded up the Rangoon river with the Hon. Company's cruisers 'Mercury' and 'Thetis,' and three companies of the 41st, embarked in the flotilla and row boats, for the purpose of making a diversion in favour of any attack which might take place by land. Commander Ryves also accompanied Sir Archibald Campbell with three flotilla gunboats and the pinnaces of H.M. ships 'Larne' and 'Sophie.'

The start was made at five a.m., and, in two hours, the 'Mercury' and 'Thetis,' with the gunboats and pinnaces, anchored abreast of Kemmendine, and opened a heavy fire on the stockades. The squadron had not long been under fire, when Commander Middleton, of the 'Thetis,' was mortally wounded by a cannon-shot which carried off his leg. Commander Ryves, who was on board her—as the gunboats and pinnaces were directed to rendezvous round the 'Thetis'—assumed temporary command of the 'Thetis,' though, as he says in his despatch, "Sir Archibald Campbell, having embarked on board the Hon. Company's cruiser 'Mercury,' all orders to the cruisers and flotilla proceeded from him." When the stockade was reduced, and the enemy's fire silenced, the troops landed and burnt the works, before the arrival of the two columns proceeding by land. At three p.m., the enemy being in great force, the troops were re-embarked, when the cruisers and flotilla weighed and returned to their former anchorage. In his despatch of the 4th of June, reporting this success, the Commander-in-Chief states that he had already captured from fifty to sixty large cargo boats, which were being cut down for transport purposes, and were calculated to carry, on an average, a complement of sixty men each. There still remained the enemy's fortified camp and stockades at Kemmendine, which the general determined to attack with a

HISTORY OF THE INDIAN NAVY. 415

strong column, for not only was it necessary that the neighbourhood of Rangoon should be cleared, but the numerous fire-rafts which the Burmese sent down the river, occasioned the most imminent risk to the shipping, and kept the naval force in a constant state of harass. Sir Archibald, accordingly, moved upon the stockades, on the 10th of June, with three thousand men, four 18-pounders, four mortars, and some field pieces; and a portion of the naval force was also employed under Lieutenant Fraser, R.N., who had been placed in temporary command of the 'Thetis.'

The following is that officer's report of his proceedings in co-operating in the attack on the great stockade at Kemmendine, which was reduced by artillery fire, the enemy evacuating when the troops advanced to storm:—" In compliance with your orders, on the 9th instant, at eleven p.m., at the commencement of the flood-tide, I proceeded up the river in the Hon. Company's cruiser 'Thetis,' accompanied by the 'Jessy,' six of the gun flotilla, six row-boats, and the Malay proa you were pleased to put under my command.* At two a.m. the 'Jessy' and the row-boats took up the position assigned them, about three-quarters of a mile below Kemmendine. The 'Thetis' was anchored at the entrance of a creek about the same distance above Kemmendine, and abreast of the stockade from which the gun was taken on the 3rd instant, but which had been greatly strengthened. The gun flotilla were to have been placed abreast of the opposite point, forming the entrance of the creek (distinguished by a pagoda), on which, since the 3rd, there has been erected a formidable stockade; but in consequence of the ebb-tide making against them, with the exception of the 'Robert Spankie' and two others, they failed in their endeavours to take up their position, and were brought up a short distance below the 'Thetis.' About ten a.m., the batteries opened their fire against Kemmendine; the stockade on the Pagoda point, at the same instant, commenced a fire of musketry, and from four small pieces, apparently 4 or 6-pounders, upon the 'Robert Spankie' and the other two gun vessels opposite to it, which was returned by them and kept up on both sides for upwards of an hour. The stockades abreast of the 'Thetis' not having fired a shot the whole time, and observing that the flotilla did not succeed in silencing the other, I took advantage of the flood-tide just then making, to drop abreast of it in the 'Thetis,' and after a fire of half-an-hour, so far silenced the enemy, that from that time they only fired an occasional musket at intervals when we had ceased,

* About three hundred Chinese and Malay sailors had recently joined the combined force at Rangoon, and some time afterwards five hundred Mugh boatmen, natives of Arracan, arrived from Chittagong, to assist in transporting the army up the Irrawaddy.

but altogether so badly directed that we had only one man wounded, belonging to a row-boat at that time alongside the 'Thetis.' Having observed a great number of boats, many of a large size, collected about two miles above us, and considering it possible that at night, during the ebb, they might attack any of the flotilla that remained in advance, when we, from the rapidity of the current, could not render them any assistance, I thought fit to shift the 'Thetis,' at the last of the flood, about a quarter of a mile above the point, directing the flotilla to drop with the ebb below the stockade on the opposite point, which they accordingly did. At noon on the 11th, observing the signal agreed upon, when the General wanted communication with us to be made, I sent an officer to answer it, who returned with intelligence of the troops having possession of Kemmendine, and with a request from the General, that two of the gun flotilla and two row-boats might be left at that place; I accordingly directed the flotilla, with the above exceptions, to proceed to Rangoon. At six p.m. the 'Thetis' weighed, and, with the boats ahead to tow, began to drop down the river."

In trying to avoid a large fire raft, composed of several country boats fastened together, the 'Thetis' grounded on the bank of the river, where she remained all night, during which she received some shots from the stockades. At daylight on the 12th, Lieutenant Fraser succeeded in floating her, when she proceeded down the river and anchored at Rangoon. The total loss sustained by the British in this affair, was sixteen killed and one hundred and twenty-two wounded.

Soon after, Lieutenant Greer, First Lieutenant of the 'Mercury,' assumed command of the 'Thetis.'

About this time H.M.S. 'Sophie' was ordered to Calcutta to procure supplies and seamen, as owing to sickness, such was the shorthandedness of H.M.'s ships, that Commander Marryat reported on the 14th of June, that he had not a commissioned or warrant officer capable of doing duty; as regards the crew, he added:—"I am afraid that we shall lose many men before we leave this place. The heavy and incessant rains, the unwholesomeness of the water, and the impossibility of procuring fresh provisions, forcibly point it out as the grave of a large part of the Expedition." Previous to the 'Sophie's' departure for Calcutta, six 32-pounder carronades were taken from her and mounted, with four of the 'Larne's' guns, on board the Hon. Company's transport 'Satellite,' formerly a sloop-of-war, which was manned with every effective officer and man from the 'Larne,' and placed under the command of Lieutenant Dobson, R.N., and rendered good service during the subsequent operations.

The Burmese General having received orders from the

"Golden-footed" monarch, his master, to make a grand attack upon the British lines, the enemy crossed the river above Kemmendine, from the Dalla to the Rangoon side, and, on the morning of the 1st of July, three columns of one thousand men each, moved towards the British right, while the jungle in front of the Dagon Pagoda and along the whole extent of the line to the left, was occupied by a large force. But their attack was weak, and, dispirited by recent defeats, they gave way before an assault made by the Commander-in-Chief in person, who reported that twelve thousand of the enemy were engaged. A writer in the "Quarterly Review" (Vol. xxxv., p 516), speaking of the silence of the military historian of the war, as regards the co-operation afforded by the naval portion of the Expeditionary Force, of which, indeed, there is no mention in Sir Archibald Campbell's despatch of the 11th of July, says:— "Major Snodgrass seems to have forgotten the part which the Navy bore in repulsing this large force; and that, when, to distract our operations and destroy the shipping, not fewer than fifty-three of their huge fire-rafts, protected by gunboats, were sent down the river towards the fleet at the same time, all of these were, by uncommon skill and exertion, turned off and rendered harmless. And the officer by whose exertions was effected this happy issue out of a great danger that threatened the shipping, was Mr. Lindquist, of the Company's service." Lieutenant John Marshall, R.N., author of a "Narrative of the Naval Operations in Ava," says of this young officer:—"The activity and zeal of Mr. Lindquist, commanding the row-boats stationed at Kemmendine, was very conspicuous on this occasion." About the same period Captain Hardy, of the 'Teignmouth,' then stationed just within the bar, and employed in examining a creek to which Captain Marryat had directed his attention, destroyed eleven large country boats, some already loaded, and some loading, with stone, for the purpose of blocking up the entrance to the river.

After the action of the 1st of July, the enemy continued to receive reinforcements until it was said thirty thousand men were assembled near Rangoon. The British Commander, therefore, determined, notwithstanding the incessant rains, to bring the newly-arrived Burmese General, Soomba Wongee, to action, and, on the morning of the 8th of July, despatched a strong column by land under General McBean against Kummeroot, about five miles from the great Pagoda, while he embarked with a second column to attack a commanding point upon the river above Kemmendine, in communication with the enemy's stockaded camp, and not only obstructing the navigation of the river, but affording an excellent situation for the construction of fire-rafts, in the handling of which the Burmese were great adepts. "About a mile above Kemmendine," says

Major Snodgrass, " the river separates into two branches; the point of land where they divide is bold and projecting, and commands a long reach under it. Upon this point the enemy's principal stockade was erected, provided with artillery, and defended by a numerous garrison. On the opposite bank of either branch, stockades and other defences were erected, enfilading the approach to the principal work, and all mutually defending each other." In consequence of the strength of these works, Sir Archibald Campbell resolved first to try the effect of mortar practice. " In the event of this not succeeding," he says in his report, " I consulted with Captain Marryat upon the employment of such vessels as he might select to breach. The shells were thrown at too great a distance to produce the desired effect, and the swampy nature of the ground would not permit of any advance. The 'Satellite,' the Hon. Company's cruisers 'Teignmouth,' Captain Hardy, 'Thetis,' Lieutenant Greer, and 'Jessy,' Captain Poynter—the whole under the command of Lieutenant Fraser, of H.M.'s ship 'Larne,' now took their stations according to a disposition made by Captain Marryat, and opened a fire which soon silenced that of fourteen pieces of artillery, besides swivels and musketry from the stockades, and, in one hour, the preconcerted signal of 'breach practicable' was displayed at the mainmast head." The troops, as previously arranged, entered their boats on the signal being hoisted, and the assault was delivered by two columns under Colonel Godwin and Major Wahab, who carried all before them. The Commander-in-Chief says :—" To the officers and men of the breaching vessels every praise is due; and I much regret that severe indisposition prevented Captain Marryat from being present to witness the result of his arrangements." General McBean also captured seven stockades in the most brilliant style, and the result of the day's work, as reported by the Commander-in-Chief, was the capture of ten stockades, thirty-eight pieces of artillery, forty swivels, and three hundred muskets. The enemy also left on the field eight hundred dead, among them Soomba Wongee, and two other chiefs of the first class. The remainder, deprived of their leader, fled in confusion to the rear, there to await the arrival of the King's brother, the Prince of Sarrawaddy, said to be advancing with seventy thousand men. The loss on the part of the British was four killed and forty-seven wounded.

In acknowledgment of the services rendered by the naval force, the Commander-in-Chief wrote to Commander Marryat as follows, on the 9th of July, 1824 :—" I request you will accept my very best thanks for your able arrangement and disposition of the vessels employed in the attack of the enemy's stockades yesterday, and I beg you will also do me the favour of conveying them to Lieutenant Fraser, R.N., Captain Hardy, and the officers in command of the Hon. Company's cruisers, 'Thetis' and 'Jessy.'" On the 13th of July Commander Marryat dropped the 'Larne'* down as far as the Dalla Creek, on her way to the mouth of the river, from whence she returned, with the sickness much decreased, on the 27th of the same month.

On the 19th of July the Commander-in-Chief despatched a column of troops, by land, to disperse the enemy then gathered at Keykloo, about twelve or fifteen miles distant from Rangoon, and himself embarking in the 'Diana,' proceeded with six hundred men in the flotilla, up the Puzzendoun Creek, but, owing to the impassable state of the roads, the land column was forced to fall back, and Sir Archibald returned after an absence of three days. Having learned that the Governor of Syriam, or Pegu, had constructed some works and assembled a force on the banks of the river of that name, he proceeded thither on the morning of the 4th of August, with six hundred troops, and the Hon. Company's brig, 'Jessy,' and the 'Powerful,' sloop, employed as a mortar vessel. The soldiers landed under the fire of these two vessels, and, having crossed a deep nullah, which was bridged by Commander Marryat and part of the crew of the 'Larne,' the enemy's defences were carried after a brief resistance. A portion of the force then captured the Syriam Pagoda, and altogether, during the day, twelve guns were captured with a loss of only eight wounded.

Considering the impossibility of immediately engaging in operations in the direction of Ava, Sir Archibald Campbell judged it advisable to employ a portion of the combined forces under his command, in reducing some of the maritime provinces of the Burmese Empire. Accordingly, an Expedition was directed against the province of Tenasserim, comprising the districts of Tavoy and Mergui, as containing a valuable tract of sea coast, and one likely to afford supplies of cattle and grain. For the reduction of these places a force was despatched under the command of Colonel Miles, C.B., consisting of his own regiment, the 89th, and the 7th Madras Native Infantry; also the Company's cruisers, 'Teignmouth,' 'Mercury,' 'Prince of Wales,' 'Thetis,' and 'Jessy,' besides three gunboats, two row-boats, and six transports, the whole being under the

* On the 11th of July, Commander Marryat wrote to the Commodore:—"I must now call your attention to the condition of H.M's. ship 'Larne,' whose crew I am sorry to say have been rendered quite inefficient by disease. Since we have been on this Expedition we have had one hundred and seventy cases of cholera and dysentery. We have had thirteen deaths; we have now thirty patients at the hospital on shore, and twenty on the sick list on board; our convalescents are as ineffective as if they were in their hammocks; they relapse daily, and the surgeon reports that, unless the vessel can be sent to cruise for a month, there is little chance of their ultimate recovery. When I sent away the Expedition under Lieutenant Fraser on the 7th instant, I could only muster three officers and twelve men fit for duty."

command of Captain Hardy. The Expedition sailed from Rangoon on the 26th of August, and arrived at the mouth of the Tavoy River on the 1st of September.

Colonel Miles says in his despatch, dated Tavoy, 27th of September:—" Having advanced with the large ships as far as the depth of the water would allow, I found it necessary to distribute the troops embarked on the Hon. Company's cruiser 'Teignmouth,' and transports 'Argyle,' 'Indian Oak,' and 'Marianne,' among the smaller vessels and boats of the fleet, myself and staff proceeding in the Hon. Company's cruiser 'Jessy,' which, drawing the least water, was appointed to lead. These arrangements having been effected, on the 4th instant we advanced, but from the difficulty of the navigation of the river, full of shoals, and in many parts only to be passed at the top of high water, together with the obstacles by which the enemy attempted to impede our progress, by sinking their largest boats in shallow places, and stockading it across one of the narrow channels, it was not till the 8th, about noon, that we anchored within three miles of the fort. I had, prior to this, despatched a summons for its unconditional surrender, and no reply having, at that time, been received, I proceeded with Captain Hardy and my staff to make a reconnaissance within a short distance of the works. This object had just been accomplished when it was perceived that three war-boats, full of men, were pulling along-shore, apparently for the purpose of cutting us off. In this they, however, failed, and on our regaining the 'Jessy,' I directed two guns to be fired, and they instantly retired with great precipitation. The tide serving in the evening, the whole fleet arrived within gunshot of the place about ten o'clock at night, when two or three shots were fired from the fort at our headmost ship, the Hon. Company's cruiser 'Prince of Wales,' but without effect. At an early hour on the morning of the 9th, two Burmese came on board, and brought me a communication from the second in command, stating his readiness to seize or destroy the Mayhoon, or Governor of the Province, or to obey such orders as I might dictate. Immediately, on receipt of this, an answer was returned to say I was on the eve of advancing, and that he was to be taken and confined until my arrival, which was in about two hours after. All was directed, and at one o'clock p.m. we were in possession of the fort, pettah, and all the defences of the place without opposition. The population is very great, and from the strength and extent of the works (all built of brick, and very high), our loss must have been very great had any defence been attempted. The annexed copy of my orders, issued on the 10th instant, the sketch of the fort and pettah, herewith sent, together with the return of ordnance, ammunition, and military stores, will, I trust, give you some idea of the importance of our acquisition. The capture of the Mayhoon, his brother and family, with his principal adherents, completely weakens the enemy, and places us in a commanding situation to cripple any exertions in this quarter. Where everything has been so happily accomplished, I have but to add my sincere and heartfelt thanks to Captain Hardy, of the Hon. Company's Marine, who commands the naval part of the Expedition, for his cordial co-operation, and the unceasing labour and fatigue he experienced in sounding the river, and directing the movements of the ships, whose officers and crews exerted themselves to the utmost."

Three hundred and seventy soldiers, with the 'Mercury' and a gunboat, were left at Tavoy for the protection of the place, and the remainder of the combined Expedition sailed for Mergui, where they arrived on the 6th of October. Colonel Miles describes as follows the operations that ensued, in his despatch of the 9th of October:—"My first care was to send a summons to the town for its unconditional surrender, but instead of a reply, at half-past eleven o'clock, their guns opened a heavy fire upon the Hon. Company's cruisers, who had previously taken their position in front of the enemy's batteries, mounting thirty-three pieces of heavy ordnance. The practice on our part was so good, that in about one hour the whole were silenced." In the meantime Colonel Miles had assembled all the available troops in the boats of the squadron, which effected a landing to the right of the town, and a party of H.M.'s 89th Regiment greatly distinguished themselves in escalading the walls, when the enemy lost five hundred men. Mergui was a place of considerable strength. Colonel Miles says :—" Their batteries were placed on the brows of the different hills, commanding the shipping. From the best information I have been able to collect, the enemy had three thousand five hundred men in arms. On our first gaining possession the whole population fled ; but in the course of the night and the following morning, great numbers came in, and are now following their several avocations." The loss sustained in the capture of Mergui was six killed and thirty-six wounded, and thirty-seven guns and one hundred and six swivels were captured in the city. Leaving part of the Madras troops to garrison Mergui, and some of the flotilla, Colonel Miles and Captain Hardy returned with the remainder of the force to Rangoon in time to take part in the important operations about to commence.

In the month of September some sharp fighting took place in the Dalla Creek, some distance up which was Thontai, capital of the province and the retreat of the Rangoon people, and in this the boats of the 'Larne' did good service, while the gunboats and mortar-vessels also rendered assistance. The gun-vessels, row-boats, and soldiers left in

defence of the works captured on the 8th of August, were assailed every night by large bodies of the enemy, who kept up a fire from the surrounding jungle, whilst the energies of the seamen in the boats were directed to watching, grappling, and towing away the fire-rafts. On the night of the 5th of September, the Burmese made a desperate attempt to overpower the flotilla stationed up the Dalla Creek, and three officers of the Company's service, Messrs. Crawford, King, and Frances, commanding the gun-brigs, 'Kitty,' 'Narcissa,' and 'Tiger,' highly distinguished themselves. Commander Marryat says, in his despatch to Sir Archibald Campbell, of the 8th of September:—
"In compliance with your request for a detail of the circumstances which occurred in the attack on the Dalla stockade, made by the Burmese on the morning of the 6th instant, I have the honour to inform you that, at midnight of the 5th, a straggling fire was heard in that direction, and shortly afterwards a rocket was thrown up—the signal previously arranged with the detachment, in case of immediate assistance being required. With the advantage of a strong flood tide, the boats of H.M.'s sloop 'Larne' proceeded rapidly to the scene of contention, where a heavy fire was exchanged. As our approach could not be perceived from the smoke, we cheered, to announce that support was at hand, and had the satisfation to hear it warmly returned, both by the detachment in the stockade and the crews of the gun-vessels. It appeared that the attacks of the enemy had been simultaneous, the gun-boats laying in the creek having been assailed by a number of war-boats, while the detachment on shore had been opposed to a force estimated at one thousand five hundred to two thousand men. Upon our arrival we found the enemy on shore had not retreated, but still kept up a galling fire. The war-boats, which had endeavoured to board the 'Kitty,' gun-brig, had been beaten off by the exertion and gallantry of Mr. Crawford, commanding that vessel, and were apparently rallying at a short distance up the creek, with a determination to renew the attack, but on perceiving our boats advancing ahead of the gun-brigs, they made a precipitate retreat. Although from their superior speed, there was little probability of success, chase was immediately given, and five of the war-boats which had been most severely handled, and could not keep up with the main body, were successively boarded and captured. Many others appeared to be only half-manned, but we could not overtake them, and the pursuit was abandoned about four miles above the stockade. The spears remaining in the sides of the gun-brig, the ladders attached to her rigging, and the boarding netting cut through in many places, proved the severe conflict which had been sustained; and I trust you will be pleased to recommend the very meritorious conduct of Mr. Crawford to the considera-

tion of the Right Hon. the Governor-General in Council. Great praise is due to Mr. J. King, of the 'Narcissa,' and Mr. Frances of the 'Tiger,' for the well-directed and destructive fire which they poured into the war-boats; and I trust, as an eye-witness, I may be allowed to express my admiration of the intrepid conduct of the officer commanding the detachment on shore. The loss of the enemy in this attack cannot be correctly ascertained, but frŏm the number of dead in the boats captured, and the crippled state of many others, it cannot be estimated at less than two or three hundred men." The Commander-in-Chief says in his despatch, of the 9th of September, to the Supreme Government:—"All accounts concur in bearing testimony to the resolute conduct of Mr. Crawford, in defending his vessel, the 'Kitty,' against superior numbers, although wounded early in the attack; and I beg leave to bring his name to the favourable notice of the Right Hon. the Governor-General in Council."

On the 9th of September, Lieutenant Fraser, R.N., was sent to search for the passage up to Thontai by way of the Dalla Creek, but, after an absence of three days, he returned without being able to find it. While on this service, Mr. Lindquist, commanding a detachment of row-boats, was wounded by a musket-ball. Owing to the sickness* on board H.M.S. 'Larne,' of whose original crew only twenty-seven remained, Commander Marryat proceeded to Penang, and did not return to Rangoon until the 24th of December, 1824. On the 15th of September, Captain Henry Ducie Chads, who had arrived from England in H.M.S. 'Arachne," assumed command of the naval forces at Rangoon. Much was expected from this officer, who had immortalized himself by his noble defence of H.M.S. 'Java,' of thirty-eight guns, in her memorable action, on the 30th of December, 1812, with the United States ship 'Constitution,' forty-four guns, after the death of Captain Lambert had placed him in command of the British frigate, and it may be added that, on all occasions, Captain Chads proved himself equal to his reputation as a first-class officer and seaman.

Captain Chads commenced his service in Burmah by proceeding, on the 19th of September, upon Panlang, where the enemy had established a post, with the 'Satellite' and 'Diana,' the boats of the 'Arachne' and 'Sophie,' and a flotilla of nine gun-boats and sixteen row-boats, of the Company's Marine, together with five hundred troops under Brigadier-General Fraser. The Expedition having attacked and captured several stockades,

* At this time the European troops fit for service were reduced to less than one thousand five hundred effectives; seven hundred and forty-nine men had died, and upwards of one thousand had invalided. The fatality among the native troops was not less, but the officers and men of the Company's cruisers at Rangoon, owing to their being acclimatized by service in these seas, did not suffer to anything like the same extent.

returned to Rangoon on the 27th of September. Early in October, a detachment of troops was repulsed with heavy loss, in attempting to escalade the entrenchments surrounding the Pagoda of Keykloo; and, at the same time, another detachment, under Major Evans, embarked in a flotilla of gun-boats, one of which was fitted as a bomb-ketch, accompanied by the 'Satellite' and 'Diana,' under the immediate command of Captain Chads, and carried the breastworks and stockades, which formed the defences of the village of Than-ta-bain, about thirty miles distant from Rangoon. In this affair Lieutenant (the late Admiral Sir) Henry Kellett highly distinguished himself, though the storming party of soldiers carried off the honours of the day. Sir Archibald Campbell, having determined to occupy the city of Martaban, an Expedition was fitted out, the naval portion of which, under the command of Lieutenant Keele, of the 'Arachne,' consisted of seven row gun-boats, one mortar-vessel, six gun vessels, all of the Company's service, thirty men from the 'Arachne' and 'Sophie,' and an armed transport having on board four hundred and fifty troops, the whole being under the command of Lieutenant-Colonel Godwin. On the 29th the flotilla opened fire on the city, and at five o'clock on the following morning, a portion of the troops and the seamen stormed the forts and other defences, when sixteen guns and a large amount of war *matériel* were captured.

Some good service was done at this time by the officers and men of the Hon. Company's frigate 'Hastings,' which was stationed at Cheduba. A military correspondent at Cheduba, writes in a letter dated August 12th:—"I took a sail in the Company's frigate, 'Hastings,' on the 17th and 18th of July, to look at a stockade of the enemy's on the north-west point of the Island of Ramree, and also to destroy some boats said to be collected in a creek near it, and in which it was apprehended they would take a run over to destroy the villages, and disturb the natives on this island opposite their point, and return before daylight. The distance is eight or ten miles across. We anchored some distance from the point, which we have named 'Hastings Point,' in honour of the ship and her first action. Soon after daylight on the 18th, the gun-boat, the launch of the ship, having an 18-pounder carronade on board, with the two cutters having a part of the Bombay European Regiment on board, were sent to reconnoitre the shore and sound towards it. The beach was soon covered with natives when they perceived our boats approaching, and they commenced a sharp fire from musketry and some guns, until by signal orders, we returned to the ship by seven a.m. I think our gun-boats and musketry surprised a few who will no longer tell the tale. The stockade, and a long line of entrenchment, was discovered by the reconnaissance in a small bight of land, near the place where the boats had their brush. Soon after breakfast, Captain Barnes weighed anchor and stood in towards the shore, and anchored in four and a-half fathoms water within half-gun shot of it. A spring was soon got on the cable, and the broadside of the 'Hastings' brought to bear on the place, and I doubt not several of them bit the dust, so tremendous was the fire, and the guns so elegantly directed. We gave the name of 'Barnes' Bight to the place, in honour of our gallant commander, and returned to the anchorage by noon."

The following is an extract from a letter by Captain Barnes, to the address of the Secretary of the Supreme Government, dated the 21st of September, 1824:—"I have great pleasure in transmitting to you, for the information of the Right Honourable Lord Amherst, Governor-General in Council, an account of a daring and successful attack made by two cutters belonging to the Hon. Company's frigate 'Hastings,' under my command, on four boats* belonging to the enemy, on the coast of Ramree, and trust that my entering somewhat into detail will be excused, as I am anxious to do justice to the officers and men, who so gallantly achieved the dispersion of the enemy, whose numbers were so disproportionate to their little force. On the morning of the 10th instant, at daylight, the look-out at the masthead announced three large boats to be in sight, close to the shore of Ramree, and about five or six miles distant from the frigate, rowing to the southward. I immediately directed the two ten-oared cutters to be manned and armed, and sent six marines in each, placing both boats under the command of Lieutenant Harrison, second of the frigate, Mr. Graves, master's mate, being in charge of one boat, with orders to bring them alongside, if possible. Some time after the cutters had left the ship, I observed a fourth boat, and could plainly perceive they were all full of men. Our launch unfortunately being absent watering, I manned and armed the two boats belonging to the pilot brigs 'Meriton' and 'Planet,' with European seamen and marines, and despatched them to the assistance of the cutters; but owing to the start they had of them, and these being very heavy-pulling boats, they were not able to assist in the capture, which I cannot better describe to his lordship than by transmitting the modest letter of Lieutenant Harrison, describing the affair."

The following is the report of Lieutenant Harrison, dated the 10th of September, 1824:—

"In pursuance of your orders of this morning, I proceeded with the two cutters under my command, in pursuit of four

* The following description of a Burmese war-boat will convey an idea of their size, and formidable nature. "The boats were somewhat of the structure of a canoe, about eighty feet in length and seven in breadth, gilt outside and painted red inside, carrying fifty-two oars, and capable of holding, with the greatest safety, at least one hundred and fifty men."

boats belonging to the enemy, as seen from the 'Hastings,' pulling along the Ramree coast to the southward. After a smart pull of about six miles, I had closed with the chase so near as to enable the cutter, under the command of Mr. Graves, to intercept the two sternmost boats of the enemy, while I succeeded in turning the two boats in advance ; they then seemed inclined to receive us warmly, by giving loud cheers, which was immediately returned by our seamen and marines, with their accustomed spirit. A fire of musketry now commenced on both sides, and the enemy, perceiving our intention of laying them on board, immediately beached their boats ; we pursued so closely as to enable us to do considerable mischief. Three boats were captured and towed into deep water, six of the enemy made prisoners, and the fourth boat, I regret to say, was bilged and rendered useless. So precipitate was their retreat, that they left everything behind, and amongst various articles, a great number of arms of all descriptions have been captured. I feel much pleasure in bringing to your notice the zeal and exertions of Mr. Graves, to whom the highest praise is due, as well as the satisfactory conduct of everybody employed, particularly the seamen, whose great exertions in pulling deserve my best thanks, and although the second division of boats were not up at the commencement, I have every reason to suppose they aided in enabling me to effect my purpose without the loss of a man; as the enemy could not be estimated at less than four hundred effective men. Their loss in killed and wounded I have no means of ascertaining correctly, but I should imagine it to exceed sixty."

The following letters describe further operations undertaken by Captain Barnes, with the seamen and marines of his ship, and of the 'Investigator,' which, though employed in the survey of the Arracan coast, under her distinguished Commander, Captain D. Ross, was, for a time, engaged in hostilities. The first is from Captain Barnes, dated the 19th of October, 1824 :—" Captain Ross, of the Hon. Company's Marine, and commanding their ship 'Investigator,' having delivered into my charge, on the 7th instant, a division of gunboats, five in number, under the direction of Captain Finucane, of H.M.'s 14th Regiment of Foot, I thought this additional force might be employed to advantage for the purpose of covering a landing of troops on the north part of Ramree, for the purpose of destroying some stockades and breastworks the enemy possess on the sea-face; and as I had learnt that the Burmahs had some strong defences at a short distance inland, I applied to Lieutenant-Colonel Hampton for the aid of two hundred Sepoys, which that officer was pleased to grant, and on the evening of the 14th, the troops being embarked on board the 'Hastings' and 'Planet,' pilot brig, we weighed and proceeded to our position. The frigate drawing too much water to approach the shore near enough for her guns to prove useful, I placed the gunboats close in shore, abreast of the enemy's works, and in the morning disembarked the whole of our force, consisting of two hundred Sepoys of the 40th Regiment, commanded by Captain Vincent, twenty-six European Marines, and fifty-seven European seamen of the Hon. Company's frigate 'Hastings,' and forty European seamen, volunteers from the Hon. Company's ship 'Investigator,' under the command of Lieutenant H. Wyndham, first of the 'Hastings.' I went on board the 'Elizabeth' gunboat, to give such directions as I might think requisite. A smart fire was kept up by the boats on the enemy, who showed themselves in force, and fired smartly on the boats, but with the exception of one shot from a large jingal that hit the 'Burrampootra,' and a few musket-balls that struck the 'Megna,' which was placed by her gallant commander, Mr. Boyce, so close to the bank it was hard to miss her, no accident occurred, the whole of the enemy flying into the jungle as soon as the troops landed, leaving their jingals behind them. The position held by the enemy was exceedingly strong and well-chosen, being composed of a well-formed breast-work fronting the sea, with a nullah of considerable width between it and the high sandbank forming the shore; the tide flowing into the nullah, so that the place was capable of good defence. The rear of the stockade was also entrenched at the distance of about 100 yards, and that backed by a thick jungle. As the force, about noon, moved into the interior, and being unable from my weak state of health to march with them, I beg leave to give the remaining account of the reconnaissance in the language of my first-lieutenant, who commanded the nautical party on shore.

"I have much pleasure in mentioning that, on the morning of the 16th, Mr. Midshipman Laughton landed about a mile and a-half to the south of our first position, and, with the crews of the 'Burrampooter' and 'Irrawaddy,' burnt a chowky belonging to the enemy, who fled on his appearance. Hoping that this diversion may meet the approval of the Right Honourable Lord Amherst, Governor-General in Council."

The following is Lieutenant Wyndham's Report to Captain Barnes of his reconnaissance on the island of Ramree:—"In obedience to your orders of the 16th instant, I proceeded on shore with the seamen from the 'Hastings' under my command, to co-operate with Captain Vincent, in the destruction of the enemy's stockades. The landing of the force having been effected in sight of the enemy, without opposition, about one mile to the southward of Umlabeen, I was joined by Lieutenant

Lloyd, with forty seamen from the 'Investigator.' A large body of the enemy were seen in their trenches half a mile to the southward, but immediately our force was put in motion, they disappeared among the jungle, and we then occcupied a breastwork guarding the road to the interior. A short halt was made for arrangements and the guides to be landed. At noon we were again put in motion, and commenced our march to the stockades along a narrow pathway, admitting, in many places, only two abreast, and intersected with rivulets. In about twenty minutes we were upon the spot of the expected stockade, but the enemy had previously demolished it, leaving nothing but a few of the large posts standing at its angles, and the intrenchments not filled up. From this place we pushed forward one and a half miles more, and came upon a well-constructed stockade, capable of containing four thousand men, with a double fence round a sand breastwork, and well filled up between with pointed bamboo stakes inclining outwards, and I regret to say that William Williams, seaman of the 'Hastings,' was severely wounded by one of them running into his foot. Here again the enemy fled upon the approach and firing of the light troops in advance, when our party triumphantly entered the gates and took possession. A small jingal, with a pair of colours were taken, and the stockade set on fire, which consumed the whole of the interior buildings; and from the explosion of some concealed powder, did damage to the breastwork and outer fences. From this we marched on the left, and destroyed another large stockade, which had no outwork, but a breastwork inside the stockade, about four feet six inches high, and barracks sufficient to contain three thousand men; from hence we marched down to the beach and occupied our former position within the breastwork, and slept under arms for the night. About half-past three o'clock next morning, we were aroused from our slumber by the enemy, who commenced an attack on our picquets. We received them with cheers, and every one was at his post instanter. The enemy, when they found us on the alert, and our picquets commenced firing upon them, retreated immediately to the woods, and nothing more was seen of them. We continued under arms till daylight, and then commenced a circuitous march of about four miles to the northward, and passed three villages in the rear of Umlahbeen; but as they appeared to be Mug habitations, with no work of defence about them, they were not destroyed. We then marched towards the sea, and came up in rear of the breastworks, which the frigate under your command, upon a former occasion, drove the enemy from. We proceeded along the beach to the position held by us during the night, where we halted, refreshed the men, destroyed the buildings, and embarked the force. I have much pleasure in bringing to your notice the good conduct of the officers and seamen you did me the honour to place under my command, and I feel confident had the enemy stood, they would have shown themselves to be British seamen."*

In November, 1824, Captain Barnes died from the effects of climate. In him the Company lost a gallant, zealous, and enterprising officer, who, though he knew the great risk he incurred in going on service, volunteered at Bombay to take command of the newly-launched frigate in her first commission, when his services were gladly accepted by the Government. Captain Hardy, having given over charge of the 'Teignmouth' to Captain Goodridge, succeeded to the command of the 'Hastings.' Not less brave and energetic than his predecessor, Captain Hardy had already frequently gained the approbation of Captain Marryat and the Commander-in-Chief. At this time a large number of seamen were shipped at Calcutta for the 'Hastings,' which became very efficient under its new Captain, and First-Lieutenant, Mr. Henry Wyndham. Other changes in the command of the Company's ships, necessitated by the death of Captain Barnes, were the promotion of Lieutenant Moresby, first of the 'Prince of Wales,' to the temporary command of the 'Mercury,' in the place of Captain Goodridge, until the arrival of Lieutenant Anderson, then Master-Attendant at Mangalore.

Encouraged by the successful results of the operations undertaken at Ramree in October, Colonel R. Hampton, commanding the troops at Cheduba, contrary to the advice of Captain Hardy, determined to undertake the reduction of the whole island. Accordingly, a party landed on the morning of of the 3rd of February, 1825, and proceeded to attack the defences by land, whilst the gun-boats effected a passage up the creek leading to the harbour, across which strong stakes were planted. In consequence of the treachery of the guides, the troops, after a fatiguing march, found themselves in a thick jungle, at a considerable distance from the stockades, and it became necessary to return to the beach before the evening, without effecting the object of the attack. As the troops retired, the Burmese kept up a scattered fire from the jungle into which they had been driven, and from some entrenched positions; but

* Captain Vincent commanding the troops, in concluding his Report to Colonel Hampton, says:—"Though it may be considered presumption in me to speak of the merits of any other branch of the Service than that to which I immediately belong, I cannot, in the present instance, avoid bringing to the notice of the Lieutenant-Colonel the highly meritorious conduct of the officers, seamen, and Marines of the Hon. Company's frigate 'Hastings,' and surveying ship 'Investigator,' who acted in conjunction with the troops, not only as regarded their readiness to meet every obstacle which the nature of the service led us to expect, but likewise in their steady and prompt obedience to the rigid rules of discipline, which the peculiar nature of the enterprise rendered so essentially necessary to be observed."

upon the junction of the reserve with two 6-pounder field pieces, this annoyance was checked, and by six in the evening the party re-embarked without further molestation.

The following is the report by Colonel Hampton, dated Cheduba, the 8th of February, 1825:—" Captain Hardy, commanding the Hon. Company's frigate 'Hastings,' having sent me two Burmese prisoners taken in Ramree Island on the 22nd ultimo, by a party sent on shore from that vessel, and having from those individuals obtained what I considered sufficient information regarding its localities, defences, and means of resistance, as to justify my making a descent on the island with a view to its capture, I addressed him on the subject, stating that if he would make arrangements for the transportation of part of the force under my command, I should be most happy to join him (Captain Hardy being at this time most actively employed in surveying and reconnoitring the harbour and creek of Ramree), and had not the least doubt, provided the information proved correct, that with his cordial co-operation and assistance, we should neither find much difficulty nor trouble in accomplishing the object. Captain Hardy came over to Cheduba on the 27th, and, after a short consultation, although he was of opinion that our European force was not sufficient, yet he was unwilling to throw any obstacle in the way, the business was determined on.

"By five p.m. on the 29th, the detachment—forty-eight artillerymen, with two brigades of guns, and five hundred and twenty of the 40th Regiment Native Infantry—was embarked on board the depôt ship 'Francis Warden,' the armed brig 'Planet,' and the flotilla of gun-boats. The brig having the artillery on board, sailed that afternoon, and, on the following morning, the remainder of the vessels got under weigh, but from light and variable winds, and the intricacy of the entrance into Ramree harbour, we did not reach the mouth of the creek until the morning of the 2nd instant. At one p.m. Captain Hardy, accompanied by Major Murray, Captain Hull, commanding the Artillery, and my detachment staff, Lieutenant Margrave, went for the purpose of examining the localities of the creek, and to ascertain the landing-place which had been pointed out by one of the guides. About five p.m. the party returned, and reported that the plain pointed out appeared a favourable spot for landing at high water, and just above it the creek was strongly staked across. About three hundred yards further up the creek, there was a second row of stakes much stronger, and defended by a battery, from which the enemy opened a heavy but ill-directed fire upon the boats, from jingals and musketry. About half a mile up the creek, beyond the second row of stakes, the angle of the stockade was visible. Arrangements being made for landing the troops as early in the morning as possible, to benefit by the flood tide, the distance from the vessels to the landing-place being about four miles, by half-past nine a.m., nearly the whole force was landed without opposition. I immediately formed a column, of the strength specified in the margin,* with the view of attacking the enemy in flank, and driving him from the breastwork which defended the creek, to enable Captain Hardy to proceed up with gunboats, to remove the stakes, and to accompany the troops to the principal stockades, leaving Captain Skardon with the reserve of about one hundred and eighty men, and the two brigades of guns, under Captain Hull, to act in concert with Captain Hardy, as circumstances might render it necessary. The column of attack, I regret to say, was led by the guides in quite a different direction to the place I wished to carry, and had to surmount obstacles never contemplated from the information received. The gallantry of the party, however, overcame every difficulty which presented itself, and drove the enemy out from all his entrenched positions at the point of the bayonet, obliging him to take shelter in his usual place of resort—the jungle, from which a galling fire was kept up, until he was dislodged by our troops. It now being half-past three p.m., the detachment, quite fatigued and exhausted for want of water, and finding that it was totally impracticable to advance by the road pointed out, the jungle being so very close as not to admit of a file of men abreast, and lined by the enemy, who had now opened a fire upon our rear, we were about five miles distant from our boats, without any possibility of communication, and it appearing evident that we had been most treacherously deceived, it was deemed prudent and advisable to return to the boats, so as to arrive in sufficient time to recross the nullahs, which had so greatly impeded our advance. The enemy reoccupied every hill and plain as we quitted, and continued firing on us from jingals and matchlocks, until checked by the arrival of the reserve, when a few well-directed rounds from the 6-pounder field-pieces dislodged them from their lurking places, and effectually silenced their fire, which enabled us to re-embark the whole force by six p.m. When every man composing the force did his duty, it is difficult to discriminate individual merit, but I should consider myself wanting in duty, were I not to bring to the notice of his Excellency the gallant conduct of Lieutenant Bell, of the Bombay European Regiment, commanding the Marines, and of Lieutenant Coxe, commanding the light company of my own regiment, who were conspicuously forward on every occasion, showing an example to their men which did them honour and

* Marines of the 'Hastings,' thirty; seamen, sixty; 40th Regiment Native Infantry, three hundred and thirty, also six men of H.M's. 54th Regiment. Total four hundred and twenty six.

credit. To Captain Hardy, who commanded the naval part of the force, and who was engaged with the gunboats during my absence endeavouring to remove the stakes and force a passage of the creek to the enemy's breastwork, and whose officers and seamen exerted themselves to their utmost, my sincere and grateful thanks are due, as well as for his cordial co-operation and assistance on every occasion, wherever the public service required it." In this affair Mr. Graves, master's mate of the 'Hastings,' and five men were killed, and twenty-two wounded,* of whom some died.

Captain Hardy says, in his report to Commodore Hayes:—
"The 'Henry Meriton' has been detained to convey to you and General Morrison, the result of the operations against Ramree, which, I regret to say, have failed, from causes which Lieutenant-Colonel Hampton will more properly explain. I am happy to say the Lieutenant-Colonel speaks in high terms of the good conduct and bravery of our seamen and Marines; and I beg to recommend all the officers under my command to the notice of Government as deserving every praise for their exertion and valour on every occasion. Previous to this attack with the military, we had, with a party of seamen and Marines, under Lieutenant Wyndham, several skirmishes with the enemy, and had succeeded in defeating them in two separate attacks, and in taking and burning two of their villages, strongly defended by five hundred men sent from Ramree for the purpose. I reconnoitred the creek under a smart fire, and gave the Lieutenant-Colonel the result of all my observations, and also every professional information connected with the service. Enclosed is a return of our killed and wounded; our boats suffered from the enemy's shot. I further beg to acquaint you, that the ships and vessels under my orders at Cheduba, have been actively employed on the enemy's coasts and possessions since I took command.

"The cutter 'Matchless' is now going into Chebuda Creek, to undergo repairs and caulking, after which I intend examining Chandwah, and some of the creeks on the eastern side of Ramree Channel, that are said to lead into the Irrawaddy, unless called up to Arracan. By this opportunity I have the pleasure to forward to you a plan of Ramree creek, channel, and harbour, as surveyed by my orders by Lieutenants Wyndham and Harrison, assisted by Mr. Carless,† master's mate of this ship, and beg to recommend those officers to your consideration, as deserving notice."

Throughout the Burmese War a flotilla of gunboats was

---

* Among the casualties were two soldiers of H.M's. 54th Regiment, who had volunteered their services, together with five comrades embarked, for the benefit of their health, on board the Hon. Company's armed cutter 'Matchless,' then commanded by the famous Lieutenant Waghorn.

† The late distinguished surveyor, Commodore Carless, I.N.

employed in Assam, assisting, where practicable, the column under the command of Brigadier Richards, and was of essential aid in the operations.

An opportunity of earning distinction was afforded to one of the Company's cruisers, which was turned to advantage. On the 3rd of June, 1824, as the 'Vestal,' 10-gun brig, commanded by Lieutenant James W. Guy, brother of the surveyor, was under weigh near the island of Shahporee, at the mouth of the Naaf river, accompanied by two gunboats, under Midshipmen Laughton and Boyè, of the Bombay Marine, a fleet of one hundred Burmese war-boats, all armed with guns and filled with men, hove in sight. The enemy's boats, owing to their overwhelming force, were so confident of success, that they hailed the little cruiser, and demanded her surrender and that of the gunboats. The reply to this request was volleys of grape and canister, and, after a sharp action, the Burmese were glad to make their escape, having sustained a loss of fourteen warboats and one hundred and fifty men.

The following is Lieutenant Guy's report :—" Shortly after I weighed anchor and stood down the river, I saw about one hundred war-boats drawn out in a line off Mungdoo Creek. On our nearer approach a canoe was despatched, with five hands in her, ordering me to surrender the vessel or they would take her by force, and kill every man on board. This message I answered by a broadside from my great guns. They kept up a smart fire for about ten minutes, then retreated into Mungdoo Creek; the two gun-boats, under Messrs. Laughton and Boyè, chased them upon this, and poured in several well-directed showers of grape and canister, which did great execution; they then returned, after having taken four prisoners from the above-mentioned canoe.

"I then tacked and stood towards Shahporee island, under which several boats lay. They endeavoured to escape, but finding themselves cut off by the gunboats, they ran their boats on shore and fled into the jungle, but not before numbers were destroyed by the volleys of grape poured into them from the gunboats. The rest of the boats having escaped, I stood for the new stockade, fired a broadside into it whilst passing, then ran down and anchored off the south-eastern point of Shahporee Island for the night. I should imagine about twelve or fourteen boats were destroyed, as I observed them floating out of Mungdoo Creek after the attack, completely shattered by the great guns. I also beg leave to report the great zeal and activity evinced by the officers on board the vessel, as also the high-spirited conduct of Messrs. Laughton and Boyè, each commanding a gunboat."

The Governor-General says, in his despatch of the 14th of July, to the Secret Committee:—" The enemy were completely foiled, and received a severe and memorable chastisement from the 'Vestal' and her gunboats, whose fire destroyed several of their war-boats in the Naaf, and committed terrible havoc among the crews and the troops who lined either shore, expecting to find the vessels an easy prey. The cruiser and gunboats immediately after made sail for Chittagong, where they arrived in safety on the 7th ultimo."

We will now detail the services rendered by that portion of the Bombay Marine, which assisted in the operations on the south-east frontier and in Arracan, conducted by Brigadier-General Morrison, C.B., of the 44th Regiment, an officer who had greatly distinguished himself during the war in Upper Canada. The naval force, which was placed by the Supreme Government, under the command of Commodore John Hayes, who, notwithstanding his age, relinquished his comfortable post of Master-Attendant at Calcutta to proceed on active service, consisted of the following ships and gunboats:— The 'Vestal,' ten gun brig; the surveying ships, 'Research' and 'Investigator,' fitted with ten guns; the six gun brigs 'Helen,' 'Henry Meriton,' 'Planet,' 'Sophia,' and 'Asseerghur;' the 'Trusty,' ketch, six guns, and steam-gun-vessel 'Pluto,' six guns; ten pinnaces, each carrying two guns, and eight divisions of gunboats—each of ten gunboats, carrying a 12-pounder carronade—besides transports and country boats. In addition to their crews, the vessels and boats carried a flotilla Marine, about six hundred strong.

A portion of General Morrison's force* proceeded in January, 1825, to Coxe's Bazaar, where the flotilla under Commodore Hayes also rendezvoused. A detachment made the four marches from Coxe's Bazaar to the grand estuary of the Naaf,† and the heavy Artillery and the greater portion of the Infantry were conveyed thither by the flotilla. A delay arose in the arrival of the latter, due to a heavy gale of wind which it encountered, when some of the native boats and gunboats were stranded, and one officer and some men were drowned. The force continued in camp at Tek Naaf until the 31st of January, 1825, just a month from the period of quitting Chittagong. Before

* General Morrison's force consisted of the 1st, 2nd, and 5th Brigades of the British Army, with Brigadier-General McBean (second in command), and Brigadiers W. Richards (26th Native Infantry), C. Grant, C.B., (54th Regiment), and Fair (10th Madras Native Infantry). The troops consisted of H.M's. 44th and 54th Regiments; the 26th, 42nd, 62nd, and 49th Bengal Native Infantry; the 10th and 16th Madras Native Infantry; Bengal Artillery, eight 9-pounders, four 12-pounders, four 5-inch howitzers; Madras Artillery, four 9-pounders; also six companies of Pioneers; levy of Mugh Pioneers; 1st and 2nd Light Infantry Battalion, and 2nd Regiment Local Horse. The total of effective fighting men numbered nine thousand three hundred and forty-three.

† The Estuary of the Naaf, some three miles broad, separates the province of Chittagong from the Kingdom of Arracan; across this inlet were situated the extensive stockades of Mungdoo, the first Arracan post, at which it was supposed the enemy would make a stand.

this date the troops on board the ships and vessels had arrived, also those which had followed by land, except the 42nd Native Infantry. On the evening of the 1st of February, appeared a Divisional Order for the following troops to hold themselves in readiness to cross the estuary :—H.M.'s 54th Foot, one hundred men of H.M.'s 44th, the 26th and 62nd Bengal Native Infantry, 10th Madras Native Infantry, two companies of Mugh Light Infantry, four companies of Pioneers, and the Bengal field battery of guns. This force was divided into two divisions; the first, under General Morrison, was to proceed to the Mungdoo creek and storm the stockades, whilst the other, under Brigadier-General McBean, was to land lower down and intercept the fugitives, or act as circumstances might render necessary. The embarkation commenced at five o'clock in the morning, and by eight the troops were all on board the boats, and the artillery on the rafts in tow of the 'Pluto' steamer.

On the British force effecting a landing on the opposite shore of the estuary of the Naaf, the Burmese, acting on the well-known Hudibrastic maxim, beat a hasty retreat over the mountains, leaving the invaders to take undisputed possession of their stockades of Mungdoo. Here were found a great quantity of grain, several war-boats, one about ninety feet long, and a small ship on the stocks.

A considerable force was sent in pursuit of the flying Burmese through the forests, but without avail. After a halt of many days at Mungdoo, General Morrison pushed on through dense forests and grass plains, or by the sea-shore, to the Myoo river near its embouchure, where it is some three or four miles broad.

Commodore Hayes, commanding the flotilla, left Mungdoo on the 16th of February, having arranged with General Morrison that he was to take on the major part of the fleet, including half the gunboats, to the Arracan river, with General McBean and Brigadier Fair's brigade, consisting of H.M.'s 54th, the Madras 10th Native Infantry, and left wing of the 16th Native Infantry. The Commodore also directed Captain Crawford, with the other half of the gunboats and Mugh boats, to proceed to the Arracan river, for the purpose of joining General Morrison, who was proceeding to its entrance with the main body of the army.

On the morning of the 17th, the Commodore cleared the Naaf to join the transport ships destined to convey the above-mentioned advance brigade to Arracan, but, at one p.m., a violent storm commenced from the northward, which raged round the compass until the morning of the 19th, and prevented the embarkation of the troops in question. Commodore Hayes, before quitting Mungdoo, had despached, on the 10th instant, a small squadron of vessels,* under command of Lieutenant

* 'Asseerghur,' 'Pluto,' 'Thames,' and 'Africa' gunboats.

Armstrong, of the Bombay Marine, to explore the entrances of the Myoo and Arracan rivers, in communication with General Morrison; and, feeling anxious for their safety, he proceeded in quest of them, with the 'Research,' 'Vestal,' 'Helen,' 'Trusty,' 'Osprey,' and 'Gunga Sauger,' two transports, and five commissariat sloops, leaving Captain Crawford to follow with the gunboats.

On the 21st he was joined to the eastward of the Myoo, by Lieutenant Armstrong, who reported as follows, in a letter dated the 21st of February, 1825:—"I proceeded with the vessels to the supposed latitude of Mosque Point (20° 14'), and finding the entrance of a river, which, from the correctest information we possessed, led me to believe it to be the Arracan river, I entered, crossing over a bar one and three-quarters and two fathoms low water, and after a slight survey, discovered a stockade that might give annoyance to the vessels in passing. I landed with Lieutenant Coote, a detachment of H.M.'s 54th Regiment, a party of the Bombay Marine Battalion, and the European crew of the 'Pluto' On perceiving us, the enemy fled; it was situated in a strong position, being on a point with a jungle in the rear. On the 16th, the spies belonging to the Quartermaster-General's department, being closely pursued by the Burmese, were obliged to retreat to the vessels. They informed us we were in the Miou River, on which information I proceeded to the south-eastward in quest of the Arracan river, which we entered on the same night. On examining the river, the pilot I had obtained informed me of a new stockade commanding the channel, about eight miles from the entrance, to which we proceeded with the 'Asseerghur,' 'Pluto,' and gunboats. After firing a few shots we landed, and found it deserted. It was not quite finished, in a very strong position, and had the day before been garrisoned by five hundred men, and had employed the villagers around two hundred days to build it. It is 100 yards square and full of barracks, the whole of which we burnt (named by the natives Patinga). On the 20th, the spies gave me information that the Governor of Arracan, with one hundred war-boats and two thousand men, was coming down the river to attack us that night. I moved out into the centre of the river, and kept the people under arms all night. This morning, hearing guns in the offing, I proceeded out to join the fleet. Mosque Point is situated in latitude 20° 5' 40" north, being nine miles to the south of the situation given by the "East India Directory" (which is 20° 15' north) about east-south-east from the Miou River.

Lieutenant Armstrong reported to the Commodore that the people were much alarmed, and insisted on being taken off, and as it was requisite to give them immediate support and protection for the general good of the Service, Commodore

Hayes determined to proceed into the Arracan river without loss of time, and, accordingly, entered it the same evening with the vessels above-mentioned. On the 22nd, the Commodore was joined by a Moonshee, employed by Captain Drummond to procure intelligence of the enemy's proceedings, who informed him there was a stockade halfway to Arracan, called Chamballa, or Keung-peela, erected by the Burmese to defend the water approach to the capital; that it contained only one thousand Burmese fighting men, and would easily fall if speedily attacked; that the principal Mugh chieftains were confined in the stockade, as pledges for the fidelity and good behaviour of the inhabitants, and that if liberated, all the country would make common cause with the British, thus greatly facilitating military operations.

Believing this information to be correct, the Commodore determined, with the small means at his command, to attempt the capture of the place, and despatched a messenger to General Morrison with an intimation to that effect.

Accordingly, on the 23rd, he stood up the Prome Pura Khione, or branch leading from the Oratung River to Arracan, with a squadron* consisting of the 'Research,' commanded by Lieutenant Armstrong, during the absence of Captain Crawford with the gunboats; 'Vestal,' Lieutenant Guy; 'Asseerghur,' 'Helen,' 'Trusty,' 'Pluto;' and the gunboats 'Asia,' 'Osprey,' 'Thames,' 'Gunga Saugor,' and 'Africa.' There were also embarked in two transports, a detachment of the 54th Regiment, and details of Native Infantry.

At two p.m. they came in sight of the enemy's works at Chamballa, which immediately opened a heavy fire upon the

* The following was the military and naval force present in this affair, of which all were not, however, engaged:—The Hon. Company's ship 'Research,' ten 12-pounders, Commodore Hayes, Lieutenant Armstrong, Acting-Commander, in the absence of Captain Crawford. Hon. Company's cruiser 'Vestal,' six 12-pounder carronades, four brass long 18-pounders, commanded by Lieutenant J. W. Guy. Hon. Company's brigs 'Asseerghur,' six brass 6-pounders, two 12-pounder carronades, W. Warden commanding; and 'Helen,' six brass 6-pounders, J. W. Higgins commanding; Hon. Company's ketch, 'Trusty,' six brass 3-pounders, J. Royce commanding; Hon. Company's steam gun vessel 'Pluto,' four brass 24-pounder carronades, two brass long 6-pounders (not in action), T. C. Minchall commanding; Hon. Company's gun pinnace 'Osprey,' two 12-pounder carronades, Mr. Oakshot, gunner, in charge; Hon. Company's gunboats 'Gunga Saugor,' one 12-pounder carronade, Charles Montriou, Master's Mate of the 'Research,' in charge; 'Thames,' two 24-pounder carronades, Richard Kent commanding; 'Africa,' one 12-pounder carronade, C. R. Richardson, third officer of the 'Research,' in charge; and 'Asia,' one 12-pounder carronade, Charles Avery, Boatswain's Mate of the 'Research,' in charge. Also the Hon. Company's transports 'Asia Felix,' S. Jellicoe, commander; and 'Isabella,' F. McNeil, commander. The troops consisted of:—Detachment H.M.'s. 54th Regiment, under Captain Grindley, forty; detachments of 10th and 16th Madras Native Infantry, Captain Tolson, commanding, one hundred and seventy; Marines in the flotilla, one hundred; Calcutta Militia, twelve; and 11th Bombay Native Infantry, eighteen. These, together with the seamen in the different vessels, one hundred and forty men, made a total strength of four hundred and eighty-eight soldiers and seamen.

'Gunga Saugor,' and 'Vestal,' the headmost vessels. The 'Research,' with the Commodore on board, was soon within half-pistol shot, and commenced a heavy cannonade and fire of musketry upon the stockade and breastwork, which was returned by the enemy with great regularity and spirit. On ranging to the northern end of the stockade, with intent to anchor and flank it, as well as to allow the other vessels to come into action, the Commodore found his ship raked from forward by another stronger battery and stockade, of which he had no previous information, and the strength of the enemy was greater than had been anticipated, amounting, as was subsequently ascertained, to three thousand men, commanded by the son of the Rajah of Arracan, and other chiefs of rank. After a severe engagement of two hours' duration, the tide beginning to fall, Commodore Hayes was obliged to wear round and drop down the river. The 'Research,' 'Asseerghur,' 'Asia Felix,' and 'Isabella,' took the ground, and remained fast for several hours near the batteries; but the enemy made no attempt to fire at or molest them. The loss in this attack was severe. Amongst the killed were Mr. Rogers, second officer of the 'Research,' and Major Schalch, a distinguished officer of the Company's service, commanding an extra pioneer and pontoon corps attached to the army, who was on board the 'Research' for the recovery of his health. He was struck while standing on the poop by a musket ball in his breast, and died on the morning of the 25th. He was an officer, says Horace Hayman Wilson, "of high scientific attainments, as much admired for his talents as for the amiability of his disposition." On receiving his wound, he fell into the arms of the Commodore, exclaiming, "I am a dead man," but lingered for two days in excruciating pain, imploring the bystanders to shoot him through the head, and put an end to his sufferings. "The old Commodore," writes Captain Bellew, of the staff, describing this hot day's work, "was a genuine 'heart of oak,' as brave as a lion, time not having reduced the temperature of his blood much below the boiling point."

In this action two officers and four men were killed, and thirty-two wounded, of whom five died. The Commodore* attributed his failure to the unexpected number and strength of the stockades, regarding which he had been deceived, his information inducing him to understand there was only one; also to the tide falling in the course of the engagement, and the breadth of water diminishing in consequence, the vessels were cramped for room to manœuvre, which resulted in some running aground.

* The following is Commodore Hayes official letter of the 25th of February, detailing the action at Chamballa :—
"On the 23rd, at two p.m., came in sight of the stockade (as it was called

In concluding his report of the action to the Governor-General, Commodore Hayes says:—" I have to bring to your erroneously). At three p.m. made the signal No. 1. Soon afterwards the enemy opened his fire upon the gunboats, ' Gunga Saugor ' and ' Vestal,' the headmost vessels; when the ' Research ' got within half-pistol shot, we commenced a heavy cannonade and steady fire of musketry upon the stockade and breastwork, which was returned by the enemy with great regularity and spirit (his musketry in particular being tenfold that of our whole force). On ranging to the northern end of the stockade with intent to anchor and flank it, as well as to allow the other vessels room to come into action, we found ourselves raked from forward by another stronger battery and stockade, which we had no idea of, nor were the latter works known to our informants, which may be the case, considering the rapidity with which the Burmese throw up their works of defence. I am not inclined to impute treachery to our informants, although it is difficult to suppose them ignorant of such important works. Finding myself disappointed, and our best men falling fast, wore round and ranged up again from the southward, in like manner as before covered the other vessels engaged, and ordered them off, after a severe conflict of two hours' duration. Seeing that any further contest was a useless waste of the lives of my brave companions (as we neither had men enough to keep the place if taken, nor sufficient means to land them with effect, owing to the absence of the ' Pluto ' steam gun-vessel, upon which I had calculated upon landing one hundred men on the beach, under her commanding battery), having seen the whole clear, wore round again. On hauling to the wind, grounded about half-a-mile from the stockade, as did the ' Asseerghur ' and ' Asia Felix ' transport, the ' Isabella ' transport having grounded previously did not join in the action. The contest terminated about 8 p.m., and although the vessels mentioned remained in the position, they grounded until three a.m. next morning. The enemy did not attempt to fire at any of them, which shows the crippled state he was reduced to better than any other comment; in fact, the river part of the stockade and breastwork was completely battered down, and the works deserted by the enemy, who retreated into his other stronger hold, so that our possession of the deserted one would have availed us nothing, as we could not have maintained it with our small force, and left the vessels capable of defence. I grieve to state, in the first instance, the premature fate of my valued friend, Major Schalch, who was mortally wounded by my side on the front part of the poop, and fell into my arms; he lingered in great agony until half-past three this morning, when his gallant spirit fled for ever. In the next place, I have to lament the loss of Mr. Rogers, second officer of the ' Research;' the other lamented disasters are detailed in the casualty reports, herewith submitted for his Excellency's information, the whole of which were occasioned by the enemy's musketry, although he fired from several pieces of ordnance and numerous jingals. To account for our loss, I need only add that the river part of the Burmese works is not more than musket range across, and that the ' Research ' was never without pistol shot while in action with the enemy on the 23rd instant.

"I am impelled by a sense of common justice due to the troops, to express my admiration of the steady and gallant conduct of H.M's. 54th, the Madras details of the 10th and 16th Native Infantry, the 11th Bombay Native Infantry, and Calcutta Militia present on this occasion; and I humbly presume to recommend Captains Grindley and Tolson, and the officers under their command, to his Excellency's consideration. Lieutenant Coote, of H.M's. 54th, fought by my side, and a more gallant officer I have never seen in action. The gunboats were admirably served and exceeded my expectation, as did the ' Trusty ' and ' Asia Felix ' transport. All the officers and men of the larger vessels of war did justice to the high character I had previously formed of them, and every effort which can be drawn from courage, zeal, and ability, may be confidently expected from the whole on the most arduous service hereafter.

" P.S.—While writing the above disastrous report, I was visited by Mharne, the Jemadar of Oratung district, who says he made his escape from Chamballu when we drove the enemy out of the southern stockade; he added that several more Mugh heads of villages got off at the same time, that there were three

Excellency's particular notice the very gallant conduct of the following officers—viz., Mr. Royce, commanding the 'Trusty,' and Captain Jellicoe, of the 'Asia Felix' transport, who remained with their vessels off Chamballa a considerable time. I am the more indebted to Captain Jellicoe than any other person, as I had no reasonable pretension to expect such assistance from him. With regard to Mr. Royce, the case is different. I expected much able aid from him, in consequence of his established character for undaunted courage and zeal in the service. Mr. Kent, commanding the 'Thames,' first-class gunboat, greatly distinguished himself, as did Mr. Charles Ramsay Richardson, of the 'Hastings,' in the 'Africa;' Mr. Charles Montriou,* in the 'Gunga Saugor;' Charles Avery, of the 'Asia,' gunboat, and Mr. Oakshot, in charge of the 'Osprey,' gun-pinnace; the whole of the crews of vessels just mentioned are equally entitled to the most favourable notice of his Excellency. In consequence of the loss of the second officer of the flag-ship, I have been enabled to promote Messrs. Richardson and Montriou to the situations of second and third officers of the Hon. Company's ship 'Research,' as a just reward for their gallant conduct on the occasion in question, and trust such proceeding will meet his Excellency's approbation."

After several routes for the march on Arracan had been discussed, it was at last determined that the army—except the portion, including the 54th Regiment, on board the vessels in the Oratung,—should proceed in the gunboats and other craft from Myoo Mooa to the plains on the left bank of the Arracan River. Accordingly, on the 4th of March, the General and Staff embarked, and, leading the way in the 'Osprey,' pinnace, crossed the broad waters of the Myoo, and entered the Arracan river near the Oratung Pagoda, a large Buddhist temple, which occupies the summit of an eminence, and is visible at some distance from the coast; on the arrival of the troops it was

thousand Burmese soldiers opposed to us, besides pressed Mughmen, and that they retreated into the stronger fort or stockade. He further observed that the three stockades communicated with each other for such purpose ; by his account there were five Shoee Tees, or Golden Chattahs, Nackoonda, the Ramoo conqueror, the Rajah of Arracan's son, and other inferior chiefs. All the Mungdoo and Loodhong troops were posted therein to retrieve their lost character, and the Commander of Mungdoo was in triple irons. He earnestly entreated that we would not leave them to the rage of the barbarous Burmese. I told him we were not going farther, that in two or three days we should return with a sufficient force, and take Chamballa ; that I merely came to Oratung for water, &c., for the troops and vessels, which was indispensable for our farther proceedings; that if the vessels had been supplied, I would not have lost sight of Chamballa for a moment. We are now only four short reaches from it (none of three miles in extent), at the most commanding station of the river ; the creek close to us, to the westward, runs into the Miou, near the General's head-quarters; we completely cover the Arracan river, from its entrance to this station, and alike intercept all communication to the northward."

* The late Captain Montriou, I.N., the distinguished surveyor.

found that some of Commodore Hayes' seamen had taken possession of the temple by hoisting the Union Jack on its highest point. A portion of the force was disembarked on the island of Chankrain, opposite to which lay the Commodore's ship with the other cruisers and transports at anchor. On the 25th of March, the entire army, consisting of eight regiments, with artillery, was assembled at Kray Kingdong, a few miles distant, excepting the 5th, or Madras, Brigade, and the small column left at Chankrain. The naval portion of the force, under the command of Commodore Hayes, consisting of several pilot-vessels and armed brigs, ten pinnaces, and a large number of gunboats, performed good service during the succeeding operations, and the seamen, who were landed to co-operate with the army, appeared to be inspired with the zeal and enthusiasm of their gallant old chief.

The following were the final arrangements for the co-operation of the Marine in the advance upon the Burmese provincial capital of Arracan, made by Commodore Hayes in conjunction with General Morrison, and here we may note the perfect harmony with which the military and naval chiefs worked together throughout these operations:—

The 'Helen,' six guns, Mr. Higgins, and 'Trusty,' six guns, Mr. Royce, and half the 5th division of gunboats, were stationed at the southern part of Chamballa Reach, to support the troops left in possession of Chankrain Island, and eventually to take possession of Chamballa stockades on the enemy's moving towards Arracan. The 'Sophia,' six-gun brig, with the other half of the 5th division of gunboats, was left to support the detail of troops left at Kray Kingdong, and to protect the transports; the 8th division of gunboats, and 'Pluto' steam vessel, six guns, were stationed under Captain Crawford, in advance with Brigadier Grant. The 1st and 7th divisions of gunboats, under Commodore Hayes' personal command, with the 'Research' and 'Asseerghur,' and the transports, 'Isabella,' 'Brougham,' 'Goliath,' 'Jessy,' and four Commissariat sloops, with the guns, ammunition, and provisions, were to proceed up the river, and form a junction with the army at Mahattie, near the capital. On entering the river, the Commodore received a despatch from Mr. Higgins, commanding the detachment of the flotilla in Chamballa Reach, stating that the enemy had evacuated the stockades, and that he had, agreeably to his order, occupied them, and awaited further instructions. In consequence, Commodore Hayes directed the 'Sophia' and gunboats at Kray Kingdong, immediately to join Mr. Higgins, and instructed the latter officer to proceed with the whole detachment up the Chamballa Reach to Arracan, and cause a diversion in that quarter.

In the direct road between the British army and Arracan,

lay a low range of wooded hills, through which ran a narrow defile, called the Pass of Paduah; this debouched near an open plain intersected by two or more rivers, and fronting the strongly fortified post of Mahattie. Here at Paduah resistance was expected, and the General determined to force the pass and advance on the capital without further delay. The whole of the troops were consequently divided, at Kray Kingdong, into four columns, and advanced on the morning of the 26th of March. The first column, under Brigadier Grant, was instructed to force the right pass; the second, under General Morrison, to attack the centre; the third, commanded by Captain Leslie, H.M.'s 54th Regiment, was ordered to proceed in the gunboats and turn the enemy's position and intercept their retreat; the fourth column, under Brigadier Walker, 54th Regiment, was instructed to act as a reserve. Some sharp fighting took place with the enemy at the foot of the hills, and the troops, crossing the bed of the tidal river, finally took post behind some works, in a large open plain opposite Mahattie, designed by the Burmese as the great bulwark to defend the land route to the capital, as the stockades of Chamballa were to protect the water approach.

Buddhist temples and other religious structures crowned the heights within the peninsula of Mahattie, the horse-shoe edge or outer line of which, was defended by trenches, embankments, and abattis. On the morning of the 27th of March, the whole force, in battle array, marched down to attack this position. After some sharp firing on both sides, the enemy were dislodged, and joined their comrades across the river. As the columns advanced, the Burmese opened a fire of cannon, musketry, and jingals, with little effect, which was returned by the British artillery, the flotilla, under Captain Crawford, participating with equal resolution and effect. Thus firing, the main body of the troops steadily moved up to the brink of the river, which separated them from the Burmese lines. In a short time General Morrison ordered Brigadier Colquhoun Grant to ford the river with his Brigade, and attack the right and rear of the enemy's position, which was done with alacrity, and soon the Burmese were in full flight.

The Army remained at Mahattie two days to prepare for the move on Arracan, the defences of which were rumoured to be of a very formidable kind, both natural and artificial. Meanwhile Commodore Hayes, with the 1st and 7th Divisions of gunboats and the larger vessels, finding that, owing to want of water, the latter could not approach within six miles of Mahattie, left the 'Research' and 'Asseerghur,' with a native crew, and one warrant officer in charge of each, and, proceeding in the gunboats 'Osprey' and 'Gunga Saugor,' effected a junction with the army on the afternoon of the 28th. Having communicated with General Morrison, and ascertained that the gun-boats could not approach the capital within range of their guns, it was determined that the seamen and marines should land under his personal command, and act with the army, taking with them two 24-pounder carronades and the requisite ammunition. Accordingly, Commodore Hayes landed two 24-pounders, and put himself at the head of seventy flotilla seamen, besides officers and warrant officers, together with the crews of the gunboats present, amounting in all to two hundred and fifty European seamen. " We succeeded," he says in his despatch, " by great exertions in dragging the guns and carrying the shot and ammunition on the men's shoulders to the camps, where we arrived at seven p.m. on the 29th ultimo, Captain Crawford being previously detached with the 8th division of gunboats to endeavour to approach Arracan by a channel between Mahattie and the Chamballa Reach ; perhaps it is here necessary to observe that the gunboats brought up the mortars, howitzers, and two 24-pounder field guns, with all their requisites to Mahattie."

The 31st of March was the day fixed for the march on Arracan. The troops quietly assembled some time before daybreak, in the order laid down by the General; Brigadier-General McBean commanding the column.

Commodore Hayes furnished from the flotilla the following details:—For the advance attack, under Brigadier Richards, Lieutenant Armstrong, Mr. Howard, Mr. Montriou, Mr. Keymer, two warrant officers, and thirty seamen; for the supporting column, under Brigadier-General McBean, Captain Crawford, Mr. Warden, Acting-Lieutenant Richardson, Mr. Pruen—the late Captain Pruen, I.N., who died in June, 1875—Mr. Jackson, four warrant officers, and forty seamen ; while he himself accompanied the Commander-in-chief with the main body of the army.

The column moved on over rough-ploughed ground until they reached a wide plain, when the curtain of fog and mist, which had hitherto enveloped the hills, rolled away, displaying the whole extent of the Burmese position, formed on the scarped, and stockaded summits. " A more picturesque *coup d'œil,*" says Captain Bellew, " cannot be imagined. Above, the Burmese posts, and the dusky array of their defenders, the gleam of the gilded umbrellas, and the white volumes of smoke emitted from the stockade and embrasure ; below, our splendid force, spreading across the plain, the bayonets of the infantry glistening in the rays of the morning sun, the pennons of the irregular horse gaily fluttering, and, to complete the picture, a body of blue jackets from the flotilla determined to share the fun, hauling along two ponderous carronades with the Union Jack floating over them."

The moment the Burmese caught sight of the army,

debouching, they cheered lustily, and a gun opened fire from a lofty conical hill, on the extreme right of their defences, which stretched in an undulating line for a great distance; it was replied to by the British guns, and soon the firing became general on both sides. Brigadier-General McBean, who commanded the advance, halted on reaching a bank fringed with wood, near the further end of the valley, and close to a pass leading into a basin in which the town is situated; from this point, which lay within gunshot, and was cannonaded by the Burmese, but with little effect, he detached a party, composed of European and Native troops, to storm a low hill flanking the mouth of the pass. This small force, which consisted of men of the 54th Foot and 1st Bengal Fusiliers, the whole led by Major Kemm, moved off to the point of attack, plunged into the woods at the base of the hill, and were soon seen emerging on the steep, scarped portion which rose above them; but they were unable to make any way, owing to the heavy fire of the enemy, and were forced to retire. Something like a check was also received in the pass, where Captain French, commanding the 10th Madras Regiment, was killed, and Captain Fitton, of the Pioneers, lost a leg. General Morrison, also, had a narrow escape, a ball having struck the scabbard of his sword, causing his horse to rear and throw him. After these mishaps a good deal of firing from the artillery and mortars was maintained on the Burmese lines, which caused several conflagrations and explosions of gunpowder; but it ceased after a few hours' duration, leaving the enemy still masters of their long line of scarped eminences. The force now encamped as far out of gunshot as possible, and further plans had to be considered for the reduction of the place.

It was at length decided that Brigadier Richards, with a force of about one thousand men, including Lieutenant Armstrong's party, from the 'Vestal,' should make a night attack on the conical fortified hill* on the extreme right, which formed the key to the enemy's position. At the same time, in order to divert the attention of the enemy from this point, a battery was constructed for four mortars, two 24-pounders, which the seamen of the flotilla had landed and dragged with infinite labour to the front, and six smaller guns. "At half-past seven that evening," says the General, "ground was broke, by three o'clock the battery was finished, and before daylight completely armed, when the guns opened and continued during the day a heavy cannonade, which had the effect of checking the enemy's fire, though it was not entirely silenced."

At the hour fixed for the assault, all being hushed, the party

---

* This eminence was afterwards called Richards' Hill, from the Brigadier, who became General Sir William Richards, K.C.B., and died on the 1st of November, 1861, when he was the Senior Officer of the Bengal Army.

quietly paraded, and, led by Brigadier Richards, set out through the woods for the point of attack. The path the column took, was often very narrow and difficult of ascent, and, in one place, where there was a lake or sheet of water on one side, and a lofty precipice on the other, the troops could only advance by single file. But their gallantry was rewarded by complete success, and soon the fortified position was stormed, when they made the preconcerted signal, by firing one or more rockets. The whole of the troops then advanced, and the British flag floated over the defences of Arracan. The loss in these last affairs was about thirty killed and one hundred and twenty wounded, including six or seven officers.

The entry of the army into Arracan caused a scene of great confusion. One quarter of the town took fire and was burnt to the ground, and there was some looting, though the plunderers were made to disgorge their booty in passing through a gate of the town leading to the camp. Colonel Bucke, with the Light Infantry Company of the 54th, and some of the Light Infantry Battalion, was sent in pursuit of the fugitives, but the detachment returned in a few days, and, having caught the jungle fever, died off nearly to a man.

In his official despatch of the 2nd of April, General Morrison speaks of the services of the flotilla in the following terms:— "Commodore Hayes has, on all occasions, rendered an aid the most effectual, and had it not been for the assistance afforded by the flotilla under his command, the arrival of the force before Arracan would have been almost impracticable. Every exertion was made by him to co-operate, and when insurmountable obstacles prevented the further approach of the gunboats to the scene of action, he landed two 24-pounders, and, with the British seamen, dragged them and their appurtenances a distance of five miles to the encampment before Arracan, rendering them available for any service on which they could be usefully employed."

Commodore Hayes, in his official report to the Military Secretary of the Commander-in-Chief, dated Pondoo Prang Plains, Arracan, the 2nd of April, 1825, says of the officers and seamen under his command:—"I have every reason to be proud of the gallantry and good conduct of every officer and man under my command with the Arracan Army. Lieutenant Armstong has invariably distinguished himself ever since the flotilla left Coxe's Bazaar." Soon after these operations, this gallant and zealous young officer died of fever brought on through over exertion.

By these successes, Arracan and Cheduba, two of the four provinces of Arracan, were cleared of the enemy, and it only remained to dislodge them from the remaining divisions of Sandoway and Ramree. Accordingly, General McBean and

Commodore Hayes, having determined on a second attack upon the island of Ramree, a small force* was embarked in the flotilla, which weighed early in the morning of the 17th of April, and, being favoured with a fair breeze, anchored on the night of the 18th, within three miles of Cheduba roads. The squadron, having taken in a supply of water at Low island, proceeded to the entrance of Ramree creek, and, on the following morning, the troops were landed. The numerous rows of stakes the enemy had driven across the creek, presented so formidable and effectual an obstacle that the seamen were occupied two hours in clearing a passage for the small boats. General McBean and the Commodore marched towards the town of Ramree with the advance, under the command of Captain Shelton, of the 44th Regiment—an officer who attained an unenviable notoriety as second in command of the Army under General Elphinstone in Affghanistan in 1841-42—and the town was occupied without any opposition.† Eight companies of the 40th Native Infantry, with a detachment of artillery from Cheduba, under the command of Major Murray, were left in the island, and General McBean and Commodore Hayes then proceeded upon other service. Of the latter officer the General writes :—" To Commodore Hayes I am most indebted for his hearty co-operation upon all occasions, and feel the fullest confidence from his able assistance."

On the 28th of April, the military and naval chiefs arrived at the entrance of the Sandoway River, up which the boats, with troops on board, rowed about eight miles, Commodore Hayes leading, until, at dusk, they came upon a stockaded entrenchment; the enemy had also constructed breastworks in commanding points, and had staked the river below the entrenchment, but left a space sufficently wide for the boats to pass. The troops were landed for the night, but were re-embarked early the next morning, and the whole force was in progress up the river at four o'clock. No opposition was made to their passage, and, soon after seven, the stockades at Sandoway were in their possession. After destroying the works the troops were re-embarked, and the boats returned to the ships at the entrance of the river. General McBean, in concluding his despatch, adds:—"I

* Four 6-pounders, two 5½-inch howitzers, and two 5½-inch mortars; four companies each of H.M's. 44th and 54th Regiments; and eight companies each of the 40th Bengal Native Infantry and 16th Madras Native Infantry.

† "The road," says the General in his despatch, " had to appearance lately been made, and was commanded in every part by fortified heights and well-constructed entrenchments. The creek is practicable for boats to the town at high water, distance from its entrance about seven miles—by land, from the great entrenchment, considerably less. The enemy, to protect him against a landing by the creek, had thrown up a long line of entrenchments upon the bank, constructed with great judgment, and made particularly strong by the numerous traverses placed in all directions. The defences of the town consist in a stockade of considerable extent and some strength, situated about the centre of it, this being protected by several forts upon hills, and one of them completely commanding the road by which you approach."

have to repeat how much I owe to Commodore Hayes, and my admiration in him of the good effects of a zealous and animated example for enterprises."

The occupation of the entire province of Arracan, fulfilled one important object of the war, and afforded a valuable diversion in favour of the march on Ava; but it was not found practicable to carry out the chief object, that of effecting a junction, across the mountains, with Sir Archibald Campbell's Army. Several reconnaissances were made with the view of proving the practicability of such a march, but without avail. But though the success that rewarded the forces operating in this portion of the Burmese Empire was complete, and gave the British undisputed possession of the province, the Burmese were avenged by the terrible losses their victors incurred while occupying their provincial capital of Arracan and other points. The malaria engendered in these fetid swamps and gloomy forests swept off the officers and men of the army and flotilla in hundreds, and of those who returned to India and England, few escaped without carrying away with them the seeds of the fatal "Arracan fever."

We will now resume the history of the campaign of the main, or Ava, portion of the Expedition, under the command of Sir Archibald Campbell, so far as relates to the services of the Bombay Marine, taking up the thread of the narrative from the month of November, 1824.

On the 7th of that month, Lieutenant Greer, commanding the Hon. Company's cruiser 'Thetis,' while proceeding from Elephant Point to Rangoon, with a guard of only six marines, greatly distinguished himself by beating off two large Burmese boats, each carrying between thirty and forty armed men, every one of whom were killed, several falling by his sword and pistol. Lieutenant Greer says in his report to Sir Archibald Campbell, dated the 14th of November:—"I have the honour to report that, on Saturday, the 7th instant, at eleven a.m., I left the ship in a row-boat, with a guard of six Sepoys of the Bombay Marine Battalion, for the purpose of waiting on the Senior Officer at Rangoon. Abreast of a small creek, a little below Bassein creek, six war-boats pulled out and stood up close along till abreast of Bassein creek, when eight more boats of the same description joined them; they then came out and endeavoured to cut us off by pulling across the river, ahead of the row-boat. I kept up a constant fire from the 12-pounder and musketry until two of the boats came alongside, when I immediately jumped on board of them with the Sepoys, and succeeded in bayoneting every man; in one of the boats there appeared to be a chief, whom I shot in the act of darting a spear at me. The other twelve boats were coming close up, but, seeing the fate of the two, made off towards the shore, upon which I kept up a smart fire while within range. I am sorry to state that during the action one Sepoy and one row-boat man were severely wounded, the former in two places. In each of these boats were from thirty to forty men. I cannot conclude this Report without recommending strongly to your notice, the gallant conduct of the Sepoys of the Bombay Marine Battalion in leaping into the enemy's boats, and for the destructive and well-directed fire they kept up on the approach of the enemy, whereby great numbers were either killed or wounded before they came alongside. The conduct of the row-boat men deserves every praise." Stimulated by the encouragement and example of Lieutenant Greer, the conduct of these Native boatmen affords a striking contrast to that always attributed to them in previous actions, where they could not be got to face the enemy.

Lieutenant Marshall, R.N., speaks as follows of one of the consequences of this affair, on which, however, we will make no comment : " The bold and determined conduct of Mr. Greer, was duly appreciated by Sir Archibald Campbell and Captain Chads, who were well aware that the capture of even a single boat would have been a source of the highest exultation to the Burmese, and emboldened them to give further annoyance on the river. Unfortunately, the seeds of jealousy respecting the command of the Hon. Company's naval force in Ava had previously been sown in Calcutta; and Mr. Greer's gallant exploit was followed by a painful correspondence, in the course of which, however, Captain Chads most firmly and successfully supported the dignity of His Majesty's service."

It was right that the senior naval officer should be jealous of the dignity of the Royal Service, which, however, was never assailed; but the honour of the Company's Naval Service was equally dear to its officers, and was guarded by the authorities at Calcutta, who, probably, had not forgotten the still more "painful correspondence" that took place during the Java Expedition, when Commodore Hayes vindicated the honour of his Service and received the support of the Governor-General.

During the month of November, owing to the improvement in the weather, the health of the British forces improved, and preparations were pushed on for the advance into Ava; meantime the Burmese had not been idle. The "golden-footed" monarch had recalled from Arracan, Maha Bundoola, a general of undoubted capacity and resource, who had long before, at Ramoo, inflicted a disaster upon a small British force. Bundoola had concentrated his legions at Donabew, and, before the end of November, arrived before Rangoon with an army of sixty thousand men, of whom thirty-five thousand were musketeers, with a considerable train of artillery and a body of seven hundred Cassay horse ; this vast army, a portion of which arrogated to itself the title of "Invulnerables," was animated with a resolve speedily to end the war by driving the small British force into the sea. Sir Archibald Campbell, however, calmly awaited his antagonist, and, before the 1st of December, had constructed redoubts and other defences, in which his small force was distributed to the best advantage, while a column was held in readiness for moving to the support of any menaced point or for attacking the enemy. The advanced post at Kemmendine, some three miles from Rangoon, which was occupied by the 26th Madras Native Infantry and a detachment of the Madras European Regiment, under the command of Major Yates, was supported on the river by the Hon. Company's cruiser 'Teignmouth,' Captain Goodridge, which had thus the post of honour, and some gunboats. "This post," says Major Snodgrass, "was of great importance in preventing the enemy from attacking Rangoon by water, or launching from a convenient distance the numerous formidable fire-rafts he had prepared for the destruction of our shipping." Commander Ryves, the senior naval officer in the temporary absence of Captain Chads, placed the 'Arachne' about one and a-half miles in advance of the shipping at Rangoon to enfilade the Madras lines.

The grand attack of Bundoola's army, which had approached to the very edge of the jungle within musket-shot of the Great Pagoda, was delivered on the 1st of December, the first efforts being directed against the British advanced post at Kemmendine. Major Snodgrass says:—

"The day had scarcely dawned when hostilities commenced with a heavy fire of musketry and cannon at Kemmendine, the reduction of that place being a preliminary to any general attack upon our line. The fire continued long and animated; and from our commanding situation at the Great Pagoda, though nearly two miles distant from the scene of action, we could distinctly hear the yells and shouts of the infuriated assailants, occasionally returned by the hearty cheer of the British seamen, as they poured in their heavy broadsides upon the resolute and persevering masses. The thick forest which separated us from the river, prevented our seeing what was going forward; and when the firing ceased, we remained for some time in some anxiety, though in little doubt as to the result of the long and spirited assault. At length, however, the thick canopy of smoke which lowered over the fierce and sanguinary conflict, gradually dissolving, we had the pleasure of seeing the masts of our vessels lying at their old station off the fort, a convincing proof that all had ended well on our side."

The military historian then describes the conflict that raged on this eventful day before Rangoon,—the skill with which the

Burmese soldiers entrenched themselves, and the signal gallantry with which the 13th Light Infantry and 18th Madras Native Infantry, under that fine soldier, Major Robert Sale, drove them out of their cover and destroyed their arms and entrenching tools. Major Snodgrass continues :—

"During the day repeated attacks on Kemmendine had been made and repulsed, but it was not until darkness set in that the last desperate effort of the day was made to gain possession of that post. Already the wearied soldiers had lain down to rest, when suddenly the heavens and the whole surrounding country became brilliantly illuminated by the flames of several tremendous fire-rafts floating down the river towards Rangoon; and scarcely had the blaze appeared, when incessant rolls of musketry and peals of cannon were heard from Kemmendine. The enemy had launched their fire-rafts into the stream with the first of the ebb tide, in the hope of driving the vessels from their stations off the place; and they were followed up by war-boats ready to take advantage of the confusion which might ensue should any of them be set on fire. The skill and intrepidity of British seamen, however, proved more than a match for the numbers and devices of the enemy; entering their boats they grappled the flaming rafts, and conducted them past the shipping, or ran them ashore upon the bank. On the land side the enemy were equally unsuccessful, being again repulsed with heavy loss, in the most resolute attempt they had yet made to reach the interior of the fort. The fire-rafts were, upon examination, found to be ingeniously contrived, and formidably constructed, made wholly of bamboos firmly wrought together, between every two or three rows of which a line of earthen jars of considerable size, filled with petroleum or earth-oil and cotton, was secured; other inflammable ingredients were also distributed in different parts of the raft, and the almost unextinguishable fierceness of the flames proceeding from them can scarcely be imagined. Many of them were considerably upwards of 100 feet in length, and were divided into many pieces attached to each other by means of long hinges, so arranged, that when they caught upon the cable or bow of any ship, the force of the current would carry the ends of the raft completely round her and envelope her in flames from the deck to her main top-masthead, with scarcely a possibility of extricating herself from the devouring element. With possession of Kemmendine, the enemy could have launched these rafts into the stream, from a point where they must have reached our shipping in the crowded harbour; but while we retained that post, they were obliged to despatch them from above it, and the setting of the current carried them, after passing the vessels at the station, upon a projecting point of land, where they almost invariably grounded; and this circumstance, no doubt, much increased Bundoola's anxiety to drive us from so important a position."

On the night of the 30th of November, and again during the night of the 1st of December, the 'Teignmouth' had been driven from her position off Kemmendine by fire-rafts, when she dropped down below the point, to return to her station again, on the first occasion to participate in the furious fighting of the 1st of December, and again, on the following morning, when, says Captain Chads, " she was constantly engaged with the enemy's war-boats, which had long guns in their bows and annoyed her a great deal."

Captain Chads returned to Rangoon on this day, and ordered the 'Arachne's' pinnace, under Lieutenant Kellett, and three more gunboats, under Mr. Midshipman Coyde, to take up their stations off Kemmendine, and, on the following day, still further to strengthen Major Yates' garrison on the river, H.M.S. 'Sophie,' with three more gunboats, proceeded off that post. "With the ebb," says Captain Chads, "the enemy again brought fire-rafts down, not lighting them until within a very short distance of the ships, with their war-boats firing their shot over them, to prevent the approach of our boats. The 'Sophie' cleared them, but the 'Teignmouth' was touched, and on fire for a short time without damage."

As the enemy's boats had become very bold in their attempts to fire the 'Sophie' and 'Teignmouth,' a force was sent against them, consisting of seventy seamen, under the orders of Lieutenant Kellett, of the 'Arachne,' Lieutenant Goldfinch, of the 'Sophie,' and Lieutenant Clarke, of the 'Teignmouth,' embarked in three ships' boats and six gunboats, under Midshipmen Pickey, Coyde, Scott, Murray, Boscawen, and Lindquist. Pulling up the river at early morning they came upon the enemy's war-boats, and, says Captain Chads, " boldly made a dash upon them, notwithstanding their great number and size." The enterprise was completely successful, and seven war-boats were captured, some measuring 83 feet in length, pulling fifty-two oars, and carrying a 9-pounder. The chase was continued three or four miles up the river, when the boats returned with the prizes, and towing a large floating stockade. Captain Chads says:—" I enclose a report* of this gallant attack, which

* The following is Captain Chads' Report :—
" Captain Ryves, having thought it practicable to surprise the enemy's war-boats, who were annoying the ships with their long guns very considerably, placed the whole of his disposable force of Europeans, about seventy in number, under the orders of Lieutenant Kellett of this ship, and Lieutenant Goldfinch, of the 'Sophie,' Lieutenant Clarke, of the Bombay Marine, with Messrs. Pickey, Coyde, Scott and Murray, midshipmen, Mr. Clarke, and Messrs. Lindquist and Boscawen, Bombay Marine, in charge of the gunboats. The force was put into the three men-of-war's boats and six gunboats, and, as the men went down on the morning of the 4th inst., shoved off, and pulling up on the contrary side to the war-boats, by daylight came abreast, and boldly made a dash at them, not-

G G 2

will again bring to your notice officers I have already mentioned to you for their good conduct. The result of this defeat of the enemy's war-boats has been highly beneficial, not one having ventured within gun-shot since. The two ships, however, have had their hands quite full in keeping up a constant fire on the enemy attacking Kemmendine, and throwing up works against them, to mount guns in, which were dismounted as soon as got up, without their having done any material damage."

The Commander-in-chief, having determined to attack the enemy's left wing on the morning of the 5th of December, requested Captain Chads to move up the Puzzendoun Creek, during the night, with the flotilla to cannonade their rear as a diversion to the main attack. Captain Chads, accordingly, proceeded, on the evening of the 4th, with the whole of his disposable force, consisting of the 'Diana,' steamer, 'Powerful,' mortar-vessel, three gunboats, and several merchant boats, with about forty Europeans, and, dropping down to the mouth of the river, waited till the last of the flood—about four o'clock—when he took up his station off the village of Puzzendoun. At six he opened fire from all his vessels, and made every appearance of landing, which brought the enemy down in great force, when their loss from shell fire was very considerable. At seven o'clock, by previously concerted signal from the Pagoda, he ceased firing, and, the troops advancing, the enemy were driven from every point in the utmost confusion, their guns and ammunition falling into the hands of the victors.

On this day (the 5th) Captain Chads sent the 'Powerful,' mortar vessel, to Dalla, and a few shells from her quickly dispersed the enemy, who were strengthening their defences in that quarter. On the following morning, the enemy renewed his attacks upon Kemmendine, when the mortar-vessel proceeded there, and, says Captain Chads, "rendered the post very

withstanding their great number and size. They were taken by surprise, but did not run until our boats were within pistol-shot, when their confusion was great, and they fled with all haste keeping up a smart fire; their large boats with heavy guns were fixed on by our boats, and from the fire of grape were soon unmanned and captured. Lieutenant Kellett came up with some of the first with heavy guns, and Lieutenant Goldfinch, passing him whilst taking possession, captured the boat of the commander of the war-boats, with the flag, her crew running into the jungle. The chase was continued three or four miles, when Lieutenant Kellett judged it prudent to secure his prizes, having an enemy of considerable force in his rear, up another branch of the river.

"The result of this gallant exploit was the capture of seven large war-boats, four of which carried long nines in the bows; and on their return they cut adrift and brought down a large floating stockade from Pagoda Point; and what adds to the value of the service is, that it was performed without the loss of a man. Lieutenant Kellett's conduct on this and on former occasions speaks for itself, and I trust will meet with its due reward. Lieutenant Goldfinch is a valuable officer, and merits every praise; and Lieutenant Kellett reports the high gallantry of Lieutenant Clarke and the midshipmen commanding the boats, and of every individual under his command. The largest war-canoe was 83 feet long, 12½ feet broad, 5¼ feet deep, pulling 52 oars and carrying a 9-pounder."

essential service, and relieved the garrison considerably." The enemy's war-boats appeared still in considerable numbers, and, on the 7th of December, made a final attempt to fire the ships of war. They were very busy all the morning constructing the fire-rafts, and, with the strong ebb, brought them down in such numbers that they stretched " nearly across the river, and consisted of upwards of twenty-six rafts and eight large boats all lashed together; but they were afraid to venture very near, and fired them earlier, so that the squadron suffered no injury." At noon the British troops assaulted the enemy's lines, and Maha Bundoola's vaunted soldiery were driven panic-stricken from their entrenchments with the loss of five thousand men and two hundred and forty guns.

Sir Archibald Campbell, in his despatch of the 8th of December, speaks in high praise of the conduct of the officers and men of the Royal Navy and of the Company's Marine, during the six days' heavy fighting since the 1st of December. He says:—" A division of the enemy broke ground in front of Kemmendine, and for six successive days tried in vain every effort that hope of success and dread of failure could call forth to drive the brave 26th and a handful of Europeans from this post, while tremendous fire-rafts and crowds of war-boats were every day employed in the equally vain endeavour to drive the shipping from their station off the place." Further on he says:—" The attacks upon Kemmendine continued with unabated violence, but the unyielding spirit of Major Yates and his steady troops, although exhausted with fatigue and want of rest, baffled every attempt on shore, and Captain Ryves, with H.M.S. 'Sophie,' the Hon. Company's cruiser 'Teignmouth,' and some flotilla and row-gunboats, nobly maintained the long-established fame of the British Navy, in defending the passage of the river against the most furious assaults of the enemy's war-boats, advancing under cover of the most tremendous fire-rafts, which the unwearied exertions of British sailors could alone have conquered."

Captain Chads, the senior naval officer, in his despatch to Sir Archibald Campbell, of the 10th of December, speaks in the following terms of the conduct of the Company's officers:—" In the attack on the enemy's war-boats, Lieutenant Kellett speaks in high terms of the gallantry of Lieutenant Clarke, and Mr. Boscawen, of the Hon. Company's cruiser 'Teignmouth,' and Mr. Lindquist, in charge of the row-boats; this latter young officer I have also had reason to be much pleased with."

The following is a Copy of the proceedings of the Hon. Company's row-gunboats, from the 26th of November to the 10th of December, 1824; from the former date up to the 2nd of December this portion of the flotilla was engaged, under command of Captain Chads, in co-operating with some troops, commanded by Colonel Miles at Pegu, and after that date in assisting the 'Sophie' and 'Teignmouth' in the defence of Kemmendine:—

"November 26.—At two p.m. left Rangoon with eleven row-boats, under the immediate orders of Captain Chads, R.N., for Pegu. At four p.m., received sailing instructions to lead next to the boats belonging to H.M.'s ships. At half-past seven p.m., in passing Syriam fort, enemy fired great guns and musketry; passed on without noticing it. At ten p.m. anchored in a direct line across the river. Men-of-war's boats on the starboard and larboard bows, flats, &c., with troops and artillery in the rear, closed in by two row-gunboats.

"November 27.—At half-past three a.m., weighed and proceeded up; men-of-war's boats ahead, flats astern, river shallow and narrow; two row-boats closing in the rear. At eleven a.m. anchored close on the starboard shore, the rear-guard some distance astern. At three p.m. all boats arrived. At four p.m. weighed and proceeded up. At six p.m. anchored in six feet of water, taking up the same position as yesterday.

"November 28.—At daylight weighed and proceeded up; at noon came to a small village named Abo, made fast to the shore; river fifteen or twenty yards broad, fordable at low water.

"November 29.—At nine p.m. proceeded up, enemy fired a few muskets from several villages. At one p.m. arrived at Pegu, landed the troops, and received orders to bring up twenty men to assist in dragging forward the artillery; reconnoitring, returned and reported the place to be evacuated by the enemy; re-embarked the artillery, and anchored for the night; river forty yards broad, and fordable at low water.

"November 30.—At noon despatched four row-gunboats, under the orders of Captain Chads, to reconnoitre* up the river; embarked all the troops, having previously hoisted a white flag in the ancient city of Pegu; at four p.m. reconnoitring party returned; proceeded down, four boats being ordered as a rear-guard; grounded several times during the night.

"December 1.—At ten a.m., Commodore made signal to close and anchor; at three p.m. weighed and proceeded down; at eight p.m. passed three vessels with foraging party on board; at nine p.m. Commodore made signal to close and anchor.

"December 2.—At three a.m. weighed, and proceeded down; at daylight heard a heavy firing in the direction of Dagon Pagoda; at eight a.m. arrived off Rangoon, and found it

---

* This reconnaissance was made with the object of ascertaining whether a high road existed to Prome.

besieged by the enemy; disembarked the troops, and anchored in advance of the fleet, forming a direct line across the river. At noon manned seven row-boats with seamen from the 'Arachne,' and received orders to despatch them to reinforce Kemmendine. At two p.m. received orders to proceed with two row-boats, to communicate with the foraging party, for the purpose of recalling the troops, then marching across the country with cattle; at four p.m. anchored abreast of Puzzendoun Creek. At seven p.m. observed some of the enemy's boats reconnoitring; when within grape-shot distance, opened fire on them, which caused their immediate retreat. At eight p.m. gun vessels of the foraging party came down and anchored; went on board and held a communication with Captain Jones, 89th Regiment; learnt he had one hundred men escorting a herd of cattle in a direction for the entrenchments. On the flood, dropped up about two miles, and despatched a Mugh, who volunteered his services for a small sum, to prevent the escort advancing.

"December 3.—At seven a.m. foraging party came down abreast the vessels, embarked them and made sail for Rangoon; received orders to proceed immediately to Kemmendine; at eleven a.m. arrived at Kemmendine, found it closely besieged by the enemy, six war-boats within bow-shot annoying the shipping then riding flood; having eight row-boats, anchored them on the 'Sophie's' starboard quarter, brought the cables aft, and got the guns to bear up the river. At seven p.m. enemy sent down two fire-rafts, and accompanied them in the rear with war-boats, keeping up a heavy fire of great guns and musketry on the boats and shipping, which did no damage except cutting away the 'Sophie's' after-shroud on the starboard side; kept up a smart fire from the row-boats and bow-guns of the Hon. Company's cruiser 'Teignmouth;' fire-rafts passed clear of all; in the course of the night, enemy made three attacks on Kemmendine stockade; row-boats' position advantageous for flanking the right of the stockade.

"December 4.—At three a.m. all boats alongside H.M.'s ship 'Sophie;' at 4.30 a.m. left for the purpose of attacking the enemy's boats, laying about one mile above their entrenchments; our boats pulled up, all silence, astern of each other on the larboard shore, enemy occupying the starboard; at daybreak Burmese sighted us from their boats, and opened a smart fire of six-pounders and musketry. Lieutenant Kellett in the 'Arachne's' pinnace, and commanding, issued orders to form a line, and advance to board; the line being formed without the least confusion, gave three cheers and advanced, firing; the enemy also advancing, and never did I witness a better spirit and cheerfulness in the row-boats' people than on this occasion. In ten minutes we got within grape-shot distance, and then confusion commenced in the enemy's boats; they pulled in shore, and made for the jungles; we then advanced, as fast as possible, without regard to the line, and took possession of seven boats, three of which had 6-pounders in the bow; one with a 9-pounder, and three with muskets, spears, &c., in great number; and also took the flags, one of which was red, bordered green, Brahmin goose in the centre; in the boats with guns were found one hundred round shots and five barrels of inferior powder. As soon as we were in possession of the enemy's boats, we gave way for the 'Sophie,' but in passing their entrenchments, experienced a volley fire of musketry; but three cheers from a British sailor has a powerful effect on inexperienced warriors, and invariably inspires them with fear. I regret to say that one war-boat escaped us. Two attacks on Kemmendine stockade this day, but shipping and boats quiet, otherwise than flanking the stockades; notwithstanding the duty of this day, fortune favoured us all—not a man was touched.

"December 5.—At nine a.m. returned to Rangoon in No. 6, for a supply of ammunition, having fired about four hundred and fifty rounds since the 3rd inst.; at three p.m. returned to my station with four hundred rounds; the enemy all silent afloat during the night, but mounted two 6-pounders abreast of the Hon. Company's cruiser 'Teignmouth,' with which they hulled her several times. Row-boats at anchor in their station.

"December 6.—Row-boats at anchor in their station; at eight a.m. enemy made a desperate attack on Kemmendine stockade, but were driven from both flanks by the 'Sophie's' and boats' guns; at nine they retired with three horrid yells.

"December 7.—At seven a.m. enemy sent down twenty-six rafts of split wood, lashed together, placing six large boats on them filled with petroleum oil; war-boats in the rear firing at the shipping and boats. All boats away to tow rafts clear of the ships, and then let them go; lost two iron grapnels in the rafts.

"December 8.—At four a.m. steam vessel arrived from Rangoon; at five a.m. made all boats fast astern of her; at 5.30 p.m. proceeded up in chase of the enemy's boats, but unfortunately could not fall in with them; no firing from the enemy's lines. At seven p.m. received orders to proceed to Rangoon with all boats except four; at eight p.m. received orders from Captain Chads to be ready to start at midnight.

"December 9.—At one a.m. rendezvoused alongside the transport ship 'Good Hope,' waiting the flood to attack Dalla; at 1.30 left, and proceeded up Dalla Creek; anchored by the stern, and fired on the enemy's flank, shot from our troops falling about and in the boats very thickly. Troops having routed the enemy, weighed and proceeded to the China Wharf. At daylight commenced transporting a reinforcement with the artillery to Dalla; at one p.m. left with six boats to make a diversion on the enemy's left flank. Troops proceeded out to attack them on the right; at three p.m. anchored in shore off H.M.'s ship 'Arachne.'"

In the General Orders of the Governor-General in Council of the 24th of December, his lordship paid a tribute of thanks to the naval portion of the forces engaged in Burmah, though the manner in which all the officers of the Royal Navy who distinguished themselves, were singled out for commendation, while not one belonging to the Company's Service was individually mentioned, must have been particularly painful to the gallant men who had borne equally with their brethren of the Navy, the hardships and dangers of the protracted operations. Probably, as the Supreme Government had no opportunity of judging for itself as to whether these latter had, not less honourably than the officers of the Royal Service, done their duty, the General Order was, as is often the case, merely an echo of the despatches and notifications of the Military and Naval chiefs, in which but meagre thanks were rendered to the Bombay Marine. The following is the extract from Lord Amherst's Orders, alluded to:—"The Governor-General in Council seizes this opportunity of expressing his warm acknowledgments to Captain Chads, of H.M.'s ship 'Arachne,' the senior naval officer at Rangoon, and to Captain Ryves, of H.M.'s ship 'Sophie,' for their distinguished personal exertions, and requests the former to convey to the officers and crews of H.M's ships, of the Hon. Company's cruisers, as well as the officers and men of the transports who volunteered their services, the sense which Government entertains of their gallant conduct in the several actions with the enemy's war-boats, when they so conspicuously displayed the irresistible and characteristic valour of British seamen."

Notwithstanding his crushing defeat, Maha Bundoola did not lose heart, but, gathering the *débris* of his shattered forces, returned to Kokeen within four miles of the Dagon Pagoda, and prepared to resume the offensive. At this time the advanced post at Kemmendine was still held by Major Yates' little force, strengthened on the river by H.M.S. 'Sophie,' Commander Ryves,* the Hon. Company's cruiser 'Prince of Wales,' Lieutenant W. S. Collinson, the 'Powerful,' mortar-vessel, the 'Diana,' steamer, a detachment of seamen under Lieutenant Kellett, and three gunboats under Mr. Lindquist.

* Commander Ryves, who was left at Rangoon when the army and flotilla proceeded up country, was invalided in the following April, and the 'Sophie' left Burmah in May.

On the 14th of December, Burmese emissaries succeeded in setting fire to Rangoon in several places at once, by which one quarter of the town was burnt. On the 15th Sir Archibald Campbell attacked the enemy with three columns, and, in less than fifteen minutes, drove them in utter rout from the formidable entrenchments they had been at so much pains to construct.

The remainder of December passed away without any occurrence of importance, except that the army received large reinforcements and the navy was strengthened by the arrival of about twenty of the Company's gunboats from Chittagong.

In order to leave no enemy in his rear before advancing upon Ava, the preparations for which were nearly complete, Sir Archibald Campbell, on the 11th of January, 1825, detached a small Expedition, under command of Colonel Elrington, against the old Portuguese fort and factory at Syriam, which the enemy had rendered a tolerably strong post. Accordingly, two hundred men of the 47th Regiment and a party of the 1st Battalion Madras Pioneers, were embarked on board two divisions of gunboats, respectively under the command of Captain S. T. Finucane of H.M.'s 14th Regiment and Lieutenant J. H. Rowband of the Bombay Marine, together with forty-eight seamen from H.M.'s ships, under Lieutenant Keele. The detachment landed close to the fort, and were subjected to a heavy fire while a bridge was thrown across a nullah by the sailors, which was returned by two of the gunboats which had been brought up the creek. The bridge completed, the enemy's works were stormed, when Colonel Elrington, advancing on the following morning, carried the Syriam Pagoda. The loss on this occasion was one officer (Ensign Geddes) and one man killed, and three officers and thirty-two men wounded; four guns and twenty jingals were found in the works.

On the 22nd of January, H.M.S. 'Alligator' arrived at Rangoon, and Captain Alexander, as senior officer, assumed the chief command from Captain Chads. Shortly after the defeat of the Burmese Army on the 15th of December, Sir Archibald Campbell, from motives of policy, issued a Proclamation to the Peguers, and having contrived to introduce a copy into the enemy's stockaded lines at Paulang, it had the desired effect of detaching the major part of the army, who retired into the Dalla district with their arms. Sir Archibald despatched a column to support them against the attacks of the Burmese force which had followed them, and the whole flotilla was also employed, for four days, in protecting our new allies, whose families came flocking into Rangoon in thousands. As the Commander-in-chief deemed it necessary, before commencing the attack on Ava, to dislodge the enemy's advanced division from their defences on the Lyne river, on the 5th of February he directed Colonel Godwin to proceed with a column to Tantabain for that purpose; the naval force co-operating, under the command of Captain Chads, consisted of the 'Satellite,' 'Prince of Wales,' 'Diana,' fifteen row-gunboats, seven boats belonging to H.M's ships, and several flats. The Expedition arrived, on the 6th, before the enemy's works, which were cannonaded and stormed with trifling loss, though defended by two thousand men and thirty-six guns. On the following day the two branches of the Panlang river were reconnoitred, and a large number of the enemy's war-boats and fire-rafts destroyed. Some of the troops were left to occupy the captured stockade and also the 'Prince of Wales,' with four gunboats, to assist in its defence.

At length, the preparations being complete, the British forces set out upon their long march for Ava. The land column, which was to move in a direction parallel to the Lyne river, under the personal command of Sir Archibald Campbell, quitted Rangoon on the 11th of February, its numerical strength being thirteen hundred European infantry, one thousand Sepoys, two squadrons of cavalry, a troop of horse artillery, and a rocket troop. This column, for which only sufficient carriage could be provided for the conveyance of from twelve to fifteen days' provisions, was to strike the Irrawaddy at the nearest accessible point, for the purpose of co-operating with the Marine column, proceeding up the Panlang channel to that river, in driving Bundoola from Donabew, should its aid be required. This column, which was placed under the command of Brigadier-General Willoughby Cotton, consisted of eight hundred European infantry, two hundred and fifty Sepoys, one hundred and eight Artillerymen, and twelve of the rocket troop. The flotilla that was to convey this force, was commanded by Captains Alexander and Chads, and consisted of the 'Satellite' and 'Diana,' two mortar-vessels, six gunboats, thirty armed row-boats, about sixty launches, flats, and canoes—all armed, except the flats and canoes, with one or two 12 and 24-pounder carronades—and the boats of H.M.'s ships, manned by about one hundred seamen. A third division, under Major Sale, numbering seven hundred and eighty soldiers of H.M.'s 13th and 12th Madras Native Infantry, with H.M.S. 'Larne,' Captain Marryat, and the Hon. Company's cruiser 'Mercury,' Lieutenant Anderson, was directed to reduce Bassein, after which it was to join the other columns. The rest of the army, numbering three thousand seven hundred and eighty one effectives, chiefly Sepoys, and one hundred and thirty-four convalescent Europeans fit only for garrison duty, remained to hold Rangoon.

The main column marched on the 11th of February, and was

followed, on the 16th, by the water column; but, before
detailing the services of the Marine with the latter throughout
the arduous campaign that ensued, we will briefly refer to the
capture of Bassein, in which the 'Mercury' participated.

After a tedious voyage the Expedition arrived off the mouth
of the Bassein River on the 24th, and, on the 26th, weighed
and stood in for the river—the 'Mercury,' owing to her light
draft of water, leading. At noon the first stockade commenced
firing, and shortly afterwards, the 'Larne' and 'Mercury' took
up their positions within a hundred yards; the enemy's fire
was soon silenced when the troops landed and destroyed the work
and guns. The ships then proceeded to the next stockade, and,
says Major Sale, "the effects of the guns from the 'Larne' and
'Mercury' were as decided as before;" these works were also
destroyed and the guns spiked. The Expedition proceeded up
the river on the following day, and ran past four deserted
stockades, three of which stood in commanding situations on
the island of Negrais. From this point, the stream being very
narrow, and the wind strong and contrary, the ascent became
extremely arduous; the ships often getting on shore and towing
and warping day and night, till the evening of the 3rd of
March, when they anchored about three miles below Bassein,
which had been almost entirely burnt to the ground by the
people, who had then deserted it. The troops were landed,
and, a few days later, Major Sale made a reconnaissance to
Lamena, about one hundred and forty miles distant, with three
hundred soldiers, and seventy seamen, proceeding up the river
in boats and bivouacking at night upon the banks. The villages
as well as Lamena, were found to be deserted, and, on the 23rd,
the force returned to Bassein with several war-canoes. On the
15th of April Captain Marryat assumed command of the
'Tees,' twenty-six guns, and, in May, finally quitted Burmah.

The water column, under Brigadier-General Cotton, having
left Rangoon on the 16th of February, burnt several stockades
on the 17th and 18th, and, on the following day, arrived before
Panlang, the extensive stockade of which, though of great
strength and garrisoned by three or four thousand men, was
captured after a feeble resistance, the flotilla co-operating by
their fire with a shore battery of three mortars and two guns.
At Panlang stockade a post was established, and the 'Satellite'
remained behind to assist in its defence, as her draft of water
caused her to take the ground. On the 25th of February the
General, with the flotilla, proceeded to Mezle, about ten miles
from Panlang, and, on the following day, reached a point
eighteen miles higher up, where the shallows commenced and
the larger vessels grounded. On the 27th it was found
necessary to unload the 'Diana' and gun-vessels, for which
purpose boats were allotted, and the remainder of the flotilla

joined the advance division in the Irrawaddy. Early on the morning of the 6th of March, the whole of the flotilla, having entered the main stream on the previous evening, got under weigh, and took up a position about two miles below Donabew, while General Cotton and Captain Alexander proceeded to reconnoitre. "It was evident," says the General, "that the enemy had prepared to receive us below his position, having a succession of formidable stockades, commencing at the Pagoda, and continued increasing in strength, until completed by the main work, which is lofty, upon a very commanding site, surrounded by a deep abattis, with all the customary defences. The guns appeared to be numerous, and the garrison were seen in crowds upon all the works."

A summons to surrender was first sent to Bundoola, who commanded in person, and, upon receipt of a refusal, General Cotton made a reconnaissance with one hundred and sixty men of the 89th Regiment, covered by the light division and some row-boats. The enemy's war-boats retired under the guns on the opposite side, and, during the reconnaissance, says the General, "the enemy kept up a heavy fire from about thirty pieces of cannon, many of heavy calibre;" and the precision with which they were directed, surprised the British officers. General Cotton would have preferred assaulting at a point above the main stockade, but, owing to his having only six hundred available bayonets, he considered that it would not be advisable to divide so small a force in attacking a garrison estimated at twelve thousand men. "I had," he says, "no option but that of landing below the whole of the works, attacking them in succession, while the flotilla defended the river." At sunrise on the 7th, five hundred men were formed into two columns, and, under the fire of the guns and rockets, advanced upon the first, or Pagoda, stockade; nothing could withstand the headlong valour of the troops, who carried the work under a heavy fire, inflicting an enormous loss on the enemy. The second defence was 500 yards distant from the Pagoda stockade and the same distance from the main work which commanded it. Some guns and mortars, with a fresh supply of rockets, were brought up and opened fire, and when it was thought that a sufficient impression had been made, a column of two hundred men, under Captain Rose, 89th Regiment, advanced in two parties to the storm. But the enemy, who reserved their fire, opened it now from all parts of the face of the work with such destructive effect that Captains Rose and Cannon of the 89th Regiment, and many men were killed, and a large number wounded. Seeing that the attack had failed, the General directed the assaulting column to retire, and landed two 8-inch mortars and four 12-pounders from the gunboats, to strengthen the battery, and, in the evening, General Cotton, seeing the impossibility of carrying the works with his small force without the certainty of incurring heavy loss, decided to re-embark his force and await reinforcements. Accordingly the guns and stores were re-shipped, and, after spiking the enemy's cannon, the troops proceeded on board the flotilla at two a.m. on the 8th. The flotilla then dropped down to Youngyoun, and re-occupied the strong position from which it had moved on the 6th, while the wounded were sent down to Rangoon. In this check the British loss was two officers and sixteen men killed, and four officers and one hundred and seven men wounded and missing; of these the Navy had two men wounded, and the flotilla two killed, and Mr. A. F. Derby, commanding the gunboat 'Amherst,' and ten men, wounded.

In the meantime the land column had forded the Lyne river, and marched on to Sarrawah, where they distinctly heard the cannonading at Donabew, and concluded that the place had fallen. Sir Archibald Campbell, accordingly, proceeded on to Uandeet, about twenty-six miles above Sarrawah, where he learned of the repulse at Donabew, upon which he immediately commenced a retrograde march, and, by the 18th, had crossed his whole army over the Irrawaddy at Sarrawah, on rafts.

On the 25th Sir Archibald arrived before Donabew, but as the works were found to be much too extensive to admit of being invested, a position was taken up, and, on the following day, ground was broken at an old pagoda about 300 yards from the enemy's defences. On the 27th the 'Diana,' towing one mortar-boat, four gun-vessels, and a number of flats with provisions and breaching guns recently brought from Panlang, proceeded up the river, "under all the fire of the fort," and anchored on the left of the land column. "During the heavy cannonade that took place between the boats and the stockade," says Major Snodgrass, "Bundoola, who was superintending the practice of his artillery, gave his garrison a specimen of the discipline he meant to enforce in this last struggle to retrieve his lost character and reputation. A Burmese officer being killed while pointing a gun, by a shot from the flotilla, his comrades instantly abandoning the dangerous post, could not be brought back to their duty by any remonstrance of their chiefs, when Bundoola stepping down to the spot, instantly severed the head of two of the delinquents from their bodies, and ordered them to be stuck up upon the spot."

While forcing their way past the stockade,* the flotilla was

---

* Major Snodgrass describes the work as follows, "The stockade of Donabew extended for nearly a mile along a sloping bank of the Irrawaddy, its breadth varying according to the nature of the ground from 500 to 800 yards. The stockading was composed of solid teak beams from 15 to 17 feet high, driven firmly into the earth, and placed as closely as possible to each other; behind this wooden wall the old brick ramparts of the place rose to a considerable height, strengthening the front defences by means of cross beams, and affording a firm

under a heavy fire for an hour and a-half, but had only six men wounded; one of the gun-vessels received a shot between wind and water, but was run ashore, which she fortunately reached before she filled. On the 28th, while the working parties were making approaches towards the place, " the steam-vessel, and some light boats," says the military historian, " pushing up the river after the enemy's war-boats, succeeded in capturing nine of them." The batteries being at length completed and armed with the heavy ordnance brought from Panlang, on the 1st of April a heavy fire was opened upon the enemy's works at intervals during the whole day and succeeding night, the Burmese making but little return.

On the following morning, when the fire was resumed, two Lascars, who had been taken prisoners, came running out of the fort with the astounding intelligence that Bundoola had been killed on the previous day by a rocket, and the whole garrison had fled or dispersed during the night. The troops now advanced and occupied the formidable stockade, on which were found mounted one hundred and thirty-nine brass and iron guns, mostly of small calibre, and two hundred and sixty-nine jingals. The British loss was eleven killed and sixty wounded, including two officers. " Since we have been before Donabew," wrote the General in his despatch, " eleven of the enemy's large class war-boats have been captured by our advanced boats under Captain Alexander's immediate orders, making, with others evacuated by their crews, thirty-eight first-rate war-boats now in our possession; and I have every reason to think that only five of the large squadron the enemy had stationed at this place have succeeded in escaping. A vast number of other boats of an excellent description have also fallen into our hands."

On the 4th of April Sir Archibald Campbell resumed his march for Prome, and, by the 12th, had recrossed the Irrawaddy at Sarrawah, where he was joined by Brigadier McCreagh with reinforcements. In a letter to the Commander-in-chief, dated " 9th of April, 1825, on board the Hon. Company's steam-vessel ' Diana,' " Captain Alexander speaks as follows of the services of the flotilla:—" The conduct of the Hon. Company's flotilla I have the pleasure to command, has been such as to merit my warmest praise; their hardships, privations, and fatigue for the last six weeks have been borne with cheerfulness, and their conduct against the enemy's

and elevated footing to the defenders. Upwards of one hundred and fifty guns and swivels were mounted on the works, and the garrison was protected from the shells of the besiegers by numerous well-contrived traverses and excavations. A ditch of considerable magnitude and depth surrounded the defences, the passage of which was rendered still more difficult by spikes, nails, holes, and other contrivances. Beyond the ditch several rows of strong railings were next interposed, and in front of all an abattis, 30 yards broad, extended round the place."

works and war-boats, steady and creditable. The officers commanding divisions of gunboats and vessels, have my best thanks, particularly Captain Finucane, H.M.'s 14th Regiment, whose zeal and activity has always been conspicuous. I request you will be pleased to recommend these officers, whose names are specified below, to the favourable attention of the Right Hon. the Governor-General in Council.

"Gunboats.—1st Division, Captain Finucane, H.M.'s 14th Regiment; 2nd Division, Lieutenant Laughton, Bombay Marine; 3rd Division, Lieutenant Rowband, Bombay Marine; 4th Division, Mr. Lindquist; 5th Division, Mr. Hutton. Gun-vessels.—' Swift,' 'Sulkea Packet,' ' Elizabeth,' ' Saugor,' ' Tiger,' and ' Emma.' Mortar-vessels.—' Powerful ' and ' Tom Tough.'"

General Cotton continued his route by river, and, on the 24th of April, the Commander-in-chief established a communication with the flotilla, which was anchored a short distance below Prome; he soon concerted measures with Captain Alexander for an attack upon that place, which, however, was found to have been evacuated and set on fire by Prince Sarrawuddy. The stockade was of great strength, and in the different works were mounted one hundred and one guns. The inhabitants now gradually returned to Prome, and confidence was restored throughout the country—a matter of prime necessity, as supplies were urgently needed for the army, which made preparations for passing the rainy season, which sets in early in June. Cantonments were laid out, a large fleet of canoes was soon placed at the disposal of the commissariat for the purpose of forming a depot of provisions at Prome, and two divisions of gunboats, armed with 24-pounder carronades, which had come up the Irrawaddy by way of Bassein, having arrived from Commodore Hayes' squadron in Arracan, all the gun-vessels were stationed at regular intervals, so as to afford protection to the supply boats.

In consequence of reports of the advance of the Burmese army, General Cotton, on the 13th of August, proceeded in the 'Diana,' with some gunboats and fifty soldiers, to reconnoitre their positions, and, on the 15th, discovered them at Meaday, forty miles up the river, where they had entrenched themselves, having their boats ranged underneath. The enemy opened fire from sixteen guns, which was returned by the flotilla, "to make them develope their whole force," estimated by the General as between fifteen and twenty thousand men. On the 6th of September a mission arrived from the King of Burmah to propose terms of peace, and, in conformity with the request of the Commissioner, Mr. Robertson, Sir Archibald Campbell deputed two officers to confer with the Burmese Commander-in-chief. Several meetings took place between the British representatives and the Kee Wongee, or prime minister, and, ultimately, a conference was arranged between the Kee Wongee, accompanied by another chief, and Sir Archibald Campbell, when an armistice till the 17th of October was agreed to. But the only object of the Burmese statesmen and generals was to gain time to collect an army, and, after further meetings, and a prolongation of the armistice till the 2nd of November, the duplicity of the Burmese officials became apparent, when preparations were made for a hostile advance upon the capital. On the 22nd of September, Commodore Sir James Brisbane, a highly distinguished officer, who had acted as Lord Exmouth's flag-captain at Algiers, and had been appointed Naval Commander-in-chief in India, in succession to Commodore Grant, arrived at Prome, accompanied by Captain Chads from Rangoon, and bringing with him the boats and seamen of the 'Boadicea' frigate. On the 7th of November, Captain Alexander, late senior officer, died at Rangoon, and was succeeded in the command of his ship, the 'Alligator,' by Captain Chads, who was directed to remain with the flotilla in the Irrawaddy.

Early in November, the Burmese forces advanced upon Prome in three divisions: the right, under Sudda Woon, consisting of fifteen thousand men, having crossed the Irrawaddy and moved forward on its west bank; the centre, thirty thousand strong, commanded by the Kee Wongee, moving along the left bank, accompanied by a large fleet of war-boats; and the left division, of fifteen thousand men, led by Maha Nemiow, a veteran general lately sent from Ava to direct the operations of the entire army. In addition to these three corps, a reserve of ten thousand men, commanded by Prince Memiaboo, the king's half-brother, occupied a strongly fortified position at Mellown, while another division was ready to oppose an advance from Arracan. To meet these vast hosts, the British general could only muster, including the garrison of Prome, a force of six thousand one hundred and forty-eight effectives, a small column being required to hold in check a force which threatened Rangoon, the garrison of which consisted of one British and several Native regiments.

The campaign, upon which the destinies of an ancient empire depended, opened unfavourably for the invading army. Two brigades sent to dislodge Maha Nemiow's army at Wattygoon, suffered a disastrous repulse on the 15th of November, which so encouraged that general, that he changed his cautious tactics, and, advancing boldly upon Prome with the other corps, surrounded the town. The first brush with the enemy took place on the 25th of November, at Padoung-mew, on the west bank, where they made an attack on some works. Lieutenant Kellett was in the act of pushing off with the row-boats, but instantly returned, and commenced so well-directed a fire from the works and the boats' guns, that the enemy were forced to retire with heavy loss. Between this period and the end of November, Colonel Godwin's detachment and the flotilla cleared the left bank of the river for fifteen miles below Prome. As the Burmese leaders appeared unwilling to take the offensive, on the 30th of November arrangements were made for attacking the three corps in detail, beginning with the Kee Wongee's extending from Napadee, five miles from Prome, to the village of Simbike, upon the Nawine river, distant eleven miles, which was to be the main point of attack. Accordingly, early on the 1st of December, Sir James Brisbane commenced a heavy cannonade with the flotilla on the enemy's posts upon both banks of the Irrawaddy, attracting his attention to that point, while Sir Archibald Campbell marched with the rest of his force upon Maha Nemiow's division. The troops were formed into two columns; one under General Cotton, marched direct on Simbike, and the other, under the Commander-in-chief, crossed the Nawine river, and moved along its right bank, for the purpose of cutting off his retreat from the Kee Wongee's corps. The operations were completely successful; the veteran leader was killed, and his entire force, including a *corps d'élite* of eight thousand Shans, was routed with great slaughter and dispersed. During the night a message was sent to Sir James Brisbane, to request him to be in readiness to move forward with the flotilla, as soon as the troops were seen debouching from the jungle in front of Napadee, for the purpose of co-operating in the attack upon that position. The army moved early on the morning of the 2nd, and, after two hours' march, opened a communication with the flotilla, and, at the same time, drew up in front of the stockaded heights of Napadee. The 87th Regiment carried one of the stockades in the rear, when the enemy withdrew from his advanced position. The flotilla now moved forward, and opened a heavy fire upon the enemy's works on both banks of the river. The main attack then advanced under a heavy fire, and carried the positions on the summits of the hills in succession; the flotilla meanwhile pushed past the heavy batteries on the banks of the river, and succeeded in capturing nearly three hundred boats, with large quantities of ammunition and stores. The corps of Sudda Woon, on the right bank of the river, still remained in position, and, on the 5th of December, it was attacked by General Cotton's division, after the guns of the flotilla, assisted by a mortar-battery and some rockets, had silenced the enemy's fire. During the operations between the 1st and 5th of December, the British lost only twenty-nine officers and men killed and one hundred and thirty-three wounded.

In a letter to the Admiralty, dated the 3rd of December, Sir

James Brisbane says of the Company's Marine under his orders:—" I have much satisfaction in stating, that the whole of the officers and men employed in the flotilla, conducted themselves throughout this service in a manner that reflects the highest credit on each individual, composed, as this force is, of varied establishments. The officers of the Hon. Company's Marine vied with those of the Royal Navy in gallantry and exertion." The same officer, in a letter to the Commander-in-chief, eulogised "the highly-distinguished conduct of the officers and men belonging to that branch of the flotilla which is in the service of the Hon. Company. It is extremely gratifying to observe, that on this, as on other recent occasions, they have uniformly vied with the boats of the squadron in zeal, gallantry, and exertion. Indeed, since my arrival at head-quarters, I have derived no small satisfaction at the promptitude, good order, and regularity which have been conspicuous in the details of the flotilla. One common feeling animates the whole of the force, which has produced the happiest results." The Governor-General in Council, on the receipt of the despatches of Sir Archibald Campbell and Sir James Brisbane, writing to the latter of the "distinguished share" in the operations of the 1st, 2nd, and 5th of December, borne by the Hon. Company's flotilla, and the "important aid and support" they rendered to the Commander-in-chief, expressed to the Commodore his "high gratification that the conduct of the officers and men of the flotilla had merited and received his approbation."

Sir Archibald Campbell marched on the 9th of December, with one division of the army for Meaday, where it was supposed the enemy would concentrate his shattered legions, by Watty-goon and Seindoop, while the column under General Cotton marched three days later by Neoun-ben-zeik to Meaday, upon a road running parallel to the river, so that he might keep up a communication with the flotilla. Owing to the rapidity of the current, and the numerous shifting sandbanks, it became necessary to track the heavier boats as far as Yondoun, and at Meong Sir James Brisbane formed a junction with General Cotton. The enemy had erected very strong posts at Pettoh and Paloh, where in some places the channel of the river obliged the flotilla to pass within 200 yards of the banks, but they abandoned these works without firing a shot. Meaday was reached on the 17th, but its strong stockades were found to be evacuated. The army proceeded towards Mellown on the 21st of December, and, on the 26th, a messenger, with a flag of truce, was brought in, and stated that a commissioner, called Kolein Menghie, had arrived from Mellown, with full powers from the King to treat for peace. On the 29th, the army arrived before that city, which was defended by a succession of stockades, extending between one and two miles along the river bank, the principal one, which lay exposed to view on the face of a sloping hill, appearing to be about a square mile in extent, full of men, and mounting several guns. As the flotilla came up the river, led by the 'Diana,' having Sir James Brisbane on board, the enemy's boats tried to escape, but the Commodore, passing close under their works, without a shot being fired on either side, anchored above the principal stockade, thus cutting off the escape of the boats.

The first meeting between the Burmese envoys and the British Commissioners—Sir Archibald Campbell, Sir James Brisbane, and Mr. Robertson, of the Bengal Civil Service, was held on the 1st of January, and, on the 3rd, a treaty of peace was signed, subject to ratification by the King of Ava. So assured did the prospects of peace now appear, that, on the 6th, Sir James Brisbane issued a memorandum to the Naval portion of the Expedition, thanking the officers and men for their conduct during the war. In this Order his Excellency eulogised "the officers of all descriptions, for their prompt obedience, unwearied exertions, and gallantry, which they had conspicuously displayed throughout the late campaign. The various materials of which the flotilla was composed," he continued, "brought together for one grand object, might have occasioned frequent collisions between the members of different Services, had not a spirit of emulation pervaded all ranks, surmounting all difficulties, and producing a universal feeling of harmony and good-will. The Commodore will long remember, with feelings of the highest gratification, the period which he has commanded this branch of the Expedition, and the personal acquaintance it has afforded him with individual merit. The Commodore begs the officers, without distinction, to be assured that he has brought under the notice of their superiors his opinion of their merit, and the brave men who have served with them, giving, as they have, the most striking examples of activity and exertions, under the greatest privations in open boats."

There were at this time fifty-six of the Hon. Company's gun-vessels and row-boats, forming five divisions, and the officers attached to these divisions were Lieutenants Laughton and Rowband, and Messrs. Lindquist, Crawford, Ravenscroft, Robson, Power, Leggatt, and Cooper. The Royal officers were Lieutenant Nagle of the 47th Regiment, and Mr. Winsor, R.N. Sir James Brisbane, owing to failing health, was forced to relinquish the command of the flotilla to Captain Chads, to the regret of all those who had served under him, and, proceeding to Penang and New South Wales, died at the latter colony on the 19th of December, 1826.

The gallant Commodore was premature in issuing his General Order on the conclusion of peace, for the King of Ava declined to ratify the treaty, and, after the usual exhibition of lying and duplicity on the part of his envoys, at midnight on the 18th of January, hostilities were recommenced. Batteries were constructed before Mellown, and heavy ordnance landed from the flotilla; and, at eleven a.m., twenty-eight guns and mortars opened fire upon the enemy's works, which was continued for two hours, by which time the troops intended for the assault were embarked in the flotilla at a point above the chief stockades. But, notwithstanding every exertion of the boats' crews, the current carried Colonel Sale's* brigade, consisting of the 13th and 48th Regiments, to its destined point of attack, before the three other brigades could reach the opposite shore. Colonel Sale was wounded in his boat, but, without waiting for the arrival of the other columns, Major Frith, who succeeded to the command, moved forward, and carried the formidable stockade by escalade; a second brigade cut up the flying foe, and the other works were occupied without opposition. Prince Memiaboo had fled as Colonel Sale's brigade moved to the assault, but in his house was found the treaty of peace of the 3rd of January, which had never left Mellown, thus proving that the negotiations were a mere blind. In the works were captured seventy-six guns, ninety jingals, and a large amount of arms and ammunition; also in the river eighteen war-boats, fifty-nine other boats, and between two hundred and three hundred canoes. The British loss was only nine men, including four in the flotilla, killed, and thirty-four, including nine in the flotilla, wounded. The Commander-in-chief expressed his earnest thanks " to Captain Chads and every officer and man of H.M.'s ships and the Hon. Company's flotilla."

On the 25th of January, 1826, the army left Mellown for the final advance on the capital, and, on the 30th, one of the gunboats struck, and bilged, upon a bar with only five feet of water, over which the rest of the flotilla passed in safety. In the meantime the King, terror-struck at the fall of Mellown, sent Dr. Price, an American missionary, and Assistant-Surgeon Sandford, of the Royal Regiment, to open negotiations for a fresh treaty, and Sir Archibald Campbell agreed to halt at Pagahm Mew for twelve days; but, upon the 8th of February, when within a day's march of that place, he received certain intelligence that the King had resolved to stake all upon one pitched battle, and that an army of between sixteen thousand and twenty thousand men, under a savage warrior, styled Nee-Woon-Breen, or King of Hell, had taken post in that city to bar his passage to the capital. On the following day, the small British army, which, owing to the absence of a brigade at Toundwain, only numbered fourteen hundred men, marched

* After the capture of Bassein when the reconnaissance up the river by the H.C.S. 'Mercury,' showed that it was not navigable, Colonel Sale proceeded to join the main army under Sir Archibald Campbell.

forward and encountered the enemy, eight thousand strong, drawn up within three miles of Pagahm Mew. Sir Archibald Campbell at once boldly attacked the centre, and, breaking through, routed and dispersed the enemy with great slaughter. This was the last action of the war, and the only one in the advance up the Irrawaddy in which the flotilla was not engaged. The army continued its march to Yandaboo, only forty-five miles from Ava, where, on the 24th of February, 1826, a peace was finally signed, which is known in history as the Treaty of Yandaboo. By this instrument, besides the payment of one million sterling, as an indemnity for the expenses of the war, and other provisions, the King ceded in perpetuity the province of Arracan, including the divisions of Arracan, Ramree, Cheduba, and Sandoway, and also that portion of the province of Tenasserim, which includes Ye, Tavoy, and Mergui, as far as the Martaban river.

On the day following the signature of peace, Captain Chads issued the following General Memorandum to the officers and men under his command:—" I feel the highest gratification in announcing to the flotilla, that the unwearied exertions, gallantry, and zeal of the officers and every individual composing it, have been crowned by an honourable peace, and in resigning the command of it, I beg to express my unfeigned thankfulness for the alacrity and cheerfulness with which this arduous service has been performed, and the personal attention which I have at all times experienced will ever be remembered by me with most pleasing and grateful thanks." In a letter of the same date, addressed to Sir Archibald Campbell, Captain Chads especially recommended Lieutenant Laughton, of the Bombay Marine, to the favourable notice of the Supreme Government, "his conduct and ability on all occasions, from the very commencement of the war, having met with the constant approbation of his superiors and the esteem of all others." Lieutenant Rowband, who had accompanied the flotilla to Pagahm Mew, was despatched in a gunboat to Rangoon, with four sick officers and eight seamen; but it was not until the 8th of March, when a sufficient number of boats had been provided by the Burmese government, that the European regiments, with the greater portion of the artillery, commenced the return by water to Rangoon, the remainder marching to Prome, or proceeding overland to Aeng in Arracan, which was reached in eleven days.

Sir Archibald Campbell, with Mr. Robertson, embarked in the 'Enterprise' steamer, and proceeded to Calcutta, where he landed on the 5th of April, 1826. Most of the British regiments returned to the Bengal and Madras Presidencies, and small garrisons were left at Pegu and Rangoon, until the payment of the balance of the indemnity. H.M.'s ships also quitted the country, and the maintenance of peace on the vast seaboard with its populous cities, was entrusted to the Bombay Marine and a flotilla of gunboats.

The Governor-General in Council, by General Orders, dated the 3rd of August, 1826, granted to the officers and men engaged in the Burmese war, a donation of six months' batta to those who had served for a period of not less than twelve months, and half that amount to such as had served a less period. On the 19th of October, 1827, a second General Order was issued from the same authority, stating that the Court of Directors had authorised the issue of a second donation of batta of a like amount to the forces engaged in Ava and Arracan, " as a token of the favourable sentiments they entertain of the brilliant services achieved." The officers and men of the flotilla who had not shared in the benefit of a previous Resolution of the 19th of November, 1824, awarding extra allowances while on service, were included in this distribution.

On the conclusion of the war, the Governor-General[*] in Council issued General Orders, of which the following paragraph refers to the service rendered to the State by the Bombay Marine:—

"The conduct of that portion of the naval branch of the Expedition which belongs to the East India Company, has been exemplary and conspicuous for gallantry and indefatigable exertion, and it has fully shared in all the honourable toils and well-earned triumphs of the land force. The Governor-General in Council experiences the most sensible gratification, in offering to Commodore Hayes, to Captain Hardy, Senior Captain of the Bombay Marine, and to the several commanders and officers of the Bombay cruisers, which have been employed in the Irrawaddy, and to the officers in command of the armed brigs and divisions of gunboats, the cordial thanks of Government for their zealous and meritorious services. Although not commanding in person the Hon. Company's naval force in the Irrawaddy, Commodore Hayes has amply entitled himself to the special notice and consideration of Government on this occasion, since it was mainly owing to his professional and unremitting exertions, that the armed flotilla from this port was so efficiently equipped, and thus enabled to acquit itself in a manner which has repeatedly been honoured with the approbation of his Excellency the Naval Commander-in-chief of His Majesty's squadron in the East Indies, and the officers of the Royal Navy, under whose orders they have been em-

---

[*] Lord Amherst was advanced to the dignity of an earldom, and Sir Archibald Campbell was created a baronet for his successful conduct of the war.

ployed in conjunction with the armed boats of His Majesty's ships."

A Resolution of thanks was passed by the Court of Directors on the 24th of November, 1826, and by the Court of Proprietors on the 13th and 19th of December following, to the Military and Naval Forces of His Majesty and the Hon. Company, of which the last paragraph is to the following effect:—
"Resolved unanimously—That the thanks of this Court be given to Commodore Sir James Brisbane, C.B., and to the captains and officers of His Majesty's and the Company's ships, who co-operated with the Army in the Burmese War, for their cordial, zealous, and most useful exertions, and to the crews of His Majesty's and Company's ships and boats employed in that service, for their spirited and intrepid conduct on all occasions, and that the Commander of His Majesty's ships on the India station be requested to communicate the thanks of this Court to the officers and men under his command."

But the most highly prized honour was the Vote of Thanks of the House of Commons on the 8th of May, 1827, and of the House of Lords on the 14th of May, to the gallant officers and men lately engaged in the arduous operations in Burmah, in which the following paragraph bore especial reference to the Naval force:—

"Resolved, *nemine contradicente*—That the thanks of this House be given to the several captains and officers of His Majesty's and the East India Company's Naval forces, employed in the late operations against Ava, for their skilful, gallant, and meritorious exertions, which greatly contributed to the successful issue of the war.

"Resolved, *nemine contradicente*—That this House doth highly approve and acknowledge the services of the Seamen and Marines, serving on board the ships of His Majesty and the East India Company, employed in the late operations against Ava, and that the same be signified to them by the captains of the several ships, who are desired to thank them for their gallant behaviour."

So far the captains and officers of the Bombay Marine had only cause for gratulation, and even when Commanders Mitchell, Chads, Marryat, Studdert, and Ryves received post-rank, and every lieutenant and passed midshipman belonging to the 'Alligator,' 'Arachne,' and 'Larne,' besides others of the 'Liffey,' 'Boadicea,' and 'Sophie,' many of whom had seen little service, and some none at all, in Burmese waters, received their promotion, they had no cause of complaint, for theirs was a seniority Service, and the rules as to promotion admitted no modification; but it must have aroused feelings of bitterness, when Captains Marryat, Chads, and Ryves were awarded the C.B., and no officer of similar rank in the Bombay Marine, though five cruisers had served throughout the entire operations, was deemed worthy or eligible for that honour. The claims of Commodore Hayes could not be overlooked, and he was subsequently created a Knight Bachelor, an honour of little consideration when conferred for war services, but it must have been galling to that veteran seaman, who had served his country on shore and afloat since the year 1782, and to the Service of which he was so distinguished an ornament, that, though holding relative rank with the officers of the Royal Naval and Indian Military Forces, and having independent command of the squadron serving throughout the war on the Arracan coast, he was denied the insignia of even the lowest grade of the Order of the Bath.

CHAPTER XIV.

1826—1830.

Changes in the Constitution of the Bombay Marine—The succession of Superintendents—The Flotilla on the Arracan Coast—The Blockade of Berbera—The *matériel* and *personnel* of the Service in 1827—Discussion at the India House on the Condition of the Marine—Remodelling of the Service—Appointment of Captain Sir Charles Malcolm, R.N., as Superintendent—Formation of the Service into a Marine Corps, and its anomalous position as regards Martial Law—The Report of the Finance Committee—Trial of Commander J. C. Hawkins for Slave Dealing—Steam Navigation, and Overland Communication with the East—Commander Wilson and the First Voyage of the 'Hugh Lindsay'—Titular Change of the Service to "Indian Navy."

DURING the Burmese War, one cruiser of the Bombay Marine was employed at Penang, and four, besides the surveying ships, 'Discovery' and 'Psyche,' maintaining the peace of the Persian Gulf; and during the same period the usual convoy was provided for the Surat vessels trading with Mocha, and other ports in the Red Sea.

The commissioning of the new frigate 'Hastings,' on the outbreak of the Burmese War, had necessitated an augmentation of officers. Four passed midshipmen, then called masters' mates, were promoted to lieutenants, and an additional surgeon was posted from the Army, the Marine always being supplied with medical officers from the military establishment. By an Order, dated the 12th of April, 1824, the Governor of Bombay abolished the rank of commander, and increased the number of senior and junior captains to twelve of each rank.* A change was also made in the retiring allowances of officers who had served twenty-two years in India.†

* The following were the officers affected by the promotion: Junior Captains R. Morgan, G. Walker, Daniel Ross, and W. T. Graham to be Senior Captains; Commanders W. Maxfield, P. Maughan, D. Jones, W. Arrow, H. Hardy, C. J. Maillard, J. Crawford, R. E. Goodridge, and First Lieutenant Thomas Tanner to be Junior Captains.

† The following is the Government Order alluded to:—

"Bombay Castle, September 30, 1824.

"The Hon. the Governor in Council is pleased to publish for general information the following Extract from the Hon. Court's despatch of the 20th of August, 1823, amending the regulation of the 1st of August, 1798, for granting retiring pensions to the officers of the Marine.

Para. 7. "Being of opinion that it is desirable that the total amount of retiring

In 1823 a small brig of 192 tons, and carrying eight guns, was added to the Service; she was called the 'Palinurus,' and no more appropriate name than that of the pilot of Æneas could have been given to the little vessel, as for nearly forty years she was employed as a surveying vessel, and in her confined cabins were worked out the observations which formed the basis of the beautiful charts for the production of which the scientific officers of the Service were so famous. In 1824, was launched the 'Elphinstone,'* sloop-of-war, of eighteen guns and 387 tons, and, on the 18th of July, in the following year, a second sloop-of-war, of 420 tons, and eighteen guns, was added to the Service, and named the 'Amherst.'† In 1826, a third ship, called the 'Clive,' was launched, and, in the following year, a fourth, named the 'Coote,' both of these being built on the same lines as the ' Amherst.'

In 1825, a change took place in the office of Superintendent, by the resignation of Captain Meriton, who had greatly distinguished himself in the Company's mercantile marine—or "regular service," as it was called—to distinguish it from the "freetraders." Captain Meriton had held the post of Superintendent since the year 1813, when he succeeded Captain Money, a man of enlightened views and great administrative capacity, who had also served in the Company's mercantile marine. Captain Meriton was a man of undoubted ability and integrity of purpose, but he was unpopular in the Service, and, instead of striving to elevate the Marine, sought to subordinate its officers

allowance to your Marine officers should be definitively fixed, we have with that view revised the regulations, and have resolved :—

Para. 8. "That the retiring pay to Marine officers, who have actually served in India twenty-two years or upwards, be as follows, viz. : To the Master Attendant and the Commodore, after having served five years in either of those stations, £450. To Captains of the First Class, or Senior Captains, £360. To Captains of the Second Class, £270. To First-Lieutenants, £180.

Para. 9. "We have further resolved that Marine officers retiring from ill-health, after ten years' service, before they have completed that of twenty-two years, be granted one half of the retiring allowance of their rank as specified in the last paragraph."

In August, 1826, the retiring allowances of the Junior Captains were increased to £293, and of First-Lieutenants to £191 12s. 6d.

* The 'Elphinstone' and 'Clive' were in existence at the date of the abolition of the Indian Navy in 1863, and were as staunch and seaworthy as on the day they passed out of the hands of Mr. Nowrojee Jamsetjee, the Company's builder at Bombay, though they had never been laid up, but were always in commission.

† The 'Amherst' was so called after the Governor-General, as was the 'Hastings' launched in the previous year, after the late Governor-General. Other ships of the Marine were named after successive viceroys, as the 'Teignmouth,' in honour of Sir John Shore (afterwards Lord Teignmouth), the 'Mornington' after Lord Wellesley, and the 'Auckland,' many years later, after the nobleman of that name. The 'Elphinstone' was called after the Governor of Bombay, the Honourable Mountstuart Elphinstone; the 'Clive,' after Lord Clive; the 'Coote,' after Sir Eyre Coote; and the 'Falkland,' after Lord Falkland, Governor of Bombay.

to the members of his own former Service, notwithstanding that, with the exception of the captains of the Company's trading ships, none of the officers held relative rank with the army—a privilege conferred on the Bombay Marine by the Regulations of 1798, and confirmed by the Warrant of the Prince Regent in 1814. Thus it happened that, though Captain Meriton was an honest servant to his masters in Leadenhall Street, he never commanded either the confidence or regard of the Service, as did his predecessors, Messrs. Dundas and Money, the two first Superintendents of the Bombay Marine.

Captain Meriton was a consistent opponent of any augmentation of the Service, or increase of benefits such as were from time to time granted to the army, and, as the Marine refused to join in any agitation for increased emoluments or privileges when such a course was proposed by the sister Service, and as it had no representative in the Court of Directors, being the only public service unrepresented in that august assembly—it happened that, while the claims of the Army received consideration, those of the Bombay Marine were systematically evaded. Individually, few officers had special cause of complaint, but collectively all were dissatisfied, for Captain Meriton possessed none of that *suaviter in modo*, which is as necessary in the head of a service as the *fortiter in re*; thus, remarkable for his great charities, he was the reverse of urbane, and during the twelve years of his tenure of office was never known even to invite an officer of the Marine to his table. On the other hand he was a laborious, conscientious servant, and, if he exacted much from his subordinates, never spared himself, but reduced the expenses of his own office and did all the work single-handed. He was also a first-rate seaman and strict disciplinarian, but, nevertheless, the Service was relieved at the resignation of so unsympathetic a head. Captain Buchanan, also of the "regular service," succeeded Captain Meriton, and, during his tenure of office, was much liked for his social gifts and the attention he paid to the officers; he was just also, but on the other hand took little interest in advancing the Service. He revived the post of Assistant-Superintendent, and threw fresh vigour into the surveys, in which he always took a decided interest. In this he found a warm supporter in that great Governor and good man, Mountstuart Elphinstone, to whose initiative, indeed, was due the surveys of the Persian Gulf, the Concan, the Red Sea, and other hydrographic labours undertaken by the Marine.

After the Burmese War, the sloops-of-war 'Teignmouth,' sixteen guns, 'Mercury,' fourteen guns, 'Prince of Wales,' fourteen guns, and the ten-gun brigs 'Vestal' and 'Psyche,' were condemned and sold out of the Service, and, besides the four eighteen-gun ships already mentioned, which were added to the Service between the years 1824-27, a fine ten-gun brig of 255 tons, called the 'Euphrates,' was launched in Bombay dockyard, on the 30th of June, 1828.

On the 22nd of September, 1825, the Hon. Company's sloop-of-war, 'Amherst,' eighteen guns, and brig 'Palinurus,' eight guns, proceeded to Mandavie, accompanied by four transports taken up to convey troops for the suppression of the predatory bands of Meyanas in Cutch, and on the borders of Guzerat. The "Cutch Field Force," as the division was designated, numbered seven thousand men of all arms, including H.M.'s 6th Regiment, the whole being under the command of Brigadier M. Napier of that Regiment. Trouble was apprehended with the Scinde princes, and hence the strength of the force, but the demonstration was sufficient to avert a collision, and the only losses experienced by the Expedition were due to an outbreak of cholera.

During the year 1826 a flotilla of gunboats was maintained on the coasts of Arracan and Tennasserim, under the command of Lieutenant J. H. Rowband, who was first stationed at Rangoon until its evacuation by the British troops, after payment of the second instalment of the indemnity, in the terms of the treaty. This flotilla was divided into two divisions, respectively commanded by Lieutenants C. Sharp and A. H. Nott.* The former officer, with the first division, which was stationed on the Tennasserim coast, was actively employed on the Salwein, protecting the villages on the Moulmein, or British, side, from the attacks of bands of Dacoits acting in conjunction with a rebel chief, Oozenah by name, whose stockade was situated inland. Lieutenant Sharp then proceeded to Tavoy and Mergui, and was engaged in making a cursory survey of the coast as far as the St. Martin's River. Lieutenant Sharp, who was authorised to proceed by land to Siam, and explore the intervening country, surveyed the St. Martin's River for a distance of about fifty miles, but, being unable to obtain guides, was forced to return without accomplishing his self-imposed task. During this service, this energetic young officer made a rough survey of many hundreds of miles, taking soundings, bearings, and latitudes, which was all the means at his disposal permitted, and a copy of this survey, with remarks,

---

* These two officers, with Captain G. Robinson, who served throughout the war as midshipman and lieutenant under the orders of Commodore Hayes, in the 'Vestal,' 'Research,' and 'Hastings,' are the only three surviving officers of the Bombay Marine who participated in the Burmese War. Captain Sharp retired from the service in July, 1839, with a commander's pension, and proceeded to New Zealand, where he served the Government for seventeen years, in the several capacities of sub-treasurer, postmaster of a district, harbour-master, collector of customs and emigration officer, and finally retired in 1866 on a pension. Of Captains Nott and Robinson we shall have occasion to speak again.

was sent to Government. In June, 1829, the flotilla was reduced, and Lieutenant Rowband alone remained to conduct the duties. Lieutenants Nott and Sharp returned to Calcutta, and, in the following December, arrived at Bombay, where the latter was appointed First-Lieutenant of the 'Clive,' then commissioned by Commander John Croft Hawkins, and about to proceed to the African coast on her memorable cruise; and Mr. Nott became Senior Lieutenant of the new steamer 'Hugh Lindsay,' fitting out under the command of the late Commander John Henry Wilson, for her even more memorable voyage to Suez.

In February, 1827, a small squadron, consisting of two of H.M.'s ships and the Honourable Company's sloop-of-war, 'Amherst,' was employed under Sir Gordon Bremer, of H.M.S. 'Tamar,' in blockading Berbera* and the adjacent portion of the African coast opposite Aden, for the purpose of punishing, and exacting restitution from, the Soomalies, who, in 1825, had plundered an English brig, called the 'Marianne,' and murdered the greater portion of the crew, the captain, mate, and a few seamen alone escaping to Mocha, whence they proceeded to Madras. The Soomali chief and people agreed to the demands made upon them, paying a portion of the indemnity then, and promising to discharge the whole demand by instalments within two years. Before this agreement was concluded, it was necessary to land a force, and Berbera was burnt after a skirmish, in which the British experienced some slight loss. This was the first occasion in which these lawless people came into collision with the Bombay Marine, but, unhappily for them, it was not the last. The stipulation as to the payment of the indemnity within two years, was not carried out, and, in 1832, we find that the Hon. Company's brig, 'Tigris,' commanded by Lieutenant Nott, was employed blockading the coast; indeed one or two of the ships of the Indian Navy were, from this time forward, particularly after the acquisition of Aden, constantly "looking in" at Berbera and other places on the Soomali coast, for the purpose of keeping the police of these waters.

As the close of 1827 marks the commencement of a new era in the history of the Service, we will briefly show what the

* The town of Berbera lies at the head of the harbour, which is the only sheltered one on the coast, and varies in size and population according to the season of the year. Thus, between the months of October and March, the place presents the appearance of a fair, and the people number at least fifteen thousand souls. At this time the tribes from the interior bring their commodities for exchange with the Banian merchants who flock from Mandavie, Porebunder, and Bombay, or the more humble traders from Yemen, Bahrein, and Grane. The first notice we have been able to find of Berbera, is contained in a paper entitled "Information on the Town of Barbera, situated on the East Coast of Africa," by Lieutenant R. Ethersey, I.N., which was printed in the "Transactions of the Bombay Geographical Society," vol. i. p. 286.

personnel and *matériel* were on the 1st of January, 1828. The ships at that date, consisted of the 'Hastings,' thirty-two guns; the four eighteen-gun sloops-of-war, 'Elphinstone,' 'Coote,' 'Amherst,' and 'Clive;' the fourteen-gun sloops-of-war 'Ternate,' 'Benares,' and 'Aurora'; the brigs 'Antelope,' fourteen guns, 'Nautilus,' fourteen guns, and 'Thetis,' ten guns; and the ten-gun brig 'Euphrates' (on the stocks). Besides these there were the 'Discovery,' six guns, surveying vessel; the brig 'Palinurus,' eight guns; the schooners 'Vigilant' and 'Zephyr,' six guns; a bomb-ketch, and about six or seven pattamars and other smaller craft. The strength in officers, and their pay, was as follows:—

One master-attendant on the captain's list, 30,000 rupees per annum; one commodore, 24,000 rupees per annum; eleven senior captains, average pay, 1,000 per month; twelve junior captains, 700 rupees per month; thirty first-lieutenants, drawing two rupees three annas a day when in command, or the allowance of their appointments, in addition to their pay of 150 rupees per month; twenty-two second-lieutenants, drawing from 82 to 122 rupees per month; and forty midshipmen whose monthly pay was from 30 to 50 rupees.

There were also some lucrative staff appointments at this time, lucrative that is, when the scale of pay awarded to the Service is considered. The Marine Board* consisted of the Superintendent, who was not an officer of the Service, the master-attendant, the commodore of the harbour, and the senior captain, who also latterly held the office of boat-master and agent for transports; they met on the Tuesday and Friday of every week, with a secretary and accountant, a post held by a lieutenant. One of the officers of the Service also held the office of deputy judge-advocate-general, with a staff allowance of 200 rupees per month, which was abolished by order of the Court, on the 14th of August, 1832. In addition to these offices, the prizes held out to the veterans of the Service, were the posts of commodore at Surat and in the Persian Gulf, and master-attendant at Calcutta, which had been held for a great many years by Commodore Hayes.

The year 1827 was to see a radical change in the constitution of the Service, but, though greater advantages were held out to the officers, these promises were never fulfilled in their integrity.

* We find by referring to the Marine General Orders that, in 1828, the following officers were appointed members of the Marine Board. "September 26, Captain Richard Morgan appointed to succeed present Master-Attendant and Inspector of Port, and to be second member of Marine Board. Captain William Graham to be General Agent for Transports and Boat-Master and third Member of Marine Board." "January 7, 1829, Captain P. Maughan to be Captain of Mazagon Dockyard and Member of Marine Board, in succession to Captain Walker deceased." On the 25th of September, 1828, we also find that Captain George Grant was gazetted to be senior officer at Surat, an office formerly held by a Commodore with a high salary.

During the year an important discussion took place at the India House, which sheds a light on the position of the Bombay Marine at that time; this state, which may be said to represent its normal condition during the two and a-half centuries of its existence, will be most aptly described as, *friendless in Leadenhall Street, and neglected in India*. That the officers of the Service, under the unfavourable conditions brought into notice by the chief speaker on this occasion, maintained the efficiency of their ships and crews, affords the highest possible testimony to their *ésprit de corps* and devotion to duty.

On the 22nd of February, 1827, a requisition to the Directors for convening a General Court of Proprietors, to inquire into the condition of the Bombay Marine, was drawn up and signed by nine Proprietors, among the signatures being such names as Mr. Joseph Hume, M.P., Dr. J. B. Gilchrist, Colonel Hon. Leicester Stanhope, General William Thornton, and Captain Maxfield, of the Bombay Marine, an officer distinguished alike for his scientific attainments and his character, and who, during his twenty-four years' service, had obtained the recorded thanks of Government on ten different occasions. In accordance with this requisition, a Special General Court of Proprietors was held at the India House in Leadenhall Street, on the 14th of March, under the presidency of the Chairman, Sir G. A. Robinson, Bart. Captain Maxfield introduced the subject in a lengthy and able speech. He first read a letter from an anonymous writer, signed "An Anti-Meddler," in which the writer warned him to desist from "persisting in the course he was now pursuing at the India Office," adding, "it is said you pique yourself on being a good shot; be not too confident, it will not be sufficient to serve you. You had better reflect in time before it is too late."

After observing that he treated such "silly threats" with disdain, Captain Maxfield continued his speech, from which we will make some extracts:—"Were he to say that, since the Order the Court of Directors, in 1798, they were obnoxious to the charge of neglect with respect to this Corps, he should be borne out by evidence; but in order to save time he should commence with a few extracts from a letter of Mr. Money, Superintendent of the Marine, to the Bombay Government in answer to some sweeping censures passed on that unprotected corps, in the letter of the Court of Directors of the 8th of April, 1806. They were to be found on the records of the Court; and, unless something had been done to remedy the evils which Mr. Money complained of, and brought to the notice of the Directors in 1807, or twenty years ago, then he must contend that the charge of neglect was fully proved. In the ninth paragraph of that letter, Mr. Money said, 'Permit me on a subject so materially interesting to the department committed to my trust, to state, with all respectful deference to the

Honourable Court, what I conceive to be the causes of every defect and deficiency in the Marine character and institution. The want of a code of laws enacted by legislative authority has been and continues to be the promineut defect of the Marine establishment. It is only necessary, I humbly conceive, to refer to a description of the duties expected from the Marine, as given by the Honourable Court, in their public letter under date of the 1st of August, 1798, to render it manifest, without a waste of argument, that a Corps having such services to perform, should be vested with legal authority, and its discipline upheld by the power of a legal tribunal. The Honourable Court, in the second paragraph of the letter referred to, have stated the following to be the objects of the establishment of the Marine force. 1st. To protect the trade from port to port. 2nd. To defend the Company's trade and possessions. 3rd. To transport troops, &c. 4th. To make nautical discoveries. 5th. To convoy packets. It must be very evident, upon the most superficial review of these duties, that their effect and creditable execution depend upon professional knowledge, public zeal, and strict discipline and subordination.

"'The next principal defect in the Marine establishment results, in my humble judgment,' continues Mr. Money, 'from the low estate to which the officers' comparative rank is reduced. By the old regulations of the Company, yet unrepealed, the commanders of their regular ships from Europe take their rank between a captain and a major in the army. By the order of the Honourable Court already referred to, it was directed that, in order to preserve due respect and attention to the officers of the Marine, who on important occasions are associated with the military, corresponding rank should be assigned as follows :—" The commodore to rank with a colonel in the army; captains of ships of twenty-eight guns and upwards, or senior captains, with lieutenant-colonels, junior captains with majors, first-lieutenants with captains, &c." This distinction, supported by a code of martial law, would have given to the Marine Corps all the vigour and spirit which it could be rendered capable of expressing; but by subsequent resolutions, the corresponding rank was virtually abolished, and the code of laws which the Supreme Government so strongly recommended, and which the Honourable Court declared, upon a conviction of its necessity, that it was their intention to procure, has never been obtained. On the 22nd of May, 1804, the Honourable Court was pleased to direct that the commanders of their regular ships, whose corresponding rank with the military rested between that of a major and a captain, should precede all the captains of the Marine, having the comparative rank of lieutenant-colonels of the army. Whatever of respect and attention the orders of 1798 were calculated to produce, has been completely extinguished by the regulations of comparative rank of 1804. By them, an officer who has served the Honourable Company in a profession strictly confined to arms, and from which the advantage of trade of any description are rigidly excluded, who has arrived at a rank corresponding with that of a lieutenant-colonel in the army, which he has held for a period of fourteen or fifteen years, finds himself compelled to yield precedence to the commander of a regular ship, ranking below a major in the army, who perhaps has not been ten years at sea, who but a short time before may have been (and I believe it has been the case) a mate of a ship at this very port, and whose ship at present the captain of Marine may be destined to convoy. These circumstances, combined with the want of a code of laws, precludes the mind from aspiring to a respectable rank in society, they tend to depress every feeling of laudable ambition, and blight, by their natural operation on the character of men, all that *esprit de corps* which is so much to the public advantage to encourage and cherish, and which has led to the aggrandisement of all other military services.'

"Mr. Money's letter," continued Captain Maxfield, "then entered into a comparative statement of the pay and pension of the Marine with the Company's Army, illustrative of the neglected and depressed state of the Marine. But knowing that more pay was not all to which an officer attached value, he did not think it necessary to quote farther. Perhaps it would be said, that the Court of Directors were anxious to obtain a code of laws for the Government of the Marine, but that they wanted power to effect that object. He was willing in charity to suppose that such was the case; but then came the question, if they were really disposed to render the Marine efficient and respectable, why had they avoided doing that which was unquestionably in their power? Did they frame any regulations for its better management? Did they issue any orders to construct vessels adapted to accommodate the unfortunate crews who were crammed into them? Did they repeal or explain their inconsistent orders of 1804? Or did they adopt any measures whatever to remedy the palpable evils pointed out in the Superintendent's letter? No! The pay of their Marine officers did not admit of a comparison with the other branches of the Company's service. The pay and allowance of a Marine captain was only 360 rupees per month, while that of a branch pilot at Calcutta, was 700 rupees per month, or 850, when sent beyond the Sandheads. But even this pittance was not secured to the captains of the Company's Marine; for by the orders of the Marine Board at Calcutta, of March 30, 1814, the captains of the Marine were rendered accountable for all advances made to any of the crew on the Company's account, and the loss sustained by desertion was deducted from the pay of the captains. A rule so illiberal was not applied to any other branch of their service, nor was it to be found in any other service whatever.

"Every liberal-minded man must suppose that the officers of the Bombay Marine were governed by some specified rule. That, however, was not the case; and, therefore, he entreated the attention of the Court to a few facts which would enable gentlemen to arrive at just conclusions. Early in April, 1818, a commander and all the officers of one of the cruisers were placed under arrest, on charges framed by Mr. Meriton, the then Superintendent of Marine. The usual forms of trial having been gone through, the proceedings were sent to Government on the 8th of that month. As they were not considered satisfactory, the Court were ordered to re-assemble, and to put certain questions, which was accordingly done; and the proceedings in the second instance were also forwarded to Government. From that time, until the 28th of November, the prisoners were kept in suspense, when they were again called before the Court. By the Court they were informed that the Government had directed certain questions to be put to them, to which they were expected to give explicit answers. The Commander begged to know whether he stood before the Court as a prisoner. This plain question the Court could not answer, but merely repeated the purpose for which they were assembled. The Commander stated his readiness to answer any question which the Government might think proper to put to him, after they had given their final decision on his case, but declared that he would give no answer while he appeared before the Court as a prisoner. The proceedings were then closed a third time, and sent to Government, by whom a final decision was given some time after, and notwithstanding the punishment which he had previously suffered, the Commander was further suspended until some time in 1819. Now it was hardly possible to conceive that any public authority could have resorted to such capricious measures, which were as repugnant to every species of judicial proceeding as they were opposed to every liberal and honourable feeling. Having said so much for the practice of Marine Courts, he would next advert to their composition. As the facts which he was about to state were to be found on the Company's records, he took it for granted that they would not be denied. Lieutenant Boyce, of the 'Mercury,' was, in 1812, put under arrest by his commander, Lieutenant Blast. The Superintendent assembled a Court in order to try him, on which he placed two of the officers of Indiamen as members. Lieutenant Boyce, be it remembered, held a commission, but these two gentlemen held no commission, and belonged to a merchant ship; they could not, therefore, be expected, from their habits, and the different duties they had to execute, to be proper judges. The degradation and insult offered in this instance to the Marine officers, were evident and studied, because there was no want of Marine officers to form a proper Court."

After alluding to the sale of the 'Mornington,' twenty-two guns, "for two-thirds of her probable value," Captain Maxfield continued :—

"When she was got rid of, the largest vessel remaining was the 'Teignmouth,' of 250 tons, which, in H.M.'s service, would have only ten or twelve guns; but she was absurdly crammed with eighteen guns, and at one time, twenty. It was as injudicious as cruel so to equip her, as it rendered her unsafe, and in the event of capture insured the disgrace of whoever commanded her. The rest of the vessels were of the same stowage, except that they were much smaller, and one, the 'Ariel,' a brig of 160 tons, carrying ten guns, was so crank that she overset and sank in a squall in the Persian Gulf, and of her crew only three men were saved. These were facts which could not be denied, and which the records of that house fully established. In October, 1814, the 'Vestal' being under orders to carry despatches to Bussorah, her commander, Lieutenant Phillips, was directed to receive on board (by the orders of the Superintendent) a certain number of bales belonging to private merchants at Bombay on freight. That officer represented the utter incompetency of his vessel to carry any cargo, as it was with difficulty he could stow his provisions and water for the crew. His objection was overruled, and the bales sent on board, which he (sooner than deprive the crew of their wretched accommodation) stowed in his own cabin. By the orders of 1798, all freight except bullion was prohibited to be carried in the Company's cruisers; but this disregard of orders by the Superintendent, brought into the Bombay Treasury the pitiful sum of 160 rupees. The 'Vestal' was a small sharp brig, 160 tons burthen, mounting ten guns, and scarcely able to carry ten weeks' provisions and water; and, as the Superintendent long commanded one of their large Indiamen, he could not plead ignorance of the utter inability of the 'Vestal' to carry any cargo whatever, and his motives therefore could not be mistaken. What was the consequence? Not mere discomfort to the unfortunate commander, but death. The 'Vestal's' cabin was very small, and had neither port nor scuttle. The Persian Gulf, they knew, was dreadfully unhealthy. Such stowage induced a liver complaint, and an officer of distinguished merit, who had served for nearly twenty years, fell a victim—not to the cause of his country, but to injustice and cruelty. Now it was well known to all who heard him, that in every kind of ship or vessel, from the privateer to the collier, some difference of accommodation was allotted to the persons serving on board; but the Superintendent, to give a death-blow to the Service, thought to confound all ranks; he therefore ordered that the berth allotted to the midshipmen of the 'Vestal' should be taken away, and the midshipmen put into the lieutenants' cabin. Now the lieutenants' cabin on board the 'Vestal' was only nine feet by seven feet, and as there was no other, the surgeon was necessarily obliged to live and sleep in it also. Such was the wretched den into which the Superintendent ordered the midshipmen to be crammed also, putting health and comfort out of the question. Their Marine officers had no remedy; and if the pigs had been ordered to be put there also, they must have submitted or resigned the Service. It happened, however, that the surgeon belonged to the Army, and was protected by its rules and regulations from such abominable injustice; and he wrote to Government, complaining that the accommodation allotted to him in the 'Vestal' was worse than that provided by Act of Parliament for slaves during the slave trade. The Superintendent took fire at the reflection, and preferred charges against him; but as a military officer could not be punished without sufficient grounds, a court-martial saved him, and very properly remarked on the conduct and evidence of the Superintendent. This conduct, however, obtained approbation and support, and he continued in office as long as he pleased. The Directors could not plead ignorance of the facts he had related, unless they were guilty of neglecting to read the papers sent to this country. But supposing that in the multiplicity of business and the incessant application to foster private claims, no time was found to attend to their insignificant Marine, still the executive body could not deny that they were almost knee-deep in Marine memorials, not one of which they ever condescended to answer, or probably even to consider. He held the public correspondence in his hand, and abstained from reading it merely to save time; it was, however, on their records, and could not be denied.

"It might be supposed by some utterly ignorant of the merits or claims of the Bombay Marine, that it deserved such treatment, or that it had forfeited all claims to attention; it was therefore with reluctance that he was compelled to advert to its conduct as a public body, of which he was probably one of the least worthy members. First, then, on the score of fidelity and attachment to their country, the Marine were eminently conspicuous; and it could not be denied that when the Company's Army, with arms in their hands, urged their claims to equal rank with H.M.'s troops, and invited the Marine to follow their example and join them, the latter declined so doing. The Army obtained the most liberal consideration, while the

Marine was unnoticed. He had heard it said, that the Marine deserved to be so treated for not joining the Army. If so, it would serve as a lesson in future to regulate the claims of military bodies, and teach the just value of demands unaided by power. Now for patriotism. In 1799, a subscription was set on foot towards carrying on the war, as a test of public opinion. It was liberally supported in this country, and was also effectively carried on in India. Most of their servants, Civil, Military, and Marine, subscribed towards it; but Captain Selby, of the Bombay Marine, subscribed the whole of his pay during the war. He stood a solitary example of such devotion in the Company's Service; and continuing to serve, he sacrificed his life in their employ. He would not tire them with a detail of the numerous instances of gallantry and devotion which he could adduce of your Marine officers under such evident disadvantages and discouragement; suffice it to say the repeated testimonies of His Majesty's officers in favour of their good conduct, afforded some consolation to their wounded feelings; and the existence of those testimonies on the Company's records could not be denied. He would now assert, without fear of being denied, what might be justly deemed a proud proof of devotion by any military body in the world. In no one solitary instance had the British colours ever been lowered from the peak of one of their miserably ill-manned cruisers to any enemy of inferior, or even of equal force, while they had often proved successful when combating a superior foe. But supposing such military ardour and patriotism of no value in the estimation of the Company, he would address them simply as merchants, and ask if disinterestedness on the part of their Marine officers in preferring the Company's interests to their own, could establish any claim?"

Captain Maxfield then recounted the circumstances, already detailed, under which Commodore Hayes, with the noble disinterestedness for which he was remarkable, refused to permit the captains of his flag-ship, the 'Malabar,' and of the 'Mornington,' to make prizes of two large Chinese junks, bound from Batavia to Amoy, having on board Dutch property to the value of £600,000, but directed their release on the grounds that their retention might be prejudicial to the interests of the State. After citing this order, Captain Maxfield continued:—"Now the above order afforded a good illustration of the impolicy of the orders of the Court of Directors in 1804. Suppose for one moment that Commodore Hayes had not been present, but that one of their regular ships had been in company, it was not possible to believe that the commander would have presumed to issue such an order, and still less likely any captain of their Marine would have attended to it if they had. The man who made such a sacrifice to promote their interests was not then worth one shilling, nor did he believe that he was at this moment. His disinterestedness and gallantry, of which their records possessed abundant proof, would, in any other service but their Marine, have obtained for him honour and distinction. The two officers to whom the order to release the junks was addressed, submitted a memorial, which he believed shared the usual fate of Marine memorials. But if the feelings of the Marine officers, their character and efficiency, were of no value in the Company's estimation, it was worth while to estimate its consequences by another test; let them therefore try it by pounds, shillings and pence. In 1812, the presence of a single cruiser of twenty guns, although badly manned, prevented a war with the Burmese, and obtained ample reparation for an insult offered to the Company. At that time there was as good occasion for a war as since; but Lord Minto sent the 'Malabar,' of twenty guns, which was lying at Calcutta, to support the arguments of the British Envoy at Rangoon.

"Now, the want of a respectable cruiser in Bengal in 1823, previous to our rupture with the Burmese, compelled the Bengal Government to equip and send a pilot-schooner* into the river Naaf, as a measure of naval defence, when its feeble and unwarlike appearance encouraged rather than repressed the aggression of the Burmese, who seized the commander and carried him off; and they augmented the grounds of a dispute, which precipitated us into a war that had entailed an expense of upwards of twenty millions sterling, and the loss of thousands of our brave and valuable troops. On their present Superintendent of Marine, Mr. Buchanan, he should offer but one remark; he had just given the command of the 'Hastings' frigate, and the 'Ernaad,'† the largest ships in the Service, to two mates of the country service, which was no less an act of injustice to the Marine officers than of disregard for the Company's interests." Captain Maxfield concluded by moving for a series of papers, sixteen in number, tending to bear out the different statements he had made.

Colonel Hon. Leicester Stanhope, of the Royal Army, who had served with the Bombay Marine at the capture of Dwarka in 1820, and elsewhere, and was, therefore, a good judge of their value, seconded the motion, and said in the course of his remarks:—

"His gallant friend was no factious character—he was no disappointed individual, coming into that Court for the purpose of opposing the conduct of the Court of Directors; no, he was one of their oldest and best officers, who had received the thanks of the Company nine or ten times in public Orders.

---

* This was the 'Phæton,' which was recovered at Martaban when that place was captured by Colonel Godwin on the 30th of September, 1824.

† The 'Ernaad' was a transport, not a ship of war.

He here wished to mention a particular circumstance with which his gallant friend was intimately connected. His gallant friend had mentioned the capture of two China junks, which had been given up in the most disinterested manner by Commodore Hayes. Now, his gallant friend was present on that occasion, and he had, in consequence of the restoration of those vessels, lost a very considerable share of prize money, the one-eighteenth or one-sixteenth of £600,000. With respect to the Bombay Marine, they must be all aware that it was one of the oldest branches of the Company's Service; and, as his gallant friend had truly stated, never was there an instance of any ship belonging to the Bombay Marine having lowered her flag to an enemy of equal force. Under these circumstances, he thought that their Marine Service ought to be a subject of interest to that Court. He could not help lamenting what he conceived to be the indignity offered to this useful Service. In the first place, he thought it was unfair to deprive the officers of that rank which they formerly held. This led to a very ridiculous occurrence. It happened that Commodore Hayes and his wife dined with the Governor-General. The Commodore having the rank of Colonel, the Governor-General thought it was proper to lead out Mrs. Hayes to dinner, conceiving that the precedence was due to her. This set the senior merchants' hearts on fire, and they in consequence wrote long letters home to the Court of Directors. They pondered over this weighty matter; and at last they came to the resolution of uncommodoring the Commodore. Now, Mr. Wynn, who had been in the habit of considering questions of precedence, and who was nightly occupied in explaining them in the House of Commons, thought this was very unfair, and therefore he reversed their proceeding. This was no laughable matter, when they considered that an indignity was offered to an old and meritorious officer, whose brow was covered with wounds and honours.

"It was a very fair subject of complaint that there was no martial law for the Government of the Bombay Marine. Did they ever before hear of a civilised society, especially a military society, without some species of law for its government. He always understood that, in the military profession, the law ought to be more strict and rigorous than elsewhere. He must ever view, as a gross act of injustice, the placing captains of the Bombay Marine under the commanders of Indiamen. He knew the captains of the Bombay Marine were most distinguished men; perhaps they were the most scientific men ever employed in the Naval Service. And he conceived that it was really putting the cart before the horse, to place the captain of a ship of war under the command of the captain of a merchantman. It was an absolute indignity to the Service, and he thought his gallant friend was right in withdrawing his labours from a Service which was so much degraded. Now he would tell the Court what the reason of this degradation was. The fact was plainly this : The Bombay Marine was not represented on the other side of the bar; but the other service —the merchant service—was so represented; for he believed that no less than four Directors had been captains of East Indiamen. Those captains came constantly within the influence of the Court of Directors, but the captains in the Marine service were quite removed beyond that influence."

The Chairman of the Court of Directors, in reply, entered into a lengthened defence of the conduct of the late Superintendent, Mr. Meriton, and stated that " for a great length of time, he admitted even for years, the Court had been sedulously engaged in endeavouring to effect the improvement of the Bombay Marine, and that many difficulties had occurred in the progress of their efforts for that purpose; difficulties occasioned by the peculiarity of the naval service of this country, which entertained a kind of jealousy of any interference on naval subjects." He did justice to the character and conduct of the Bombay Marine, but denied that it was neglected, saying that the Court had " gratuitously " increased the emoluments of the officers since the year 1798, when the gallant officer and others had entered the Service. He concluded by moving:—" It having been declared from the Chair, that measures are in progress for improving the condition of the Bombay Marine, and for placing it on a footing more consonant to the merits and services of that distinguished corps, this Court is disposed to give confidence to the correctness of the statement thus given from the Chair, and considers it, therefore, both injudicious and inexpedient to force a premature discussion of the subject on this Court, until the details of the proposed plan come regularly before it."

The Deputy Chairman (the Hon. H. Lindsay, M.P.) seconded this amendment, and did justice to the "able and effective manner in which the Marine performed its duty." Sir C. Forbes advised Captain Maxfield to withdraw his motion, and, after paying a high tribute to his honourable and disinterested conduct, continued :—" He concurred in all that was said, on each side of the bar, as to the merits of the Bombay Marine. He believed that a more deserving set of men, as public servants, did not exist, and he was only sorry that circumstances did not allow them to have done as much as, he was sure, they could have done. He greatly regretted that some mark of distinction had not been granted to officers who had so greatly signalized themselves. With respect to Commodore Hayes, every person who knew him would admit, that he was one of the most disinterested men in the world; and he believed that the order which he issued in reference to the China junks, was one that very few men besides himself would have sent forth. He conceived that such conduct must have recommended him strongly to the Company. He thought that the giving up of those junks was extremely proper, and he only wished that the same sort of liberality had been displayed on other occasions."

That eminent scholar, Dr. Gilchrist, said in the course of his speech:—" It had been asserted that the Bombay Marine had no right to complain, because the officers entered into the Service under certain stipulations as to pay and allowances. But did not military men enter the Service under certain stipulations? and did they not all know that something had occurred by which the pay of the Army had been increased? Did not many military officers now get more than was stipulated for when they entered the Army? Had the Bombay Marine been represented, as it ought to be, in the Court, by one or more members of the body behind the bar, he was pretty well convinced they would not have such grounds for complaint."
Another speaker observed, " one sentiment at least appeared to be unanimous on all sides of the Court, that of doing justice, and giving merited distinction to the Bombay Marine. All parties strove to confer upon that Corps the honour which was due to it. The disadvantages under which that Service laboured had been felt and known for a considerable length of time."

In concluding his reply upon the discussion, which ended adversely to his motion, Captain Maxfield said:—" Before he concluded, he could not omit to mention the kindness and consideration of many of His Majesty's naval officers, with whom the Bombay Marine had been especially associated on service. In most instances (and he spoke from experience), the British Navy had exhibited a degree of sympathy, feeling, and liberality towards the officers of the Marine, which the orders and treatment of the Court of Directors were but little calculated to produce. The gratuitous consideration and liberality of that gallant corps formed a striking contrast with the conduct of those whose duty it was to uphold and cherish the Bombay Marine, rather than to neglect and degrade it. That Marine was employed on the most arduous service, and yet the Court of Directors took no measures whatever to man or equip them efficiently. It remained solely dependent on the efforts of a commander to obtain a crew, as if the vessel belonged to him and not to the State. The individual in command received no aid from the Court of Directors or the Government abroad; he was left to his own resources, and frequently had he been obliged to rob their merchant ships of part of their crews, that he might man the cruisers which he commanded. He thus always procured a crew, and he would rather run the risk of being dismissed the Service for distressing the Indiamen, than he would take the chance of being without the means of defending the ships he commanded, and of upholding the honour of the colours which he carried."

It would appear that the discussion at the India House, had the effect of quickening the Directors in bringing forth the scheme for the reorganisation of the Bombay Marine, which had been so many years in a state of incubation, as we find that a letter, dated the 31st of October, 1827, was addressed to the Governor of Bombay, ordering the remodelling of the Service. The letter commenced by saying, that relative rank with the Royal Navy had been obtained, and martial law was hoped for in the ensuing session of Parliament; that a captain of the Royal Navy would be appointed Superintendent, and the senior officers would have retirement on the Senior List in England, with pensions equivalent to colonels, and off reckonings, amounting in the aggregate to £800 a-year. The strength of the Service was fixed at five captains, nine commanders—a rank which, abolished three years' before, was now restored—forty-six lieutenants, and sixty midshipmen. Three twenty-four-gun ships were to be built, and other vessels if required, and a steamer was also ordered. The pay of the officers was fixed at the following rates:—

Five captains, at 932 rupees per mensem; nine commanders (afterwards increased to twelve), 722 rupees per mensem; fifteen senior lieutenants, at 252 rupees per mensem; thirty-one junior lieutenants, at 147 rupees per mensem; sixty midshipmen, at 50 rupees per mensem.

But, though the numbers of each rank was made known to the Service, the pay fixed by the Court was kept a secret; at least the officers were never made acquainted with it, neither was any increase given for at least one year, when the following scale was put into operation. The total sum per mensem allowed by the Court, would amount to 24,661 rupees, or 295,932 rupees per annum, but the Government only paid the following amounts:—

One captain, at 900 rupees per mensem; three others, at 800 rupees per mensem, and, if a fifth was employed, one at 600 rupees per mensem; nine commanders, at 500 rupees per mensem; fifteen senior lieutenants, at 150, afterwards 175, rupees per mensem; thirty-one junior lieutenants, at 120, afterwards 145, rupees per mensem; sixty midshipmen, at 50 rupees per mensem. The total amount per mensem was thus 18,520 rupees, or 222,240 rupees per annum.

Thus the officers of the Bombay Marine were, by some cause that looks singularly like taking a mean advantage of their ignorance and weakness, mulcted of 6,000 rupees of pay monthly, as sanctioned by the Court; and Government could congratulate itself on "conveying" to their own uses—perhaps we might with justice use a stronger epithet, but we will adopt the euphemism made famous by "ancient Pistol"—nearly a lac of rupees, the salary of their hard-worked and inadequately-rewarded servants of the Bombay Marine. The Service, being unaware of the liberality of the Court, bore the injustice without appealing; and, writes a deceased officer, to whose unpublished jottings of the history of the Service we have had access, "it was only while compiling these papers that it came to my notice, when examining the report of the Finance Committee, appointed by Lord William Bentinck, where all is openly and officially stated. Even that Committee was ignorant of the officers not receiving the pay offered by the Court, for though they recommended the reduction of the number of the officers, yet they did not touch the amount of pay, which was not, even in their most clipping mood, thought by them too much."

How different was such treatment to that conceded to their powerful Civil and Military services. Had the Court granted an increase of pay to these branches of the public service, it would have been quickly published in Orders, or have come to their knowledge through some friend in the Court, but the Bombay Marine was uninfluential and unrepresented in Leadenhall Street. It simply did its duty, and did it well, as all allowed, but not for it were the sweets of "interest" or the honours of the Bath, and when it was awarded a boon in the shape of increased pay, this was withheld from it, while, on the other hand, the reduction of the senior ranks was strictly carried out in the terms of the Order.

In addition to the reduction of one commodore, seven senior captains, three junior captains, and six lieutenants, it was ordered that no officer was to hold a shore appointment, with the exception of three or four posts, which were specified, without retiring from the Service. The Bombay Government found it necessary to add two captains to the number authorised by the Court, and, in writing home, stated that the commanders were insufficient; the result was that the captain's list stood at seven, being still five less than were authorised in 1824, and, in the following year, the commanders were increased, by orders of the Court, to twelve. In other grades the numbers remained unaltered until the year 1838. The pecuniary value of the Court's boon, in granting the four senior captains pensions of £800 per annum, may be made apparent in a few words. The commodore and master-attendant were entitled to £450 each, and the two senior captains to £360 each, making a total of £1,620, so that the increase amounted to £1,580. But by the reduction of one commodore and five captains, Government saved 5,000 rupees a month, or £6,000 a year, besides the £7,000 per annum of pay sanctioned by the Court, but withheld by the Government.

We said only such portions of the Court's despatch, as suited the convenience of the Government, were published for the information of the Service. Thus, by a General Order, dated "April 30, 1828," the Governor in Council published the following extracts from the Court's letter of the previous 31st of October, with a copy of the King's Order, conferring on the officers of the Bombay Marine "the privilege of taking rank with the officers of the Royal Navy:"—

"Para. 2. You are aware that for some time past we have been endeavouring to attain for your Marine an authorised code of laws, and a defined rank relatively with the Royal Navy.

"Para. 3. We have the satisfaction now to acquaint you, that His Majesty has been graciously pleased to pass an Order in Council, conferring on the officers of the Bombay Marine, within the limits of the Company's charter, the privilege of taking rank, agreeably to their several degrees, with the officers of the Royal Navy, but under the condition that all officers of any rank in the Royal Navy shall have precedence of all officers of the same rank in the Bombay Marine, and that officers of neither Service shall have any command whatsoever over the ships, officers, and men of the other Service, unless under special orders to that effect from their respective Governments.

"Para. 4. We transmit a copy of His Majesty's Order, and we desire that you will promulgate it for general information. It is scarcely necessary to add, that the rank now fixed by His Majesty for the Bombay Marine relatively with the Royal Navy, carries with it the privilege of relative rank with His Majesty's and the Company's troops in India."

The following is the Order of His Majesty George IV., referred to above:—

"At the Court of St. James, the 30th of June, 1827. Present, the King's Most Excellent Majesty in Council.

"Whereas, there was this day read at the Board a Memorial from His Royal Highness the Lord High Admiral, dated the 12th of June instant, in the words following, viz.:—

"Whereas, in consequence of a communication with the Chairman and Deputy-Chairman of the East India Company, I am of opinion it may be expedient to confer on the officers of the Bombay Marine, within the limits of the East India Company's Charter, the privilege of taking rank agreeably to their several degrees with the officers of the Royal Navy, but under the condition, that all officers of any rank in the Royal Navy, shall have precedence of all the officers of the Bombay Marine of the same rank, and that the officers of neither Service shall have any command whatsoever over the ships, officers, and men of the other Service, unless under special orders to that effect from the respective Governments. I beg leave, therefore, most humbly to submit to Your Majesty, whether Your Majesty will not be most graciously pleased, by your Order in Council, to confer upon, and to grant to, the officers of the Bombay Marine the said relative rank and precedence, in conformity with the foregoing proposition.

"His Majesty, having taken the said Memorial into consideration, was pleased, by and with the advice of his Privy Council, to approve thereof, and to order, as it is hereby ordered, that the officers of the Bombay Marine, within the limits of the East India Company's Charter, do take rank agreeably to their several degrees with officers of the Royal Navy, under the restrictions and upon the conditions proposed in the said Memorial; and His Royal Highness the Lord High Admiral is to give the necessary directions herein accordingly."

The following is a copy of the warrant of the Duke of Clarence, dated the 12th of June, 1827, permitting the ships of the Bombay Marine to wear the Union Jack and pennant:—
"By His Royal Highness the Lord High Admiral of the United Kingdom of Great Britain and Ireland, &c., &c. Whereas I have deemed it expedient that the ships of the Bombay Marine shall be granted the privilege of wearing, in addition to the Red Ensign which all ships belonging to His Majesty's subjects should legally wear, the Union Jack and a long pennant, having St. George's Cross on a white field in the upper part next the mast, with a red fly; I do, therefore, by virtue of the power invested in me, hereby warrant and authorise the Union Jack and pennant above described, being worn on board the ships of the Bombay Marine accordingly."

As by the new regulations it was decided that a captain of the Royal Navy should be placed at the head of the Service, in November, 1827, Captain Sir Charles Malcolm, C.B.*—a brother of Admiral Sir Pulteney Malcolm and General Sir John Malcolm, who had been sworn in at Bombay as Governor of that Presidency, on the 1st of November in that year—was appointed to the post of Superintendent by the Court of Directors. On this occasion, the "Times" stated that H.R.H. the Duke of Clarence, the Lord High Admiral, had declared his intention not to interfere in the choice of an officer, declaring that "it would be unhandsome and might be invidious in him to meddle with the patronage that belongs to the Court." In making this appointment, the Court decided to confer on the then Superintendent of the Bombay Marine, a pension of £800 per annum, although

* Sir Charles Malcolm was one of three brothers, known as "the three knights of Ribblesdale." The family seat is Burnfoot, near Langholm, where is a statue of Sir John Malcolm. The representative of the family is now Mr. W. E. Malcolm, who resides on the property close to the house where the brothers were born. Sir Charles had seen considerable service in the great war, and was present, in his brother's ship, at the cutting out of vessels at Manilla in 1798. He was knighted in 1826, by Lord Wellesley, when Lord-Lieutenant of Ireland, and was now forty-five years of age.

that gentleman had served but little over eighteen months, and might have been employed in another capacity—the post of Master-Attendant at Madras, with equal emoluments and less work, being just at that time vacant; the excuse of age could not be pleaded, as eighteen months make little difference in a man's capacity for work, but the Court wanted the Madras post for another protégé. Accordingly, at their meeting of the 5th of December, 1827, the Court granted Captain Buchanan a pension of £800 a year, as compensation for the loss of the emoluments attaching to his office, and the resolution conferring this retiring allowance, mentions that his retirement and the appointment of Sir Charles Malcolm, were made "in consequence of the grant by His Majesty of defined rank to the officers of the Bombay Marine, and in reference to the intention to subject that corps to Naval discipline."

The proposed pension was strongly opposed by Captain Maxfield, who was seconded in his opposition by Mr. Hume and others; and it was pertinently asked why Captain Buchanan's services—he being comparatively a young man, fifty-four or fifty-five—were not utilised in some other office, as happened in the case of Mr. Anderson, a former incumbent. Finally, Colonel the Hon. Leicester Stanhope wound up the debate, by emphatically declaring that the "whole proceeding was a job, and nothing but a job." Nevertheless, the Court carried their resolution by a majority of thirty-eight to twelve: but independent public opinion was against them, and when the grant came up for confirmation on the 19th of March, 1828, upon a question by General Thornton, the Hon. H. Lindsay, the Chairman, agreed to add to the resolution the words, "so long as Captain Buchanan shall be out of employment."

Sir Charles Malcolm was sworn in at the India House on the 6th of February, 1828, and entered upon his duties at Bombay* in the following month of June, when the new system came into operation. The commodore, master-attendant, and two senior captains, quitted the active list on their pensions of £800 a year, others left the Service, and some died, so that by the close of the year the reduction was complete, and there were no supernumeraries. By an order of the Governor in Council, dated the "18th of October, 1828," it was directed

* Sir Charles Malcolm sailed from Gravesend in the 'Duchess of Athol,' Captain Daniels, which anchored in Bombay harbour on the 1st of June, 1828, without touching at any place. Among the thirty passengers were the following midshipmen, called "volunteers," for the Bombay Marine:—A. H. Gordon, W. Jardine, C. D. Campbell, G. Quanbrough, Tweedell, and E. W. S. Daniell. Also J. Thacker, M. W. Lynch, and Richard Walker, who were proceeding to join the Pilot Service, but were transferred to the Bombay Marine. Mr. Tweedell was drowned within a few weeks of joining the Service, having, it was supposed, fallen overboard in his sleep out of a gun-port where he was last seen sitting to cool himself. Mr. Thacker also died on board the 'Benares' shortly after joining the Service, from the effects of the climate of the Persian Gulf.

that the Superintendent should have the rank of major-general, with "all the honours due to the rank."

Sir Charles Malcolm entered upon his duties under the happiest auspices. His brother, Sir John Malcolm, was Governor, and, without exception, the officers of the Service were favourably inclined towards him, and were gratified that an officer of the British Navy of his name and distinction should be placed at their head. Sir Charles was a kind-hearted man, with abilities far above the average, and he was a gentleman in every sense of the word; he also vigorously prosecuted the surveys which were inaugurated by the enlightened policy of the late Governor, Mr. Mountstuart Elphinstone. He took a warm interest in the welfare of the young officers, sought to elevate the moral tone among them, and stopped the allowance of ship's grog they hitherto received, substituting wine instead. Though his motive—a desire to prevent drunkenness—was laudable, he insisted on the youngsters having wine, and, moreover, buying it at a particular firm and at a fixed price. This wine system ceased in 1832. Equally arbitrary, though well-intentioned, was his choosing the agents to whom the midshipmen should entrust their savings, with the unfortunate result that the house failed in 1838; had he restricted his interference to the circular letter he issued to the commanding officers, recommending the midshipmen to their care, and advising the latter to deposit their savings in an agency, instead of spending them, he would have shown more discretion. On the whole, however, it may be said that his public conduct, like his private character, was always blameless, and that he was a good administrator and wise Superintendent.

One of the first acts of Sir Charles Malcolm was to improve the discipline of the Service, which had deteriorated, owing to the anomalous position occupied by the officers, and the want of a code of laws, by which the will of the Governor and Superintendent were paramount. Thus, in former years, though a Court of Inquiry was held, it was not at all unusual for the verdict of the Court, which acted more as a jury, to be set aside by Government, who would decide and punish as seemed to them best. Mr. Elphinstone, on becoming acquainted with this system, provided a remedy, so far as lay in his power, by creating a penal code from the Naval articles of war, and the officers comprising the Court not only found a verdict, but pronounced judgment, the Government only exercising an approving power, and in no case after was that power employed except on the side of mercy. This system, introduced in 1825, had just begun to be felt and appreciated, and Mr. Elphinstone had made strong appeals to the Court to procure martial law for the Service, when he quitted the country and gave place to the new Governor, Sir John Malcolm. At length martial law was conceded to the Service, but it came under a "questionable guise," and with certain anomalous provisions as to convening courts-martial which are inexplicable, and appear to be contrary to the dictates of common sense.

In order that their Marine might be placed under the same provisions as to martial law which were applicable to their Army, the Court of Directors decided upon the extraordinary course of forming the service into a Marine Corps, and giving the officers military as well as naval commissions; accordingly, early in 1829, the Service underwent another, and the most singular, but not the last, of its numerous metamorphoses. The following is the order in question:—

"Bombay Castle, April 3, 1829.

"The following extract of a letter from the Hon. the Court of Directors in the Marine and Forest Department, dated the 10th of September, 1828, together with the resolution of Council in the same department of the 24th ult., are published in General Orders:—

"Para. 2. We have the satisfaction to acquaint you, in reference to the expectation expressed in our despatch, dated 31st of October, 1827, Paragraphs 6 and 7, that an Act has recently been passed for extending to the Bombay Marine the provisions of the 4 Geo. IV. cap. 18, being the law which regulates the Company's Army.

"Para. 3. Six copies of the Act accompany this despatch; and in order that the Corps may have the benefit of it without delay, we desire that you will forthwith embody its officers into a regiment, to be called the Marine Corps, under the command of the Superintendent, with the rank of Major-General, in which corps you will invite the petty officers and seamen to enlist.

"Para. 4. The military commissions of the officers are to be of the ranks to which they are respectively entitled, under our orders dated the 1st of August, 1798, which fixed the rank the officers of the Marine were to enjoy respectively with the officers of the Army, and the dates of the Military commissions are to correspond with those of the Marine commissions.

"Para. 5. You will cause it to be distinctly understood by the Superintendent and all the officers under his command, that the Marine officers are not, in virtue of their military commissions, to exercise any interference, nor to possess any claim or right to any advantages which may be exclusively enjoyed by the Army, nor to receive any addition whatever to their allowances.

"Para. 6. That there may be no misunderstanding regarding the nature of the commission, we have caused a form to be prepared by our law officers, which is forwarded in the packet for your guidance.

"Para. 7. We further desire that no fees be taken upon the commissions to be so granted to the officers of the Bombay Marine, as officers of our Army.

"Para. 8. You will observe that the Act of 4 Geo. IV., by the provisions of which the Marine will hereafter be governed, requires a larger number of officers to constitute courts-martial, than it will be practicable to collect from the limited number of officers belonging to the Marine; the deficiency must in every case be supplied from among officers of the Army, who are not to derive any pecuniary advantage from the performance of that service. You will at the same time perceive, by the Act 4 Geo. IV., cap. 81, sec. 30, that the appointment of courts-martial must, in all cases, be in the officers commanding His Majesty's forces."

"Minutes, March 24, 1829.

"In pursuance of the foregoing instructions, the Hon. the Governor in Council is pleased to direct that the officers of the Bombay Marine be forthwith embodied into a regiment, to be called the Marine Corps, under the orders of the Superintendent of Marine, with the rank of Major-General, into which corps the Governor in Council is pleased to authorise the Superintendent of the Marine to invite the petty officers and seamen to enlist."

By this anomalous transformation, the Service became neither "fish, flesh, nor fowl;" neither an Army, nor a Navy, nor even a corps of Marines.

None of the officers had ever cause to complain of the provision by which military officers—in the event of a paucity of officers of their own Service—served on their courts-martial. But the most extraordinary part in this arrangement was, that the Superintendent, or Major-General, at the head of the new "Marine Corps," as it is styled in all orders, had neither power to convene a court-martial of any description, or to approve or disapprove of the proceedings of any court; so that in cases of insubordination in warrant, or petty officers and seamen, he was obliged to adopt the humiliating course, of applying to the Commander-in-chief of the Bombay Army to convene a General Court-martial. Thus we find that on the 2nd of November, 1829, a court-martial, presided over by Captain R. Morgan, of the Marine, was convened at Bombay, to inquire into certain charges for "insubordinate and disrespectful conduct" on the part of Lieutenant W. Bowater, of the Hon. Company's ship 'Elphinstone,' preferred against him by his commanding officer, Captain F. W. Greer and that the sentence of the Court, which was dismissal from the service, was confirmed by the Commander-in-chief of the Bombay Army, Lieutenant-General Sir Sydney Beckwith, K.C.B. The same system was in vogue until, in 1847, the Superintendent was transformed into a Commander-in-chief, and hoisted his broad pennant in Bombay harbour as a first-class commodore. Scarcely had the measures of 1828 for the increased efficiency of the Service, as a war marine, been inaugurated under the fostering care of a distinguished officer of the Royal Navy, than their utility was seriously impaired by a development which affected both the discipline and status of the Service. This step was the enactment by Government, in August, 1829, of rules and regulations, whereby the Service was transformed from a Marine established for purely war purposes into one of a hybrid character. A regular packet service was to be established, and the Company's steamers were to run at stated intervals between Bombay and Cosseir, carrying passengers who were to pay 1,200 rupees for the passage either way. " Passengers taking servants with them were to pay in addition, 150 rupees for a European, and 75 for a native." The charges for overland postage from Bombay, were to be as follow:— " If the letter or packet weighs not more than one rupee, four rupees. If it weighs more than one rupee, but not more than two rupees, eight rupees. Ditto more than two rupees, but not more than three rupees, twelve rupees; and so forth, four rupees for each additional rupee weight up to twelve rupees, beyond which weight no packet will be allowed." As a rupee weighs about three-quarters of an ounce, this makes the charge twelve rupees, or 24s. per ounce.

During the year 1829,* orders were issued that the larger

* At this time of great changes and General Orders, the following order, dated Bombay Castle, 2nd February, 1829, addressed to Sir Charles Malcolm, Superintendent of Marine, should not be omitted a record in these pages :—
"It having been brought to the notice of the Hon. the Governor of Bombay Fort and Castle, that masters of country vessels, and merchant vessels, and ships within the harbour of Bombay, have hoisted pendants and assumed other distinctions, in contravention of H.M.'s proclamation bearing date 1st January, 1801, and the Governor of H.M.'s Forts and Castles being directed by H.M.'s said proclamation on their observing any ship or vessel belonging to any of H.M's subjects, wearing the flag commonly described as the Union Jack, or any of the distinction Jacks in the said proclamation mentioned, unless such ships or vessels shall have commission of letters of marque or reprisal, or shall be employed in H.M.'s service, to cause such flag, pendant, Jack, or ensign, to be seized, and to return the names of the master or commander of such ships and vessels wearing such flag, pendant, Jack, or ensign, contrary to H.M.'s aforesaid proclamation, unto the Judge of H.M.'s High Court of Admiralty, for the time being. The Hon. the Governor of the Fort and Castle of Bombay, is pleased thereby to enjoin you to carry the provisions of the above proclamation into effect, as far as regards the ships or vessels within the harbour of Bombay; and you are hereby directed to seize, or caused to be seized, by officers of the Marine Service of Bombay, such flag, pendant, Jack, or ensign worn by any ship or vessel within the harbour of Bombay, contrary to H.M.'s said proclamation, and to return to the Hon. the Governor the names of the respective masters of ships or vessels so offending."

ships were to be officered on a new system, in order that their efficiency might be increased, ships being formerly sent to sea with a paucity of officers. Each ship was to have one captain or commander, three lieutenants, one master (generally a *passed* midshipman), and five midshipmen; but, unhappily, in too many instances, this order was a dead letter, as the necessary complement of officers was not forthcoming. In the preceding year, a regular commissioned class of pursers was introduced, these officers entering the Service as captain's clerks; this was a much required innovation, for many of the pursers hitherto employed were not very reputable members of society. Under date of the 30th of September, 1828, the Governor of Bombay wrote home, proposing that pursers should have the same pensions as lieutenants, that is, £190 a-year after twenty-two years' service, and £125 after ten years; and the Court of Directors approved the proposal in their despatch of the 31st of December, 1829.*

But these officers had a just cause of complaint in the title they bore, of "purser" and "captain's clerk," and, though they repeatedly memorialised to be denominated "paymaster" and "assistant-paymaster," like their brethren in the Royal Navy, the Court refused the boon. It may be said that the grievance was a sentimental one, but, allowing this, as no extra pay was involved, the Court might have conceded the privilege which gratified a meritorious class of their servants, who fulfilled important public duties and were of sufficient numerical strength to be entitled to consideration, for we find that, at the date of abolition, in 1863, there were on the active list eleven pursers and twenty captain's clerks.

* In the year 1836 the following Orders of importance relating to pursers were issued by the Governor in Council.—

The first, dated the 28th of November, had reference to the General Order of the 11th of August, 1835, and prescribed the mode in which the detail|duties assigned in that Order to pursers were to be conducted.

The Second Order, bearing the same date, was the publication of the following letter from the Court of Directors, dated the 25th of May, regulating the passage-money and furlough allowance :—

"In your letter of the 27th of November, 1835, you transmit a memorial from Mr. Purser Joliff, praying, on behalf of the pursers of the Indian Navy, that the Court will grant them the same passage-money and allowance, on sick certificate to Europe, as have been granted to lieutenants, with whom the pursers rank, and you recommend the application to our favourable consideration. In our despatch of the 31st of December, 1829, para. 29, we approved of the principle and amount of the remuneration to the pursers, submitted for our sanction in your letter of the 30th of September, 1828. That principle recognised the grant of retiring pensions to pursers, upon the same scale, and under the same regulation as obtained in the cases of lieutenants of the Indian Navy. (Note—After twenty-two years £190 a-year; after ten and less than twenty-two years, £125.) You have assigned satisfactory reasons to induce us to extend the furlough regulations to the pursers, and we authorise you to admit them to the benefit of those regulations accordingly, classing them with lieutenants. (Note—Their pay will be £165 a-year.)

"We decline to grant passage-money to the officers of the Indian Navy."

On the 20th of April, 1829, an addition was made to the Service in the 'Tigris,' which was launched at Mazagon dockyard. The 'Tigris' was a ten-gun brig, of 258 tons, 93 feet in length "between perpendiculars," 26 feet extreme breadth, and with a height between decks of 5 feet 10 inches. She was commissioned by Commander John Sawyer, who, early in August, proceeded in her up the Persian Gulf, and succeeded in effecting the direct passage against the south-west monsoon in nineteen days, instead of sailing by the long, circuitous route known as the Southern passage,—" a feat of seamanship," writes Captain Tanner, " then known to have been often attempted but never before accomplished by any navigator."* For this service the Bombay Government expressed their high gratification, under date of the 27th of June, 1830.

In the same year as the 'Tigris' was launched, a small six-gun schooner, called the 'Royal Tiger,' was added to the Service, and, in 1832, a sister schooner named the 'Shannon.'

In November, 1827, the Hon. Company's schooner, 'Zephyr,' while cruising against pirates in the Straits of Singapore, fell in with twelve piratical proas, which she at once attacked, and succeeded in sinking or dispersing the whole of them. Two natives, belonging to a boat recaptured from the pirates, stated that an European boat's crew of six men had been murdered by these pirates a few days before the 'Zephyr' fell in with them. This statement was confirmed not long after, when the only survivor of these men, who had deserted in a boat from the ship 'Inglis,' in Singapore, was brought to Penang by a native chief, and stated that he had been wounded, but had managed to escape with his life by swimming ashore, the remaining five of the boat's crew being either speared or killed in the water while attempting to escape.

No event of any great importance occurred in 1828.† In

* Captain H. A. M. Drought puts forward a claim to the honour of having been the first to make the direct passage to the Gulf, on behalf of Lieutenant Haines. He writes to us:—" The 'Benares,' Lieutenant S. B. Haines, sailed from Bombay in the beginning of June, 1829, and made the direct passage to Muscat in eighteen and a-half or nineteen days. On her return spoke the 'Tigris,' Commander Sawyer. I was a midshipman on board the 'Benares' at the time."

† The following is the description of the uniform sanctioned in July, 1828, by the Governor in Council, for the officers of the Bombay Marine, so as to assimilate the dress more to that of the Royal Navy :—

"Captains above three years,—Coat, blue cloth, blue stand up collar, sloped in the front, one and a-half inch gold lace round the top and front, a slashed sleeve with blue three-pointed flap, three buttons and holes, blue cuff, one and a-half inch gold lace round the top and down the front edge, pocket flaps with three points, no buttons, skirts lined with white kerseymere, two rows of buttons in the front, ten buttons in each row, the two rows to be three inches apart, from the front of the button-hole to the centre of the button, the skirt to begin at one-sixth of the circumference from the front edge, two buttons on the hips and two on the bottom of the plaits, the button to be raised, gilt, one inch in diameter,

October, Commander John Betham, commanding the Hon. Company's ship 'Coote,' had a fracas with the Sheikh, or Governor, of Bushire, which might have entailed unpleasant consequences but for that officer's promptitude. Some of the crew of the Hon. Company's ship 'Amherst' having deserted, Commander Betham sent a messenger to the Governor, politely requesting him to order the surrender of the men; the Sheikh, however, beat the messenger, and seized the boat's crew, whom he threw into prison. Thereupon Commander Betham landed

inducted with a round rim, within the rim an anchor and a cable, above the anchor a lion rampant supporting the crown. Two gold naval epaulettes, with forty bullions each, on the strap an anchor and cable two inches long, above the anchor a lion rampant supporting the crown, one and a-half inches in height, embroidered. Waistcoat, single-breasted white kerseymere, jean or linen, nine buttons of half-inch diameter, same pattern as on coat. Trowsers, white jean or linen. When blue cloth trowsers are worn, to have gold lace down the outside seam, same width as on the coat, to be worn over short boots. Cravat or stock, black silk. Hat, cocked, the flap ten inches in the back, eight and a-half inches in the front, six inches at each corner, bound with black silk, two and a-half inches wide, showing one inch and a quarter on each side, with a black cockade, six inches wide, looped with four gold bullions three and a-half eighth of inches wide, the two centre twisted with a button of the same size and pattern as that on the coat, tassels with five gold and five blue bullions each. Sword and scabbard, blade the same as the regulation for the Infantry, with naval handle, substituting the lion for the crown. Belt, blue silk tape, two inches width, ornaments plain, gilt—clasp plain square, gilt with a circle wreath, within the wreath, the anchor and cable, with the lion above, of silver. Knot, blue and gold rope, twenty-three inches long, with blue and gold vellum basket-work head, and twelve gold bullions; a piece of the same sort of cord fourteen inches fixed to the hilt. Captains under three years.—The same as above, epaulettes without the anchor. Commanders.—The same, epaulettes plain. Lieutenants.—The same, with one inch gold lace, one epaulette on the right shoulder. Hat, loop, two gold bullions twisted. Pursers.—Same, without the lace on each side the collar, two anchors and cable across, saltierwise, embroidered in gold. Hat, cocked, the same, without the gold bullion, loop to be of black silk, twisted. Midshipmen.—Coat, blue cloth single-breasted (A.D.C. cut) ten buttons on the front, three on the cuff, four on the skirt, lining white silk, white piece of kerseymere on the collar, three quarters of an inch width, three inches long, twist button-hole, with a button. Waistcoat, trowsers, cravat or stock, cocked hat, and swords the same as lieutenants—dirks may be worn. Undress coat, blue cloth, plain round collar, with half turned lappels, ten buttons on each side, three buttons on the cuff, four on the skirt, lined with white silk, with the epaulettes of their rank. Undress.—Officers when on leave in the neighbourhood of their ships, or on such duty as in the opinion of their immediate commanding officer, or of the senior officer on the spot, do not require them to appear in the regular uniform above described, may wear in lieu thereof, a short blue single-breasted great-coat, plain stand up collar, sloped front and appropriate button. Gold lace strap, with or without the epaulettes. A round jacket, stand up collar, sloped front, may be worn of either cloth, silk, or camblet of the navy blue (no other colour), nine buttons on the breast, gold lace strap the same as on the coat, epaulettes are not to be worn, lining, white silk. A round blue cloth cape, with capi, band of gold naval lace, two inches width (except midshipmen), who are to wear a worked black silk band, the same pattern and breadth of the lace, crown of the cap twelve inches in diameter. Epaulettes, lace, buttons, and ornaments, naval pattern, having the lion instead of the crown. Patterns or drawings, of each of the before-mentioned articles of dress, are to be seen at the Superintendent's Office, and it is directed that no article shall, after this date, be made of any other pattern. Articles which have been already made of a different pattern to the foregoing, may, however, be worn till the 1st of June, 1829."

every available man from both ships to attack the town, which quickly brought the Governor to his senses; alarmed by this display of promptitude, the prisoners were given up, and an ample apology was afforded.

This officer was arraigned before a court-martial in January, 1829, on charges preferred against him by Sir Charles Malcolm, for disobedience of orders, " in not having taken on board his ship three months' supply of biscuits, pursuant to a verbal order given him by the Superintendent in or about the end of July, 1828." Other charges were for taking on board only one month's supply; for asserting in an official letter, that the biscuit was " such abominable trash, that he could not expect the ship's company would eat it;" and for subjecting the Government to unnecessary expense, by purchasing two months' supply of biscuit elsewhere, with " the intention of deriving a private and dishonourable advantage." The Court found Commander Betham guilty of all the charges, except as to the dishonourable intent, and acting under the "penal articles established by Government," martial law not being granted until the following April, they recommended that he should be dismissed the Service, though they expressed a hope that he would receive " favourable consideration" from the Governor, owing to extenuating circumstances, and "his long and meritorious services." Sir John Malcolm, however, confirmed the sentence, but recommended the Court of Directors to grant him the pension of his rank. Commander Betham, who was an able writer, and had interest in Leadenhall Street, memorialised the Court of Directors against this decision, on the ground that five out of the seven members constituting the court-martial, were his juniors, and succeeded in procuring a reversal of the sentence. The decision of the Court inflicted a heavy blow on the authority of Sir C. Malcolm, but the constitution of the court-martial was certainly irregular and unjustifiable, as there was no want of military officers in Bombay to constitute a Court. The case created much controversy at the time at Bombay, and many hard words were bandied about, and uncharitable motives imputed among those chiefly concerned.

During the year 1829, the 'Hastings' and 'Antelope' were employed at Penang, in the suppression of piracy; the ' Ternate,' and several gunboats, in Bengal, and other vessels in surveys and the general routine of the Service.

It would seem as if the Bombay Marine was regarded as a *corpus vile*, on which experiments could be made, without limit, and so little regard had the authorities for its efficiency, which, of course, could not but be impaired by the frequent changes made in its constitution, that we find the new Governor-General, Lord William Bentinck, who had made reductions in every branch of the public service, directing the Finance Committee assembled at Calcutta, under the presidency of the late Right Hon. Holt Mackenzie, to inquire into the whole question of the Service. The Committee's labours extended over the years 1829-30, but it would appear, by the eighth paragraph, that they only examined two officers of the Marine, and their ignorance of the duties and utility of the Service is glaringly displayed, in the seventh paragraph, in which they state, " neither are we aware of any service for a ship-of-war in the Red Sea." Considering that the exports from the Bombay Presidency to ports in the Red Sea, were of the annual value of twenty-four lacs, and that the trade from Calcutta and other places was of an equal value, this is an extraordinary statement to have emanated from a committee of financial experts, who, possibly, could not be held to apprize at their correct value the prestige attaching to the presence of ships-of-war in that important inland sea. A summary of British relations with Mocha and other places in that part of the East, which we shall lay before the reader later on, will show the fallacy of the conclusions at which the Committee arrived, and upon which the Government wisely declined to act. Those conclusions were the abolition of the Service and the employment of a squadron of Royal Navy ships, although they were fain to allow in their third paragraph, on the showing of Admiral Gage, that the Navy could not do the work at less expense. Perhaps the key to the hostility that always existed in the Supreme Government towards the Service, may be ascribed to the fact that a minor Presidency enjoyed the honour of having the Indian Marine under its orders, though this was due to the circumstance that Bombay harbour was the only port which could be employed as the head-quarters of a naval service, and so it had remained since the Company first acquired the island by cession from the Crown. We will now take leave of this Report of the Finance Committee, as its essential recommendations were not acted upon, and Sir John Malcolm refuted its mis-statements and lame deductions in an able Minute.

In the year 1830, Captain Thomas Tanner—whose name has so frequently appeared in these pages as one of the most eminent and scientific officers in the Service, one who was as ready with his sword as with the " pen of a ready writer," or the sextant of a practised observer—laid the Service under a debt of gratitude to him, by founding, under the auspices of the Bombay Government and the Court of Directors, the Pension Fund, for giving annuities to officers' widows and children. For the trouble he incurred, and the skill he displayed, in drawing up the tables and making the arrangements, the officers of the Service presented Captain Tanner with a piece of plate of the value of one hundred guineas.

The year 1830 was memorable for two events—a trial for

piracy of a distinguished officer of the Service, who was made a scapegoat for the sins of others, and the first voyage of a steam vessel from Bombay to Suez, under the command of an officer of the Bombay Marine, an event, the importance of which can scarcely be exaggerated.

Commander John Croft Hawkins, arraigned on the extraordinary charge of piracy, was one of the most able officers of the Service, and had repeatedly received the thanks of Government; indeed, it was his zeal for the public welfare, in carrying out the orders conveyed to him by his official superiors, that induced this high-minded officer to commit an act which was technically of an illegal character, and fraught with most grave consequences to himself. The case created a great stir, and aroused strong feelings of partisanship throughout the press of India. Our duty, as the historian of the Indian Navy, is simply to chronicle facts, and to lay before the public, letters, hitherto unpublished, from which they will be able to form an opinion as to whether, on the one hand, Commander Hawkins exceeded or mistook his instructions, and on the other, whether his official superior, the Superintendent of the Indian Navy, abandoned to his fate an officer who, with rare loyalty, sacrificed himself in order to screen his chief.

Commander Hawkins was posted to the 'Clive' in April, 1829, and, in the following month, proceeded to the Persian Gulf, whence, after visiting Muscat and Bassadore, he returned to Bombay in September. As at this time there was a deficiency of European seamen in the ships of the Indian Navy, and the supply of lascars, hitherto shipped at Gogo, in the Gulf of Cambay, failed to fill the vacancies, Commander Hawkins was selected to proceed to the coast of Africa, for the purpose of shipping black boys, who were to be trained for the Service. The 'Clive' at this time carried an armament of sixteen 32-pounder carronades, and two long nines, with a crew of ninety-four Europeans, including three lieutenants, master, purser, surgeon, six midshipmen, captain's clerk, gunner, boatswain, carpenter, apothecary, the rest being petty officers and seamen; she had in addition a detachment of Marines, and one boat's crew of native seamen, shipped for the purpose of saving the Europeans from exposure to the sun, in the generally unhealthy climate experienced on the coast of Africa.

The following were the sailing instructions addressed to Commander Hawkins, signed by Sir Charles Malcolm, and dated the 4th of January, 1830:—

"Sir,

"It having been deemed expedient by this Government, as per enclosed copy of a letter from Mr. Secretary Willoughby, under date of the 10th of December, 1829, to raise seamen for the Honourable Company's Marine from the coast of Africa, and the adjacent Islands, you are (after having performed the instructions contained in my letter, No. 20,* of 1830, of this date) directed to proceed to the coast of Africa and islands in its vicinity for that purpose, and adopt the best means of entering for the Service as many able-bodied lads as you can, in age from twelve to eighteen, free from all disease and bodily infirmity, and of that compact symmetry best calculated for seamen.

"You are authorised to employ (on reasonable terms) an agent to assist you in this duty, and to give these lads the bounty agreeable to the regulations, or a reasonable sum more should that not be thought a sufficient inducement. You will rate these lads as marine boys on board your ship, and pay the strictest attention to their morals, and the speedy attainment of their profession; and you will perform this duty with the greatest delicacy and consideration, and avoid as much as possible giving umbrage to the Mahometan Government, as upon the success of this measure, the efficiency of the Hon. Company's Marine Service will very materially depend.

"You will keep a private journal of every transaction that occurs during your cruise, which will be forwarded to me on your return, with a report on what you consider the best means of engaging these lads for the Service. You will visit the island of Socotra going and coming, and report on the anchorage at both sides of the island, with such facilities or advantages as it may possess for forming a coal depot on it for the steam navigation between this and the Red Sea.

"You are to engage no more than sixty of the boys, as that number will be sufficient for the present.

"You are to instruct Lieutenant Peters (in conjunction with the master) to make a useful survey of such ports and harbours at Socotra and other places, as may be useful to navigation in general, but to detain the vessel as little as possible from the more important duties on which you are engaged.

"I have the honour to be, &c."

During the course of the subsequent trial and the recriminations attendant thereupon, frequent reference was made to other secret instructions, and though none were produced at the trial or made public at a later date, yet from a reference by Commander Hawkins, in a letter addressed to Sir Pulteney Malcolm, to "a private disclosure," and a correspondence "shown to some friends in the heat of the moment," and also from a passage in a letter from Captain Cogan, Assistant-Superintendent, writing on behalf of Sir Charles Malcolm, where there is a suspicious reference to "documents emanating in any way from you to his prejudice,"—all these together justify the

* This letter directed him to proceed to Bassadore, in the Persian Gulf, and land stores and provisions for the use of the squadron.

inference that something more passed between the two officers than ever came to light.

Commander Hawkins sailed from Bombay on the 5th of January, 1830, and, on the 20th, anchored in Bassadore roads, where he found the Hon. Company's sloop-of-war 'Ternate,' Commodore W. S. Collinson; on the 23rd, having delivered the stores for the use of the Persian Gulf squadron, he proceeded to Muscat, where he arrived on the 30th. The 'Clive' remained at Muscat till the 6th of February, Commander Hawkins having, during the interval, laid in with difficulty, owing to the absence of the Imaum at Zanzibar and the unsettled state of the country, a supply of wood and water, and also apprehended three miscreants, belonging to a brig, who had confessed to the murder of the captain and officers. On the 6th of February Commander Hawkins[*] sailed from Muscat, and, on the 13th, sighted the island of Socotra, of which he made a cursory examination, landing at some places, including Gollanseer; having gained the information necessary to enable him to report upon the facilities possessed by the island as a coal depot for the projected line of steamers, Commander Hawkins bore up for the southward on the 25th of February. On the 3rd of March he arrived at Brava, and, on the 8th, anchored at Zanzibar, where he received a warm welcome from the Imaum, whose capital of Muscat he had saved from destruction by fire in the previous year, for which service his Highness had presented him with a handsome sword.

Commander Hawkins sailed from Zanzibar on the 19th of March, and, after visiting various places on the coast in furtherance of his mission to ship boys for the Service, he proceeded to Lindey,† where he anchored on the 28th of April. At Lindey he found a whaler, the master of which applied to him for assistance to keep his unruly crew in subjection. Com-

---

[*] Commander Hawkins says in his Journal of the cruise of the ' Olive ' :—
"On the 8th, having run close in abreast of Cape Jube, shoaled very suddenly from twenty fathoms to seven, and then five, then steering to the southward, had regular soundings from five to eight and twelve fathoms soft mud. At two p.m. saw the wreck of the ' Oscar,' (a) hauled in for it, lowered a quarter-boat, and sent an officer to examine; but the surf was too high to venture on board, from which it may be concluded the coast is always difficult to land on, we having been on it at different periods, and each time a high surf, although the weather was quite moderate in the offing. We observed from the ship, as well as from the boat, that the Arabs had pulled down her topsails, ripped off her upper deck, and completely stripped her of copper. They had huts erected close to the spot, and sheds under which they were building boats, supplied with necessaries from the wreck."

† Lindey River, in lat. 9^0 59' S., long, 39^0 45' E., is about 22½ leagues to the north-west of Cape Delgado; it is a fine river, with several villages on its banks, the principal of which, called Lindey, lies, with its fort, on the west bank.

(a) The 'Oscar' was wrecked near Ras Roos, between Ras Jibsh (called above Ras Jube) and Ras El Khabbeh, on the Arabian coast.

mander Hawkins exchanged one of his seamen for two of the mutineers, and, on the 4th of May, one of the whaler's men having again been insubordinate, he sent for the master and crew on board the 'Clive,' and punished the delinquent with three dozen lashes. Being short of supplies, on the 5th of May, Commander Hawkins proceeded on shore with a party of men, when the natives, who have the reputation of being very treacherous, attacked him. Commander Hawkins exhibited great forbearance, but, at length, when he was himself wounded, and the safety of his men was imperilled, he fired and drove the enemy off, when he succeeded in reaching the boats without loss.* On the 8th of May Commander Hawkins proceeded with

---

* The following extracts from Commander Hawkins's Journal detail his proceedings between the 8th of March and 5th of May :—

"On the 7th of March passed Pemba Island; on the 8th, at sunset, saw Zanzibar Island from the deck, and at two a.m. anchored in twenty-eight fathoms, off the north end of the island. At sunrise weighed, and at four p.m. saw the shipping at anchor off the Imaum's palace—saluted him with nineteen guns. On the 10th of March, paid his Highness a visit of ceremony, and was received with great honour and kindness, his Highness insisting on supplying all the wants of the 'Clive' during our stay. On my return on board, a boat-load of bullocks, goats, vegetables, and fruit, in the greatest abundance, were sent, and during our stay we were frequently supplied in the same liberal manner, and also with wood, and offer of water. Nothing could exceed the attention of his Highness; I could only assure him of the pleasure it would give me to represent his friendly conduct to the notice of my superiors.

"March 19th. Having completed our wood and water, weighed and proceeded to the southward—his Highness having kindly ordered us a pilot, who, on quitting, could not be prevailed on to accept of remuneration. On the evening of the 20th, shoaled suddenly on a small bank, from twenty to four and a-half fathoms rocks and sand; bore up to the westward, and immediately deepened to thirty fathoms.

"On the 7th of April came-to in twelve fathoms, under the lee of Isle Langa, immediately to windward of Cape Delgado, having experienced very strong currents and fresh winds from the southward—some days gaining a few miles, on others losing as many. Found here several large boats, two with horses, belonging to the Imaum of Muscat; they had been here some days, having quitted Zanzibar before our arrival, and, in consequence of the strength of the current could not proceed. The Naquedar having represented that he had nothing to hold water, having his tank stove, I directed him to be supplied with two sixty-gallon casks. I remained at this anchorage till after the springs, in hopes the wind would shift or become more moderate. On the 17th of April weighed, and worked southward, but found, on standing in shore, we had lost ground; would have got into our old anchorage, but could not fetch it, and to avoid the loss we should sustain were we to remain under weigh all night, anchored off a reef projecting from Cape Delgado in six and a half fathoms. At daylight on the 12th weighed, and again attempted to work to the southward, but finding we lost ground considerably, bore up, and anchored in Hambreezy Bay, (a) in eleven fathoms. Remained here till the 27th April, it blowing hard from the southward in squalls, with a great deal of heavy rain; filled up with water collected from rain in pools opposite the ship, opened a communication with the natives up a salt water river, from whom we obtained supplies of fowls and pumpkins in quantities sufficient for the ship's company. There were in the river great numbers of the hippopotamus; but although we wounded some, were not fortunate enough to kill any. At this place I was visited by an Arab Sheik, named Nasser bin Easser, to

---

(a) Probably off Mizimbary Island on the north side of Rovuma Bay.

the object of his cruise, and, between that date and the 30th of May, shipped thirty negro boys. He says in his journal :—
"May 8th. Entered for the Service seven boys, rated them whom I communicated the object of my visit. He informed me that he was the Imaum's vakeel from Keelwar to Ibo, where the Portuguese Government commences. He assured me he would do all in his power to assist me—that at Lindey, where he resides, he could insure me all that I required, and that he would return after two or three days. In this he failed; but as I saw not the least chance of getting to Mozambique or Madagascar, I was fain to endeavour to obtain the object of the voyage at Lindey, in prosecution of which I bore up for that river on the 27th of April, having procured a pilot at Mickindamy,(*a*) where we anchored for the night.

"Next day, the 28th, arrived at Lindey; found here a whaler, the 'Ann Elizabeth,' nineteen months from London. Commenced filling with wood and water, of both of which there is abundance. May the 1st, the master of the whaler having applied to me for assistance, his crew being unruly, two having deserted, and two refusing duty, sent an officer on board to harangue them into better order, and to threaten punishment (having apprehended the two deserters through the Sheikh, who had returned from Toonga, and sent them on board). On this day received a visit from the Sheikh and his brother, Mahommed bin Easser; saluted him with three guns. On conferring with him, he agreed to do all in his power towards our wishes. May the 2nd, found it necessary from the stay we were likely to make at this place to put the crew on half allowance of biscuits and flour. May the 3rd, having another application from the master of the 'Ann Elizabeth,' as also from two men—foreigners—to do them justice, the master came on board with them. He wished to discharge them (they volunteering for the 'Clive'), they refusing their duty, and using threatening language; but the ship being short of hands, he could not spare them, though apprehensive of bad conduct at sea. I agreed, much to his satisfaction, to let him have one volunteer from the 'Clive' in lieu of the malcontents, and this, I trust, will meet with the approbation of Sir Charles Malcolm, Superintendent, as I had nothing in view but the furtherance of the Service. May the 4th, one of the original deserters having again deserted and given himself up on board the 'Clive,' I sent for the master and crew of the 'Ann Elizabeth,' and punished the deserter with three dozen lashes for frequent desertions and refusing his duty.

"May the 5th. I went with a party of officers and men, in the launch, with the intention of opening a communication with the natives for supplies, and to explore the country. We had arms in the boat; having proceeded twelve or fifteen miles up the river, we remained for the night in the boat, and in the morning landed, having but four muskets, and the men with cutlasses, not wishing to alarm them by appearing in force. After walking about four or five miles to the top of a hill, we came to some of the habitations of the natives, but the most of them fled at our approach. On our talking with an old man, and explaining what we wanted, he appeared satisfied, and conducted myself and some of the men to the top of the hill where the country was well cultivated and populous; but meeting with a party of twelve or fifteen men, they threatened us from some high groves, into which they had immediately jumped on seeing us, that they would let fly their arrows if we did not go away; and as no explanation would satisfy them—they being concealed from our view—we retired, but on joining the rest of the party, that had remained half-way down the hill, at the first houses, we were attacked by between forty and fifty with bows and arrows, spears, and large stones, which latter they threw with unerring aim. I was extremely loath to fire at these poor creatures until I was struck several times with stones, all the time begging them to desist, and that we would go away. But finding they gathered boldness on my clemency, and having received a severe contusion on the head, I fired, and brought their chief down. On this they again rushed up to the rear of our party, and nothing but pointing the

―――――――――――――――――――――――――――

(*a*) Probably Mizimbary.

on the books, Marine Boys. A report came to Lindey that in our late affray one of their chiefs and another man was killed, as also one wounded. I begged the Sheikh to send and explain to them, as also to say if the wounded man was sent to Lindey the surgeon would attend him. May 10th, sent the agent in the launch with a native crew down the coast, to Keelwar to expedite the service. May 11th, entered one boy; May 14th, entered one ditto; May 15th, entered five ditto; May 18th, entered thirteen ditto; May 22nd, entered three. May 23rd, having no less than twenty on the sick list, myself and two officers in the number, with sudden fever, weighed and dropped down the river. May 24th, having procured pilots for Keelwar,* weighed and stood down the coast; at five p.m. anchored off Kiswara River in sixteen fathoms. Daylight, weighed and stood along the coast for Keelwar; when we anchored for the night, sent an officer on shore to inquire for the launch—she had quitted the same evening for Zanzibar. Daylight weighed, and stood out between the reefs which perfectly enclose the harbour. There is here abundance of provisions and fresh water, and the best anchorage on the coast, having plenty of water and good holding ground. The Sheikh was very civil, and said he had not been visited by an English ship since Captain Owen had been in the 'Leeven.' On the 29th of May arrived at Zanzibar. The Governor, Seyyid Hamed, and the young prince, son of the Imaum of Muscat, behaved very kindly, proffering services, and sending off a large supply of fruit, goats and vegetables, which were very acceptable to the sick. On the 30th the launch returned with four volunteer boys.

"On the 7th of July left Zanzibar; on this day buried two seamen, and on the 10th of June, to my very great regret, Mr. Gilbert, purser, died, a young man I highly respected for his amiable, gentlemanly manners, and complete professional knowledge. June 11th, buried three seamen, and in the evening died one of the most promising young midshipmen in the Service, Mr. Thomas Pitcher. Still had on the sick-list nineteen Europeans and six natives, and, unfortunately, in consequence of the great number seized with this fever, our medicines ran out. Making prodigious way, in consequence of

---

muskets kept them from attacking us with their spears. I had the mortification to find that only two of the four muskets would go off. I was obliged to fire again, several of us being knocked down and nearly stunned by the stones. I received another blow on the head, which obliged me to order another shot to be fired, which wounded a man. I imagine that perceiving the certain effects of our fire, and that we did not fire often, but were retreating to the boat, after seeing us close to it, letting off their arrows and throwing stones at us the whole way, and that our strength was not diminished—for we had observed their counting us—they retired. I had much satisfaction in retreating without loss, and could have wished our opponents equally fortunate, although everything was done to avoid the contest. Two of our little boys were interpreters and behaved faithfully."

* Also known as Quiloa.

a current of eighty miles a day. June 14th, in consequence of a strong easterly set out of the Red Sea, found ourselves considerably to leeward of the west-end of Socotra island, although I had steered to make Abdul-Coory; bore up to round the East Cape. Here we experienced a very high sea and strong monsoon. In hauling round the east end of Socotra found the reef and bank to extend much further to the southward and eastward, and very dangerous; I should judge from ten to twelve miles—Horsburgh says two leagues. June 15th, it blowing at times in such heavy gusts as to endanger the masts, splitting our sails and carrying away our gear, so that we were fairly blown off. Remained till eight a.m. on the 16th, when bore up, finding we had lost ground. At this time I was suffering from a severe relapse of fever; 17th, the first-lieutenant reported that a quantity of provisions were spoiled by a leak in the store-room. Sold the effects of the deceased officers and seamen; 18th, buried a seaman. On the 22nd of June, at 7.40, anchored off the Apollo Pier."

Commander Hawkins was utterly ignorant of having committed any illegality in shipping the negro boys—the only point in which he had exceeded his instructious arising from some of the number being of a more tender age than was authorised; had the money been paid to them in the shape of bounty, even though it had been afterwards handed over to their masters, he would have evaded the law—but such double-dealing was foreign to his nature. The children under twelve cried to accompany the other boys, and, being of a kind-hearted disposition, he engaged them also. He says in a narrative of the subsequent proceedings, addressed to Admiral Sir Pulteney Malcolm, the brother of Sir Charles, and written while in England, towards the end of 1831:—

"On the 26th of July, 1830, I was first made acquainted with the intended prosecution of the Supreme Court, by Sir John Malcom, while on a visit to him at Dapoolie. His brother, Sir Charles, had a long conversation with me, and I told him I would go down and try and put a stop to it, by affording any explanation the Grand Jury might require, at the same time giving him to understand he might rely on my prudence. On my arrival at Bombay, the case had proceeded too far, and as it was believed by the opposing faction,* that I had received some

---

* By this term is meant the party friendly to Sir John Peter Grant, who had entered upon a course of hostility towards Sir John Malcolm and his Council, which became more virulent when, by the death of his colleagues, he became the sole occupant of the Judicial Bench at Bombay. Subsequently, by a notification of the Bombay Government of the 13th of September, 1830, Sir John P. Grant was "recalled from Bombay by an order of the King in Council to answer complaints made against him by the Hon. the East India Company." We will not refer to the merits of this unhappy dispute further than to say that it was generally understood in Bombay that it was in order to embarass the Governor of Bombay

orders, my lawyers and friends strongly urged me to criminate the Superintendent. I invariably answered that I had received no other orders but such as had already appeared before the Court. I had not been more than twenty-four hours in Bombay before warrants were out for my apprehension, no less than seventeen true bills having been found. I was obliged to go over to Angria's territory, which put me to great expense, especially as I had at the same time to advance large sums to lawyers, and retaining fees to my counsel; however, as I thought that the less communication I had with Sir C. Malcolm the better, I drew what was necessary from my agents, under the firm persuasion I should be repaid. About the middle of August Captain Cogan* came over to see me on the part of Sir Charles Malcolm, and having ascertained the course I meant to pursue, he acquainted me that he was authorised to assure me of the support of Sir Charles Malcolm and the Government collectively and individually; that I should not suffer in any way, that I should have the 'Clive's' pay, and even added, that I should not be removed from the Island of Bombay, if convicted. I replied I would undergo anything rather than criminate Sir Charles; that he was a sailor, one of our own cloth, and would not deceive me. I will here add that my feelings of regard for Sir Charles determined me to adopt this course rather than divulge to a soul how far he was to blame. His brother, Sir John Malcolm, at Dapoolie, had a good deal confounded me by asking me questions as to how the boys were procured, but even to him I did not choose to reveal the truth. I need not inform you how long I was kept in suspense and anxiety awaiting my trial to commence, or to what inconvenience I was put in pecuniary matters, for although I thought Sir Charles might have put so much confidence in me as to offer me assistance, I was persuaded his only reason for not doing so were apprehensions lest I should incautiously mention the source from whence I derived support. In October I arrived at the Mahableshwar Hills, where I received a letter from my lawyer (marked A) to which I replied (see Letter B). These were

and his brother, the Superintendent, that Commander Hawkins was prosecuted. Sir John Grant was soon afterwards appointed one of the judges of the Supreme Court at Calcutta.

* The Assistant-Superintendent.

(A) "Mr. Morley appears to be satisfied that your only resource is to satisfy the jury that you acted in obedience to what you believed were the orders and intentions of Sir Charles Malcolm and the Government, and that you should lay before him (Morley) your secret report, and all official orders from Sir Charles Malcolm, or by his directions all accounts of monies you expended to procure the boys, your report of those expenses, all private conversations between you or any person acting under you respecting the manner of procuring the boys, and the names of the witnesses who were present at such conversations. Morley also further advises you to prove Sir Charles Malcolm's seeing the boys, the date of the 'Clive's' arrival in Bombay, and that no censure was passed on you. All the foregoing advice I received from Morley yesterday, and I send it you almost

shown privately to Sir John Malcolm, and I heard he was much pleased with my determination, and the reply I had written. During all this period, from the end of July, I was without pay, and latterly without any resources whatever; but I was averse to make any direct application for pecuniary assistance to Sir Charles, as I expected to have everything finally settled to my satisfaction."

Commander Hawkins was arraigned before the Supreme Court presided over by Sir John Awdry, on Monday, the 28th of March, 1831, and the trial lasted on that and the two following days. The Counsel for the prosecution were the Advocate-General, Mr. Le Mesurier, and Mr. H. Morgan; and for the defence, Mr. Morley and Mr. Hill. Eighteen true bills were found by the Grand Jury, and the indictment contained four counts. The crime charged in the first count was, for conveying from a certain place off the island of Zanzibar to Bombay, certain persons—here were given the Christian names and surnames of the thirty boys Commander Hawkins received on board the 'Clive' at Lindey, and the four brought to Zanzibar in the launch, of which total, one died and one was drowned on the voyage. The second count was the same as the first, only stating that the names of the persons conveyed were unknown. The third and fourth counts were the same respectively, as the first and second, only stating that the conveying was *for the purpose of the persons conveyed being treated as slaves.*

Commander Hawkins pleaded "not guilty," and, the day being far advanced, the Court was adjourned until Tuesday, when the trial commenced before a dense throng of excited and attentive spectators. After the opening address by the Advocate-General, Lieutenant C. Sharp, first of the 'Clive,'

---

verbatim, that you may consider it and write me by return of post, that I may lose no time in communicating the tenour of your reply to him."

(B) "Of course Mr. Morley gives me such advice as he thinks best, and in so far does his duty by me, for which I return him my thanks; but I must now inform him, through you, that if he cannot defend my cause strictly on the grounds of my own innocence, without throwing even the shadow of blame on either Sir Charles Malcolm or Government, he cannot do me the slightest service, and I would sooner plead my own cause, with your assistance in the examination of witnesses. I have no secret instructions, nor have I any private conversation to swear to, or to have evidence. I must stand on the plain merits of the case, which never as yet have been *fairly* inquired into. Morley beforehand appears to have decided my case as gone, without such aid as I have not to produce.

"Sir Charles did not see the boys till after the disturbance in the Supreme Court, at least if he did, not in my presence. Neither did I receive approval or censure, except in taking some of the boys younger than I was ordered. I cannot for a moment admit that I believed I was obeying the orders of Government in doing that of which I am accused, and which accusation I repel and defy. The only report I sent him was a private journal, which was before the Grand Jury, and which merely mentioned I had engaged thirty-four at a bounty of thirty-five and a-half dollars each."

was called as the first witness, and stated as follows in the course of his cross-examination :—" The boys were not treated like lascars, but their treatment was precisely the same as that of English boys. The Superintendent of the Indian Navy came on board and inspected the boys on his return from Poona about a month after our arrival in port. Captain Cogan, assistant to the Superintendent, came on board two or three days after our arrival. Nothing more was said to the boys than what I said, that if they came on board for five years, for which period the bounty was usually given, they might afterwards return to their own country if they wished."

The Advocate-General admitted the good treatment received by the boys. Mr. Fraser, the surgeon, and Mr. Peters, second lieutenant of the 'Clive,' were also examined as to the facts of the shipment of the boys, and the latter deposed that some thousands of dollars were taken on board at Muscat, and disbursed at Lindey. The native syrang who brought the four boys in the launch to Zanzibar, deposed that "they came willingly," and that they used to leave the boat and return without compulsion. Mr. Willoughby, the Secretary to Government, and Captain Cogan, were examined as to the correspondence between the Governor and the Superintendent; and the sailing instructions issued by the latter to Commander Hawkins were produced. Several of the African boys were then examined, and it was elicited from two of them that they received no money, but were ordered by their masters to proceed on board the 'Clive.' They had, however, received pay regularly since. This closed the case for the prosecution, and, on the following morning, the prisoner, we are told, "stood up in the bar, and in a loud, firm, and almost triumphant tone of voice, read his address," which, as was afterwards announced by his Counsel, " was written by him without any communication with them, and that they were quite ignorant of its purport, till they heard it delivered in Court."

His object in addressing the Court himself, and not, in the regular course, leaving the conduct of his case in the hands of his Counsel, was due, as is shown in his correspondence with his solicitors, to a fear lest his Counsel might compromise Sir Charles Malcolm or Government. For the same reason the Captain of the 'Clive' declined to call witnesses on his behalf. Such self-sacrificing loyalty is as rare as it is noble.

On the conclusion of Commander Hawkins' defence, which is too lengthy for insertion here, some evidence was produced as to the humane character he had always borne, and then the judge charged the jury, who gave a general verdict of "guilty," but with a strong recommendation to mercy in consideration of the peculiar circumstances in which he had been placed.

In reply to a question put to them by the judge, the jury stated their belief to be (1), that the boys came willingly on board the 'Clive;' (2), that they were obtained by purchase.

On the 12th of April, the judge passed sentence on Commander Hawkins, who was condemned to "be transported to the east coast of New South Wales for the term of seven years."

On the following day the negro boys, brought by the 'Clive' from Zanzibar, were taken before the Senior Magistrate of Police, and informed, through an interpreter, that they were to consider themselves at perfect liberty to go where they pleased. They were given to understand that the usual bounty would be paid them if they would return on board ship; but that, in case they wished to go back to their parents, care would be taken to send them to the country from whence they came. A large number selected to return to the 'Clive.'

Commander Hawkins continues as follows his narrative of the transactions, addressed to Sir Pulteney Malcolm:—

"You will see by the paragraph in my letter, of the 24th of April, 1831, to your brother (marked E) that I was reduced to great difficulties. After my conviction your brother visited me in gaol, and told me he hoped I should get my back pay, and my memorial complied with; but he gave me no promise of support in case it should fail. However, I thought it best to

(E) "My dear Sir,—

"The Government have decided I am only to get lieutenant's pay to the time of conviction, and then no pay whatever, with the exception of the month and seventeen days I held command of the 'Clive.' I have deferred writing till this has been settled, as I daresay you have to determine what will lay in your power to do for me in a pecuniary point. I may now look on myself as a ruined man, as the sum I have to receive is only adequate to pay a most pressing debt due to Mr. West, taken up by him when I was last in Bombay to save me from gaol, and which at that time I was assured I should have it in my power to pay from my expected promised wages of the 'Clive.' As for myself, I have nothing, but am in debt at least a couple of thousand rupees, in addition to the sum due to Mr. West, which I feel bound in honour to pay, he having become bail for me. Having placed implicit confidence in getting the whole of my arrears, as in command of the 'Clive,' I gave him to understand he should have the money to a *certainty*. There is no provision made for me while I remain at New South Wales, and it may be for seven years. This is exactly my situation at present. I need scarcely remind you how frequently you have promised to support me in the event of this unfortunate affair taking an adverse turn. It is hardly, I trust, necessary to put you in mind how frequently it was pledged my pecuniary affairs should not suffer. At that time they did not in the least operate in swaying me to adopt the honourable course I may safely assert I pursued. Although you know how far it was in my power to have proceeded in a different way, you know how well I have preserved silence even to my most intimate connections, and also how I have taken the load off your shoulders and put it on my own. I therefore look to you for that support you are bound in honour to grant me. Trusting in which I remain, &c.

wait till the Government had decided. The officers of the Indian Navy had come to the determination of making up a purse, regarding with commiseration my undeserved and distressing situation. This was confined to the Service at my own particular request, and was to be strictly regarded as a loan; but how shall I paint to you, Sir, my indignation, when I found your brother proffered a smaller sum than brother officers of my own rank enjoying not a fifth of his income. I restrained as much as possible my feelings, and then wrote the last letter (marked E).

" He was then on the Mahableshwar Hills, apparently to be out of the way, which circumstance was warmly animadverted on.

"In consequence of the letter* (marked F) he came down to Bombay, and entered into the agreement (marked H), but on the 15th of May, the day the 'Coote' sailed from Bombay, I had my drafts on Messrs. Forbes (into whose hands the money was to be paid), returned dishonoured, and to this day I am left in uncertainty whether the agreement has been fulfilled or no, nor do I care; for I do assure you it was not the money I required so much, although I was in such poverty as to require small loans from my acquaintance—it was from your brother's want of gratitude, and I told Captain Cogan, who was the mediator between us, that if the Court of Directors reimbursed my expenses, every farthing of his money should be returned.†
I also conditioned that I should make a private disclosure to my friends of the whole circumstances. I concealed nothing from him; I acquainted him who had seen the correspondence, as I had shown it to some friends in the heat of the moment, for, although I had kept every little thing a most profound

---

* This letter is couched in strong language, which, however regrettable, is not to be wondered at under the circumstances; it is too long for insertion.

(H) The following is the agreement referred to :—

"May 4th, 1831.

" My dear Hawkins,—

" Respecting the assurances made by Sir Charles Malcolm through me, viz., that you would not suffer in a pecuniary point of view, let your trial take whatever turn it might,—he now wishes to fulfil the pledge as far as lies in his power, and has determined that you shall have five thousand (5,000) rupees, paid by him to your agent now, and after the expiration of two years from this date, should you not be pardoned, he will remit you annually the sum of three hundred pounds (£300) sterling during the remainder of your sentence. In coming, however, to this arrangement for your benefit, he wishes you to clearly understand that in the event of any documents emanating in any way from you to his prejudice, he will of course consider this arrangement void.

"Yours sincerely, R. COGAN.

" Approved, Charles Malcolm."

† Sir Pulteney Malcolm said in his reply of the 26th of December, 1831 :—
"I consider it out of the question your repaying to Sir Charles the money which he gave you."

secret from every living soul during all my suspense and anxiety, I was at last tried beyond my patience."

Lord Clare,* the Governor of Bombay, tried to induce Commander Hawkins to remain in prison at Bombay until the King's pleasure was known as to the granting of a free pardon for which application would be made to His Majesty; his lordship sent an aide-de-camp to the unfortunate officer, and, after the latter had decided to undergo the sentence, he sent him again with a message that he should sail in a ship of the Indian Navy, and that a brother officer should be his gaoler, with instructions to treat him as an officer and a gentleman. Accordingly, Commander Hawkins sailed for Sydney on May 15th, 1831, on board the Hon. Company's sloop-of-war 'Coote,' Commander Pepper. The 'Coote' touched at Madras, where Commanders Pepper and Hawkins were fêted for three days by the community, and thence she proceeded to Batavia, where Commander Pepper found despatches of importance awaiting to be forwarded by the first ship to England. The Captain of the 'Coote' said to his charge, "here's a glorious opportunity to go straight to England," and, though Commander Hawkins was averse from this course, fearing that it might be considered as done at his instance, and thus prejudice his case, the former took upon himself the responsibility, and, accordingly, to England the 'Coote' proceeded. Commander Pepper had with him a copy of the petition to the King sent by Lord Clare, and signed largely by officers of the Indian Navy and of the Military and Civil services, and also the letter from his lordship to the Governor of Sydney, requesting that Commander Hawkins might be treated as a gentleman, and with these he hastened up to London. Lord Melville, to whom he showed them, immediately proceeded to Windsor, and obtained an interview with the King, who promised to grant Commander Hawkins a free pardon,† and graciously commanded that he should appear at the next levee.

Commander Hawkins obeyed the royal mandate, when His Majesty received him with great kindness, and conversed with him. The Directors asked him how soon he would be ready to return to his duty, upon which he replied that he should memorialize the Hon. Court for six months' leave to recruit his health, which had suffered in the prison at Bombay, and then he should again memorialize for a further period of six months, and also for his full pay as captain of the 'Clive' for the time of his confinement and passage to England. And he succeeded in obtaining these demands, thus showing that his masters

---

* This nobleman was the schoolfellow and friend of Lord Byron, regarding whom he wrote the exquisite stanzas in his "Hours of Idleness."

† This document was addressed to the Governor-General, and was dated from St. James's Palace, on the 9th of November, 1831.

exonerated him from any charge beyond error of judgment.*
In their letter of the 29th of February, 1832, to the Bombay
Government, stating that the Royal warrant for Commander
Hawkins' pardon had been issued, they reviewed the conduct
of the parties concerned, in the following terms :—

"Para. 6. On a review of the whole transaction, we do not
think that the conduct of Mr. Hawkins ought to be confounded
with those which form the ordinary course of a traffic in slaves.
He was not actuated by mercenary motives, but, as it would
appear, by a genuine though misguided zeal for the performance of a public service for which he had been specially
selected. Relying on the obvious tenor of his instructions, he
engaged in the enterprise, anxious only to prove himself worthy
of the trust reposed in him.

"Para. 7. The apology for his conduct, which he attempted
to derive from the benefit conferred on the youths whom he
purchased, cannot be admitted on any social principle of
morality, nor on any enlightened view of the public interest;
yet it may be acknowledged that it was sufficiently plausible to
perplex and mislead the judgment of a man probably not much
practised in the consideration of such questions, and taught by
his professional duty to execute rather than to canvass the
order of his superiors.

"Para. 8. At the same time, he is entitled to the benefit of
the fact, that, in the fulfilment of those orders, he conducted
himself with all the humanity compatible with the nature of
the mission.

"Para. 9. There is undoubtedly a distinction to be drawn
between wilful delinquency, and an honest, though heedless,
zeal for the public service.

* The following is a copy of a letter addressed by Sir John Malcolm to the father of Commander Hawkins, dated the 1st of October, 1831 :—
"I have received your letter of the 18th September. I can give you the most satisfactory account of your son, Captain Hawkins ; he is an excellent man and a good officer ; he erred from the want of a knowledge it was hardly possible for him to possess, and in the zealous and honourable performance of his duty vio-lated the *words* of a statute which was never meant—I must believe—to apply to a case where the decided object was to liberate, not enslave—and to improve and elevate degraded and miserable creatures, and in all probability to render them, after the service of a few years, the happy instruments of benefiting others of their countrymen. Of the causes which have led to the disappointment of these expectations I will not speak, but merely inform you that your son has been pronounced by the judge to leave the bar without a stain upon his character. The Government have given him his full pay and allowance, and propose to request his pardon ; for this also there are petitions from the inhabitants of Bombay and from his own Service. It will, I make no doubt, be granted the moment the Government despatch is received, for the Court of Directors see his conduct in the same favourable light. In short, my dear Sir, however distressing the sentence, the whole affair has given your son an opportunity of displaying a character that will, I trust, promote his future success in life—in my brother, Sir Charles Malcolm, and myself he will ever find warm friends.
"P.S.—You are at perfect liberty to communicate to any person the sentiments expressed in this letter."

"Para. 10. It is not without much concern that we advance to the further observation, that the immediate employers of Mr. Hawkins cannot justly be acquitted of a grave responsibility for the measures, for the execution of which he was involved. Mr. Hawkins was despatched to enlist young men at those ports which are notoriously the great emporia of the slave trade on the eastern coast of Africa. It ought not to have escaped those who so despached him, that there were dangers peculiarly incident to such an expedition, unless conducted with the utmost circumspection; it was obvious that such enlistments would not be distinguished by the natives from their ordinary traffic, and that the two things would become identical in reality as well as appearance.

"Para. 11. In the instructions addressed to Mr. Hawkins, he was desired to perform the duty with delicacy and consideration, and to avoid as much as possible giving umbrage to the Mahomedan governments; but not a solitary caution was given to him to be careful to observe the slave laws, which the due execution of his orders placed him in the most imminent danger of violating.

"Para. 12. These observations illustrate the imprudence with which the Government engaged in such an enterprise, and the negligence with which they omitted to take any precaution against so probable a result as that which followed."

By letter of the 15th June, 1832, the Court presented Commander Hawkins with £400 "to meet the expenses of his return to Bombay," and on his arrival there, Lord Clare, to whom he had addressed a petition, granted him relief, subject to the confirmation of the Court, to the extent of 9,287 rupees, to reimburse the legal expenses incurred on his trial. In November, Lord Glenelg, President of the Board of Control, requested him to proceed overland to India with important despatches on the prospect of a Dutch War. Commander Hawkins consented with alacrity, and immediately started in the depth of winter, by way of Vienna, Constantinople, and thence through Armenia, by Tabreez, Teheran, Shiraz, and Bushire, to Bombay. Writing from Tabreez on the 26th of December, 1832, he says: "I arrived here yesterday in time for Christmas dinner, and go away to-morrow. I have accomplished my journey quicker than it has ever been done before; crossing the mountains with the thermometer 34 deg. below zero, and the icicles for the last fortnight hanging in thick clusters to my upper-lip, the breath from my nostrils freezing as quickly as emitted. My boots were not taken off for a fortnight, and the Tartar dead beat half way, and unable to proceed with me. Numerous adventures which I have no time to describe; in all thirty-seven days on the road from England, and I had reached half way in six days from Constantinople, and in that period only laid down to sleep twice." He arrived in safety at Bombay after surmounting many difficulties and undergoing great hardships; and Lord Glenelg spoke in eulogistic terms of his "talents, public spirit and energy." Soon after his arrival, Commander Hawkins was reappointed to the command of his old ship, the 'Clive.'

The second event of importance in the year 1830, already alluded to, Commander Hawkins' trial being the other, was the inauguration of steam communication between Bombay and Suez, for which an officer of the Service is entitled to the chief credit. In 1829, there was launched at Bombay, for the Marine, a small steam vessel of 411 tons, called the 'Hugh Lindsay,' which had a long and serviceable life of thirty years. The 'Hugh Lindsay' was not by any means the first steamer that had appeared in the East, but she was unquestionably the first to demonstrate the feasibility of the overland route, so far as the most important link – the sea passage between India and Suez – was concerned, and for this her captain, the late Commander J. H. Wilson, is entitled to high honour. The first proposal we have been able to ferret out, for the establishment of overland steam communication, was in the year 1822, and we read the following in a letter which appears in the "Asiatic Journal" of May in that year : – " A Captain Johnston has suggested a plan for opening an intercourse with India by means of steam vessels, and the details he has furnished respecting it are so specious, and all the obstacles in the way of its success are so admirably disposed of, that it is astonishing the projector has not been deluged with contributions or subscriptions already, and that a steamer is not unloading in the port of Suez." What would the writer, who wrote this half in irony, say of the steamers now at the port of Suez and the other ports throughout the East! Lieutenant Johnston, R.N., was commissioned to proceed to Calcutta, with the object of forming a company for working one or more vessels on the Suez line, but the scheme fell through. A proposal was then made to run steamers by the old route of the Cape of Good Hope, and funds were obtained by subscription in order to carry out an experiment.

In our account of the Burmese war, mention has frequently been made of the 'Diana,' which—under charge of her engineer, Mr. Anderson—was of such essential service throughout the operations on the Irrawaddy. In January and February, 1827, other steamers, the 'Irrawaddy' and 'Ganges,' were launched at Kyd's dockyard, at the same slips that gave birth to the 'Diana;' and a year or two later, a third, called the 'Hooghly,' was added to the Company's service. But these were all river steamers, and the first sea-going vessel propelled by steam, was the 'Enterprise,' built in England, by means of the subscription raised to further Lieutenant Johnston's views. She was a ship of 500 tons, and having two sixty-horse power engines, with copper boilers extending across the ship, and seven furnaces, each seven feet in length. The 'Enterprise,' under command of Lieutenant Johnston, carrying only passengers, and having 300 tons of coals on board, sailed from Falmouth on the 16th of August, and arrived at Calcutta on the 9th of December, having performed the voyage under sail and steam combined, in one hundred and fifteen days ; a performance that was considered by no means satisfactory by the mercantile community, at a time when the splendid ships of the Company frequently covered the same distance in ninety days. On her arrival, Government purchased the 'Enterprise' for £40,000, and she was sent to Rangoon. She was of considerable use in towing ships between Calcutta and the newly-acquired provinces, and, on one occasion, carried the Governor-General; ultimately she was brought round to Bombay by Lieutenant Denton, of the Service, and was to have made the experimental voyage to Suez, but circumstances prevented it.

The origination of the overland route between India and England, though generally credited to the late Lieutenant Thomas Waghorn, is claimed with equal justice by others. Mr. R. W. Crawford has stated, that it was due "to the community of Bombay, as represented by the Bombay Steam Committee," though, whoever first suggested the scheme, it is a matter of fact that the honour of being the first to demonstrate the possibility of communication by steam between Suez and India, is justly due to an officer of the Service.

Mr. Waghorn, to whose energy and perseverance the establishment of the overland route through Europe and Egypt, is chiefly due, was born at Chatham in the year 1800. At the age of twelve he entered the Navy, and, before he was seventeen, had passed his examination in navigation for a lieutenancy, being the youngest midshipman who had ever done so. He did not receive a commission, however, and, on being paid off in 1817, sailed as third mate of a merchant ship bound for Calcutta. He returned to England, but, in 1819, was appointed to the Bengal pilot service. In 1824 he volunteered for service in Burmah, and for two and a-half years commanded the Hon. Company's cutter 'Matchless,' which formed a part of the squadron under the orders of Commodore Hayes. Mr. Waghorn's name first appears in connection with steam navigation between England and India, at Calcutta, in 1828, when he advocated a renewed attempt by the Cape route, that made by Lieutenant Johnston, in the 'Enterprise,' not being regarded as very favourable. A public meeting was held at Calcutta on the 30th of July, 1828, at which Sir John Hayes gave his warm support to Mr. Waghorn, who published a letter* in the Calcutta papers, detailing his plan for a line of steamers by the Cape. In consequence of the support he received from the subscribers to the Steam Navigation Fund, Mr. Waghorn left Calcutta for England in October, 1828, accredited by the Committee to persons of official standing at Madras, Ceylon, Mauritius, the Cape, and St. Helena.

On his arrival in England, in April, 1829, Mr. Waghorn endeavoured to stir up popular feeling in favour of his project in the principal cities of the United Kingdom, but without much success. It is true, the mercantile classes connected with India and some high public functionaries, applauded his scheme, but the Post Office authorities were doggedly opposed to steam navigation, and the Court of Directors, with the exception of Mr. Loch, were lukewarm in the cause, though they voted the necessary steam machinery for one vessel. After waiting for several months, in October, 1829, he was summoned by Lord Ellenborough, then President of the Board of Control, to proceed to India, through Egypt, with important despatches for Sir John Malcolm, and also to report upon the practicability of the navigation of the Red Sea. Accordingly, Mr. Waghorn left London on the 28th of October, 1829, crossed from Dover to Boulogne, and reached Trieste, *viâ* Paris and Milan, on the 8th of November, a distance of 1,242 miles, performed in

---

* In this letter Mr. Waghorn says:—"I propose that the vessel for the intended experiment should be in size about 280 tons, in model like the 'Monarch' and 'Sovereign,' Norway packets, which are remarkable for the three qualities most essential in every vessel, but above all in a steam one intended for a very long voyage, viz.: stability, buoyancy, and fast sailing. The masts of the vessel I would have fitted after the fashion of the row boats in this river, to strike when required. The yards to be very square, but of the lightest possible dimensions, so as to spread a large quantity of sail, without too much top weight; even the canvas itself is to be of the lightest quality consistent with strength. The rigging of the masts and yards to be so fitted that in four hours they may be got up or down. The vessel to be schooner rigged on a wind, and square when before it. In order that the whole space of the vessel under hatches may be available for fuel, and more particularly the shifting of it below as ballast, her only accommodation for officers and crew, will be a roundhouse on deck. With regard to fuel, she would stow 40 tons in tanks, and the rest, about 200 tons in all, in bulk. The tanks, when emptied, will be filled with salt water, for ballast; by a peculiar contrivance, already arranged with the engineers at home, this water could run into the vessel, and be thrown out again by the engine in light winds, so as to increase speed, and fill again at pleasure. The plan of sailing will be, according to my present views, as follows:—"The vessel will start from Falmouth with the mails for Madeira, Cape, and Isle of France, touching at Trincomalee and Madras, in the south-west monsoon, to land letters, but, if possible, without anchoring. At Calcutta she would remain only ten days for the mails, calling at Madras on her way back, and remaining a few hours there." He elsewhere states the capital required to commence the undertaking at £12,000, exclusive of the cost of the engines. Taking the number of letters brought out by the 'Undaunted' frigate as a criterion, he calculates that the receipt, for letters only, out and home, would amount to £4,137. He says: "I believe the public are already convinced that I may succeed in the passage I contemplate, viz., out and home, from Falmouth to Calcutta, in six months (stoppages included), calling at

eleven days. He was nineteen days going by sea, in a sailing vessel, from Trieste to Alexandria, a distance of 1,265 miles; proceeding to Rosetta by donkeys, 33 miles; to Cairo, 150 miles, by boat; and to Suez, 72 miles, by camel. He arrived there on the 8th of December, being nearly twelve days on the journey, including a delay of three days. He waited at Suez, in expectation of the steamer 'Enterprise,' which he understood had sailed from Bombay to that port, and left, on the 9th, in a native boat, for Cosseir, which he reached on the 13th, and, after a further delay of five days, proceeded to Jiddah (a distance of 660 miles from Suez) which he reached on the 23rd of December. The time occupied in getting to Jiddah from London, was thus forty-one days sixteen hours. At Jiddah he learned that the 'Enterprise' was not expected, and, after waiting eighteen days, he again sailed for Bombay in a native baghalah, but the same day was taken out of her by the Hon. Company's cruiser 'Thetis,' which arrived at Bombay on the 21st of March, 1830.

Another rival worker in this field was Mr. J. W. Taylor, agent of some capitalists in London, and brother of Major Taylor, Resident at Bagdad, who set off from London on the 21st of October, 1829, seven days before Mr. Waghorn, reached Calais the same day, and Marseilles on the 28th. He sailed for Malta the same day, and arrived at Alexandria on the 8th

---

Madeira, Cape, Isle of France, Trincomalee, and Madras, carrying mails to and from these places when the season of the year will permit, both out and home. I would at these places, except Madras, have my depots for coals." At the meeting of the 30th of July, 1828, Mr. J. A. Prinsep was of opinion that Mr. Waghorn could not succeed in bringing the vessel out in less than eighty-five days, and that letters might be conveyed from Calcutta to Cosseir in twenty-nine days, thence to Cairo in two days, and thence to London in twenty-three days, going the entire distance in fifty-four days, instead of eighty-five days. Captain Johnston made a few remarks on the circumstances which he considered tended to the partial failure of the 'Enterprise' in making her voyage to India within the specified time. He spoke of Mr. Waghorn, from personal knowledge, as an individual of persevering industry and unshaken self-possession in the hour of danger; and he said he considered that if any person could carry the projected speculation into effect, it would be Mr. Waghorn. He said he felt convinced that a vessel of proper dimensions would make the voyage in seventy days; but, at the same time, he was certain she would never pay the necessary expenses. He differed from Mr. Waghorn on one part of his plan. The machinery for a vessel of 280 tons would be 100 tons, and if he added 180 tons of coal to make up her registered tonnage, she would be too heavy at leaving port; he would, therefore, suggest to Mr. Waghorn the expediency of having another depot of coals, so that the vessel may at no time be too deeply laden, and he may be better able to ensure success. The meeting came to the resolution that "should no speculation promising greater or equal success be undertaken before the 10th of February, 1829, the unappropriated fund for the encouragement of steam navigation shall, under proper security, be applied for the purpose of enabling Mr. Waghorn to carry his plan into execution." Mr. Waghorn stated that the support he had received and been promised did not make up the amount of the outlay (including £1,000 of his own); and that he was about to proceed to Madras, Isle of France, and the Cape, for further encouragement; but that, if he failed to raise the sum specified, he should not attempt the experiment.

of November, in eighteen days from London, earlier by seven days than Mr. Waghorn. He departed from Alexandria on the 28th of November, and reached Suez in nine days; that is, five days quicker than Mr. Waghorn performed the journey. The whole time actually consumed in travelling from London to Suez, was thus only twenty-seven days. He quitted Suez on the 9th of December, and also arrived at Bombay, in the 'Thetis,' on the 21st of March, performing the journey from London to Bombay (exclusive of stoppages) in forty-six days.

Mr. Taylor—who, unlike Mr. Waghorn, was a consistent supporter of the Red Sea route, in preference to that by the Cape, though his plan of combining steam tugs with sailing vessels was impracticable—left Bombay for England, viâ Bagdad, on the 2nd of May, 1830, in the Hon. Company's ship 'Amherst,' which conveyed him to Bussorah. Taking with him some packets of letters from India, he quitted Bagdad about September, 1830, being accompanied by some Englishmen, including Lieutenant Bowater, who had lately been dismissed from the Service for disobedience of orders. The intention was to survey the course of the Euphrates from Bir to Hillah, with a view to the establishment of steam navigation, and the party proceeded in safety as far as Mosul; but, within three marches after leaving it, they were attacked by a large body of Yezedis. At the first attack their guards fled, but the Englishmen stood their ground, and killed some of the robbers, who, exasperated at this loss, made a desperate onslaught, when Messrs. Taylor, Bowater, and Aspinall were slain, and the three remaining Englishmen succeeded with difficulty in escaping with their lives. Thus untimely fell the first projectors of the Euphrates Valley route of steam communication with the East, a line by which many competent persons, including Mr. W. P. Andrew, its veteran and able supporter, and Captain Felix Jones, of the Service, are of opinion railway communication is destined to be accomplished at no distant date.

Lord Wellesley, that greatest of Indian Viceroys, fully appreciated the advantages of speedy postal communication between England and India, and, so early as the last years of the eighteenth century, established a fortnightly communication between Bombay and Bussorah, by means of the cruisers of the Bombay Marine. From Bussorah, under the supervision of the Company's Resident, Arab carriers, mounted on dromedaries, kept up a regular communication with Aleppo, from whence Tartars—called, says Colonel Chesney, "life and death Tartars"—carried despatches to and from Constantinople. In 1837, Colonel Chesney, after making his successful descent of the Tigris and Euphrates in the little steamer 'Euphrates,' tried to induce the Indian Government to reopen this " dromedary dawk," with the increased advantage of a line of steamers to run between the two ports of Bussorah and Bombay; but he was before the age, and the Governor-General was as clearly behind it. Lord Auckland was not a Wellesley, and we are told by Chesney, "that he thought it advisable to postpone the opening of the overland route, and that he was not prepared to carry out his previous intention of placing steamers on the river Indus."

We find that in 1798, Lord Nelson* communicated the intelligence of his victory of the Nile to the Bombay Government, by the overland route, viâ Bagdad, the Company's cruiser 'Fly' bearing the officer he had despatched with the news, from Bussorah to Bombay. Some years after that date, the Red Sea route, viâ Cosseir, came into vogue, and a regular communication was established by the Company's cruisers between that port and Bombay, though despatches continued to be sent also to the Persian Gulf, as we find that the 'Ternate' arrived at Bombay on the 22nd of February, 1833, with overland despatches from Bussorah. By the Red Sea route many distinguished officers had journeyed to England, or joined their appointments in India, proceeding from Cosseir in the Company's cruisers. Among the number we may mention the Commander-in-chief at Bombay, Sir Miles Nightingall, who proceeded home by this route, in the 'Teignmouth,' in 1819, accompanied by his wife. In December of the same year the 'Prince of Wales' took a party to Cosseir, returning thence to Bombay early in March, 1820, with Captain Sadleir, who had been sent on a mission to Ibrahim Pasha, after the Expedition to the Persian Gulf against the Ras-ul-Khymah pirates in the preceding year. In 1825, Sir Hudson Lowe—Napoleon's custodian at St. Helena—proceeded to take up his appointment as Governor and Commander of the Forces in Ceylon, by the Cosseir route; and, in November of the same year, General Sir Charles Colville, Commander-in-chief at Bombay, returned to England as far as Cosseir in the 'Palinurus.' Sir John Malcolm had gone home by this route in December, 1821, in the 'Teignmouth,' the 'Antelope' having quitted Bombay in the preceding month with some more of his party and the despatches, which were regularly transmitted by Cosseir, the remainder of the route to Ghenna being made on camels, and thence to Alexandria by the Nile.

Mr. Mountstuart Elphinstone, in 1823, was the first to make a distinct official proposition for the establishment of steam communication between Bombay and England, viâ the Red

* The great Nelson always maintained friendly relations with the East India Company, and it is an interesting fact, of the truth of which we have been assured on high authority, that some years before this period, when the future victor of the Nile and Trafalgar was in embarrassed circumstances, he was a candidate for the appointment of Superintendent of the Bombay Marine.

Sea, and, in 1826, he renewed the proposal, but the Court were unwilling to act upon the suggestion. On relinquishing the Government to Sir John Malcolm, this far-seeing statesman proceeded to Cosseir in the 'Palinurus,' on the 15th of November, 1827, accompanied by a large party, including Mr. and Mrs. C. Lushington.* The first lady to undertake the overland route from England to India was Mrs. Elwood, wife of Lieutenant-Colonel Elwood, of the 3rd Bombay Native Infantry, who made the journey in 1825, and speaks of herself, in her highly interesting and graphic work,† as "the first and only female" who ventured upon that route.

As Mr. Waghorn himself states, it was not until 1826 that his attention was first turned to steam communication, and then, and for many years subsequently, he was an advocate of the Cape route; indeed, on the 17th of April, 1830, only four weeks after his arrival in Bombay by the Red Sea route, we find that, at a public meeting of the merchants and inhabitants, he still advocated the Cape route to Calcutta, in preference to that by the Red Sea, treating the latter merely as a *pis aller*, while his rival, Mr. Taylor, spoke strongly in favour of the Red Sea route. Proceeding to Calcutta, he was present at a meeting held on the 24th of June, at which Sir John Hayes again advocated his cause. On this occasion both Lieutenant Johnston and Mr. Waghorn spoke; the latter detailed his proceedings, and declared his intention to proceed to England, whence he would shortly return. Meanwhile an event had happened which perfectly demonstrated the advantages to be derived by the Red Sea route.

On the 20th of March, 1830, the day before Mr. Waghorn arrived at Bombay in the cruiser 'Thetis,' the Hon. Company's steamer, 'Hugh Lindsay,' sailed from Bombay on her great experimental voyage, commanded by Commander John Wilson. This officer was in command of the sloop-of-war, 'Coote,' a vessel of higher rate than the 'Hugh Lindsay,' and, though the distaste for the service was general, he volunteered to take command of the steamer then on the stocks, and fitted her out for sea. As he says in his pamphlet, "I was the staunch assertor that the Red Sea route was *the one* which must become, through the means of steam, the high road to India, and I was stimulated by a desire to be *the first steam navigator of the Red Sea*." The gallant officer performed the trip with signal success, and, when the disadvantages under which he laboured are taken into consideration, the achievement

---

* Mrs. Charles Lushington published an account of her journey to England *viâ* Mocha, Cosseir, Luxor and Thebes.

† *See* "Narrative of a Journey Overland from England by the Continent of Europe, Egypt, and the Red Sea, to India, including a Residence there, and Voyage Home, in the years 1825, 1826, 1827, and 1828." By Mrs. Colonel Elwood. Two vols. London, Colburn and Bentley, 1830.

may be regarded as one of the most remarkable on record. This will be readily conceded, when we consider the conditions of the experiment. The 'Hugh Lindsay' was a steamer of only 411 tons, with two eighty horse-power engines, built to carry five and a-half days' consumption of coal, and drawing eleven and a-half feet of water, while she was required to perform a voyage of 3,000 miles, of which 1,641 were across the Indian Ocean to the first coaling station at Aden. To enable her to effect this long flight, she took on board sufficient coal for eleven days, for which purpose more than two-thirds of the space abaft, intended for accommodation, and also half of the forehold, were filled with coals; this, together with stores and provisions for the voyage to Suez and back, no less a distance than 6,000 miles, increased her draught of water to thirteen and a-half feet, and it is certain her safety would have been seriously imperilled had she encountered bad weather. Previous to undertaking the voyage, a collier brig, laden with 600 tons of coal, under convoy of the 'Thetis,' had been despatched to the Red Sea, so that a supply was ready stored at Aden, Jiddah, and Suez. The experiment was a triumphant success; Aden was reached on the 31st of March, the whole distance having been covered *under steam alone*, and the 'Hugh Lindsay' arrived with only six hours' consumption of coal in her bunkers. Commander Wilson called at Mocha to deliver despatches and at Jiddah for coal, and arrived at Suez on the 22nd of April, having been thirty-two days and sixteen hours, including stoppages. From Suez he forwarded the despatches and the mail of three hundred and six letters, together with a despatch to the India House reporting his arrival, and enclosing a copy of his log, which was printed in the appendix to the evidence taken before the Parliamentary Committee of 1834.*

* After receiving voluminous evidence, the Committee of the House of Commons arrived at the following Resolutions on Steam Navigation in India :—
1. That a regular and expeditious communication with India by means of steam vessels is an object of great importance to Great Britain and to India.
2. That steam navigation between Bombay and Suez having, in five successive seasons, been brought to the test of experiment (the expense of which has been borne by the Indian Government exclusively), the practicability of an expeditious communication by that line during the north-east monsoon has been established.
3. That the experiment has not been tried during the south-west monsoon, but that it appears from the evidence before the Committee, that the communication may be carried on during eight months of the year, June, July, August, and September being excepted, or left for the results of further experience.
4. That the experiments which have been made, have been attended with very great expense, but that, from the evidence before the Committee, it appears that by proper arrangements the expense may be materially reduced; and, under that impression, it is expedient that measures should be immediately taken for the regular establishment of steam communication with India by the Red Sea.
5. That it be left to His Majesty's Government, in conjunction with the East India Company, to consider whether the communication should be in the first

On his return voyage Commander Wilson called at Cosseir, Jiddah, and Mocha, and reached Bombay on the 29th of May. It appears from the 'Hugh Lindsay's' log, that the voyage to Suez was accomplished in twenty-one days and eight hours, and the return to Bombay in nineteen days and fourteen hours. The total time occupied in the passage there and back was seventy days, but the preceding was the time she was *actually under steam*, during which she traversed 5,928 miles, being at the average rate of somewhat less than six miles an hour; a surprising result, when we consider that she was two feet deeper in the water than was intended by her builder, and consequently was much out of trim. For this achievement Commander Wilson received the thanks of the Bombay Government.

So far the credit of having shown, by practical demonstration, the feasibility of running steamers between Bombay and Suez,

instance from Bombay or from Calcutta, or according to the combined plan suggested by the Bengal Steam Committee.

6. That by whatever line the communication be established, the net charge of the Establishment should be divided equally between His Majesty's Government and the East India Company, including in that charge the expense of the land conveyance from the Euphrates on the one hand, and the Red Sea on the other to the Mediterranean.

7. That the steam navigation of the Persian Gulf has not been brought to the test of experiment; but that it appears from the evidence before the Committee, that it would be practicable between Bombay and Bussorah during every month of the year.

8. That the extension of the line of the Persian Gulf, by steam navigation on the river Euphrates, has not been brought to the test of experiment; but that it appears from the evidence before the Committee, that from the Persian Gulf to the town of Bir, which is nearer to the Mediterranean port of Scanderoon than Suez is to Alexandria, there would be no physical obstacles to the steam navigation of that river during at least eight months of the year; November, December, January, and February, being not absolutely excepted, but reserved for the results of further experience.

9. That there appear to be difficulties on the line of the Euphrates from the present state of the countries on that river, and particularly from the wandering Arab tribes, but those difficulties do not appear to be by any means such as cannot be surmounted, especially by negotiations with the Porte, Mehemet Ali, and the Chiefs of the principal fixed tribes; and that this route, besides having the prospect of being less expensive, presents so many other advantages, physical, commercial, and political, that it is eminently desirable that it should be brought to the test of a decisive experiment.

10. That the physical difficulties on the line of the Red Sea appearing to be confined to the months of June, July, August, and September, and those of the river Euphrates to the months of November, December, January, and February, the effective trial of both lines would open a certain communication with the Mediterranean in every month of the year, changing the line of steam on both sides according to the season.

11. That it be recommended to His Majesty's Government to extend the line of Malta packets to such ports in Egypt and Syria as will complete the communication between England and India.

12. That the expense of this experiment by the 'Euphrates' has been, by an estimate which the Committee has subjected to the examination of competent persons, stated at £20,000, which includes a liberal allowance for contingencies, and the Committee recommend that a grant of £20,000 be made by Parliament for trying that experiment with the least possible delay.

is due to Commander Wilson, but the experiment would, in all probability, have long borne no fruit as regards the establishment of the overland route, but for the unbounded energy of Mr. Waghorn. As soon as he became convinced of the superiority of the Suez route—which was not until some time after he left Calcutta, where it appears he still advocated the Cape route, notwithstanding Commander Wilson's successful voyage—he threw into his advocacy of the new line all the admirable energy and perseverance for which he was so conspicuous. Turning his attention to the speedy mail communication afforded by the overland route, he felt that nothing could compensate for the loss of time caused by the Cape voyage. Early in 1831, he resigned the Company's service, as he says in his pamphlet, "the better to further the object of steam navigation between England and India." He returned to Bombay on the 12th of July, 1833, and again proceeded to England, and, after giving evidence before a Parliamentary Committee, went out to Egypt in October, 1835, and, after many years of arduous labour, in which means and health were sacrificed, succeeded in establishing the overland communication through Egypt.*

* Mr. Waghorn proceeded to Egypt not only without official recommendations, but, as he says, "with a sort of official stigma upon his sanity." The Government officials pronounced the Red Sea unnavigable; the East India Company laid documents before Parliament, showing that the scheme was impracticable, because coals cost £20 a ton at Suez, and took fifteen months to get there. Waghorn soon removed this objection, by carrying coals on camels' backs to Suez at £4 3s. 6d. a ton. At the outset of his endeavours to carry his point, which occupied many weary years, his attention was directed to that extraordinary man, Mehemet Ali, whom, above all others, it was necessary to conciliate, as his will and pleasure were supreme in Egypt. Mr. Waghorn having entered the service of the Pasha, conciliated his esteem, and then, knowing that a regular traffic could not be carried on across the desert between Cairo and Suez without the permission of the Arab tribes, lived in their tents for three years, and induced them to exercise forbearance, and permit the passage through their midst, of that mysterious thing, the overland letter-bag. His next step was to prevail upon the Pasha to open a house of agency at Suez, and to establish caravanserais at points between that dreary locality and Cairo. Mr. Waghorn subsequently built houses at the latter city and Alexandria for the reception and safe deposit of the letters. On the completion of his arrangements he had the gratification of conducting from Bombay the Earl of Munster and a party of officers, by the new route across the desert, and through France to London. Mehemet Ali was so pleased with what had been effected, that he continued to permit every existing facility during his war with this country in 1840, and for the protection thus afforded to the Indian mail, he received on its conclusion the thanks of the merchants of this country. The result of Mr. Waghorn's exertions was the establishment of a communication from India, by Egypt and Marseilles, to England, occupying about thirty-five days. This was the route used for letters, and available for travellers also, with the alternative of the steamer *viâ* Gibraltar. Unfortunately, the French were at this time animated by hostile feelings to England, the two countries having taken different sides in the Syrian war. Indignant at the annoyances thus experienced, Mr. Waghorn determined to try if it was possible to find another and equally convenient line of transit across the continent. After encountering numberless obstacles, and receiving a rebuff from the British Government, to whom he applied to assist him in establishing the Trieste route, he was more

From this it appears that Mr. Waghorn's services in furthering the overland communication, which is such a boon to England, were incalculable, but when his advocates call him the "pioneer" of steam navigation, they do a grave injustice to Captains Johnston and Wilson. The former performed the first voyage round the Cape in a steamer, and the latter the first by the Suez route, under steam alone, and ultimately Commander Wilson's reports to the India House, his pamphlet, published on the 19th of June, 1833, but more than aught else, his seven voyages in the 'Hugh Lindsay,' demonstrated the fact, that the steam communication between England and India was a *fait accompli* and had passed beyond the region of cavil or experiment. But it was many years before this happy con-

successful with the Austrian and other Governments. After two years passed in maturing his plans, Waghorn, who was promoted to a lieutenancy in the Royal Navy in 1842, was enabled, in 1845, to see his efforts rewarded with success. Having made the necessary preparations, he sailed for Alexandria to receive the mail, which started from Bombay on the 1st of October. This was brought as usual by steamer to Suez, thence by Arab couriers across the desert to Cairo, and up the Nile and canal by steamers to Alexandria. Off this place, Mr. Waghorn awaited the mail, in the Austrian steamer 'Imperatore,' and it was placed in his hands on the twentieth day of its transit from Bombay. The steamer, notwithstanding the heavy weather which it encountered, arrived at Dwino, near Trieste, after a passage of six days and thirteen hours. From thence he made his way by post-chaise from Dwino through Innspruck, Ulm, and Bruchsal, thence to Mannheim by railway, and from the latter place to Bergen by steamer down the Rhine. Being prevented by an accident from continuing the voyage, he landed and posted to Cologne, whence he proceeded to Ostend by railway. Here the 'Herne' steamer waited to convey him to Dover; and he arrived in London by train, after one of the most rapid journeys ever made across Europe. Despite delays and accidents, the entire distance was accomplished in ninety-five hours and forty-five minutes. On the 1st of October, another mail had been despatched from Bombay, with extra speed, by the Marseilles route, in order to see which would first reach London. Mr. Waghorn had, however, anticipated its arrival by two days. This triumph of rapid travelling, as it was justly considered at that time, was entirely accomplished by private enterprise. The proprietors of the 'Times' supplied the pecuniary means, and Mr. Waghorn did the rest. He had commenced his negotiations with Mehemet Ali in 1833, but not until twelve years later was the scheme on which he had set his heart accomplished in its entirety, and a mail was brought from Bombay to London in thirty-five days. The Government and the East India Company, compelled to acknowledge their own miscalculations, united in starting an opposition. Superseded in his mail traffic, Waghorn set about providing easier means of transit, and more comfortable accommodation for the few travellers by the new route from East to West. He may be said to have created the passenger traffic, but again was superseded by an influential company under the patronage of the Government and the India House. Foiled in his every attempt, impoverished and in debt, he applied for assistance to discharge the obligations he had contracted in the public service. After wearisome delay, the East India Company granted him a pension of £200 a-year, and the Government did the same, but neither would pay his debts. The pensions, therefore, were handed over to his creditors. His constitution was shattered, and he expired in 1850, having only drawn the first quarter of the Government pension, and eighteen months of the Company's. His widow was left in distress, but the East India Company gave her an annuity of £50, while the Government awarded her £25, which was afterwards increased to £40 a-year. A memorial has been erected at Suez to Lieutenant Waghorn by the French Suez Canal Company.

summation was brought about, and the successive steps are of interest, and should be briefly recorded in the history of the Service which achieved this great result. Sir John Malcolm, in co-operation with his brothers, Sir Charles and Sir Pulteney—the latter then Naval Commander-in-chief in the Mediterranean, who assisted to the extent of his power on the European side of Alexandria—continued the efforts of his predecessor, Mr. Elphinstone, in promoting steam communication between this country and India by the Red Sea route, and the two former, recognising the fact that a survey of that sea must be a preliminary to action, entrusted the duty to Captain Elwon, commanding the 'Benares,' and Lieutenant Moresby, in the 'Palinurus,' assisted by an efficient staff of officers.

The survey of the Red Sea, of which a detailed account will be given in another chapter, was commenced in October, 1829, and Commander Wilson sailed in the 'Hugh Lindsay' in the following March. It had been intended that this great experiment should be made by the 'Enterprise,' and, in May, 1829, Lieutenant W. Denton, of the Indian Navy, brought her round from Calcutta to Bombay, but her boilers were found to be worn out, and the 'Hugh Lindsay,' then building, was substituted. The narrow escape she had of expending all her coal before reaching Aden, showed that the distance was too great for a steamer of her carrying capacity, without an intermediate coaling station, and, accordingly, a coal depôt was established at Maculla, on the coast of Arabia, about two hundred and fifty miles nearer Bombay than Aden. On the 5th of December, 1830, the 'Hugh Lindsay' started on her second voyage, this time having as a passenger Sir John Malcolm, who was returning to England, accompanied by his suite. She touched at Maculla and Jiddah, and reached Cosseir on the 27th of December, "making," Sir John Malcolm says in a letter, "twenty-two days and some hours from Bombay, of which they had spent nearly six at Maculla and Jiddah, an average of seven miles an hour from Bombay." "A pleasanter voyage," adds Sir John, "was never made." At Cosseir Lord Clare, the new Governor of Bombay, embarked, and returned in the 'Hugh Lindsay' to India. Commander Wilson started on his third voyage on the 5th of January, 1832, and reached Suez on the 4th of February, having made the passage in twenty-one days sixteen hours actually steaming. The mail, consisting of seven hundred and nineteen private letters, reached England without any steam in the Mediterranean, in sixty days from Bombay. On the 14th of January, 1833,[*] the 'Hugh Lindsay' started on her fourth

---

[*] In this year a young civilian proceeded to Bombay by the Cosseir route, who was destined to rise to the highest distinction. This was Sir Bartle Frere, Bart., G.C.B., G.C.S.I., late Governor of Bombay, and now at the head of the Government of Cape Colony.

voyage, although, on account of the great expense of coal—which, it appears from the Report of the Calcutta Steam Committee of November, 1833, was Rs. 46,250 per voyage, the receipts from passengers and letters averaging only Rs. 14,225—the Court of Directors had desired the Bombay Government not to send her again, "except on emergency." On her return from Suez, she brought London news fifty-nine days old—an unprecedented feat in those days. In February, 1836, Commander Wilson was appointed Comptroller of Bombay Dockyard, having made seven voyages to Suez, and one, in May, 1834, to Bassadore in the Persian Gulf with the mails, thus having the double honour of being the pioneer of steam navigation in the Red Sea and Persian Gulf. In 1838, he retired from the Service, but, from that date to the day of his death, in December, 1875, never recived any acknowledgment, honorary or otherwise, for his great services in promoting steam communication between England and the East.

The Governor of Bombay in Council, in accepting his resignation of the Service, said that he "had much satisfaction in acknowledging on this occasion the long and meritorious services of Commander Wilson, more particularly those which he has rendered in the first introduction of steam communication by the Red Sea." Sir John Malcolm, writing to him on the 31st of January, 1832—to ask his acceptance of a pocket chronometer, "as a light mark of my friendship and esteem, as well as of the sense I entertain of your kindness, when I had the good fortune to be in a vessel under your command"—adds, "I have done my best to promote the steam navigation by the Red Sea, but your exertions and that of others in the honourable Service to which you belong, will do more to further this natural object than all the efforts of us land-lubbers."

On the 1st of May, 1830, the following Government Order was published, in which the claims of the Bombay Marine to be officially designated the Navy of India, a claim they had made good by two centuries of arduous and faithful service, were at length recognised :—"Bombay Castle, May 1st, 1830. In accordance with a communication from the Hon. the Court of Directors, the Hon. the Governor in Council is pleased to announce, that the Bombay Marine will henceforward be denominated the 'Indian Navy.'"

APPENDIX A.

LIST OF THE INDIAN NAVY IN 1830.

MARINE BOARD:

CAPTAIN SIR CHARLES MALCOLM, KT., C.B., R.N . *Superintendent.*
„   RICHARD MORGAN . . . . . *Master-Attendant.*
„   WILLIAM GRAHAM . . . . . *Boatmaster.*
LIEUTENANT JOHN HOUGHTON . . . . *Secretary and Accountant*
CAPTAIN GEORGE SIMPSON . . . . . *Marine Storekeeper.*
WILLIAM C. BRUCE, ESQ. . . . . . *Marine Paymaster.*
LIEUTENANT ROBERT COGAN . . . . { *First Assistant to the Superintendent.*

LIST OF OFFICERS:

Rank.	Names.	Date of Commission.	Remarks.
Captain	Charles Keys . . .	Oct. 1, 1808	Senior List (at Home).
„	James Jeakes . . .	July 15, 1812	„ „ „
„	John Lawrence . .	Sept. 30, „	„ „ „
„	John Pruen . . .	Sept. 9, 1821	„ „ „
„	Sir John Hayes, Kt .	Nov. 11, 1807	Master Attendant, Calcutta.
„	Richard Morgan . .	April 12, 1824	„ „ Bombay.
„	Daniel Ross . . .	„ „ „	Marine Surveyor, Calcutta.
„	William Graham . .	„ „ „	Boat-Master.
„	Henry Hardy . . .	Mar. 11, 1827	On Furlough.
„	John Crawford . .	April 3, 1828	„
„	Thomas Tanner . .	Oct. 1, „	Mazagon Dockyard.
„	Charles F. Grice . .	May 1, 1829	On Furlough.
Commander	John Betham . . .	June 21, 1824	
„	Wm. S. Collinson . .	June 19, 1826	{ Commodore, Persian G 'Ternate.'
„	George Minchin . .	Mar. 11, 1827	Manickapatam.
„	George Grant . . .	Mar. 18, „	Senior Officer, Surat.
„	Henry Windham . .	April 3, 1828	Commanding 'Amherst.'
„	Frederick Greer . .	Oct. 1, „	„ 'Elphinstone.'
„	Thomas Elwon . .	Jan. 30, 1829	Survey of Red Sea, 'Bena
„	George Barnes Brucks	Mar. 24, „	On Furlough.
„	John Pepper . . .	May 1, 1829	Commanding 'Coote.'

APPENDIX.

Rank.	Names.	Date of Commission.	Remarks.
Lieutenant	Richard Kinchant	April 22, 1823	On Furlough.
,,	Robert Cogan	May 4, ,,	First Assist. to Superintenden
,,	William Macdonald	,, 4, ,,	Master Attendant, Mangalore
,,	Edward Wm. Harris.	,, 9, ,,	Timber Agent, 'Malabar.'
,,	John Sawyer	,, 9, ,,	Commanding 'Tigris.'
,,	William Rose	July 10, ,,	On Furlough.
,,	Samuel Richardson	Mar. 1, 1824	,,
,,	John Henry Wilson	,, 1, ,,	Fitting out 'Hugh Lindsay.'
,,	J. Croft Hawkins	May 23, ,,	Commanding 'Olive.'
,,	William Denton	June 21, ,,	,, 'Euphrates.'
,,	John Houghton	Aug. 19, ,,	Secretary and Accountant Marine Board, Marine Jud(Advocate, and Draughtsm
,,	John McDowall	Nov. 10, ,,	On Furlough.
,,	Robert Moresby	Dec. 10, ,,	Survey of Red Sea, 'P(nurus.'
,,	Richard Lloyd	July 9, 1825	Survey Department, Calcutta
,,	Robert Lowe	Sept. 2, ,,	On Furlough.
,,	William Lowe	April 24, 1826	'Coote.'
,,	John Harrison	June 10, ,,	Commanding 'Antelope.'
,,	Charles Wells	,, 19, ,,	'Ternate.'
,,	Jos. H. Rowband	Jan. 2, 1827	Commanding Flotilla in Arra(
,,	William Igglesden	Mar. 11, ,,	On Furlough.
,,	Stafford B. Haines	,, 18, ,,	Superintendent of Quarantin(
,,	George B. Harrison	May 10, ,,	'Coote.'
,,	Thomas E. Rogers	June 21, ,,	Assistant-Surveyor, 'Palinur(
,,	William Bryon	,, ,, ,,	On Furlough.
,,	George Laughton	Sept. 2, ,,	Survey Department, Calcutta
,,	Edward B. Squire	Feb. 21, 1828	'Amherst.'
,,	Curtis Clark	May 31, ,,	'Ternate.'
,,	Thomas Clendon	Nov. 10, 1824	Signal Officer, Lighthouse.
,,	George Pilcher	Dec. 10, ,,	On Furlough.
,,	Henry Warry	May 27, 1825	'Coote.'
,,	H. N. T. E. Pinching	July 6, ,,	Assistant-Surveyor, 'Benare
,,	Edward Wyburd	,, 9, ,,	'Euphrates.'
,,	Hugh Rose	May 10, ,,	'Coote.'
,,	George Harvey	,, 15, ,,	'Nautilus.'
,,	W. Rigden Hayman	Sept. 2, ,,	'Antelope.'
,,	Anthony H. Nott	Oct. 29, ,,	'Amherst.'
,,	William Hodges	April 18, 1826	'Ternate.'
,,	Alfred S. Williams	,, 24, ,,	Survey Department, Calcutt(
,,	Philip Lewis Powell	May 8, ,,	On Furlough.
,,	Chas. R. Richardson	June 19, ,,	,,
,,	Charles Sharp	Jan. 2, 1827	'Olive.'
,,	John P. Porter	Mar. 11, ,,	'Thetis.'
,,	Henry H. Whitelock	,, 27, ,,	'Nautilus.'
,,	Stephen Newnham	Sept. 2, ,,	On Furlough.
,,	Hen. Nelson Poole	Feb. 21, 1828	'Amherst.'
,,	William Bowater	May 31, ,,	'Elphinstone.'
,,	George Boscawen	Mar. 24, 1829	Survey Department, Calcutt(
,,	Thomas G. Carless	May 1, ,,	,, ,, ,,
,,	George Peters	July 20, ,,	'Olive.'
,,	James R. Wellsted	Dec. 10, ,,	Survey of Red Sea.
,,	Henry B. Lynch	,, 18, ,,	Persian Interpreter, Per(Gulf.

APPENDIX.

Rank.	Names.	Date of Appointment.	Remarks.
Midshipman	J. P. Sanders	May 27, 1823	'Elphinstone.'
,,	W. H. Wyburd	,, 27, ,,	On Furlough.
,,	Henry A. Ormsby	June 7, ,,	'Amherst.'
,,	Fred. Thos. Powell	July 8, ,,	'Benares.'
,,	George Robinson	,, 8, ,,	'Elphinstone.'
,,	J. Langford Pruen	June 7, 1824	On Furlough.
,,	F. D. W. Winn	,, 7, ,,	'Benares.'
,,	Richard Ethersey	Oct. 6, ,,	'Coote.'
,,	E. Shepherd Smith	June 5, 1825	'Nautilus.'
,,	Jas. Anthony Young	May 3, 1826	'Benares.'
,,	Charles Parbury	,, 3, ,,	On Furlough.
,,	G. B. Kempthorne	June 4, ,,	'Euphrates.'
,,	John Jas. Frushard	,, 4, ,,	'Antelope.'
,,	Richard Harrison	,, 12, ,,	'Amherst.'
,,	Hen. C. Boulderson	Aug. 31, ,,	'Nautilus.'
,,	Fred. Parry Webb	Feb. 17, 1827	'Elphinstone.'
,,	Griffith Jenkins	May 11, ,,	'Coote.'
,,	Sergison Nott	,, 11, ,,	'Clive.'
,,	Rt. Dalgleish Swan	June 13, ,,	'Euphrates.'
,,	John Wood	,, 13, ,,	'Clive.'
,,	Chas. Wm. Down	,, 13, ,,	'Coote.'
,,	Charles Montriou	April 11, ,,	Survey Department, Calcutta.
,,	John Glen Johnston	June 2, ,,	'Benares.'
,,	Francis Whitelock	,, 12, ,,	'Ternate.'
,,	Frederick Jones	,, 12, ,,	'Antelope.'
,,	John Jas. Bowring	Aug. 29, ,,	'Ternate.'
,,	James F. Prentice	Oct. 26, ,,	'Euphrates.'
,,	Thomas Beahen	Dec. 24, ,,	'Clive.'
,,	George Quanbrough	May 25, 1828	'Coote.'
,,	John W. Young	,, 25, ,,	'Elphinstone.'
,,	John Buckle	,, 25, ,,	,,
,,	C. Francis Warden	June 5, ,,	,,
,,	Thos. W. Pitcher	July 1, ,,	'Clive.'
,,	Alex. Hen. Gordon	,, 1, ,,	'Nautilus.'
,,	Walter Jardine	,, 1, ,,	'Euphrates.'
,,	Chas. D. Campbell	,, 1, ,,	'Benares.'
,,	Edw. W. S. Daniell	,, 1, ,,	'Amherst.'
,,	Thos. Wm. Dent	,, 1, ,,	'Coote.'
,,	James Felix Jones	,, 14, ,,	'Palinurus.'
,,	Harry H. Hewett	,, 14, ,,	'Amherst.'
,,	John Shaw Grieve	Sept. 2, ,,	'Euphrates.'
,,	John Stephens	Oct. 21, ,,	'Clive.'
,,	Wm. Chas. Barker	,, 13, ,,	'Euphrates.'
,,	Arch. Macdonald	,, 20, ,,	'Clive.'
,,	W. Christopher	Jan. 1, 1829	'Benares.'
,,	Hen. A. M. Drought	Mar. 8, ,,	'Amherst.'
,,	Wm. E. L. Campbell	May 19, ,,	'Elphinstone.'
,,	Arthur Whitburn	,, 10, ,,	,,
,,	Robert Riddell	,, 14, ,,	'Benares.'
,,	William Fell	,, 19, ,,	'Ternate.'
,,	Alfred Offer	June 6, ,,	,,
,,	Alan Hyde Gardner	,, 2, ,,	,,
,,	Joseph S. Draper	July 3, ,,	'Tigris.'
,,	Henry Green	,, 3, ,,	,,
,,	James Rennie	Dec. 10, ,,	'Clive.'
,,	Benjamin Hamilton	Aug. 26, ,,	'Amherst.'
,,	Rodk. McKenzie	Sept. 6, ,,	'Elphinstone.'
,,	Thomas Reid	,, 6, ,,	'Euphrates.'
,,	John Hollis	,, 6, ,,	—
,,	Christie Hewett	,, 6, ,,	—

APPENDIX.

VOLUNTEERS, PILOT SERVICE,

DOING DUTY AS MIDSHIPMEN, SUBSEQUENTLY TRANSFERRED TO THE SERVICE.

Names.	Remarks.	Names.	Remarks.
John Bird	'Thetis.'	John Sheppard	'Amherst.'
Sid. Ham. Buckler	'Elphinstone.'	J. Samuel Thacker	'Benares.'
Wm. John Garrett	'Palinurus.'	Michael Wm. Lynch	'Ternate.'
Robert Waller	,,	George Hitchings	—
Richard Walker	'Amherst.'	—	—

LIST OF THE HON. COMPANY'S MARINE VESSELS
ON THIS ESTABLISHMENT.

Names.	Description.	Guns.	Names.	Description.	Guns.
'Amherst'	Ship	18	'Hastings'	Frigate	32
'Antelope'	Brig	14	'Nautilus'	Brig	10
'Benares'	Ship	14	'Palinurus'	,,	4
'Olive'	,,	18	'Royal Tiger'	Schooner	6
'Coote'	,,	18	'Ternate'	Ship	14
'Elphinstone'	,,	18	'Thetis'	Brig	10
'Euphrates'	Brig	10	'Tigris'	,,	10

APPENDIX B.

VESSELS* BUILT IN BOMBAY DOCKYARD, FROM 1736 TO 1863,

COMPILED FROM THE DOCKYARD RECORDS AND OTHER SOURCES.

Year.	Name and Description.	Guns.	Tons.	For whom built.	Year.	Name and Description.	Guns.	Tons.	For whom built.
1736	'Drake'—grab	14	—	H.C.S.	1764	'Restoration'—ship	24	—	H.C.S.
,,	'Success'—ketch	14	—	H.C.S.	,,	'Wallace'—ship	—	—	—
1737	'Prince Augustus'—grab	14	—	H.C.S.	1768	'Princess Royal'—grab	14	—	H.C.S.
1738	'Resource'—grab	14	—	H.C.S.	,,	'Queen'—grab	14	—	H.C.S.
1739	'Bombay'—grab	24	—	H.C.S.	,,	'Princess Augusta'—grab	14	—	H.C.S.
1740	'Success'—galley	—	—	H.C.S.	1769	'Hunter'—ship	14	—	H.C.S.
1741	'Defence'—ketch	14	—	H.C.S.	,,	'Griffith'—ship	—	—	—
1747	'Shaw Pedro'—grab	—	—	—	1770	'Alexander'—ship	—	—	—
1749	'Nesbit'—ship	—	—	—	,,	'Sky'—cutter	—	—	—
1750	'Bombay'—frigate	32	—	H.C.S.	,,	'Swallow'—ketch	14	—	H.C.S.
,,	'Mary'—ship	—	—	—	,,	'Phœnix'—ketch	14	—	H.C.S.
1751	'Indian Queen'—ship	—	—	—	,,	'Syren'—ship	—	—	—
1753	'Penny'—ship	—	—	—	1772	'Wolfe'—galivat	6	—	H.C.S.
1754	'Revenge'—frigate	28	—	H.C.S.	,,	'Britannia'—ship	—	—	—
,,	'Eagle'—snow	16	—	H.C.S.	,,	'Louisa'—ship	—	—	—
,,	'Euphrates'—ship	—	—	—	1774	'Royal Charlotte'—ship	—	—	—
,,	'Success'—ketch	14	—	H.C.S.	,,	'Nancy'—ship	—	—	—

* Those built for the Royal Service have the letters H.M.S. after them; those for the Hon. Company, whether of the Naval or Mercantile Service, H.C.S.; the remainder being either private merchant ships or uncertain. All the earlier vessels, described in the list as "grabs," were built, we believe, for the Bombay Marine. Three ships of the name of 'Bombay' appear in the above list, of which the last, launched in 1793, was the thirty-eight-gun frigate which, in 1805, was handed over to the Royal Navy, with the 'Cornwallis,' fifty-six guns, the ships being re-named respectively the 'Ceylon' and 'Akbar.' The list has no pretension to absolute accuracy.

APPENDIX.

Year	Name and Description	Guns	Tons	For whom built
1775	'Betsy'—snow	14	—	H.C.S.
„	'Byramgore'—ship	—	—	—
1776	'Industry'—schooner	—	140	—
1777	'Nerbudda'—schooner	14	200	H.C.S.
„	'Swallow'—packet	14	—	H.C.S.
„	'Brazil'—snow	14	—	H.C.S.
1778	'Amphitrite'—snow	14	—	H.C.S.
„	'Bencoolen'—snow	—	181	—
„	'Panther'—snow	—	747	—
„	'Britannia'—ship	—	188	—
„	'Sea Horse'—pilot vessel	—	—	H.C.S.
„	'Mermaid'—pilot vessel	—	—	H.C.S.
1780	'Hermanis'—ship	—	—	—
„	'Defence'—luggage boat	—	189	—
„	'Intrepid'—snow	14	—	H.C.S.
„	'Hornby'—ship	—	—	—
1786	'Milford'—ship	—	655	H.C.S.
1787	'Cornwallis'—snow	14	—	—
„	'Johanna'—snow	—	70	—
„	'Jay'—snow	—	868	—
1788	'Shaw Ardaseer'—ship	—	—	—
„	'Cyrene'—ship	—	—	—
„	'Tazbux'—ship	—	—	—
1789	'Shaw Municher'	—	—	—
„	'King George'	—	—	—
„	'Bomanean'	—	—	—
„	'Hannah'—ship	—	—	—
1790	'Lowjee Family'—ship	—	926	—
1792	'Sarah'—ship	—	935	—
„	'Born'—ship	—	—	—

Year	Name and Description	Guns	Tons	For whom built
1793	'Stromboli'—bomb-ketch	—	68	H.C.S.
„	'Bombay'—frigate	38	639	H.C.S.
„	'Antelope'—brig	14	199	H.C.S.
„	'Fly'—brig	12	176	H.C.S.
1794	'Upton Castle'—ship	—	675	—
„	'Hoogly'—pilot vessel	—	150	H.C.S.
„	'Abercromby'—pilot vessel	—	147	H.C.S.
1795	'Alert'—brig	8	85	H.C.S.
1797	'Asia'—ship	—	736	—
1798	'Comet'—brig	10	115	H.C.S.
„	'Philip Dundas'—brig	—	187	—
1799	'Scaleby Castle'—ship	—	1216	—
„	'Teignmouth'—sloop-of-war	16	257	H.C.S.
„	'Mornington'—sloop-of-war	22	350	H.C.S.
„	'Kaikusroo'—ship	—	1045	—
„	'Seringapatam'—ship	—	336	—
1800	'Cornwallis'—frigate	56	1363	H.C.S.
„	'William'—ship	—	393	—
1801	Yacht for Governor	—	—	—
„	'Ternate'—sloop-of-war	16	257	H.C.S.
„	Water boat	—	67	—
1802	'David Scott'—ship	—	749	—
1803	'Tazbux'	—	737	—
„	'Pack-Horse'—luggage boat	—	161	—
„	'Alexander'—ship	—	746	—
„	'Charlotte'—ship	—	672	—
„	'James Sibbald'	—	—	—
„	'Cambrian'—ship	—	705	—
„	'Estombole'—ship	—	441	—
1804	'Admiral Rainier'—luggage boat	—	102	—

APPENDIX. 539

Year.	Name and Description.	Guns.	Tons.	For whom built.	Year.	Name and Description.	Guns.	Tons.	For whom built.
1805	'Prince of Wales'—sloop-of-war	14	248	H.C.S.	1814	'Victor'—brig	18	384	H.M.S.
,,	'Pitt'—frigate	36	872	H.M.S.	,,				Imaum of
1806	'Mercury'—sloop-of-war	14	185	H.C.S.	,,	'Caroline'—frigate	36	575	Muscat.
,,	'Nautilus'—brig	14	185	H.C.S.					
,,	'Sylph'—schooner	8	78	H.C.S.	,,	'Flora'—Bengal pilot vessel	—	186	H.C.S.
1807	'Benares'—sloop-of-war	14	230	H.C.S.	,,	'Guide' ,, ,, ,,	—	189	H.C.S.
,,	'Salsette'—frigate	36	885	H.M.S.	,,	'Sophia' ,, ,, ,,	—	189	H.C.S.
,,	'Bombay'—ship	—	1126	H.C.S.	1815	'Torch'—light vessel	—	174	H.C.S.
1808	'Thomas Grenville'—ship	—	889	H.C.S.	,,	'Wellesley'—ship	74	1745	H.M.S.
1809	'Charles Grant'—ship	—	1246	H.C.S.	,,	'Zebra'—brig	18	385	H.M.S.
,,	'Aurora'—sloop-of-war	14	247	H.C.S.	,,	'Sphynx'—brig	12	239	H.M.S.
,,	'Vestal'—brig	10	159	H.C.S.	1816	Water-boat	—	—	—
,,	'Ariel'—brig	10	160	H.C.S.	,,	'Planet'—light vessel	—	174	H.C.S.
1810	'Psyche'—brig	10	180	H.C.S.	,,	'Cameleon'—brig	12	239	H.M.S.
,,	'Thetis'—brig	10	185	H.C.S.	,,	'Amphitrite'—frigate	38	1064	H.M.S.
,,	'Minden'—ship	74	1681	H.M.S.	,,	'Buckinghamshire'—ship	—	1349	H.C.S.
,,	'Balcarras'—ship	—	1406	H.C.S.	1817	'Henry Meriton'—pilot-brig	—	190	H.C.S.
1811	'Minerva'—ship	—	985	—	,,	'Melville'—ship	74	1767	H.M.S.
,,	'Abercrombie'—ship	—	1288	H.C.S.	,,	'Trincomalee'—frigate	46	1065	H.M.S.
,,	'Hannah'—ship	—	457	—	1818	'Malabar'—ship	74	1715	H.M.S.
1812	'Ann'	—	788	—	1819	'Seringapatam'—frigate	38	1152	H.M.S.
,,	'Herefordshire'	—	1279	H.C.S.	,,				Imaum of
1813	'Buffalo'—luggage boat	—	59	—	,,	'Shah Allum'—frigate	56	1111	Muscat.
,,	'Nerbudda'—grab	—	—	—					
,,	'Taptee'—brig	—	—	—	1820	'Jane'—pilot-vessel	—	170	H.C.S.
,,	'Ernaad'—timber-ship	—	557	H.C.S.	1821	'Vigilant'—schooner	6	72	H.C.S.
,,	'Cornwallis'	74	1767	H.M.S.	,,	'Bombay'—gunboat	—	—	H.C.S.
,,	'Eliza'—pilot vessel	—	189	H.C.S.	,,	'Ganges'—ship	84	2289	H.M.S.
,,	'Cecilia'—pilot vessel	—	191	H.C.S.	1822	'Madagascar'—frigate	46	1164	H.M.S.
1814	'Thames'—bomb-ketch	—	102	H.C.S.	,,	'Nancy'—brig	—	163	—

540
APPENDIX.

Year.	Name and Description.	Guns.	Tons.	For whom built.	Year.	Name and Description.	Guns.	Tons.	For whom built.
1823	'Palinurus'—brig	8	192	H.C.S.	1833	'Jamsetjee Jeejeebhoy'—ship	—	555	—
,,	'Hastings'—frigate	32	566	H.C.S.	,,	'Two Sisters'—brig	—	277	—
1824	'Elphinstone'—sloop-of-war	18	387	H.C.S.	1834	'Mahi'—schooner	3	157	H.C.S.
,,	'Asia'—ship	84	2289	H.M.S.	1835	'Nerbudda'—cutter	2	49	H.C.S.
,,	'Caledonia'—ship	—	742	—	,,	'Margaret'—cutter	2	61	H.C.S.
,,	'Clairmont'—ship	—	328	—	,,	'Maldiva'—cutter	—	23	H.C.S.
1825	'Amherst'—sloop-of-war	18	420	H.C.S.	,,	'Cardiva'—cutter	—	27	H.C.S.
,,	'Sea Horse'—pilot-vessel	—	188	H.C.S.	,,	'Mootnee'—for River Indus	—	42	H.C.S.
,,	'Mermaid'—pilot-vessel	—	188	H.C.S.	,,	'Taptee'—brig	—	172	H.C.S.
1826	'Clive'—sloop-of-war	18	420	H.C.S.	,,	'Nancy'—brig	—	179	H.C.S.
					,,	'Lady Grant'—brig	—	239	—
					,,	'Sir Herbert Compton'—ship	—	346	—
,,	'Liverpool'—ship	74	1715	Imaum of Muscat.	,,	'Bombay'—schooner	—	62	—
					1836	'Ardaseer'—ship	—	422	—
1827	'Mountstuart Elphinstone'	18	611	H.C.S.	,,	'John Fleming'—ship	—	514	H.C.S.
,,	'Coote'—sloop-of-war	18	420	H.C.S.	,,	'Megna'—Bengal pilot-vessel	—	201	H.C.S.
1828	'Pownah'—pattamar	6	43	H.C.S.	,,	'Saugor' ,, ,,	—	200	H.C.S.
,,	'Bheema'—pattamar	6	55	H.C.S.	,,	'Krishna' ,, ,,	—	200	H.C.S.
,,	'Euphrates'—brig	10	255	H.C.S.	1837	'Rajasthan'—ship	—	600	—
,,	'Bombay'—ship	84	2285	H.M.S.	1838	'Cavery'—Bengal pilot-vessel	—	200	H.C.S.
,,	'Hormusjee Bomanjee'	—	757	—	,,	'Colleroon' ,, ,,	—	182	H.C.S.
,,	'Sir Charles Malcolm'—ship	4	866	H.C.S.	,,	'Constance'—schooner	3	40	—
1829	'Hugh Lindsay'—steam-sloop	10	411	H.C.S.	,,	'Snake'—iron river-steamer	1	350	H.C.S.
,,	'Tigris'—brig	6	258	H.C.S.	1839	'Mary Gordon'	—	705	—
,,	'Royal Tiger'—schooner	6	120	H.C.S.	,,	'Victoria'—steam-sloop	4	204	H.C.S.
,,	'Andromeda' (or 'Manilla'?) frigate	46	1166	H.M.S.	,,	'Comet'—iron river-steamer	2	149	H.C.S.
1831	'Calcutta'—ship	84	2298	H.M.S.	1840	'Meteor' ,, ,,	2	397	H.C.S.
1832	'Shannon'—schooner	6	87	H.C.S.	,,	'Planet'—iron river-steamer	2	335	H.C.S.
,,	'Earl of Clare'—ship	—	904	—	,,	'Satellite' ,, ,,	2	335	H.C.S.
1833	'Ruparel'—water-boat	—	—	—	,,	'Medusa'—steam-sloop	3	432	H.C.S.
,,	'Sultana'—ship	—	312	—					

APPENDIX. 541

Year.	Name and Description.	Guns.	Tons.	For whom built.	Year.	Name and Description.	Guns.	Tons.	For whom built.
1840	'Ariadne'—steam-sloop	3	432	H.C.S.	1852	2 pilot-boats, coal-boat, and 'Curset-jee'—flat	—	—	H.C.S.
,,	'Auckland'—steam-frigate	6	946	H.C.S.	,,	A schooner (for Collector of Customs)	—	155	H.C.S.
1842	'Semiramis'—steam-frigate	6	1031	H.C.S.	,,	'Lady Falkland'—iron steamer	—	494	H.C.S.
,,	5 coal-boats; and 'Colaba'—light-vessel	—	—	H.C.S.	1853	'Falkland'—corvette	18	49	H.C.S.
1843	2 coal-boats, 1 mud-boat and 1 flat-boat	—	—	P & O Co.	,,	A light-vessel	—	114	H.C.S.
1844	Coal-boat; bridge of boats, Nos. 1 to 60, for Scinde, with platform	—	—	H.C.S.	,,	'Augusta'—schooner	2	—	H.C.S.
,,	'Napier'—iron river-steamer	3	445	H.C.S.	1854	'Ethersey' flat; and pilot-boat	—	1800	H.C.S.
,,	'Conqueror' ,,	3	299	H.C.S.	,,	'Assaye'—steam-frigate	10	1800	H.C.S.
,,	'Meanee' ,,	2	208	H.C.S.	,,	'Punjaub'—steam-frigate	10	1800	H.C.S.
1845	'Sutledge,' 'Beas,' and 'Ravee'—Indus flats	—	664	H.C.S.	1855	'Georgiana'—schooner	2	90	H.C.S.
,,	'Grapler'—buoy-vessel	—	—	H.C.S.	,,	'Emily'—schooner	2	90	H.C.S.
1846	2 coal-boats and water-boat	—	—	H.C.S.	,,	'Goolanar'—steamer	—	215	H.C.S.
1847	A steamer	—	500	—	,,	Barge for the Governor	—	51	H.C.S.
,,	A coal-boat	—	—	—	1856	Barge for Commander-in-Chief, I.N.	—	26	H.C.S.
1848	'Ferooz'—steam-frigate	8	1440	H.C.S.	1857	'Charlotte'—schooner	2	167	H.C.S.
,,	'Nerbudda'—brig	16	420	H.M.S.	,,	'Lady Canning'—steam-sloop	4	527	H.C.S.
,,	'Jumna'—brig	16	420	H.M.S.	,,	Pilot-schooner; cargo-boat; 2 dredging-vessels; 2 bunder-boats; water-boat; 2 pilot-boats and 2 warp-boats for Kurrachee	—	—	H.C.S.
,,	'Meanee'—ship	80	2298	H.C.S.	1859	'Clyde'—gunboat	3	300	H.M.S.
,,	A pilot-boat	—	—	H.C.S.	1860	'Hugh Rose'—gunboat	3	300	H.M.S.
1849	A pilot-boat and coal-boat	—	619	H.C.S.	,,	'Hyderabad'—flat	—	394	H.M.S.
,,	A steamer	—	—	—	1862	Governor's barge	—	51	H.M.S.
1850	'Nerbudda'—cutter	—	62	H.C.S.	,,	Commander-in-Chief's barge	—	36	H.M.S.
,,	A ferry-boat and coal-boat	—	—	H.C.S.	,,	A light vessel for Ceylon	—	169	H.M.S.
1851	'Indus'—iron river-steamer	2	522	H.C.S.	,,	2 pilot-vessels	—	—	H.M.S.
,,	'Jhelum' ,,	2	499	H.C.S.	1863	Dredging-vessel for Aden and 2 pilot-vessels	—	—	H.M.S.
,,	'Chenaub' ,,	2	499	H.C.S.					
,,	'Falkland'—steamer	—	1159	—					
,,	'Zenobia'—steam-frigate	6	1003	H.C.S.					

INDEX

EAST INDIA COMPANY, H.M. AND OTHER SHIPS

ACTAEON	HMS Sloop	1/230
ACTIVE	Gun Boat	1/411
ADVICE		1/143
AFRICA	Gun Boat	1/435,437,440
AFRICAINE	HMS Frigate	1/228,230
AKBAR	HMS	1/237-238
ALCESTE	HMS	1/251,271
ALERT (ex L'EUGENIE privateer)		1/234-235
ALERT	Schooner	1/203,215,261. 2/7
ALLIGATOR	HMS	1/458,465,472
AMHERST	Gun Boat	1/462
AMHERST	Sloop	1/475,477-479,502,524
ANGELICA	Transport	1/352
ANGLESEA	French Pvtr	1/82,102,116,120
ANN	Transport	1/352
ANNE	Grab	1/92,107,124
ANSON		1/120
ANTELOPE	Gallivat	1/117
ANTELOPE	Gun Brig	1/117,192-193,199,215,262,265,277
		1/280,288,302-303,305-307,309,347
		1/348,350,370,390-391,394-395,398
		1/479,503,525. 2/20,182
APOLLO	HMS	1/140
APOLLO	French Pvtr	1/119
ARACHNE	HMS	1/423-424,449,451,455,457,472
ARGYLE	Transport	1/420
ARIEL	HMS	1/187. 2/538-539
ARIEL	Gun Brig	1/226,229,236,238,265,277,325,330
		1/345,351,367-370,484
ASCENSION		1/5-6,8,25
ASIA	HMS	1/298,411. 2/4,15
ASIA	Gun Boat	1/437,440
ASIA FELIX	Transport	1/437-440
ASSAYE	Schooner	1/215,391-392,394,398. 2/68
ASSEERGHUR	Gun Brig	1/434-438,441-442
ASTREA	French Frigate	1/229-230,378

542   HISTORY OF THE INDIAN NAVY.

AUCKLAND	Steam Frigate	1/475,541. 2/131,135,137-138
		2/140,150,154-155,157,168-169
		2/179,193,297,306,312,316,336
		2/379-382,429-430,434,452,464
		2/493,532,534,538-539,548-549
AURENZES		1/93
AURORA	Sloop	1/226,228,230,238,250,252,256
		1/257-258,260,268,276-277,281
		1/325,330,340,351-352,354,360
		1/378,479. 2/53,235
AURORA	HMS Frigate	1/173
BANTAM		1/58
BARRACOUTA	HMS Sloop	1/237,256,258
BASSEIN	Snow	1/313-315
BEDFORD		1/81
BELISARIUS		1/254
BELLONE	French Frigate	1/230
BENARES	Sloop	1/226,229,263,265-268,274-275
		1/285,288,302-303,305-306,309
		1/337,350-353,379,403,406-408
		1/479,495,501,531. 2/11,29,31
		2/69-72,76-78,317
BENJAMIN	Yacht	1/82
BERENICE	Steam Sloop	1/284
BERKLEY CASTLE		1/77-78
BETSY	Schooner	1/375
BHOWANY	Pattamar	1/275
BLENHEIM	HMS	1/235
BLESSING		1/52
BOADICEA	HMS Frigate	1/226,229-230,465,472
BOMBAY	Galley	1/105
BOMBAY	Frigate (1750)	1/120-122,127-128,130,134,137
		1/141,156,176,178,181-182
BOMBAY	Frigate (1793)	1/199,206-207,213,215,220-221
		1/226,229,235,375,397
BOMBAY	HMS (84 guns)	1/298. 2/4
BOMBAY CASTLE	Transport	1/352
BRIDGEWATER	HMS	1/134
BRIDGWATER		1/253
BRITANNIA		1/94,205
BROUGHAM	Transport	1/441
BRUNSWICK		1/202
BUCHEPHALUS	HMS Frigate	1/237
BUCKINGHAMSHIRE		1/283
BURRAMPOOTRA		1/427
CAESAR		1/74
CALCUTTA		1/254-255
CAROLINE	HMS Frigate	1/237,325,331,333
CAROLINE	French Frigate	1/227
CARRON	Transport	1/352
CASTLEREAGH		1/221
CATHERINE		1/92
CENTURION	HMS	1/206

INDEX. 543

CERES	East Indiaman	1/108
CEYLON	HMS Frigate	1/229-230
CHALLENGER	HMS Sloop	1/342-346. 2/1-2
CHARLES		1/25-26,29-30,47
CHARLES II		1/72-74
CHARLOTTE		1/100
CHIFFONNE	HMS	1/189,325-326,331
CLIVE	Sloop	1/475,478-479,505,507-509,512
		1/513,515,517,520. 2/2-3,11
		2/43,104-105,131-132,164,201
		2/217,235-236,297,326-327,336
		2/337,339,341,354-356,359-360
		2/362-364,373,393,510,518-519
		2/521,523,535,538-539,548-549
CLORINDE	HMS Frigate	1/230
CLOVE		1/10
COMET	Brig (1798)	1/210,215,394
CONDE DE RIO PARDO	Transport	1/352
CONCORDE	HMS	1/225,398
CONWAY	HMS	1/349
COOTE	Sloop or Corvette	1/475,479,502,517,526. 2/5 2/11,72,75,96-97,118-120,122 2/136,168,177-178,183,193,197 2/321,323,326,392,523
CORNELIA	HMS Frigate	1/230,245
CORNWALL	Transport	1/352
CORNWALLIS	Frigate (1800)	1/208,215,226,230
CUMBERLAND	HMS	1/134,141
CURLEW	HMS	1/351-352,360-361,371
CYBELE	French Frigate	1/202,204-205
DAEDALUS	HMS	1/399
DALHOUSIE	St Transport	1/275
DARLING		1/25
DART	Gun Boat	1/275,379
DASHER	HMS Sloop	1/237
DEFENCE		1/25,73,78
DEFIANCE	(1715)	1/94
DEFIANCE	(1735)	1/147
DERBY		1/131
DERIA DOWLUT	Pattamar	1/275,339-341
DESPATCH	Bomb Vessel	1/134
DIANA	HMS Brig	1/236
DIANA	Steam Paddle	1/412,419,423-424,452,457,459 1/460,462-464,468,520
DIANA	Transport	1/352
DISCOVERY	Survey Vessel	1/404-408,410,474,479
DOLPHIN	Ketch	1/37,185
DORIS	HMS Frigate	1/230,237
DOROTHEA		1/81
DORRELL		1/81
DOVE	Grab	1/67
DRAGON = RED DRAGON		
DRAKE	Bomb Ketch	1/127,134,168,171,176,183

HISTORY OF THE INDIAN NAVY.

DRAKE	Snow (1787)	1/208,215
DUCHESS		1/200
DUGUAY TROUIN (ex PRINCESS ROYAL)		1/205
DUKE OF AQUITAIN	HMS	1/144
DUKE OF CLARENCE		1/200
DUKE OF YORK		1/284
DURRUCK		1/178,375
EAGLE		1/31
EAGLE	Snow	1/166-168,170-171,178,375
ECLIPSE	HMS Sloop	1/230
EDEN	HMS	1/347-351
EDWARD BONAVENTURE		1/4
ELIZA	Pilot Vessel	1/411
ELIZABETH	? / Gun Boat	1/77,174,427,464. 2/251
ELPHINSTONE	Sloop	1/475,479,498. 2/9,11,18-21 2/23,41,104-107,133,169,185 2/186-187,189-191,201,297,303 2/305-309,311,318-319,325,328 2/386,501,523,534-535,538,548 2/549-550
EMMA	Gun Vessel	1/230,411,464
ENDEAVOUR	Survey Vessel	1/195-200
ENTERPRISE	Steam Vessel	1/470,520-521,523,531
ENTREPENANT	French Brig	1/230
EPERVIER	HMS Sloop	1/285
ERNAAD	Storeship	1/302,309,352,412,487. 2/119 2/391
EUPHRATES	Brig & Survey Brig	1/477,479,524,528. 2/11,36-43 2/45,47,50,97,100-101,103-104 2/126,128,133-135,185,193,297 2/318,328,339,341,387,395-397 2/404,407,417,420-421,523
EUROPA		1/199
EXETER		1/202
EXPEDITION		1/8,25
EXPERIMENT		1/190
FAIZ REMAUN	Transport	1/352
FAZL KEREEM	Transport	1/349
FALKLAND	Sail Corvette	1/475. 2/295,297,326-328,337 2/339-342,345,347,351,354-356 2/359-360,362-364,368,373,393 2/417,538-539,548-549
FAME		1/94
FAVOURITE	HMS	1/189
FISGARD	HMS Frigate	1/323
FLETCHER	Transport	1/180
FLORA	Brig	1/401
FLY	Gun Brig	1/203-204,215,222-223,225,233 1/398,525. 2/8,329
FOX	HMS	1/273,318,391. 2/183,237-237 2/241-243,246-247,253-255,257

INDEX. 545

		2/262-263,265,270,277
FOX	Schooner	1/185
FRANCIS WARDEN	Depot Ship	1/430
FREAK	Brig	1/401
FURY		1/320,326,330-332,377
GANGES	HMS	1/298
GANGES	Steamer	1/520
GLENELG	Transport	1/352
GLOBE		1/12,25-26,28
GOLDFINCH	Gun Boat	1/411
GOLIATH	Transport	1/441
GOOD HOPE	Transport	1/456
GUARDIAN	Frigate	1/127,133-134
GUEST		1/5
GUNGA SAUGOR	Gun Vessel	1/411,436-440,464
HALIFAX		1/108
HANNAH	Transport	1/352
HARRINGTON		1/108
HART		1/31
HARPY	HMS Sloop	1/237
HARRIER		1/253
HARWICH	HMS	1/82,86,173
HASTINGS	HMS	1/82,86,173. 2/257
HASTINGS	Frigate	1/298-299,411,413,424,426-427
		1/429-432,440,474-475,477,479
		1/487,503. 2/53,181,183,199
	Receiving Ship	2/218,232,234,296,314,317,396
		2/523
HAWK	HMS Sloop	1/173
HEATHCOTE		1/146-147
HEBE	Gun Boat	1/411
HECATE	HMS Sloop	1/230,237,255-256,258
HECTOR		1/5-7,10,17,21-22,25
HELEN	Gun Brig	1/434,436-437,441
HENRY MERITON	Survey Ship	1/398,400,425,432,434
HERBERT		1/77
HESPER	HMS Sloop	1/230,237
HINDOSTAN		1/198
HOOGHLY	Steamer	1/520
HOPEWELL		1/51
HOSEANDER (OSIANDER)		1/12-13,25
HOUGHTON		1/205
HUGH LINDSAY	Steam Sloop	1/478,520,526-528,530-531.
		2/11,25-26,41-42,50-53,56
		2/57,69,75,99,138,170,256
		2/339,364,373
HUSSAR	HMS Frigate	1/237,256
HUNTER		1/61,63,67,72,173
ILLUSTRIOUS	HMS	1/230,237-238
INDIAN OAK	Transport	1/420
IPHIGENIA	HMS Frigate	1/228,230,378
INSPECTOR	Schooner	1/407

HISTORY OF THE INDIAN NAVY.

INTREPID	Snow	1/209-210,215,394
INVESTIGATOR	Survey Ship	1/401,426-429,434
IPHIGINIE	French Frigate	1/230,378
IPHIGENIA	(late British)	
IRIS	HMS	1/381
IRRAWADDY	Gun Boat	1/427
IRRAWADDY	Steamer (1827)	1/520
ISABELLA	Transport	1/437-439,441
JAMES		1/12,25-26
JAVA	HMS	1/423
JEMIMA	Transport	1/352
JEHANGIRE		1/202
JESSY	Brig/Transport	1/352,411,415,418-420,441
JONAS		1/37-38
JOSIAH	Ketch	1/80-82
KENT	HMS	1/134,174
KINGFISHER	HMS	1/134
KING WILLIAM	Galley	1/104
KITTY	Gun Brig	1/411,422
LA CHIFFONNE = CHIFFONNE HMS		
LA CONFIANCE	French Pvtr	1/232-234
LA FORTUNE	French Pvtr	1/223,225,397
L'EUGENIE	French Pvtr	1/233-234
L'HIRONDELLE	French Pvtr	1/235
L'INDIENNE	French	1/137
LANNERET		1/52
LARNE	HMS	1/411,414,416,418-419,421-423
		1/459-460,472
LAUREL	HMS Frigate	1/227
LEANDER	HMS	1/398
LEDA	HMS	1/237,240,256
LEOPARD	HMS	1/197,219,399. 2/213,551
LES FRERES UNIS		1/215,254,262
LIFFEY	HMS	1/411,413,472
LION		1/24-25,37-38
LION	HMS	1/198,237
LIVELY	Schooner	1/236,274,319
LIVERPOOL	HMS	1/351-352,354,356,359,361,366
		1/385-386. 2/15
LIZARD	HMS	1/82
LONDON	Sloop	1/31,37,117
LYON		1/25
MADAGASCAR	HMS	1/298
MAGICIENNE	HMS	1/228
MALABAR	HMS	1/298
MALABAR		1/229,231,238-240,256,258,260
		1/263-265,276-277,287,486-487
MALACCA	HMS Frigate	1/256
MANILLA	HMS	1/298
MANCHE	French Frigate	1/230
MANCHESTER		1/178,375

MARIANNE	Transport	1/420
MARY		1/82
MARY	Gun Boat	1/411
MARY	Transport	1/331
MATCHLESS	Armed Cutter	1/432,521
MAY		1/253
MAYBOON		1/61,172
MEGNA		1/427
MENELAUS	HMS Frigate	1/230
MERCURY	Sloop	1/226,246-247,249-250,263,274 1/325,342,345,350,351,365,371 1/411-414,416,419,421,429,459 1/460,469,476,483. 2/75,391
MERCHANT'S HOPE		1/17,20,22-23,25
MERITON	Pilot Brig	1/425
MERMAID	Pilot Vessel	1/143
MINDEN	HMS	1/237
MINERVA	HMS	1/204
MINERVE	French Frigate	1/230
MOCHA		1/80-81
MODENA		1/73
MODESTE	HMS Frigate	1/237-238. 2/143-145,147-154
MOINEAU	French Frigate	1/202
MONSOON		1/93
MONTAGU		1/119
MORNING STAR		1/101,261
MORNINGTON	Sloop	1/215,221,231-234,238-240,253 1/262-263,276-277,317,325-326 1/330-332,393,475,484,486
MOSQUITO		1/236
NAMUR	HMS	1/140,143
NANCY	Transport	1/180
NARCISSA	Gun Brig	1/411,422-423
NASSAU		1/78
NAUTILUS	Sloop	1/205
NAUTILUS	Brig	1/226,238,265,269,280,284-294 1/322-323,325,330,331-332,351 1/353-354,360,379,385,479. 2/3,11,30-31,34,73,524
NEPTUNE		1/180,208
NEPTUNE'S PRIZE		1/118
NERBUDDA		1/235
NEREIDE	HMS Frigate	1/226,228,230,322
NEWCASTLE	HMS	1/141,143-144
NEW YEAR'S GIFT		1/17,25,
NISUS	HMS Frigate	1/230,237
NONSUCH		1/205
OLD JAMES		1/55
ORIENT	Transport	1/352
OROOLANG	Schooner	1/193
ORPHEUS	Transport	1/352
OSIANDER = HOSEANDER		1/12-13

OSPREY	Gun Boat	1/436-437,440
OTTER	HMS Sloop	1/226,229
PALINURUS	Brig	1/475,477,479,525-526,531.
		2/11,30,69-74,80-81,104,164
		2/178,214-215,395,397,413,524
PANTHER	Snow	1/195-198,200,215,389,391-394
		1/397-398. 2/68
PASCOA	Transport	1/352
PEACOCK	U.S. Sloop	1/285-294
PEMBROKE	HMS	1/140
PEPPERCORN		1/9,11,16,24-25
PERSEVERANCE	HMS	1/187
PHAETON	HMS Frigate	1/237
PHAETON		1/411,487
PHOEBE	HMS Frigate	1/230,237
PHOENIX	Ketch	1/276
PHOENIX	Gun Boat	1/411
PHOENIX	HMS	1/245,256
PLANET	Brig	1/425,427,430,434
PLUTO	Gun Boat	1/434-437,439,441. 2/79,150
		2/151-153,241,246-247,255,258
		2/287,292-294,488-489
POWERFUL	Mortar Vessel	1/411,419,452,457,464
PRESIDENT		1/71,97
PRESIDENTE	HMS Frigate	1/237
PRINCE OF WALES	Sloop	1/226,274,277-278,294,297,299
		1/300,325,327,330,337,371,373
		1/381,383,385,402-403,411,419
		1/420,429,457,459,476,525.
		2/391
PRINCESS	Galley	1/105
PRINCESS ANN		1/78
PRINCESS AUGUSTA	Grab	1/215,225,392-393,397
PRINCESS CAROLINE		1/147
PRINCESS CHARLOTTE	Transport	1/270
PRINCESS ROYAL	Grab	1/199,204,205,215
PROCRIS	HMS Sloop	1/237,246-247,256,258
PROTECTOR		1/128-131,133-135,140,142,144
PRUDENTE	French Frigate	1/202,204-205
PSYCHE	Gun Brig	1/226,230,238,265,347-348,351
		1/371,381,404-406,410,474,476
		2/33
PSYCHE	HMS Frigate	1/237
PULTENEY		1/108
QUEEN		1/173
QUEEN	Ketch	1/215
QUEENSBOROUGH	HMS Frigate	1/141,144
RAISONNABLE	HMS Frigate	1/226
RANGER	Brig	1/157-161,180,182,186
RED DRAGON		1/5-7,12-14,25,71,74
RESEARCH	Survey Ship	1/400-401,411,434,436-442,477

RESISTANCE	HMS	1/206-207
RESOLU	French Pvtr	1/205
RESTORATION		1/118,135
RETURN		1/55,72
REVENGE		1/61,66-67,72,172-173
REVENGE	Frigate	1/133-134,137-138,142-143,156
		1/157,166,174,176,179-180
REVOLUTION		1/78
ROBERT SPANKIE	Gun Boat	1/411,415
RODNEY	Ketch	1/215,274
ROEBUCK		1/31
ROEBUCK		1/52
ROMNEY HMS		1/219
ROSE		1/25
ROYAL ADELAIDE		1/179
ROYAL ADMIRAL		1/180
ROYAL MERCHANT		1/4
ROYAL TIGER	Schooner	1/501
SALAMANDER	Bomb Ketch	1/119,146
SALSETTE	HMS Frigate	1/298. 2/4
SAMARANG	HMS Sloop	1/237
SAMARANG	Dutch Ship	1/251
SALISBURY	HMS	1/134
SATELLITE	Sloop	1/416,418,423-424,459-460
SAUGOR = GUNGA SAUGOR		
SCALEBY CASTLE		1/231
SCARBOROUGH		1/86
SCIPION	HMS	1/237,240. 2/180
SCORPION		1/204,261
SERINGAPATAM	HMS Frigate	1/298
SEVERN		1/86
SHANNON	Schooner	1/501
SHARK	Gallivat	1/146
SILLY		1/177
SIR FRANCIS DRAKE	HMS Frigate	1/237,243
SIRIUS	HMS Frigate	1/226,228
SLANEY	HMS	1/411-413
SOLOMON		1/12,17,25
SOPHIA	Gun Brig	1/401,411,434,441
SOPHIE	HMS	1/411,413-414,416,423-424,451
		1/453-457,472
SPEEDWELL	Sloop	1/153
STAG	HMS	1/173
STAR	Brig	1/210-211,213,215
STAUNCH	HMS Brig	1/230
STREATHAM		1/227
STROMBOLI	Bomb Vessel	1/326,332
SUCCESS	Ketch	1/78,97,166,168,170-171
SUFFOLK	HMS	1/206
SULKEA PACKET	Gun Vessel	1/411,464
SUNDERLAND	HMS	1/144
SUPERB	HMS	1/179
SUPPLY		1/52
SUSAN		1/5-6

HISTORY OF THE INDIAN NAVY.

Name	Type	Pages
SUFFOLK	HMS	1/206
SUFFOLK		1/232
SWALLOW	Ketch	1/128,130,134,163-164,176-177,394
SWAN		1/25
SWIFT	Sloop	1/210-213,215,261-262
SWIFT	Gun Boat	1/411,464
SYBILLE	HMS	1/234-235
SYLPH	Schooner	1/226,236,274,279,294,297,320 1/321,324,377,399
TALBOT		1/210,394
TAMAR	HMS	1/478
TEES	HMS	1/460
TEIGNMOUTH	Brig	1/215,221,225-226,235,246-247 1/250,256-258,260,265-266,268 1/273,277,280,351,353,365,371 1/373,381,387,393,397,399,411 1/413,417-420,429,449,451,453 1/454-456,475-476,484,525. 2/391
TERNATE	Sloop	1/212,215,225,265-266,271-273 1/275,325,331-332,397,399,411 1/479,503,507
THAMES	HMS	1/197
THAMES	Mortar Vessel	1/302-303,306,309,435,437,440
THETIS	Gun Brig	1/226,229,238,265,276-277,294 1/347-348,409,411,414-416,418 1/419,447-448,479,523-524,526 1/527
THOMAS		1/10
THOMAS		1/82
TIGER	HMS	1/134,143
TIGER	Gallivat	1/118,146
TIGER	Brig	1/168,171
TIGER	Gun Brig	1/411,422-423,464
TIGRIS	Brig	1/478,501. 2/10-11,20,27-28 2/31,34,36-40,42,50,72,74-76 2/97,106,136,164,212-213,297 2/298,313,317,318-321,326,328 2/336,387,523,548-550
TOM TOUGH	Mortar Vessel	1/411,464
TOPAZE	HMS Frigate	1/302-306,309
TRADE'S INCREASE		1/7,9,11-12,25
TRITON	HMS	1/138
TRIUMPH	Bomb Vessel	1/128,134
TROUBRIDGE	Transport	1/256
TRUSTY	Ketch/Gun Boat	1/434,436-437,439-441
UNDAUNTED	HMS Frigate	1/522
UNICORN		1/25
UNION		1/8
UNITED KINGDOM		1/230
UPTON CASTLE	Transport	1/352
VENGEUR	French Pvtr	1/205

VENUS	French	1/229
VENUS		1/261,394
VESTAL	Gun Brig	1/226,229,238,276,279,325,330
		1/342,345,351,381,385,405,411
		1/434,436-439,444,476-477,484
		1/485
VICTOR	French Cvtte	1/229-230
VICTORIA	Frigate	1/105,147
VICTORY		1/94
VIGILANT		1/202-203,376
VIGILANT	Sloop	1/479
VIPER	Bomb Vessel	1/128,134
VIPER	Snow	1/215,225,376
VIPER	Brig	1/313-315
VOLAGE	HMS	1/256
VULCAN	French Brig	1/205
WARLEY		1/199
WARREN	Bomb Vessel	1/134
WARWICK		1/119
WASP		1/226,262
WELLINGTON	Gun Boat	1/246-247
WEYMOUTH	HMS	1/141
WHALE		1/37,41
WILLIAM	Survey Brig	1/401
WILLIAM PITT		1/205
WOLFE	Gallivat	1/182-183
YOUNG BARRACOUTA	Gun Boat	1/246-247
ZEPHYR	Schooner	1/274-275,479,501

INDEX

EAST INDIA COMPANY & R.N. OFFICERS

ADAM, Sir Charles	Capt	1/234
ALDERTON,	Capt	1/72
ALEXANDER,	Capt RN	1/458,463,465
ALLEN,	Lieut	1/330
ANDERSON,	Capt	1/177
ANDERSON,	Lieut	1/429,459
ANDERSON,	Engineer	1/520
ANDERSON, J.	Asst Surgeon	1/404
ANDREWS,	Capt	1/73-74
APPLEGATH,	Capt	1/199
ARMSTRONG,	Lieut	1/436-437,443-445
ARROW,	Lieut	1/226
ARROW, W.	Cdr/Jnr Capt	1/474
ARTHUR, James	Lieut/Commander	1/279,294,351,362
ATKINSON,	Lieut RN	1/305
AVERY, Charles	Bosun's Mate i/cmd	1/437
BAGWELL,	Commodore	1/107
BAIN,	Capt RN	1/237
BAKER, Charles	Actg Lieut	1/210
BARNARD,	Captain	1/350
BARNES,	Capt	1/411,425-427,429
BEAVER,	Capt RN	1/230,237
BENDY,	Capt	1/177
BENNETT,	Lieut	1/322,392
BERLEW,	Commodore	1/97
BERTIE,	Vice Admiral [RN]	1/230-231,244
BEST, Stephen	Lieut	1/209
BEST, Thomas	Capt	1/12-15,17,25
BETHAM, John	Commander	1/502-503
BICKERTON, Sir Richard	Admiral [RN]	1/179
BISSET,	Capt	1/399
BLAIR, Archibald	Mid/Lt/Capt	1/185-188
BLANKETT, John	Rear Admiral [RN]	1/219,399
BLAST,	Lieut	1/274-275,279-280,483

BLYTH,	Capt	1/41
BOND,	Capt	1/208
BOSCAWEN,	Admiral [RN]	1/140
BOSCAWEN,	Midshipman	1/451,453
BOWATER, W.	Lieut	1/498
BOWEN,	Capt RN	1/245,256
BOYCE, Charles	Lieut	1/265,284-285,288-294
		1/427,483
BOYE, Charles	Midshipman	1/405,433
BRANGWIN,	Capt	1/78
BRIDGES,	Captain	1/343-344
BRIGGS,	Capt RN	1/230
BRISBANE, Sir James	Commodore RN	1/465-468,472
BROUGHTON,	Capt RN	1/230,237,244
BROUGHTON, Gabriel	Surgeon	1/51
BRUCKS, George B.	Lieut/Commander	1/353,362-363,373,404
		1/405-406,408
BUCHANAN,	Capt	1/136,476,495
CAMPBELL,	Lieut RN	1/354,356
CAMPBELL,	Capt IN	1/304
CAMPBELL, C.D.	Volunteer/Mid	1/407,495
CANNING,	Capt	1/205
CARRUTHERS,	Lieut	1/314
CARLESS,	Master's Mate/ Commodore IN	1/432
CAULFIELD,	Capt RN	1/230
CHADS, Henry D.	Commander/Capt RN	1/423-424,449,451-454
		1/456-459,465,468-470
		1/472
CHEAP,	Capt	1/205
CHILD, John [Sir]	Admiral	1/73-76
CHITTY,	Midshipman	1/367
CLARKE,	Lieut	1/451-453
CLEMENT, W.L.	Lieut	1/404
CLIFTON,	Capt	1/177
COGAN,	Lieut/Capt	1/295-296,506,512,514
		1/516
COGAN, Robert	Lieut	1/404-405
COLE,	Capt RN	1/237
COLLIER, F.A. Sir	Capt/Cmmdre RN	1/351,353,358,360-361
		1/363,367
COLLINSON, Sir Richard	Admiral [RN]	1/396
COLLINSON, W.S.	Lieut/Commodore	1/402-403,411,457,507
CONSTABLE,	Capt I.N.	1/33
CONSTABLE, C.G.	Lieut	1/405
CONYERS,	Capt	1/246
CONYERS,	Lieut	1/330
CORBETT,	Commodore RN	1/322
COOPER,	Midshipman	1/468
CORBET, Robert	Capt RN	1/226,229
CORNISH,	Admiral [RN]	1/143-144
CORNWALLIS,	Commodore	1/187
CORNWALLIS, Hon W.	Rear Admiral	1/204

Name	Rank	References
COURT, Charles	Lieut/Capt	1/191,213,225,391,393
		1/394,396-397,400
COYDE,	Midshipman	1/451
CRAIG,	Lieut RN	1/230
CRAWFORD	Capt RN	1/237
CRAWFORD, John	Lt/Cdr/Capt	1/391,393-395,400-401
		1/411,422-423,437,441
		1/442-443,474
CRAWFORD,	Midshipman	1/468
CRAWFORD, R.W.	?	1/521
CRIDDLE,	Midshipman	1/391
CURTIS,	Capt	1/177
DALRYMPLE, Alexdr.	Hydrographer	1/189-191
DANIELL, E.W.S.	Volunteer	1/495
D'ARCY,	Midshipman	1/367
DASHWOOD,	Ensign	1/295
DAVIDSON,	Capt	1/265-266
DAVIDSON,	Lieut	1/330
DAVIS, William	Capt	1/5
DEANE, Robert	Lieut/Capt	1/231,238-239,245,254
		1/255-256,260,261-265
DELANO,	Midshipman	1/195,197
DENTON, William	Midshipman/Lieut	1/268-269,392-393,404
		1/521,531
DENTON,	Actg Lieut ex Mid RN	1/321
DERBY, A.F.	Midshipman	1/462
DILLON,	Capt	1/401
DIXON,	Capt	1/253
DOBSON,	Lieut RN	1/416
DOMINICETTI,	Lieut	1/294-295,297,300,402
DOWNING,	Lieut	1/93,97,99
DOWNTON, Nicholas	Capt	1/17-23,25
DRURY,	Capt RN	1/237,256
DUFF,	Midshipman/Lieut	1/268,367
DROUGHT, H.A.M.	Midshipman/Capt	1/408,501
EATWELL, W.	Capt	1/265-268,285,287
EDGCOMBE,	Capt RN	1/230,237
EDGELL,	Capt RN	1/230
EDWARDS,	Capt	1/93
ELLIOT, Hon George	Capt RN	1/237,256
ELWON, Thomas	Lieut/Capt	1/302,309,408,531
ETHERSEY, R.	Lieut IN	1/404,478
FAITHFUL, J.	Lieut/Commander	1/265,302,351,362
FALCONER,	Purser RN	1/173
FALLON,	Asst Surgeon	1/373
FARQUHARSON,	Capt	1/294-296
FESTING,	Capt RN	1/237
FIELD,	Capt	1/176
FRAMPTON,	Capt	1/106
FRANCES,	Lieut ?	1/422-423
FRASER,	Lieut RN	1/415-416,418-419,423

FRASER,	Surgeon	1/514
FREEMAN,	Capt RN	1/246
FROST, Henry	Lieut	1/207
FROST,	Capt	1/232-234
GARRAWAY,	Gunner	1/367
GILBERT,	Purser	1/510
GLEN, Joseph	Surgeon	1/368
GOLDFINCH,	Lieut	1/451-452
GOODRIDGE, R,E,	Cdr/Jnr Capt	1/411,429,449,474
GORDON, A.H.	Volunteer	1/495
GORDON,	Capt RN	1/229-230
GOWAN,	Lieut	1/320,377
GRAHAM, W.C.	Lieut	1/321-322
GRAHAM, Wm.T.	Jnr/Snr Capt	1/474,479
GRANT, Charles	Commodore CB,RN	1/411,413,465
GRANT,	Capt	1/279-284
GRANT, George	Capt	1/479
GRANT,	Midshipman/Lieut	1/274-275,278-279
GRANTHAM, Sir Thomas	Senior Capt	1/72
GRAVES,	Master's Mate	1/425-426,432
GREENWAY, W.C.	Lieut	1/351,362,367-368
GREER, F.W.	Lieut/Capt	1/416,447,498
GRIFFIN,	Commodore RN	1/139-140
GRUBB,	Lieut	1/387
GUY, James W.	Lieut	1/267-268,332,411,433 1/437
GUY, John M.	Lieut (Surveyor)	1/404-405
HAINES, S.B.	Lieut	1/404-407,501
HALL,	Commander/Capt	1/177,209-210,238,351 1/360,362
HALL, J.	Lieut	1/265
HALL,	Lieut	1/332
HAMILTON, W.J.	Capt	1/253
HAMILTON, Alexdr.	Capt/C-in-C	1/39,41,49,77,86,94 1/99,102-103
HAMILTON,	Lieut	1/234
HARDY,	Lieut	1/274-275
HARDY, (1811)	Lieut	1/399
HARDY,	Actg Lieut	1/391
HARDY, H?	Capt	1/411,417-418,420,421 1/429-432,471,474
HARLAND,	Commodore	1/89
HARLAND, Sir Robert	Admiral [RN]	1/173
HARRIOTT,	Midshipman	1/209
HARRIS,	Capt RN	1/237,243
HARRISON,	Lieut	1/425,432
HASWELL, Thomas	Lieut	1/195-196
HATLEY	Capt RN	1/226
HAWKINS,	Capt	1/6,8-10,13,25,
HAWKINS, John C.	Lieut/Commander	1/402,478,505-508,511 1/513-520
HAY,	Midshipman	1/332

INDEX. 557

HAYES, Sir John	Volr/Commodore	1/180-181,183,200-204
		1/210-212,220-222,235
		1/238-242,244,262,376
		1/432,434-435,437-439
		1/441-443,445-446,448
		1/464,471,473,477,486
		1/488-489,521
HEATH,	Capt	1/73
HEATHCOTE,	Capt RN	1.237
HEATHCOTE,	Lieut IN	1/186
HENDERSON,	Capt RN	1/230
HENRY, William	Lieut/Capt	1/210,394
HEPBURN,	Lieut/Capt	1/265,287
HEWETT, H.H.	Midshipman	1/387
HEWITSON,	Lieut/Capt	1/225,246
HIGGINS, J.W.	Lieut	1/437,441
HILDER,	Capt	1/75
HILLYAR,	Capt RN	1/230,237
HIPPON, Anthony	Capt	1/12
HOARE,	Capt RN	1/237
HORSBURGH,	Hydrographer	1/189,191
HORSBURGH,	Capt	1/396,398-399,405
HOUGH, Samuel	Capt	1/120-122,135
HOUGHTON, John	Lieut	1/404-405
HOWARD,	Midshipman	1/443
HUDDART,	Capt	1/191
HUDSON,	Capt	1/205
HUGHES, Sir Edward	Admiral [RN]	1/137,178-179,181,187
HURST,	Actg Lieut	1/391-392,394
HUTTON,	Midshipman	1/464
HYDE,	Capt	1/71
INCHBIRD,	Lieut	1/105-106,108,112-114
JACKSON,	Midshipman	1/443
JACOB, W	Lieut	1/304,308
JAMES, Sir Wm.	Commodore	1/125-134,137-138,144
JAMESON,	Capt RM Bn ?	1/375
JARDINE, W.	Volunteer	1/495
JEAKES, James	Capt/Commodore	1/274,330,340
JELLICOE, S.	Commander/Capt	1/437,440
JOHNSTON,	Lieut RN	1/520-521,526,530
JOHNSTONE,	Commodore	1/178
JOHNSTONE,	Midshipman ?	1/367
JOHNSTONE,	Boatswain ?	1/368
JONES, D	Lt/Cdr/Jnr Capt	1/265,302,309,474
JONES, Felix	Capt	1/524
JOSEPH, Benjamin	Capt	1/25-26,28
KEELING,	Capt/Admiral	1/6-8,24-25
KEELE,	Lieut RN	1/424,458
KELLETT, Sir Henry	Lieut/Admiral	1/424,451-453,455,457
KELLY,	Capt RN	1/237
KEMPENFELDT,	Capt RN	1/141
KEMPTHORNE, G.B.	Lieut	1/404,407-408

KENT, Richard	Lieut	1/437,440
KEYMER,	Midshipman	1/443
KEYS,	Capt	1/390-391
KINCHANT, John C.	Lieut	1/266,275
KINCHANT, Richard	Lieut/Capt	1/340,383,385
KING,	Lieut ?	1/422-423
LANCASTER, James	Capt/Adm/Gen	1/5
LAUGHTON,	Lieut	1/427,433,464,468,470
LEE,	Capt RN	1/173
LEGGATT,	Midshipman	1/468
LESLIE,	Capt RN	1/256
LEY, James. 3rd Earl of Marlborough		1/55
LEWIS,	Capt	1/106
LINDQUIST,	Midshipman	1/417,423,451,453,457 1/464,468
LINDSAY, Sir John	Capt RN	1/173
LITTLETON,	Commodore	1/84,102
LLOYD, Robert	Lieut/Commander	1/401-402,427
LOCH,	Capt RN	1/347,351
LORD,	Midshipman	1/255
LOWE, W.	Lieut	1/404
LUARD,	Capt	1/177
LUMLEY, J.R.	Capt RN	1/302,306-309
LYE,	Capt RN	1/230,237
LYNCH, H.B.	Lieut	1/404
LYNCH, W.	Volunteer	1/495
LYNNE,	Capt RN	1/230
MACDONALD,	Mid/Commander	1/235-236,238,250,252 1/256,259,261,274,276 1/319
MACDONALD,	Lieut	1/411
MACDONALD, D.	Capt IN	1/231
MACK,	Capt	1/283
MACKAY, D.	Capt RN	1/256
MAILLARD, C.J.	Lt/Cdr/Jnr Capt	1/351,354,362,474
MAINWARING	Lieut	1/223
MALCOLM, Sir Pulteney	Admiral	1/232
MALCOLM, Sir Charles	Capt CB, RN	1/494-496,503,505,511 1/517-518,531
MARGRAVE,	Lieut	1/430
MARRYAT, Frederick	Commander/Capt RN	1/411,416-419,422-423 1/429,459-460,472
MARSHALL, John	Lieut RN	1/417,448
MARTIN,	Capt RN	1/141
MASCALL,	Midshipman	1/185
MASKAL,	Lieut	1/406
MATTHEWS,	Capt/Commodore	1/94,101-102
MAUDE, Hon J.	Capt RN	1/189
MAUGHAN, Philip	Lt/Cdr/Jnr Capt	1/394-395,404,474,479
MAXFIELD, W.	Lieut/Cdr/Capt	1/390,392,394,398
MAUNSELL,	Capt RN	1/237

MAXFIELD, W.	Commander/Capt	1/238-239,276,390,392
		1/394,398,474,480,482
		1/486-487,489-490,495
MAXWELL,	Capt RN	1/271-272
MAYSTON, Robert	Lieut	1/286,288,291
McCLUER, John	Lieut/Capt	1/187,189-192,195-200
		1/403
McDOWALL,	Lieut	1/305
McNEALE,	Capt	1/104-105
McNEIL, F.	Commander	1/437
MEARS,	Lieut	1/399
MERITON,	Capt	1/475-476,489
MICHIE, Jonathan	Lieut	1/195-196
MIDDLETON, David	Capt	1/8
MIDDLETON,	Lieut	1/280
MIDDLETON,	Commander/Capt	1/411,414
MIDDLETON, Sir Henry	Capt/Admiral	1/6-7,9-12,25
MILLS,	Lieut RN	1/356
MINCHAL, T.C.	Lieut	1/437
MINCHIN,	Capt	1/67
MITCHELL,	Capt	1/205
MITCHELL, C.	Commander RN	1/411
MITCHELL,	Commander/Capt RN	1/472
MITCHELL, C.E.B.	Lieut	1/404
MOFFAT,	Lieut RN	1/353
MONEY, William T.	Capt	1/218,255,263-264,475
MONTRIOU,	Capt	1/191
MONTRIOU, Charles	M's Mate/Lieut/Capt	1/400,437,440,443
MOORE, John	Commodore	1/137,156,176
MORESBY, Robert	Mid/Lieut/Cdr	1/267,402,409.429
MORESBY,	Lieut	1/531
MORGAN, Richard	Jnr/Snr Capt	1/474,479,498
MORIATY,	Lieut RN	1/305-306
MULLION, Thomas	Midshipman	1/404
MUNDAY,	Master's Mate	1/267
MURRAY,	Midshipman	1/451
NEVILLE, Viscount	Capt RN	1/230
NEWPORT, C.	Capt	1/25
NICHOLSON, William	Lieut	1/210
NICHOLSON,	Surgeon	1/196-197
NORTON,	Capt	1/256
NOTT,	Lieut	1/477-478
NUNN, Radford	Capt	1/115-117
OAKSHOT,	Gunner	1/437,440
ORMSBY, Henry A.	Lieut	1/404,407
OWEN,	Capt RN	1/237,245
PAKENHAM,	Capt RN	1/206-207
PARBURY, Charles	Midshipman	1/407
PARKER,	Capt RN	1/230
PASSWATER,	Capt	1/94
PATERSON,	Capt RN	1/230
PAVIN,	Capt	1/253

PEACHEY,	Capt RN	1/237
PELLEW, Fleetwood	Capt RN	1/237
PELLEY,	Capt RN	1/237
PENNY,	Capt	1/177,183
PEPWELL,	Capt	1/26,29-30
PEPPER,	Commander	1/517
PETERS,	Lieut	1/506,514
PETERS, George	Midshipman	1/405
PHILLIPS,	Lieut	1/238,330,484
PHILIPS,	Lieut	1/255
PICKET,	Commodore	1/206,397
PICKEY,	Midshipman	1/451
PILCHER, George	Midshipman	1/405
PINCHING, H.N.	Lieut	1/404,406-407
PITCHER, Thomas	Midshipman	1/510
POCOCK,	Vice Admiral	1/134-135,140-143
POPHAM, Sir Home R.	Capt RN	1/219
PORTER,	Lieut	1/185
POWER,	Midshipman	1/468
PRICE,	Capt	1/163-164
PROCTER, John	Lieut	1/190,195-196
PRUEN,	Lt Commanding	1/158-161
PRUEN,	Midshipman/Capt IN	1/443
PYM,	Capt RN	1/226
QUANBROUGH, G.	Volunteer	1/495
RAINIER,	R/Adm & V/Adm [RN]	1/206,231
RAVENSCROFT,	Midshipman	1/468
RENNIE,	Capt RN	1/230
REYNOLDS,	Capt RN	1/237
REYNOLDS, R.	Lieut	1/387
RICHARDS,	Commodore	1/86
RICHARDSON, Chas.R.	Lieut	1/400,437,440,443
RICHARDSON, Isaac	Actg Lieut	1/210
RICHARDSON, Isaac G.	Capt	1/208
RIGBY,	Capt	1/115
RINGROVE,	Lieut	1/190-191
RITCHIE, John	Capt	1/187-188
ROBINSON,	Capt RN	1/237
ROBINSON,	Lieut	1/185
ROBINSON,	Lieut	1/384
ROBINSON, G.	Capt	1/477
ROBSON,	Lieut	1/294,297,302,307
ROBSON,	Midshipman	1/468
ROGERS, W.E.	Lieut	1/404-405,438-439
ROGERS, Thomas E.	Lieut	1/404
ROPER,	Capt	1/205,394
ROPER, George	Capt	1/210
ROSS, Daniel	Lieut/Snr Capt	1/474. 2/3,10,13,83-85, 2/135,202-203,210,398
ROWBAND, J.H	Lieut	1/404,458,464,468,470 1/477
ROWLEY, Josias	Commodore RN	1/226-230,245
ROYCE, J.	Lieut	1/437,440-441

INDEX. 561

RYVES, G.F.	Commander RN	1/411,449,451,453,457 1/472
SADLER,	Capt	1/253
SALMOND,	Capt	1/251
SALTER,	Midshipman/Lieut	1/314,330
SANDERS, J.P.	Lieut	1/404
SANDILANDS,	Capt	1/115
SARIS, John	Capt	1/11-12
SAWYER, John	Commander	1/501
SAYER,	Capt RN	1/237,240,242,245,256
SCOTT,	Lieut	1/210-211
SCOTT,	Midshipman	1/451
SEALY,	Capt	1/256,265
SEAWRIGHT, Edward	Lieut	1/353,363
SELBY,	Capt	1/191
SEYMOUR,	Lieut	1/296
SHARP, C	Lieut	1/477,513
SHARP,	Surgeon	1/193
SHARPEY, Alexander	Capt	1/25
SHAXTON,	Capt	1/63
SHERIFF,	Capt	1/156,177
SHILLINGE,	Commodore	1/31
SKINNER,	Lieut	1/190-191
SMEE, Thomas	Lieut/Capt	1/209,399
SMITH, T.	Boatswain	1/332
SNOOK, Samuel	Lieut	1/195-196,199
SPRY, W.	Asst Surgeon	1/404
SQUIRE, E.B.	Midshipman	1/404
STEVENS,	Commodore RN	1/140-141,143
STIFFE, A.W.	Lt IN	1/33-36
STOPFORD, Hon Robert	Rear Admiral [RN]	1/237,240,244
STREET,	Capt	1/230
STUDDERT,	Commander/Capt	1/472
SUFFLET,	Capt	1/6
SWAN,	Capt	1/47
SWANLEY,	Capt	1/47
TANNER, Thomas	Lieut/Jnr Capt	1/189,238,280,308-309 1/323,347,370,403,474 1/504
TAYLOR, A.D.	Lieut IN	1/191,399
TAYLOR, William H.	Lieut	1/210
TAYLOR,	Lieut	1/320,326
THACKER,	Master	1/407
THACKER, J.	Volunteer	1/495
THORPE,	Ensign	1/65
TOLSON,	Capt	1/106
TOMKINSON,	Capt RN	1/230
TOPPING,	Capt	1/188
TOVEY,	Capt	1/134
TUCKER, Nathaniel	Capt	1/199
TWEEDELL,	Volunteer	1/495
VASHON,	Capt RN	1/391

VERNON, Sir Edward	Admiral [RN]	1/177
VINCENT,	Capt	1/427
WAGHORN, Thomas	Lieut	1/432,521-524,526,529 1/530
WAINWRIGHT,	Capt/Commodore RN	1/189,231,325-332,336
WALES,	Capt	1/235,396
WALKER,	Commander	1/238
WALKER,	Commander/Capt	1/474
WALKER, Richard	Volunteer	1/495
WALPOLE,	Capt RN	1/351,361
WARDEN, W.	Midshipman	1/437,443
WARREN	Capt/Commodore RN	1/82,84,237
WARRINGTON	Capt USN	1/285-294
WATERWORTH,	Midshipman	1/370
WATKINS, James	Lieut/Commander	1/226,238,279,330
WATSON,	Vice Admiral [RN]	1/132-136,138-140
WATSON, John	Commodore	1/149,154-156
WATSON,	Lieut	1/351,362
WEDDELL,	Capt	1/41
WEDGEBOROUGH, John	Lieut/Capt	1/190-191,194-199
WEEKS,	Capt	1/94
WELLSTED, J.R.	Lieut IN	1/403-404
WHEATEL,	Lieut	1/255
WHEATLEY, John	Capt RN	1/385-386
WHITE, (1790)	Lieut	1/397
WHITE, Robert	Lieut	1/389,394
WHITE, Robert	Midshipman	1/194-196
WHITELOCK, H.H.	Midshipman	1/404-405,408
WILDEY,	Capt	1/73
WILLOUGHBY,	Capt RN	1/226,228
WILLS, William	Surgeon	1/122
WILSON, John H.	Lieut	1/305
WILSON, Henry	Capt	1/192-194,199
WILSON, John H.	Commander	1/478,520,526-532,530 1/531-532
WINN, F.D.W.	Lieut	1/404,407
WINSOR,	Midshipman RN	1/468
WOODCOCKE,	Capt	1/41
WRIGHT,	Capt	1/74
WRIGHT,	Lieut RN	1/305
WYBORNE,	Vice Admiral	1/73
WYNDHAM, Henry	Lieut	1/427,429,432
YOUNG,	Capt	1/56
YOUNG, James	Midshipman	1/407

www.ingramcontent.com/pod-product-compliance
Lightning Source LLC
Chambersburg PA
CBHW031747220426
43662CB00007B/309